Simon Mark Smith's Autobiography - Volume One - Love, Hate and Knowledge

Simon Mark Smith

Simon's Diary Volume One - Love, Hate and Knowledge

Copyright © 2024 Simon Mark Smith

Hardback First Edition April 2024

ISBN: 978-1-7385202-9-9

Details

Author: Simon Mark Smith

Book cover design: Simon Mark Smith

Editing and proofreading: Pauline Smith

Printer: Ingram Spark

Disclaimer

The events and conversations in this book have been set down to the best of the author's ability, although some names and details have been changed to protect the privacy of individuals. Some portions of this book are works of fiction and in those sections, any references to historical events, real people, or real places are used fictitiously. Other names, characters, places, and events are products of the author's imagination, and any resemblances to actual events or places or persons, living or dead, are entirely coincidental.

Sexual and Violent Content Warning

This book contains explicit sexual and violent content, where possible some warning will be given, however, in some instances, there may be none.

Web Links

Please note that any links included in this volume were working when the book was published but may not work in the future.

Contact Details

Publisher: Simon Mark Smith or Simon Mark Smith's Literary Executor

70, Royal Parade, Eastbourne, East Sussex, BN22 7AQ, UK

Website: www.simonsdiary.co.uk

Email: info@simonsdiary.co.uk

For my partner, and sweetest friend,
Gillian Toft
And my children.

Acknowledgments

There are always too many to mention when it comes to acknowledging all those who played a part in the creation of a work. Firstly, though, I would like to thank Pauline Smith who helped complete the final edit and went through the arduous task of correcting and proofreading every word on every page. I would also like to thank my partner, Gillian Toft, for casting her eye upon these pages and giving me feedback too.

As you can imagine, many people influenced the content of this book. I was going to write, "I wouldn't know where to start", but I do, so a special thank you to Ann, Paul and Aiden Ellis, Lee Batty, Veronica Pakenham, Julia Robertson, Eileen O'Brien, Ian Fletcher, Rachel Kearney, John McVicar, Steve Venus, R. Finney, Greg and Jackie Gregory, Naomi, June, Amanda, Monica, Joanna, Gianna Williams, Diana Bremner, Joseph Waters, Eddie, Miri and Jonathan Shruster, all my Rachailovich, Smith and Ellis family relations, my father, Boris, my mother, Angela, my step-father John and, of course, my brother, Stephen Hill.

Also, I have been blessed by the kindness of others throughout my life, both directly and indirectly, and without their kindness, I doubt I would have ever had anywhere near as rich a life as I did. So, I would also like to thank not only all those I am aware of but those I was never to meet too.

Simon Mark Smith - February 2024

Contents

Foreword

Whenever I start reading a book, I tend to see the Foreward as a bit of an inconvenience. With that in mind, I'll keep this brief. Firstly, I have used a stylistic format that interweaves sections from different times and subject matter. At first, you may find this a little jarring. However, if you persist, you'll get used to it quickly and hopefully find it a thought-provoking approach. Secondly, I partly wrote this to preserve and pass on lessons I learned throughout my life, especially regarding relationships. But it's also about a relationship between myself and you, the reader. Thirdly, this was meant to be the first of a series of at least three volumes. Alas, as you will discover, I doubt that will come to be, but such is life. Lastly, as I came to publishing this and the other three books I've been working on, there was a feeling of time being very limited. Therefore, I did have to rush to get them published. So, if at times you come across errors, please forgive me.

With all that said, I hope you enjoy this, and thank you for taking the time to read it.

Chapter 1
No Man's Land

2005

This evening I was sitting in a Polish restaurant with a friend. I told him I wanted to start this book with a brief history of my family. He said I should start with an impact.

The Greeting

I want you to imagine you're at a social gathering and someone behind you says, "I'd like to introduce you to my friend." You turn around to see a man about 5 foot 3 inches tall, with short, cropped hair, slightly Mediterranean-looking and dressed in black. The man smiles at you, you smile back and put your hand out to greet him. He pulls his right arm forward, but it stops just beyond the elbow joint and just above the end of his arm, a small finger protrudes which forks into two fingers. You're not quite sure what to do, but politely you take a hold of his arm wondering what it will feel like. He then brings his other arm forward which also ends close to where the elbow would be, this one however doesn't have any fingers coming out of it at all. As he places it on your hand gently, you're struck by how normal it feels, even though you're entirely out of your comfort zone.

He, of course, is me. I say, "Hi, I'm Simon, what's your name?"

1914 – 1917 Corners of Foreign Fields – Part 1

My maternal great-grandfather was called John Frederick Smith and as was common back then he named one of his sons John Frederick too. When his name-sake son was just 19, World War 1 broke out, so along with many of his friends he joined the march to the battlefield, hopeful of a quick resolution and the chance to prove himself. However, within months the reality of his situation dispelled those expectations, especially when the initial land battles quickly led to trench warfare and a stalemate that would last for years. For him though, his situation enveloped both his external and internal worlds in a darkness he'd never previously faced and as each day passed, his mind increasingly wandered back to the life he'd left behind, and with it the realisation he hadn't appreciated just how much he loved it.

He woke one October morning to find the sun warm on his face. Though his feet were wet through, as they had been for days, he pretended he was back paddling in the mudflats of a Bournemouth beach a few summers ago, joking with friends in the late afternoon sun, and looking forward to their guest house evening meal.

For all the discomfort of trench life, there was a lot of joking between some of those same friends who'd been stationed with him. Much of their humour centred around the dire food they'd endure, but the daily routine was still marked out by their meals, and the evening one was nearly always looked forward to.

But still, the air was heavy and cold, and the silence of no man's land continually unnerved them as it reminded them of why they were there.

I can't tell you why John Frederick found himself in the middle of no-man's land, but it was nighttime and both the mist and smoke meant he couldn't see much further than a few yards ahead. Disorientated, all he could do was assess his surroundings as best he could while taking slow, careful, silent steps forward. The fact the Germans were not spraying the air with machine gun fire meant they too had soldiers in the vicinity, so, at any moment he was sure he might be faced by one of them, and then what? Would they shoot at each other, end up on the ground fighting to the death, or just back off into the cover of the night?

In the distance, John heard the crack of a single shot, and as he turned his head to the side, he realised he was on his back in the mud. He tried to sit up but couldn't and feeling warm liquid running across his neck to his shoulder he realised he'd been shot.

He wanted to try crawling back to the trench, but aside from not knowing which way that was, he could barely move, so, he lay there hoping he'd be rescued. Shouting for help might bring the enemy to him, so he waited in silence.

From the darkness, a figure approached but within seconds he realised it was a German soldier. Desperate to escape the soldier's bayonet he pushed himself backwards, but there was nothing he could do.

On another battlefield, a much vaguer attack occurs. This time to Samuel Rachailovich, my father's father. The details are unknown but the resultant trauma, shell shock, still reverberates through history to this moment for me.

The Appearance of Family

In 2005 genealogy via the Internet was in its infancy so my maternal family history only appeared to me as a series of glimpses that came from other family members at first. The earliest were myths of an aristocratic girl eloping with a stable boy and family names being changed as a matter of necessity, but no explanations were ever offered. By the time our family got to the mid-1800s, the memorable figure was a dominant East-End matriarch called Rosa who died in 1961 aged 93. My mother told me she was a buxom, vivacious, and stern character.

From the late eighteen hundreds, the view became more photographic, faded black and white images of the two families, the Ellises and Smiths, both living in Fulham, London, posing in the backyards of terraced houses, next to boats on the Thames, on beaches on seaside holidays, at weddings, and in photographic studios. Even now, there's a picture of my mother's father on her living room wall. He's young, dressed in a soldier's uniform, his eyes look through the picture at us in the here and now, and next to it, there's another photograph of my mother's mother, Ethel May, who sits serenely in a large wooden chair.

These are the pictures they were happy for others to see, but their concern with how the public viewed them and their family had as much impact on me as the bullets and bombs that destroyed a part of Samuel Rachailovich.

2005 – London

A couple of years ago I went to a spiritualist demonstration in Belgrave Square in London. One of my neighbours, Denise, had suggested we pop in on the off chance. As soon as it started the demonstrator came up to me and said, "I see an old lady." I wasn't impressed and thought, 'Well it's likely, given I'm not that young, my grandmother is dead, but if you want to impress me, tell me her name.' As if she'd heard my thoughts she said, "Her name is Ethel, and she wants to say sorry, she also says you write a lot, I see you writing music and painting too". Denise and I looked at each other as the demonstrator, who was already walking toward someone else turned to me and added, "Well, she wants me to make it clear to you that she's sorry, can I leave that with you?"

My mind jumped back to the moment when in 1976 my grandmother was on her deathbed in hospital after having suffered a stroke. She beckoned me toward her, I hesitated but my mum shoved me forward and as I approached her, she put her hand on my face. I was about 11 years old and some of my cousins were looking on, most likely worried I was going to do something highly inappropriate, but this time I stood there feeling very embarrassed. Years later, I came to realise she was most likely trying to tell me she was sorry. Sorry for letting the public image of our family be more important than my welfare. Back then, I had no idea she had anything to be sorry about, nor did I think my, or my family's past, had any bearing on my present or future either, but, of course, it did.

March 1965 - Epsom District Hospital, Surrey, England.

Silence falls across the theatre. Two women look up from a child. One of them passes him to his mother. She looks at him and says, "Poor thing."

Summer 1964 - London

"Angela is late, she's always late." These words echo through Angela's mind as the coach pulls out of Victoria Bus Station and sets off on its journey through Europe to Croatia.

To me, timekeeping is a symbol of maleness and those who have problems with organising time are often wrestling with the world of boundaries, the world of the

4

archetypal father. Somewhere in Angela's past, she decided, as so many harangued children do, to withdraw into her own protective world, to step out of time. At 24 she looked in her make-up mirror, carefully adjusted her hair and finished putting on her lipstick.

"Is everybody happy?" The tour guide shouted to his audience.

"Yes," they shouted back in unison, and indeed for that circus moment, everyone was.

1940s

Angela was born of an unplanned pregnancy. Her parents had already had three children. One of them, Neville, had died of meningitis four years before she was conceived. Perhaps it was Neville's death and her mother's sense of mortality that brought about the "accident" that gave Angela life. But the residue of not being planned for meant her eldest brother resented her, especially when she got to her teens, and he sensed her rejection of the boundaries that meant so much to him and his father. Her sister, on the other hand, became a surrogate mother to her while her mother, though caring, was rarely, if ever, affectionate.

Angela was a pretty child, as was her sister, and her father had a soft spot for her, but that changed as she did. When she started to become a young woman and liked the attention she received, he disapproved. For Angela, 'home' was the domain of her controlling father, while the outside world was full of possibilities, desire, and 'love'.

1964

As Angela glanced over the top of her make-up compact, she saw the tour guide looking at her through the driver's mirror. Instead of looking away politely, he stared at her. Angela felt a bit drunk for a moment, closed her powder case, turned away and looked out the window.

1964

The tour guide's ability to see into a woman's heart, to see an opportunity for seduction, didn't mean he could see anything more than the opportunity itself. It may have appeared as if he was seeing deeply into her soul, but he could barely see or understand anything of who she was, and what's more, he didn't want to. Perhaps this is what fathers instinctively sense about other men approaching their daughters, they know it's a dance of lies, but try as they might to warn their girls, they still don't understand that it takes two to dance these choreographed steps. The seducer and seduced are each other's perfect gifts.

When the tour guide touched Angela with his eyes, he could feel her need to be seduced. She knew he was watching her. She could see his image wavering in the glass of the coach window. She arched her back a little as she stretched for a moment.

The Tour Guide

Every few weeks during the summer, the tour guide would take a new party of travellers around parts of Europe. Each journey would bring him countless opportunities for seduction. Just as a stage hypnotist seeks out the susceptible from a crowd of onlookers, the tour guide could tell within seconds who would be more likely to come his way.

Just as he didn't see deeply into their heart, they never took in who he was either. It was a thrilling act of love, a playing out of the connection we all yearn for.

On one journey, the tour guide took a party of 45 women and seduced 24 of them. He said no sooner had one left his room than another would be knocking on his door. Like something from a 'Carry on' movie, the tour guide, who knew Sid James in real life, would adjust his dressing gown, light up another cigarette and beckon the next, slightly 'distressed' woman in.

Telling me this story, years later, its meaning was insignificant to him beyond making me laugh, but I couldn't help but be impressed and sad all at once.

2005 - Maria

I tell Maria, a friend of mine, about this in Tinto's Café in Fulham, as we sip on our chai lattes. She says many lonely women want sex so they can feel loved. But for me, I feel some know they are not being loved, and outside of the excitement, simulation, and stimulation, somewhere behind this "act of love", there's also an act of desperate sadness, anger, and maybe some hate too. A cry of frustration for the lack of understanding and acceptance that never came their way.

2005 - The Microwave

I was at the Tour Guide's apartment the other evening. He told me his microwave was making sparks. I thought it might just need cleaning but when he showed me the bright flame that shot across the inside when he turned it on, I told him he'd need to buy a new one, and if he wanted, I could order one over the Internet there and then. He looked at me slightly bemused. The Internet was as much a foreign land to him as his past was to me. We were from different worlds meeting briefly in the present.

1914 – 1917 Corners of Foreign Fields – Part 2

The German soldier said something, grabbed John and pulled him so they looked at each other face to face.

Chapter 2
Boris

1914 – Fulham

For John Smith's parents, John Snr and his wife Susan, life continued pretty much as it had done before their son went off to war. There'd be moments when they'd think of him and worry, but, along with most of the country, they expected the war to be over and their son to be back by Christmas.

Susan was preparing breakfast, poaching eggs, and buttering bread, as John came down the stairs of their dark terraced house in Fulham. Just as he got to the bottom step an envelope fell from the letterbox to the floor. The youngest of their children, William, picked it up and handed it to his father, but as he took it he froze.

"What is it?" William asked.

His father, still motionless, seemed to wake suddenly. "Go help your mother."

William pushed his lips together and did as he'd been told while John put the letter in his pocket and joined him and Susan in the kitchen. He sat down and proceeded to eat his breakfast in silence.

"You alright?" Susan asked.

John looked at her and nodded, but as soon as the children left the house, he took the letter from his pocket and showed it to her. As they sat together, she read it aloud to him.

Their son's dog collar had been found on a dead German soldier, and that, along with his disappearance, had led his senior officers to register him as missing in action, presumed dead. Susan reached out to John and grabbed his hand, and looking into his eyes said, "I'm telling you now, he's not dead. I'd know if he was, I'd feel it."

1934 – Boris Aged 7 – Rēzekne – Latvia

Boris gathered the last crumbs of latke (a kind of potato pancake) from his plate, then seeing his mother's back was turned, his mouth still full, he tried for a quiet exit. His eldest sister, Betty, thought otherwise, and grabbed him, "Listen you little," she paused to restrain herself, "if you make jokes about my finger again you won't make it to your eighth birthday!" She pushed him away and attempted to slap the top of his head. He ducked and roared with laughter as he made a hasty, far less discreet getaway. By the time his mother shouted after him, he was gone. She dried her hands, walked to the front door, and called his name again, but he was up the road, waving from a cart he'd jumped on bound for the town. It was raining so Boris pulled some straw over himself and through it told the cart driver he was going to the theatre.

"When I grow up, I shall sing to you from the stage to thank you for this lift."

The driver laughed, "If your mother ever gets hold of me, I doubt I'll be around."

When they reached the town Boris made his way to the theatre, walked past the queue, and took the side alley where, unseen, he scaled the wall to a second-floor window. Once inside he found a single empty seat between two couples knowing both would think he belonged to the other. As everyone joined in the sing-alongs Boris fantasised about being on stage singing, acting, and leading the audience one day too.

After the show, Boris looked out for people from his neighbourhood and casually joined them for the journey home. Again, he managed to hitch a lift where he sang to his captive, but drunkenly appreciative, audience as the snow fell.

When Boris got home the door was locked. He shouted up to the little window in the attic where he knew they'd all be sleeping.

"Mum, let me in. I'm freezing."

No answer.

"Please, it's snowing. I am sorry."

No answer.

Boris felt the tears rising, sniffed them back, looked at his inevitable bed for the night, the kennel, got in, and as the temperature dropped further, he pulled the dog close and took refuge in sleep. The next thing he felt was the dog scrambling to get out and his mother pulling both out into the cold. It was then the beating began. As she smacked and screamed at him, he cried for her to stop, but she continued until eventually, he could only surmise she didn't love him anymore.

———

Boris's mother, Esther (nee Berzin), had dark piercing eyes and long black hair with roots that went all the way back to the Jewish tribes of the Levant. When Boris was a kid he'd walk the streets in Rēzekne where sticks, stones and hurtful words would be thrown at him for being a Jew. He'd hurl those stones and hurtful words straight back at them, but no matter how hard or far he flung them, they'd burn a hole in him that could only be filled by a yearning for justice.

When Esther beat him, she would scream, "Boris why do you do these things to me?" He would tell her he loved her, but the more she beat him the more the lure of the external world, the intrigue of the night, and the excitement of danger carved a path for him to follow.

If Boris was a child in today's world he'd probably be labelled as having some kind of syndrome such as Attention Deficit Disorder and most of the other mothers in the school would be thinking what he needs is a good beating, but for Boris, the beatings were bad and certainly didn't make him good.

———

1928 - Rēzekne, Latvia

Boris's earliest memory was of being two years old when he was carried into a dark room to see his dead grandmother, Yudas, (Judy/Nechama), who was covered in a sheet and surrounded by candles. The significance of this death wasn't apparent at the time, but her passing set off a chain reaction that links to my own first memory, this being one of sitting in a hallway, looking at the doors of a nursery waiting for my mother to pick me up. As soon as the doors would open, my mother would walk in, pick me up and I'd nuzzle into her neck and hair as she hugged me.

When Esther's husband's parents had been alive the whole family lived in one of many houses the family owned. But when, in 1928, Boris entered the blacked-out room of his grandmother's wake, darkness fell upon the whole family. Boris's grandfather had died shortly before Yudas, so, she'd thought it a good time to release the capital in the properties and share it amongst the family members. Within days of doing so, though, an exceptional rise in inflation meant all that money wasn't worth the paper it was written on and within weeks they moved from being landlords to land-poor.

A few years after Yudas died, Samuel decided to go to South Africa to find work with the aim of establishing a new home for his family there. He left his wife to look after Boris and the two elder brothers Rudie also known as Hymie, (I know, it's confusing) and Eliezer. There were also two daughters, one, Betty, had been born in 1914 and was already grown up. The other, Batia, was only six. Before leaving for South Africa, Samuel took Batia to Riga, the capital of Latvia, to visit an aunt and exhausted by the long train journey she fell asleep soon after their arrival. Riga was an exciting city for a six-year-old girl and her father had promised her a tour the next day, but when she woke, he was gone. Later that morning her aunt informed her she'd be staying with them for a while. Of course, Batia was devastated, but I'm getting ahead of myself here. Don't worry, I'll tell you more about her another time.

Shortly before moving out of their old, previously owned house, Boris, who slept in the attic, fell down the attic stairs and damaged his testes. Thirty-two years later this accident would be used to try to deny the accident that created me, but a court-ordered blood test denied the denial and a settlement was agreed upon.

Within a few months, Esther had lost her home, her financial security, and a husband who'd left her with three sons to care for, one of whom seemed determined to command, demand and self-harm!

August 2005 - The Microwave

I've ordered a microwave for Boris, the Tour Guide, now. It's taken me a few days to get around to it, however, there's a pleasure in buying for other people. Like casual sex with no consequences.

1930 - Rēzekne, Latvia

The disappearance of Samuel meant Boris's waywardness would go unchecked further and consequently triggered a chain of absentee fathers that stretched through me and possibly beyond.

When Samuel arrived in South Africa, he immediately shirked his responsibilities and acted like a single man once more. As Esther was left to fend for herself, she slowly grew ill while at the same time, Boris and his brothers experienced their childhood under the encroaching clouds of World War 2.

1936 to 1939 - Rudie

Rudie, aka Hymie, was Boris's eldest brother and in many ways was his opposite. Boris once told me he was his father's favourite because they were both the black sheep of the family, but when it came to white sheep, none were ever as luminescent as Hymie. Fortunately for the rest of the family, Hymie sensed their need to escape Europe, so, he decided to make his way to South Africa where he'd join his father and remind him of the original plan.

Six years had passed since Samuel had left his family to fend for themselves but within two years of Hymie arriving, they'd saved enough money to buy tickets for Esther, Eliezer, and Boris to join them. Meanwhile, Boris's sisters had both settled in Riga, so, they chose not to go to South Africa.

1938

Soon after arriving in Johannesburg, Boris's mother, already emaciated and ill from the journey, collapsed and was diagnosed as having breast cancer. Boris told me that in her last weeks, she screamed in agony and begged to be put out of her misery. If there was pain relief, they couldn't afford it.

Her desire to get her children to safety, to a better life, had been fulfilled, but for her, beyond that, there was no consolation and within days she died.

Soon after, Hymie told Boris a psychic had told him they would come to South Africa and their mother would die before 1940.

"Why didn't you tell me?" Boris asked.

13

Hymie sighed, "What good would it have done?"

2005 - The Homeless

I often have people say to me that because I have short arms it makes them appreciate their lot is not so bad after all. At one time I used to work with homeless people, and I'd occasionally hear them say they thought they'd "had it bad" 'til they saw me. Yet, I'd be thinking about how much better my life was compared to theirs. But when I think of the likes of Esther, her mother, or her 13 dead siblings, I realise just how lucky most of us are.

One advantage I have found of appearing burdened with a tragic life is homeless people begging on the street rarely ask me for any money. Instead, they wave at me and greet me as a brother in arms, even if it's a shorter one than normal.

On my first day working in a homeless people's resource centre, I even got away with hurrying everyone away at closing time with, "Come on you lot, haven't you got any homes to go to?"

1930s - Johannesburg

Once Esther died, Samuel had Boris put into a local orphanage, but Boris ran away, so, his father let him live at home, even so, he spent most of the time on the streets. Sixty-two years later I sat and watched Boris cry because he couldn't stand to be kept in hospital any longer as he recuperated from a stroke. For Boris, feeling restricted was an anathema. Ironically, he didn't find the army restrictive, so by the time he was 14 and World War Two had broken out, he leapt at the opportunity to join the struggle.

Along with a lot of other young men, he queued in the heat of the Johannesburg midday sun and eventually stood in front of Colonel Molineux who asked him his age. Boris told him he was seventeen, but he was informed he'd still need his father's signature, at which point Molineux handed him the form. Boris went away for a couple of hours, signed it himself, then returned it and within weeks was serving as a medical orderly on the front line in Kenya and Abyssinia against the Italians.

I have a photograph of Boris taken during this period, and he looked like me when I was 14, only he was wearing a soldier's uniform that looked too big for him, while

14

I dressed up like Fonzi from *Happy Days*. We both looked seventeen by the way, but I just used my mature looks to get into pubs, rather than battlegrounds.

As the weeks went by, Boris befriended another soldier from Johannesburg who sent a letter back to his girlfriend expressing his concern that Boris didn't seem to have anyone back home. Feeling sorry for him she sent Boris a parcel for Christmas. Perhaps this act of kindness jogged Boris's feelings of connection to his family and noticing this, his friend got his girlfriend to let Boris's father know where he was and reassure him he was safe. A few weeks later Boris's captain, Finley Edgington, entered Boris's tent and told him they'd received a report that Boris had signed up fraudulently. Boris went very quiet. Edgington said, "I know you don't want to go back, and we all like you and don't want you to go either, but if you say nothing, we'll have no alternative but to send you back immediately. But if you say this is true and you want to stay then we can send a request back to your father asking for permission for you to continue in the army. If he says no then we'll have to send you back but that might take weeks before we get the orders, which will be better than going today." Boris opened up to him, and after several weeks of waiting, he was indeed ordered to return home, which he did so, begrudgingly. However, as soon as Boris turned 16, he re-enlisted but this time was sent to India, where at first he was in the Tank Corps and later involved in moving horses and mules.

One of the other members of his company had also been a school friend named Barney Smith. One day they were summoned to a meeting at the transportation depot. Their Commander asked for volunteers to go on an expedition that involved travelling by boat. Barney stepped forward, no doubt anticipating a pleasant day out, but Boris grabbed him and told him not to go, so, Barney took his advice. The boat was sunk and everyone on it died, including the Commander. One day I met Barney, and Boris said, "Hey, Barney, remember when I saved your life?"

Barney said, "Of course, I do."

"Well," Boris added, "When you die leave some of your money to my son Simon here."

Barney looked at me and said, "Don't you worry Simon, I'll remember you."

But he didn't.

1997 - Psychic or Psycho-Neurotic

Incidents such as Boris saving Barney's life are possibly just coincidences to which we attach greater significance than we should. Still, there have been many such coincidences in my life that I find hard to dismiss so readily. Consequently, I can't help but be a little open-minded to there being more to them than meets the eye. I shall share some of these incidents with you as we go on, but in the meantime here's one, and yes, it's a bit tenuous, but it'll do to get started with.

I didn't get to meet Boris until I was in my mid-thirties and had only ever written one poem which mentioned him. In it, I wrote the line, "Am I psychic or neurotic?" During our first-ever meeting, I videoed Boris who looked at the camera and said, "Am I psychic or psycho-neurotic?" And as he said those words the poem came back to me. I can't prove there's such a thing as telepathy, or pre-cognition, or the ability to speak to the dead, but this aspect, the world of the sixth sense, is one that both Boris and I seem to have had some experience of, yet both of us doubt it is real too.

While we may share that gene, there are two others that he didn't hand down to me. One was his aptitude for languages, he speaks around 12 of them to a practical standard, (which means he speaks them well enough to chat women up with), and the other is his thick mop of hair. I used to think I'd like to have his linguistic skills. OK, I speak English, a bit of French, a tiny bit of Japanese and a lot of Rubbish, but now, as I'm balding I think I'd prefer the hair!

2005 - Radio Show

Yesterday evening I went to a Radio 4 recording of a comedian called Adam Bloom. During the warm-up he interacted with the audience and at one point pointed out my hair was receding, I nodded at him and agreed it was. As I looked at him, I thought he looked Jewish, and his name was probably a shortened version of Bloomberg, although I may be wrong, and because of that, I felt there was some kind of kinship between us. Of course, I am not Jewish, especially in terms of Jewish doctrines, because my mother was not Jewish, but to a Nazi, I'd be one. Even among my non-Nazi-non-Jewish friends, once they're aware of my Jewish heritage, they often treat me as if I am Jewish. The issue of being Jewish has had very little impact on me, still though, I enjoy the idea of having links to such a contentious part of the world's population, even if I don't wholly belong to it either. Ironically when I was a child, I was quick, along with everyone I knew, to use the term "You Jew!" in a derogatory manner, never suspecting I was, technically speaking, Jewish too.

July 2005 - The Hilton

A few years ago, I walked onto the balcony of my room at the Hilton Metropole in Brighton and spoke to my mother on my mobile phone. As we chatted, she told me about a time when she'd stood outside the same hotel as a child and heard her father spit out the words, "See that woman coming out of that place, the one in a fur coat and all those jewels, she's a Jew!" And another time, when she shopped in London's Oxford Street, her parents would warn her not to go into some of the shops there as they were owned by Jews who would "drag you in and not let you go until you've bought something."

1940s - Unknown Soldiers

Boris shoots his gun at a soldier's head. This is the real unknown soldier, the one soldiers know they've killed, who they will know for the rest of their lives even though they'll never know who they were. They are the ones they do not mention, who they try to forget but remember, who they hope will greet them at Heaven's gates and forgive them.

When Boris returned from the war, he knocked on his father's door and an English woman answered, it turned out she was Samuel's new wife. Boris told her who he was, but she wouldn't let him in and suggested he come back later when Samuel was back. Boris went up the street to his aunt's house and returned later as requested. As he approached, he could hear the English woman and Samuel arguing about her not welcoming his son in, which to him was tantamount to a mortal sin, even if this was a tad hypocritical given, he hadn't helped Boris when he was a child. It wasn't long after this incident, and partly because of it, they divorced. However, maybe all wasn't as it seemed because a short while later, Samuel married for a third time. This time it was to a large German woman whom Boris seemed to like, which must have been a bit of a relief to Samuel, given his new policy on getting his kids' approval when it came to wives.

Boris, like so many soldiers after the war, found he was at a loss when it came to what to do next. He was unqualified, inexperienced and restless. At first, life became a series of exciting adventures, bouts of drinking, gambling and getting women to sleep with him. As hard as he tried, he wasn't prepared to fit into 'civvy-street', so, he joined a fun-fair and worked as a showman in a gambling tent.

If you've seen the film Big Fish, you might think there's a similarity between my father's story and the main character's. The significant difference though is that Big Fish wraps itself around a love story, but I don't have one to share with you about Boris. Boris and I occasionally argue over whether I should give as much as I do when I love someone. It is an abomination for him to feel needy, let alone tell a woman about such feelings. Perhaps it was his dislocation from such feelings that made him so attractive to women. After all, it can be very off-putting to experience neediness in another, as I've often found out and still haven't learned to curtail. So, maybe it was the brief, fun, and non-entangling relationship Boris offered to most of his prey that drew them to him so readily, except of course, when things didn't go to plan, and they fell pregnant.

1946-48 - Moving On

The fun-fair work was seasonal, so Boris decided to join the merchant navy during the winter months, and for the next few years migrated back and forth between these two worlds.

In 1948, partly as reparations for the Arab anti-Semitic position throughout World War 2, and partly due to Zionist pressure on the League of Nations to find a solution to the "Jewish problem", along with a whole host of other factors, it was agreed to create the State of Israel.

The surrounding Arab States of Jordan, Syria and Egypt made it known they wouldn't tolerate this, so, as the date for Israel's independence approached tension mounted on all sides. Boris's brother Eliezer lived on a kibbutz in the middle of Israel and was also a member of the Palmach, a strike force set up in 1941 to protect Palestine from the Nazis by the British Military and Haganah. The British trained some of them as "special operations soldiers" to help the British invade Syria and Lebanon, but in 1942 the British victory at El-Alamein meant the Palmach was no longer of any use, so it was officially disbanded. As a result, the whole organisation went underground.

The call to arms came to Boris who jumped aboard the Danish-owned and Israel-bound ship, the Birkalandis, which was mainly a cargo ship but also carried 15 other passengers who also had the same intention. As soon as they arrived, they were all loaded onto a truck and taken to a camp. Within days, Boris was given the position of machine gunner, firstly on the back of jeeps but later in armoured cars.

Whatever one's position regarding Israel, one can't help but admire that in this instance the Israelis fought off a three-sided attack by opponents who seemed to have the upper hand.

2005 - Research

I am around at Boris's drinking tea and writing notes about this time in his life. My partner, Monica, has decided we ought to split up, so, I'm spending more time with my family and using writing this as an excuse to go around more regularly than normal. "Finally," I think, "I can get some exciting war stories from Boris", but he's not having it. Next time I'm going to bring a bottle of Scotch and some truth drugs!

1946 - Boris and the Seamen Strike

After World War Two, Boris went back to the navy mainly bringing Jewish refugees to Israel from Morocco and Marseilles. While waiting on the docks Boris noticed that all the black Jews were being turned away from working on the boats. He'd become involved in the Communist party in recent months, thinking that it might help his sister Batia who was trapped in Russia if he was seen as part of the system, and due to this involvement, he'd become more aware of some of the social injustices around him. Watching these men being turned away left him seething with anger so he decided to do something about it.

Most of the waiters, cleaners and general dogsbodies on his ship were non-Jewish Italians, so, Boris spread a rumour about a possible attack by an anti-Semitic organisation on the route back to Israel. The casual staff thought better of the risks involved and didn't come to work on the departure date. When the ship got back to Israel Boris went straight to some of the local left-wing papers and got a few articles published calling for a demonstration demanding that black Jewish people should no longer be discriminated against by these companies. Within hours of publication, the local hotels were warned off letting Boris reside with them and told him so. As a result, Boris managed to wangle spending the next few weeks sleeping in the prostitutes' quarters.

When he told me this bit of the story I did wonder if this was all an elaborate tale to explain why he spent so much time with prostitutes during this period, but he showed me a few newspaper articles relating to this incident so just to be sociable I'll take his word.

Come the day of the demonstration he and a few hundred striking seamen started their protest. Two policemen approached Boris, both holding sub-machine guns at their waists pointing toward him. He walked up to them and filled with anger said in a hushed but vitriolic tone, "You can kill me but these guys all have long knives, and it won't be long before you feel one go through your back if you do!" Their guns lowered slowly, and they backed off as one said, "You can have your say, but make sure there's no trouble." Soon afterwards a few black Jewish people started to be employed by the shipping companies involved. But for Boris, it was time to lay low, that's if you don't consider laying in the prostitutes' quarters low already, so he sailed to England. Nowadays, telling such a story would probably have levelled at it, 'white-saviour syndrome' but for Boris, that sense of injustice had come from his own experiences of being persecuted, rather than a need to feel virtuous while simultaneously diminishing the power of those he was trying to help. Remember, no good deed goes unpunished.

1952 - London at First Sight

When it came to London it was love at first sight for Boris. It was exciting, it was grimy, and it was full of potential, so it wasn't long after he arrived that he discovered a scam where he could use people he knew who worked in South Africa House to help him develop a "fast-track" system for those with the cash to not only get their immigration papers sorted but also a place on a boat. For this Boris would get the fee from the "clients" and a commission from the boat operators. A good little number, but the secret of a long life is knowing when it's time to leave, so, Boris cut his profits and took a ride upon a boat bound to Canada.

1940s - Canada

In just a few days upon arriving in Canada, Boris arrived in Nova Scotia, took a train to Montreal, found accommodation in a religious Jewish family house, and got a job in a factory. After week one the foreman sacked him for shoddy work so Boris went to the boss and gave him a sob story that his work was shoddy because he hadn't eaten for days so the boss gave him another chance. The factory was making parts destined to be used in the Korean war so it was working 24 hours a day. Boris came in on the night shift and watched how they did it. He asked how many of these items they'd make in an hour and was told about 20. So when Boris was creating 28 per hour by the end of his first "educated" day he got a sharp warning from his fellow workers. Ever the communist, Boris thought, "Fuck them, I need the dough" and compromised a bit by dropping down to 26 units per hour. At the end of the week, he was called into the boss' office. "What now?" he thought, but to his surprise, he was given a pay rise and an apology from the foreman who sacked him in the first place. Needless to say, Boris still wasn't popular with his workmates.

It was a bad winter; work relations were frosty, and his hosts were not much warmer. Boris would lie in bed at night and could hear:

"Mary, you like it?"

"Don't bother!"

"Mary, you like it?"

"Don't bother."

"Mary, you like it?"

"Yes, I like it"

Boris laughed and blew smoke rings up to the ceiling.

After a few months, Boris realised he didn't like working in the factory anymore and decided it was time to sail off into the sunset.

He noticed an Israeli ship was coming into the local port and needed a qualified oiler, (whatever that is), so Boris contacted the boat company and made his way to meet it, but the ship was nowhere to be found. Boatless and cold Boris looked through the telephone directory and called a local Rabbi. He told him that there was a boat coming in a few days which was the first to come to this port from Israel and what a wonderful gesture it would be to throw a welcome party for them. The Rabbi, probably feeling somewhat cornered agreed. Boris met up with, befriended and lodged with him for the few days wait.

When the boat arrived it only had a few Israelis aboard, the rest were English, however, the gesture didn't go unnoticed, and Boris had in the process ingratiated himself with his new crewmates. One of them, the boson, was a black Jew whom Boris had previously got a job for, but as he went to greet Boris, Boris put his finger to his mouth because he also recognised the chief purser as someone he'd antagonised during the strike. The Purser half-recognised Boris but couldn't place him at first but a few days later he did and immediately telegraphed ahead that he was on the boat.

Boris was in the engine room when the boat pulled into Haifa. Four police officers came down and started to arrest him, but Boris informed them that because he was sailing on Canadian Articles, they couldn't arrest him until he was on shore. In fact, he told them to fuck off, but he did present a good legal case as well.

He was put on open arrest and the shipping company boss came to see him to ask what he was up to. He explained that he didn't intend to cause any trouble, so an amnesty was agreed.

Advert Break

For ducking, diving and boat engine driving $2000

For high productivity and low popularity $1000

For having a party thrown in your honour and for standing up to the boss.

Priceless and jobless.

End of Advert Break

Leaving South Africa

With an adventure under his belt and a wad of money in his pocket, Boris flew to South Africa. If travel makes you look at your hometown with a different perspective that is especially true when there have been dramatic changes in the meantime. In the intervening years, South Africa had brought in Apartheid which essentially legalised racism. It came as quite a surprise to Boris who had suffered at the hands of anti-Semitic peers as both a youth and adult to suddenly find that he was part of the oppressive regime. In an attempt to make amends, Boris endeavoured to have sex with an equal number of women from all ethnic groups. This, however, did not go down well with the authorities.

One evening, Boris visited a black neighbourhood, got a bit drunk and started to make his way home alone. Ahead of him, two young black women were being noisy, laughing and shouting at boys. Then a small group of police officers turned towards them and one of them shouted, "Shut up you black bitch".

"Hey, don't talk to them like that!" Boris retorted.

And within seconds the police officers started to beat Boris with their sticks. Even though being inebriated meant Boris didn't feel the full force of the law at that precise moment, he was bedridden for several weeks as a result of his injuries.

When Boris eventually came out to play again, he was preoccupied with this incident. So much so, that he decided to seek out his revenge. As it turned out though, it wasn't to be as calculated an affair as he'd probably hoped for. Instead, just by coincidence, he saw the officer who'd shouted at the women walking towards him down a side street. Boris ducked into an alleyway where he saw a metal bar and decided to make the best of a bad job. No one else was around so as the officer passed the alley Boris stepped out and smashed the bar across the back of the officer's head. Fortunately for Boris, the officer did not turn around and ask what he'd done that for but conveniently dropped to the floor where Boris crashed the bar down upon his collar bone, which he heard a crack from and then hit him a third time across his back. Boris looked around for witnesses, but there didn't seem to be any, so, he walked away calmly.

Boris's eldest brother still lived in Johannesburg and was a minor celebrity as a long-distance (100 km) runner and jewellery shop owner. Also, Boris had become quite well known to the police when he worked in the fun fair as he'd been the one bribing the police to let the fair gamble. The hot-headed and radical Boris knew he wasn't anonymous enough to get away with this act of retribution, so, he decided to go back to England.

He'd often tell people he left South Africa because of Apartheid, but the fear of being prosecuted for attempted murder was the real one.

1914 John Smith Jnr – Fulham

After the letter arrived John's parents tried to hide the truth from the rest of the family, but it was obvious something bad was in the air, everything felt loaded with more than its own weight. The kids spoke amongst each other and surmised something may have happened to their older brother, but they knew that if he'd been killed, they'd have been told by now, so this left them a little perplexed.

Crookham Road was one of many that angled off Fulham Road, so consequently was generally a quiet residential street. But 4 days after the letter arrived the clatter of horses' hooves and the sound of a soldier giving orders in the early evening brought the family to the front room window where, given it was already dark, it was hard to make out what was going on. But what was now clear was two of the soldiers were marching up to the front door. John Snr and Susan, now filled with dread looked at each other. When the soldiers knocked on the door John and Susan took each other's hands and made their way to them.

As the door opened the soldiers took off their hats and asked if this was the residence of John Frederick Smith, father of John Frederick Smith. When John nodded, one of the soldiers asked if they could come to the cart to identify their son before the orderlies brought him in. John and Sarah looked at each other and almost knocking the soldiers off their feet bustled past and rushed down to what they hoped was their son. When they got to the man, they looked at him, his face was swollen and bearded and for a few seconds they wondered if there'd been a mistake, but as the man opened his eyes he quietly said, "Mum, dad, what are you doing in France?" Susan, crying now looked at the orderlies, "Yes, it's my son John. Please bring him in." As they did, Susan held his hand and talking to the cold winter night sky kept repeating, "I knew he wasn't dead."

It would be a few days before John became strong enough to tell of what had happened, and of course, there was no explanation as to how he'd become registered as missing in action, but his last memories from the battlefield included being shot, falling into the mud and a German soldier approaching him. He thought he was just about to be killed but instead, the soldier, who was tall and had a big beard, helped him get comfortable, gave him some water and took one of his dog tags with him when he left.

"I couldn't understand a word he was saying, but I knew he didn't want to hurt me. I don't think he wanted to hurt anyone. And... and when I realised that at that very moment, I knew I didn't want to hurt him either. If I could have, I'd have shaken his hand and hugged him in thanks."

John Snr interrupted, "I'm sorry to tell you son, but I think he might be dead. They found your dog tag on his body and that made them think you'd been killed."

John Jr pushed his tongue under his bottom lip and barely able to speak, whispered, "I owe him my life."

Susan stroked his forehead, "We'll always be thankful for his kindness John, and we'll say a prayer for him every night for the rest of our lives. We'll never forget him."

John Jr nodded, bit his lip, and furrowed his brow."

Chapter 3
Angela

1942 - First Memories

Angela's first memory was being held in her mother's arms while she pointed at the distant anti-aircraft gunfire glistening amongst the stars. For her first three years, most nights were spent sleeping in the air raid shelter which, shaped like an old gipsy caravan, caused her to imagine travelling to mythical worlds as she'd fall asleep, and some nights she was sure she did. But one morning the ground shook her awake as a bomb fell nearby, when a badly damaged Luftwaffe plane kindly emptied its payload as it descended, blowing in the windows of her house, and knocking a few tiles off the roof. Angela's brother, Sydney, came back a few hours later saying he'd found the burnt-out plane and removed the papers from the bodies of the crew. No doubt his ability to act with such cold efficiency also contributed to his later success as a bank manager.

1940s - The Cost of Bombs

Between 1985 and 2004 I lived in a flat in a terraced house in Fulham, London. During World War Two it was bombed when, once again a shot-up German bomber careered towards the river Thames. As with the one that crashed near my mum's place, this one's crew also emptied their bombs as well, etching upon the landscape a line of craters, fires and tales of devastation that ended in the ultimate crash course of arrivals.

One of the bombs they jettisoned, an incendiary device, landed on the house I lived in on Bronsart Road, which set it on fire. This was forty-two years before I moved in, I hasten to add. The fire brigade turned up, extinguished the smouldering roof, and found the air raid shelter in the backyard full of black-market petrol. The owner was summarily arrested and charged while the bodies of the crew were buried in the cemetery just behind the house.

My next-door neighbours in the mid-1980s, Nellie, Elsie, and Claude, told me this story. At the time they were still shuffling to the outside toilet through wintry nights and cleaning themselves at the kitchen sink. For them, the 1940s and 80s were but a moment apart from each other. World War Two did not end in 1945 but continues to fade around us today. Just as the Big Bang Theory proposes there's a background hum of radioactive "noise" crackling around the universe as a direct result of the initial singularity, the same goes for most of our traumas. There's a symphony of hums within us that continually reminds us of the sufferings that originally touched us.

During the last years of Elsie and Claude living together, having been married for fifty years, he became demented and abused his wife verbally. She would come around to my place crying in her nightgown because she didn't know how to cope, saying she'd had fifty wonderful years with him, but never imagined it would end like this. That's the thing about endings, apart from us being sure there will be one, the 'how' and 'when' tend to come to us very unexpectedly.

2005 – Our Unappreciated Potency

Many of us feel we have no potency or effect on others, but even when merely passing someone we may enter their mind's internal dramas and affect them without us ever doing or saying anything apart from just being there. To think, a look we give someone, or the words we say have no effect, isn't realistic at all. We're continually affecting the world and those around us, even if we believe we've gone completely unnoticed.

I used to hide my arms when I was in public, but now I think people seeing me will probably provoke some questions and feelings in their minds. Of course, I can't control where their thoughts go, or if it's ultimately a good or bad thing, but just as if I'd skimmed a stone across a pond, I know I'm sending ripples out, and there's something very satisfying about that.

Angela – 1950s

Angela didn't do particularly well at school. From puberty onwards, she had the added complication of an undiagnosed condition, Narcolepsy, which manifested itself as sudden periods of drowsiness. This combined with her lack of interest in a subject made learning very difficult, however, where she did have some talent was in her artistic pursuits, especially dancing, ice skating, and painting. When I was at Art College, I had a lecturer who said that make-up artists were latent painters, so, I'd better add to Angela's list "latent sculptor" because at 15 she left school to become a hairdresser.

Angela Cutting a Girl's Hair.

When Angela was nine years old, she noticed a boy called Ian and immediately fell for him. He was older than her but by the time she was fourteen, they started seeing each other. Ian, who was studying art, adored her, as she did him, but one day, as if a comedy songwriter was pulling the strings of fate, the son of the local greengrocer caught her eye too, so she dumped the Artist and pulled out a plumb. A short while later realising the mistake she'd made, she dumped the greengrocer's son and got back with the Artist. This time though the Artist's vision of his muse was damaged, so, while still enthralled by her beauty, he began to notice the differences between reality and his dream girl. Then one day, as they made love, she felt like he was no longer thinking about her and sure enough, a short while later he left her and moved on forever.

Angela was devastated. If one of the first stages in dealing with trauma is denial, then it was here she became stuck. For Angela, the dream became one of her and the Artist reuniting but while she harboured this, she couldn't accept that he was gone. The space in her heart for a new love was still occupied by her dream man and as Freud phrased it, she was "trapped in the grave" of a relationship. Unable to move on to pastures new. With her heart still engaged to an absent 'other', her body found solace in acts of love and hate, and this is where my father came in.

If Angela represents the face of a coin that doesn't let go of those we love, then Boris represents the other, the one that can't ever hold on to anyone. This is the bad penny that's passed from one generation to the next, the hard currency of love between parents and their children, and when some of it is counterfeit, then it may be perceived as a lack of love. If both my parents had their issues, then my perception of not being loved enough was about me, but in reality, it was all about them. Even so, there was no way I was ever going to get away with it unscathed.

Angela – 1958

When Angela was eighteen, she became pregnant. Knowing full well her parents would have been mortified, she went to a back-street abortionist who used a syringe to pierce her embryonic sack, and unsurprisingly, when she got home afterwards, she started to feel very ill. A doctor was called who quickly worked out what had happened and suggested to her parents that by using the excuse that she was mentally unfit to be a mother, they could legally obtain an abortion through a private clinic. So, her parents hurriedly got a Harley Street doctor to create the necessary paperwork and within two days the matter was dealt with. But for Angela, who was already making emotional connections with the "baby", it was far from over. While in the recovery unit, she tried to see the children who'd just been born but was pulled aside and told to go back to sleep. When she came home the sense of shame and failure bore down on her so powerfully that she was unable to grieve. However, years later she saw Mr Moppet, a "psychic", who, maybe taking a calculated guess, referred to there being a child, "who was alright," and whether this was just a lucky break as far as he was concerned, it was also one for Angela too, because it allowed her to cry about this episode for the first time finally.

For me as well, the abortion was significant because when my mother realised at twenty-four, that she was pregnant again, she decided she couldn't go through another abortion and knew before we ever met, she wanted me.

Chapter 4
The Ending of a Beginning

The Church Spire

I have often seen that church's spire from my window but until this morning I'd never heard its bells. Everything right now feels like it's in slow motion. We walk from the house, across the road, to the car and as we get there a couple pass us pushing a child in a buggy. I get in the car as you lean over the passenger seat organising your bags, a car passes too close, too fast. I feel its danger. "What would happen if they lost control?" I say, but you're not sure what I'm going on about. We set off, the first two speed bumps hurt you, so, I slow down, and on these quiet Sunday morning roads, we make our way.

A Few Days Earlier

Driving home I call to see if you're still at the house, you ask me how long I'll be, "I'll be there in 5 to 10 minutes". Normally when I come home, I call out to say hello but this time I don't. There's just silence and as I get to the top of the stairs, you're sitting on the sofa in the dining room, cigarette in hand. I want to greet you with a kiss, but your poise says not to. You nod towards the table. I'm not sure what I should be looking at, but as I scan the clutter, I see a pregnancy test showing a positive result. I ask you how you feel, and you say, "Nothing".

I walk towards you to hug you, but as I bend down, I knock the ashtray over you. As I clear it up, I ask if you feel this was symbolic, you half laugh, "Yes, it's a fucking mess".

---

200 Yearning Texts

Over Christmas, you'd gone on holiday with a friend and somewhere amid 200 yearning text messages, you'd asked me to, "come inside you" upon your return. To play, as you put it "Russian Roulette between the sheets." So, after picking you up, we made our way to yours, handed each other the revolver, clicked back the hammer, and pulled hard on the trigger.

In the logical madness of passion, I wanted you to fall pregnant. A month before you'd previously come on late and told me you'd started to get used to the idea. But this time, you didn't think it'd be possible anyway as you were still on, so we spun the chamber without fear. The next day I came inside you again, but this time you looked shocked and scared as if I'd betrayed you, so from then on, we returned to playing safe. For some who lose at Russian Roulette, when the bullet hits the brain, there's probably a moment when they think the gun didn't go off.

Unspoken Words

As the month drew on you felt as if you'd ovulated, but then started feeling smothered and sensing that, I felt scared. You went off sex and I felt even more insecure. Up till then, I thought we'd be together for a long time, but these changes said otherwise. You started to feel pain in your groin and womb, and your breasts felt tender, but still, we both reassured each other your period was late due to stress. In my gut though, I knew.

When we spoke about it and you said you hoped you weren't pregnant, I asked if you were thinking about an abortion and when you said you were, my heart sank. You made it clear, you didn't want a child now, but I also heard those extra unspoken words, "a child with you."

Blindsided

Later in the evening, after the pregnancy test, you searched the internet for information about terminating a pregnancy and came across the Marie Stopes website. They had a 24-hour, 365 days a year, telephone line which you called. Within minutes you'd booked an appointment for the following day. Several times as you browsed the website the page just closed without any obvious reason. I'd never seen it do that before, so, took it as a sign we shouldn't go ahead, but you didn't see it that way at all. You asked me what I wanted, so, I told you I didn't want to terminate "it". But I loved you so would support whatever your decision was. Then, as we got into bed, I kissed each of your breasts and your stomach. You asked me what I was doing. I said I was kissing "it" goodbye. Unsurprisingly, you told me you found it disturbing and I wasn't helping matters, especially given you were only just keeping it together and you started to cry. Of course, I look back at this moment from the future and see what I did as cruel and cringe, but even now I kind of understand us both simultaneously, these were desperate times and my love for you was still based on a love for myself. We both saw a future beckoning and neither of us wanted it.

It was clear we had very different objectives and instead of us both taking on board that maybe we also shared some common ground we took our positions and saw each other as a little blindsided. You turned your back and went to sleep, but in the night you reached out.

The Next Day

The system at the Marie Stope's Centre did not lend itself to anonymity. Just like any doctor's waiting area, we were all on show to each other. First, we were called in to pay the consultation fee, then a doctor asked what the reason for the termination was. My partner said she felt, "physically and emotionally unfit to go through a pregnancy". The doctor wrote the words down without question. Counselling pre-and-post-termination was offered, but my partner opted for the latter only.

Even though it was me who'd pointed out the centre's 24-hour telephone line and therefore instigated the "fast track" approach in the first place, I justified it to myself because I didn't want to be part of a process that terminated a foetus with a functioning nervous system. If we delayed further, it may have been a matter of weeks before the termination could be arranged. Still, I hadn't quite expected it to be within 12 hours. Nervous system or not, week 1, 8 or 28 it still felt like a possible human to me.

The next job for the doctor was to scan the womb using an ultrasonic device. I'd had a number of children before, so, I was used to seeing foetuses of 14 weeks upwards, and I was dreading seeing anything that resembled those previous images. My partner asked me if looking would be a good idea. I felt that if I saw a human-like figure I would have had to ask my partner to re-evaluate the situation. However, what the doctor zoomed in on was a small floating dot. To me, this half-formed shape that floated in silence wasn't a human-shaped embryo, nor was it a connected nervous system, but instead a mass of potential. I convinced myself my future child was not going to feel anything, but I was still haunted by whether it had a soul or not. I looked at my partner and reassured her that what was there wasn't going to suffer physically. But I didn't know, not really.

After the scan, my partner had to provide a urine sample, but she hadn't drunk anything for hours, and as she may have had to have a general anaesthetic, the 'nil by mouth' rule had to be followed. The consequence of that was there was a very slim chance of her peeing. We both went into the disabled loo together, as this had been the nature of our relationship, very intimate, very 'get to know who you really are'. Finally, she managed to fill the file.

Once the initial assessment was completed there was a short walk from one building to another a few streets away. My partner referred to the street as, "Termination Terrace," where all the neighbours watched the comings and goings. As we got to the building there were several doors to choose from, I opted for the wrong one, whereas my partner got it right the first time. Once in, the same people who'd gradually left the previous building were also waiting. It was like a scene from Kafka's *The Trial*. Eventually, the time came for my partner to go upstairs, we kissed goodbye, told each other we loved each other, and then, once she was gone, I was told to come back at 4 p.m.

I walked to the front door where another man was going out too. As the door closed behind us, he adjusted his coat, I sighed and said, "It's an awful thing this." He looked at me and nodded, "Yes, it is".

"Do you want to come for a cup of tea with me?" I asked.

He nodded again, and said, "That's a good idea".

We went for our tea, exchanged our stories, and through our time together – one of those immediate connection meetings – I felt and reported to him my pangs of awful loss and wondered at which moment the termination was taking place. He said he was wondering the same.

Shortly after returning at 4 pm, my partner emerged, a little bit shaky and smiling as usual. The journey home was gentle.

Later that evening my friend Denise knocked on my door and asked if I wanted to come to a party. I said I couldn't because my partner was ill. She looked at me with a concerned look and said, "Don't forget your friends."

The next day my sons came around to play and understandably my partner didn't want to join in. To her the place was a mess, nothing was organised in a good way for her and when we'd been out a bit earlier she felt the crowds too threatening, and worried about being bumped into. At that point, she snapped at me that I wasn't paying attention to her needs.

After my kids had gone back to their mum's and she was still clearing up I went into a room away from her, but a bit later she came up behind me and put her arms around me and sobbed. She said sorry for having a go so I told her it was alright, that I understood and hadn't taken it personally. We went into another room and sat together, and for the next hour or so talked and broke into crying fits as the feelings of grief began to strike home. No matter how logical the justification, the doubts, fears and awful feelings of loss kept sweeping over us. Later, we cried less but the little things that set off the thoughts and feelings surrounding this were everywhere.

Needless to say, in time, the relationship ended, and even now I feel one day I'll have to face my unborn child and ask for forgiveness. But then the same may be true for both my sons and daughters who got to live too.

The Doors of Unreality - 1958

Angela wakes from a dream where she hears a baby swaddled in a basket crying from the doorstep of her parent's house. She gets out of bed, walks downstairs and opens the front door but there's no one there. She goes back up to her bedroom, and as she steps onto the landing, she sees her mother watching her from her doorway. "What are you doing?" her mother asks. Looking up, Angela answers, "I thought I heard someone at the door." Her mother scowls, "What at this time of night?" "I must have dreamt it," Angela says quietly. Her mother shakes her head in disbelief, "Now, go back to bed before you get a cold."

Dream

I woke from a dream where I was back in the termination assessment clinic but had to go through a doorway because I was scared of a Dalek patrolling the area. Once through the doorway, I found myself in an unending wasteland. I felt like I'd been banished from the Garden of Eden and wanted to go back through the door, but the Dalek kept screeching, "Exterminate!" and I knew if I was to face it, I would die.

———

Chapter 5
The Myth of Trust

Outliving the Myth of Trust

Billy Bragg, the politically inspired singer-songwriter, once wrote about outliving the myth of trust. I recently had a few friends read over the first drafts of this and they all questioned the validity of Boris's stories. I told Boris this and he suggested that maybe I tone down his stories so people would find them easier to believe. But I guess, in a way, you're going to have to trust that as far as I can I'm going to be as honest with you as I can be. If anything, there will be times when I have toned things down, both for legal reasons and the protection of those also involved. I realise trust is a hard-earned and fragile commodity, so I hope you'll at least accept, I'll try my best.

The Pros and Cons of Snooping

One day I was in a hotel room in Israel with my father and Barney Smith, when I told them I was going somewhere for five minutes and left my PDA in audio record mode. When I got back, I let them know what I'd done and asked if I could have a listen. They said yes. Most of the conversation involved Boris telling Barney about my mother, which was quite interesting. However, listening in on someone talking about oneself or reading someone else's diary is something I've learnt through painful experiences to be a precarious pursuit. Even so, I can sometimes still feel a bit tempted to do it, especially if I believe something is amiss when it comes to myths and truths.

When I was seventeen, I looked at a girlfriend's diary and saw the words "The bastard. Simon came around". Once I saw this, I couldn't contain myself and asked her about it. She showed it to me and I realised that the words "the Bastard" referred to the previous few lines' rant about a teacher. The full stop between Bastard and Simon made all the difference, but in my glance, I didn't notice it. In that situation, I not only revealed my paranoia but also made it very clear I'd pried. I also discovered that firstly, I wasn't strong enough to burden myself with a secret, and secondly, the cost of snooping was far more emotionally tolling than it was worth.

The Brutality of Honesty

Tonight I was out with Monica, well we've just split up and are trying to remain friends. We were sitting in a theatre bar chatting with a mutual friend when I needed to go to the toilet, so, I turned my phone to silent because my ex hates its petulant ring and walked away. When I returned, I picked the phone up to turn its ringer back on and realised it was recording. At that moment, I was torn between letting them know it had recorded them and waiting to have a listen later. As I thought it through my ex said, "Why are you recording us?"

"For fuck's sake!" I thought to myself.

I hadn't cared about whatever they were likely to say about me, I was just being a bit nosey, or paranoid, but now, with this happening I finally understood she and I had outlived the myth of trust, and this was the end.

In time though, I realised what mattered more was whether I had any trust in myself, and it was clear right then I didn't. I'd had therapy and found it hard to be completely honest, and likewise, I wasn't totally open in many of my other relationships, including the one with Monica. With that in mind, I realised trusting in myself was going to be something I'd have to develop if ever I was to ask it of others.

In the following pages, the honesty may at times be brutal, but at least you'll get a sense I'm trying my best to be as truthful as possible.

Chapter 6
Monica

2023

When I first started writing this book, I wasn't quite sure where it was leading. There was a plan, but artworks tend to direct their creators to places they never originally considered.

As things developed the book turned into two main volumes, the first is partly an exploration of love, while the second touches on belief systems and ideologies. Love still weaves through the second volume, as it does most things, but this first volume was an attempt to work out what it was I kept doing that would destroy every romantic relationship I had. As it turned out, the answers were far more linked to fundamental ideologies than I could ever have imagined, and I hope may surprise you too.

It's going to be quite a while before we get there, sorry, but this chapter is one of many that touch on the relationships that fell by the wayside. Even so, in their way, all of them helped me realise the path I was following wasn't working.

Part 1

The Depths I'll Go To

I had just started a new job and was sitting in my office when Monica, the Irish girl who worked downstairs, came up to see how my co-worker and I were settling in. At first, we chatted together but I got a phone call so sat down and looked at her, subtly of course, while she and my office mate chatted. As I looked, I was struck by the beauty of her long brown hair and the curve from her waist to her hip, and even then, laughed at myself at the depths I go to when assessing a potential partner.

A few days earlier I'd spoken to Monica for the first time and on finding out that she was from Ireland I told her about a friend of mine falling in love with an Irish girl. In that instance, due to neither of them being willing to move to each other's hometowns, they went their separate ways. Soon after though, the girl got married to someone who she didn't love and visited my friend before and after the wedding where they both declared their feelings to each other. However, faced with reality, they still went their separate ways again but this time they realised they weren't so certain of their decision. When I got to the end of the tale, there was a pause, then Monica looked at me as if to say, "And?"

A few weeks later there was a leaving do in a local pub for one of the other workers. I was only able to stay a short while as I had to go off to teach an evening class, however, just before setting off I sat next to Monica and threw a few jokes her way.

She looked me in the eye and laughed, "Are you flirting with me?"

"Yes," I said, "Is that okay?"

She laughed again, "Yes, sure!"

Without hesitating I added, "So does that mean you'll come back to my place later?"

She pushed her tongue into her bottom lip, smiled and said, "Yeah okay."

We swapped numbers and after I'd finished my class I returned to the pub. She was still hanging around but wanting to keep our meeting secret she pretended to her friends that she was going to make her way home alone, so, they dropped her off near a station, which was way beyond my road. From this point, she had two main routes she could have taken. One was the main road, the other was a quieter, slightly more dangerous and darker back street. She took the latter. I could see her walking down the dimly lit path so drove to a point where another road joined it and as she walked in front of me, I flashed my headlights. At that moment she'd been delving into her bag for her phone, but instead put her fingers into a loose tomato and as she jumped because of my flashing lights she squashed it. As she walked over, she waved her tomato fingers at me with a massive grin on her face and got into my car.

We went back to my apartment, which was a temporary place I was renting between selling and buying some properties. The place was a mess, chaotically filled with my belongings all waiting to find a home. I asked her if she wanted a drink or should we not bother with the civilities. She said she didn't need a drink, so we lay on the single mattress on the floor and began to kiss. We made love that night and it felt good, but when she told me she was just looking for a bit of fun I replied, "We never know what's around the corner."

A few days later she came around again and over the next few weeks, we met regularly, grabbed clandestine kisses at work, went for breakfast at a nearby greasy spoon Café, and as a sign of solidarity, shared a dish of apple crumble.

OK, she was my type physically, so that helped, and there was something between us, plus we made each other laugh a lot. But after about a month she got a bit fed up with my nonchalance and one evening at a restaurant, made it clear we wouldn't be having sex that night. I shrugged and said I understood, but as far as I was concerned, I wasn't bothered either way.

Two days later she came around again, and this time we made love and chatted till the early hours. From then on when we weren't together, she'd call me to say goodnight, and as we did more and more things jointly, I started to fall for her which expressed itself, partly, by finding it almost unbearable to be away from her. Things must have been serious, as I even let her drive my car – and then one morning, somewhere in the autumn mists, I told her I was falling in love and she said, "Yeah, I feel the same way as well. I love you too."

I'm not sure if scent and taste are one of the fundamental pillars upon which relationships are built but I'm certain they can create a barrier if we find them disagreeable. Some mornings I would push my face into Monica's armpit because I loved the smell of her sweat so much. In theory, we're supposed to get to know those we feel might be a good partner, and from those we learn to trust and like we may find our partners. But in reality, most of us spend more time and effort considering which tomatoes to buy at a supermarket than working out who we should get involved with.

With the Internet, we can go on dating websites which use categories and criteria to work out who's more likely to be compatible with whom, but that doesn't take into consideration factors such as chemistry or whether bodies feel right together, and I certainly haven't found any scratch and sniff dating sites so far. And while it's easy to dismiss the importance of the feel of someone's skin or lips upon our own, when it doesn't feel right it may ultimately tip the balance when it comes to commitment.

At the other extreme, there are nightclubs or pick-up joints where it's all about visual and sensual cues, followed by sexual ones, along with chemistry and lastly, if it lasts long enough, personality. The thing is, by the time you've had sex with someone for a while, a strong bond may have formed, even if you don't necessarily get on with them. There's a reason it's called making love.

One afternoon, I told my co-worker I'd met someone but wasn't sure about them and was considering ending the relationship but seven days later, I felt committed to Monica!

We'd had seven weeks of playing around which included speaking to each other nearly every night, buying a new bed together and getting to know each other sexually. Then one morning as we made love I looked into her green eyes, which seemed much brighter than usual and felt the sex was no longer just sex, but we were now connected on a far deeper level.

A couple of days later I got food poisoning and spent the night being violently sick, the next day Monica came to me during her lunch hour and brought me some fruit and drink. She tentatively leant towards me, probably a little worried she might catch what I had, and I gently stroked her face and said thank you. I also told her that her tights had a nice pattern on them to which she laughed and said she appreciated the appreciation.

So, after lots of making love, weeks of chatting, doing romantic things together, looking into each other's eyes, and feeling cared for, the weight was beginning to bear down on me, and I liked it.

If I were to buy a lottery ticket and the first 4 numbers that came up matched my ticket, I'm pretty sure I'd get excited. A rush of adrenalin and subconscious hopes of being rich would start coming to the surface. Then when the next two non-matching numbers appeared I'd almost certainly go through a momentary feeling of despondency. Isn't this a micro-metaphor of what happens when we fall in love? We have a subconscious checklist of who we dream to be united with, and as we get to know someone we tick or cross the boxes until, one way or the other, the "evidence" mounts up for or against them. And sometimes, no matter how well the checklist goes or not, we still connect with someone, and just can't understand why.

Somewhere during that transitionary week, my checklist seemed to be coming on nicely, and there'd been enough good sex, affection, and connection to allow me to let go. What I wasn't aware of though was a great wash of emotions emerging from the shadows, waiting to have their say.

When I told Monica I'd fallen in love I sang the chorus from Elvis's song, "I want you, I need you, I love you" and as I crooned those words Monica curled her lip, Elvis-style, and said, "I love you too."

I looked at her and reflected, "I wonder at which point in a relationship one would feel devastated if the other person was no longer in our life because I would feel devastated if you weren't around anymore?" She told me she felt the same way too.

So seven weeks into the relationship and after a slightly rocky start we were both together with similar feelings towards each other. She felt like a friend, we enjoyed making love with each other, and to me, there was a promise in the air that she might be "the one".

The Night of the Knight and the Nightmare

I have had this kind of strange sleepless night before with previous potential part-ners. It was a night when I wanted to get out of bed and walk away. I knew if I did, it would be over, and as much as I didn't want to hurt their feelings I was over-whelmed with nausea, claustrophobia, and a fear of being trapped.

Monica was going to an important interview the next day, and she'd have been very annoyed if I had walked out. So, I lay there thinking the pillow was uncomfortable, the walk to the loo was difficult in the dark and something deep down was wrong.

I struggled for a while, and then Monica woke up and asked if I was okay. I told her I was uncomfortable, and she helped adjust the pillows. Her caring nature – she was the knight in shining armour – tipped the balance and I stayed knowing from then on, I was there for the duration.

On another occasion, just before her birthday, she called me to ask if I'd pick up a book from work and bring it to the pub. I was just about to get in the shower and then make my way to a class I had to teach before joining her. But I said to myself, "If you love her then you'll forget the shower and go get the book." So, I got dressed, raced out and picked it up for her. She also felt that if I loved her, I'd go get it, so, fortunately, I'd made the right decision. In the box marked devotion and prioritisation, she placed a big tick.

When I came to the pub after my class Monica wasn't surrounded by loads of friends but instead was sitting next to a male co-worker who was running his fingers through her hair. Because our affair was a secret, he didn't know we were partners, but I was confused as to why she didn't stop him. I sat there seething with anger, while Monica looked at me as if to say, "Sorry, but I can't stop him." I felt a rush of rage because she didn't have the wherewithal to stop him and couldn't see how much it affected me. So, on the way home, I told her how I felt, and she brushed it aside saying he was just being affectionate.

I put the first cross on my checklist in the box labelled, 'Does she set out the boundaries to other men'. I didn't realise at the time how much it had affected me but to keep things running smoothly I took on board her points and threw mine aside. Things continued to run well for another week or so until she told me she was going for a drink with an ex-lover of hers because he might have some work for her. Had I not seen Monica letting her co-worker fondle her hair I might have felt less unsettled but now I wondered if she would be able to fend off an attempt at seduction. I didn't really know her then, and when I told her of my doubts, she couldn't understand them. The child in me who fears being abandoned, who thinks anyone who loves me will go away, started to see Monica as possibly untrustworthy. Could she be trusted? Could I be? My insecurity coupled with her having different boundaries from me, opened a crack in the relationship that would become so wide we'd eventually fall out of love through it.

A few days later she informed me she had promised a friend she would go on holiday with her in a few weeks. As she told me my heart sank. I was certain this would be hard for me to cope with, but I knew asking her not to go just wasn't an option.

The following week I moved out of the temporary accommodation into my new home and it felt as if we were moving in together. I asked her to consider living with me, but she declined, saying she had already done that with someone else and it resulted in her staying in the relationship because of practicalities. "How sensible," I thought, but really, I just wanted her to throw caution to the wind. If she loved me as madly as I did her, being sensible wouldn't come into it. I realised she wasn't feeling the same strength of feelings as I was, but what I didn't see was my love for her, wasn't love. Still, my irrational self recognised an imbalance between us and knew there'd be "trouble ahead", but what I didn't question was whether the lack of love was mine, not hers.

I tried to continue to be nonchalant about the holiday, but it started to cast a shadow over our future. On the day she was going to meet her friend to book the ticket I dropped her off on the High Street and just as we were going to say good-bye, a man went past with a wayward hairstyle. Monica looked at me, made her eyes big, raised her eyebrows and said, "Now that's a hair don't". We both laughed. But as she walked to the travel agents I wanted to call out, "Don't" but how could I? I couldn't. Even so, I knew our relationship wouldn't be the same ever again. As I drove home I saw her walking up the road with her friend, so, I beeped my horn and symbolically neither of them looked up.

The logic, or illogic, of my insecurity, was this. Monica went to bed with me very quickly, she was going on holiday with another woman who I didn't know, to a resort that was well known for being a young people's sexual hook-up place, and given I knew they'd possibly drink quite a bit, (Monica liked drinking to get drunk), then she might end up having sex with someone else. Behind this set of thoughts was the feeling that I am not potent enough for someone else to ever want to be faithful to and alongside that, was the doubt I could ever be faithful, even to someone I believed I loved dearly. This is partly the inheritance of my childhood DNA and family history that continues to set a path of self-destruction in the present.

I didn't see Monica for a few days after the "booking day" and when she next slept with me, I felt worried I might accidentally hit her with my arm, so I moved a safe distance away from her. I went to therapy and talked about this and during the session, we covered some ground about a violent boyfriend my mother had had, and how I felt that if I'd ever go that way, I'd want to kill myself. I started to cry and continued to do so after the session. I sent Monica a message telling her how I felt, and she said she couldn't bear to be away from me and wanted to come and help. When she came around, I told her about some of my past and she cried too and then I told her about my fears about her going away. I explained my "psycho" illogic and she reassured me she wasn't like that but, for all her reassurance, all I had was a childhood of abandonment, three months of love and her word of the "truth". And in the back of my mind was the knowledge I'd just manipulated her into being my saviour when that should have been my job.

Of course, Monica's attempt to rescue me did reassure my doubts to a degree, especially as she'd come to my self-inflicted and self-indulgent rescue. But when troubled with a bucket with a hole in it, no matter how often you top it up, it still feels empty in time.

That weekend, obviously trying my best to firm up my crumbling foundations, I bought her a diamond ring. Up till then, I had never bought a woman a ring in my life and while we might not have been engaged, this, for me was as close as I'd ever got.

As the holiday approached my doubts and her re-assurances continued, but by the time she was waving me goodbye from the airport I had become a clingy faded version of the person she'd fallen for. Not surprisingly she started to go off sex with me, saying it was pre-menstrual pain putting her off, but I knew my behaviour had something to do with it. I felt I was now at the mercy of my insecure self and its agenda was to push Monica away. I felt unable to stop myself from being needy, which in turn made being strong enough to overcome it even harder, and faced with my self-destructive shadows taking control, I was filled with even more fear and insecurity.

———————

When she was away, we were in constant contact almost, mainly engineered by me, because if I didn't hear from her within five hours I'd start to worry she'd forgotten me. At times while she was away, I missed her so much I cried, but of course, my need for constant reassurance began to weigh down upon her.

She missed me too, maybe not as much as I was missing her, but as the days drew on her commitment to our relationship seemed to become firmer, so, by day five she was suggesting that all bets were off, all her cards were on the table, she was willing and able, she loved me with all her heart and, as you already know, she asked, "Did I want to play Russian roulette between the sheets with her?"

"Yes," I said, "I would."

———————

Part 2

When Monica came home from the holiday, we made love that night, unprotected and again the next night – but even though her period still hadn't finished she became pregnant. We didn't know this at first but over the next week her sexual feelings waned, then one morning she snapped at me, and I told her off for doing so. She cried and said my anger made her doubt whether we should be together. I was shaken, because for me, saying, "Just because you're tired doesn't mean it's okay for you to talk to me like that," didn't warrant such a devastating reaction, but to her, it did.

She felt she'd tried so hard to reassure me over the weeks before, during, and after going away, that this was an unappreciative slap in the face. I felt that although she'd made an effort, that didn't warrant her being able to shout at me without a reaction. After all, her help was a gift, not a pre-paid deal. After a day or so, she calmed down, but from this point on the relationship changed into one where the dynamic of distancing, pursuing, threats of separation and making up, took over from the fun-loving one we'd known previously. This continued for about 4 weeks until we discovered she was pregnant and the next day, again, as you know, she had an abortion.

If you asked me what traits I loved about Monica it was her humour, her sense of irreverent fun, and her child-like playfulness. We would spend many hours talking into the early hours, and then lie in together so breakfast in bed would start as the sun was setting. But as I became more insecure, I'd repeatedly direct the conversations toward the relationship itself. Initially, our time together had been a friendly, sexy one, but that was now lost, and the new one was dark, intense and about jealousy, possessiveness and freedom. The focus was no longer on love but on the imbalance between our feelings, and the lack of freely given love and sex. After the abortion, her sexual desire vanished, and she told me she didn't fancy me anymore. It was then I started to spiral down into a dark depression. My childhood fears and lack of trust dominated the landscape of our world and every week the relationship dropped down a notch until by the week of my birthday we got to the point of no return. I questioned her trustworthiness once too often and she stopped saying she loved me.

For the next four months, we tried to salvage the relationship. And so it went on, me trying to persuade her to stay and her feeling more and more constricted. Then just as I thought things were beginning to feel better, I dropped her off at the underground station where she was going to meet with the friend she went on holiday with, and a feeling washed over me that this would be the last time I'd say goodbye to her as my girlfriend, and, at first, a quiet, shocked, acceptance took hold of me.

That night I dreamt her friend was sitting astride me attempting to have sex with me. I told her she was just trying to split us up. In her hands she held my penis, which in the dream had been split down the middle and, I stress this was a dream, was the shape of a wooden spoon. The message, at least partly, was I thought her presence would stir things up between us and cause a split, and sure enough the next day when I greeted Monica with a kiss, she turned her head away.

Later, she came around to my place and told me that the look I gave her when she'd turned her head away had angered her, and if she didn't want to kiss me hello, I should accept it. As I drove her back to her place, the conversation became darker. She spoke of how she felt that just because things had picked up lately between us, that didn't mean she felt any differently towards me, i.e. she still didn't fancy me. She said if it hadn't been for the doubts cast in her about how genuine her feelings were due to the abortion, she'd have split up with me a long time ago, but now she was sure she couldn't love me the way I needed to be loved. I asked if she wanted to split up, and she said she didn't know, but then we didn't see each other for a week. During this time, she felt happier not seeing me and I felt more and more devastated. I sent her an email asking her to wait until things were more stable between us before making a decision but when we met up, she was determined to call it a day, and so on a sunny Monday afternoon we split up.

She felt the damage had been too much for such a short-lived relationship and didn't want to go on. We decided, partly because we felt there was a possibility of a friendship between us, and partly to do with the practicalities of working together, that we'd try to remain friends. This meant having a one-month safety zone of remaining faithful while we (mainly I) tried adjusting to the new relationship, during which we'd see each other socially a few times.

Keep Sake

I dropped off Monica's bits and pieces that she'd had at my place. We hugged goodbye on her doorstep, her head turned away enough for me to get the message that she wasn't feeling close, and she asked if I wanted "our ring" back. I said I wanted her to have it to remember us by. She said, of course, she'll remember us. Then she made a joke about Zsa-Zsa Gabor and her attitude to men and diamonds, and I laughed.

I said, "Well it's not the end but just a change in the relationship" and she agreed, well she would because she was instigating it. As I was getting into the car, she said something, but I didn't hear it properly, so I asked her to repeat it thinking it was something funny, but on the third try she shouted: "I was just saying thanks for the lift". I said, "Bye darling, I love you," and then drove off while she moved bits from the hallway up to her room. She didn't want me to go into her place. Ever since making love to her and getting her pregnant just after Christmas, I was never invited to stay the night again.

On the way home, I felt sick thinking about not being able to make love to her again, not feeling her naked body against mine and the awful thought that in time, possibly in a month or so, she'd be in bed making love with someone else. I hoped by then I would have let go of her, but right then, that didn't feel possible.

When I got back to my place, I realised my attempt at getting rid of reminders of her wasn't going to work. The bed was "our bed", we'd bought it together, and she chose the colour and headboard. The lamp was one just like she had in her place. There are now two bins, one normal one and one for recycling, that was her idea. There are some DVDs she said she'd come to watch with me and a couple of other things that hurt to look at right now.

Just before I went to bed she texted me, "I know you're hurting and I'm sorry darl x".

Next!

After almost two months apart, much of which was filled with pain-filled mourning, I woke up one day and was glad, for both our sakes, that we were no longer together. And so, it came to be, I was ready for my next attempt at love and its inevitable failure.

Chapter 7
Simon - 1964 to 1969

Part 1

Simon - 1964

Soon after realising she was pregnant, Angela made her way to Victoria Coach Station. This was where my father's tours would start and end and eventually found him surrounded by a throng of well-wishing women. She pulled him aside and told him what had happened. He said "Let's talk" so, they went back to his place.

The most important decisions in life tend to be made between two people in bed. Well, that's what Billy Bragg knowingly crooned to me once, and it certainly resonated with me. Likewise, that night, when Boris asked Angela to live with him, she refused his kind offer unless it involved marriage, which he, in turn, declined. So, the next day they went their separate ways.

As Angela began "to show", her mother had her stay in a "mother and baby" clinic. In 1964 unmarried mothers were severely stigmatised, so, for all concerned, having them disappear for a while was seen as the best course of action.

I was born in Epsom District Hospital, at 3 pm on March 18th, 1965. It was a sunny Thursday and the mottled pattern of light coming through the trees danced around the walls, but when I first made my entrance or exit, all in the theatre became still and fell silent. Angela immediately knew something was amiss, and as the nurse passed my naked bloody body to her, she looked at me and cried, "Poor thing". While said with compassion, I'm glad I couldn't understand her back then, otherwise, my self-esteem would have taken a dive from the outset.

My mother was beautiful, and not just to me, her biased son. She was affectionate and loved me. She'd get on her knees and hug me, she loved me, oh yeah, she loved me, but there were times when it wasn't like a rock, but tidal water. I felt her love all around and deep inside me, yet for a lot of the time she wasn't there.

From the day the midwives showed me to her, I was put in a nursery where she would come once a day to feed, clean and hug me. The sensation of knowing what it's like to be loved but to yearn for it because it isn't there enough has haunted me far more catastrophically than having short arms and deformed legs ever did. Of course, one could argue that having a disability meant it was far easier to have me institutionalised, especially as my mother's mother, Ethel, was also shamed by my illegitimacy, alien blood, and disability, and didn't want anything to do with me, so without her mother's support, Angela had no option but to have me put into "care".

Even so, my mother would visit me nearly every day and I'd respond accordingly but the long gaps between meetings meant that as the loving commenced so too would the fear of it ending. Instead of a regular pattern of feeding and loving followed by short moments alone and then being heard if I was to cry, what I experienced were countless long bouts of being left alone.

It's hard to know what really went on in my mind but it's probably reasonable to assume that the fear of being abandoned was likely followed by anger at being ignored. Even today I can still feel those feelings rise from the depths, as an overwhelming fear and collapse of any internal strength.

My mother was not abusive, but a victim of circumstances. In 1965 the state did not recognise how important it was to keep children close to a parent and even though there were people who did, my mother, as in love with me as she was, was not one of them and had little idea of what damage was being done.

I spent the first two and a half years of my life living between the nursery, Roehampton Hospital and my grandmother's house, where I was allowed to stay occasionally, and to me, that was home. My mother would come to see me at the nursery about four evenings during the week and both weekend days. When I recently asked her about this, she got a bit defensive and couldn't understand why I didn't appreciate how much effort she'd put into seeing me then. The point I wanted to make to her was simply, that the irregularity and "long" gaps will likely cause problems for most young children, but even so, that was still better than being abandoned totally, which for some at the time was the logical answer. "If it upsets him to see her go, maybe it'd be best for him to not see her at all." As one social worker put it to my mother.

1965

Soon after I was born a friend of my mother suggested that given my father was "foreign" – he held a British passport but was technically South African, and originally from Latvia – it'd probably be best to get him to pay her a lump sum rather than have him agree to regular payments and then disappear. So, my mother started legal proceedings against him.

My father hated the thought of being forced into anything so decided to fight her and on top of that was angered because the summons to the court was delivered to his office and that resulted in him being summarily sacked for playing around on the job. How little they knew. So, feeling coerced and humiliated Boris went to court with the defence that he was not able to have children due to an accident he'd had as a child that damaged his testes. However, he omitted to tell them he'd already had a daughter.

The court ordered blood tests and as they sat in the waiting room of the clinic, neither my mother nor my father spoke to each other. My mother said she would have, but her mother was with her, so she felt inhibited. Then when it came to the day of the proceedings my father made an offer of a one-off payment of £400, which was about one-fifth of the price of an average house back then. My mother accepted it and put it into a savings account where it gradually lost its worth and was one day spent on something insignificant.

My father got to hold me for a few minutes in court, and then, Angela and Boris, my mother and father, went their separate ways.

When Boris would see children with short arms later in life, he'd call the name "Simon" to see if they'd react and when he painted pictures, he'd put a little figure somewhere on the canvas as a memorial to me. But for Boris that was the limit of his involvement as a father. He did try to find me on several occasions, but they were half-hearted attempts. For Boris, it was more convenient not to be involved. My original reaction to this was as to be expected, but later in life I experienced a similar situation and came to understand just how hard it is to connect to a child when there's so much resentment flying around. It's easy to say it shouldn't make a difference, but it does.

Part 2

Surgery

I had been born with the fibula, the small bone, in each of my lower legs, missing which consequently resulted in my feet turning out. At six months old, I was taken to Roehampton Hospital in the south-west reaches of outer London where surgery was performed to fuse my ankles throughout the following year. When I was brought in from surgery my mother sat next to me, watched me twitching in my sleep and cried.

Simon and Angela at Roehampton Hospital.

Roehampton Hospital had been one of the centres in the world where after both World Wars, soldiers could be put back together again, well at least partially. For me, throughout my childhood, it became a second home. Half hospital, half factory it was built around an old mansion and its gardens. Situated in the far corner of the hospital was the ward I stayed on. At first, it was known as C.P.U. but this was later changed to the Leon Gillis Unit, (L.G.U.). Over the years it had additions built on, but its original layout was a square room with a column in the middle of it. This was where we played and ate, and another square room next to this one was where we slept. There was a further corridor which went off from that room to the kitchen, bathrooms, and staffroom.

The square room we slept in had about 9 beds sticking out from the walls and next to each of them was a small bedside cupboard. On top of each bed would be a fleece which was dyed a strong hue of either gold or purple. Above us on the very high ceiling were blue round lights that stayed on throughout the night and illuminated the internal world of anyone who slept there as a child for all their remaining days.

52

At about four years old, a girl I was friends with was put into my cot one morning. She snuggled up to me under my Golden fleece which was all very cosy, but then she started telling me the blister on my foot was going to get bigger and bigger until it was as big as the room, at which point it would explode. I screamed out in fear, which resulted in the girl being removed and told off by the nurse. I guess some patterns start very early on.

Simon, aged about four, playing on a climbing frame.

Chapter 8
Simon - 1969

Barnardo's - 1967

Background politics tend to have a far greater effect than those taking place in the open. Likewise, when it came to where I was allowed to live as a child, the same was true. Well-meaning but detrimental agendas were playing out behind the scenes that would come to play their part in scarring me for life.

My mother lived with her mother, Ethel May, at 30 Ruskin Drive, in Worcester Park, a suburb of South West London. The hospital and nursery where I stayed were ten miles away, so journeying to visit me daily was still practically possible, however, my next place of residence was to be in the northeast suburbs of London, which was a far harder place for Mum to get to.

Angela Holding Simon.

At the time it was made clear this was the only option available, but, as I discovered when I acquired my records many years later, this proved to be part of a plan to get me away from my mother. One particular social worker had taken an immediate dislike to Mum and the report didn't hide why. Firstly, my mother having a child out of wedlock was almost unforgivable in her eyes, and secondly, she believed Angela to be stupid, fanciful and irresponsible. For instance, when my mother said my father had told her he was Spanish and Russian, the social worker asserted Angela was talking rubbish. As it turned out, what he said was a half-truth, as the Spanish side came from what he believed to be his mother's Sephardic roots and the Russian, his father's Ashkenazi ones. As it turned out, when I got a DNA test my Jewish heritage was completely Ashkenazi. But, anyway, as far as this social worker was concerned, it would be better for me not to see my mother.

Simon in front of JCH.

The result of this social worker's machinations was I was moved, at just two and a half years old, to a Barnardo's home in Woodford Bridge known as John Capel Hanbury (JCH). So, instead of an hour-long journey to visit me, it would now take between five to six hours for each round trip. Consequently, from then on, we'd only see each other on alternate weekends and some holidays.

2005

I have friends who have had childhoods which were far worse than mine. Yesterday I spoke to one who had been systematically sexually abused for ten years from the age of three, and when the abuse was discovered, her parents turned on her for bringing the family's name into disrepute. So, I'm well aware my story is mild compared to many others, however, that's my point, you don't need a massive tragedy to bring you into a world of instability, and you shouldn't feel guilty just because your past wasn't as bad as others.

The place I mistook for JCH.

In 1987, soon after I'd got my first car and was looking for any excuse to drive it, I decided to go to the old Barnardo's home I'd stayed in. I wasn't quite sure of where it'd been situated, but eventually, I found a building that resembled it, although since then it had been converted into a posh-looking restaurant. It was winter and the sky was already darkening everything to a faded blue. I stood there feeling a bit tearful. I was almost tempted to push my face up to the glass and mime taking a mouthful of food as one of the customers put their fork in their mouth to see if I could get a sympathy meal.

Fortunately, someone walked past me just as I started to approach the window. "Excuse me," I said, "but do you know if this was the old Barnardo's building?"

It turned out they used to work for Barnardo's and the place I was talking about had been knocked down to make way for a housing estate quite a while back. I wiped the tears from my eyes and drove home vowing from then on to keep my sentimental outbursts to places which were definitely the right ones.

1967 – JCH – Barnardo's

The John Capel Hanbury (JCH) "home" had originally been a hospital. It had large double-fronted doors opening onto the main entrance hall with corridors going off to the left and right. These led to what were originally wards, but when I was there, were either play areas, dining rooms, or dormitories, at the end of which were smaller, 'end rooms'. The one at the end of our dormitory had a black and white television in it and a doorway leading to a fire escape from which I'd wave goodbye to my mum as she'd set off on her arduous journeys home.

To the front of the building there was a large lawn with a driveway running up to the main entrance and to the right of the building a more modern, portacabin-type, annexe had been added. This was where our school room was, and beyond that were other mysterious places.

The corridor to the dormitory upstairs had a bathroom with light-blue-coloured walls, a colour that'd come to haunt me later in life. Due to my right foot being so twisted, most of my weight was taken on the side of my big toe which would regularly result in the skin blistering, becoming hard and in time cracking open. Not a pleasant thought I know, but worse than the crack itself was I'd be taken into this blue room every evening where surgical spirit would be applied to the skin on my feet. The stinging sensation was extremely painful and eventually, knowing what was coming I'd have to be dragged in screaming.

My mother often tells me I was happy when I was in JCH and on the whole, I was. The place was a mixture of Victorian values and flower power. The matron and her deputy walked around followed by their Labradors, while most of the female workers were long-haired, miniskirt-wearing hippies. The male versions had beards, but apart from that, they looked similar, bar the miniskirts. Well, in public anyway.

A few years ago, I met up with one of my teachers from JCH, Ms Parker, and she showed me some photographs she had from those times. One of them was of her sitting in front of a small group of children, she was wearing a miniskirt and her long slim legs curved around her. One of the children in front of her was me and the look on my face was one of awe.

From my adolescence to my early thirties, I found I was drawn to leggy women with long dark hair, my mother on the other hand was blonde and voluptuous. So, as I grew up, I seemed to have a split idea of the type of women I was drawn to. I do realise that as a man I'm drawn to most women, however, I seem to have these two very different looks imprinted in my mind. For instance, the voluptuous blonde type draws me in with her breasts and hourglass figure, but I carry a severe mistrust of her desire to be with me, while the dark-haired slim woman pulls me in with her dark eyes and beautiful face and is enigmatic from the outset. She is the unattainable, the object of unrequited love. Even so, both dance around my issues of yearning and jealousy, or more accurately I dance around them.

1969 -Dreams and Reality – Memories are Made of This

One morning one of the hippie workers came to help me get up and ready for breakfast. I told her that this was a special day for me as I was going to have breakfast with Matron. I said that after I was dressed, I was to have my breakfast put on a tray and then proceed to the Matron's quarters. So, we did so.

Standing at the Matron's door I was filled with feelings of privilege and excitement, especially at the thought of being able to stroke her dogs, who I loved. As the door opened, she stood there, glaring at us in her dressing gown. "That's very informal," I thought, "how nice".

"What's going on?" She asked.

"I've brought Simon down for breakfast, as instructed," said the hippie helper. Unfortunately, it was the hippie helper who was just about to be had for breakfast. Matron, who must have been a frustrated actor bellowed, "By whom?" The helper looked down at me for help, "He told me you'd said he could." Matron had obviously once played a cunning interrogator, "And you, you believed him, did you?" The helper clasped her hands together, "Well, I did, he was very convincing and he was so excited about seeing you." The matron gulped, then straightened her back a little, "Don't be ridiculous girl, we don't have breakfast with the children, whatever next."

I was both confused and overwhelmed with shame at the same time, not only did I suddenly realise the invitation may have been a dream, but I had also betrayed this poor kind-hearted woman. I started to cry. The Matron looked down at me and pushed her lips tight together. She sighed, then offered to let me come back later to give the dogs a biscuit each. I sniffed back the tears and said, "Thank you." Needless to say, my relationship with the helpers took a bit of a nose-dive from then on.

The line, as any good philosopher will say, between dreams and reality is a thin one. So, as I grew up and recalled incidents from my time at JCH it would sometimes be hard to tell if they'd been real or dreamt. It's often said that as we get older our lives feel like a dream. So here are a few memories which I wasn't sure were real or not.

1969- The Picnic

One day our long-legged teacher, Ms Parker, took us to the field at the back of the school. About four other children and I sat on a faded turquoise tarpaulin. We pretended we were on a boat, calmly sailing across an ocean, all went well till I thought I'd try running on water and made a bolt for the corner of the field. I could hear Ms Parker calling for me to stop, but there was no looking back, this was it, freedom was just a few strides away. The error in my plan lay in the fact that I had quite short legs, unlike our gazelle-like teacher, who had, as you already know, very long ones. So, my fate was very much sealed from the outset. Still, even in the face of certain failure, there can, at times, also be an overwhelming urge to laugh hysterically. Running with the ever-approaching figure of Ms Parker over my shoulder, was an adventure well worth the consequences. Was this my father's nature literally running through me? Thirty-six years later, Ms Parker laughed about this incident over a reuniting lunch in her house in York. So that memory was real unless we both dreamt it. Maybe being picked up and held close to her on the journey back to "the boat" made it all worthwhile. Possibly, for both of us even.

Back on the tarpaulin, we watched a bull in the next field running in circles, bucking and generally going a bit mad. We soon started feeling a bit agitated especially as some of us had bright red clothes on. To our surprise and fascination, an older child, no doubt another Barnardo's escapee, ran into the field and taunted the bull. Predictably it decided to chase after him. As you can imagine, we were all a little disappointed when the boy got away unscathed. Now that bit might be real, it felt real, but when I asked Ms Parker about it, she didn't remember anything, but she was probably busy drawing up lesson plans for our next week's study. So, we'll leave it as a possibility.

As we played on, one of the others shouted, "There's a snake". We looked around and indeed a small orange snake approached us. We all moved out of its predicted path and then watched it slip under the tarp. We jumped or rolled off the mat and called for help. A few moments later Ms Parker came to the rescue and pulled up the mat, but the orange snake was nowhere to be seen. We looked at each other wondering if the snake was on one of us or worse still inside our clothes. Well, no one else thought that until I suggested the possibility, at which point there was general pandemonium and screaming.

For years, I thought this must have been a dream, and when I recounted it in therapy, you can imagine the field day we had with that one. "An orange snake you say?" But now, I've concluded it may well have happened. About a year ago I came across something about an orange snake-like worm in the UK on the Internet, and it was with this in mind that I started to question whether it might have been real after all. So, the other night I attempted to track down the existence of an orange snake in the UK on the net, but I couldn't find anything that vaguely resembled what I'd seen. I then had a Gestalt moment – I studied them in Teacher Training but I'm still not sure what they are, maybe one day it'll come to me. – Instead of using the word "orange" I inserted "golden" and behold a plethora of results came back. Apparently, in the UK we have a lizard that has no legs, - a lizard with a disability, I like that – so it looks like a snake, but it's known as a Slow worm. –

Confused? – Anyway, the young Slow worms are a golden colour with a black line. If you're wondering what the difference between a snake and a lizard without legs is, the lizard has eyelids, not that I'd want to be close enough to find out.

So, was it a dream? The answer is, I don't know, but there's certainly evidence to suggest it might not have been. In this instance, it doesn't really matter, but my reason for making an issue of it is that our childhoods, and indeed a lot of our adult lives, merge the worlds of dreams and reality, yet we rarely question the accuracy of our memories.

2005

I was talking to one of my friends the other day and she was telling me about how when a new boyfriend told her he'd started to have deep feelings for her she could almost physically feel a wall between them appear in front of her. I said she may have some issues from her past that might be worth paying attention to. Her father had gone away when she was five, so I mentioned that the incidents around her parent's separation might have affected her. "No, I'm sorry," she said "but that's just nonsense. It was the best thing that could have happened. They weren't happy together. Anyway, I can't remember anything about my father."

I said that the fact that she had no memories of him before his leaving the family home could be significant, and the words "It was the best thing that could have happened. They weren't happy together" were not those of a five-year-old but of an adult, possibly her mother or herself, attempting to make the best of the situation. The thing is that for many of us, the memories that have a profound effect on our present are not ones we can always easily recall but instead come to us via smells or physical sensations.

One such memory I carried with me from a very early age, would often come as I tried to get to sleep. I'd see a small spot in the distance hanging over me and sense it was approaching me slowly. At the same time, I would feel as if a large object was bearing down upon me, smothering me whilst getting heavier and heavier. The feeling of fear that accompanied this sensation was almost unbearable and would often result in me getting out of bed and seeking reassurance.

One night I woke from this "dream" in the dormitory at Barnardo's to find the night nurse snoring, her head resting on her arms on the table. I walked up to her and tried to wake her, but she didn't, so I went back to my bed and tried to get back to sleep, only I kept hearing a voice inside me saying, "The wolf, the wolf, the wolf". This continued for a long time. I wanted them to hush but they wouldn't and the more it persisted the greater the fear I felt. I also noticed I could simultaneously hear other words or thoughts going on below those words and a more controlled conversation taking place above them. This internal chatter, perhaps it was a din, was something I possibly created as a reaction to the unbearable silence of waiting for Mother.

That night I wasn't brought to tears but instead, I felt frozen with terror. Sitting on my bed I knew there was nowhere to run. That sensation of fear is one I know well now and can range from a humming cold sweat to a shaking body, fast heartbeat, profound sweating, heavy arms, aching knees, tight throat, tense chest and a heavy-hearted sensation. Even as an adult, these feelings are hard to cope with but for a child, they must have been overwhelming.

If having one's feet on the ground, and feeling grounded, are terms we use to describe being more in contact with what's real, as the words "understand" and "understood" also suggest, then feeling light and high above the ground, point to a feeling of being detached from reality. Sometimes I'd have awful dreams of being blown in the wind and tossed around in the sky and would feel sick from the sensation of my stomach churning. Just before they'd come, I'd often know such a dream was just about to start and unable to wake myself would feel utter dread.

1969

I was about four when, one morning one of the helpers, a woman with long dark hair was getting me dressed. I asked her if she was a witch, and she laughed and said, "Yes." So, wanting to know more I asked if she ever got together with other witches, to which she said yes again. Excited by this I told her I was curious to know if, when they met up, they were naked. To my delight, she told me they were. I was feeling very sexually curious about the prospect of lots of women being naked, so enquired if she could use her magic powers to make me small enough to fit into a keyhole thus enabling me to watch them. I can't remember what her reply was, I was probably too engrossed in the thoughts I was having. Nowadays she'd probably be in jail, or be dunked in the sewage of social media, but they were simpler times back then, and even now I look back and remember her fondly.

That friend of mine, the one I mentioned a bit earlier. The one who felt a wall appear between her and her new boyfriend as he proclaimed his love for her. I want to return to her because today I've been thinking about the pursuer-distancer dynamic and its profound effect on people's relationships, including mine. I tend to feel that because of my past, I'm more prone to this dynamic, however many others seem to suffer at the hands of it too, so, I thought it worth a mention.

This dynamic mainly occurs as one person distances themselves in a relationship and the other reacts, almost involuntarily, by pursuing them more than they were previously. The problem with this dynamic is as soon as it comes into play in any significant way, the relationship between both parties becomes inhibited, often so much so, that it's no longer about who they are, but the dynamic itself. Although one could argue the dynamic is who we are, in practical terms, neither party continues to relate to the other without the presence of the dynamic and at that point the relationship, as it had been, ends.

For my friend, the one with the wall, her feeling of relief of getting rid of her pursuer far outweighed the feeling of loss of someone who, up to that moment, had been a pleasure to be with. It's as if the pursuer-distancer part of her took her real self and cast it aside.

As I grew older, I realised that many of my relationships couldn't avoid being affected by my feelings from the past, but, even so, there are some dynamics which nearly all of us are prone to, no matter the quality of our childhoods. Probably ever since humans have walked the earth, they've been dealing with emotions linked to what is known as the "romantic illusion". Whether you see this in terms of biology or metaphysics, deep down you're still likely to harbour a romantic illusion which generally manifests itself in ideas about there being a soulmate or someone with whom we can feel whole again. In other words, a dreamy idea about relationships that bears little resemblance to what most of us experience in reality. There may be moments within relationships that have us feeling as if we are at one with our partners, but generally speaking, this isn't our day-to-day experience of "being together".

In medieval times the notion of romantic love was set out clearly in stories that have been handed down throughout the ages and still echo through such modern-day "classics" as 'Star Wars' and 'Lord of The Rings'. In our society, the idea of having a good relationship has almost become the new religion. We are duty-bound to feel we ought to be happily ensconced with someone else and through this relationship we will feel reconnected.

Many of our films climax with a reunion that brings most of us to tears and even the word Religion is derived from words that mean "reconnected". Even the prevalent idea of what happens to us when we die includes a moment of being drawn into the light where we submit our individuality so that we can be reconnected to a feeling of immense Love or God. When I was growing up there were slogans everywhere saying "God is Love" so I suppose it's no surprise that there's an overlap still.

For many people, the reality of their relationships with their parents was a real, day-to-day, hustle and bustle of family life. But for me, it was a romantic illusion. I didn't know what it felt like to be part of a family, all I had was, little glimpses and a dream. The problem with yearning for a dream is you can never feel satiated because, of course, the dream can't ever be acquired.

As for the romantic illusion, I'll come back to it again throughout these chapters as it's such an important part of who we are.

1970

One weekend when I was five, a local policeman took me out for a drive in his Panda car, probably named because it was painted in blocks of white and blue. There aren't blue and white pandas, but the police probably thought that associating themselves with pandas would be a good public relations exercise. I imagine the panda community must have been up in paws about it. Anyway, the policeman told me as we pulled up outside a house that I was to wait in the car while he went inside and made some ice cream. I waited for what seemed to be an interminable time and when he did come out the ice cream was nowhere to be seen.

As a five-year-old one doesn't question the local bobby but years later, well tonight, it struck me that he had probably entered the house to do a bit of undercover private investigations into his own romantic illusion, and I was just his excuse. If he'd come out with a choc-ice, I'd have been happy to play along, but as they say, there's a thin blue line between the goodies and the baddies and while I didn't want to judge, I did want to let him know I was rather disappointed. And you wonder why I'm so cynical.

1970

It's hard to get across the sense of family that existed between me and some of the other children who I stayed with during this period because so few stories come to mind, but there was a bond between us. I'm not sure how much this says of the human race, but my first experience of hysterical laughter was around the breakfast table when a small blond-haired girl – possibly called Paula – farted and I said it was an "eggy". All of us had tears rolling down our cheeks. I guess at four or five years old it's ok to be immature. However, I'm sad to say that even last night I was laughing hysterically as I did an impression of someone who had lost their ability to focus on what they were trying to say, as they breathed in somebody else's wind. To those of you who have matured beyond such airy humour, I salute you.

Lee-Roy was also a co-captive at JCH. He was black and walked with a limp, as we both did. One day there was a summer storm which we both got caught in on the front lawn. We decided to dance in a circle while the warm rain fell upon us and the staff called us from the main entrance. We ignored them knowing full well they didn't want to get wet, or risk being struck by lightning, and given Lee-Roy wore callipers on his legs there was a strong chance anyone near him would. Left alone, we played in the rain for ages. Nowadays it would probably be seen as a little presumptuous and racist to associate Lee-Roy with Africa, but back then I was more concerned with finding my own roots than looking good, and perhaps my desire to do an African dance was motivated, well at least partly, by having been told my father was South African. I didn't know what this meant, but any association with Africa was significant to me.

One day my mother and I were on a tube train. Just opposite us, a black man sat reading a paper minding his own business. I looked at him and said, "Excuse me, but are you my daddy?" I'm not sure how long the gap was between me saying that and my mother whacking me and snapping, "Of course not!" But I'd say it was pretty fast. The man laughed and looked at me and then at my mother, and said, "I don't believe we've ever met, so I don't think so. However, I think if I had, I would most certainly have remembered".

"Thank you," I thought "at least someone around here can deal with a simple question".

My mother apologised and got off at the next stop even though it wasn't the one we were going to. I imagine she was tempted to leave me on the train, but much to my possible father's relief, she didn't.

The lack of a father played on my mind. Even watching a group of contortionists on television who had come from South Africa had me getting my body into all kinds of small places for years afterwards. I have managed to stop myself nowadays but sometimes seeing a small suitcase does get me a little excited.

2005 - Hello Cruel World

As the song goes, there is "a time to kill", and today was one of them. The air was dry-hot, we had prepared our weapons, gone through the plan and worked out what to do if it went wrong. David, who was heading the first strike, laughed and said, "Run and keep running". I hate running.

The only way in was through our enemy's well-guarded entrance. Our main strength was daring, and a lethal combination of nerve gases. David crept up quietly while I kept watch. They didn't even see him place the nozzle of the pipe in position. He released the trigger and the gas poured in.

We are talking seconds from when he hit the trigger to when the first soldier tumbled out of the mouth of the entrance and down to the ground. David almost escaped unharmed but one of the first to exit took a swipe at the back of his leg. I wanted to shout out, "Watch it!" but I didn't want to direct attention my way. It was too late though; he nicked the back of David's thigh. David kicked him and the little bastard dropped and writhed around in silent agony.

We both retreated to a safer position to watch the results of our work. One by one they staggered out, white specks appeared around their faces, as they blindly followed the source of fresh air, but by the time they got outside they just dropped, hit the ground, their bodies in convulsions, and within minutes they were dead.

I'd like to tell you that I felt some pity or sadness for them, but I didn't. One of their kind, if they can be called kind, had hurt me as a child, and another had ruined a meal out one night. From early childhood, I was indoctrinated to hate them, and throughout my lifetime they conformed to my stereotypical views. I can't help it, I hate wasps. Call me a speciesist if you like.

The other night I had left the light on in the kitchen and hadn't closed the window properly. Later on, I noticed about 20 wasps walking forlornly across the floor. The redundant wasp's nest I'd seen in the attic last December now had a new one next to it. I'm going to have builders do a loft conversion soon, so I thought it best to get rid of the wasps before I got into a situation where they'd all be running away from the job in panic.

I got the local pest controller around. His name was David, and we set to work. I don't know how we got around to discussing his sexual preference, but we did, and it turned out he's a sadomasochistic domination and bondage master. He even has a website. I could see by the way he enjoyed killing the wasps and didn't complain too much about being stung that this was undeniably the perfect job for him. I have to admit I too enjoyed watching them die, but I don't need to get dressed up in leather or rubber to do so.

2005

It's well known that much of our humour is based around cruelty. When a monkey smiles, its teeth are not bared in delight but aggression and I'm the first to admit I have a very dark streak of cruel humour, but I still try my best not to hurt people's feelings when making jokes, in other words, I do it behind their backs. Like most of us, when we're confronted with a difficult situation, we tend to deal with it through humour and, sometimes when faced with a person who looks different, like me, people will often cope by making a joke. Nowadays, I tend to forgive people for this trespass within certain limitations, but it wasn't always so. To me, it's okay to laugh at stereotypical tropes and jokes as long as we consciously realise that's what they are and we should at least temper such beliefs with a bit of common sense, and decency. However, I wasn't always so tolerant.

Near JCH there was a local infant's school which I was invited to attend. During break time a group of children surrounded me and started calling me Captain Hook because I was wearing artificial arms with hooks on. Not seeing the funny side of it I attempted to make them stop by swinging my arm toward one of them at speed. There was a clunk, followed by a thud as his body hit the ground, and then there was some wailing, well actually quite a bit of wailing. The other children, however, fell silent, which, as far as I was concerned, was a good result. I wasn't invited back the next day, or any other day as the experiment hadn't gone quite as well as hoped. But for me, I'd learned a valuable lesson, and that was violence can be an answer sometimes, even if it isn't the right one but a right hook one.

1969

During the summer holidays, a group of JCH kids and staff would stay a few weeks in Clacton, a seaside town not far from the Thames estuary on the east coast of England. This was a place where occasionally when the tide went out, there'd be hundreds of stranded jellyfish covering the beach. Along with them, there'd be the crabs too, lots of them. It was the stuff of nightmares, so much so, that one night during our stay I dreamt of a crab chasing after our minibus (I'm almost certain it was a dream), and lastly there were the wasps to top it off. At one point I was pretty sure a wasp stung me, but one of the hippie helpers told me I hadn't been stung and as she had such a pretty face, I was inclined to believe her, so I soon recovered. Even the fallen red berries along the pathway from our hotel to the beach were poisonous but at least the blossom wasn't, but that didn't taste too good. Given all the natural threats posed by Clacton, I couldn't help but think Matron had sent us on a "survival of the fittest" quest. What she probably wasn't aware of was when the younger staff members took us there, it was like being part of a 60's hippie genre film such as, "Easy Rider". There were journeys in the back of trucks with their orange plastic windows. The drivers would slalom as they knew we loved being thrown around in the back. Then there were the late-night parties on the beach with campfire-cooked food, guitar-playing singers, dancing in the firelight and waking up with long-haired men and women sleeping on the floor in the guest house next to us. One morning I woke up with a bearded, half-naked, man lying on the floor next to me. He sat up and said, "Hi man," to me, then someone entered the room and passed him a mug of extra sugared black coffee. He looked at me, I was probably still staring at him as I had no idea who he was, and held the mug towards me saying, "Go on, try it, it's coffee, have you ever had coffee before?" I shook my head. The woman who'd brought the mug in told him I was too young for coffee, but she was too late, I'd taken a swig. It was delicious and I wanted more. "Hold on soldier," he said pulling the mug from me, he took a mouthful, then let me have the sugary remainder.

1970

By the age of five, the world had shown me that it was a dangerous place, where people could be cruel, and while I hadn't been totally abandoned, I was aware that for much of the time I'd have to cope without family support. I'd also learned destroying threats through anger could be of use, and the feeling of control doing that was a powerful sensation. In time, actually a long time, I learned that understanding and letting go could be a far more creative and less self-damaging means of dealing with these situations, but still, even now, I can often get flashes of fury.

2005

Last night a man in a car drove at me on a roundabout so I made sure I didn't give way to his aggression. His forcefulness had nothing to do with me until I let it, but something in me must have wanted to connect with him and all he symbolised. To me, he was a bully and I wanted to stand up to him, but I know it's not my job to rid the world of such people, that'd be exhausting. Still, though, I couldn't let it go. Whether it's something biological, sociological or related to childhood experiences that makes some of us more aggressive than others, I don't know, but what I can tell you, is not far below the surface lies a rage inside me, especially when it comes to bullies and wasps.

1970 - Auto-Contact

At five years old I was moved into a more formal class setting in JCH. I sat near the front of the class and could feel the hot sunlight upon my face through the glass. I noticed a reflection of the sun on my artificial arm's hook. I put it up close to my eye so I could see into the reflection and what I saw looked like a field of grass. While the teacher spoke, his words became distant as I drifted into this green and not-unpleasant land. At the same time, a small piece of nylon string used to help my hook open and close touched my face. As I moved, it stroked me and as it did that, I fell further into a world of sensuous pleasure. If the people I depended on could not be with me or offer physical affection then I would have to provide my own comfort and escape.

Within the "self-help" community there seems to be a consensus that when it comes to being happy, being so in one's skin is a fundamental prerequisite, but regarding being independent, that's far less clear-cut. The point I'm getting at is, there's a difference between being happy in our own company and being independent and it's easy to get confused by the two. There was a time when being independent was seen as something to strive for and to a degree we all need to feel we can cope on our own, but that's just it, it's to a degree. In reality, we need other people, whether it's to bring us up, educate us, build the infrastructure we use, and so on. And on a more personal level, most of us need understanding, connection, friendship, family and love. With that in mind, it might be better to think more in terms of being interdependent rather than dependent or independent. We don't get to choose our families, and some say our friends are God's compensation for that, but how do we choose our friends and lovers if we repeatedly choose badly? If that keeps happening, we're eventually going to end up asking ourselves why. Is it simply a case of there not being any good people for us to find, or are we drawn to making bad choices? I shall come back to that question in later chapters but one thing I realised looking back to my time in Barnardo's was I came to find the things that'd sustain me when I was alone both back then and for most of my life.

In JCH there was a playroom in which we'd be placed for both a treat and a punishment, but to me, it was always a pleasure because there was a wind-up gramophone available. I'd sit listening to old records while watching dust move through the beams of sunlight through the gaps in the curtains. I had my own audio-visual show going on. And then there was my interest in the visual arts, which started very early too. When they sat me at a table with a paintbrush, paper and paint I'd be happy for hours. At four years old I won a national painting competition with a painting called "Mummy and Simon". I even got a spot on the national news. The interviewer asked me about the painting but all I wanted to talk about was a toy aeroplane I'd just got which could be swung around in a circle and "would actually fly." It seems I wasn't able to tell a story without going off on a tangent even then. So, both the process and results of painting made spending time alone doing it very rewarding.

Away from the playroom, there were other areas of interest. There was a small hut-type house on the grounds which I'd try to 'do up', if only in my imagination. This I now see as the start of my interest in property development and right next to the hut was an old wreck of a car we'd play on, yep, you've guessed it, I love driving cars, it's very meditative. We also had a sandpit, but apart from going to the beach and occasionally building sand sculptures, I don't think it had a profound influence. So, there you have it, my passions as an adult were pretty much mapped out by the age of five, and nearly all of them resulted from spending time alone. Except of course flirting with women, which as can be seen from the photo of me making eyes at Miss Parker, also started at a very young age.

When I planned out this chapter, I wanted to discuss the truth behind things, not just what is in front of us, but the underlying factors that are so often obscured. I was particularly interested in the factors that come into play in our relationships, especially those that stop us from relating honestly with one another. Even the word "care" was a paradox to me as a child because while it was used to define the place I lived in, the care I yearned for couldn't be found there. Well, not to the same extent as the type I'd experienced at home.

From the outset, there was a discrepancy between the meaning of people's words and their actions, and being a victim of this resulted in me having a mistrust of the words people used, especially those who were supposed to be caring. Beyond those early years, and possibly throughout my whole life, I've experienced the contradiction of "care". Sometimes it can be with the best intentions that people offer help with what they think is best for me, but in reality, it isn't. And anyway, we all know what the road to Hell is paved in.

For example, at five years old, a non-hippie older helper saw I had a very runny nose as a result of hay fever, and within minutes she'd tied a load of tissues together and made them into a kind of necklace that went around the back of my head, across my face and under my nose. When Matron saw this, she ordered me to take it off. I almost thought about bursting into tears to see if I could get another bone-feeding treat with the Labradors but thought better of it. Under her breath, I heard her snarl, "Something has to be done about that woman." Needless to say, it was a time before unfair dismissal was around and the non-hippie inventor was never seen by me, or possibly anyone else, ever again. Come to think of it, those labradors were rather portly.

This experience of being offered aids and adaptations continued throughout my life, and as we shall see later it did have some devastating results. I grew up with a serious mistrust of any adaptation being offered to me and aimed for a life where I barely relied on any piece of equipment if I could help it. Even now, when people ask if my car's been adapted, which they often do, I say, "Yes, I've had an extremely loud and expensive stereo system installed."

What I learned from this was that the first step in caring for someone is to try to find out what their needs are. I'd often have people inventing adaptations for me which were not only of no benefit to me but were not necessary in the first place. To them, I had a problem, and their way of caring was to offer solutions, but most of the time I found my own way to do things and instead of working with me they felt they knew best. To many that may come over as ungrateful, but it wasn't a case of me not appreciating their motives, I did, but there was also a sense of not being listened to. And then there'd be the opposite situation, where someone offered a solution, but their motives were not good at all. I'll come back to that another time, but if you want the short version have a listen to my song 'Grateful'.

This sense of things not being as they seemed also came from the relationship with my mother, possibly long before I ever arrived at JCH. The big discrepancy was, that I couldn't understand how if my mother loved me as much as she said she did, she could leave me alone in this place. One winter evening I waved goodbye to my mother from the JCH TV room fire escape and as we blew kisses at each other, she cried and I sobbed uncontrollably. The care worker who was with me told me to come inside and stop crying, that my mother would be back next week and if I stopped, I could stay up and watch The Virginian, a cowboy programme on television, so I did as she said and stifled my tears. The next day someone gave me a toy tractor as a consolation prize but the plastic it was made of smelt awful. I informed someone else and they told me not to be so ungrateful. I soon came to understand that saying what you think, and expressing what you feel, is bad and should be discouraged, so, slowly I learned, as you probably did too, that both the word and world of truth are not as welcome as you may think. Even now I hate the thought of people close to me lying, and yet I am an expert at doing it myself, so, obviously, I know it has its uses.

There's a line in the original version of my song. 'This is Me', which goes, "You may say it's a problem I've got but I'd rather be hated for who I am than loved for who I am not". (If you think Kurt Cobain wrote those lines he didn't, it was me.) But not everyone thinks it's a good idea to be honest. When I asked Monica what she thought of white lies, she said, "They are neither good nor bad. They are essential." But to hear her say that unnerved me because generally speaking, I'd rather argue than deal with a lie, unless, of course, it's about an infidelity, in which case I'll lie.

1969 and 2005

One day as a group of us Barnardo's kids and our helpers sat out on the lawn to pod peas when I found one with a maggot in. From then on for the next year or so I squashed every pea before eating it to check it was maggot-free.

A year ago, I got ill after eating some grilled sardines. Up until then, they'd been a regular favourite with me but after that single bad experience, even the smell of them made me feel nauseous. You've probably had similar ordeals. My point is, I have often heard people doubt whether negative childhood experiences affect us, but for me, if just a single upset stomach can – even in adulthood – then it's not so hard to believe traumas in childhood could have profoundly damaging repercussions throughout our lives.

My stay at Barnardo's was, on the whole, both traumatic and pleasant for me, but still good enough for me to feel sad when I came to leave. My last image of JCH was rather cinematic because a whole group of children and workers came to see me off. As we pulled away in the black cab, I waved goodbye through the back window, and they waved back and shouted, "Goodbye Simon," and then as we turned the corner they were gone. The woman next to me told me to sit down, and if I stopped crying, she'd take me to eat fish and chips as a treat. I did as I was told and just like in one of those creepy thriller movies, she, the social worker who unbeknown to me at the time wanted to get me as far away from my mother as she could, put her arm around me and told me not to worry, I was going to a better place.

Chapter 9
The Paradox of Memory - 1969-70

1969 - Worcester Park

Throughout my years in care, I'd regularly stay with my mum who lived in her mother's house in Worcester Park. Ruskin Drive was the road we lived in, and it was situated at the top of a hill from which the main high street ran down steeply to the station at the bottom. I still have vague memories of journeying up and down the hill in my pushchair. When I was about five Mum got a car but up until then, we travelled by public transport. Sometimes Mum would carry or push me, but I'd often trail behind her when she couldn't carry me any further. I'd call out to her to wait for me, and she'd stop, turn around, and tell me to hurry up.

1969 - The Social Worker

When the social worker realised my mum wasn't going to be put off by such a long journey, she pushed for me to be moved to a home even further which was well over 90 miles away in Chipping Norton, just north of Oxford.

2005 - Worcester Park

Worcester Park still looks pretty much as it did back then. Sometimes, if I'm nearby I'll drive through it for nostalgia's sake. At one point, about ten years ago, I thought about buying the house we'd lived in. In fact, I dreamt it was for sale, so, I went to look at it the next day and sure enough, it was. But the urge to buy it was probably more about the desire I had as a child to be permanently housed there, than based on any sound current reason. Mind you it's trebled in price since then so maybe I should have bought it after all.

The Paradox of Memory

Much of what we do in the present is influenced by memories from the past, but the paradox is there are so many we can't consciously remember, and yet they continuously whisper to us.

I wanted to buy the house ten years ago and came up with a few good reasons why, but those underlying feelings surrounding my motivations were not obvious without a bit of analysis.

1935 - Worcester Park - Dream

I once had a dream in which I was a kind of Charlie Chaplin tramp-like figure who walked past my grandparent's house soon after it had been built. There was still a lot of sand around the property from the building work and a couple – my grand-parents possibly - were planting vegetables in the front garden. I stopped and asked them if I could have a drink of water. The woman went into the house and called me from a small window at the side of the building from which she passed me a glass. I could feel she was a bit nervous, so I drank it quickly, thanked her and went on my way. When I woke up, I wondered if there'd ever been a window in the side of the house, so, when I next saw Mum, I asked her and she confirmed there'd been one in the pantry. I'm sure I'd have seen it too, but my conscious mind had completely forgotten about it.

There was also another interpretation I didn't see at first, and this was one that linked to me asking gran for a glass of water when I was a child, and when handing one to me, she'd always say, "Now don't upset it," even though I never did. By the way, the cup would always be half full. Of course, some may see it as being half empty, but maybe the glass was just too big. Anyway, on a more serious note, perhaps in my subconscious I related her reaction to me asking her for a glass of water as making me feel second-class and consequently 'homeless'.

I don't remember my grandmother being at all affectionate towards me. What stuck in my mind was she made me feel I had to keep my distance from her, that I wasn't welcome and barely tolerated. One day I started to cry because I thought I'd broken a toy when I heard her say "What's he crying about now?" I looked up at her and said, "You bitch" in baby language, which fortunately she could no longer speak. This as well as a lot of other similar instances may also have been what she was apologising for from her deathbed.

However, there were other times when the notion of "my enemy's enemy" applied, or maybe it was something else. For instance, one day, soon after Mum bought her first car, she reversed into Gran's driveway and caught her tail-light on a post. As I got out of the car Mum warned me not to say anything to Gran. I nodded as accomplices do, however, as soon as Gran opened the front door, I looked at her, in full angelic pose, my arms stretched up to the sky, and said "Mummy told me not to tell you, but she has just crashed the car into the gate post". Maybe I thought I could finally win her over by becoming an informer, but instead, both of them stared at me with a "No one likes a tattle tale" look.

Besides this tension between Gran and I, the family home was filled with love, as far as I was concerned. Gran's way of showing love was, so my mother tells me, through offering practical help. She would occasionally make me a drink of milk with sugar, which I loved and probably paved the way for my present-day taste for sickly drinks such as Chai latte and snowballs and dental bills.

Simon and Angela's symbolic shadow.

Mum was a different story. Perhaps the lack of tactile affection she'd experienced drove her to shower me with it. Bedtimes had a particular routine. Firstly, Mum would give me a drink which signalled bedtime was coming, so I'd take as long as possible to finish it, and even when I'd accidentally done so too quickly, I'd mime sipping from it for a good while longer. Once Mum finished whatever she was watching, she'd look down at me and raise her eyebrows and smile, pick me up and carry me upstairs to my bedroom where I'd jump from the windowsill onto the bed. Then I'd do a roly-poly and get between the cold sheets. I still prefer a cold bed now, and back then I'd kick the hot water bottle away from me if one had been put in.

Mum would read to me for a while after which I'd lay down and we'd rub noses together (Eskimo kiss), then there'd be a butterfly kiss, which involved either flickering eyelashes together or stroking the other person's face with one's eyelashes, and finally a kiss and a cuddle. As Mum would go out of the room, I'd ask her not to close the door properly and insist she didn't switch the hall light off. After she'd gone, I would look at the pattern of the wood in the cupboard doors or the flower design in the curtains and see faces which would scare me, so, I'd close my eyes and swing my head from side to side as I'd drift off.

This rocking of my head was something both my grandmother and one of my children, have done too. Is it genetic or just a case of many people doing it? Whatever, I'm sure it hasn't helped as far as my bald patch goes.

Extended Family - 1970s

My mother's older sister, Yvonne, and her husband, David, would throw a Christmas party each year when I was a child. The whole extended family including the great aunts and uncles, their children, - my Mum's cousins, - their partners and, of course, their children would all be invited too.

Uncle Albert was a memorable relation, with a large personality and physique to match. I quite liked him especially as he'd give me money, not that I'm easily bought or anything. He'd put coins in my Christmas pudding when I wasn't looking and buy some of us premium bonds. These were savings certificates that also acted as lottery tickets. Later it turned out that he wanted the lot of them back and had been using us as a means to dodge tax. He'd been the chief concierge at the Trocadero in London so, no doubt had to find a way to launder his non-declared tips.

He also wasn't one to go without ruffling a few feathers either and went out in style when, as he approached his last days, he fell for a woman who helped "care" for him and decided to leave everything to her, including the house he lived in which had been partially owned by his siblings. Still, while she got the house, the rest of us managed to hold on to a few of our premium bonds.

Every Christmas three generations would come together, have polite conversations, then go away none the wiser. For us kids though, Christmas meant new toys, or if we were unlucky, items of clothing or a leg-shaped cardboard cut-out with a few chocolate bars held in place to it by some red or blue netting. Sometimes we had to do the churchy bit too, but we accepted this as a somewhat necessary evil given Father Christmas was technically a religious figure.

1970 - Aged Five

I woke up in the early hours of Christmas day and found a pillowcase full of presents at the end of my bed which Mum, sorry I mean Santa, had left for me. The first parcel I pulled out was an odd shape, it had a long thin bit as well as a bulbous part so given it was so dark and I couldn't see anything I felt my way around the object while slowly tearing the paper from it. The more I unwrapped it, the more I was convinced it was a toy trumpet so by the time I'd stripped it bare, I thought it worth blowing down it as hard as I could, but the only sound I heard was the pressure in my ears nearly bursting my ear drums. The lack of an early morning bugle call was probably fortunate for Gran and Mum, who were either still sleeping or blindly opening their presents too. Eventually, I left it and went back to sleep. In the clear light of day, all was revealed. It was a red elephant-shaped money box whose trunk I had been blowing. And that your honour, is the case for the defence.

1969

The thought of how cold the house was, gives me a nostalgic warm glow now, as does the smell of toast and bacon cooking. Well, that just makes me hungry, but I also associate it with home. The kitchen was the main warm room in the morning during the winter and it was there Gran would get dressed, so, I'd have to wait in the hallway till she'd let me in. Once in I'd sit at the table and Mum would serve up cornflakes in blue and white striped bowls, then a boiled egg and bread soldiers. I even have memories of Mum doing the "Here comes a train, now open up the tunnel [my mouth] and let it in."

Perhaps home became an unrealistic version for me because not only did I idealise it in relation to being in care, but also Mum was able to give me more attention as our quality time together was so limited. There was an unsaid deal, something along the lines of, "If you give me lots of attention when we're together I won't make a fuss about you not being there for me when we're not." But this required me to split off my anger from my feelings of missing her. Still, that rage would surface from time to time, deal or no deal.

1969

There's a sudden silence, Mum is kneeling and holding her head with one hand as she cries. I am looking on, having just kicked her hard just above the eyebrow with my built-up shoe. Five-year-olds can deliver a hard kick. Even now I feel a great sense of guilt and sorrow toward my mother for this. How could she understand where the motivation for such an attack came from? Likewise, I recognise the frustration and sense of betrayal that lay behind my traitorous action.

Strewn across the floor was the debris of my coveted electric car racing track, which I'd smashed up during the same tantrum. By breaking it, I had taken myself hostage and looked at my mother for the ransom. However, when she pointed out the obvious truth, that it would serve me right if it didn't work anymore, I struck out at her, because she didn't understand. The silence that came from this emotionally shocked and physically stunned moment has stretched out through my life and serves as one of the many reminders that wrap themselves around me to contain the un-containable anger that both drives and destroys me. What boy would dare to strike his mother if his father was at their side?

I have often felt that I am at the mercy of my destructive self. Perhaps this kick was aimed at sending a message beyond the obvious one of, "I hate you and want to kill you right now." It might also have been a call to control me, to get me a father so I wouldn't be like this! To be blown around by a storm of emotions can be very frightening for anyone, let alone a child. Whether there was any basis in reality for me to believe a father would have made a difference, I can't tell, but to live in a home without a father, certainly left me feeling that something was lacking.

1969 - The Social Worker

In a way, the social worker's issue about me not having a father was something Mum wanted to address too. She did what she could to find a good man but firstly, those who would have been okay about there already being a disabled child on the scene tended to be quite caring types and Mum's self-destructive inclinations didn't tend to find them attractive, and secondly, the memory of Ian still blocked her from falling for anyone properly. Instead, short-term flings with bad boys were the only form of excitement she could indulge in. With that in mind, you may think the social worker had a point, but the bond between Mum and I was very powerful, so to try breaking it carried its risks too.

1969 - Boyfriends

When Mum brought boyfriends around for me to meet, I would view them as potential daddies. I didn't have a conscious checklist I'd run through, but if they were willing to play with me that would normally qualify them in my eyes. One such man was Mick. Unbeknown to me at the time he fancied Mum, but she wasn't having it, which meant he wasn't either. I don't think I helped matters when one day Mum told me to have a bath with him, don't worry back in those days child abuse just didn't exist, did it? So, I was ok. Unfortunately, Mick wasn't. Mum stood outside the bathroom while we all chatted when I decided to shout, "Oooh yuk, Mick has a horrible-looking tongue between his legs". There was a brief pause while Mick gave me a look that said, "I've played with you for hours so I could get into your mother's knickers, how could you betray me with such a revelation, even if it is true?" Mum burst out laughing, which translated as, "I wasn't sure about Mick, but now I definitely am".

A few years later, Mum had another boyfriend, Michael, who took me into a public loo where he decided to have a pee too. Don't worry the only abuse was adult abuse. On seeing his penis, I hollered at the top of my voice, "Goodness your tail is massive!" to which he quite proudly replied in a raised voice, "Yes, it's a good eight inches". Of course, nowadays such public announcements would have the loo door broken down in seconds by a lynch mob, but back then he just got a pat on the back from his fellow loo-goers while for the rest of the afternoon, Mum got a lot of knowing looks from their wives.

1970

One of my favourite pseudo-dads was Colin who was the husband of my Mum's friend, Val. They had two daughters but showered attention on all of us equally when we were together. He even let me sit on his lap and steer his Lotus Elan (I called it a Lotus Lamb) sports car up and down his street. Colin would spend hours playing with me but alas he was already taken.

Colin took me to Battersea Funfair one afternoon where he introduced me to a shooting range. Everything was ok until he let me aim the gun. I didn't understand what a target was so shot at the prizes. Colin laughed but the stall holder was not amused.

When I got older Colin told me how as he carried me on his shoulders people would openly say nasty things about me and he'd want to get into a fight with them, but that wasn't feasible right then.

Simon in front of Colin's Lotus "Lamb".

On one occasion at Colin and Val's place, Mum showed off a new pair of black and white check trousers she'd just bought me and warned me not to get them dirty as we played in the garden. The first thing we did was eat some of the tomatoes growing in the vegetable patch, so, Mum called me and asked if I'd been eating Colin's tomatoes. I denied it so Mum showed me my tomato-stained face in the mirror. It was then I suddenly recalled a brief incident where a tomato may have accidentally passed my lips and as I trotted off, I could hear her laugh, and say something about me getting into politics when I got older, but she laughed too soon as things were about to take a turn for the worse.

When I returned to the garden we decided, to play pretend families which involved sitting on wicker chairs in a circle facing each other and shouting out what we had to pretend to do. Someone told me to pretend to go to the loo, so I did a straining face. (I think you know where we're going). My shit mime brought rapturous laughter from the others, so, I did it again, this time with a little bit more gusto. There's method acting and then there's a thin line between reality and make-believe and I crossed it. "Oops I've just poohed myself," I said. The other children laughed even more. With a rather serious look on my face, I shouted, "No I mean it." I didn't think it was a good idea to stand up, so I asked for someone to get my mum. The look of disgust on her face as she helped me change back into my old trousers is etched upon my soul. "They're ruined!" she said with venom. I wanted to tell her about a good washing powder I'd seen advertised on TV, but thought it better to just stay quiet... "Still", I reassured her, "I didn't get any grass stains on them."

1969

Home not only existed within the actual building but spread out to the domains of other family members, friends and neighbours. Apart from the occasional boyfriend, Mum had a close circle of friends, and most of them had children of a similar age too. Her sister Yvonne had three daughters; two who were of a similar age to me, Druscilla and Caroline, were playmates. The older one, Sarah, once played her recorder at my fourth birthday party, and was technically booed off stage. I have a feeling that put her nose out of joint, and given the large age difference of three years, we were destined not to be that close. However, in adulthood she always made me laugh, and in time I came to love her just as I did all my cousins.

I was particularly close to Druscilla and even asked Mum if I could marry her when I got older. Apparently, in law, you can, but it also requires the other person to agree to it too and due to her not sharing the same desires I was forced to make other arrangements! Anyway, Druscilla, Caroline and I would often be left for hours to play together. Caroline was the youngest and consequently got bullied, but Druscilla bullied me too, so it was pretty equal, well okay it wasn't, but as I thought Druscilla was beautiful, I didn't mind. The story of my life!

Mum's brother had two daughters. They lived around the corner, but we hardly saw them, mainly because he found Mum's waywardness an anathema. Whenever we visited, he would grunt hello, and that was as far as the conversation with him would go. But his daughters, Christine and Nechama were very friendly and the memory of them bringing a chocolate egg with a creamy white and yellow filling to me for Easter thrilled me for years. That was my first experience of mythical food. Mythical food is something you eat which tastes beyond delicious but never tastes as good ever again. About six years later I had a Cadbury's Cream Egg but, of course, it wasn't as good as the one my cousins gave me and even now if ever I eat one I'm left feeling disappointed, wondering what magical egg it was they gave me that day.

The problem with cousins is no matter how much you love them, your parents, well in my case, my Mum, will often compare them to you. Telling you how great they are and how shit, in comparison to them, you are. So, after a while, you can't help but resent them a bit. When I was informed their parents did the same to them too, that made me feel a lot better, even if it did come a bit too late and was probably not true.

1969

Having family members living very close by is not so common nowadays, but back then my family mainly lived within a few miles of each other, and visiting relatives was a big part of the weekly agenda. Even now my mother tells me off for not calling her regularly enough. For her, it is a rejection because visiting family members is a sign of caring, whereas for my generation a sign of caring is to leave each other well and truly alone. The word 'Kindness' has in it the word 'Kin' and in this, there lies a warning to us all.

1970

One day when I was five, I wanted to ride my tricycle up and down the road in front of Gran's house. Mum stood in front of me and listed what I should be careful of including such things as, "Don't talk to any strangers, if someone offers you a lift then come and tell me at once, and if someone says they've come to take you to see me, run away as quickly as possible," and so on, including warnings about offers of sweets and ice cream (which got my hopes up). By the end of the list, I got off my tricycle and said I'd rather play in the back garden. However, there's only so much appreciation of the scent of grass that a child can take, especially as peddling on grass is hard work. So, I decided to explore the end of the garden. This is where the shed and vegetable patches were.

Between them, a maze of pathways crisscrossed and divided the different areas, so I marched and peddled along them. From nowhere, a voice said, "Hello Simon", I looked up and over the fence, a neighbour's head was looking at me. It was Mr Bertie. Mum walked towards us, picked me up and chatted with him for a while, then passed me to him. I'd often spend hours with Mr Bertie, his wife and their white Scotty dog. There must have been a connection between people with pets and those who liked looking after kids because the neighbours on the opposite side of the road, the Marchmonts, also looked after me although they had cats. In fact, people with dogs tended to be more fun. I base this on the evidence of Mr Bertie being playful while Mrs Marchmont was strict. Also, to prove my theory with undeniable empirical evidence, Mum's friend Nechama had a cat called Sooty, and a dog called Kim, who, by the way, had puppies. Just having puppies made Nechama's place magical, especially when we, that's her son Peter and I, spent a whole morning pulling sugar puffs – a breakfast cereal – out of their fur after they'd got into the cereal box. I rest my case. Pets, especially dogs, indicated a receptive environment.

At five years old I was forced to wear artificial arms which meant when I wanted to stroke people's pets, I couldn't feel their fur unless I put my face to them. This would often get me a stern warning from any adults nearby because of the dangers of being so close to a potentially dangerous animal, but I was never attacked. I'd regularly be told that animals who tended to keep away from people would often warm to me. I still have this gift now, sadly though, it doesn't apply to snakes but does attract the homeless and mentally ill.

2005

The days of passing kids over the fence are bygone ones for most people now, we live in a world where time after time even family members have often proved to be a danger to them. The other night I visited a friend who lives on a boat in Chelsea Harbour, her main living area is a room that has a glass front and burgundy red walls that curve around. We sat watching a Russian animation based on a lullaby that says something along the lines of"

"Go to sleep, little one, for Mama

If baby won't go to sleep

The big wolf will come and eat him".

As we watched it, I remembered my early fixation on the Wolf. The irony is that wolves tend not to attack people. However, people focused their attention on external enemies to avoid the terrible truth about our real greatest threat, our lack of control.

I read the bit I wrote about "adult abuse" a few paragraphs back to a friend the other day, and as a result, she told me how her mother had been a paedophile and had farmed her out to other paedophiles from when she was three years old. My friend, who's now 50, has only recently been able to talk to others about this. For her, the Wolf was the least of her worries. A few years ago, I stroked a wolf and its fur was the most beautiful I'd ever felt. I don't wear artificial arms now, so I didn't need to bury my face into it: I wanted to, but I wasn't quite up to taking the risk.

1970

Beyond the end of Gran's garden, stood three very tall conifer trees. I would sit in the garden and look at them, seeing them as giants bearing over us. I'd most likely be playing with my Action Men, which were soldier dolls – I stress they were not only soldiers, but elite scar-on-the-face types so there could be no mistaking that this wasn't a pursuit likely to result in overt homosexuality, but just to make sure, they didn't have any penises. So, the giant trees looked on at me and I would look on at my brigade of post-op transsexual soldiers. There was a certain feeling of order to it all.

1971

One day a doctor from West Park, the psychiatric hospital where my Mum worked as a hairdresser, took me to a shop with his girlfriend to buy an action-man diving suit. I could feel him playing at being a daddy, but his girlfriend wasn't so involved. If this was what it was like to have a father, then I wanted more of it. A few weeks later I asked Mum if I could see him again and she told me that sadly he'd committed suicide. I asked her what suicide meant and she explained that he'd been so unhappy he'd killed himself. She put it down to the pressure of his medical exams, but thinking about it now, I'm sure there was more to it than that. At that time, of course, I couldn't understand how someone so nice could take themselves away from me and in the hope of creating a kinder world, I told Mum that I would never kill myself. "Suicide", I said, "That's the last thing I'd ever do."

1971

The garden was a place for driving my trike, exploring, setting up Action Man battles and lying in the paddling pool while Mum got the hose and aimed cold water at me. Gran would leave jam jar traps out for wasps. You see just like the Bush Family's battle with Saddam, my war on wasps was part of a trans-generational conflict.

The garden with its apple tree, the old shed with curtains painted on the window, and the birdbath were all remnants of a grandfather I never knew. This was his domain, a world he once lovingly tended to, and was now maintained by Gran,

84

possibly partly as a memorial to him. A photograph of him sat on the mantelpiece in the front room. He was a ghost of the dream I yearned for, maybe he watched over me or maybe it was me who, like a ghost, now haunted his garden. One of my cousins told me she remembered him pushing her sister's pram, which back then was seen as a bit unseemly for a man, but he didn't care and was always very affectionate to her and her sister. He'd have probably found the whole issue of me being born very difficult, but I wonder if he'd have ever come around and learned to love me too.

My Grandfather

When I was 23, I painted a large triptych. The central painting was called "Garden Stories", and had a shadowy figure, (my grandmother), standing under the apple tree, while buried beneath the garden were my grandfather and their son, Neville, who'd died from meningitis as a child. Inside the house was the home of Mum and Gran, but outside had been the world of the men in my family, but now, they were all gone.

Garden Stories - Oil on Canvas (6x6ft).

1969 - Making Up is Hard to Do

Whenever we were going to go anywhere, Mum would take what felt like an interminable time to do her hair and make-up. Sometimes I would sit and watch her. If I did, she'd brush her hair up, so it looked like bunny ears and pull a rabbit face at me in the mirror. Even now I like watching whoever I'm going out with putting their make-up on, but instead of making a funny face they just tell me to get lost.

The routine of home life doesn't generally lend itself to the exciting subject matter of a book but there were odd moments when it may. For instance, when I was about four, I put Mum's bikini on and walked up and down in front of her feeling a bit sexually excited about doing so. I didn't grow up to be a transvestite and I doubt even that momentary experience gives me an insight into what it feels like to be interested in that realm.

Then there was Gran telling me not to come into the kitchen because she was getting changed, I got a chair and stood on it to look through the keyhole, but then I thought, "I don't want to see Gran undressed." For a change, I made a sensible decision and got down.

Amongst other indiscretions, I occasionally ate a few of Gran's grapes without asking and played with the light switch at the top of the stairs but at that point in my life, I didn't seem set on a path of crime and misdemeanours.

Then, of course, there'll be the experiences shared by many people of my age, such as hiding behind the couch when Dr Who was on TV, or the coldness of a house without heating, especially the cold loo, or being washed in the washing-up bowl in the kitchen. Even if all that stuff isn't interesting reading, the routine, and boisterous regularity of family life, was what I yearned for when I was in care. From waking in the morning and finding toys to play with, being dressed, having breakfast, more playing, maybe some magic painting, which involved putting water on a page and watching colours appear, or colouring in pictures of exciting furry animals, and then, with me dressed up in my new spaceman suit, complete with a green visor helmet, going out to visit a relative and playing with their toys too. Then when we'd go shopping, we'd pass the mirror shop at the top of the high street where I'd play in front of the bendy ones, or we'd pop into the toy shop and occasionally get a treat. Normally a model aircraft would keep me quiet for hours and sometimes there'd be very special occasions when I'd be taken to the cinema where I'd get upset if there weren't any aeroplanes involved in dog fighting, no matter what kind of film it was. If Mum wanted to go out for an evening, I'd stay at her friends' places where their kids and we'd build camps and play with each other's toys. I'd fall asleep but wake slightly as Mum carried me to and from the car in a wash of orange streetlights, then wake up the next morning in my own bed. If home is where the heart is then home spread out to Mum's friends, their homes and their children. When I came home from "care" (the Home) I felt like everywhere we went together was home.

---

17 July 1969 - A Day in the Light Of

Light streamed through the gap between my curtains. For a moment I was transfixed by it, but the call of duty was greater. Downstairs my Action Men awaited their missions, so I crept down to them. Mum was still sleeping but Gran was up and sitting in the kitchen. I said hello as I passed her and she briefly looked up at me. The back room was where my toy box was so by definition this was MY playroom. When I wasn't there, it was the dining room. It had a burgundy/red wine-coloured carpet, and on the fireplace were ornaments, including china horses, porcelain deer and red glass vases. There were also French windows that opened onto the garden. I played until Mum, who'd finally got up, called me to the kitchen.

I ate cornflakes while Mum cut out some tokens from the cereal box. Cereal boxes, labels on marmalade jars, and Hot Wheels racing cars had perpetual offers for "free" items. When I'd eaten most of the cornflakes Mum poured the rest of the milk into a cup and I drank it. One particular morning, Mum was talking when she suddenly made a strange sound. I looked up to see tea gushing from her nose, she stood up and made her way to the sink, still coughing. The paper she had been reading was soaked. Mum cleaned herself up then came back to the table and said:

"Sorry Simon."

"Are you alright Mummy?"

"Don't worry darling, the tea just went down the wrong way. Come on let's get ready."

Gran added, "You won't be late back, will you?"

Mum wanted to see one of her friends who lived behind some shops around the corner. To get to her flat we had to walk up a large black wrought iron staircase. Mum and her friend talked while I played with my Action Men. This friend didn't have any children, so I was left to my own devices, so, when an ice cream van sounded its music nearby, I dutifully begged Mum to buy me one, but she refused. Instead, her friend offered me an ice pop, which was an ice lolly you squeezed out of its plastic wrapper as you ate it. It was so cold that I had to scrape it with my teeth. No doubt this was a deliberate ploy by the adults to keep me busy for half an hour while they chatted. After their catchup we made our way home, stopping at the mirror shop again for a quick play, as the toy shop was closed. When we got back, I played in the garden while Mum stood in the kitchen putting on make-up and doing her hair. I have tended in my adult life to go for women who put on a minimal amount of make-up and have plain hairstyles. This is possibly due to the nausea I'd feel after the initial 10 minutes of waiting.

"Are you ready yet?" I'd ask.

"Are you still not ready?" Gran would ask.

"How much longer are you going to be?" We'd both ask.

"I'm so bored Mum," – that'd be me saying that, in case you're getting confused.

"Can't you see I'm going as fast as I can?" Mum'd be getting quite irritated by now.

I bounced off back into the garden followed by a stern warning, "Don't you get your clothes dirty, young man!" Gran would be sitting waiting in the front room, reading and rustling her Daily Mail paper.

The shift of power between children and their parents generally takes place gradually. A parent stands over and protects a helpless child and if all goes to plan the child eventually stands over and protects a helpless parent; what a comforting thought that is. Similarly, Mum had recently bought a car, a Singer Chamois, so Gran was beholden to her for lifts. If Mum wanted to take a little longer to do her hair then she did, and there was nothing we could do about it.

Gran's youngest brother, Eddie, had a daughter, Marianne, who was having her 21st birthday party. Nowadays this would probably be celebrated in a nightclub under the influence of copious amounts of alcohol but back then it was a sedate affair. When we got there, I realised it was the same lot who'd got together at Christmas, but this time there was no Christmas pudding to get rich quickly from, so, I turned my attention to Uncle Binks, who was an ex-RAF type with a handlebar moustache to show for it. To the adults present, Uncle Binks was a bit of a pain, but to me, he was quite magical. He had me believing there were crocodiles in the pond. So much so, I wouldn't go out into the garden. In fact, I started crying at the prospect of being made to do so.

Marianne's brother, Paul, had his soon-to-be-married girlfriend, Ann, with him. She had long black hair, and big brown eyes and was wearing a white and mauve miniskirt. She came up to me and said, "Come on darling there aren't any crocodiles out there," and as she gave me a cuddle I was, I have to say, persuaded and let her carry me outside. I wouldn't meet Ann again for another nine years but both of us carried this moment with us for the rest of our lives.

As the sun shone on this family occasion, it shone on me. The light of a family's love, even if it isn't a strong one, is a precious commodity when most of the time you live under a shadow. As the afternoon drew on, I was jogged into remembering Mum would be driving me back up through London to JCH and might if I was lucky put me to bed and kiss me goodnight there, but the next morning she would be gone. Even the toy robots and battery-operated cars she'd bought for me could not make up for the mundane existence of family life that I knew I was missing.

1969 - The Social Worker

When Chipping Norton was suggested as a suitable alternative to JCH, Mum put her foot down and demanded I be placed somewhere nearby. The social worker, probably sensing Mum was getting an inkling of what was going on, then mentioned a children's home about 20 miles south of where Mum lived, which on the surface looked like a gracious compromise. However, unbeknown to my mother, that place was run by friends of the social worker, and they already had a plan in place to make life very difficult for us.

Chapter 10
Pastens

Pastens

One night when Monica was on holiday still and I was driving home to London from a dinner party in Kent. As I sped along hard windy country roads, I climbed a steep hill and sensed I'd once known this road. When I reached the top, I realised I was right next to the place the social worker had brought me three decades years previously

This new "home" was called Pastens. Originally, in 1946, an orphanage was situated here but the old house burnt down in 1958 and five years later the buildings I lived in, the ones I was now pulled up next to, were opened. Pastens was situated on the Surrey/Kent border, in a leafy semi-countryside area called Limpsfield.

JCH had been run by Barnardo's, but Pastens was a National Children's Home, an organisation run by the Methodist Church. I don't remember much about being shown around the place the first time, but I did meet the two women who ran it. They were stern figures with gull-winged glasses and immaculate wavy hairstyles. Don't be fooled though, the only coolness they displayed came in the form of Victorian harshness. Likewise, the buildings were soulless too, with blank walls painted in sickly pink or pallid green colours, and an atmosphere drenched in the scent of disinfectant. No doubt purposefully echoing the notion of 'Cleanliness being next to Godliness'. A phrase attributed to John Wesley, the co-founder of Methodism.

The place did have a few redeeming features though, amongst which was its garden. It had at least four descending large terraces, the last of which we weren't allowed to enter. We were told it was overgrown and full of snakes and even as a child I couldn't help but wonder if it was the original Garden of Eden.

After the introductory tour, to my relief, I was dropped off at my mother's, but it would be Roehampton Hospital where I'd be spending most of the summer break. I was to be operated on, the main aim of which was to straighten my right foot.

1970 - Roehampton Hospital

A few days before the operation was to take place Mum took me to Roehampton Hospital to help get me settled in and ready for the surgery. The woman who ran the ward was called Sister Gwen Mears. She'd looked after me there since I first visited it when I was six months old and had taken a keen interest in my welfare, not just when I was on the ward, but also when she'd visited me in the nursery in Epsom. On that occasion, she found I'd been left alone for many hours and had a go at the staff there for being so negligent.

Gwen later became the matron of Roehampton Hospital and went on to receive an O.B.E., however, her first love had been working on the ward I'd come to. At that time, it was known as CPU and had originally been set up to help deal with children who had disabilities caused by Thalidomide. Later its specialisation spread to include limbless children generally, as well as many other forms of disabilities. It was then renamed the Leon Gillis Unit (LGU).

1966 - Cut Off

In many ways, the children of Thalidomide, and the ensuing generations of other disabled children became the unwitting guinea pigs for some of the doctors at Roehampton Hospital, and while I have the utmost respect for many of them, there were a lot of mistakes made resulting in many of my peers bearing both physical and mental scars.

I too almost became a victim when the doctors at Roehampton asked my mother if she would give them permission for my finger and both my feet to be amputated, even though I was barely six months old. Fortunately, she said no. Their reasoning behind my feet being taken away was I could have artificial legs fitted to both legs which would overcome the difficulties I faced as a result of my clubbed feet. It's hard to tell if this would have been beneficial, however, I would have always relied on prosthetic feet to walk with and the psychological impact of that may have been just as impactful as the difficulties I'd come to face as I was.

With regards to my finger, the only reason given for having it removed was its appearance. It was, and still is unsightly, but it's extremely functional, so, I'm glad to have it. My finger and I are friends. I once cried in a dream where I was offered normal arms because I knew I would lose my finger if the transplant went ahead.

A friend of mine who was born with similar arms and short legs to me also had a finger that sprouted from close to her elbow as well, but hers was removed before she ever got to find out if it might have been of any use. Her parents were pressurised into giving permission for her feet to be amputated so artificial legs could be fitted more easily, but they declined the 'buy one get two free' special offer, tempting as it was.

Many other children who had parents who blindly followed the doctor's orders, as well as those children who'd been handed over to the authorities, and therefore had no parents to defend them at all, were operated on without question.

Often the main criterion for doing such operations was to effect a more cosmetically acceptable image rather than to improve functionality. For instance, some could walk even though their legs wouldn't bend. For them, having their ligaments cut resulted in them being neatly sat in a wheelchair, which ironically was now a blessing, given they could no longer walk.

The distrust between the medical world and the disability political one was partly due to this period of butchering. The stem of the problem arose from the power doctors had when it came to not only making decisions about 'solving' functional and cosmetic issues relating to disabilities but also whether certain disabled people should live or die. This was particularly pertinent during the 1980s when the government in the UK changed the law regarding abortion time limits. For non-disabled foetuses, the time was decreased significantly, whereas, if a foetus was found to have a disability, it could be aborted at any point right up to the moment just before birth. The main criteria used to determine whether this should happen or not was based on the doctor's judgement as to whether the child's quality of life would be worth living. But how could most doctors determine this?

When the mother of my sons was first pregnant, we went to meet her obstetrician. As soon as we sat in front of him, he openly expressed his disbelief that this could ever have been a planned pregnancy. Firstly, he presumed there was a risk my disability was hereditary, which it is not, secondly, I would not be able to be a supportive father because of my disability, and thirdly, if my child was born with the same disability then its quality of life would be so awful it wouldn't be worth living. Given my life has been such a rich tapestry I begged to differ with his opinion, as I politely made clear to him.

Had my mother ever had an ultrasonic scan when she was pregnant with me, I'm pretty sure the pressure applied by medical practitioners to abort me would have been immense, so it was fortunate for me she didn't.

1970 – Life on the Ward

When Mum dropped me off at the hospital, she told me she'd come to see me the next day. We kissed goodbye and waved to each other as she walked down the corridor and out of sight. Still a bit sad, I went to the TV room where I quietly sat on the floor and proceeded to pick my nose and eat it. This was possibly taking self-sufficiency a bit too far, which I soon realised as a din of disgust emanated from those around me. I looked up at them in horror, still not fully aware of my faux pas. A slightly older boy with no arms at all, Christopher, who was sitting nearby, looked at me and said, "Don't you know if you eat your bogeys they'll turn into worms and eat your brains out". I have to say I was quite disturbed by this and swallowed my last ever bogey once and for all.

I must have looked distressed because the other mothers and children started to laugh. I got up, slightly tearful by now, and attempted to walk out of the room. As I did Christopher grabbed my pyjama bottoms with his toes and pulled them down.

Abandoned, with my brains being munched at by bogey-worms and my pyjama bottoms around my ankles, I lurched at Christopher with a pyjama-constrained foot carefully aimed at his head. He pushed me away with his legs while the other mothers pulled me from him. He laughed, I screamed in rage, and Sister Mears came in to see what all the commotion was about. She gave the other adults in the room her look of death, pulled my pyjamas up and carried me to the kitchen where she got a block of ice cream out of the freezer, sandwiched it between two wafers and passed it to me. I sniffed back my tears, bribe accepted.

The next day Christopher and I were a bit quiet with each other until a new toy was brought in. This was a traffic light that could be switched on by pulling and pushing buttons below it. The green light one was very stiff and neither of us could lift it. I looked up to see a nurse who'd just entered the room and asked her if she could help us. She was about the same size as us, in other words, she was a midget. That probably isn't the politically correct term, by the way, but her nurse's uniform was what caught my eye.

"Oi miss!" I said, "Can you come and do this for us please".

She came over with a big grin on her face and helped us with the lights.

"What's your name?" I asked.

"Murphy," she said.

"Thank you, miss."

This was Murphy's induction into the world of looking after disabled kids and this moment was one she'd carry with her from then on as one of those, "I'll never forget when…" stories that she'd always tell me whenever we met later.

94

Another nurse, Mary Colohan, also took me under her wing during this time too. She was very tall, leggy, and had long black wavy hair, with a Pre-Raphaelite-looking face and deep red lips. She would often carry and hug me, so, in return for this, I gave her a nickname that stuck with her from then on. "Mary Lamb" was my first love or at least the first I can recall. I would yearn for her when I left the hospital and when I'd return, I'd feel heartbroken if she wasn't working there.

When I was twenty-two, we'd get to meet again and I still felt a bit of a spark for her, but, alas, to her I was still that five-year-old who touched her heart with affection and life with a nickname. Still, I did try as hard as I could to seduce her, just for old times' sake, but she wasn't having any of it!

———

For most people, the association of going to a hospital is a negative one, but for me, and many of my peers, Roehampton was half home and half horror house. When I got older and experienced normal hospital stays in pain, I soon changed my opinion though.

———

1970 - Pre-Med

On the morning of the surgery, the sun shone brightly through the gaps in the curtains, which were still drawn, no doubt to help keep me calm. Unbeknown to me, I was to be sedated with an injection known as a pre-med. A nurse came into the room and asked me to turn on to my front, which I did. She pulled my pyjamas down then I felt something cold being wiped on one of my buttocks which was soon followed by a sharp pain. I jerked suddenly, the syringe tore my skin slightly and the needle broke. The nurse swore, I screamed, and Sister Mears ran into the room. When she saw what had happened, she tried to reason with me to let her get the needle, out but I wasn't too inclined to go with that plan, so, she called in reinforcements.

Within a few minutes, I had people holding my legs, arms, torso, and head down, and given I was only five, I couldn't help but feel quite proud of myself as I write this. Anyway, by this time I'd managed to get myself into growling mode and continued to struggle against my oppressors. Eventually, I heard Sister Mears say that it was impossible to do anything. "Success!" I thought. However, just as I started to relax, she came up to my face and said if I let her do what she had to do, then she'd let me do an injection. That seemed like a fair swap, so, I said, okay as long as I could do it to her. She agreed, although a little too quickly for my liking.

Still held down, she got the first needle out and put an unexpected second one in, this time successfully. Now it was my turn. It was then Sister Mears informed me she wasn't going to let me inject her after all.

"You bloody bastards", I thought, "You inflicted pain and lied to me, and if that's not adding insult to injury what is?" Or something along those lines in a five-year-old's words. As a compromise, they allowed me to inject a teddy bear which got its vengeance because as I pushed the plunger down on the syringe the liquid squirted back out into my face. This wasn't one of my days and I should have known then the surgery wasn't going to go well.

———————

The procedure involved breaking the bones in my ankle, repositioning my foot, inserting metal rods, known as pins, to keep my foot in place, and then plastering me up. A few months later, the plaster was removed as were the pins and a new cast with a rubber foot sole was put on under anaesthetic so I could try walking. The bones were supposed to fuse together in a good position, but they didn't. By the end of it all, my foot was still quite twisted, and I mainly continued to walk on my big toe.

I'd spent nearly all this recovery time at Roehampton. Mum would visit me most days but at one point she went on holiday with Janet, one of the staff nurses from the ward. I felt a bit angry about her going off and even though she bought me a bag with an Olympic logo as a present, I wonder if this served as a catalyst for my feelings of jealousy to become more infused in me.

I can't recall consciously thinking Mum had abandoned me for someone else, but it may have possibly crossed my mind. After all, if she wasn't with me then who might she be with? The idea of her having time for herself which may lead to her being a better mother for me never crossed my mind, but, for a 5-year-old, I guess that's probably a little too much to expect.

———————

Contained

As my relationship with Monica approached its death knell, she bought me a bag because she didn't like me carrying my paperwork around in plastic carrier bags. Maybe to me, the memory of Mum buying me the Olympic logo bag was echoed in this gesture too. The symbolism being around the notion of things being held, contained, in a container that didn't show what was inside.

I always analysed everything and wanted to expose what was being said or meant because I felt something was being hidden and perhaps, I sensed both Mum and Monica didn't want these things to be visible. These may, of course, be the thoughts of a paranoid mind, but it's possible I'd got that way because there was at least some truth in it.

2005 - Dream of Escaping the Nazis

The other night I dreamt I was in charge of a group of captives trying to escape from the Nazis. The significant factor was we could go back in time and attempt an improved escape whenever we made a mistake, a bit like the film, "Groundhog Day" and eventually, we hatched a plan that worked.

As I grow older and see the mistakes I've made, I also see the opportunities I now have to do things differently and possibly with a more successful outcome. The problem is, sometimes, even though I know what I'm doing isn't going to help matters, I still do it anyway.

1970 - Pastens – The Long Haul

When Mum brought me to Pastens she was shown where I'd be sleeping, the gardens and the lounge. She was then asked not to come back for a month. This was, the social worker explained, so I could acclimatise to my new environment. But mum wasn't having that and insisted she would return in two weeks and given I was there on a "voluntary" basis, there was nothing the evil social worker could do about it.

As Mum pulled off that day, I stood on the porch crying uncontrollably. I have no memory of what, if anything, consoled me, or what happened next at all, but the feeling of loneliness shook me to the core. Now with children of my own, I couldn't imagine leaving them alone for such a long time and no doubt for Mum too it must have been very painful.

The Others

Most of the other children residing with me in Pastens, and there weren't many of them, had either learning difficulties or had been neglected, subjected to violence, or sexual abuse. There were two sisters who seemed to have a genetically related learning disorder, and then there was Janet, Tracey and Paul. For just the six of us, there was a matron, several "nurses", a cook, and her husband, who was the gardener.

1970 - School Stuff

My new school, St Peter's Church of England Primary School was situated just over half a mile away from Pastens. It was built of sandstone and had stood there for over a hundred years. We had to wear a uniform which included grey shorts, a shirt, a grey sweater, a school tie and a cap with Saint Peter's Keys embroidered on it. To the front of the school there was a playground that faced the main road and surrounding the school were fields, a golf course, and woods.

Every morning we'd be lined up in the playground and would march into the classroom to a tune played on the piano by one of the staff members. We'd approach our desks and when the music stopped, we'd take our chairs down and sit on them.

My teachers were not quite sure of my needs and didn't spend too much time working out what they might be. Instead, they presumed what they were and came up with what they imagined were appropriate solutions. While this was all done with the best of intentions, being given extra-large exercise books – as in they were almost larger than me – and being kept in during break time so I wouldn't get injured, were not gratefully accepted by me and within a few weeks, I was penning my great works in the same size books as all the other kids and playing contact sports in the playground with everyone else.

Perhaps a good indication of having good schooling is we don't remember much about the place. So outside of playing in the woods, sliding down a big embankment on a journey to the local town, staying in the classroom during dark stormy afternoons, saying hello to the lollipop man (who was on TV one evening talking about how dangerous the road was) and winning the egg and spoon race but losing the sack race, on sports day, all that remains are a couple of mildly traumatic events.

The first was of a girl shunning my advances. I don't remember her name now, but she had blonde hair and was pretty. When I asked her if she'd be my girlfriend she laughed and walked away. This became somewhat of an annoying pattern throughout my life, hence my penchant for brunettes.

The school was around a 25-minute walk from Pastens, well, it was when a member of staff would push me in a buggy through the woods. However, if I tried walking it, it'd take about an hour. On most days when we came out of school, the staff member would be waiting there with the buggy for me and reins for Paul and Janet.

One day I'd acquired an apple and wanted to eat it before being pushed back to Pastens, so, I stood in the corridor eating it when Janet, my co-inmate at Pastens, came to tell me to hurry up. I told her I'd come when I finished the apple. She then let me know that she'd be telling the woman what I'd said. I looked her in the eye, a look Martin Scorsce would be proud of, then kicked her very hard on the shin. We looked at each other for a moment as her eyes welled up with tears and then came the shrieks. I ate the apple as soon as I could and marched out of the school with Janet limping and screaming behind me.

"He just kicked me!" she shouted through her tears.

"Did you Simon?" The care worker asked.

"Well, she hit me first!" I lied.

Janet paused in disbelief, "No I didn't!" she yelled.

She looked to the care worker for support, who saw through my complicated web of deceit, grabbed my arm and sternly said, "Listen, Simon, you shouldn't kick girls, or boys come to that matter, in fact, don't kick anyone." So, like those couples, the ones you see in cars who've just had a row, both looking out of their windows, Janet and I sat together in the buggy this time looking away from one another the whole journey back to Pastens.

Boris - 18th October 2005

I gave Boris a lift this morning. He looked at me and said, "Sometimes I look at you and wonder if I was as stupid as you when I was your age and you know what, I think I was!" We both laughed and he said, "The apple doesn't fall far from the tree".

2005 - Sleep Patterns

I do not remember how my first live-in girlfriend would fall asleep. Sometimes I'd hold her hand and wake from some strange, almost nauseous dream, where, for instance, I had to make a ring of match sticks in the ground, to find I was making love to her. In our last days, I looked upon her body, which had become quite thin after a period of depression and knew in a short while I would no longer see her anymore.

A year later I was sleeping regularly with someone else, she would cuddle up to me for a while as she drifted off, and as she did, she'd start to feel irritated, so she'd tell me to either stay or go. I wasn't ready to sleep yet, so I'd get up and work for a few hours after which I'd get back into bed with her, where she would wake a little and welcome me into her arms.

At first, my next lover and I didn't sleep next to each other. I didn't want her to, but as I started to fall in love with her, I would come to bed even if it was too early for me and fall asleep anyway. I would lie in the half-light of the morning, looking at her beautiful face and wanting to touch her but not wishing to wake her up. Sometimes I would see her body as if it was a prison wall then one day, she said she preferred to sleep alone so we granted each other her wish.

Monica was next, she'd lay and chat with me for hours until we got tired, and the conversation would fade away. I'd move away from her as I'd get too hot and she'd reach her arm out, maybe touching my face or arm. In the middle of the night, we'd cuddle up to each other and in the morning, she wouldn't want to talk for a while. Then there'd be times when we could spend all day in bed, looking at the internet, snacking and sleeping.

And now, in 2005, there's someone else. The first night we spent together I was drawn to her by the way we slept together. I would wake with her lips touching my mouth, or her arm wrapped around mine, or her breath breathing in and out of me. This conversation between our bodies spoke to me of the depths my heart will go to find dreams in reality.

Kate – Late September 2005

One evening after work, a friend from another department invited me along with 8 of her friends to a Japanese restaurant in Soho. Finally, after the pain of recovering from splitting up with Monica, I realised I felt I was back to normal.

A woman called Kate sat opposite me, she had long brown hair, was tall, and had a strong London accent. As the night went on, we kept making each other laugh, so, when the meal ended, I asked if she wanted a lift home. She did, but she had her bike with her so, I said we could try fitting it in my car and with a bit of breaking the laws of physics and probably the land too, we got it in.

Initially, we went back to her place, where we ended up kissing, and then went out again to meet one of her friends, who immediately made it clear she didn't understand what we were doing with each other. Then after dropping her off, Kate came back to my place as the sun rose and got into bed with me.

For the next few months, we'd meet up a few times a week, then one day I realised I'd stayed at her place for some time, and we both acknowledged we were going out with each other. All was going well till she mentioned she'd have to go on holiday with the friend who hadn't approved of me that first night. I got a sense of deja vu, and not surprisingly, once again, started to feel anxious.

November 2005

I have just spent the last two weeks sleeping next to Kate nearly every night. This morning, I dropped her off at a station with the disapproving friend and from there they made their way to the airport. They are going on holiday for a week. I went back to her place to get some of my belongings and as I walked out, I looked back into the early morning rooms as if I might never see them again.

I'd made it clear to Kate that if she becomes sexually involved – which to be specific, covers anything from a drunken kiss to an affair – then I won't see her anymore. It's not so much the act itself, that I possibly could forgive, but it's my inability to cope with mistrust. I need a woman who marks out the boundaries of our relationship to other people without me interjecting and I want someone to love me enough that they don't need anyone else. Typically, though, these are all qualities I tend to lack myself.

A friend of mine recently told me his wife would be "confounded" if he ever got involved with someone else. I was touched by that notion. But with all these rules and hopes, if I'm incapable of following them myself, how can I expect someone else to do so too?

1970 - Tearing Us Apart

When I stood crying at the doors of Pastens I probably cried because I knew I'd miss my mother, I'd miss home. I knew I'd feel isolated and vulnerable, but perhaps worst of all, I also felt an amount of hatred toward my mother for leaving me there, and maybe that upset me too. To feel such anger towards the one I loved meant in time I'd tear myself from her and, even now, the same process often fills me with anxiety as an adult. I have fallen for Kate but if she "betrays" me then I would have to dislocate myself from her, yet, in the process I'd lose someone I've come to love too.

2005 - The Cyclist Dream

I had a dream a few months ago about a girl on a bike careering towards me on a road. She nearly bumped into me, so I shouted at her as she cycled off. She turned around and put two fingers up at me.

One of the things that came to me after this dream was, if I see someone coming at me, I have a choice to either get out of the way or remain in their path and increase the risk of getting run over.

From the moment I met Kate, she had a bike with her, and I couldn't help but associate this dream with her.

2005 - Jealous Guy

It's been a day and a half since Kate went away. My mind has been wandering all over the place and my body is filled with fearful sensations. Cold sweats, weakness, aching, nausea, and a lack of hunger.

A couple of months ago, before we met, I was feeling pretty good. I had, as I said at the time, got over separating from Monica, and was enjoying life. However, over the last few weeks, the relationship with Kate has deepened to such an extent that both of us feel there's something potentially significant going on. The feelings I have for her are so strong that the thought of being with someone else sexually is almost repulsive. So, if she has the same feelings for me then I'd feel secure, but I can't hold on to that belief for some reason. Instead, I visualise her getting drunk and getting involved with somebody else.

1970 - Seeing Red

When I was in Pastens, I didn't know what sex was. I would sometimes play with the girls and get them to let me put my head on their stomachs. I sensed that this was both naughty and intimate so tried it on with all the girls in the home, still, the idea of looking at or playing with each other's private parts was not yet in my mind. One night though I was put to bed in a room upstairs with a girl I'll call Tracey. It was still light outside and one of the care workers came upstairs to tell us to get to sleep. After she'd gone, Tracey called me to her bed and told me to look between her legs. When I did, I saw a red hollow and smelt a strong odour. She asked me to touch her there, but feeling scared and perturbed I ran back to my bed. Years later Mum told me that Tracey had been a victim of sexual abuse. Back then, the lack of intimacy in my life was mitigated slightly by putting my head on a tummy, but for Tracey, at five years old, it was already found via genital stimulation.

1970 - Echoes

So, at five years old I was playing the girls around me off against each other. It wasn't deliberate, it was more a case of wanting to have access to all of them but not being sensitive or caring about how they felt. One can excuse a five-year old but whenever I feel like I want attention from lots of women nowadays I justify it by believing I'm not connected with anyone. As soon as a woman comes along who feels like she's enough for me, I don't want to see any other women at all. Well, not until things start falling apart; again, this might have been something I learned at age 5. The woman who could have been enough, my mother, wasn't available, so, instead, I found echoes of her in those around me. It's easy to blame one's mother, after all, if it's not one thing, it's your mother, but lots of people are unfaithful even though they had loving and devoted parents. So, maybe infidelity is caused by multiple reasons.

2005 - Shallow Grave

A few years ago, I read some notes compiled about me by one of the matrons at Pastens and in them she said I was shallow, craving attention and affection from anyone willing to show me any. When I read that my heart went out to the child that had been me and, of course, felt like killing the matron.

1970 - Maria

There were a few relationships between me and others at Pastens that did have some depth to them. Firstly, there was Janet and Paul who for almost two years were my "siblings" and then there was a couple of night staff who would cuddle us before we went to sleep.

One was called Maria, she had long dark hair and olive skin. I thought she was beautiful and became very attached to her. She would talk to us in our beds, put her arms around us and kiss us goodnight. Perhaps it was because she looked after us through the night that meant she could see our need for intimacy. She would watch us fall asleep, see our bodies move or hear our voices call out as we dreamt and, to both us and her, she was our only protector through the darkness. Even though she wouldn't see us in our daily routines, perhaps her view allowed her to see our core identities, which were most likely those of lost children.

Her heart reached out to us, and we grabbed hold of her with all our might. But, one night she put her arms around me and told me she would be leaving soon and not coming back. I started to cry and asked her not to go, but she told me she would be getting married and moving somewhere else. Recently my mother told me she could have kept in contact with Maria but didn't see the need.

2005 - Straight on till Morning

For many years I have led a nocturnal life. I tend to find I can work for hours without a break during the night and early hours. I don't feel lonely and have no desire to communicate with others during this time, which I'm sure is a big relief to my friends. The opposite is true of daytime though. I find it hard to get on with work, I want to meet up with friends, and I am very easily side-tracked. Given the night can be so isolating, it seems a bit of a paradox, but maybe it's the feeling that there was someone there for me if I needed them at night when I was a child that's behind this. Perhaps though, maybe I keep busy at night because going to sleep then would remind me I'm still one of the lost children.

2005 - Silence

In one of my songs I sing, "Silence, they say is golden but sometimes it's deadly too, so why is it so quiet tonight, between me and you?"

Over the last few days, Kate has telephoned me from Turkey, and just by the sound of her voice I've felt reassured that she hasn't been unfaithful to me while she's been away. Tonight is her last night away and she hasn't called me. I wasn't expecting her to, but the silence allows my mind to fill in the gaps with every scenario it can come up with.

Some people think it is what is done or said that has the most profound effects on our lives, but in a way, what is acted out in action, or said in the heat of the moment tends to paradoxically be a result of silence or inaction. As we lie down to sleep our minds find long periods of inactivity and fill the time with dreams. When we are awake, we do the same, but when we wake from dreams, we tend to automatically differentiate between what was dreamt and what is real. However, when we dwell within our imagination within non-sleep silence spells, we can become very unsure as to whether what we are considering is real or just fantasy.

When I play chess, I tend to use the time my opponent takes thinking, to work out what their next move will be. When I'm in a relationship I try to imagine what my partner might say. When, in chess, my opponent makes the move I thought they'd do, I tend to react very quickly, moving my piece almost immediately. This has the effect of making me look like a very quick thinker and tends to intimidate them, especially if they're a beginner – a good player will probably think I must be a beginner - especially given most of the time I get it wrong. When I start to imagine what might be said in a relationship, which I know is not a competitive game even though it can be, I start to feel what I would've felt, had those words been said. The residue and mental exhaustion that ensues are also accompanied by a belief that what's been imagined is the truth.

If everyone I love goes away, then I cannot help but presume that those I will come to love will go away too. Consequently, I'm constantly on the lookout for warning signs that this is going to happen, and it's no different tonight. The silence could be a sign of anything, it might have no meaning at all, but I automatically see it as a bad sign and go through the pain of fear and dread without knowing anything for sure. If silence might be golden or deadly it might also be nothing more than what it is, nothing. But when you've been damaged, even nothing doesn't go unnoticed.

1970 - Death

One day I was colouring in a picture with felt tips when one of the care workers told me the ink was poisonous. A few minutes later I ran to her screaming hysterically because I'd put the ink end into my mouth and thought I would die. Fortunately, she reassured me I'd survive, so, I continued with my masterpiece.

I can't remember thinking about death before this time, I'm sure I did, but the notion of having to die one day didn't tend to fill me with dread unless, of course, I was in the midst of perceiving I was just about to die, in which case there was a fair amount of panic.

Possibly being made to go to church twice on a Sunday and attend Sunday school pretty much softened the blow of realising death might well be the last thing in a chain of meaningless events we ever experience.

One of the churches we went to was a large traditional one. We had to sit quietly, but apart from that, and the pile of cans of food, vegetables and bread that appeared at the Harvest Festival I hardly have any memories of it. The other church was small and made of corrugated iron sheets, and had a tall, thin, greasy-haired vicar who spoke vehemently of damnation to his flock. Again, I have no memories of what was said, but when it came to their harvest festival there was a much smaller pile of gifts on display.

Religion for me between five and seven was where we listened to stories, sang songs, and gently avoided the issues that underpin the reason for religion existing in the first place. You know, death, despair, and God knows what else. The church though still underpinned our community as most activities for kids took place in the church hall. The school was a church school, and the community festivals were organised by the church and so on. Even Pastens was run by the church. But still, there was no escape: materialism, sex, and violence were dominating factors even in my little 5-year-old world. I would lie in bed in the summer evenings, the bright sun blazing through thin flowery curtains, calculating how long it would take to save up my ten pence per week pocket money to buy a toy gun. If the coast was clear I'd jump into bed with one of the girls for a quick cuddle and exploration, and when pushed, I'd think up violent ways to get back at members of staff who'd unfairly "oppressed" me. So, no change there then.

1986 - Janet

When I was 21, I found Janet, who'd been adopted by a family who came to the home to help occasionally. At 21 she was working as a shop assistant in a department store and seemingly happy, but she didn't want to talk about those times, in fact, they were pretty much a blank to her.

1971 - Pastens

Janet and I once sat on stage together and dressed up as the black and white minstrels (I'll probably get cancelled for doing that so don't tell anyone) and sang, "If you were the only girl in the world". I mimed it – about a verse out of sync – and she gazed on lovingly at me in front of everyone in the Christmas Show at the church hall. She didn't remember that, or that just like an old couple, we'd bickered and fought many times, or that we'd hugged and played with each other's bits, bathed, slept, and shared the pain of the oppressive regime together. To her, it was all a blank. I even told her how my bullying of her had filled me with guilt as I got older, but she didn't remember the apple incident at all. Was it all a dream? Well, the newspaper cutting of the singing on stage said not, but the rest might be.

The Staff

I had been naughty, and Sandra, one of the new helpers wasn't having any of it. We were now at the point where the victim was strapped, metaphorically, to the bed and the evil angel of death, Sandra, was about to administer the death sentence, normally the removal of sweet rations. As if I'd suddenly taken on James Bond's persona, I calculated just how hard and where exactly to deliver my death kick.

"Don't even think about it!" Sandra warned.

"Fuck!" I thought, or at least I would have if I'd known the word. "Great, a bloody mind-reading Nazi... what next?" I turned over and sulked for ten minutes, at which point Sandra re-entered the room and said, "Right if you're going to play nicely you can come back in."

I wonder how often a child has actually waltzed back into the room there and then and said, "Thank you, I can see your point of view and I'm genuinely sorry to have mucked you around, please don't hesitate to scold me again if ever, and I hope it never comes to it, I am disobedient in any way again".

Perhaps some genius sociopath managed it, but for the rest of us, muttering under our breath as we shuffle slowly back is about all we can muster.

1971 - Liver

"If you don't eat your dinner you'll stay at the table until you do."

This fascist was new but old in years (She was probably 40). Her hair was grey, and her heritage Indian. She looked soft but was as hard as the liver she was forcing me to eat. I don't think I was a fussy eater, but she'd deemed I had to be shown who was boss. I cried as I placed the leather-textured morsel in my mouth. But in the end, she won. Although for years after I didn't eat the stuff but when I did, maybe 20 years later, I discovered I liked it.

Differentiating between a child genuinely not liking a certain food and just playing a power game is probably not so hard to determine and perhaps it was exactly these scenarios that helped British prisoners of war resist being tortured. After all, some might say eating British food is good enough training in itself.

1971 – Pastens - Ear Infection

In the middle of the night, a light shines in my eyes.

"The doctor is here to see you."

Something hard digs into my ear

I scream out in pain

I'm crying

Nauseous crying

There's a taste of cough mixture

Then sleep.

1970 – Pastens - Dr Who

"At home my mother lets me watch Doctor Who," I cry out in protest.

"Well, she shouldn't," the gull-winged glasses commandant shouts.

"But it's the last of the series." I implore.

"There's no Doctor Who Simon! It will give you nightmares."

The gardener's dog, a golden retriever walks up to me. I hug it. As I walk along the path outside there's wool on the fence, left by itchy sheep. I want to make a ball of wool from it and use it to find my way home.

1972 – Pastens - Seventh Birthday Party

Mum has come to my seventh birthday party at Pastens. I've been allowed to invite one friend from school. Mum too has also brought a friend along with her. It turns out his name is Michael. He's tall, dark, thin, and wears glasses. Just before Mum leaves, she asks me if I'd like to live with her after the summer. The idea of being with Mum all the time and escaping Pastens filled me with joy and hope. It was as if all my wishes were just about to come true, but you know what they say about wishes.

Chapter 11
Roundshaw

1972 – First Morning on Roundshaw

Mum calls me into the kitchen, as the song, *Concrete and Clay*, is playing on the radio. "Come on, come and eat your breakfast, hurry up, you're going to be late for school."

19th October 2006 – Fulham – Sands End

Tonight, I'm teaching web design at a local adult education college in Fulham. There's a football match at the nearby Chelsea Stadium so there's heavy traffic and finally, when I get to the college, there's nowhere to park, so I drive around looking for a space when a van comes up behind me. At first, I think it's being driven by a fellow tutor but it's not and as I proceed at about 10 mph the driver starts to flash his lights and honk his horn at me. I shout out to him that I'm looking for somewhere to park, to which he shouts back, "Fuck off you prick". So, I slam my brakes on and drive even slower.

2006 - May The Force Be With You

My sons have just started at a new school, and they've already had a taste of bullying. When they told me today about it, I wanted to get the kid involved and threaten him into submission but instead, I told them to reason with him. They said they've already asked him to try and understand how it feels for them to be subjected to his behaviour, but he just replied, "I'm not you, so I can't understand." I then recommended they speak to the teacher again and if that didn't work, come back to me. Their mother interjects, "That's enough for God's sake, I don't want them getting into trouble." The boys look at me and wink, sometimes force may have to be met with force.

19th October 2006 Fulham – Sands End

I'm driving very slowly in retaliation to the aggressive driver behind me. I try to let go of the anger that's welling up inside of me so decide to take the first available turn to get out of his way. Instead of driving on though, he follows me. Unperturbed, I continue looking for a parking space while he continues to shout at me. I then see a space which won't be any good for parking in, but I pull into it all the same. This is more of a gesture of, "OK if you want a fight come on then." He pulls up beside me and blocks me in.

I get out of the car and watch him take a long spirit level from his back seat. I feel no fear, I'm calm, almost too calm. I'm thinking that I might be able to take him, and if he swings the spirit level at me, I'll try to either block, ride or take the blow and then, if I get close enough, I'll kick him with my artificial leg across his knee or shin. As he approaches me, he sees my arms and stands still, and then in a genuinely apologetic tone says, "Sorry mate."

I reply, slightly indignantly, "I was just trying to find somewhere to park".

"Yeah sorry, yeah you were trying to park, sorry" He places his hand affectionately on my shoulder, says sorry once again and then walks away.

Perhaps for him, it was a relief to find a way out and to show a better side of his nature, and for me too, as calm, and as unshakable as I was, I preferred the realisation that we were both real humans after all, not some violence crazed characters from a Tarantino film fantasy.

Roundshaw 1972

Roundshaw, the word means ring of trees, was a housing estate ten miles south of Central London, built on top of part of what had been the original Croydon Airport.

London is based in the centre of a naturally formed geological basin which the River Thames flows through. For those travelling to London from the south, the sight of the city as they came over the rim of the basin, even hundreds of years ago, was almost the same view I could see as I stood outside our new flat for the first time. In the hazy distance, I could see St Paul's Cathedral glinting in the sun.

Powell Close.

When I first visited our flat on Roundshaw the sun shone bright on the white concrete walls, and given anything would have looked good in that light, I was taken. Roundshaw was a meeting of the past and future – the old airport, its runways all around us, and these new modern homes. It offered me an escape from care and a dream come true in which I could finally live with Mum full-time.

During this visit, my friend Peter and his mother Judith came along too. However, Peter and I wandered off and managed to get lost within a few minutes. There were tower blocks, concrete decks, patches of grass, walkways and stairs, and to the untrained eye, they all looked the same. In desperation, we called for our mothers who heard our cries and called back.

Roundshaw symbolically welcomed me to a world where I would come to lose myself and no matter how much I cried for help, there'd be no way back.

113

Dream 20th December 2005

I'm standing in my neighbour's garden on Roundshaw. In real life, the neighbour who was called Bill, died a long time ago, but his second wife continued living in his flat for many years after so I would visit her once every couple of years, and every time I did, the place always looked exactly as it had done in 1972. Yellow flowery wallpaper, brown smoked glass tableware and a glass-topped table.

In the dream though things were slightly different. Scattered across the garden, which was now slightly overgrown, were items from Bill's life, including a box full of board games. I decided that if these things were going to be thrown away, I should take some for myself, but as I did, three men passed by and began to look through the debris too. As I watched them, I found a photograph of Bill when he was young. I told the men how I used to sit on his shoulders and stroke his hair and as I relayed this to them, one of them started to cry and that made me cry too.

I then walked into his flat where a woman startled me. I tell her she reminds me of Bill's first wife, and she laughs at my lack of diplomacy because she is young and his wife was old. I look at the debris again and realise that what looked like rubbish was actually valuable after all.

1972 – June - Visiting Roundshaw Junior School

I am standing in front of a class of children. The headmaster, who's next to me, says, "This is Simon and he shall be joining us next term", I feel like hundreds of faces are staring at me. A couple of the girls let out exasperations of pity.

1972 - Roundshaw - September

My next visit to Roundshaw, the one where Peter and I got lost, took place a couple of months later. Mum was already moving in by then. These first visits occurred on sunny summer days, but by the time I moved in it was September and the days were already getting darker.

As I couldn't walk far, and Roundshaw was a sprawling mass of concrete decks, Mum bought me a bike to help me get around. The decks were made of large slabs of concrete, most were about ten metres wide and some hundreds of metres long, and nearly all of them were positioned above parking garages or roadways. To the edge of each deck would be doorways to apartments and next to them a cupboard where people could put their rubbish. Opposite the doorways would be a wall and beyond that, a twenty-foot drop. At each end or regular intervals, stairs and ramps would take the inhabitants from terra-firma to terror firmer!

114

Five Powell Close.

Roundshaw had already gained notoriety among the local surrounding community, where if you were from Roundshaw you were seen as, at best common, but, more likely dangerous too. Given the estate had recently featured on the national news because milkmen refused to service the area for fear of being robbed, their concerns were probably justified.

I was completely unaware of Roundshaw's dark side at first. Instead, I smelt the newness of the paint, got dazzled by the sunlight on the lino throughout the flat, and bathed in the joy of finally being able to live with Mum at last in our own home.

The smooth surfaced decks particularly lent themselves to being cycled on, so, for my first few ventures alone I rode in front of our doorway and due to our deck being a thoroughfare to the shops, it didn't take long for the little boy with short arms to become known all over.

As I peddled up and down, mothers pushing their children, stray dogs and other children passed me too. Within the first hours of playing outside a gang of children passed and taunted me for having stabilisers on my bike. So, I got off it and tried to detach the stabilisers, which were bolted on.

A few doors down from our place I saw an old man looking at me.

"Excuse me mister but can you help me take these off please?"

He came over, crouched down and told me that he would if my mother said it was ok. I told him I'd ask her when she got in, so he nodded and went back inside. As far as I was concerned this was an emergency and I wasn't prepared to wait, so, as soon as he was gone, I went at the bolts with my teeth.

Years later the old man, Bill, the one in the dream about debris in his garden, told me he'd watched me from his window in disbelief. The stabilisers were off within minutes, and I would no longer be persecuted for not being able to ride a bike properly, but instead, it would be because of my arms.

Powell Close.

2001 - Conflict of the Oppressed

When I was thirty-two I was cycling along a road in Fulham when I heard some loud laughter. As I looked across, I saw three teenagers pointing and laughing at me. I did a U-turn and pulled up next to them. They looked on, still laughing, so, I said, "I shouldn't have to put up with this kind of behaviour when I go out, should I?"

I looked at one of them who was tall, stocky, and mixed race and said to him, "How would you like it if someone called you a nigger?"

He shouted, "Are you calling me a nigger?"

I calmly said, "No, I'm just pointing out that you wouldn't like it if someone called you a nigger."

"Right," he said, "I'm going to teach you a lesson."

He threw off his jacket and shouted, "I'm gonna knock your lights out."

I felt very relaxed and looked at him.

"The moment you touch me will be the last time you'll be free to live in Fulham, I'll make sure you're beaten up every day until you can no longer bear to stay here. I know you live in Sherbrooke Road." This technique of "psyching someone out" was one of the first things I'd learned on Roundshaw.

He seemed a bit disturbed, especially as I knew where he lived, so he picked up his jacket and walked off cursing me. I cycled home, but when I got in my rage started to pump through me. I told my partner at the time, what had happened, and she said she'd come out with me to find him. So, we got in the car and drove around the streets until we saw him. I pulled up and leant out the window. "See this car," I shouted, "this will be the last thing you see if I feel like getting you, you should be careful who you threaten you fuckin' cunt."

A couple of days later I saw him standing in my street looking up at my house. I went to my kitchen put on an arm band, slid a knife up it and walked downstairs. Faced with someone threatening me or my loved ones I wouldn't hesitate to push a knife through their face or chest and move it around to make sure they could no longer function.

Somewhere in the dark garages and sparkling decks of Roundshaw, I learned that being ruthless was the best way to deal with threats. Sometimes, though, I would find myself hurting someone in a fight, they'd be screaming out in agony, and I'd feel sorry for them and want to stop. I knew I had to teach them a lesson, but a part of me hated this world of violence.

When I opened the door, he was gone. I had my arm pulled towards my back to hide the long blade. If he'd confronted me both our lives may have taken a very different direction and deep down, I knew it wasn't worth it.

Later that evening, I thought it best to find a different resolution so visited a friend who I thought might know him. He said he did, and he'd have a word. A few weeks later I was driving down Sherbrooke Road when a person on a bike pulled out in front of me. I slammed my brakes on and as I came to an emergency stop, I realised it was the same guy. We looked at each other and I gave him a, "See I told you," smile. He almost smiled back.

A few weeks later I heard he'd been put in prison for punching a policewoman in the stomach. Somewhere, he had his own story to tell, but I didn't like the way he wanted to tell it, so I didn't want to hear it.

When I was forty-one, nine years after this all happened, one of the girls from the group who'd initially laughed at me, served me in a chemist. I wondered if she remembered the incident. Maybe she was thinking the same thing. A few days after that, I saw her walking an old lady home and as I passed by, I heard her tell the old lady that "it was nothing at all."

Outside of not wanting to be psychologically attached forevermore to this guy, being imprisoned, or possibly losing my soul, the thought of killing him wasn't too unappealing. Although, I might have felt differently in reality.

1972 - Roundshaw

My murderous violent temper was already bad before I got to Roundshaw, but once there it was honed to a far greater degree.

My First Fight on Roundshaw

I cycled down a ramp from our deck to a grassy area. In front of me was a group of children who started laughing and calling out, "Oi! You! Where are your arms? Hey, where's your arms?" I had just moved from a provincial village and the worst swear word I knew was, "bastard". So, with as much vehemence as I could summon, I told them I thought they were, "Bloody bastards". They laughed at me and started to imitate my middle-class accent and shout out, "No arms" over and over again.

I cycled over to them, got off my bike and started to chase them. They got out of the way, then formed a circle around me and started to taunt me further. As I'd run at any one of them, they'd move out of my way, swarm-like, so in frustration, I started to cry.

One of the boys yelled, "Oh poor little crybaby". I looked at him and spat in his face. Fortunately, for me, my saliva landed in his eyes. He put his hands up, slightly blinded and leant forwards. I ran at him and kicked him in the head as hard as I could with my built-up medical boot. There was a clonking sound, he fell backwards, rolled in a ball and clutched his head. A few seconds later he got up, tears streaming, screaming in pain, and shouted, "I'll get my mum onto you."

The other kids stopped taunting me and stood in silence as he ran into one of the doorways. A few seconds later a well-built blonde woman came out dragging him by the arm. When she saw what had happened, she smacked him around the head and told the other kids they should be ashamed of themselves. She knelt down, wiped the tears from my face and invited me into her house to get cleaned up. I went in and was introduced to her Turkish husband and three other children. After a short while I was playing with them all and through them was introduced to the other children from the block. What I learned that day was having an aptitude for violence not only stopped the taunting but also earned respect and friendship from the kids on Roundshaw.

1972 - Roundshaw

When I went into my victim's house, I entered not only a foreigner's home but also an environment which was foreign to me. It was a family home. A mother and father who seemed to love each other, 4 children, two girls and two boys, and a

118

myriad of pets, all living together within this small council house. To add to the strangeness of the scene, the whole place had been decorated in a Turkish style.

The youngest daughter, Sema, wanted to show me her cat's new litter of kittens and asked if I wanted one. When I got in that evening, I asked Mum if we could have one, but she said no. The next day Sema turned up at our front door with one of the kittens in her pocket. She went up to my mother and said she had something to show her. Her hand came out of her pocket with a tiny black kitten curled up in her palm. My mum let out a sigh of resigned debilitation and from their family home, I was given an opportunity to experience the joy of a pet. That night, I named the little black kitten Ginny after a cat mentioned in a book that had been read to me in care.

1972 - First Day at Roundshaw Juniors

My first day at school was marred by two main events that related directly to my disability. Both involved my clothing. The first one was caused by the occupational therapists at Roehampton Hospital cutting a hole in the groin of my trousers so I could get my penis to poke out through it when I needed to go for a pee. The problem was, as with most penises, mine seemed to have a mind of its own and decided to pop out during my first hour of class. Not able to get it back in myself I walked up to the teacher and asked her to do it for me. She got quite flustered and told me to go away and not to be so silly. I don't remember how the issue was solved but I did feel humiliated in front of my whole class, especially as some of them were making gestures of exasperation or disgust. The other incident involved playing football. We were told to put on our football gear, so, I went into the changing room full of pride that I had a Chelsea kit and couldn't wait to get out there with the rest of them. The problem was, I took so long trying to get my boots tied up that the class was over before I was even changed. Possibly this event turned me against football for the rest of my life and consequently, by not being interested in the world of football, I also segregated myself from an important part of male culture. From then on, I'd sit out of break time footie matches and chat to the girls sitting on the sidelines. While the boys in my class developed skills in kicking a ball around, I learned how to talk with girls and most of the time, it didn't involve football. One of the girls I'd talk with was called Jackie, she took a shine to me which somehow ended up with her being my girlfriend for a few days. She even came to my home one day where Mum and Michael created an elaborate tea ceremony. Possibly my proposal of marriage and a further offer of fathering copious amounts of children gave her the wrong impression, so, when we arrived at school a few days later she told me I wasn't her boyfriend anymore. My reaction was to kick her hand, maybe it was symbolic, as in wanting to damage something that she had that I didn't. Her hand or her heart possibly, but when I was later informed I'd broken her finger, I felt the condemning gaze of my peers fall upon me. Even now, the shame of physically hurting a girl fifty years ago, still gnaws at the heart of me.

2006 - Perfect Stranger

There's a new guy who just started at my work. One of my friends who'd come into my office today told me she thought he was the most beautiful man she'd ever seen. Even in his wheelchair, he sits almost as high as I do standing. I told Kate about this good-looking man, and she laughed, "So, what's wrong with him then? There's got to be something." As they say, nobody's perfect, not even a perfect stranger.

2006 - Dream - Starbucks the Eighth Wonder of the World

I've just had a dream about Boris in which he has had to move out of where he lives. We're talking on the phone. I try to guide him to where I'm waiting with a few other people.

"Where are you?" he asks.

I explain that he'll "Have to walk to the end of the high street, then go up a hill, and there's that building with the dome, do you remember it?"

In real life, this building would be the eighth wonder of the world but in my dream, it's the roof of a Starbucks coffee house.

As soon as I wake up, I wonder if Boris has just died. I'm feeling guilty because I haven't seen him for a few days. I shall ring him shortly just to check he's still with us. I do so, and he is.

During the call, I tell him I've just been accepted as a member of The Chelsea Arts Club, a prestigious London club that's renowned for being hard to become a member of. He's not impressed at all. There's no pleasing some parents.

1972 - Roundshaw - Michael

A few weeks after moving in with Mum and Michael, I tried to open their bedroom door, but it was locked. When I knocked and called out, I was told to go away. A day or so later, I came home and found Michael was in too. He was pointing an air pistol at a photograph of a woman, his ex-wife, Sue. He pulled the trigger and where her face had been a hole appeared. He reloaded and took another shot.

Michael had been a soldier and was now a photographer. He'd been brought up in Yorkshire within a strict family, joined the army as part of the medical corps and after leaving he became a nurse. He then suffered a brain haemorrhage which resulted in him having surgery. As a result, the scar tissue on his brain caused him to have blackout-type fits and unbeknown to us at the time, extremely violent, psychotic episodes. Perhaps the fact that he had been stopped from seeing his daughter by his wife should have been a big red flag.

For someone from a strict family, the behaviour of a precocious child, erm that's me I'm talking about, (I know, it's hard to believe), was particularly riling for Michael.

1972 - Michael's Temper

Michael has me pinned to the floor; his hands are around my throat.

"And if you ever tell your mother I'll kill her in front of you and then I'll kill you. Do you understand?" Michael then turned me over and smacked his hand across my backside.

This all started when he confronted me about going out to play with my friends. A bit earlier I'd crept down the stairs, I knew Michael was to be avoided, so, I opened the front door and almost walked off, but still in my pyjamas, I knew I couldn't. I decided to close the door quietly, walked back up the stairs and went back into my room.

Mum had gone to work, and Michael was sleeping on the couch in the front room because after months of bullying us, Mum had finally managed to get him out of the bedroom, but not the flat.

The first time I'd witnessed Michael's temper occurred one Saturday morning as I sat on my bed playing. I heard raised voices and then a yelp from my mother. I picked up my milkshake and walked to the doorway. Michael was shouting at Mum about using his towels which, he claimed she had made damp when she knew she wasn't allowed to touch them. I heard a thud and Mum crying then the bathroom door opened.

Michael faced me and said, "What are you looking at?" I was frozen to the spot, but I still wanted to see if Mum was okay. He stepped towards me, picked me up and threw me across the room. I landed against the bed which partly cushioned the fall but still winded me, while the milkshake went everywhere. Once I could breathe, I wanted to cry but Mum walked in, and in silence, with tears streaming down her face, hugged me and cleaned up the mess. A few days later I came home from school and found Michael decorating the lounge. This would become a familiar pattern over the next year.

The second incident involved Michael grabbing me by my arm and throwing me under the table. This happened in front of Peter, the friend I'd got lost with months earlier. Michael had been watching an orchestra performing on the TV while Peter and I imitated the conductor which made us laugh hysterically. Michael told me to stop being stupid, I continued, and within seconds was flung to the floor. I continued to laugh but I wanted to scream out for help.

When Michael went for Mum the next time, I shouted out that I would tell sister Mears from Roehampton Hospital about him if he continued hurting us.

1972 - Michael - A Step Too Far

So, after getting past Michael and then returning to my bedroom in my pyjamas, I heard Michael call me. I walked to the landing. "Did you go outside earlier?" he asked.

"No," I replied.

"Don't lie, I know you did because you left the door open".

I clearly remembered shutting the door but perhaps in my efforts to be as silent as possible, I hadn't let the catch of the lock click into place correctly.

"Right, I'm going to teach you a lesson," he said as he grabbed me, his hand around my throat. "So, you're going to tell Sister whatever her name is about me, are you?" He spun me over and his hand came down hard on my bottom. "Well let me tell you that if you ever do, I'll make you wish you'd never been born." Another smack hit me. He spun me around again, placed his hands around my throat and squeezed. "And if you ever tell your mother I will kill her in front of you and then I'll kill you. Do you understand?"

I was crying in shock but managed to summon a yes.

"Now get out of my sight, go on, go out and play with your friends if you want, I don't want to see you." As I walked away, he kicked me up the backside, so I slid and fell over at the top of the stairs. Still, in my pyjamas, I got out of the house as quickly as I could, and as I shut the door behind me, I saw a group of friends talking nearby. I walked up to them, wanting to tell them what had just happened but instead, all I could do was burst out crying. They looked at me, completely confounded. It was then I realised there could be even greater levels of loneliness than those I'd experienced in care.

A bit later Michael called me in and fed me.

One night soon after the first attack I was allowed to stay up to watch a film called *Mutiny on The Bounty*. The story follows a mutiny against an overly harsh ship's captain and his subsequent return and persecution of his mainly innocent crew.

That night I experienced what is known as a night terror. This is like a nightmare but includes sleepwalking as well as a certain amount of consciousness. Even now, 32 years later, I clearly recall having to find my mother to tell her the ship we were

122

on was going to sink and she must get off as soon as possible. She told me I was dreaming so I pleaded with her to wake me up. She continued to speak to me and then got me into bed where I soon went back to sleep.

A few nights later I had a similar nightmare, but this time it was about a train that was just about to crash. "Please mummy you've got to get off," I begged.

If Michael had banned me from telling Mum directly then my subconscious tried a different tack, only it was far too subtle for anyone to understand. Mum didn't kick Michael out, maybe she would have had she been aware of his violent abuse of me but it's also possible she'd have been too scared to do anything anyway.

Almost a year passed when, to our delight, we came home, and he had gone. The relief stayed with us for months, but about six months later there was a loud knock on the door and when I looked down the stairs through the glass door, I recognised Michael's form and told Mum it was him. She uttered, "No" in disbelief, but still answered the door. I went to bed and the next day he was there, back on the couch sleeping.

That evening I went to the Roundshaw community centre and watched people doing karate in the main hall. I stood in front of them and copied what they did. I had seen the TV series Kung Fu and dreamt of being able to defend Mum and me from Michael's attacks. Well, actually, I dreamt of killing him.

1972 - War and Love

There must have been a volcano that had erupted somewhere in the world around this time because beautiful sunsets seemed to be all the rage. From the exact spot where I cried in front of my friends, you could see St Paul's glimmer in the distance, and as summer frayed into autumn and the nights drew in cold around us, our adventures on the old runways of Croydon Airport became, as Peter Gabriel put it, games without frontiers.

The domain of kids, especially those brought up on a council estate, lacks limitations when it comes to inhibitions. That can be a good thing, especially when it comes to making new acquaintances. For instance, asking a stranger of a similar age, if they want to play with you is perfectly acceptable when you're a child, but when it came to playing war games, it was a whole different story.

The war games we played were far more war than play. Firstly, there were real trenches with sheets of metal laid over the top to form tunnels. Secondly, real artillery was fired across the battleground in the shape of stones, firework rockets, bangers and/or any other fireworks that could be stolen from the local shops, and thirdly hand-to-hand combat included quite extreme violence, again including various weapons. The pleas of one kid who I'd crept up on, and held a brick over, went unheard by me. This was war, so, I let the brick go and watched as he curled up in a ball crying.

There were also large old air-raid shelters which we'd dare each other to enter. They were pitch black inside and smelt of piss and dampness. I once fell over in one, landing knee-first on some barbed wire. Given how unsanitary they were I'm surprised I didn't get gangrene.

Lynette and Dan

After one evening's exciting game of war, I returned home at around nine pm to find my mother hysterical with anger. She'd called the police, allegedly, and was not going to let me play out anymore. So, from then on, well at least for a while, I went directly from school to a babysitter called Lynnette.

Lynnette's flat was dark, smoke-stained throughout and filled with the smell you get when you leave a gas cooker on too long. The flame was partly continuously lit to not only cook us the nightly beans on toast but to also keep the cigarettes she continuously had hanging from the corner of her mouth alight.

Lynnette's husband Dan often sat in a chair in the kitchen dressed in his full Teddy Boy regalia, which even in 1972 was rather passé. Whenever they spoke to each other it'd be in the poetic form of resentful argumentative rhythms. I didn't realise at the time, but this possibly had a lot to do with Lynnette recently revealing she was pregnant which, had Dan not had a vasectomy shortly after the birth of their previous child, may have been something to celebrate.

Mum might have got me out of the killing fields of Roundshaw, but now I was immersed in the deadly feuds of a struggling marriage. I didn't like being there and I didn't like Lynnette, who seemed to have me there merely to make money and I could tell her heart was not in the job, the home, or the marriage.

1972 - A Day in the Trenches

I wonder if the type of breakfast one chooses is partly influenced by genetics. My Gran nearly always cooked breakfast when I visited. Her day started in the kitchen because that's where she'd get dressed in the warmth of the cooking range. Perhaps having a cooked breakfast was as much a choice related to stoking the oven in the morning as it was a need to eat.

For me, though, I don't wake up feeling hungry but by lunchtime, I'll often have an English breakfast. For my mother, however, breakfast was important when it came to starting the day. Cereal was the mainstay, while cooked breakfasts were for days when we weren't in a rush. Throughout the winter though, it was a plate of porridge covered in sugar surrounded by a moat of cold milk that'd greet me.

The problem with porridge was, five minutes after leaving the house I'd find my bowels stirring with an unstoppable force that'd often result in returning home for an emergency poo, much to mum's anger. The memory of the incident in the garden while wearing my new trousers probably meant she wasn't prepared to take such risks anymore.

"Oh Simon, I've got to get to work. Why do you always want to go to the loo just when we have to leave."

If I'd made the connection between porridge and an overwhelming need to have a bowel movement, I could have pointed the finger back at her, but I didn't.

There's a snugness about walking to school in the darkness of a winter morning, seeing a friend from school and trotting up to join them. This morning it was a boy with wavy auburn hair called Michael, there were a lot of Michaels around back in those days. I could have changed his name to make it easier for you, but I know how much you like a bit of gritty reality.

As we approached Roundshaw's shopping centre I asked him, "Shall we go to the supermarket and see what toys they've got?" Within minutes we were in the shop, bleak and bright with its yellow strip lights, while the darkness of the winter morning sky still pushed against the window. The place was full of freezer cabinets but in the middle was a stand that displayed toys, records and other things.

What interested me this morning was a magnet set. We both sat on the floor and started playing with whatever we could get out of the boxes, meanwhile one of the cashiers kept a close eye on us. About a minute later, a man in a white uniform approached us and asked if we intended to buy something. Given we had no money it wasn't likely. "We're just looking," I said, and as the man turned his back and huffed, Michael slipped a magnet set into one of my pockets.

We walked out slowly looking pissed off about our playtime being abruptly ended, while the man and woman nodded to each other while saying something disparaging about us. As we got close to the school, Sevin, the boy I'd kicked in the head, joined us and told us about a dead dog he'd just seen. It was still early, so, we went to have a look. The dog was a sandy-coloured mongrel who we'd often seen roaming the estate. By this point, we weren't the only children gathered around and as we stared at the pool of blood that had dribbled from its mouth, and its long grey-purple tongue draped on the paving slab, someone in the crowd remarked how much it looked as if it was sleeping. The sun was rising and, in its light, we pretended our breath was smoke, and watched it rise like a ceremony for the dog's soul. There was a strange silence which was broken a few seconds later by the sound of someone running towards us.

As the steps got closer, we turned and the boy, almost unable to speak for being out of breath, told us he'd just seen a woman commit suicide by jumping off Instone, the tallest building on the estate. Once he was able to speak more coherently, he informed us a man who'd seen what had happened told the congregation around the body that he'd come out to get his milk and said hello to his neighbour, but within a few seconds she'd climbed onto the balcony wall, looked across at him, and before he could say anything, let herself fall. After she hit the ground, she was still alive for a few minutes. Her body was motionless, but her eyes kept looking around and her mouth quivered a bit, and, "Then," he said, "she became still.

As this story was relayed to us an RSPCA van pulled up to take the body – of the dog – away. If there'd been a policeman at the scene, he'd have said something like, "Come on, move on, there's nothing to see here," but there wasn't. Still, once the body was taken, we continued our reluctant pilgrimage to school. When we got there, children were still playing outside in the low-cast sun and long-shadowed playground.

A few of the kids were taking running jumps onto iced-up logs so they could skate the length of them. I decided I wanted to have a go too, but as I tried, a boy from the year ahead, Mark, pushed me off. I decided to run at him, a bit startled, he tried to put his arm around my neck. Unfortunately for him, he didn't quite get the position he hoped for, and I bit his arm as hard as I could. The more he tried to shake me off the deeper my teeth went in. I was screaming in temper, well as much as you can with an arm in your mouth, while he was screaming in agony. Mrs Gee, one of the teachers screamed from a window for us to stop fighting, but by the time she got to us, blood was trickling down Mark's forearm and we were both crying. His tears were as much a result of the shock of me managing to bite through his Parker coat sleeve as they were the pain he was feeling. Whereas mine had somewhat abated when I saw the damage I'd done and couldn't help but take a little comfort from it.

Mrs Gee managed to separate us but decided this was a matter for the headmaster to adjudicate. At first, recriminations between Mark and myself were met with calm commands to be silent but once we'd hushed ourselves, we awaited our fate.

"Wait outside."

Mrs Digsall, Mrs Phillips, and Mrs Spall were the secretaries, playground attendants, and nurses amongst many other things, so after a few minutes Mrs Digsall came to clean us up, dress Mark's wounds and reprimand us too.

The secretaries weren't quite as frightening as the headmaster, but they came a very close second. When we finally re-entered the Head's office, he asked us what had happened, lit his pipe, shook his head in disbelief then warned, he'd be watching us, and with that, we were sent back to our classes.

16th June 2006 – Chelsea Arts Club

This evening I took Kate to the Chelsea Arts Club for a meal. The set menu offered a starter of either tomato soup or crayfish. Thinking the latter would be something like a small dish of prawns in a mayonnaise sauce I went for it. Instead, the waiter bought us two plates with six little monsters on them that I wouldn't want to see in a nature film let alone eat. I looked around me to see people on other tables happily dissecting and tucking into their large insect-like prey and came to realise that being brought up on an estate in South London didn't necessarily mean you'd end up having a harder constitution than a middle-class person brought up in the quiet suburbs. I realised then it's no wonder it's the middle-class celebrities who tend to do so well when it comes to endurance-type programs such as, I'm a Celebrity Get Me Out of Here. One glamour model who ate jungle food such as worms, and kangaroo testicles in order to win her fellow contestants a good meal didn't seem to hesitate as she bit into the innocent crustaceans. Had I known she was just licking the tip of the iceberg when it comes to disgusting delicacies in middle-class circles, I might have held back on giving her so much credit.

1973 - Don't Cry Over Spilt

One evening Mum took me along with her to get a Chinese takeaway about a mile from home. As we waited for our food, I decided to do my then-normal routine of showing the owner some of the kicks I'd learned from watching the karate class. As I did, they'd get their relatives from out of the kitchen and ask me to show them my, "feet of fury" in action.

Feeling buoyed by the adulation at the takeaway we marched from the garage below our flat where Mum had parked, when the bag holding the food gave way. Mum and I stood almost crying over the spilt meal. But you know what Confucius says about spilt Chop Suey.

1973

Sean was one of the hard kids from the year above me. I was beginning to recognise there were those at school who wanted to fight and those who preferred to remain quiet, and by doing so managed to avoid getting into ruts with others. Sean thought he was a fighter and he wanted everyone to know it.

One day, on the way to Lynnette's after school, I decided to pop into the community centre where there was a lounge and snack shop. Lots of the other kids from school hung out there, so I thought I'd join them. Within minutes of arriving, Sean said something derogatory to me which I retaliated to, and within seconds he was sitting on my chest, trying to punch me in the face, but every time his fist came down, I put my arms in the way. By this point, I was in full-blown temper mode, with tears of anger streaming down my face, but still, I didn't take my eyes off him. As he raised his arm high above his head and looked for an opening to strike me, I brought my foot almost up to my head and then crashed my heel into his eye. He clasped his face, screamed and within a second was no longer on top of me but writhing around in agony. The crowd around me looked on in disbelief. Not only was the victor younger and smaller than Sean but he had short arms. That was the moment when a consensus amongst my peers started to develop. It wasn't so much I was tough, but more a case of being more dangerous than I looked.

2006 - Strange Fruit

Tonight, Steve, the friend I mentioned in the very first paragraph of this book, and I pulled up in my car outside his home. Just as we came to a halt, I heard a cracking sound and then felt a splat of something hit me. At first, I thought it was a gunshot, then I realised it was a bird in the tree above us that had been startled and in retaliation, shit upon us. As I drove off, I started to feel as if I was dreaming. The music didn't seem to sound right, my mobile phone kept lighting up and I felt very uneasy. Just as in one of those films where the twist at the end reveals the main character is dying, and suddenly realises the reality they've experienced throughout the film had been made up by their dying brain. I too wondered if the crack I'd heard was a gunshot and everything I perceived after that was my brain offering me a softer touchdown to the afterlife. Fortunately, it was just one of those strange thoughts, and I didn't die then. Unless of course, the near-death experience was real and is lasting a few years.

1973

As I stood looking at the dead dog, I didn't realise Roundshaw was encircling me, creating a new reality inside me. One that created new values, while the old, "me," was laid out to die. My fall onto the concrete decks of Roundshaw had paralysed me too. Life on the estate came at a cost that meant you weren't allowed to live fully. Just like in the film *The Matrix*, people are farmed in order to power the system which in turn offers a pretence of living as a kind of payment, even though it's never openly revealed. Likewise, council estates are a way of keeping a resource (human beings) available for whenever the system should need it. Such as a war, or a potential workforce.

1973/4 - Andrew

Children with heart defects were kept in during lunch breaks or games at our school. Most kids with anything "wrong" with them tended to be wrapped in cotton wool whether they needed to be or not. The $a + b = d$ lack of thought process that leads to disabled kids being seen as delicate is the start of the perception that disabled people must be judged with a different yardstick. The consequence of that though leads to more serious issues later on, most of which result in a lack of equal opportunities for disabled people. But I'll come back to that another time.

Andrew Wilson was a thin, almost white-haired, and slightly blue-lipped boy who played in the library during games and lunch breaks because he had a hole in his heart. Perhaps because my classmates were playing a lot of football at the time, I decided to play with my Action Men in the library with Andrew too. Throughout the winter and even in the summer months Andrew and I would often sit at a table in the library and play together. The library also acted as a corridor from the secretary and headmaster's offices to the gym/assembly/dining hall, so we started to become friendly with the staff too.

The headmaster, Mr Garriock, was tall, wore glasses, had white hair and smoked a pipe. He exuded quiet authority, rarely shouted, read stories to us all every morning during assembly and inspired a desire in the kids, well me at least, to impress him.

At the school disco, we played a game where he would stop the record playing, by the way, he was the DJ, and over the microphone gave us an instruction to do something like lie on the floor or raise an arm in the air. The last person to do the action had to sit out. Eventually, only a few of us remained on the dance floor. When he asked us to stand on our left foot, I put my right foot on my left whilst my competitors balanced on one leg. I could see him look at me and wonder what I was up to, and once he saw my response told the rest to sit down. For once in my life, I won something. I don't remember the prize but his desire to train me to pass the eleven-plus grammar school entrance exam may have been borne of this incident.

If Mr Garriock was a kindly man, he was protected by his hench-women, Mrs Digsall, Mrs Phillips, and the smoulderingly good-looking Mrs Spall. These three sat at the main entrance to the administrative area like the three-headed dog of Hades. Everyone, even the caretaker feared them. Andrew and I had a lot of contact with them and possibly because we looked a little vulnerable and sweet, we were taken under their wing. Even the Mafia couldn't have provided better protection.

2005 - The First Question

The issue of how I manage to go to the loo is often brought up by strangers on our first acquaintance. Nowadays I tend to quip back that if they hang around, they'll get to see for themselves. The question of how I masturbate often also comes hand in hand with the loo question too. That query will normally get the "where there's a willy, there's a way" joke, or "I use my mouth", or I admit I do have a problem reaching, then reach up above my head.

1973 - Pee Time

Walking back from school one sunny early summer afternoon I found I was desperate to have a pee. I found a quiet spot in the garages but couldn't undo my trousers. I decided to go to one of my fellow schoolmate's places as he lived very close by. Richie was one of the few black kids who lived on the estate, so, I knocked on his door and his father answered. I explained to him I needed help going to the loo and I was desperate. He looked at me and started to shout at me, telling me to go away. I walked off, at first slightly distracted by the shock of what had just happened, but realised this reprieve gave me enough time to make my way to Lynnette's. The problem was, as I got closer the feeling of desperation increased exponentially, so by the time I got there I'd reached "legs crossed" mode.

I knocked on the door but there was no answer. I knocked again and then a few more times. She still didn't answer. I started to cry then a minute or so later her door opened. We looked at each other. I told her I was desperate for the loo but as I uncrossed my legs, the warm pee poured out and down them, possibly spurred on by my anger at her not answering the door quickly enough. Although to be fair, gravity was more likely the greater force.

At first, the feeling of relief outweighed the fear of the repercussions, and possibly the look of fear on my face touched Lynnette's conscience. Instead of telling me off, she told me not to worry and beckoned me toward her. The Vikings had a saying about such moments. It goes something like, "He who pisses in his shoes will not have warm feet for long."

As I got older my arms grew longer in proportion to my upper body so by about nine years old, I could reach my penis and trousers. Until that time, I was reliant on help. At eight years old, it wasn't an issue that worried me too much. So, in answer to any queries regarding pissing and wanking, I can reach, but thanks for your concern regarding such matters.

1973 - Roundshaw - Thursday Special

One of my teachers once told me the US had been built on a society that was polarised between criminals and religious fundamentalists from the outset.

As we, the criminal kids from Roundshaw fought our way through life, religious people from the outside world wanted to save us. As we'd play in the park a group of young adults sat in the sun playing guitars and singing. In time we'd ride up to see what was going on. They'd invite us to join them and at first, we'd ride off thinking they were a bit weird but after a few weeks, we became so acclimatised to them that we joined in singing with them. We'd meet them every Thursday and listen to their stories, sing along, pray and never question if God was real or not. This club was called Thursday Special and was run by the local Pentecostal Church.

How they managed to get us into their Church I don't know, they probably used the cold and ever-darkening evenings as an excuse, but for at least a year and a half, many of us regularly went to Church even if the next day we'd be involved in stealing, fighting or swearing. When Elvis sang about lying, cheating, and stepping on people's feet, but how he was now saved, he also sang to us the story of our theological path to God.

2006

Last night I watched a film in which the central character, Borat, finds himself in a Pentecostal church. From the outside, the speaking in tongues, the laying on of hands, the writhing on the ground and running around uncontrollably, looks extremely disturbing and comical. But when we were kids, we didn't see that sort of behaviour, instead, there was a slower propaganda machine working upon us. It wasn't particularly malicious. The criticism I'd level at it was the same as I would of nearly all political or religious groups -that the only truth important to them is that which supports their point of view -. Even so, for them, we were to be saved. Not by the truth, but by hook or by crook.

1973 - Religious Camp

And so it was with our Thursday Special sessions. We would sit in the park, and sing songs, such as "Give Me Oil In My Lamp" and "When The Saints Go Marching In" and they would tell us stories from the Bible. They would test our faith by asking us to fall backwards so that they could catch us although most of us would take a quick peep over our shoulder to check they were there. They would tell us about having dark hearts, and temptations but, if we loved God and Jesus and were good to others, as we would have them be good to us, then we would be welcomed into the Kingdom of Heaven when we died. And a giant Jesus in the clouds would have a place at his right hand, even if there was a lack of love in our lives. That God and Jesus would always be there, in reserve, for us.

During the summer months, the church would take us to a camp in Bonsall, a small village near Matlock in Derbyshire. This is where we'd be further inducted into the way of Christ. Just before we got on the coach that would deliver us from evil, my mum told me to make sure I looked after the new clothes she'd just bought me. I kissed her goodbye and with God's speed, we were on our way on the 150-mile-long journey. When we finally arrived in a field with some wigwam-type tents with no covers on the ground and a few log cabin huts on the edge of the field, we were slightly disturbed and possibly subconsciously transposed this to what might be in store for us when we arrived at Heaven's or Hell's gates. When it came to working out which we were now in though, we weren't sure.

After a quick introduction to those in charge, we were shown to our tents which were green with green canvas camp beds, and told to get our stuff ready, have a wash and then go to the tabernacle, which was a large marquee in which we were to meet everyone else. Soon after entering, we were asked to pray and then the main pastor introduced himself, his wife and daughter, Caroline. Immediately, one of the older boys from our group, I'm pretty sure it was a kid called Terry, shouted out "Yeah Caz the spaz". There was a moment's pause and the pastor continued. No doubt everyone had been informed that we were a rough lot and our conversion into good folk was a priority.

To help in this matter we were split into several groups, and we were informed the group with the most points would earn a prize, most probably a Bible, at the end of the week. Points could be earned by doing chores and deducted for misbehaviour and swearing. If you've ever watched South Park, the cartoon series, and seen how often they swear, then you'll have an idea of the colour and quantity of our, the Roundshaw kids, language.

Terry had come to the camp with his two younger brothers Andrew and Michael. Michael was in my class at school and was known on the estate as being from a hard family. Within the first two days, I'd had fights with all three of them. Unfortunately, when I went for the older of the three, I ran along the top of a couple of bunk beds in one of the dormitories fully intent on kicking him in the head. As I got closer, he gave me a bit of a concerned look and just as I went to deliver my attack, I ran straight into a beam and almost knocked myself out. I was dazed and laid out spread-eagled upon the bed, and as I started to cry, I heard them laughing. I was still in temper mode and started to shout out obscenities and threats at them when one of the staff came in and restrained me. He took me to a group of women sitting on the other side of the field and asked them to look after me for a while.

Each day we'd be taken on an outing, such as visiting caves or going for walks in beauty spots. For children such as us, there was a problem when it came to identifying what beauty was. Maybe it was our age but also our whole value system revolved around excitement and distraction. Beauty didn't play much of a part in our lives. The caves were not particularly of any interest except that there was an inherent danger about caves and to be under such a threat gave us a sense of bravery.

A few days into the week we visited Matlock, the nearest big town. One of our activities involved going swimming. Just before swimming, we'd looked around the shops and I was mesmerised by a toyshop which had a model railway displayed in its window. I went in and immediately an underwater mask with a built-in snorkel caught my eye. I bought it and decided to try it out in the local swimming pool.

At first, I played around in the shallow area but soon decided to try it out in the deep end. I jumped in along with another boy I'd just met, but as soon as I hit the water I felt the mask, which was over my nose and mouth fill up with water. I quickly made my way to the side of the pool, but there was no bar along the edge to grab hold of, nor was there a drainage channel, so I tried to reach for the side of the pool and hoist myself up, but there was such a large gap between the water level and the edge I couldn't pull myself out. My new "friend" looked on laughing, no doubt thinking I was clowning around, so realising I was on my own I tried to pull the mask off. By this time, I was beginning to breathe in the water and started to cough and splutter. It was then I felt myself relax, and looking down at the bottom of the pool, said to God "I didn't think I was going to die this soon, but if that's your will I'm ready." I started to blank out, everything went fuzzy, my vision went speckly and just as I thought that was it, the lifeguard pulled me out and asked if I was alright.

The mask was off me, I coughed uncontrollably and cried a bit. I told her I was okay, and thanked her, then looked at my new "friend" in disgust even though he was now looking a bit more concerned. The lifeguard told me to go to the children's pool, so I did. When I got there I dived in head first and bumped my head on the bottom of the pool. I let myself float to the surface, got out and rubbed my head better. After swimming, we were allowed to visit the fun fare, which was quite a small affair, but feeling ravenously hungry I decided to have some almost luminous green candy floss.

All went well until the next day when I thought I better show one of the people in charge my luminous green poo. All Hell broke loose. Firstly, I was moved to a dormitory and put in the care of the five girls sleeping in it. In turn, they thought I should be tucked up in bed which was where I spent the day under observation. Food was brought to me and concerned visitors came in now and again to see if I was okay. I failed to make the connection or tell anyone about the previous day's green candy floss and that morning's poo, so I was pretty concerned for myself too.

That evening the logistics of where I should sleep became an issue. I was given the choice to either sleep in a bed by myself or share a bed with one of the teenage girls. Just as I was unable to see nature's beauty, I was also unable to feel sexual attraction and the thought of sleeping next to someone filled me with horror, especially at the thought of what would happen if I were to wet the bed. That hadn't happened since the psychopath Michael lived with us, but still, it was a bit of a concern.

Before going to bed one of the older girls helped me get ready, but just at the point when I was completely naked, I jumped in the air, spun around, gyrated my hips, wiggled my penis up and down and shouted, "Tom Jones, Tom Jones". The girls looked, gasped for a second or two, then shrieked and covered their eyes. The one helping me pulled me back towards her and admonished me and I laughed as she told me not to do it again.

The next morning over a breakfast of porridge, one of the three brothers taunted me about sleeping with the girls and to protect their honour, I thought it best to attempt to leap across the table to land a kick, punch or bite. One of the staff grabbed me and took me outside. He tried to tell me about another way, about turning the other cheek but it fell upon deaf ears. While speaking to me he helped me climb over a stone wall and walked me across a field. I felt my feet get wet and he showed me the dew on the grass and the fields around us and the world God had made for us. But when you live in a concrete jungle where those around you seem to come from Hell and make you feel like you've got to be on guard all the time, you can't help but wonder if God might have forgotten all about you.

———

On the last day, we were called together to find out which team had done the best, not surprisingly we didn't win, but when my name was called out to receive the prize for best boy camper of the week, I was more shocked than anyone. This was my first taste of being judged by a different yardstick because of my arms. My position now is I'd rather fail on an equal footing than succeed because I have a disability. This isn't to appear more heroic, it's simply because there is little pleasure in being praised for just being diligent. That's like saying ten out of ten for trying but only one for succeeding. The noble failure is still a failure at the end of the day.

When I got home, I showed Mum the Bible, and she was very impressed but less impressed by the loss of most of my new clothes. They'd been left in the tent when I was transferred to the girls' dormitory. In just one day I felt what it was like to reach the heady heights of success and the pain of falling from it.

———

Chapter 12
Betrayal

Betrayal lies at the heart of love

1973 – Roundshaw

Something hit the ground. I looked down to see one of my toy soldiers, sprawled, gun in hand, across the lino. The friend I was saying goodbye to looked at me and smiled. At first, I was confused about where it had come from but then, still grinning, "my friend" looked at me and let the whole platoon fall from inside his coat.

My politically aware Action Man radioed ahead. "We have one man, sorry person, down…" "Who is it?" I radioed back. "I'm sorry sir, I know this is a bit of a cliché, but it's Truth".

It was "us and them", and "you and me". This was the dislocated sense of community that underpinned our neighbourhood on Roundshaw. There was a sense that people outside the estate saw us as "a bad lot", and we were the enemy and definitely their enemy. But given my enemy's enemy was all around me, linked by the label of being the underclass, we were connected, whether we wanted to be or not.

Where we lived was rough, and many of us lived by the sword, knuckle duster, knife, shotgun or fist. Those that did thought they were tough and everyone else was soft and scared of them. Those who lived outside of the estate were the haves, we were the have-nots, so, resentment festered in both us and them.

My "friend", the soldier stealer, saw me as "a have" and therefore I was a legitimate target. The victim makes a victim.

2006

All I need is the air that you breathe and for you to love me

I used to think that at the root of most "evil" acts you'd find betrayal. Even in the bible, the devil falls from grace as a result of an oscillation of betrayal.

An oscillation of betrayal is where one even very small perceived act of betrayal, whether it occurred or not, is then met with another, normally slightly greater one. In turn, this volley continues until eventually, a cataclysmic one takes place. In relationships, if you follow the path of a break-up backwards, you'll find it often starts with the perception of miniscule betrayals.

To feel betrayed normally requires an expectation. Whether an expectation is just or unfair is a matter of debate, but all the same, expectations stand nose to nose with betrayal. Some people might say that at the heart of our suffering, it's not betrayal, but expectation. I wonder though if it's also a matter of truth and understanding, or more accurately, a lack of them. We suffer because we are unable to truly understand what has happened to us, or those who've betrayed us and why.

This probably isn't much help really; I mean if we can't get to the truth of hardly anything we might as well make the most of feeling betrayed. At least that saves us from battering ourselves for having expectations and lacking understanding of the bigger picture, and let's face it, feeling resentful is much more satisfying in the short term.

2006 – Kate

I came in tonight; I was home later than I said I'd be. When I got in Kate had kindly kept some food back for me. I said I was sorry that I was late and as I passed her, I hugged her, she told me to eat my food as it was getting cold. I continued to maul her a bit and she repeated that I ought to eat up.

136

As I sat down to eat, she told me how annoyed she was that I didn't stop hugging her when she'd asked. The proceedings then took a turn for the worse because I felt she was making a meal of the incident. She told me I wasn't listening to her, I said she was being overly controlling, and within seconds the whole evening was ruined.

November 2006

A year ago, I sat in my kitchen while Sean, a neighbour and friend who'd already done building work for me over the preceding 20 years, went over the plans and schedule of works an architect had drawn up to develop the property I'd recently bought. He told me that it would cost from £55,000 to £75,000 depending on what was included. He said as I was a friend, he'd only charge me a fee for acting as a coordinator, and he'd fit the electrics within this fee. Outside of that, of course, I'd have to pay the workers' wages and materials. I agreed and just after Christmas, the men started working on my place. I started the project with £38,000 in the bank and realised that I'd have to borrow the remainder.

Sean told me that the job would take 16 weeks but by the 12th week I'd spent £45,000 on wages, materials and his fee and we were nowhere near finishing the job.

When I talked to Sean about it, he said, "Well you obviously can't afford to finish the job, can you? I've got some friends who might buy it from you."

I went back to my mortgage company which lent me a further £25,000 and told Sean I could afford to finish it after all. A few weeks passed, and after a further £10,000 had been paid, very little progress was made.

So, Sean and I sat in a café and went through the remaining jobs and what I'd have to budget for. Within a week, a job he'd told me would cost £2,500 came in at £5,500. At this point, I made it clear that I needed accurate quotes for the remaining works. He told me to write out a list of what I thought remained, he'd write one too and we'd agree what jobs needed to be done and that he'd be held to those prices.

I typed up the job list and left it on-site for him. A few days later one of the large burly workmen came up to me and said, "You're a cunt for writing that list".

I asked why he thought that.

"Well, who are you to say what needs doing and how long it'll take."

"I'm just doing what Sean asked me to do."

Another week went by and again barely anything got done.

I woke up feeling angry about being taken for a ride and on the way to the house I discussed with Kate what I should do; she took on my feelings and fed back to me how angry it made her feel. By the time I approached my house, I was extremely wound up. If I'd had a gun I'd have walked in and shot each of the builders, firstly in the kneecaps, then in the elbows and then in the stomach. Fortunately, I only had a Swiss Army knife, so the worst I was likely to do was peel off a lid from a bottle of beer and drink it in front of them.

When I got to the property, I went to find the list of jobs I'd written previously only to find it had shit smeared all over it where someone had wiped their arse on it. I asked the big burly builder if he'd done it and he said, "No it was Ron." Ron was a carpenter who was particularly slow.

I went quiet, had a pee, and just as I came out of the loo, Sean arrived. I said I needed to talk to him in private, so we went outside.

"Sean, I'm pissed off."

"Why, what's the matter mate?"

"Well, there's a few things. Firstly, I don't like being treated with disrespect by the guys. One thinks it's ok to call me a cunt, the other has wiped his arse on my documents, and on top of all this, they're taking the piss by working slowly. You said this would be almost finished two weeks ago, but there's hardly any change."

"Do you want me to pull them off the job?"

"I want what's best for me. I want the job done for the agreed price. If they don't want to work for a fixed price send them home."

"Ok, I'll talk to them."

I went off for a while and decided I didn't want Ron in my house anymore. He'd shown his true colours and was a liability to my security. What he thought of me was of no interest to me, but his actions were. So, I came back to Sean and told him I wanted Ron off the site.

"How about I run him into the ground for a week, make him do loads of the shit work and get someone else in to do the good stuff?"

"Ok do that."

The next day I turned up and the builders were packing everything away.

Sean greeted me with, "They're not willing to work for a set fee" with a, 'told you so,' look on his face.

"Well, they can get lost then, can't they?" I replied with a 'Do I look bothered' face.

The house emptied and work came to a stop. A bit later, a couple of the builders came back to me and said they were willing to work for a set fee per job, but they hadn't wanted to look like they weren't supporting the others. So, for a few weeks, the work went on.

I started to bring in people independently and paid those who'd agreed prices with me directly. As if I'd entered a completely different dimension of reality, I had people coming in on Saturdays, whereas beforehand they were leaving work early on a Friday – "POETS day" they called it, "Piss off early tomorrow's Saturday."

One of the guys I brought in independently was called Trevor, and although Sean had introduced us to each other because we were both songwriters, Sean hadn't wanted him to work on the job. However, when Trevor gave me a quote for decorating that was far lower than Sean's, I naturally went with the better price. In turn, Trevor introduced me to a tiler who also offered to do the tiling for a third of Sean's price. Sean was not happy about this and told Trevor he shouldn't be poking his nose into business that didn't concern him and should've approached him with quotes that he would decide on as he was the foreman.

Trevor is black, and it wasn't long before racist graffiti appeared on my walls.

Every quote Sean gave me came in at double the amount and took two to three times longer than expected, yet all the jobs I set up came in on budget and sooner than estimated. One Friday, as I paid the workers, Sean told me he was no longer on the job, that I had insulted him by slyly taking over. This had insulted him in front of the others. So, I pointed out that I'd now spent £90,000 and a further £30,000 worth of work was still outstanding. He said his initial costing was just a guide price. I then told him, that given he was unable to keep to any agreed price or time limits, I felt it was time for me to take responsibility. To him though, none of this mattered, his main concern, allegedly, was I'd insulted him. This became his main focus in terms of his resentment of me and from then on, whenever I'd drive past him, he'd mutter and look away from me in disgust. He walked off but things didn't end there. He kept on asking for bills to be paid for materials, some of which were not even for my job. I always tried to be fair and pay what I owed, but he didn't do the same for me.

I subsequently found out that he had a history of getting his customers into far more debt than they'd anticipated and then getting them to sell their property to him at a low price because it was unsellable, and they were desperate.

It didn't make sense. What had I done to deserve such bad treatment? Perhaps firstly there was a perception that I would be making a good profit out of this venture and secondly, the friendship between us was worth very little in comparison to his allegiance to his workers. There is, after all, honour amongst thieves. But maybe, to him, anyone stupid enough to fall for his con deserved what they got and ultimately, he had to put food on the plate for his family. Still, I couldn't help but feel betrayed and consequently wanted to strike back at him.

From the moment Sean and I parted company, I felt a strong sense of relief and striking back would have meant continuing our connection be it just emotionally. So, at least right then, I thought it best to enjoy the disconnection.

There were practicalities, as there is with most separations. I knew that I had to take over and find a way forward, but the responsibility was mine, so, over the next three months, I had to hire and fire workmen and organise everything.

If ever there was a good way to learn management skills, this was it. One of the big lessons was nearly all people you deal with will overcharge and underperform unless you make it hard for them to do so. There are good people around, but learning who you can be safely dependent on is a long drawn-out process and finding them is like finding good friends. It takes time and the ability to limit what you'll accept is ultimately, you get what you settle for.

The result of Sean's betrayal was I made a lot less money than I thought I would. Consequently, this resulted in a larger mortgage than I would have had and that meant having to work more and for many more years than I'd hoped. Also, the area I'd grown to love over a twenty-year stay became one I no longer wanted to be in because not only was Sean a neighbour, but the residue of this whole misadventure was all around me. Fortunately, I still made a profit but perhaps it was time to move off anyway. Of course, there were positives such as learning skills that might see me well in the future, but given a choice, I'd rather not have been one of his victims.

2006 – Fulham

Trevor walked past Sean the other day and said, "Hello Sean".

"Don't fucking talk to me."

"Why? What have I done to you?"

"What haven't you done to me?"

1975 – Roundshaw

I'm riding my bike through Roundshaw. There are three kids playing football. As I pass by, one of them starts calling me names. He's a boxer and has a reputation for fighting well. I continue on my way but start to feel overwhelmed by a feeling of fury. I double back and park my bike at the bottom of the stairs that lead back up to the deck where they're playing. I walk up the dark steps which smell of piss and radiate coldness. As I stand at the top of the stairs, I try to work out how to do what I have to do but needn't have worried. The ball bounces to where I'm standing. The kid walks over to it and passes me. I step out, and he turns around looking shocked, I kick him in the stomach, he falls backwards, hits the wall, drops down, curls up and tries to cry, but he can't breathe.

"That's what you get for calling me names," I shout in his face.

I walk off and from then on, he always showed me respect.

The pleasure that comes with teaching someone a lesson can easily blind one to the reality that the world is full of people who aren't going to show respect, and many of them can't be beaten into submission either. But even in my own home – even if it was a building site – I have seen what results in an enemy being let in to do whatever they want. It ends in the destruction of one's well-being. Sometimes it's a fight for respect, and sometimes it's about survival.

One of the lessons I learned from Roundshaw was how important honour was. To be a coward, well at least for me, hurt far more in the long run than standing up to a bully and getting physically hurt. I also came to realise that the maxim, "Don't be right, be clever" is well worth keeping in mind when it comes to conflict.

Sean had taken me for a ride. Either he was inept and wasn't willing to take responsibility or he'd seen me as a sucker to con. Whichever one it was, he had no respect for me. Deep down I wanted to kill him, but I also knew that letting go of all of this and seeing the positive aspects would be for the best. Forgiveness is the way to freedom, however, even now, decades later, a part of me wants vengeance.

1974 – Roehampton Hospital

A boy with no legs is sitting on my chest, while a girl with ginger hair and both short arms and legs, is lying across me, holding me down with her weight.

Clive, the legless boy shouts, "Say sorry for telling on us for smoking."

"No," I snarl.

"Say sorry or I'll hit you." His fist held high, ready to strike.

"Get off! I'm not sorry."

Clive punches me in the eye and I scream in agony. A few moments later one of the nurses pulls him off. The ginger-haired girl, Veronica, is filled with guilt and admiration simultaneously. This moment connected us and 33 years later we were still the best of friends. My determination not to submit to Clive's bullying struck her to the core.

Dream 14th November 2006

I'm sitting on the roadside, while Kate sits on a bench next to me. I'm getting dressed and putting on my underwear. A car goes by, and a middle-aged black man makes eyes at Kate. I watch him then check her out to see if she flirts back at him. I ask her if she did and she says, "No, can you imagine what would happen if I made eyes with every guy who did that to me?" she laughs, "You learn from a young age not to look back at every man who looks at you."

I'm now in my Aunt Anne's house standing in the back bedroom. A woman is in the loo and I'm hovering near the doorway of the room so I can speak to her when she comes out. Perhaps she has a partner downstairs and I want to get her alone for a moment. When she comes out, I ask her into my room. She does so and we stand in front of a mirror. She's short, petite, with big brown eyes, and short dark hair that wraps around the edge of her face. I say, "I want to tell you something, don't be embarrassed, but I've always felt something for you."

She says, "I know, and maybe in six months when I split up with Mike we could try to get together".

With that, I hoist her onto my back to show her how strong and comfortable I am. A shower is sticking out of the wall and has water pouring from it. It's pouring on us. I start to worry that the furniture and clothes strewn across the floor will get soaked, so I check if there's a plug hole in the floor. I find it but also realise that her back is wet too. She says it doesn't matter.

I don't want to wake up, but when I do, I move across the bed and cuddle up to Kate.

As I was writing this, I started to get the sensation I had as a child of the smell and taste of anaesthetic. It filled me with fear. The irony is, the anaesthetic protected me from unbearable pain, but the association I made wasn't of protection, but pain and nausea. I thought just now of how alone I would have felt when that mask went over my face, its big black overly sweet-smelling membrane felt like a hand trying to suffocate me. So much of what is good for us looks bad up close until we see it in a wider context, and no doubt the same goes for what we think is good for us. There's a kind of betrayal in that process, but who's to blame: us for our inaccurate perception, or the thing for not revealing the truth?

2007 - Actions Speak

A year and a half has passed since I walked out of Kate's place wondering if that would be the last time I'd be there. I did return though, but the relationship had changed. It didn't seem so at first, but a week and a half after she'd returned from the holiday, I started to notice it. Instead of wanting to make love on a daily basis, there was a ten-day gap. When I questioned her about it, she said I was making an issue of it by bringing it up but still, I wanted to know if she didn't fancy me anymore. Actions speak louder than words.

2007 – Marcia

Marcia is a painter. She's the partner of someone who did some work for me, and he thought I ought to meet her, so, one evening we met up at the Chelsea Arts Club. At one point Marcia and I discussed painting a picture together and as we did a man sitting nearby overheard us and told us he'd be interested in filming us doing so. Things developed and within a month we were all meeting every week, Marcia and I painting together, while Jack Pizzey, the filmmaker from the club, and his cameraman Sam Small, filmed us.

The painting's themes were mainly centred around grief. The bit of grieving after the initial mourning period, the bit which can last a lifetime, the bit where "the shadows of those we've lost illuminate our internal world". In other words, a world where we're no longer trapped in the grave of the one we love but have come to accept we have lost them, but can connect with them, at least to a degree; where we may speak with them, go walking in dreams together, hold them, kiss them goodnight, tell them we love them, know we will always love them, and one day, hopefully, be with them again.

The painting came from the pattern of brush marks we made across the canvas and ended up as a picture of a man half lying in a stream, with his eyes closed while a woman who looks as if she's illuminated stands close to him in front of a vividly coloured and stormy sky.

During the process of making this image, which has a slightly classical look to it, I decided I wanted to cut out the figure of the woman, then photograph and scan her before burning the bit we cut out. Once that was done the figure was printed out and stuck back into the same position in the painting. This was done to make a point about how important it is for us to use painting and other more modern forms of capturing images to hold on to the visual form of something or someone we've lost.

The juxtaposition of the modern and classical ways of creating images – painting and computer graphics – also highlighted how readily we look back to eras when painting seemed as if it couldn't get better, and anything since then has been seen as sub-standard. As if we too, the viewers of art, can get stuck in the grave of bygone eras.

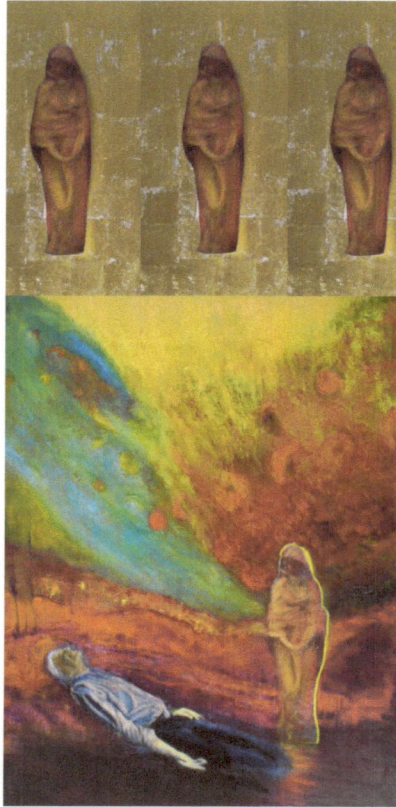

The painting I created with Marcia K Ellis.

As the film progressed the cameraman, Sam, interjected with comments aimed to stir up a reaction, such as, "Painting died after Van Gogh", or "You're just making this up as you go along, your painting is meaningless." And "van Gogh didn't need computer graphics."

At one point Sam and I had a heated discussion about how the painting would be read very differently by onlookers compared to how we'd intended it to be viewed. Sure enough, a couple of people came in and indeed, felt confused about what it was we were trying to say. Of course, there are many philosophical directions one can take regarding this matter, however, even though the air was thick with resentment from both sides, the conversation took an unexpected turn, starting with Sam asking me if I felt I'd dominated the project.

"Partly," I said.

"I think you have." He said, then paused and asked, "Do you think you're a dominant or submissive person?"

144

"What do you mean?"

"Well, a dominant person likes to take control, make decisions and have things go their way, whereas a submissive person is more nurturing, likes to take a back seat and doesn't like making decisions."

"I suppose in terms of those definitions I'm a dominating person then."

"So, what kind of women do you end up with then?"

I laugh, "Dominating ones."

"Maybe that's why your relationships don't work? A dominant person needs to be with a submissive partner and vice-versa."

I'm struck by this insight but realise I seem to oscillate between being dominant and submissive depending on the situation. "The only trouble is," I say, "If someone shows any sign of pulling away from me, I suddenly start to feel weak and become submissive."

"Ah, so maybe you attract women who want a dominant man, submissives, but then find they've got a submissive partner. No wonder your relationships collapse."

I'm almost taken in completely by the simplicity of this way of seeing things, but that thought about my changeability stops me from seeing it as the whole story. Still, there was something that resonated in what he said.

If you want to watch the video of Marcia, Jack, Sam and I, you may be able to view it on YouTube using this link: https://youtu.be/JTpTiON2p6s

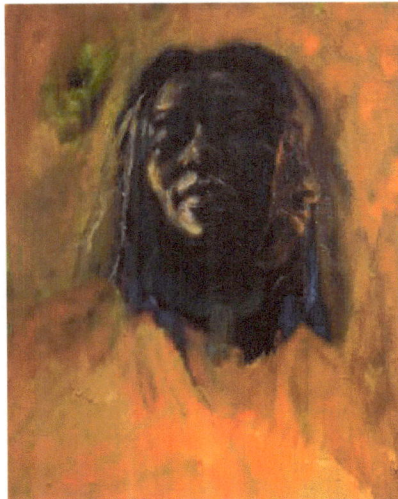

Portrait of Marcia by Simon Mark Smith.

November 2006

Kate and I had an argument a couple of days ago. I walked out after she told me she didn't find me sexually attractive anymore and I had put the dampeners on her sexual feelings towards me a year ago, when I had said that if she wasn't interested in me sexually then I wouldn't stick around. She felt it was an ultimatum whereas I saw it as an obvious point about relationships. The irony was, a year later we've hardly had any sex but I'm still here with her. After a night of being apart, I yearned to be with her and to be home. But after this last argument, it felt like an end date had been stamped upon our relationship; we might not want to see it, but we both know it's there.

The thought of not having this home together anymore and being alone in the house I've just bought on the seafront on the South Coast 60 miles away, feels scary. Even if separating might make room for a dream girl to come to me, the idea of parting from Kate fills me with dread. I can't see beyond the pain of the present, can't see the possibility of joy in pastures new and without this vision, it's so easy to get trapped in the grave of a dead relationship.

1988 - Somewhere and Nowhere

The engine is pulsating as I pull up on a side street. We're in a small town. It's dark, everything's wet but it's not raining. I get out of the car to look at the damage. There's a dent where the brick landed on the bonnet. The car was pristine until that moment. I wipe off the dirt hoping it's just a surface scuff, but it isn't.

I walk to the back of the car open the boot and pull out a large powerful air rifle which I pass to my friend as I get into the driver's seat. "OK," I say, "let's get 'em."

I'm not sure who'd started it, but all it took was a bad look. From the viewpoint of the two guys who'd thrown the brick at us, it must have been a strange sight. It's nighttime, and the sunroof is open with the passenger, like a tank turret soldier, standing up through it with a large air rifle aimed at them.

"You fucking cunts!" I shout as my friend pulls the trigger. The smaller of the two falls backwards, yelps and doubles up in agony. We drive off at top speed. The adrenalin is pumping through us and for a minute we say nothing. Then I look at my mate and say, "You got the wrong one, it was the big one who threw the brick".

"Did I?" My friend says most apologetically, "Ooh, sorry about that."

He's still holding the gun and as the messenger tends to always get it, I feel I ought to add, "Oh well not to worry, at least the other bloke will feel a bit guilty".

"Aye, there is that" he says.

1970 - The Train

When my friend was eight years old, he lived in a house on a small council estate on the outskirts of a mining town. His father was a miner and a father of six. On non-school days his mother would let the kids out in the morning to play in the fields and call them in for tea as evening fell.

A few miles away across fields of long wet grass my friend and a couple of his brothers would play amongst the coal trucks of trains that took the coal from his father's mine away to far-off destinations in "the smoke". The trucks were black and sooty and towered over the children and had buffers that would push against the next truck's buffers when they started to move. They acted as shock absorbers, but no amount of absorption could have taken away the shock my friend experienced when one day the train started to move and his right forearm became caught between two of the buffers. He screamed out but the screeching of the wheels took his cries for help and cast them into shudders. His brothers played on at first and when they realised what had happened chased the train the two miles to the depot. Every sleeper that ran along the track bumped against my friend's foot until by the end of the journey only a crushed and bleeding stump was left.

The train driver who found my friend came to the hospital to visit him every day for months; the train company however fought off any compensation claims, citing that notices warning children not to play on the tracks had been ignored.

Once out of the hospital, my friend was taken to a residential school for disabled kids. In the holidays he'd come back to his family home, but after just a few hours, would want to go back to school because at least he'd get three meals a day there, whereas at home he'd be lucky if he got one.

In my friend's hometown, life was pretty much mapped out for most people. However, there was no route marked upon it for a footless and armless man in a mining village. If a man didn't have a fully functioning body, he was a nobody. But when Margaret Thatcher closed the mines, and hopelessness filled every street, my friend realised that somewhere in this catastrophe were opportunities waiting to be found.

11th April 2007

"Please Simon, leave Kate. Not just for her sake, but for yours too." These are the words of Kate's friend to me at a party the other night. She's the one who, on the night we first met, couldn't believe Kate was even thinking about getting together with me. I know anything I say will be repeated to Kate, so, I say, "Whatever will be, will be", and she, like us, "should just wait and see what happens."

Kate and I had a big row before we set off for the party. Something had happened where I felt she'd been selfish, she thought I was being overly nasty about it, I didn't feel like I wanted to apologise and she wasn't going to forgive me. We got to a point where we had to stop speaking as we weren't getting anywhere trying to talk it out.

The next day went well though. Kate had come down to my house in Eastbourne where some of our friends joined us. We ate together, sat on the beach, chatted, went for a drive to Birling Gap, walked along the base of the cliffs, had a drink in an 11th-century pub, and then waved our friends goodbye. We curled up on the sofa together for a while, then exhausted, got into bed and fell asleep in each other's arms.

The next day the sun shone brightly, Kate went running along the shore and, once she got back, we had breakfast, then drove towards Brighton. On the way, we stopped at Alfriston and sat in a pub where we started to talk about petrol money. Within seconds we were into a full-scale argument. We left soon afterwards and continued on our journey to Brighton, still arguing, only it kept escalating. By the time we hit the traffic lights at Rottingdean, we decided it was time to split up. There was one thing we agreed on though and that was no sex and frequent arguments were not a good basis upon which to build a relationship. As we got to Brighton station, I pulled up at the drop-off point, went to the back of the car and opened the boot. Kate took out her bags and looked at me.

"Do you want to come into the station with me?" she asked.

I shook my head slowly, "It's probably better if I don't."

She put her arms around me and I felt her start to cry, at which point I felt an overwhelming sense of loss and pain. I wanted to plead with her not to go but I knew it was the right thing to do. We both held on to each other crying for a few minutes, then she walked off into the station while both of us sobbed. People could see our trembling faces, someone asked me something, but I could hardly speak. I saw Kate wave at me, so I waved back. I drove home and every few miles I got a surge of tears. This sadness, this separation, was partly the consequence of betrayal. Somewhere in the relationship, an oscillation of betrayal had started between us, starting small, it bounced back and forth between us unchecked. Eventually, I no longer wanted to listen to what Kate had to say, she didn't feel listened to, and the relationship got on a train and made its way to the smoke without us.

Chapter 13
All The Rage

August 9th 2007

I am driving to London from Eastbourne. My roof is down, the sun is shining, and I'm cruising at the speed limit, (for a change). I am on the intersection of the motorway between the south coast (the M23) and the one that circumferences London (the M25). Before joining the M25 there's another intersection which requires me to give way to cars already on it. The vehicle ahead of me brakes slightly to give way to a white car travelling at a speed that won't be making room for anyone. Just behind them, there's a blue car that could let me in but doesn't, so I brake. I'm slightly irritated but I know they've got the right of way. Somewhere in my mind, I've already built up a picture of the driver. It's a man, most likely in his 30s or early 40s, he's a bit unkempt, likes to think he's tough and wants to teach me a lesson because I'm driving a flashy car. I laugh as I realise I could be describing myself.

As we drive onto the M25 I decide I want to accelerate into the overtaking lane. I look over my shoulder, check all is clear, kick down and sweep into it. Within seconds I've caught up with the blue car and am just about to overtake it when, both he and another car which he's tailgating, pull into my lane. He'd done this without checking his mirror or deliberately cut me up. Either way, I'm forced to brake hard. The guy in the blue car has now been promoted in my mind to bully status, someone I want to stand up to. I'm thinking, "fuck you, you wanker, who do you think you are?"

I spot a gap on their inside so pull into it. Seeing a space suddenly appear in front of them as the white car ahead of them pulls away, I slowly get in front of the blue car. I don't indicate because I want to deliberately wind him up, cut him up, fuck him up. As I'm a quarter of the way into the lane I notice the nose of his car in the corner of my eye, he's accelerated and is not going to let me in. I think, "Fuck he's hard, he doesn't care if we crash, in fact, he wants to hit me, he wants to ram me. I quickly pull back into my lane. I pull in behind him as he sounds his horn and brakes hard. I shout out, "That's what you just did to me". His passenger opens his window and pulls the wing mirror in. I realise then, our car mirrors have touched. I check mine and it has been knocked out of place too, so, I pull it back into place. They decelerate and I kick down and undertake them. As I do, I mouth some obscenities at them, then drive off leaving them behind, far behind.

2007 - The Consequences of Violence

I have spent weeks trying to write this chapter. Slowly it has written itself in my mind, and the incident with the car the other day literally drove me to get on with it.

This chapter is about several issues, the first is the consequence of violence, and the second looks at classic storytelling. A few months ago I was involved in the film I mentioned in the last chapter, the one that followed another painter, Marcia, and I, as we produced some paintings together. I got a phone call a few weeks ago just as I got to the same intersection of the M23 and M25 mentioned above. During the call, I was informed the editor/cameraman, Sam, had pulled out of the project because he didn't think we had a good enough story, and he didn't want any of the film clips with him in to be included.

Maybe the ghosts of the houses that were demolished for this bit of the motorway to be built haunt drivers as they pass this spot.

Anyway, this whole episode had me thinking about how story structure could relate to this book, and whether or not what I was writing would be of any interest to anyone outside of those who already knew me.

Classic story structure follows this path. There's a protagonist, and they're normally the central character, the hero or anti-hero, (that's me by the way, although I'm not quite sure which one I am) and their path normally follows a journey that in some way resonates with the audience, and it's through those journeys, the lessons that interest us reveal themselves.

The story of the blue car and my road rage may horrify you, but at the same time, maybe you recognise this rage within you too.

There's often a shape to a story's structure which can be traced as a line on a graph. At first, it travels horizontally, then will go up or down between points of success or trouble and later return to a different level than the initial horizontal line as some kind of resolution. Along this journey, a classically founded story will reveal through its development some background information, some action, and a degree of conflict, then in its end sequences, there'll be crisis, climax and consequences. To put it simply, you will get to know a bit about the protagonist, and then through some action, there is likely to be conflict, often involving either risk or suffering for them. Finally, as you approach the end of the story, there's very likely to be more action or heightened drama where matters are sorted out or not, (as in a tragedy), and ultimately either the protagonist or at least the audience learn something from the story.

In a long story, such as this, there is a device called an arc, which is a metaphor for the development of the protagonist's character. Through a series of stories, the hero or anti-hero is led to different emotional and psychological understandings.

So why am I writing about this? Well, normally when I watch a film I can tell, almost to the second, when the protagonist's luck is just about to change, and, spoiler alert, I am just about to reveal yet another of my many falls to you.

But First... The Blue Car

I had driven about four miles since the incident with the blue car when I saw a vehicle about half a mile behind me, on the crest of a hill, flashing its lights. I was pretty sure it was likely to be a police car and I also had a feeling they might be after me. There was also the possibility that this was the blue car, in which case they might be after a fight. I didn't want to run away, but at the same time, this could become a lot more violent, so wasn't sure what to do. My exit was less than two miles away but by the time I got to it, the car had caught up and pulled in behind me. The driver flashed his headlights, so I pulled onto the hard shoulder. Deciding this might not be a good idea I pulled off. Again, they followed, but this time, the passenger pointed a police warrant card through the window at me. What I hadn't considered was the occupants of the blue car might be police officers, but they were. I pulled up on the hard shoulder and got out of my car. As they approached me, one of them put on a yellow safety vest with "Metropolitan Police" written on it. The one who got to me first had a goatee beard, was short and a little rotund.

"Do you know why we've pulled you over sir?" He asked calmly.

I felt like saying, "Why don't you tell me you fascist pig," but I refrained and instead said, "For speeding?"

He moved his hand as if asking for more, "Yes and what else?"

"And because of the incident with those guys back there."

I still wasn't completely sure if it was the same blue car, or maybe I was still in denial about the possibility of the blue car being the cops, but just to confirm my worst fears he added in a horror story tone, "We are those guys."

At this point, I wanted to fall to my knees and scream, "No!" but instead, I nodded and said, "OK."

"Was there a reason for you pulling in front of us?"

"Well, I got wound up by the way those guys, I mean you, pulled in front of me."

"But sir does the highway code not state that you should give way on such an intersection?"

"Yes, I realise that, but it wasn't at that point that I got wound up, it's when you pulled up in front of me."

He looked a little perturbed by this revelation and paused a second.

At this moment the other officer strode up and aggressively interceded, "I just want you to know that I didn't appreciate the way you tried to kill me back there."

I was still annoyed about them cutting me off so retorted, "I didn't, I tried to pull in front of you to show you what you'd done to me, I was shocked when you continued towards me, I couldn't believe it!"

"So, it was road rage?" the angry, bad cop, said.

Matter-of-factly, I replied, "Yes."

The good cop joined in again. "You do realise that what you did would easily result in you being banned from driving if we went to court."

I nodded, "I know what I did was wrong, I'm not trying to defend it. I'm prepared to face the rap".

I don't know why, but at this point, I started to try to make the best of the situation and imagined how much weight I'd lose if I had to cycle everywhere, as well as how much money I'd save if I didn't drive.

The good cop continued, "Do you have any points on your license?"

I shook my head, "No."

"How long have you been driving?" He asked.

I answered, "Twenty years."

"What's your zodiac sign?" Ok, he didn't really ask that. But then the bad cop, OK, he wasn't bad, let's just say he was a little more highly strung, asked me what I did for a living. The real answer normally goes something like, "I'm a painter, singer-songwriter, photographer, writer, web designer, computer consultant (whatever that means) property developer, and a teacher".

Instead, I just said, "I'm a teacher".

"Well," he said, "that's a good point for you."

I did wonder what jobs might have not boded so well. City traders, estate agents, and civil-rights lawyers, all came to mind.

Calming down a bit he added, "Okay we're not going to take this any further."

I wanted to jump in the air and scream, "Yehaaaaaaaaaaaaa!" but I bowed my head sheepishly and said, "Thank you." They asked me to gain as much speed as I could on the hard shoulder before joining the carriageway – I did think accelerating up to 120 mph might be taking the piss. So, instead, I drove slowly and endured them trundling past me a bit later. I was tempted to wave, then stick my tongue out at them as I went up the slip road and they continued on the motorway, but, the passenger, the highly strung one, looked sternly forward and I didn't think he'd see the funny side anyway.

2007 - Control

The next day I drove a co-worker through London and remembered how he'd converted to Islam at a time when he felt he was a bit out of control, seeing it as a stabilising force. I told him about the incident with the blue car and said that I felt it had a similar significance to me. It was a controlling force that I secretly yearned for. The part of me that is wild leads me into such dangerous situations, that I'm actually scared of it, and as a consequence I want it to be curbed.

2007 - Controlling the Controller

A few weeks ago, the mother of my sons, asked me to deal with one of them. He'd lost his temper and strewn a load of things down the stairs then locked himself in the bathroom. I walked slowly up to the bathroom and knocked on the door. No answer. I tried the door, but it was locked. "I'm going to come back in ten minutes. If you haven't cleared this mess up by then, then there'll be trouble."

I walked away and about seven minutes later returned and said, "OK this is what's going to happen if you don't clear up. I am going to return in five minutes and break the door open, come in, grab you by your hair, take you outside the house and call social services to come and get you because you can't live here if you don't abide by the rules. I'm willing to listen to what you have to say but only when you clear up this mess."

I walked away and within a minute or so he cleared up. I came upstairs and thanked him, then said I was here if he wanted to talk. But he didn't, well not right then.

There's a paradox in all of this. As I walked up and down those stairs, I was petrified that I would go berserk and beat up my child. So far, I have never hit my children, I've threatened them a few times with corporal punishment, but never hit them.

I once marched one of them into his bedroom by his hair when he wouldn't leave the living room after his mum asked him to, but as I left the room I looked back and saw he was sobbing. I felt so sorry for him, he looked so alone, that I went back and hugged him. But now as they approach their teenage years, I'm worried I'll lose it with them in a battle for power and end up destroying the love between us.

153

2007 - Take a Taxi to the Edge of My Mind

Last night I dreamt that the children were much younger, and we were on a road somewhere and one of my sons was playing up, so I threatened to make him walk home alone. In real life their mum plays along with this game, in fact, it was hers originally as her father had done it to her. But in this dream, she feels sorry for our son, so, orders a taxi which they take home together.

Out of the Blue

I am making love to a woman, her legs and arms are wrapped tightly around me. We are covered in sweat. Our bodies are sliding against each other. The movements are deep, slow, and hard. She is coming and between her breaths, she whispers, "Come, come inside me. I want you to come inside me."

The sudden twists of fate rarely come after a bout of careful thought from controlled actions, but instead from seemingly nowhere, out of the blue. But somewhere in the blue, decisions come from parts of us we barely know exist.

13th August 2007 - Second Life

A few months ago, I played around in a virtual world on the Internet called Second Life. It's a three-dimensional virtual landscape in which you can build houses, see other people, speak to them, go to clubs, sunbathe, shop, you name it.

During my first few days there I frequented a few bars. I was sitting in one, drinking virtual orange juice, speaking to three beautifully dressed Japanese women, who were actually men in real life. I realised I like sitting and chatting in bars, it's a good way to meet people. What was weird about this was, when I was sitting in a real bar in Eastbourne, a few nights later, it felt so reminiscent of sitting in the bar in Second Life. Only there were no Japanese women, just three blokes.

Via Myspace I've met quite a few people in Eastbourne since moving here last November. One such "new friend" is called Steve, and he and I have been writing songs together over the last month or so. After a typical song-writing session we tend to go out to a couple of the late-night bars around here, even though I don't drink. A fact, Steve says, which makes my antics even more inexcusable.

So far nearly every night out has ended up with us at Maxims, a bar with a night-club downstairs. When I dance Steve stands there, rotating his pelvis in slow motion laughing hysterically at me. He says it's good to see the old spirit of Saturday Night Fever is still with us.

Normally as we drive home, we take the long way which involves cruising around the town centre about five times while Steve shouts out, "Free open-top taxi, government-sponsored free open taxi" to any group of women we drive past. Quite frequently they'll shout back, "Give us a lift". Although there's always one who'll shout back, "No it's okay mate, you might murder us." Steve then puts his hand up and says with an official tone, "It's okay. We're part of a government-sponsored scheme. The government are getting local millionaires to give back to the community. So, we're out giving lifts. The only problem is we can't give lifts to other millionaires. Are you a millionaire? If you are you'll have to get out." By the end of this spiel, they're snuggled up in the back seats saying, "Don't worry mate we live in [whatever road they say] we ain't millionaires... Oooh, I ain't been in a convertible before, well not when its roof was down anyway. I hope you ain't expecting anything for this you two?"

Steve interjects in his official capacity, "Oh no we're not allowed to receive any payment for this, that would be against the spirit of the scheme."

One of them will invariably ask me, "How come you're sitting so close to the steering wheel mate, you're almost kissing the mirror?"

To which, another, less drunk one will whisper very loudly, "Shhh, he's got short arms". Normally they go quiet for a second because the one who's just been told to shhh can't believe what she's heard. A couple of curious looks later they're waving and shouting hello to strangers as we drive along. By the end of the journey, Steve has fallen in love with one of them, and much to my disbelief gets a snog from at least one of them although normally it's not the one he's fallen for.

I used to think drunken women were a danger to themselves but the other day I was put right. Steve and I had been talking to a woman in Maxims who was so drunk we started to avoid her. A bit later, she approached me and leaned forward to say something. I could feel her move towards my neck and thought, "She wants to kiss my neck, I think I'll let her." I felt her mouth open over the side of my neck, but within a second, she bit my neck so hard I thought she'd cut through to my carotid artery. I couldn't push her away because I thought that might cause even more damage and I couldn't hit her because that might make her bite me even harder. I realised I was close to being killed, even if it was by accident. I don't know if I made any noise, but had I done so, it would have been drowned out by the music. Then, after a few seconds, she started to pull me up, so my feet left the ground. At this point, I admit it, I was pretty scared. She then let go and I dropped back down to my normal height or lack of it. I put my arm to my neck to see if there was any blood, there wasn't, but then Steve, who'd just come over, looked at me and yelped, "Oh my God". Where she'd bitten me, a bulge immediately appeared alongside a large bruise where her teeth had been. Some people pay a lot of money for that kind of thing so maybe I should've been grateful, but I wasn't.

A day later we went to another bar called The Loft. I put my bag on a seat while I put my car keys in it and heard the guy at the table next to me say, "I'm gonna chin the guy behind me in a minute." So, presuming he was talking about Steve I said, "I hope you're not talking about my mate".

"Nah it's someone else."

A moment later the guy pushed me and I stumbled a bit sideways. I was holding my drink and nearly spilt it. I looked at him and he was smiling and moving in a drunken motion. I felt confused. There were five of them and just Steve and me.

At first, we moved away but then I said to Steve I was getting wound up by what had happened, so I stood right next to them again and looked in their direction. I could feel my rage beginning to bubble up. At this point, still outnumbered, I thought that if anything was to happen, we might get kicked out and banned. The reasons for not getting into a fight were stacked against me.

I eventually thought I'd wait for him to go to the toilet then follow him and while he urinated punch him as hard as possible in his spine with my sharp stump, but the damage I could do might be permanent and even I knew it wasn't worth it. So, realising I would lose too much if I tried to avenge what had happened, I concluded it best to do nothing.

A bit later we were joined by a couple of friends, so I pointed out the guy who'd pushed me to one of them. My friend stared straight at him, they caught each other's eyes and the troublemaker quickly looked downwards.

A few days later we were in the bar again and talked to the bar staff about the group of troublemakers. They said they wanted to stop them from coming in because they continually harassed others and were worried they'd lose peaceful customers like us. I was glad they couldn't read my mind.

So, Where is This Going?

Before I show you one of my many falls, I wanted you to see some of the consequences of it. They aren't particularly positive ones, in that it hasn't taught me not to be violent. Instead, it's injected me with a kind of poison, a darkness that when pushed, is ruthless, and while at odds with much of my character, can inflict violence upon others, with barely any warning.

December 2005

I'm driving in London, it's raining hard. A man walks out slowly in front of me causing me to come to a jarring halt. I beep my horn at him. He turns his back to me and sticks his arse up at me. I drive forward and push him over. He falls to the ground. He gets up. I stare at him, put my window down and shout, "I'll fucking kill you, you fucking cunt". He looks shocked. He steps out of the way and I drive off.

1989 - Somewhere Near Trouble

My friend Lee from up North and I are sitting in my flashy car. We've pulled up in front of a coach. A man gets out and approaches us. "Right lads, you've had your fun, but you better go before you get hurt."

"I tell you what," I say, "When the guy who spat on us comes and apologises, we'll go."

He shakes his head slowly, "That isn't going to happen."

I put the car into reverse then drive back behind the coach and pull up.

"I think we should go," Lee says.

"In a minute," I say.

A couple of guys walk toward us.

I speed forward and pull up in front of the coach again.

This time about 20 men are waiting there. One pulls Lee's door open, but Lee manages to close it and lock it. I spin the car around so we're facing them. They are blocking the road, both behind and in front of us. They think they've got us trapped. They're jeering, taunting and beckoning us so I drive towards them at full speed. Seeing I'm not scared of hitting them they dive out the way and end up sprawled on either side of the road. I look in my mirror as we speed off. As they get back to their feet a police panda car comes around the corner. Its blue light starts to flash so, I kick the accelerator down as hard as I can, the gear changes down and we get pushed back into our seats as the car shoots forward. Within minutes we're speeding down country lanes and I see the blue lights fading into the distance. I take a hard hairpin right turn and as fast as possible head towards Woodhead and the moors. Within minutes we get to the summit of a hill where the sun is coming up and the whole landscape is covered in snow. I want to sing 'Feeling Good', because it's a new day, and we're on top of the world.

2007 - The Unreasonable Agony of Injustice

I am currently reading "Man's Search for Meaning" by Victor E. Frankl, which is the reflection of a psychoanalyst who survived the Nazi concentration camps during World War 2. His story makes mine look like a positive walk in the park. A couple of lines struck me in terms of what I'm trying to convey about violence here. I'll paraphrase them for copyright reasons: "It's not physical pain which hurts most of all. It's the mental agony caused by the unreasonableness of injustice." Perhaps deep down I carry with me a sense of being treated unfairly, maybe being disabled has a part to play in that too, although it's more the unfairness with which people have treated me than the physical limitations of being disabled. Even Shakespeare recognised this when he wrote:

> *"In nature, there's no blemish but the mind;*
> *None can be called deformed but the unkind."*
> *Twelfth Night, Act III, Scene IV*

2007 - Trying to Appear Tough

A friend of Kate's has read some of these chapters and reckons I'm trying to sound like I'm tough. I can see that it comes over that way, but being tough is relative. Against a lot of people, I wouldn't stand a chance, but I think what I'm trying to touch on is the rage inside me.

Now, it'd be easy to blame it on my disability, or the frustration of my early years, but then my father and half-brother on my mother's side are similar too. So maybe I'll never know why I have this ruthless violent streak, but it was there from very early on, from when I kicked my mother in the head, to the Roundshaw fights, and many other times, including as an adult. It was always there and had far more control over me than it should have.

Chapter 14
Beyond Belief

2007 Late summer

I'm lying on the beach, just opposite where I live. A mermaid is sitting next to me, she looks over her shoulder and stares into my eyes.

"Come down here and cuddle up to me," I say.

She smiles, laughs a little and says, "No."

'Typical mermaid behaviour,' I think.

I can't stop myself from saying, "There's going to be something big between us."

She smiles again, and whispers, "I know."

She pushes herself back into the sea and disappears for a week, but I know she'll be back.

2007 – Theo

Theo is sitting in his flat on Roundshaw watching the Sopranos. The draw of the mob is strong. He's been playing his part too, dealing drugs and trying to get people to work for him. One of his "workers", a friend, has betrayed him.

2007 - The Wrong Impression

After I uploaded that last chapter I got quite a few concerned friends, worried that I might be giving the wrong impression. Jackie a friend since 1989 said, "You come over as really aggressive in the book, but in real life, you have a calming effect." So, to prove her wrong I went round and beat her up. Okay, okay, I didn't! Another person thought I came over as arrogant, so maybe the book isn't so inaccurate after all.

I think the point I was trying to make in the last chapter was that my innate aggressive tendencies, coupled with my experiences of hostile environments, has resulted in me carrying a dangerous ability to escalate situations. But I also have a conscience which is what some of this this chapter is about.

The incidents I'd used as examples in the last chapter happened over a long period but placed together within a couple of pages probably intensifies the impression. As with most people, as I've got older, I rarely get into dangerous situations anymore, but, still, those dynamics are never that far from the surface. So, what does all this have to do with my "fall"? I've been thinking about this chapter for months and thought it was important to define what I mean by a fall. For instance, it doesn't end up with me lying in a gutter, well not so far anyway. In a way, it doesn't end up anywhere, because it happens slowly over time and continually reverberates within me. The fall isn't so much about incidents that happen, but a shift in my perception of the world and my reaction to it.

The Glass Child

When a child is young its perception of the world is a magical one, where for example, invisibility can be attained simply by covering up one's eyes. To all those observing the child, the truth is clear to see. The child does not become invisible, and any attempts to lie are easily seen for what they are. They are so transparent, it's as if they are made of glass.

The First Casualty - 1972 Aged Seven

"Watch this." I say.

Michael, a school friend, and I are standing near the playground in Roundshaw Junior School.

"What?" he says.

"Just watch!" I laugh.

Two of the playground assistants are walking across the playground towards us. I run towards them, they look at me, I smile at them, they smile at me. I run past, then double back, pull up the prettier one's skirt and shout out "ooooohhhh" then run back toward Michael who's now got a shocked look on his face. He can see what I can't. The pretty woman is running after me and catches up with me just as I get back to Michael.

"What do you think you're doing Simon?" She yells at me.

I point at Michael and almost crying say, "He made me do it."

Michael's look of shock morphs into one of someone who's just realised they're being murdered by a friend.

Five Years later I sunbathed, next to the woman whose dress I pulled, up at Purley Way Lido, an outdoor pool, and thought she was beautiful. At one point I swam between her legs underwater. She didn't tell me off the first time but maybe she did when I tried it again.

Magic

Many adults yearn for magic in their lives, be it a spiritual connection, a magical panacea, or just romance. And even though I should know better, as much as I try to be as logical as possible, I can't stop my desire for magic to conjure up connections whenever it can in my thoughts.

Ticker Tape Vision

One day I was driving to my Father's place. He was living in Notting Hill Gate, and I was in Fulham, a few miles away. Just as I was going to set off to drive, I started to see ticker tape numbers flowing in front of my eyes. I knew immediately that they were to do with the Lottery and my father, so, I wrote them down on a small piece of pink notepaper and headed off.

When I walked into his flat, he was sitting at a table with three friends. "Simon come and put a number on this ticket we're doing." He shouted. I walked over, looked at the ticket and there in front of me were five of the numbers I'd just written down. Well actually four of them were the same, but the fifth one was slightly different. On their ticket, it was the number 23, whereas I'd seen what I thought was 25. I immediately told them what had happened and took two of them (Doris and Ivan Kurland) down to the car to verify what I'd written.

By the way, our numbers resulted in a win, but sadly it was for only £10.

1972 - Lies

It's hard to know when the lies and blame start but one day, in a frenzy of naughtiness, I launched my bike down a staircase much to the pleasure of my friends; of course, being their host, their pleasure was mine too. By the time I got to my babysitter's place, my bike was a wreck. To tuts of disgust, I told them how some boys had smashed it up. But what I didn't realise was, the more I lied, the more isolated I became.

2007 - Mermaid Tears

The next time we met, the mermaid sat right next to me; she pushed herself close to me. I leant across and we kissed.

As a child I had looked longingly at the pictures of mermaids in books, their half-revealed breasts enraptured me, and now I was laying with my bare chest against hers. The books didn't reveal their beautiful song, but as she hummed, I looked deep into her eyes and as I stared, her eyes welled up. She touched one of the tears and put it to my lips. I closed my eyes and tasted the sadness of the sea.

2007 - Theo

Theo looked at Chris, his partner in crime. "Okay, so if they don't want so much this week, they'll be back for more the next, it ain't a problem. Here's a bit extra for your personal use."

1972 - Aged Seven - Sally

About ten children have encircled me. It's just like in a film, rage seems to have muffled the sound and the image is broken. Dislocated faces come toward me, then I feel lumps of earth and grass being thrown at me. The kids are spitting, pushing and laughing.

Standing on a staircase nearby I noticed Sally, who was laughing and pointing. Sally was one of the nice girls in my class. The thought that even she was laughing at me was unbearable. It was as if the deepest betrayal had been hurled upon me. So, I decided I would retaliate with a far worse one.

I ran through the blockade and up the stairs. Sally thought I would probably run past, but I didn't. Instead, I looked at her and pulled my arm back to strike her. She screamed as I thrust my arm towards her stomach, but the disdain in my gut for what I was doing exploded throughout my whole body. I felt a sharp pain at the end of my arm as I missed Sally and hit the concrete wall instead. I was thankful. She put her hands to her face and cried, "I'm sorry" and in that moment I learnt the value of forgiveness. I looked at the end of my arm and it was covered in blood.

1975 – Roehampton Hospital

One day on the ward in Roehampton hospital a boy grabbed a cane and struck it hard across my back. I lost my temper and went for the boy who pulled the cane back to strike me again. I backed off for a second and noticed another boy who was laughing. He was standing in a special brace which held him in an upward position because he was in a plaster cast from his waist down to his feet. I ran up to him and kicked his legs until he started to scream and one of the adults, probably my mum, pulled me off.

1973 - Roundshaw

Even in the realms of fighting at the age of eight, unwritten rules existed.

A boy called Jason and I got into a fight. First, we rolled around on the ground and didn't get anywhere, then we decided we'd copy a film and trade punches in the stomach, and then I tried kicking him in the face when no one was looking, which didn't help matters. Finally, it ended when Stephen Kirby's mum intervened, at which point I burst into tears, which apparently meant I'd lost.

The old cliché of, "If you can't beat them join them," may well be the basis of gang culture. Stephen Kirby's mum was a force to be reckoned with and certainly wasn't foolish enough to let her son roam the streets. But for the rest of us, left to our own devices, the only way forward was to become part of the group. Possibly because I was an outsider, both in terms of only recently arriving on the estate and looking different, resulted in me feeling a lot of pressure to conform. Especially when it came to entering the realms of delinquency.

My friends are all crouched behind a wall which is at the end of a row of doors. They've sent me to knock on one of the doors and then run back to where they are. It's an old game known as, "Knock down Ginger."

I ring the bell and run back to my friends.

Nothing happens.

"Go on have another go," one of the boys shouts in a whisper.

I look around, "Shall I?"

"Yes, go on, go on!"

I'm laughing. It's got the same tension as an army operation. We're all pumped up with adrenalin. I creep back, as my friends' heads pop up from behind the wall. I push the bell and run back again.

Just as before, nothing happens.

"She can't be in," I say.

"Yes she is, I saw her go in." One of the others reassures me.

"Okay, I'll do it one more time."

Like some pantomime actor, I step slowly towards her door. I reach for the bell, but as I do the door flies open, an arm reaches out, grabs my hair and lifts me off the ground. The woman who's attached to the arm puts her face to mine and screams, "What do you think you're playing at?"

My friends stand up to watch. Meanwhile, I'm being lifted by my hair and dangled in mid-air. A bit shocked, I burst into tears.

"Don't give me that!" She says, loudly.

"They made me do it" I plead.

"And if they told you to jump under a bus, would you?"

I think about the philosophical implications of this question. "Erm... No"

"Well then!" She cracks her palm across my head and drops me to the ground. As I lay there, she wags her finger at me and adds, "If I ever catch you doing this again

I'll give you what for." – Listen I didn't write the script, that's what she said -.

"I'm sorry" – and I was, for years I was scared of her and didn't ever go back for a retry.

Needless to say, I did gain a bit of honour amongst my peers.

Gang Welfare

Death before dishonour is probably just as much the motto of the mob as it is with any other army. The mafia based its structure on the Roman army and in Roman times, if a unit didn't fight properly, it would be decimated which meant every tenth man in a line would have to step forward and be executed by his fellow soldiers. If you can't rule by winning hearts and minds, then fear is a pretty effective alternative.

There isn't much love between members of a gang; love is for families and most gang members are not part of a close family. However, the gang provides a kind of protective shell, which in its way is a surrogate family. Still, though, it isn't going to nurture its members as a family should. Instead, if members step out of line, they'll be met with force rather than understanding.

2007 - Theo - The Cross

Sometimes you know something's wrong, you don't want to accept it, but it just won't go away, it nags at you, until finally, the truth finds a way of making itself known.

Theo watched Chris, his so-called business partner, double-cross him, openly stealing his clients and undercutting him. Theo felt a pain in his kidneys, he couldn't breathe, he leaned against the wall and wept.

1972 - Gangland

School was another world. There were many friendly kind children, but the gang resided there too. School was like a prison, and the guards were a gang that tried to control the gangs in their care.

1973 - The Bat Kite

My mum bought me a large kite which was shaped like a bat. Sevin and I tried to get it to fly but it wouldn't. So, we took a lift to the top of one of the blocks of flats nearby known as Shaw Way and launched it from the upper walkway. It still wasn't up for going up and sullenly swooped downwards and came to rest against one of the windows. When we heard the screams from below, we burst out laughing and dragged it along the full length of the building, then before getting lynched we pulled it up and made our getaway.

Beggars' Belief

The last time I saw Sevin was when we were both 19. He was working in a hi-fi shop. Within weeks of knowing me, he'd spotted my potential and had me begging for money in the shopping precinct and when he came to my grandmother's with me on one occasion, he got me to ask Uncle Bertie if he could "lend" me some money. Uncle Bertie told me he wasn't impressed with my newfound friend. I wanted to tell him how much money we'd already made but didn't think it would go down well. Being able to go into a toy shop and buy a model aircraft with our hard begged for cash, ironically, filled us with pride. It wasn't 'til Mr Garriock, our headmaster, called me into his office to discuss the reports he'd received of me begging, that it ever occurred to me that I was doing anything wrong. At first, I was tempted to debate the finer points of being compensated for society's oppression of disabled people, but the threat of punishment seemed to instantly override any logical arguments I had on the tip of my tongue and so it was, my begging days came to an end.

1973 - Andy

Just as Sevin had developed a relationship with me that had echoed that of Colonel Tom Parker and Elvis Presley's, I developed one with a boy called Andy which had similar undertones to Lennie and George's friendship in the book, *Of Mice and Men*. Andy was both tall and strong for his age and came over as an archetypal gentle giant. Sometimes we'd walk miles together including the journey from West Park Hospital, where my mother worked, to Chessington Zoo, through snow-covered fields. By the time we got there, pretty much everything had been closed down due to the weather. Back then it was a much smaller affair compared to the multi-million theme park it has become and the proprietors felt sorry for us and opened a ride just for us. It was a rocket-shaped vehicle you sat in that would go around in a circle as well as going up and down. The problem was I wasn't held in properly and had to stop myself from falling out by grabbing the handrail with both my paws. They thought we deserved a long go and given the screams to stop, that we were enjoying every moment. Fortunately, I didn't fall out and at least I can say it was a memorable experience.

Andy seemed to become my sherpa, often carrying items for me from Wallington High Street back to my home and at one point even giving me a piggyback through a muddy field when my shoe got stuck in the mud. On another far sunnier day his duties extended to helping me capture girls when playing kiss chase in the lunch break.

For quite a while I saw myself as the brains and him as the brawn of the collaboration. However, one day we thought throwing very small bits of gravel from a bridge at cars passing below was a great idea, that was until a man came up behind us and told us he was a policeman. I believed him and gave him my real name and address whereas Andy offered false information. When the 'policeman' had gone Andy looked at me incredulously.

I did learn from this experience because a short while later I managed to set a whole field on fire with a single match we'd found. The field backed onto the park and a block of flats. Within minutes the firefighters turned up and put it out. I casually walked up to one of them and told him I'd seen some kids do it. We ended up agreeing with each other about how awful some kids can be. For months afterwards, though, I felt a sense of pride every time I saw the scorched grass there.

I'm not sure if I just lacked any imagination or compassion for the risks I created for others, or if I did it deliberately to hurt people, but this lack of empathy became a lot more dangerous later on. Even at eight years old I would say to other kids, "Does this hurt?" and though they'd plead with me to leave them alone, I'd try out some martial arts move on them and feel very pleased with myself when I saw them writhing around on the floor in agony.

It wasn't as if I didn't ever hear people talk about the danger of what I was up to or how badly I was behaving. One day, as I walked back from school, a girl called Julie asked if I wanted to be her boyfriend. I wasn't too interested but said yes anyway. During the short journey, I found a match and started trying to get it to light. She looked at me and gave me an ultimatum to stop doing that or she'd no longer be my girlfriend. That was probably one of the shortest relationships ever.

2007 – Theo

Theo and Chris would go out together late at night which cut Mira, Theo's girlfriend, to the core. When he walked into the night darkness, enveloped him. The claustrophobia that drove him out of the family home, even for just a few hours, in turn, left her surrounded by too much space. As she floated, waiting for his return she felt unanchored, and fear overwhelmed her. For Theo going out with Chris wasn't so much about rejecting Mira, but an escape of the humdrum of normality. He wanted to feel special, and being special in another person's heart wasn't enough, or maybe it was too much. Maybe the real adventure of loving another human being, of getting to know them in-depth, of putting their needs aside of his own, of fighting his more baser tendencies was an adventure too full of hardship. For him, the shallower relationships of being part of a gang, or hooking up with other like-minded easy-rider adventurers were far more inviting.

"If you go out tonight, I won't be here when you come back," she said.

He looked at her, shrugged and walked out.

2007 - Beyond Belief

I came to the beach and met the mermaid every week, and one day as we kissed, I said, "I am yours, are you mine?" She said "Yes."

But the next week she didn't turn up, and the week after there was still no sign of her. So, when, in the third week, she reappeared, I wanted to know if she truly loved me. She looked hurt that I'd even question our love, and then as she went to go, I held on to her tightly. Again, she looked hurt, but this time she looked scared as well. I could feel a distance open up between us, so slowly let go. But it was too late, she swam away, and my body filled with fear.

For months I'd go back to the place on the beach where we first kissed and wait for her. I swore I could feel I was still in her mind and felt she'd be watching me from out there somewhere. But in time, I came to accept we must allow those we love to no longer feel the same way. To be as concerned with her happiness as I was with mine. Deep down, though, I knew I didn't.

My friends waved their self-help books at me saying, "You should never lose yourself to someone else." In a way, they were right, but I also knew we should put our loved ones first. Still, finding that balance and getting beyond the virtuous words and ideals I believed in, was beyond me.

My fall, or falls, didn't just happen when I was a child but continued to have consequences for the rest of my life including causing further falls in others, and myself.

1973 - Diverging Paths

The journey that leads us to truly love someone else often starts from the other end of the spectrum, a position of self-centred self-love. Perhaps being cuddled up to my mother and other carers as a child allowed me at least some sense of being at one with another. But a child doesn't look after the needs of their carers, well not normally in any significant way.

And then maybe at five years old, or younger, there was a desire to feel the warmth of another person against me, and the stirrings of sexual desire. By eight though, the connection between being comforted and sexual stimulation was already muddled. Where essentially, I wanted to be hugged and understood, I now started to be thrilled by looking at women in flats nearby getting undressed and would hang out my window until late at night to do so.

On top of this, I discovered my erect penis was of some interest to some girls and combined with my ridiculous hole in my trousers for helping me go to the loo, I realised that I could oblige any willing spectators. Even at the school dinner table, I called across to Stella, "Do you want to see my willy?"

She laughed and said, "Go on then."

I reached into my trousers to push it through the hole but just as I did, I felt a tap on my shoulder.

"Stop playing Simon and eat up."

It was the dinner lady, Mrs Phillips.

She looked at Stella, "What are you doing looking under the table, have you lost something?"

Stella slowly repositioned herself, "Sorry miss I was looking for my pen. I thought I'd dropped it."

Alas, Stella never got to see my penis and from then on, our lives took very different paths.

Suffice to say, my sexuality was already taking a path that wasn't concerned about mutual love and care, but excitement and using others for my own gratification.

1973 - Hard

With every fight I had, a notch-by-notch change took place in me. A slow breaking of my spirit that would lead, in time, to a typical hardening of the outside while my inner world remained precariously fragile.

The kick-in-the-eye fight had put me on the map and in the running as a contender in the local fighting league and given I was already a target for kids calling me names, I would always have been destined to be involved in fights. Well, at least until I'd realised there were other ways to deal with bullies. But Roundshaw was a landscape of violence for me. There was my mother and her psychotic boyfriend Michael, the neighbours fighting with each other, and all the other kids on the estate who were vying for the reputation of being the hardest kid in their year, in their street, on the estate, in the world and so on. The estate was symbolically coated in hard concrete and everyone who lived there had to follow suit.

2007 – Theo - Oblivion Calls

Mira left, just as she said and, on the phone, later, when Theo begged her to come back, she reminded him of her ultimatum. Unable to bear the thought of being controlled by her though, it was he who put the phone down first. He then called Chris and suggested they go out in search of oblivion.

1973 Aged Eight - First Blood

Paul was a kid who, had he lived in the countryside, would have been promoted to "village idiot" at some point. God knows why, but I lost my temper with him and launched a full-scale attack. I was on top of him, kicking him, and could feel I was winning but when we both stood up at the end of the fight, someone pointed at the blood on my lip and declared him the winner.

The affront to my pride of losing to such a low-level contender filled me with shame and the importance of status within the local fighters' loser board started to concern me, while the stupidity of it all, seemed to simply evade me.

2007 – Theo

Chris was from one of the rough families on Roundshaw, but Theo wasn't from the estate and carried with him the notion of being hard because of his foreign roots. He didn't involve himself with local league tables; instead, his hardness was a matter of national pride. So much so that one day when he was convinced that Chris had betrayed him, he asked him what was going on and shoved a knife through his heart. Chris looked at him, the way a friend does when they're being killed.

1973 - A Kick in the Ear

The main reason for fighting was just to see who was the hardest, nothing else normally. Sure, somewhere in a conversation, the ball would start rolling and within minutes either an appointment for a fight was made or the battle would commence there and then. And so, with a, "You reckon you're hard, do you?" from either me or Colin, the boy who sat behind me in class when I was ten, we marched out to the playground. The chants of "fight, fight, fight," committed us to action. We eyed each other up, ran towards each other and within seconds were on the ground wrestling. We broke away and both made our way back up to our feet, but someone in the crowd pushed me over so, as I went to stand up again, Colin ran towards me and kicked me hard in my ear. The fight was over, and I lay in agony crying.

1973/4

Near to where this fight took place, I'd watched my friend Andrew Wilson collapse two years beforehand. (He's not the Andy who walked miles in the snow with me, he's the one I'd play with in the library during games.) One minute we were standing chatting, the next Stella cried out, "Andrew's having a fit." I looked down to see Andrew shaking on the floor; his lips were purple and his skin was ashen. We were used to him having fits occasionally but the teacher, Mrs Gee, picked him up by his legs and ran him into the medical room with an urgency we hadn't seen before.

Later on, rumours started going around that Andrew had died, and a bit later on Mrs Gee, crying, told us it was true. Maybe because Andrew was ill, he wasn't able to show an aggressive part of himself, so the Andrew we all knew was very gentle and friendly. When Andrew died most of the school felt a sense of loss, even though he didn't appear anywhere on the hardest kid scoreboard. As much as many of us were bothered about being tough, Andrew revealed to us we held other qualities in high regard as well.

2007 – Theo

I don't know what went on in Theo's mind as he plunged the knife into Chris, but I do know he'd lost his sense of who he was. After he'd killed him, he chopped Chris up into small packages and put them into bin liners. He then left them in his bath while he worked out what to do next, and there they remained for several weeks. During this time Theo visited my mum, drank tea with her and behaved as if nothing had happened. Then something strange happened.

He turned up on Mum's doorstep and gave her an envelope. He then asked her to deliver the letter to a man in London. Mum didn't open the letter but obligingly drove to the address and rang the doorbell. A man in a dressing gown answered the door, took the letter, thanked her then closed the door. Later that day, Theo phoned Mira and told her he was going to jump off a building. He said he was sorry, and cried goodbye to her as he disconnected the call.

He stood up, walked to the window, opened it and climbed onto the ledge. His apartment was on the second floor. Without hesitating he jumped but when he hit the ground he landed on his shoulder. Initially, he tried to get up, but couldn't and died a few minutes later.

After the police arrived, they went into his house and soon found the bins full of meat, but it didn't take them long to realise what it really was.

He did leave a few letters, one was to my mother thanking her for being so kind, but none shed light on why he killed himself. My mother, Mira, and a policewoman were the only "mourners" at his funeral.

1975/6 - Rescue Call

There was a new boy called Dale who came into our school when I was ten. During his first few days, he told me he didn't like my "style". I wasn't quite sure what he meant but I knew it wasn't a compliment. He seemed set to make his mark and wanted to be the toughest kid in our school.

As we stepped out of class one day, he pushed me, and I retaliated. The next minute we were grappling on the floor. He sat on me and tried to punch me but I blocked his punches. I then went for my normal trick of bringing my leg up to kick him in the face, but he managed to stop it. Left with no more resources to defend myself I gave in. I either let him, or he found a way to punch me in the face. I screamed out, not so much in agony, (well okay, I imagine pain played a part) but in exasperation. It was the madness of this world I'd come to live in. I was screaming for help and wanted to be rescued. I didn't want to have to fight anymore. From that beating, I not only realised my limitations but also a desire to find another way.

2007 - Tattoo

I waited many years for the return of the mermaid, but she didn't come back, so I found a way to become a merman and went into the sea to search for her. When I found her, she saw what I'd gone through, and she came back to me. We sat on some rocks and looked into each other's eyes, and it was at this point that Ms Lovelight drew us.

1976 - Bad Shot

At 11 years old I pointed an air pistol at a woman pushing a baby in a buggy walking past our flat. My school friend next to me implored me not to do it, but I ignored him and pulled the trigger then moved back inside the room. That night the lady came around and showed my mother the bruise on her back and asked me what I thought would have happened if the pellet had hit her child.

1975 - Limits

I had bought a blowpipe with darts that had suction pads on, but we found that sticking needles and pins through the suction pads allowed us to make real darts. My friend blew one into his sister's back which even I thought was going too far.

2007 - Ms Lovelight's Drawing

As I lay cuddled up to Ms Lovelight, I asked her about the tattoo on her shoulder. She said, "That's the man I'm gonna marry."

"It looks like me," I said.

"We'll see." She laughed.

"I've got a painting I did about 20 years ago in which I look exactly like the merman, it's even called, Over Her Shoulder."

"Well," she said, "the thing is my original version of the picture didn't have them touching which means they might not ever get together, you see, the tattoo isn't exactly as I drew it."

Not wanting to listen, but instead persuade, I argued, "Yes but isn't what's on your shoulder what's real, they do get it together."

"No," she said, "the original picture's what's real,"

Still unwilling to accept her way of seeing things I added, "I feel like we're going to marry."

She smiled, "We'll see."

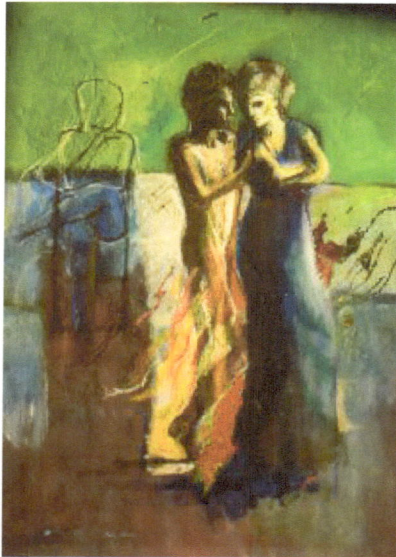

2007 - What I Mean by "My Fall"

If you want to know what I mean by "my fall" and consequently what this whole chapter is about, it's this. My ability to keep grounded, to know who I am, to know what I truly need, to have a sense of reality. All those things were nearly non-existent by the age of eleven. I was psychopathic at times, psychotic, delinquent, sexually detached and heading towards a difficult life.

Theo's fate may have been mine.

I yearn for the romanticism and magic of the mermaid story, and as for Ms Lovelight's tattoo, is it me, or is it just a coincidence? Time would be the Revelator.

2007 - In the End

I sat at my window with Ms Lovelight for hours. She lay against me and both of us said how content we felt. But when she was gone, I missed her, and one day, just sitting in the same place without her made my whole body ache. In time I realised she couldn't save me from this feeling, and it was in the passing of things that my greatest pain lies.

Just like her mermaid and merman tattoo, sometimes I feel as if I'd like to be held in an everlasting embrace of pure love. Such a thought though, reminds me of the feelings people describe when they go through a Near Death Experience. Does that mean then, that when we desire to be held in the light of everlasting love, it's a version of death, maybe a heavenly one, we yearn for, or is heaven merely a conceptualisation of our deepest desires?

Chapter 15
Gripping Dreams

It's Over

Elvis is on the radio singing 'It's Over'. Something about time not moving, so, this night of love he and his beloved shared could last forever, and that way it would never be over.

2007 - Ms Lovelight - The Ward

I stood at the doorway to the isolation unit and looked through the high-security two-panel wire mesh glass window in the door. Miss Lovelight's body lay upon a theatre bed; the ventilator moved up and down making the sound of waves.

A nurse sat near her bed reading while an orderly cleaned the floor. There was also another preparing something in the background. All of them wore masks. I pushed the intercom button. The nurse who'd been reading put her book down, walked to the door, picked up the receiver, and without looking at me said, "Hello," in a slightly pissed off, 'Not you again' tone.

"You ok?" I said.

"Yes," she said as if I was asking a stupid question.

"Any change?"

"No."

Miss Lovelight's finger twitched. As I glanced the nurse said, "It's nothing, just an involuntary action, we will have to shut the window now, sorry."

She put the intercom handset on its cradle, stood up and closed the hatch-like door across the window. As she did, I looked into her eyes and they were Miss Lovelight's, and the cleaner looked up at me, as did the other nurse. They all had the same eyes but then as the window clicked into position, I was left staring into my own eyes in the reflection. I picked up the receiver and pressed the Intercom buzzer.

Again, in the same tone, "Hello."

I said, "She loved me once."

Almost laughing she replied, "She loved being with you, that's not the same thing."

"I have a message here, on my phone. It's from her and it says: 'I'm trying to tell you I love you,' and when I told her I was hers and asked if she was mine, she said she was."

Shaking her head very slowly she said, "Well, there are different kinds of love."

I moved my head from side to side, almost in sync with hers, "I think she must love me still, somewhere inside."

She sighed, "She may have loved you, but she's gone away, and she doesn't love you anymore. She doesn't, and by the way, desperation isn't a good look on anyone, including you."

I go quiet. I hear a single tone emanating from the receiver and put it down.

2007 - The Story of the Relationship

Memories of a lost love affair get captured in slices of time; some are stationary while others flicker in the light of a bedside lamp. If I edited the months we spent together, it'd probably be entertaining for 5-minutes as a YouTube video, but, for me, I want to stretch every moment through eternity.

Question 1

Okay, you've got a choice, you've found someone you love, you're wrapped around each other, and the feeling you have inside is just right. You can "emotionally" stay in this moment forever, or you can live life normally with the risk the relationship may flounder. Either way, I can almost guarantee the good feelings won't last, but which will you choose?

Ms Lovelight - First Meeting

When I picked Miss Lovelight up for the first time, we found each other by using our mobile phones. I pulled up in my convertible car and she laughed and called it a "babe magnet". I took her to the beach and there we sat chatting till the tide came in. At one point I lay down and asked her to cuddle up to me. She looked over her shoulder, stared into my eyes and said no.

The next time we met was different. I didn't ask her to come to me, instead, she sat right next to me, snuggled up to me, our faces rubbed against each other, and we kissed.

For weeks we'd meet up and kiss and cuddle, then one day I asked her to stay the night and she did. But when we started to make love, it felt wrong. The next day I drove her to the station and both of us thought that would be the last time we'd ever see each other. But it wasn't. When we met again a few weeks later, she walked through the door, and we immediately kissed deeply; it was then we realised this was just the beginning.

We spent many hours sitting on the sofa looking out of the window, completely at peace. When we were together, I couldn't help but want to kiss her, and she'd tell me how much I loved her body, which I did. When friends would visit, she'd snuggle up to me, she'd want to look after me, as we'd pass each other we'd touch, reach out and gently caress each other and when we were apart, I'd always feel secure she'd be faithful.

One day she sent me a text saying, "I'm trying to tell you I love you," and the next time we made love I looked into her eyes and said, "I'm yours, are you mine?" She looked into mine and said "Yes". As she slept, I'd look at the tattoo on her back and kiss it. I could see the merman looked like me and felt happy that one day we might marry.

2007 - Transience

If you could choose to spend the rest of eternity held in a moment from your life, which one would you choose?

What if you could either choose to be held in a moment of your choice or experience life as a process of beginnings and endings, of acquisition and loss, of discovery and immobility, of love and heartbreak and finally, the death of those we love and ourselves? Again, which would you choose?

When Keats wrote his famous poem, "Ode to a Grecian Urn" he broached the same issue. The couple pictured on the Urn had been there for over 2000 years, held in a moment of tender yearning. They hadn't had to suffer the ravages of time or a real-life relationship but instead were caught in a moment of Eros-driven romantic togetherness, a glorious illusion.

Some people believe that as we die, we experience being drawn into a feeling of complete love. Many of those who experience this not only no longer fear death but feel hard done by in terms of having to continue to live.

Inside most of us is this quandary. Do we accept loss and live our lives full of joy and pain or do we try to escape it either through experiencing nothing or by avoiding pain at all costs? At the heart of this is coming to terms with transience, and in turn, losing our dreams and accepting loss.

The Tattoo - The Everlasting Embrace

The tattoo hung in my mind; it was like a sign from God. The couple would sit in an everlasting embrace until one day Miss Lovelight's funeral pyre would fade it to black.

Ms Lovelight - The Ending

It had been two weeks since we'd last seen each other. I was beginning to feel she wasn't interested anymore and when I told her how I felt, she went quiet, and we didn't speak for a few days. I could sense she wanted to split up and when she called me, she said she did. I told her I thought it was the wrong thing to do. A couple of days later she came to visit me, and I asked her to deny that she still felt deeply connected to me, and what we had was very special and she said she couldn't deny it. Once again, we sat on the sofa in each other's arms and after the daylight faded, she walked off.

Each night we'd talk on the phone for hours, and in time we both felt the damage was healing, and in a matter of weeks she'd come to live with me. However, on the second of January, she said all her feelings for everything, including us, had disappeared.

During the previous two years, she'd lost her home and her last boyfriend. She'd had to care for her mother for six months and recently found she had a tumour. All of it finally caught up on her and now she'd closed down. When I spoke to her it was as if I was speaking to an android and I knew then the connection and person who'd loved me had gone.

The Anatomy of My Heartbreaks

In the first moments of heartbreak, a cold fear rushes through my body but within seconds I am numb. I can see what is going to happen and though there's an element of panic still bubbling along with the numbness, I go into logical over-drive. I try to argue my corner but if there's no hope, a sad resignation sets in, and I say goodbye.

There is calmness at first, but this soon becomes a restlessness where I can no longer focus on anything and in time all that's important is the sense of loss. Consequently, I try to either regain what I've lost or distract myself from the pain of grieving. If there's a chance of re-capturing the person's heart, then I become obsessed in that pursuit and may spend months doing so, and unable to let go I become a slave to my quest. During this time, I may also wish to dampen my pain or try to find someone else to love me which normally involves seeking out inti-mate encounters to distract myself with. But even then, I end up thinking more about the person I don't have any more instead of the one I'm with and by this point, I am trapped in the grave of the relationship.

This denial is sometimes known as 'the condemned's reprieve', a prisoner who's just about to be executed will hope right up to the last moment that somehow, they'll be pardoned and get to live longer. For them though, the stages of grief probably don't get to play out to a satisfactory conclusion.

Elvis is coming to the end of the song and resigns himself to accepting he may have to force himself to say it's over. For me, that was always one of the saddest songs I ever heard him sing.

The symptoms of heartbreak are extremely painful for me. Firstly, my sense of meaning seems lost, and pleasure in previously enjoyable endeavours disappears. The day becomes a void that's better filled with sleep and dreams than living. Meanwhile, the physical sensations of heartbreak are overwhelming. A lack of appetite, a painful feeling in my chest and throat, aching legs and arms and an overall weakness set in. All of which may last for days, or weeks even.

The obsession doesn't just remain an internal issue, my poor friends have to constantly put up with listening to the same story of woe, how I feel and other reflections on the issue. To me though, it's as if I'm in a hall of mirrors and it's hard to find my way out.

In one way I feel quite lucky; I rarely harbour a great amount of anger and normally, in time, see the separation as one of those things, rather than an act of malice towards me. For many people, though, they may end up spiralling into a cycle of vengeance. If anything, the quickest way out of that is through understanding and forgiveness by accepting people's feelings change and their fickleness has little to do with us. But still, for those with other more malicious internal dynamics, such a peaceful resolution might seem an anathema.

1970 - Shattered Dreams

During my time in care, I dreamt of coming to live with my mother. The times I'd spent with her then had been full of her paying me attention and behaving well. However, when I came to live with her full-time, my dreams were shattered.

We'd moved to a rough estate, her boyfriend was violent, and her foul moods hammered me into silent submission. If I'd had a dream as a baby to be looked after in a certain way, then that dream seemed like an illusion now. So much so it's no wonder as I grew older, I came to believe if I dared to dream of anything it would end in disaster.

2007- Not To Be

I'd looked at Miss Lovelight's tattoo and thought we would marry, but it wasn't to be.

2007 - The Loss of Love and Shattered Dreams

The result of broken dreams is sadness and anger, and the result of that is the smashing of dreams and the creation of nightmares. Somewhere along our journey, we hold others responsible for our losses, and for many of us, we end up taking ourselves hostage to get back at our oppressors. We make ourselves suffer so we can look at them and say, "See, look what you did to me, you ruined my life." Consequently, whenever we feel we're on the verge of happiness we may be tempted to throw a spanner in the works and either directly, or not, bring our world crashing down around us, while deep down we're still saying, "See, look what you made me do, it's your fault, you caused this."

Whether we consciously know it, or not, there's only one way we're going to allow ourselves to be happy and that's if we find a way to forgive those who trespassed against us and for many of us we feel it's God who did so. How we do that though, is not an easy journey and for many the effort won't be worth it.

So, if I have waffled on about love, the loss of love, and the shattering of dreams, it's because much of my life and what will unfold in the following chapters revolves around these two interrelated losses. Not just for me, but for nearly all of us.

2007 - Karaoke Culture

I'm standing on a stage in a pub, it's karaoke night, and I mournfully sing the song I heard Elvis performing on the radio.

I look at the audience, some of whom are touched, some just carry on chatting, and I wonder why music no longer plays a big social part in our culture. A man once told me, it's because we've become too comfortable, that cultures where there's great social disharmony still get together and sing. We've sorted out some of our general woes and now our main suffering is a feeling of disconnection, a sense of loss, a lack of love and a general demeanour of dissolution. And for that, it's easier to stick some headphones on and suffer alone in a lack of silence.

2019 - The Ring

I spoke to Ms Lovelight on the phone.

Ms Lovelight: I heard you'd been ill, so just wanted to see if you're ok.

Me: I'm ok, thanks, much better, although I didn't like almost dying.

Ms Lovelight: I still wear the ring you gave me.

Me: What, I gave you a ring?

Ms Lovelight: Yes, don't you remember?

After the call, I did recall, in detail, buying the ring. What it looked like and what its markings meant, but the medication I was on had taken a toll on my memory. I realised my forgetting had probably broken a dream for her and maybe after the call she'd taken the ring off and thrown it in a drawer, but I hoped she hadn't. I called her a year or so later, but she didn't answer. I checked she was alive and well, via one of her sons, and she was. So, I took it that my moment of forgetting meant something to her, but that wasn't true in light of all the facts; but love-light, as with most human endeavours, tends not to be so concerned with illuminating the truth.

2023 - The Ring of Truth

I got in contact with Ms. Lovelight because I didn't want to leave her thinking I'd forgotten about the ring. She told me she hadn't thought that, but eventually had to have the ring cut off when her hand became swollen. As we neared the end of the call, I realised this would probably be the last time we'd ever speak to one another, so, feeling thankful for our connection, I said, "Goodbye".

Chapter 16
Unforgetable

Love turns everyone into imbeciles

Forgetfulness

I wake from a dream, and in a moment, it is gone. I have lived with a woman for ten years and now I struggle to remember our time together. As I drive, someone annoys me and I forget the morals I thought I lived by.

By the time I was ten, I had pretty much forgotten myself.

***

M23 – 23rd July 2008 – The Burgundy Jag - Part 1

I'm driving north on the M23 towards London and am about two miles south of Crawley. I look in my rearview mirror and see a police car speeding toward me; it's about half a mile back. Don't worry, this is a different story from the one involving the blue car. My memory hasn't got quite that bad yet.

I take my foot off the accelerator and gently move into the nearside lane; I'm feeling slightly anxious about my speed and whether they're after me. Then I notice another car, just in front of the police, it's a burgundy-coloured Jag. Its lights are on full beam too and as they pass, I quickly take a look at them, they look like elderly police officers and they're laughing. They're doing about 120 mph, so I surmise they must be important.

***

1975 - Educating Simon

Mr Garriock, the headmaster, requested my presence. When I got to his office there was a queue. I, along with two other boys, stood in silence outside his office. As I waited, I began to collate all the dodgy activities I'd got up to recently and couldn't help but wonder which of them had brought me to this corridor of doom. For each of them, I began to build defence cases along with mitigating circumstances and appropriate punishments should my opinion on such matters be requested. The two boys went in ahead of me, one after another, each coming out with tears in their eyes. The door opened and Mr Garriock called me in.

"Sit down Simon," he took a puff from his pipe. "Well, well, what are we going to do with you, Simon?" He paused, just like the man in the Condor pipe tobacco adverts. "You're a bright boy, but you keep letting yourself down. You fight, you're disobedient, and God knows what else you get up to. If you carry on like that you're going to end up in a lot of trouble. Is that what you want?"

I mouth a silent no and look down in shame.

"If you don't focus on your education, what will you have?"

I'm tempted to point out my naturally proficient criminal mind, but having such a mind means I know it's best not to.

He sighs.

"After the summer break, you'll be doing an exam, the result of which will determine the school you go to, and in turn that'll partly dictate what happens to you for the rest of your life. So, either you pull your socks up now, or I fear it'll be too late. And let's face it, you are not going to have as many options available to you as most people."

I'm like a man facing the gallows.

"So," he says, "from now until the exams I'm going to teach you a few hours a week."

And that's what happened. The fact that he was willing to pay me attention meant I felt indebted to him and so I tried my best, okay, almost my best, to do well.

It is a cliché, but the attention I received from individuals who seemed to genuinely care had an effect, and their actions found a place in my heart a long time after they'd gone. It's a big temptation for teachers to focus on students who don't need much help, but the real struggle is not lesson plans and reports but resisting that temptation and doing one's best to help those who need it too.

2008 - Bullying

One of my sons has drawn a smiley face on my touchpad.

A couple of days ago, a boy from their school threatened to follow them home and smash our windows. Their crime had been a friend of this boy had punched my son in the head from behind and my son had turned around and punched him in the stomach. The boy fell against a locker at which point a teacher intervened. The boy then felt the fight had been stopped prematurely, making it appear as if he'd lost. From then on, he'd set himself on a path of vengeance.

A few weeks later the same boy went up to a skinny bespectacled Indian boy, called him a "paki" and then with a well-placed coin between his knuckles punched the boy in the eye. The boy collapsed immediately and was unconscious for some time. His vision was permanently damaged by this attack, yet the attacker is still at the school, apparently receiving, "special attention". Meanwhile, his friends are continuing to persecute my sons.

July 2008 - Knife Crime

I'm sitting in front of a video camera; a group of youths are making a documentary on knife crime.

"Did you ever carry a knife, Simon?"

I nod, "Yes, from about 11 onwards I had a fascination with weapons and violence. I bought a large 'Green River' knife and strapped it to my leg, then tucked the handle into my sock. I wore a strap on my arm so I could hold it and continued to carry it until I was 13. What stopped me was this. I was jumping around in Roundshaw Youth Club when it flew across the floor. One of the youth workers who I liked, picked it up and went ballistic. It was his intervention and disapproval that persuaded me to stop wearing it."

"Why did you carry a knife?"

"Because I wanted to create an impression to others that I was hard, so people would either leave me alone or show me some respect."

1981 - Revenge Attack

I have cornered a boy in a stranger's porch way. He's pleading with me to leave him alone, but he's been taking the piss out of me for weeks and I know I have to teach him a lesson. I go to punch him on the nose but miss, so spin around and strike my stump hard on it. His face is covered in blood. I pull back my leg and kick him hard in the shin. He immediately drops to the ground in tears. A woman comes out from another house and shouts at me. I walk off. I feel sorry for him, but I also know this had to be done. He kept taunting me and then telling the teachers at school I'd threatened him. Which I had, but it wasn't without cause. He forgot there were other options available to me. Six weeks later he apologised to me and showed me the bruise was still dark on his leg.

M23 – 23rd July 2008 – The Burgundy Jag - Part 2

The police car is now a few hundred metres ahead of me and I can see other police cars further ahead too. There seems to be some kind of incident, I have to slow down, as the traffic is building up.

5th August 2008 - The Gloves are On

I walk into a place I'm working in today and as I do there's a group of people standing in the corridor. One of them, who always reminds me of a gangster who's gone straight, has got a couple of very large boxing gloves. "Hold on a minute mate," he says to me, "I've got an idea, put these on." He helps put them on my arms. We're standing there laughing, I do a quick karate kick towards his head. He looks impressed.

M23 – 23rd July 2008 – The Burgundy Jag - Part 3

It's difficult to know what's going on ahead. There are lots of police lights flashing, and then I notice the burgundy car is trying to get past the police cars. First, he feigns an attempt to drive up the bank to the side of the road but is blocked by a quick-witted police driver, then he tries to weave between the gap created by the movement. The police aren't having it, and four police cars ram him into the central reservation. I hold back about 100 metres in case they pull out any guns.

188

The police are all over the vehicle in seconds, opening the doors and pulling out the old geezers.

After a few minutes, a couple of other officers beckon us to drive past. As I do I see one of the burgundy Jag occupants, handsome as an ageing film star, laughing as the police handcuff him.

I can't help but wonder if these criminals were so sick with the humdrum of normal life that they couldn't stop themselves from doing one more job.

2008 - Bullying the Bullies

What do you do if your children are being threatened by someone who's shown they're willing to attack a defenceless person? My kids' mum says they should just walk away, but when one of my kids returned from the latest incident, he was pale with fear because he recognised the risk this kid posed. This stirs in me the same characteristics the boy demonstrates, but I know, that path will lead to too much destruction. If I tell you I'm more scared of what I'll do than what others may do to me, it's not me trying to be a hard man, it's me recognising that many of us have such feelings, and if we give into them then the consequences are very likely to be disproportionate.

1975 – Aged 10 - Mayfair in Paddington

My mother and I are in Paddington Station. We're waiting for a train to take me to Devon. I'll be travelling alone for the first time. We mull about for a while then, out of the blue, Mum says, "Follow me", so I do. We end up standing in front of a newspaper vendor's hut.

"Simon," she says, "I'm going to buy you a girlie magazine, you know what they are don't you?"

I nod, "You mean a porno mag."

"Yes, but I don't like that name, it makes it sound dirty and bad, and sex isn't."

"One of our teachers says porno mags degrade women."

Mum looks at me and frowns.

"Anyway," she says, "when you come back from your holiday, I'll let you look at it. The reason I'm doing this is because I don't want you to think sex or relationships are things you can't talk to me about".

I'm a bit shocked by all of this and as she points at one of the magazines to the vendor, I can't help but feel a big surge of embarrassment. The vendor put the magazine in a brown paper bag and passed it to my mother.

A bit later we walked past the station's WH Smith's shop where they were selling Monopoly board games cheap, so, Mum bought one and put it and the magazine in a carrier bag. A bit later, as she waved me goodbye from the platform, my eyes became drawn to the bag and all it had to offer. Looking back, I can't help but think the carrier should have had the words, "Simon's Future" written on it.

For many, what Mum did that day was inappropriate, however, her desire for us to feel like we could speak about sex and love did come about from my late teens onward. Again, some may say such openness isn't appropriate between a mother and son, but this will have to be a discussion for another day.

1975 – Jollymead - Part 1

200 miles and five hours later, I arrived at Newton Abbot. I'd spent the whole journey in the guard's van sitting on sacks of mail, back then that was where most disabled people were 'seated'.

Once we stopped, the guard went off for a few minutes, then returned with a man called Robbie. Robbie looked like a woodcutter from a fairy story, well he didn't have a green velvet Robin Hood cloak or an axe, but he was bearded and wore a check shirt. As he helped me get off the train, he smiled and said, "Hello Simon, welcome to Devon."

Robbie ran an outward-bound centre for disabled children on Dartmoor, called Jollymead, which my mum had sent me to for a week. When we got to the place it felt as if we were in the middle of nowhere. Jollymead was a white-walled bungalow with two large bay windows at the front while various rooms were going off from the corridors inside, including Robbie and his family's living quarters. The ones we had access to were the playroom in the left bay-windowed room, the boys' dormitory in the right-hand one, the girls' dormitory right next to the boys' one, a bathroom and a kitchen dining area. Around the house was a garden that rose above it to the left.

Once I'd been introduced to Robbie's wife Judy, and their two daughters, I was shown to my room. There were 5 beds in it but only a couple of other children were holidaying with me. A boy whose name I can't remember, and a girl called Susan.

I unpacked and was soon called to the kitchen where we were informed of all the rules and their expectations of us. To my horror, we were told we had to wash up after every meal. "Hold on a minute," I thought "We're on holiday and we're paying you to make us wash up. I don't think so." Unfortunately, I suddenly realised I wasn't just thinking these words, but speaking them. Judy wasn't impressed.

In a not very well-veiled tone of anger, she said, "You may have everyone waiting on you hand and foot at home, but here you'll be treated the same as everyone

190

else, you'll wash up or you'll be on the first train back to London." She paused to see if that's what I wanted, then added, "Everyone works as a team here, is that understood?"

I obviously didn't look too convinced, so Robbie interjected, "This isn't a holiday camp, you're here to learn. You're here to start growing up and becoming independent."

Even to me, aged ten, I got the idea this was so well delivered, that they may have already had this conversation with others on countless occasions. It may even have been a weekly ritual designed to break any revolutionary attacks before they could even begin.

"Well, no one told me that," I said.

"So do you want to go home?" Said Judy.

I shook my head.

Not satisfied with the clarity of the power structure she added, "Is that a no, I can't hear you?"

I said no very clearly.

The revolution was over!

The next day we were told to put on our swimming costumes and meet at the main gate. From there we walked along the road for 2 minutes, over a bridge and down to the riverside. We waded into the clear cold water, slowly letting it numb us bit by bit. Sue had an artificial foot which she took off, then, able to walk on her stump, joined us.

"The fish are nibbling at me." She shrieked.

"Fish! What fish!" I muttered. I'd recently seen the film Jaws and was still scared to get in the bath without clearing the bubbles first, let alone swim with fish. Yet here I was surrounded by hundreds of them.

After a few minutes, we realised the fish didn't think we were very tasty, so we splashed each other and swam across and up and down the river until Robbie told us it was time for our next activity, canoeing.

He'd probably been assessing us all this time to see how confident we were in the water. Given we were, our next exercise was practising capsize drills in canoes.

That's pretty much how most of the week went on, find our limits, then push us a little beyond them, and then the next day go a bit further.

I'd eventually return to Jollymead many times, and a few years down the line Robbie had us surviving nights by ourselves on Dartmoor in the snow in mid-March.

2008 - Christmas

I'm writing this and my legs feel like blocks of ice. It's Christmas 2008 and the credit crunch is biting along with the weather.

1975 – Jollymead - Part 2

After the capsize drills, we walked back to the house and dried off on the lawn. Sue put her towel down on the lawn and told me to lie beside her. She put her arm around me and kissed me.

When it comes to falling in love Billy Bragg puts it most aptly in his song *Life With The Lions* when he sang about hating the arsehole he became every time he saw someone he fancied. Even at ten years old, changing how I behaved when someone told me they liked me seemed the worst thing to do, but I still couldn't stop myself. Even with experience and years of self-discipline, I'm often unable to resist doing everything possible to make myself less attractive, and so it was with my first venture into adolescent love!

"Oi you two, stop your canoodling!" Robbie shouted up. "There's potatoes to peel."

With my paw in Sue's hand, we floated into the kitchen where, for the first time in my life, a chore became a joyous activity.

Of the many embarrassing traits that falling in love brings out, being overly chivalrous and humble are perhaps the most cringe-worthy. Suddenly I was no longer a street urchin but metamorphosed into an upper-class lord. Had I been able to acquire a monocle and top hat I sadly would have adorned them.

"After you, my darling," and, "Please, there's a lady in the room." All needed not to be said, but I couldn't stop myself. Instead of the naughty sexually deviant rascal, who Sue'd found attractive, she got a slightly prudish and coy pseudo-gent who was willing to wait 'til "we're married" before enjoying the kiss she offered as she pulled a sheet over our heads.

192

1975 - Jollymead - Part 3

Amongst the other activities Robbie introduced us to, were shooting, archery, survival techniques such as building shelters, cooking and identifying edible foliage, climbing rocks, horse riding, caving, learning the country code and thinking about wildlife. We also visited local tourist sites such as Princetown and Newton Abbot as well as sitting around campfires listening to Robbie telling ghost stories. For a child without a father, this was a dream come true.

In the garden, Sue paraded up and down in front of me, pouting and posing whilst I took photos. Without them, I'd have forgotten what she looked like, but with them, I'll remember her clearly forever.

The other boy staying with us, whose name and face I can't remember, had a father who worked for the Metropolitan Police. It was with him and his parents that I'd be journeying back to London. I should have been grateful but instead, I sat in silence, the tip of my tongue pushing out my bottom lip, trying with all my might not to cry. For the whole journey, the dad told his son how the policeman who'd popped in to say hello to us during our stay didn't know what real life was. How compared to the Metropolitan Police the Devon Police's job was like working in Toy-Town. Even back then I couldn't help but think he was a jerk.

2005

I recently ordered three microphones from someone on eBay. One of the microphones arrived but the other two never turned up. I emailed the seller, but he didn't get back to me. I then sent him an email from a different account to see if he'd respond and he did, so that confirmed he was ignoring me.

I thought about how to deal with this situation, yes, there was the small claims court and eBay feedback, but I doubted I'd get anywhere doing that, so, this is what I did. I bought an Internet domain name which included the words 'metropolitan police' in it. I then emailed the seller a message using the domain name email address and wrote, "I'm emailing you from work. As you can see, I'm not someone to be mucked about with, please can I have my microphones?" Technically this may have been illegal, but I got the feeling I hadn't been specific enough to get myself into too much trouble.

Within a few minutes, I received a very apologetic reply, including an offer to send me both microphones plus an extra one for free. I declined the free one but did receive the other two the next day by special delivery. As far as I was concerned, I hadn't broken the law, (although some may disagree), your honour, but by the end of it I got what I wanted, albeit at a slightly extra cost. Still, it was worth it for the speedy resolution and the pleasure of a bit of revenge.

1975 – Jollymead – The Journey Home - Part 4

When I got home, I remained very quiet but when Mum asked me if I was alright, I couldn't hold it in any longer and burst out crying. She hugged me, but when she said, "You must have had a good time." I felt resentful because she didn't understand why I was upset, which was because I was in love and missing Sue. Why couldn't she see that? At no point was there any recognition of the part I played in her lack of understanding. I'd set her up and betrayed her by communicating nothing while expecting to be understood. Perhaps this was a misguided attempt to break the bond with her now I'd found a new love, but instead of being comforted by her caring hug, I felt angry because I still needed it.

So often in life, we turn the tables on those we yearn for because we resent them for the power they have over us. It's akin to saying, I desire you, but as you won't give yourself to me fully, I'll hate you for rejecting me.

I am pretty certain this was the last time my mother comforted me as I cried. In the 1989 film *Hideous Kinky* a guru talks of teardrops being a gift from God to remind us we are human, and so, for those few minutes of crying, I reconnected with the part of me that yearns, needs to be loved and fears loss. A part I'd wanted to forget for a long time. But there was anger in the mix too, and from then on there was a distance between us caused by me.

There was, of course, the porn magazine to distract me, and although I still didn't know what masturbation was, I took some comfort in the glossy pages of the Mayfair Magazine mum had bought. There were women in it I liked the look of, and a few I didn't.

I'm not sure if it had been Mum's plan all along, but I never felt the need to buy a porn magazine as I got older. Obviously on the Internet one comes across porn, but it's never been of much interest to me. Was that because of Mum's porn policy or would it have happened anyway?

2008 - State of Misunderstanding

My mother and I haven't spoken for a while. I doubt we both know why the other isn't speaking. It's a kind of agreed-upon state of misunderstanding.

1975 – Susan M

I sat down and wrote Sue a letter which ended with "I love you". I also wrote, "I love Sue" on my schoolbooks and bought a bracelet with two hearts that had, "Sue and Simon" engraved on it. She wrote back polite newsy letters that didn't end with, "I love you." But as some people say, love isn't blind, it's just a bit short-sighted.

1975 - School

The 11-plus examination was approaching fast, and Mr Garriock made good his promise to tutor me. In turn, I did my best not to let him down. I passed the exam and was put forward to go to the local grammar school, Wilson's. The headmaster interviewed me but declined my application because in his opinion I wouldn't be able to cope with such things as science lessons because of my disability. Instead, I was offered a place at another school, Wallington Boy's Grammar.

1976 - Councillor Bassett

Roundshaw Community Centre was situated inside the top section of a rectangular concrete building, next to the shopping precinct. From the centre's entrance, a large concrete slab formed a slope down to the shops. This whole area was meant to act as the hub of the estate's communal life, but it was grey and charmless.

My mother and I sat in the community centre's vestibule waiting to meet the local GLC councillor, Phil Bassett, a tall, heavy-set man with greasy black back-combed hair.

He walked out of his office and called, "Mrs Smith?"

"Miss Smith" my mum corrected him.

"Pleased to meet you," he put his hand out and they shook hands.

"Please come this way."

We entered his office and took our seats. He reclined slightly while we sat upright.

"So how can I help you?" he asked.

"Well, I'm sorry to bother you but I didn't know who to turn to. It's just my son here, Simon, he's been refused entry to Wilson's school on account of him being handicapped." (Political Correctness hadn't landed yet).

She passed Councillor Bassett the school's rejection letter which he read and passed back.

"Well," he laughed, "I wonder why they think if Simon can't cope at their school, he'd be able to at Wallington Boys? They're just passing the buck."

Mum, relieved to hear he was on our side, smiled and said, "That's what I thought too, it's ridiculous isn't it?"

"As it goes, I'm one of the Governors at Wilson's, so I'll bring this matter up at the next meeting. If you could give me your address, I shall get back to you as soon as I can with a response."

1975 - Puberty

At ten years old I started going through puberty. During one swimming session one of my teachers came up to me in the changing room and said loudly, "My! You're a bit of a hairy monkey Mr Smith!" and promptly grabbed my talcum powder and covered me in it. The other kids in the changing room roared with laughter. Don't worry, I didn't feel abused, I kind of knew it was something to be proud of.

Along with being hairier, I started to become sexually aware. Instead of just playing hide and seek with the daughters of my mother's friends, we'd end up in cupboards or under beds touching each other. It was exploratory but not romantic, and kissing was not part of the repertoire.

Perhaps for most of us, this sex and love split is a common experience but for me, I tend to see it as a split that's almost a consequence of my mother and father's genetics. Mum was a romantic, my father a sexual predator looking for seduction and casual sex, and I became both.

2008 - Familiarity Doesn't Breed

I'm standing in a bar in Eastbourne with Steve, the one I write songs with some-times. He's introduced me to a friend of his who's just split up from her boyfriend.

"So, why did you split up? Did you leave him?"

"Yeah," she says, "we were becoming just friends."

I'm interested in this scenario, so I ask, "Don't you find that with most of your boyfriends then, that the more you get to know them the less sexually attracted you become?"

"Bloody Hell, how do you know that?"

"I think most people start off feeling very attracted to someone because they can imagine them being everything they want and at that point, it's not complicated."

She interjects, "A few months down the line and you get to see their insecurities".

We look at each other like we both know the end of a joke and I say, "Then if you start pulling away, they become needy or they bring out needy feelings in you which make you feel uncomfortable."

There's a moment of silence and then she says, "We're doomed then."

I laugh and try to reassure us both by saying, "Maybe not, maybe some people find their sexual feelings come from feeling close emotionally to someone."

"Now I'm really confused," she says, "surely that's what you feel at first?"

"You do, but it's not for who they really are."

2008 - Breaking Point

I'm at a party, a woman is talking to me, and tears are streaming down her face. No one can see but me. A moment beforehand we were chatting casually, when she mentioned her husband had been affected by the credit crunch and I asked if she was getting extra stress from him as a consequence.

"I don't know what to do, he won't talk to me. I'm sure he's having an affair but he denies it. He keeps telling me how he doesn't deserve me and I'd be better off without him. But I love him and I have for the last 18 years. We had a great phys-ical relationship now he won't touch me. I feel helpless."

I nod and say, "You need to know the truth".

"Yes I do."

"Did you get married in a church?"

"Yes"

"Then surely making a vow to God must mean something to him?"

And here is a point that many people will diverge on. Do you force yourself to abide by a commitment created by a religious regime or do you accept that, in reality, humans are fickle and cannot be forced into feeling for someone? The sensible answer is to at least try to work it out, to make an effort, but at some point, there may well be a breaking point.

"Have you mentioned counselling to him?" I ask.

She breathes in sharply, "Yes, but he won't".

I add, "It's like he's determined to destroy the relationship, most of us have a self-destruct part of ourselves, maybe that's what going on."

I pass her a napkin from the buffet table, someone says goodbye to me.

"Excuse me for one moment."

"No please don't let me stop you, I'm sorry," she says.

"I'll be back in a minute."

But when I come back, she's speaking to a couple of women and laughing.

I say goodbye to her and we never see each other again.

2005 - Boris

"You should remember the five F's." Boris says, "Find 'em, Follow them, Finger them, Fuck and forget them".

I look at him and shake my head in disapproval.

He tuts at me, "Well it's you who suffers, I never lost any sleep over a woman."

I'm curious and ask, "Do you ever feel lonely?"

"Listen I've been on my own since I was 12, I like my own company."

"Have you ever loved a woman?" I ask.

He tightens his lips in a 'that's not an easy-to-answer question" expression.

"Well, there was Rebecca, she was Eurasian. I did have feelings for her."

"So, what happened?"

"The only way she could stay here was to marry a Scotsman. So I told her to be with him because I knew I wouldn't be good for her. But I did have feelings for her. But do you remember what that sex worker in Soho once said to me?"

I quickly interject, "Yeah, I know, business is business and love is bullshit. I don't think that's true though. I think love and loss have been central to your casual approach to women."

He raises his eyebrows and shrugs a little, "Maybe, but there's nothing I can do now."

"Well, I guess you've had an interesting life," I say smiling.

He looks at me askant, "It's not over yet. I've still got to win you a million or three".

I shake my head, "I won't hold my breath".

There's a pause.

"You know Boris, I want you to know I'm grateful we met. There was life before meeting you and life after. I've learned a lot about who I am, and enjoyed being with you far more than I ever thought I would."

Boris nods.

I continue, "Do you fancy a cup of tea?"

"Go on then," he says looking a bit excited at the prospect of me finally making him a cuppa for him.

"Well," I laugh, "whilst you're making yourself one, I'll have one too".

Desolate, he moves his head from side to side, then gets up and heads towards the kitchenette.

1976 Winter

There's a knock on the door. I can see it's Mr Phil. He comes in and Mum makes him tea. He tells us he's made in-roads and thinks he'll get the decision reversed and we'll know in a few days.

He stays for hours and after he leaves Mum says, "I didn't think he'd ever go, anyway he's offered to take you to a sports event at Crystal Palace, do you want to go?"

"Yes. Are you coming too?"

"No."

"I think he fancies me. I don't want to encourage him even if he can get you into a good school."

"So, there are limits when it comes to motherly love after all." I think to myself.

1976 - There's a Price to Pay

Only two boys from Roundshaw Juniors got into Wilson's and I was one of them. But there's no such thing as a free lunch and Mr Bassett came with a price tag that I'd be paying for.

During my first year at Wilson's, he thought it would be good for me to have him teach me Maths. One day we sat in my room, and he said he'd been getting reports of me shouting out to everyone that I was a bastard.

"No, I haven't," I said.

"I know you have!" He insisted.

"But I haven't!" I protested.

He wouldn't relent, "There's no point denying it, I have proof, I have a witness."

"Who?" I asked.

"Never you mind."

I became doubtful as to whether I might have said something like that. "I don't know, maybe I did say it but I can't remember."

He sensed blood, "You did say it. There's no point denying it. Don't let me hear that you've been saying such things again. Have I made myself clear?"

We then went on to work on converting fractions into decimals, which is done by dividing the bottom number into the top one.

I kept on making mistakes – apparently – and finally I was warned if I made one more I'd be punished. I started to shake. My mother was in the front room, just a few yards away.

"I want to go," I said.

"No, you'll stay here and do this properly, I'm not having you bother your mother. Now get on with it."

So he set me a conversion to do and very carefully I got on with it. I was sure I'd got it right and beamed with relief.

"It's wrong," he said.

I couldn't believe it, "What?"

"It's wrong," he repeated, "You divided the top into the bottom. Now stand up."

He pulled my trousers and pants down and smacked me across my bare bottom 'till I cried.

"Now if I find out you've told your mother there'll be worse to follow. Do you understand?"

So, I didn't tell her until I was an adult.

When I was in my late teens, I saw Mr Bassett in Sutton Library holding the hand of a very pale and timid-looking little boy. Mr Bassett nodded hello to me and asked how my mother was.

1976 - Jollymead - Part 5

Because Mum thought I loved the holiday in Devon so much she got me booked for another week there during the Easter break. But this time the weather was bleak, and not wanting to miss an opportunity to test our resolve, one of our tasks was to sleep in bin liners on the Moors in the snow. This time Robbie wanted to push us, however, a few hours down the line even though he thought it might be going too far, so he picked us up and took us back to Jollymead. Because it was so cold and there were only three of us, Robbie and Judy let us sit with them in their living room, watch TV and cuddle up to their German Shepherd dog in front of the open fire. They also helped me find Sue's number – which in hindsight was technically aiding and abetting stalking – and arranged for her to come over for a few hours the following day. Of course, once she arrived, I turned into a blithering idiot again and probably didn't make the best of impressions, however, it couldn't have been so bad as she agreed to join me at Jollymead again the following summer.

1976 - All Set

My life was set. I'd got into a good school and it looked, well at least from my delusional vantage point, like I'd got the girl.

Christmas 2008

My son who's now 14 asks me, "Daddy, do you remember when you used to tell us you got coal for Christmas?" – that is the translated version, the original was in teenage mumble.

"No," I replied in proper adult English.

"You did!"

I'm sure I'm right, so I add, "I don't remember ever saying that. You must be getting me confused with your grandfather."

My other son interjects "No Dad, you did. Ask our Mum."

So I do and she tells me I used to tell them that if they were naughty, they'd get coal from Father Christmas.

So much for having a good memory!

———

If this chapter has partly been about forgetfulness, it's also about what is unforgettable. Our lives are both full of small and big details, incidents and other people who touch us enough that we can never forget them.

———

Chapter 17
Boris 2010

2010 - Wednesday 28th April - Early Hours

"Welcome to the Orange answering service. Please press 1 to listen to your message." I press 1.

"First new message, received at 5.40 am."

"Hello, Mr Smith." It's an exasperated voice. "I hope you have this phone with you. I do not know what went wrong. This has never happened in all the 35 years I have done this. It is awful. Your father wasn't on the plane. I don't understand. We had him there on time, it seems they just didn't put him on. We will get him on the next available flight."

Sunday – 25th April

6.18 am.

"Hello, Mr Smith" a foreign female voice comes over the phone.

"Yes." I am asleep and drowsy. I know it's a nurse as I can see the hospital number on my phone.

"Your father's condition has worsened. If you want to see him, we suggest you come soon."

Midday

Doris and Ivan are old friends of my father. They are sitting next to him; he's lying unconscious in the hospital bed. We talk for a while; they talk to my father as if he's awake. He's slumped, eyes half closed and taking little breaths occasionally.

"Do you remember Boris, do you remember when we first met?" Doris says. She then carries on as if he was nodding at her.

I walk out and go to the nurses' desk where one of them tells me his blood pressure has dropped below 90 and that's why he's in a continual state of unconsciousness now. They could bring him around, but he'd asked to not be resuscitated. I ask how long he's got. "Maybe tonight, maybe tomorrow morning."

I ask about whether they follow The Liverpool Pathway protocol. Practically that means removing monitoring machines, taking out drips and other needles that aren't involved in pain management, and making the person as comfortable as possible. The nurse tells me that they have done most of that but they are still observing him.

An hour or so later Ivan and Doris have to go, so I am alone in the yellow-walled room waiting. I get my laptop out, sit down and say, "I'm here Boris, you're not alone."

I connect to the Internet and look up at Boris, his breathing seems to have longer gaps between each breath. I can feel the moment is upon us. I stand up, put the computer down and watch him. The breaths are very small. I look at his face and notice his nose is becoming paler.

"Boris," I say, "I don't know if you can hear me but I think you're going now. I love you. We all love you, we will miss you and never forget you."

As I say this his eyes are still closed, he gasps for breath, slumps a bit and breaths no more. He is completely motionless.

A nurse walks past the room.

"Excuse me," I call, "I think my father has stopped breathing".

She nods at me and says she'll get something to check his pulse and slowly walks away. A few minutes later she connects some equipment to him and confirms his pulse had stopped.

"I'll get the doctor to come and confirm he has passed away." She says as she walks out, closes the door and leaves me in the room alone.

I kiss Boris on the forehead and stand for a while. His body is still very warm. I can't recall ever touching his skin, it feels rougher than I imagined it would.

I call Doris, and then some relatives in Israel. As I get to the end of each call my eyes well up and I can no longer speak.

As the afternoon stretches out a duty officer comes in, checks Boris for vital signs, and pronounces him dead, "Time of death, 3:50 pm" (Actually it was more like 3:40). I ask him if he'd ever found anyone wasn't dead and he says no. Then two nurses carefully wash Boris's body, redress him and lay him flat. Finally, some porters come to take him to the morgue. The nurses put him in a white body bag, place a slip of paper into a window on the bag and as I accompany him in the lift to the basement, I say goodbye.

Wednesday 28th April – Early Hours

My father died on Sunday; I was on a plane with his body on Tuesday night bound for Israel so he could be buried on Wednesday afternoon.

The previous day had been a series of duties. Go to the hospital to get the medical certification of death, then to the registry office to register the death, and then to the benefits and pension office to let them know. Contact the funeral directors; drop off the body release form for the funeral directors; talk to the coroner's office about giving an out-of-country certificate; notify the people who run the home he lives in and give them his notice to quit. Go to the bank to get control of his money to pay expenses – for now, paid on a credit card (So far: £4000 for the flight, £4000 for the burial plot, headstone, and "eternal" maintenance and £500 for his body to be transported from the airport to the grave). There is a bit of time to grieve but not much.

Wednesday 28th April – 7.20 am local time in Israel.

I have flown into Israel, and been picked up by my cousin. I tell her that as usual I have been fully checked over by El-Al security. "Tell them you have family here!" Her husband says,

I laugh, "Trust me I did"

Then a bit more seriously he says, "They don't even leave 1% room for error."

On the flight, I saw a family crying while talking to the pilot. They had a dead young man they were bringing back, and they were being informed that his body wasn't in the hold. I had been asked by the security guards not to mention my father's body was in the cargo hold as "some people are superstitious".

And so, the flight, looking out the window at hundreds of towns, looking like islands in a sea of black, the crap food, I kept what looked like a mousse till the end but it turned out to be hummus, and the achy feeling of my little legs not touching the floor. I asked for a foot stall but never heard back from the attendant. But the landing was smooth, and the audience applauded and then there was the long walk to the baggage collection and passport control. The guilty walk past customs even though there's nothing to declare and then freedom, family, a lift and sleep.

But before I could sleep came the call, Boris's body wasn't on the plane. People had come from hundreds of miles away, but the funeral was going to be delayed 24 hours. For someone who valued promptness, it was ironic that he'd be late to his own funeral.

Thursday 29th April 2010 - 11:45 a.m.

"Is it time?" I ask.

"Yes, I think so," says one of my relations.

We almost drive out of the Kibbutz, which has the appearance of a holiday village, but before we get to the armed guard exit, we take a sharp left, drive along a dusty track and up a hill to a copse of trees at its summit. We get out of the Landrover and walk into the graveyard. It's quite small, maybe 100 metres long and 30 wide. There are five rows of graves dotted with trees and mottled shadows. A group of people mull around a mound of earth. I approach them, they smile and we chat. We'll have to wait, Micha, my father's brother-in-law is late, some people want to start without him but I ask how long he'll be. I'm told 40 minutes, so, I ask, if it's ok with everyone else, we'll wait.

In time, a blue car comes speeding into the graveyard, and some of the people laugh. When it pulls up Micha is helped out of it. He's a tall old man who can barely walk. He says as he kisses me five times, "Thank you, Simon, even if I would have had to crawl on all fours I would have come."

Micha is given a seat and a plastic cup of water, and he cries. Someone puts their arm around him.

A blue van appears, and a group of men take out the coffin and carry it to the grave.

My cousin Ohad starts the proceedings. "Okay, Okay... shall we begin?"

We stand up.

Micha speaks first. He talks quietly and pauses between sentences as someone interprets his words for me.

"When we were young children in Latvia, Boris once looked at me and said 'You have slanty eyes'. So, I picked up a stone, held Boris down and banged it on his forehead for five minutes. Boris my friend, please I ask of you, please forgive me.

One day, after I married his sister, Boris came to see me off at the station. I was going to Moscow, and it was very cold. Boris offered me his coat, but I refused. As the train pulled away, he shouted to me, I looked, and he threw the coat through the window laughing. Boris wasn't just a friend, he wasn't just my brother-in-law, he was a brother to me. I couldn't have asked for better." Micha could not speak anymore.

My cousin Ohad took the reins, "There are many stories I could tell about Boris... I am going to say it in Hebrew, then say it in English for you Simon, even though you're the only person here who doesn't speak Hebrew." Everyone laughed. I didn't get my father's multi-lingual gene, nor his full head of hair one either. I did get the showing-off and flirting ones though. So as Ohad told one of many funny, almost legendary, tales about my father, I tried to think of what I would say.

Then my other cousin's husband spoke:

"I used to visit Boris when I lived in London. He had a most interesting life. But I know that the most important thing that happened in his life was meeting Simon. Without it, the last part of his life would have been very different. It gave him meaning. And we all want to thank you Simon for all the help you gave him."

Ohad then beckoned me to speak:

"I haven't prepared this sorry. My father once said to me that sometimes he'd look at me and wonder if he was as stupid as me when he was the same age, and he thought the answer was probably yes. I hope I don't fulfil that now.

Every goodbye is an echo of every goodbye and I know that when we meet like this it brings up thoughts about others who are no longer with us, but I also know that many of our tears today are happy ones as we remember the good things about Boris. [I start to struggle to speak, I don't want to cry but I can't stop myself]. What I can tell you is there was my life before meeting Boris, and my life after, and the life after is better for knowing him. I'm sorry I'll have to stop now." I started to cry uncontrollably. Someone put their arm around me.

Then the men of the family lowered the coffin, and together, almost frantically, using only their hands filled the grave within around 3 minutes. I wanted to join in, but it didn't feel right to do so, so I stood and watched.

Once the men got their breath back one of the religious ones said a prayer for Boris, then Bluma, Boris's sister-in-law (Boris was being buried next to her husband) laid a flower on the grave followed by me. As I put the red rose on the mound, I said, "Doris and Ivan say goodbye and send their love." as they had requested, I do on the phone that morning.

A bit later I placed a stone upon the grave too.

We dispersed soon after, washing our hands as we left the cemetery – another Jewish custom aimed at keeping life and death separate from each other.

Religious Jews have many rules about death and mourning. What I've been told is that normally someone does something called Shiva, which is essentially a central figure for family and friends to visit during the seven days after the death. During this time people bring stories to the person sitting Shiva for them to gain some insight into the person who died. I will be travelling to meet my relatives – a kind of home delivery service Shiva – over the ensuing week.

There are many rules that religious Jews follow, but as I am neither Jewish nor religious, I won't be following them. However, I did recognise that in many ways they help those left behind to deal with the grieving process. For instance, every good thing the grieving party does is supposed to be followed by them saying or at least thinking that they did it to help the person's soul be raised higher in a spiritual sense. Likewise, they should keep a candle burning for them for a set time.

I did say to the person who told me all of this that it rather left the destiny of the dead in the hands of a third party. She said the actions of a person's life are dealt with differently.

Monday 3rd May 2010.

Boris wasn't there when I was a child and I'm sure I carry some resentment because of that. He felt more like a friend than a father, but of course, he was my father and in time I will find my own way of grieving the loss of my absent father and latter-day friend. We had a connection, which of course continues past death, but there's still a loss, but for now, that loss hasn't shown itself fully.

I thought today that a good epitaph for Boris would be.

"He travelled far and touched many."

I'm sure he would laugh with me at that one.

Finally, as with most traumatic things in life, one is almost shifted into a far more irrational world. And so it is with death. The person who's died becomes very present in one's mind and one finds one converses with them as if they are there. There's an almost automatic acceptance of some real connection with the person beyond their death.

As I flew home – I was in a plane, I mean I haven't got that irrational yet - I lifted the blind to my window as we headed over northern France. I noticed a lot of clouds below as well as a plane we were slowly overtaking and another that crossed our path at a very fast rate below us.

I thought to myself, "So, if you're there Boris show me yourself in the clouds." I knew that even if I saw anything remotely resembling him it'd just be my mind joining up the dots, but I looked out the window anyway and immediately saw a cloud that looked just like him as he died. I watched it until my head pushed up against the glass, I couldn't see him anymore, I laughed to myself, and imagined somewhere Boris laughed with me too.

Boris February 2010.

Chapter 18
Shapes and Arcs

Dream - 9th July 2009

At the side of a slip road, somewhere near Barking, East London. A woman is lying next to a car that's on fire, she's dying. I am sitting next to her crying. I don't want her to die.

I am now driving away from the scene. I have another woman sitting next to me and say, "I feel the most beautiful pain."

My Head

Here is my head, you are panning around me, or I am spinning. It's hard to tell. I am here looking at me with you. My skin is not wrinkled yet, I am 44. My hair is receding, but lately, I have let it grow a bit longer. Normally I keep it in a crew cut style as most balding men do. Some of my hair is beginning to go white, and those hairs seem thicker and stick out. My skin is pock-marked by teenage acne. Even the word acne sounds a bit like angst. My head is like a spearhead, it's what people notice first, it's what touches them before my arms do, and it's what has guided me, both through its interior and exterior impact on the world. My head is my symbol of humanity. My head is how my spirit touches others, through thoughts, looks, expressions, words and kisses. My head is the interface of my highest and darkest feelings.

Coil

If I held a coil in front of you (like a corkscrew for example) and you were to look at it from one end you'd see a circle, from another angle you'd see a spiral and from its side, you'd see a series of peaks and troughs.

2009 - Bruce

Bruce Springsteen is on the radio saying that by the age of 11 most people have already been damaged.

26th January 2008 - Maxim's Nightclub

I'm in a nightclub in Eastbourne. It's 2 a.m. and the lights come up. I'm talking to a tall woman with long red curly hair. I glance to my right and see a woman standing nearby. Our eyes catch each other, and we look away. My friend moves and blocks my view, I move so I can see the woman again. She glances at me again. Our eyes hold on to each other. I say "Excuse me" to my friend, then walk towards the woman.

I say, "I think I better give you my card."

To which she says, "And I shall give you mine".

She's quite drunk but I try to talk with her; she has a friend with her who translates some of the slurs. "Tomorrow, when you're sober and you don't want me to contact you," I say, "that's ok". She looks at me and mouths "No, you're beautiful, you're the one". As we part she attempts to snog me, but I don't want to take advantage as she's drunk, but still, I gently kiss her goodbye.

Happiness

On a scale of 1 to 10, how happy are you at this particular moment?

10 would be the happiest you'd ever felt.

On a scale of 1 to 10, how unhappy are you at this particular moment?

Remember 10 would be a situation where you were being tortured or mortally wounded.

212

As I write this I feel as if I'm on about 2 on the happiness scale and about 1 on the unhappiness one.

I thought originally that they'd add up mathematically to a total of ten; that if I was at my most unhappy, I could not have any happiness at the same time, but, for me, I found myself feeling both feelings simultaneously.

When I'm at my happiest, it's not when I'm most happy. It's when I feel calm, connected to others, and at peace. Maybe a coolish number 6. When I'm most unhappy, it's not when I'm feeling the greatest physical pain, but when I feel a sense of separation, loneliness, and meaninglessness.

Arcs

Another shape I want to add to this visual introduction is an arc. Not the Noah kind, but something like the path a firework follows as it shoots up, then returns to earth. A parabola for all you technical types.

We often mark out our lives as a series of eras, although in my mind they're a collection of overlapping ones. Places we live, work or receive education, people we love, and political and physical states of being, all these things overlap each other throughout the course of our lives.

My mind tends to see the world in terms of visual metaphors.

Watershed

This chapter is partly about watersheds. A simple version of a watershed would be a bit of earth that divides two pools of water, but watersheds can exist on a continental scale, where water falls either towards one ocean or another. It's not a shed like a garden shed, it comes from, the term for splitting or dividing, "shedding". Symbolically it's something between other things, the place where something ends and another begins.

Summer 1976

I am eleven.

Eleven to thirteen is a watershed age. As Bruce Springsteen mentioned earlier, by eleven most people have experienced the damage that'll haunt them for the rest of their lives, and whilst most people see thirteen as the changing point, eleven is probably more poignant because it isn't marked with any ceremony, it's not even a special number. It's not a teen, it's an uncelebrated, insignificant, yet significant turning point.

1976 was infamous for its drought-like summer and long traffic jams in England.

January 2009 - Parliament Memories

I'm driving towards Parliament. A memory of sitting on Phil Bassett's shoulders aged five comes to me along with an image of a group photo of the occasion. I wonder if six years later, when meeting Mr Bassett at the community centre, either he or my mother remembered the event.

Slower Cycles

When I was a child, I would spin around and around till I felt dizzy. As I get older it feels like the cycles I follow in life become slower and bigger. As if the excitement and lows I experienced as a youth, expanded and became less intense. That is of course excluding relationships, which tend to be just as manic at any age.

Tao - Cycles

Tao (Pronounced Dow) underpins a lot of Japanese philosophy. Taoism suggests our lives and the universe follow cycles that bring us back to the same point eventually. Just as when you look down the coil of a corkscrew, you see circles, when you travel along the coil you may come to a similar position to where you started only, you're not exactly where you started, you've moved slightly along the spiral too. When you return to the same spot, you are not where you were before

214

because the passing of time creates a different perspective. Even if you start again, all you remember from your previous journey makes the same journey different.

27th January 2008 - Meeting Tracey - Part 1

"Have a look at this text I sent to a woman I met last night," I say to a friend.

"What is it?"

She reads it and laughs, "Blimey if I received that I wouldn't know what to do."

The text read, "If you want to feel the connection again contact me".

1976 - Significance

Mr Bassett has taken me to an athletics meeting where he's giving out medals. I lean towards him and say, "One day I'll be like them". I could taste my need for feeling significant. But it wasn't until I tried athletics that I came to see I was never going to be an athlete. I spoke with the mind of a child and had no idea of my limitations or power.

An Unexpected Friend

Growing up is partly about coming to terms with who we are, (or is it that we just learn not to let others know who we are?). One of the ironic things about this is, as we approach a watershed, we become full of fear, believing we'll never cope with the arduous journey across the land between seas of plain sailing. Yet somehow, we find in ourselves resources we never knew we had, and we discover who we really are through adversity, both our limitations and strengths. Adversity is often an unexpected friend.

The Journey

We had to walk from one boat to another across an arid landscape.
She looked at me.
"We've been limping for ages now."
I stopped my sea gait and replied, "We've been surviving. I'd rather limp than
*   give up".*
She sighs, "I don't think I can go on, it's not worth it".
She lays down with her back to me.
I cuddle up to her.
The sun sets.
The sky goes dark.
She's angry for a while.
Then she turns around and cuddles me.
There's a feeling of peace between us.
We fall asleep.
When we wake, she says, "I don't want to go on".
I say I do, that it doesn't feel right not to
She goes quiet.
A bit later, she says she's happy we're together.
We walk on, get to the next ship and set sail.
Soon we'll come to another crossing.
We're not going around in circles.
We're following a spiral.
But I don't know if this coil of ours,
Is mortal or if our love is eternal.

An Ending is the Beginning of Another Story

I'm reading a book at the moment about a man with a dog's head, I'm only a third of the way through it and already I'm sad that it'll end. There are the characters I met in books decades ago who I still remember like old friends.

Losing Me

The more I love someone, the more fear I have of losing them. The more I fear losing them the more I lose myself and the more they lose me.

2008 - Meeting Tracey - Part 2

The day after I sent the "connection" text I got a reply asking if I wanted to meet in a pub. So, we arranged to meet up the next day.

1976 - Roundshaw Juniors - The Last Day

I do not remember the last day of junior school and whether I was sad about it ending, but it didn't mark me. There's always that thought one has, "This will be the last time I do" such and such a thing, but stepping off this vessel was a relief, it had been an arduous journey at times.

My mother told me, "School days are the best days of your life", but they weren't for me and no doubt telling me that had me believing life was gonna be pretty awful. If anything though, living on Roundshaw meant that we'd all remain nearby, so maybe it felt like the era hadn't ended after all. It was just arcing to the ground and fading out.

1976 - Five Holidays

My mother arranged for me to have five holidays during the summer break. She almost certainly struggled to raise the money and sacrificed her pleasure for me, but at the time I probably just felt she was just getting rid of me.

Holiday 1

It doesn't matter what I do, the same curiosity about me arises in most people. How do I go to the loo, how do I masturbate, how do I have sex, how do I wash and how do I dress?

Up until holiday 1, going to the loo had been an activity that I'd received help with. Look this bit's going to be a bit difficult for both you and me, so I guess either you skip this section or we grit our teeth and bear it.

Changes

When I was in my early twenties I was sitting in a waiting room in a hospital when a man with half legs and half arms walked in. He was dressed very well and as we chatted, I found out he did a very well-to-do job. But during this conversation, he told me he had to have help with dressing and personal care. He'd always been helped and didn't realise there were ways of being more independent. I showed him a few of my techniques for dressing and he went off.

We met again a year or so later and he informed me our previous meeting had changed his life. He'd learned to dress, left his parents' home and started to live independently.

Independence

None of us are truly independent, we are interdependent. We may go through periods in our lives when we feel we're independent, but either before then or later, we're going to need others' help to support us, both physically and emotionally. So before exalting independence as the new ideal, I believe it's best to keep it in perspective.

Our value, not only to others but to ourselves can't be judged on whether we can "look after" ourselves. Throughout history, people who seemed to have been a burden have become kingpins in our society's development. Nelson, Roosevelt, Bader, and Hawkins spring to mind immediately.

Now you may think, "Well he would say that wouldn't he." But for me, the struggle has been the opposite way around. I've spent many years dealing with my desire to be independent. A Super Crip. However, we are human beings, not human doings. What shines from us is something in our being, the motivation behind why we do things. I'm impressed by Mike Tyson's physical prowess as a fighter but disturbed by his hatred. I'm just as impressed by Leonard Cohen's desire to improve his and our emotional world as I am with his talent.

I have met people who are lightly disabled, and their parents have prayed for them to die. I teach some people who can't speak properly and are only able to move their head and many people think they shouldn't live.

Holiday 1 - Catalyst

Holiday 1 is a catalyst for me.

I had been going to the Diamond Riding School for the Disabled in Carshalton for a few years. Set amidst fields and small holdings it was a world away from Roundshaw. One of the teachers from my school, Mrs Gee, would often run me to the stables in her car after school. Whilst waiting for my turn to go around the arena a million times at 1 mph I'd sit and chat to the other kids. The place smelt of manure.

We were taught to muck out the stables, put on saddles and all the other bits and pieces the girls seemed so interested in. Once on the horse or pony, we'd trot around the arena, alternating from trudging to learning how to do rising trudge (I mean trot). Sometimes the horse would break into a canter and I'd be holding on for dear life. For an extra laugh the instructor, normally a Hymie-faced man called Malcolm, would have us ride bareback. I can't tell you how much I enjoyed that.

Mainly I'd be given a docile little dark brown rotund pony called Bramble, whom I had an unspoken pact with, which was if I allowed her to do almost nothing except sniff the ground, she would not throw me off - increasingly likely the less she did.

Sometimes I'd get a chestnut horse who would delight in rearing up at which point I'd dive head-first into the sand which would result in the session ending. A great result for both of us.

Malcolm thought he'd try me out on jumping. Admittedly the jump was only about two feet high, however, Bramble would consider this a breach of our pact and would either do a Judo throw on me at the final approach or do a five-foot-high jump, banging the back of my head on her rear and then the front of my face into her neck bone. Needless to say, I wasn't a natural and didn't get too much joy from it all.

Where there's horse muck there's money, and many of the "helpers" were local rich people keeping themselves amused. Occasionally we'd be invited to their garden parties only to find their garden was bigger than our local park and it had its own swimming pools and tennis courts.

This year the riding centre decided to hold a week-long holiday. We were all to camp in the field behind the stables and go out to different places each day. This would have been far more fun if I had organised for someone to help me in the loo, specifically with regards to wiping my bottom. Sadly, I shared a tent with a helper who didn't like me, and I didn't like him, so, I wasn't going to ask him and for the first time, I felt too ashamed to ask anyone else.

Three days without going for a crap resulted in me waking in the middle of the night in severe pain and nausea. My dislike and shame were set aside, and I asked the helper in my tent if he'd help, but he looked at me from the comfort of his sleeping bag and told me to wait 'til the morning.

I then made my way across the cold damp field to Malcolm's tent, he was asleep but after I woke him, he said he'd come and help me in a minute, but I waited outside the chemical toilet because I didn't know where the actual toilet was. I was cold and the place stunk so I took myself back to my tent and finally got back to sleep. The next day Malcolm got a helper to help me, but the trauma of that night instigated an investigation by myself into how to cope with going to the toilet without someone else helping me.

If you don't have arms long enough to wipe your bottom then what do you do? There are three main approaches: Use other parts of your body, such as your foot or heel; use your environment – e.g. put some paper across the rim and side of the toilet bowl, or find another appropriate object (At this point anyone who's had me in their house is wondering what the fuck I've wiped my arse on and just for safety's sake are going to fumigate and decorate the whole bathroom); and finally one can use a purpose-built design, such as a loo with a built-in water spray and bottom dryer, a bidet, a shower, or some other kind of con-craption, sorry, contraption, that'll hold the paper and either be positioned nicely for the job or held and manoeuvred to taste. So, these are just a few of the wonderful ways in which one's bottom can be kept squeaky clean without the use of hands. Happy now? Just so you know I keep my anus so clean you could eat a meal off it.

So that was Holiday 1, a painful learning experience.

Holiday 2 - Broadstairs

We had been to Broadstairs a few years running, originally Michael the psychopath had taught me how to use a rifle sight on an arcade shooting gun there. We had also played mini-golf, and I had been allowed to watch the "Bionic Man" in the proprietor's lounge once. Aside from cutting my legs on some rocks though, not very much happened on our trips to this place.

My mother had come here with her family when she was a child and since then not much has changed. Its charm lies in the feeling it gives out of a bygone age. Italian ice cream parlours selling Knickerbocker Glories, crowded beaches, Punch and Judy shows, arcades full of penny waterfalls, fishing nets, rubber rings, bed and breakfast, and quiet cordiality.

One day my mother took me to meet the parents of Ian, the man she'd regretted leaving when she was a young woman. She dressed me in my new school uniform, I was no doubt on display, a message to her long-lost lover. We sat eating sandwiches and cakes in the conservatory. At one point the mother said that if she had me in her care she'd knock me into line. I was not impressed, and no doubt neither was my mother. A quiet and polite retreat to our single mother and son B&B room brought her dream of a reunion to its end.

I would come here again as an adult, more in passing than to stay. Even in 2005, it felt as though I'd time-warped back to the 1950s.

Torso

My Torso is turning in front of you now. My arms, as you're probably already aware end around the elbows. My chest is hairy. I am not fat, (well that's a matter of opinion apparently), but I have put on weight. When I was young my torso was well-toned. I have broad shoulders and a large chest.

My arms have defined much of what I have experienced in my life but just as they are physically placed, so metaphorically too they are a side issue. My torso defines the paradox of my life, that I am abnormal whilst normal. I am different and yet the same. My torso is the place where I feel emotions the most: my heart; my gut; my back; my kidneys; my bladder; and my stomach. One day when my heart stops, my brain may have a moment longer to live, but soon it will stop working too. My torso is where my life starts, feels the drama and ends.

2008 – January - Meeting Tracey - Part 3

I walked into the pub, the drunk woman with the business card wasn't there yet, so I went to the bar and got myself a drink. I sat near the door on a comfy chair and waited. I couldn't quite remember what she looked like, so each woman who walked in was a possible candi-date.

Holiday 3 - Four Winds

The Thalidomide Trust had developed holiday homes designed to cater for families with "children of Thalidomide". In terms of catering for any special needs, the provisions were basic compared to today's standards, but their main intent was to also provide shelter in terms of stigma.

Even though I wasn't a Thalidomide "Survivor" my mother and I were still welcome to stay at the centres.

Mum chose a guest house called Four Winds in a place called Norman's Bay. The main proprietors were a couple who'd had a son born with no arms as a result of Thalidomide. The father had been a cook in the army and the mother was a thin force to be reckoned with.

When we first arrived we had to spend the night in a caravan in the garden which backed onto the beach. Soon after getting unpacked a big storm took hold. My mother lit the little gas lights and warmed a can of something on the tiny cooker. As the lightning and thunder interweaved the gusts of wind, the swaying caravan had us cowering.

After such a long dark night came a bright fresh morning. The sun shone hard while the wind blew cold air upon us as we stepped out of the caravan. We were at the end of a long garden that ended gradually where the pebbly beach began. At the other end stood the main guest house. A square of geometric outcrops of white. At the back was a conservatory, and between us and them were various gaming props, such as a table tennis table, a pole with a string with a tennis ball attached, a table football game and other swingy things!

Mum walked down to the beach and pulled shells from the groins, brought them back and boiled them in a pan of water. She gave me a mussel to eat, but all I experienced was a mouthful of sand and grit. She pulled a winkle from a shell with a pin, "Come on," she said, "just try it". I refused, and she laughed.

We walked to the house and were introduced to the other detainees, most of whom were just about to set off back to abnormality. We'd come a day early – hence our temporary accommodation – so we were outsiders for a few hours until it was our turn to become old-timers.

Norman's Bay was a quiet place, a row of houses next to a campsite, a local shop run by two old sisters, a long platformed empty train station, a manually operated level crossing, the beach and the sea.

A road in, and when the level crossing barrier was up, a road out.

———

It was 1976, and groups of men and boys sat in darkened rooms where the sun broke through cracks in the curtains casting beams through smoke onto tins of beer. Loud cheers and groans would emanate following the plight and struggle of a

222

football team. But I was not a fan and played outside, and as mum had brought down my bike, I explored.

I don't live far from Norman's Bay now and often cross the crossing on my way to Bexhill. Now, in 2008, the person who operates it sits in a grey Portacabin, but back then the platform had a building on it – more of a shack – in which the "Station Master" had his own office and to the side of that a small waiting room. Now the platform is empty except for a small plastic "stand-in" shelter. (Update, nowadays in 2022 the crossing is fully automated).

How I managed to befriend the "Station Master" back then is beyond me now. No doubt if I did, we would have paedophiles rushing to take notes. Children, well me at least, seemed oblivious to the possible dangers of befriending adults, so back then I still did.

And so, John, the white-haired, station master, ticket seller, ticket checker, cleaner, administrator, and level-crossing operator, would make me cups of tea, tell me stories of his life and allow me to help open and close the gates. My mother would come to politely check I wasn't causing trouble, but beyond that, I was pretty much unsupervised. John would say, "I don't know why people check to see if a train's coming, we're not going to leave the gate open when a train comes, and anyway even if a train was coming it'd be so fast it'd be too late anyway."

This never reassured me and even now I always do an extra look to see if a train's coming and think of John.

The road that led eastwards from Normans Bay, was made of rough sandy-coloured concrete, and weaved around the railway track until it hit Cooden Beach. I would tentatively cycle the route and each time go a little further, so within a few days, I had managed to stray the ten miles that got me to Hastings, or more importantly, its funfair.

Each day I visited the fair, where I found one particular ride I thought I might be able to master. The challenge was to lie face down on a very large circular platform, feet outwards whilst holding on to a raised nub in the centre. The idea was to hold on tight to the central hub whilst the disk spun until either the ride came to an end, or you were sent flying off onto an array of air cushions around the edge.

On this occasion, I advised my fellow riders to hold on to the person opposite's wrists which was both good and bad advice. Bad in the sense that they all flew off almost immediately and good in the way it left me as the only rider holding on. Perhaps because my arms were so much shorter, in fact, my whole body was so much shorter, the full effect of the centrifugal force was not as strong on me, or maybe it was just that the ride's operators felt for me and didn't spin it to its full velocity, though I do remember they tried several jerky speed ups and slowdowns, but anyway I didn't get thrown off. I held on and managed to have a hold over not only the ride but all those watching. Apart from my fellow hangers-on who were probably cursing me, everyone seemed to be either impressed or somewhat moved. Had I not been disabled the feeling would have been different and, whilst I took some pride in my prowess, I felt embarrassed because I knew that there was this other, contaminating dimension. Being praised for being disabled and doing well felt like it took something away. As far as I was concerned, I just wanted to be recognised for simply doing well and that was it.

I was beginning to become aware of the duality of my situation. I would gain recognition for my pursuits, but it would be measured with a different yardstick that inevitably meant my significance was undermined, presumed lesser in some way. I was, "Good considering".

When the ride stopped the man running the ride said over the loudspeaker system, "Well done Simon" – given he knew my name I'd no doubt chatted to him too – and the "audience" applauded me.

The first week was nearly ending and Mum was going to have to leave me in the care of the proprietors for a few days. I probably would have been okay with this had I not fallen out with their son, who had even shorter arms than I. Maybe I couldn't stand being "out disabled" by him. As is usual, the cause of the fight between us is blurry now, but an underlying automatic dislike, combined with him being a bit older and wanting to exert some authority over me, led to an explosion from me when he wouldn't let me play snooker.

I ran towards him, teeth gnarling, only to be met by a good hard kick in the chest which knocked me backwards. I moved forward once again, and he kicked me again; unperturbed and slightly more angrily, I lunged at him once more. This time my teeth were gnashing. He kicked me again. And so, like a clockwork machine, we continued this dance for a further few seconds.

Nearby a blind man, who by the way was extremely good at playing dominoes, asked if everything was alright. My opponent politely said, "It's okay." And that riled me even more, and seeing the despair in my eyes, my opponent started to laugh at me. In temper and frustration, tears streamed down my face.

He taunted, "Oh is the baby crying?"

I lunged again but to no avail.

"Ooh, temper, temper!" he said in a pantomime tone.

I punched his leg out of the way which allowed me to get closer. I took a swipe at him with my arm but missed. His knee drew up and he pushed me away again.

Someone pulled me off saying, "Calm down you two."

We stood staring at one another, enemies for the rest of the holiday.

Just before Mum had left, I went to her room. She came out of the shower.

"Ooh I needed that, can you smell a funny smell?" She asked.

"No," I said.

"It's just sometimes a woman can smell more than others".

I didn't know what she meant.

"Simon, can you go to the shop and buy me some Nivea, please? You can have an ice cream".

So I walked the 50 yards to the shop. There was a different woman there. She took the money and passed me a container. I dashed back with the hand cream, which turned out to be an empty container, so Mum, not amused, sent me back with it. When I got there the woman who normally serves was there and took some persuading about what had just ensued. I stood there while she asked pointed questions as to what exactly had happened and eventually handed over another small container of Nivea whilst tutting something about "I told her not to touch anything or serve anyone".

2009 - Shop

That shop stands unoccupied now, it's moderately dilapidated but still has the word, "Shop" faintly painted on one of the external walls. One of the sisters waits out her last days in a home. In 2004 I put a note through the door saying if ever it was to come up for sale, I'd be interested in buying it, but I heard nothing.

2010 - Shop

I often drive to Normans Bay, but this time, Steve and Sue B, my girlfriend at the time, not the one from Jollymead, are with me to shoot a video nearby. I notice a For Sale sign on the old shop and take down the number of the estate agents. I look online and see it has a guide price of £235,000 which is worth considering.

A few days later I get to look inside, and I'm blown away by the potential of the place. It has four massive rooms, plus many bedrooms... it's so dilapidated that plants are growing through the windows and around the walls. If I was to sell my house and get it for the guide price I could do it up, reduce my mortgage by half and have a bigger, better home. I ask a surveyor to come around the property with me who agrees with both my calculations and ideas about its potential.

The auction will take place within a week or so, so I started calling bridging loan companies. One of my relations agreed to lend me enough money for the deposit (£30,000) so by the time the auction comes I'm ready. There's an element of gambling going on because I haven't got a mortgage in place and if I get it, I'll only have 28 days to get all the finances in place.

When the day comes Steve accompanies me to the auction, which is in the Hilton in Brighton. I have spoken to my solicitor who tells me of a man who tried to run out of an auction after accidentally bidding too high. He was chased across a park in London, tackled to the ground and made to pay the deposit. Suffice it to say, the atmosphere was tense.

As the first four properties sold a few didn't make their reserve prices. So, when it came to Lot 28, "Sunshine", Normans Bay I was a bit shocked to see the initial bids start at the guide price and steadily climb to £375,000. I didn't even bother raising my card. We got up, walked out, chatted to a couple of other people who had hoped to get it as well and went off for some lunch on the seafront.

The last few weeks had been full of fantasies about doing the place up and what it would be like to live there, but they were not to be and yet another house joined the ranks of places I occasionally pass which represent different lives I might have had.

1976 - Norman's Bay

When Mum left the next day, she bought me a fishing rod, sadly she didn't teach me to fish. So, wondering if she meant for me to be self-sufficient while she was gone I felt a mild form of panic and a bit sad. I went fishing in a brook, but didn't catch a thing.

The good thing about not having Mum there was I could stay up late watching TV and for the first time in my life, I noticed a feeling of pleasure, as I looked at the curve of a woman's hip to waist. Admittedly it was Raquel Welch, walking down a staircase wearing only a bikini in a film called Fathom. It was not so much about being turned on, but more a feeling of being drawn by the look of a woman.

The next day the proprietors took me to Camber Sands and as their 18-year-old daughter walked around in a white bikini I just stared and stared until either she or her parents told me off.

Aesthetic Appreciation

I've heard it said that as a child hits puberty they receive less physical affection from their parents and consequently look for it elsewhere, but the feelings I started to experience were different. They were nature kicking in and my perception changed accordingly. I had already felt that women were intrinsically related to romance and love, but now there was a further feeling, an aesthetic appreciation, a sexual awareness, a desire.

Fair

On the last day of this holiday, the local community held a fair that went on into the night. Our proprietor cooked ring doughnuts and shouted out that he was going for a world record. I felt so excited to be part of such a prestigious event, but then my mother, who'd rejoined me, by the way, told me he was joking, and not realising I was a fool, I felt quite disappointed.

In 2010, when I was looking around the shop to buy it, I spoke to a local man who remembered those days. He said, "That was when there was a sense of community, but it doesn't exist anymore."

This lack of community has been around for many decades now, so it's not surprising that Facebook has become so popular. After all, in its way, it's creating a kind of feeling of community. Even in the sense of my neighbours, I'm linked to a few on Facebook, so, there's a type of extra dimension of relatedness that exists between us now.

The Centre of My Body

The centre of my body is an interface too. It is where different worlds meet. The internal world comes out to the external one and it is where I can physically manifest a "connection" with an "other". I'm not sure if I should spin the middle of my body, I might end up getting arrested. But it is important in terms of procreation, making love, digestion and ridding oneself of waste. It is where the material world and the spiritual world meet. It is "between". It is between my head, which attempts to connect spiritually and my feet which touch the ground.

2008 - Meeting Tracey - Part 4

When she walked through the door, she didn't look as I had remembered at all. We got another drink and sat down to talk. She wore a big rust-coloured jumper, had brushed-back blonde hair, and was a bit out of breath.

"Hi, sorry I'm late."

"Yeah, you should be," well, I didn't say that... instead what came out was, "Don't worry, what would you like to drink?"

"A large white", God, there's so much one could say to that, I thought, but instead I waddled over to the bar and chatted up the barmaid.

My Legs

Above the knees, my legs are normal, but below them, they are about five inches shorter than they should be. Two bones normally hold the ankle joint in place for most people, but I only have one there. (My lower leg is thinner as well as shorter.) Maybe my disability or the surgery that was performed on my legs caused my lower legs to be stunted, but perhaps that was for the best. Had my lower legs been longer with just one bone, then possibly they would have been more brittle. Also being short may help me with dealing with the world with short arms – except in supermarkets of course, where I often have to scramble out of freezers I've fallen into or get released from my mountain climbing harness when hanging from top shelves. Still, even then, the frequent approaches by women offering to help me "with anything" makes it all worthwhile.

My legs are a metaphor for seeing the positive in what appears to some as negative. My legs acted as arms and hands when I was a child, and as a young man, they powered me around on a bike, protected me in fights and wrapped around the women I wanted to hold in bed. My legs are a symbol of being more than what we are defined as.

Holiday 4 - Bournemouth

There's a photo of me sitting in a wheelchair in Bournemouth, this was Mum's bright idea for dealing with the steep hills there and my leg's limitations. I don't look very happy in the photo, it wasn't so much that I felt bad about being in a wheelchair, more a case of it not being true. It's like when people say, "So, this must have been Thalidomide." Whilst nodding at my arms. What difference does it make to me whether it was or wasn't? It's just a need to be accurate that makes me correct them on the matter. However, there have been many times in my life when I was quite happy not to be too accurate, namely with girlfriends and the police.

So, I'm on holiday literally being pushed around by my mum, and occasionally creating an impression of a miracle occurring particularly when I managed to get out of the wheelchair for a quick stretch. For me though, the highlight of the holiday was watching my mum's friend, Jackie, who was staying in the same room, getting changed in front of me.

"Maybe I shouldn't undress in front of Simon," she said – I was tempted to say, "Don't be silly."

"Oh, don't worry Jackie, Simon's too young to notice." my mum thankfully reassured her.

"He doesn't look too young, he can't take his eyes off my body."

I looked away and pretended not to look at her.

Apart from that, this was a typical British holiday: guest house; beach; befriending other beach dwellers; playing with the sand; paddling in the sea; guest house dinners; TV and bed.

One family we made friends with had a beach hut, which we got invited into when it rained. The "family" consisted of a woman, her husband and two sons. Nine months later, Mum and I would return to stay with them, but by then the father had died. His sons would then show me the porn magazines and weapons their father had kept in his chest of drawers and then for fun, we threw tissues out of the window which we'd watch float down the street till they'd finally tumble to the road. We did this until the whole box was empty and we saw our mums walking up the tissue-covered road, created unbeknown to them by their artistic offspring. Perhaps the boys meant it symbolically like they wanted the tears to stop falling or maybe it was just simply interesting to watch tissues float away on the wind, and then to see our mark upon the world.

Bournemouth held a moment of significance though. Sitting on the beach near me was a deaf girl, and as we played together and communicated with each other by drawing in the sand, I felt a sense of connection with her. I can't explain "connection". How is it we know immediately, with some strangers, that we'll feel right with them?

January 2008 - Meeting Tracey - Part 5

We sat down next to each other on the pub couch. I asked her about her life.

"You're different to other men I've met." She said.

"Is that good?" I ask and laugh.

"You're interested in me, most men just tell me about themselves."

I laugh again, "Funny most people think I like the sound of my own voice too."

She looks a bit concerned, "So is it just a way of chatting women up?"

"Maybe, but you know what, I don't feel like talking about myself right now, it's not about showing you my CV. I mean you can go online if you want to find out about me."

She raises an eyebrow, "I already did."

I laugh and say, "It's about getting on, connecting, and being interested. Funny when we met, I felt a powerful draw towards you, something in your eyes, but now we're here chatting, maybe it's just a friendly connection."

She put her hand on my thigh.

"I don't know," she said.

I could feel myself feeling turned on. She leant across and kissed me.

Holiday 5 Jollymead – Dartmoor

My last holiday in 1976 was a return to Jollymead, the place on Dartmoor. Sue (not the same one as in 2010, but the one I'd met at Jollymead previously) was there, but so too was another boy. He had no hands. As the week progressed, my need for Sue pushed her towards the loving arms of this "interloper". So much so that he and I had two fights. One in which he put his stumps around my throat to strangle me, but, given the missing fingers, this turned out to be futile, so I pushed him off. The second was far more spectacular and involved a few moves I'd learned from some American TV series. This involved him running at me to push me over and me falling backwards and kicking upwards sending him flying in the air. He got up, grabbed a stone and as he pulled back to throw it at me, Robbie intervened. Needless to say, Sue went off with him and I went home heartbroken.

My Feet

I was born with two feet, but now I only have one. More about that another time. My remaining foot is twisted and only has four toes. My feet are a reminder to me of my limitations and my mortality. The foot that's gone is a part of me that has already died and is no longer here. Its absence is both a reminder of a spiritual world and a very mechanical physical one. Mechanical in terms of my prosthesis and the mechanics of my nervous system which tells me I can still feel my foot even though it died over four decades ago.

My feet connect me to the world, they get tired, they ache, and they are my trusted steeds. They remind me I am human and keep me firmly planted to the ground.

2008 - Meeting Tracey - Part 6

When we leave the pub, we walk to my car and I drive her to hers. We kiss goodbye and it feels good. We will see each other again, I know it.

1976 - Sexual Feelings

In the summer of 1976, I became sexualised, but I wasn't sexually aware. I didn't know what it was I wanted. I just knew I wanted something. A new era shot into the sky and is still arcing above me now.

I would soon be starting at a new school again. A week before my new school started, I got up early, put on my new school tracksuit and tried going for a run, but no sooner had I got around the corner than I started to feel out of breath and my feet started hurting. They were both real back then. I had the correct clothes, but something wasn't quite right. There was this idea of myself but as it came up against reality, I experienced pain and breathlessness. This was the beginning of another arc, the arc of self-awareness.

2010 August - Dream

I'm in The Chelsea Arts Club and Paul McCartney is chatting with me. I just found out that a woman I've been flirting with is his wife, so I'm feeling a little uncomfortable. Lots of people are coming up to him to ask for his autograph. I look at them all and tell them off for being rude. Then I ask if he'd like to do a bit of songwriting with me.

As you can see my Arc of Self Awareness still has a long way to go before it reaches its peak.

Chapter 19
Wilson's

Sometime in 2008 - Tracey

Nine months have passed since the day we met in the bar. I feel her fist hit my cheekbone. She's standing in front of me, shouting, shaking in anger. I can see the vitriol in her eyes. This isn't quite the end, but it's coming. I tell her not to hit me again.

I had grown up worrying that having witnessed Michael hitting my mother and me, I'd turn out to be a woman beater like him, especially given I've got such a fiery temper. Fortunately, I found I wasn't. There'd been a few times during my life when girlfriends had hit me, and I never struck them back. I'm sure I've been cruel in many other ways, but I never resorted to physical violence.

Between the beginning and end of the relationship with Tracey, there was a captivating introduction, exciting storylines, passion, and moments of connection. But then one day, a conversation broke the spell and revealed the ending's irresistible approach, which despite all our best efforts, or maybe because of them, brought us our parting. Of course, it wasn't a complete ending. We stayed friends and would meet up for a cuppa now and again. Then one day she got ill, and eventually, the illness took its toll on her and ended her life.

2014 - What's Important Now Won't Be Later

The notes I'd made for this chapter had been written in 2010, four years ago. Some of them don't feel relevant any longer. For instance, Tracey had sometimes teased me about how she fancied Ross Kemp, a TV personality, and how I shouldn't worry because she was not ever likely to meet him. I refrained from telling her I'd occasionally see him at the Arts Club in London.

Most of what was important then, isn't now, and likewise what's happening now probably won't be of much interest later, but little things and sometimes big things continue to haunt us through life.

2008 - Stories For Another Day

A few months after Tracey and I went our separate ways in late 2008, I met Sue B, and around five years later we too came to part. Stories I may tell another day, but for now, let's focus on the more distant past.

1984 – Gibraltar

I was fishing on a sea jetty in Gibraltar with some people I'd met there in 1984. I decided that cutting the head off a fish I'd just caught was the right thing to do. A few minutes later, one of my friend's mother told me not to do that again. I look back and wonder what possessed me to think it was a good idea in the first place, to put looking tough ahead of the suffering of an animal. The person who did that, well, he was me, but I am no longer him.

Sadly, my life often feels like a dot-to-dot extravaganza of cringeworthy moments. If I had written the Sinatra song, *My Way*, my version would have included, 'Regrets, I've had a lot'.

September 1976

On the 29th of September 1615, King James the First signed a Royal Charter which brought Edward Wilson's school in Camberwell into existence.

Wilson's school relocated from Camberwell to a site right next to Roundshaw in 1975, so to us locals it looked like a new school. The building was pristine and included squash courts and a swimming pool. By changing its location, it changed its identity. It had been quite a good school back in Camberwell, but here it quickly became one of the top schools in the country.

Being so close to Roundshaw meant kids from our junior school regularly went to the new school on the block to taunt the pupils as they came out. However, they soon realised this wasn't such a good idea given a lot of the kids were from Camberwell so were up for a bit of fighting, and that, coupled with them being twice the size of the junior school pupils, brought that activity to a succinct end.

1976 – Wilson's School - First Day

In September 1976, I, along with another 120 children, wearing our brand-new uniforms, black trousers, blazer, white shirt, black and yellow striped tie, and black shoes, stood in front of the yellow brick building. New kids, new bricks.

We were told that, in future though, we were not to enter the school through this entrance, but instead use the side one. But for this occasion, we marched into the main setting of our life for the next seven years.

18th October 2014 - Henry VIII and End Dates

I am approaching 50, and I've been writing this for close to ten years now. Time becomes more noticeable with age, even though it seems to slip by faster than ever. Long days, short weeks, long months, short years. What seems like distant history, for example, Henry VIII's reign, is just over nine of my life spans ago. Given how fast my life seems to have flown past, there's a sense a lot of our history was not that long ago, and how quickly things have changed in such a short period, especially over the last 50 years. This recognition of transience as I get older, where everything comes to pass, both good and bad, is still very hard to come to terms with. Especially the loss of loved ones, things and situations I hold dear. Still, at least it leads me to appreciate them more while they or I are still here. Love, time and life are beginning to show their end dates to me.

1976 - Morden Swimming Baths

I am underwater, I can hear muffled sounds down there. I come up for air and hear a whistle blowing loudly. I look towards the sound. "Yellow armbands out!" The lifeguard shouts whilst pointing at me. I'm tempted to argue I'm wearing mine on my leg, so it doesn't count, but I don't. I get out obediently.

7th September 2014

I'm at a garden party to celebrate my mother's friends, Colin and Val's 50th wedding anniversary. Whilst we're waiting for them to turn up a white-haired man approaches me.

I look at him and say, "I recognise you from somewhere".

"You should do," he says, "we sat next to each other in class for five years."

It's Robbie, he was one of the good kids from school. I was one of the bad ones.

12th March 2014 - Colin and Val

Mum and I pop in to see her friends, Colin and Val. We hadn't seen them for at least ten years but reconnected with them via Facebook and organised this meeting.

Colin, as you may remember, had been a father figure to me as a child, and both he and his wife had served as an example of a truly happy couple to me. You don't get to see too many of those in life. Someone recently told me the modern version of the wedding vows should replace the vow, "For better or worse," with, "For better or forget it".

Colin and Val bought this house close to 40 years ago. The garden was overgrown back then. Colin cut down the foliage and flattened the ground with a large roller, built an extension, knocked rooms into each other, and together he and Val held parties, brought up their children, looked after Val's mum, and lived most of their lives here. The central stage upon which their lives were acted out, was occasionally one for me too.

2012 - Revisiting Wilson's

Jeff Shaw was my form master at Wilson's for my first five years there. This meant he was the teacher in charge of our registration class until we got to 16. At that point, the pupils either left or went into the school's 6th form department.

In 1976, Jeff, our form master looked young, which, given he was only about 15 years older than us, he was. But, still, he was very much an adult to us 11-year-olds. It's been 30 years since I left Wilson's and Jeff is showing me around the school, pointing out what's changed, what's new, who's still here, who's left, and who's died.

As I looked at him, I couldn't help but notice how youthful he was. Some people become unrecognisable as time passes, but not Jeff. My mother, on the other hand, looked older than her years in her 30s. It wasn't her genetics but the clothes she wore, her hairstyle and make-up. Even now, when I look back at photos of her from then, she looks older than her years. She didn't look old for her age; it was just the culture directing her appearance.

12th March 2014 - Colin and Val's House

Mum is sitting next to Val, we're all chatting. I show Val a few tricks on her iPad. She says she knows them already, which rather steals my thunder. Then I take some photos with my phone, Mum leans over towards Val, they look old and young at the same time.

First Bad Impressions

In my first few days at school, I made a bit of a bad impression. Firstly, I told our class prefect to put his hand on the desk in front of me, and as he did, I slammed my stump down on a nerve point in the middle of the back of his hand. I didn't notice at the time, but Jeff assured me years later, that I had him close to tears. Yet another cringeworthy moment.

April 2011 - Radio 4 Interview - Part 1

A BBC Radio 4 presenter asks me questions on the phone about John Galliano, the famous fashion designer, who'd just been sacked for making racist and anti-semitic remarks.

BBC Presenter: "So what was John Galliano like at school?"

Me: "He was five years above me, so I didn't have much to do with him."

BBC Presenter: "Was there anything different about him, did he stand out?"

Me: "His hair was pretty much all over the place, in a way, he doesn't look much different now to how he looked then. I don't think he was happy being wrapped up in a uniform, so, he made sure it was never worn properly. He was definitely a fish out of water. [A Gibraltarian fish out of water, who sometimes didn't keep his head, even if he liked giving it.] He was outwardly very camp and made sure everyone knew he was gay."

September 1976 - Wilson's School – John Galliano

I'm standing near John Galliano in the corridor outside my form classroom.

"You're gay," I say, stating the obvious, with a sneer on my face.

He looks at me, "What did you just say, you little spastic?"

"Gay," I confirmed.

"Fuck off," he said as he kicked me hard up the arse. (Kicked I said). A tear came to my eye, and then the other one too and then the first one again.

April 2011 - Radio 4 Interview - Part 2

The BBC Radio 4 Presenter asks me more questions.

BBC Radio Presenter: "So how did he deal with the torments of others?"

Me: "I think he played up to it. He was gay and proud of it. I once called him gay and he kicked me. It's typical for oppressed groups to attack each other. You see it all the time. This latest incident of Galliano getting drunk and being filmed being anti-Semitic is similar to what happened between him and me all those years ago."

BBC Radio Presenter: "That's very interesting but I don't think we can use that story."

And they didn't.

1976 – First Week at Wilson's

As usual, I didn't learn my lesson from this incident and decided to call one of the senior prefects by his nickname, Dougal, because his hair curtained his face like a dog puppet called Dougal's in the children's program, *The Magic Roundabout*.

His response was to give me, "Two sides". This meant I had to fill two pages of A4 lined paper with meaningful writing. Not only that, but it had to be written on a subject. The subject he set me was, "The IMF" (The International Monetary Fund). Trust me, this brought more tears to my eyes than Galliano's kick. I spent hours copying text from the Financial Times in the school library following his directive. The upshot of this was I have gone through life with a small but occasionally useful knowledge about the IMF. Consequently, there've been occasions when I've been grateful for his punishment. I realise that does sound a bit dodgy, but at least I'm being honest.

To make matters a little less better, a few days later I was sitting in Sutton Library listening to some music with some large headphones on. At that time the library offered a music listening service. My mum came up to me, I nodded towards "Dougal" who by coincidence had just walked into the area and was approaching the counter.

"Look Mum, there's Dougal!" I said at the top of my voice (although I thought I was speaking normally).

"They all call him Dougal because he looks like a fat version of Dougal. I hate him, he gave me two sides."

My mum looked at me, pretended to take off some headphones, put her finger to her mouth and said, "Shhh!" She laughed as Dougal, red-faced, smiled at me.

The next day at school I got another two sides. I think it was on sound waves.

---

25 October 2014

I'm at home in front of my computer. This morning, I noticed an appointment in my calendar from this time next year for today. In it, I added a little message to myself, something like, "Hello from me a year ago, I wonder what will happen or if I'll even still be here."

Sometimes I go through months of playing computer games intensely. I'm going through one now. The chosen game is online *8 Ball Pool* which my daughter Leah had introduced me to sometime ago. It's a bit of a time waster and certainly stops me from being as creative as I could be. I'm not sure what causes me to do this, maybe it's an escape, or some kind of meditative state or maybe I just need times of wastefulness to drive me back into more meaningful pursuits.

When I'm playing with other people online, I often find myself laughing because of the interaction between them and myself, so part of it is about connection. But when it comes to playing proficiently, I always get to a point when I know I can't progress much further, but many other players can, and will always be far better than I'll ever be. Once virtual reality shows me the reality of my limitations, it's then I start to get back to intense writing, music production, painting, or photography. It's then that I enter an artistic stage again.

September 2007 - John and the Gateway

I am in a pub garden after a family meetup and John, my stepfather, is walking in front of me. He gets to the gate and stands there. He doesn't know how to open it. He just stands there waiting. He is in the early to middle stages of dementia. Over the next seven years, we will watch him deteriorate into another version of himself.

12th March 2014 - Wallington Surrey

Mum and I are sitting in a café. We share a similar liking for cheap greasy spoon cafes and English Breakfasts. The smell of bacon has greeted me in the morning throughout my life.

Mum's currently selling her house and going to buy an apartment near where I live in Eastbourne. We go through some of the paperwork. She is feeling overwhelmed by the idea of moving, but she's relieved to have finally decided what to do next. It will be strange to have her living so close to me.

Mum: "Is there a spiritualist church in Eastbourne?"

Me: "I think so."

Mum: "I've been going to one quite a bit lately."

Me: "Why do you go?"

Mum: "It's interesting and I feel there's something there."

Me: "Maybe."

Mum: "Oh, whilst I remember, just in case I'm ever hospitalised, tell them I'm allergic to Aspirin. Just a small amount could have a very bad effect."

Me: [I nod] "OK, I think I'm allergic to penicillin."

Mum: "Really, how did you find out?"

Me: "The last time I had some I got a rash around my waist."

Mum: "Oh."

This café we're in, it's full of people, it's almost like a circus. A couple of female traffic wardens are sitting at another table, and one of them can't stop looking at me. She's interested in my arms, probably in how I eat. She's not that pretty so I don't encourage her.

Me: "Your friend annoyed me the other day when we looked at that flat you're buying."

Mum: "Who, Sheryl? What did she do?"

Me: "Yes, her. She shouted from the balcony to those other people who'd been looking at the flat you're interested in and told them that they couldn't have it because you were getting it. I mean how embarrassing. I could have killed her."

Mum: "Did she really say that?"

Me: "Yes!"

240

Mum: "Oh dear, maybe they didn't hear her."

Me: "Maybe they just couldn't believe what they were hearing."

12th March 2014 - Later that Day

Mum is with her friend Gill.

"Shuffle the cards, Angela."

Mum shuffles a pack of Tarot cards.

The cards are placed in front of her.

Gill: "Ooh this one's interesting Angela, I don't think your move to Eastbourne is going to happen."

She shows Mum the crumbling tower card.

Mum: "I don't see why not, I mean I have a buyer for my one, and even if that falls through the company selling me the flat will buy my house at the going price."

Gill: "Well, maybe it means you need to get the building surveyed properly. Anyway, this card is more about finding power and security within yourself, instead of within material objects."

13th March 2014 - Morning

Mum, over the phone to me: "I couldn't sleep last night, I'd gone over the figures, you know, how much I'd have coming in and how much it was going to cost to live in the flat in Eastbourne and I couldn't make ends meet. It was only when I called Stephen in the middle of the night and went through it, I realised I was adding it all up wrongly. Sometimes, I'm so silly [she laughs]. So I had a sleepless night for nothing."

13th March 2014 - At the End of the Day

It was sunny today, Mum and her friends cut the grass in the front garden, had a cup of tea, and then went to the spiritualist church. It wasn't so much of a church in the traditional sense, but a grey house on the main road with a sign on it that said, Spiritualist Church.

As Mum sat down with her friend, the woman who was speaking that evening approached her. "Hello Angela, I have a message for you."

Somebody nearby started coughing which triggered Mum into coughing too. Embarrassed because she was trying to focus on what the speaker was saying, she covered her mouth, giggled for a moment, and fumbled in her handbag for a tissue. For a second, she paused, put her hand to her neck and winced. She angled her head backwards and sideways and said, "My neck's hurting. I think I'm going."

She then collapsed onto her friend who was sitting next to her.

The other people quickly gathered around, put her on the floor and felt for a pulse but could not find one. For the next few minutes, a couple of women performed CPR on her, and at one point Mum seemed to sigh. After about seven minutes the paramedics turned up, spending the next 45 minutes performing CPR. Eventually, to everyone's relief, they got her heart beating again; it was then the ambulance crew took her to the hospital.

13th March - 10 pm

I'm at my computer, trying to lay out a design. The phone rings.

Doctor: "Hello is that Simon Smith."

Me: "Yes."

Doctor: "Hi, I'm a doctor at St George's Hospital in Tooting, is Angela Hill your mother?"

Me: "Yes. Is she okay?"

Doctor: "Your mother collapsed earlier this evening, and she's currently here under sedation. We won't be sure if she's been affected until she wakes up."

Me: "Shall I come up?"

Doctor: "You can if you wish but we will probably keep her sedated for a day or so. Is your mother on any medication?"

Me: "I think she takes quite a lot, but I don't know what exactly. She did tell me to say she's allergic to Aspirin."

Doctor: "That's useful, I was just about to prescribe some for her."

Me: "Funny, she only told me about that recently. So do you think she's going to be all right?"

Doctor: "It's hard to tell, her heart did stop beating for a while. We'll be running some checks and doing some scans, but we really can't tell until she wakes up."

Me: "When will that happen?"

Doctor: "We'll try to wake her tomorrow"

I get the ward details from the doctor and call Stephen, my brother, who lives in Australia.

Phone Call with my brother Stephen

Stephen: "Shall I come over?"

Me: "I don't think you should, there's nothing we can do until we know what state she's in. I talked to a doctor earlier and they said it would be best if someone was there when she starts to come around, but they're not sure of her prognosis yet."

Stephen: "I was only just talking to her today. I told her not to over-exert herself. Why did she cut the lawn, we can pay someone to do that for her?"

Me: "I'll let you know what they tell me as soon as they do."

Chapter 20
1976 and 2014

Part 1 - 1976 - Disability Issues

9th December 2014

My house is very cold right now, the heating's broken. I'm sitting at my PC wearing a coat and hat, my feet feel like blocks of ice. Each morning, I take a cold shower but today the water was so cold it hurt. When I was a child, I would have gone into cold streams without a qualm, but nowadays I have to summon a good deal of courage before getting in that icy shower.

12th November 2014

I just watched a news item about deaf people in Uganda being treated as fools, forced into isolation and generally treated as objects of abuse. There are centres there that teach sign language, but often their parents resist sending them because they don't want to spend any money helping them. They see them as a waste.

The TV programme's approach was overly sentimental, but the issue of the isolation and abuse that people with hearing impairments endure is a big problem all over the world, not just in Uganda.

I have often thought that sign language should be part of the national school curriculum because it'd be useful for conversing silently without the use of technology, let alone helping people with issues around hearing. Maybe the deaf community's biggest impediment is not so much their lack of hearing but the rest of society's not listening to their needs.

As I watched this programme I was struck by how the lack of a solid foundation in the basics of their education meant they constantly failed to advance further. This often led to them being categorised as stupid, and this also rang a bell for me, especially as I've been thinking about how this chapter will partly cover my first year at Wilson's.

In my first few years at the school, I generally felt I was a bit of an idiot compared to my peers. As if I was missing some vital information, which I was. It was the basics, but back then I didn't know what I didn't know and hadn't grasped the importance of basics when it came to learning.

November 1976

I'd often tell Mum I wasn't the worst kid in the class. "There's someone who gets lower marks than me." But then that kid left and from then on, the only way was up... or out!

In year one at Wilson's, I didn't settle in well. The reality of being in a school that demanded hours of homework and an amount of self-discipline to learn what was requested meant I came face to face with my inadequacies from the start.

I lacked self-discipline, so it was hard for me to make myself study. That characteristic is still there in me, although at times, I do tend to knuckle down. Still, I'll often buy a book and subconsciously believe just by buying it I will somehow magically take in its contents without actually having to read it. Fortunately, I've recently found my phone will read books to me whilst I drive or do other things around the house, which means books are a part of my life again.

Some people believe that in the future we'll find a way to insert information into our brain without having to study. However, the process of studying also enriches our minds. The way we reflect on the words we read and the further thoughts that pass through our minds, not just as a direct result of the words we read, but the gaps between them too, including our wandering thoughts, all have an effect.

As I started writing notes for this chapter, I initially found it hard to remember what happened in the first year of being at Wilson's. It was as if only highlights got to remain in my memory. Yet, there must be many memories that remain dormant in our minds, as demonstrated when some get triggered from nowhere.

If humans start to live for centuries how will their brains cope with all the memories they accumulate? It only seems logical to presume the sections of our cortex that retain memories are ultimately finite. Of course, memory doesn't work like a computer hard drive, where bits of information are stored in a physical form that takes up room. Memory as far as I can understand from watching a few YouTube videos, is partly the side effect of a series of synaptic connections among the neurons in our brains getting a pulse of electrical charge along with chemicals running through them. Even if we manage to remember much more than we think we do, we all know, over time a lot of what we experience is hard to recall. Sometimes I've come across old videos of me doing something and even then, I have no memory of the event.

Some people believe that forgetting occurs in long-term memory when the formerly strengthened synaptic connections among the neurons in a neural network become weakened, or when the activation of a new network is superimposed over an older one. In turn, this causes interference in the older memory. In other words, similar experiences may well "overwrite" the previous memory.

So, if we get to live longer will we still only have the ability to recall a finite number of memories? In some ways, we create who we are by what we choose to recall, albeit subconsciously most of the time.

Sorry if I'm going on a bit about this but it's going to be relevant to what's coming up in some of the later chapters. Anyway, all of that was my excuse for not remembering much about this time in my life and writing about memory instead!

Ironically there are times when I have far too much confidence in my ability to remember. Sometimes I have what I think is a great, unforgettable idea, and decide not to make a note about it, only to find a few minutes later I can't remember it. No doubt, when I was young this characteristic, coupled with a lack of desire to get down and study, led me to start falling behind. I was keenly aware I was one of the weaker students in my year. It wasn't so much about being stupid, but more a case of not feeling motivated. Still, I seemed to be moving from one world into another. At school, initially, I relied on feeling significant by trying to be tough, renegade, cheeky, and one of the lads. This, no doubt, was my Roundshaw identity making itself known within Wilson's, but on Roundshaw, I started to become even more of an outsider. I went to Wilson's and was therefore considered a bit of a clever clog.

One evening, as I cycled home after school a boy from my junior school shoved his tennis racket handle through the spokes of my back wheel while shouting, "Alright professor!" My bike came to an abrupt stop. I got off and without hesitating punched him in the chest. He looked shocked and backed off. I stood there glaring at him for a comeback but instead, he just picked up his racket and walked away.

I no longer fitted in on Roundshaw or at Wilson's, I was in a kind of no man's land

---

1976 - Wilson's School

Wilson's was built using distinctive yellow bricks. It had a central area in front of which was the assembly hall which protruded towards the road in front of it. The main area went up two floors, (three storeys), and in the centre, a dual zig-zag staircase surrounded by glass panels led to the floors above.

To each side of the central block were two-storey wings. Beyond the one on the left, there was a swimming pool, gym and squash courts, and beyond the one on the right, a science department, and an Arts and Crafts block. To the rear and sides of the school were playing fields, tennis courts, AKA the smoking area, and a cadet building which included a rifle range.

You may have noticed I don't usually try to describe things in detail. Apart from finding such passages boring when I have to read them, I also think if someone were to draw out what was described, the outcome would probably look nothing like the original object, not unless of course it was so detailed that it took a solicitor to draw it up. Anyway, in this instance I've given a bit more detail because we'll be spending some time at Wilson's.

The headmaster was Mr Friskney, who was mild-mannered with an edge of foreboding. The deputy headmaster was Mr Massey, who was a bulldog/sergeant major type whom most people, including the staff, were scared of. Then there was the head of sports, Mr Sollis, who was short and bearded, strict but kind to those he liked. He'd been at the school as a pupil too and would often tell of being a prefect and caning Michael Caine who was a pupil at the school too. Lastly, for now, there was Mrs Hearne, who had been a rally bike champion and now taught science.

The routine for most days started with the register being taken at 8:45 by the form masters who'd also deal with any issues concerning class members. After that, all the students would make their way to the assembly hall where once everyone was gathered, a hymn would be sung, followed by a short sermon and announcements, at which point we'd vacate the hall and the lessons would begin. There'd normally be two lesson periods, a short break, another lesson, and then lunch hour. In the afternoon there'd be another load of lessons, the last of which tended to feel like it was taking forever. If you didn't have to attend a detention or weren't involved in any extra-curricular activities, you could make your way home.

Wilsons was quite strict, punishments when I first started included being hit with the cane (a stick) or the slipper (a shoe), detention (being kept in after school ended), sides (filling A4/Foolscap sheets of paper with writing), picking up waste around the school, suspension (being excluded temporarily from school) or getting expelled (being excluded from Wilson's forever). It's no wonder then that on the whole, the kids at Wilson's were quite well-behaved.

1976

Mum's mum, Ethel-May, had had a stroke and was set to live in Mum's sister's house. A few weeks after the initial stroke I got in from school and Mum greeted me at the top of the stairs.

"I've got some bad news, Simon. Gran has had another stroke and might die, we have to go and see her right now."

When we got to Gran's ward we gathered around her bed. This was when she called me over and put her hand on my face. I didn't understand what was going on but was very aware my cousins were watching me. If she was trying to say sorry it must have been very frustrating for her given I wasn't reacting accordingly.

This is my last memory of her, as a few days later she died, and I didn't go to her funeral. It was as if a funeral wasn't the place to bring a child.

In time a share of the money from her estate came to Mum who put it towards a flat in a small modern block called Sycamore Manor on Woodcote Road near Wallington High Street, about a mile away from Roundshaw.

7th December 2014 - When Do We Stop Being Who We Are?

When Gran had a stroke, she no longer communicated as she had done previously. She changed, but it was still her. The philosopher Gurdjieff went as far as saying our personality is everything that is not us. That our essence is defined by other aspects of who we are and exists from the moment of our creation. Yes, I know, that's a hard one to get your head around. A stroke takes away a chunk of what makes us who we are when it destroys a part of our brain, and yet, even if we're changed to the core, we are still us. It's as if we could change every atom of ourselves except that which is our essence, and we would still be ourselves.

Once our brain has fully died, and our body lies decomposing, even then, though people say it's just the vessel through which we live, that shell is us, and yet not us too. The same could be said of the ashes left after being cremated or the bones below our headstone. They are fragments of us, but then in many ways, we only ever presented fragments of ourselves to others anyway.

And when all that was physically us, but which isn't us too, finally disappears, we live on in the minds of those who brushed up against us when we lived, in the air that encircled us, in the words that dreamt of us and all the invisible consequences of our presence in the universe. We are not just our consciousness or that which makes up who we think we are, but also the thoughts that echo us throughout time. We may feel insignificant, but we are far more so than we can imagine.

1976 - The Calling

A few months after Gran died, I was in the living room listening to some music and heard Gran call my name. I thought at first it might have been something in the music that sounded similar, so I played back the same bit but there was nothing there. I went and asked Mum if she'd called me, but she hadn't. I presumed I must have imagined it, but close to 40 years later I still recall the sound of her voice vividly.

1976 - Lost Sons, Cigarettes and Guns

I'd sometimes bring a few friends from school back to the flat on Roundshaw during my first year at school. One day we tried smoking around the toilet and forgot to flush the cigarette away. When Mum got in, she asked me about it, and I denied all involvement. She smoked so didn't make much of it, and probably because it wasn't a big deal, I didn't try it again.

Then there was the incident of me shooting the woman in the back with an air pistol whilst a friend from school begged me not to. This was about the same time GLC Councillor Phil Bassett got to abuse me. All be it mildly compared to what many others go through.

Bassett died on 2nd August 2005. He may have done lots of good in the world but I wonder how many other kids suffered at his hands. What he did to me was relatively minor, but I still visualise the look on the child's face I saw him with once in Sutton Library in my late teens. The kid was probably no more than seven, he had a very pale complexion and looked scared and lost. When his eyes caught mine, I wondered if he recognised some understanding in mine.

1976 - Watch it

The winter of 1976 was a dark time for me. The nights were drawing in, and instead of going home to do my homework, I would jump on a 233 bus to West Croydon, then head for the "luxurious" watch department in Alders of Croydon where I'd salivate over digital watches. Eventually, I saved enough money to buy an LED one with a dark red face which would illuminate with numbers at the touch of a button. With the touch of another one, it would tell me the date. In those days this was a cool item to have and instead of being any good at my schoolwork, I thought being the first kid in the class to have a digital watch would make up for any academic failings. Twenty-five years after getting it, seeing retro watches such as this came back into fashion, I got a new battery for my one and started wearing it again. For a couple of minutes, I felt a bit hip, but then a few days later it disappeared. I didn't know whether I'd lost it or it had been stolen, but even now, I can visualise it clearly, and somewhere amongst the piles of sentimental rubbish I hoard is its turquoise velvet box, separated from its lost soul contents forever.

1976 - A Visit from the Reverend

One day Mr Jefferson, our Religious Education teacher and Reverend for the school turned up at my home. I invited him in, even though I had no idea why he'd called around. He asked me how I was and how I was finding school then told me why he was there.

"The reason I've come here is we've been discussing your application to go on the school trip to Germany and we feel it would be very impractical to have you on it because, when it came to going to the toilet or needing help doing other things, who would be responsible for helping you? It seems unfair to expect that of any of the other students or teachers for that matter to fulfil that role. Anyway, I do hope you understand and can accept this large bar of chocolate as a gesture of apology."

He pulled out the chocolate which did seem to make a bit of an impact, also he was charm personified and on top of that, Mum had been telling me that she couldn't afford it anyway. So, I accepted it graciously.

It wasn't till about ten years later that I saw it from a more political perspective. It was true I may have had more needs than others, but a better approach may have been to solve those issues without burdening people and excluding me.

On the one hand, I had Phil Bassett using me to get press coverage to help raise his political profile, and on the other, my teachers' side-stepping issues that affected my inclusion in extracurricular activities. Just to let you know, I didn't let the latter go on, but more about that later.

In my mid 20's I wrote a song called *Grateful*. Here are some of the words from it, well, the ones that relate to this point in my life:

Grateful - Written 28th October 1990

When I was a child in need of material things
The local politician would his cameraman bring
Him and the local charity would help me
Help them get some free publicity
And I was told that it was no one's fault
And I was told to be grateful
For anything they bought
But I've never seen the working class
Licking out the rich kid's ass

Or brushing the dust off the politician's coat
For getting them their rightful vote

So I don't think that I should be grateful
For the way you make me feel disabled
No, I don't think that I should be grateful
For the way, you add "dis" to able

'Cause when it comes to understanding
Here's the point of the story!
It takes more than a charity run
When it comes to change
It takes more than a program packed with fun
When it comes to brotherly love
It takes more than a sentimental song
More than a million pounds
That the last event wrung

You see, Mr Bassett didn't feel for me, nor was he interested in getting to understand what my needs might be. One day when he decided my writing might not be very legible, he saw an opportunity to not only help me but help himself get some publicity out of the situation. I wasn't aware of the negative impacts of this then, but I certainly didn't feel comfortable about it. As I got into my 20s, I was able to put the pieces together and this is what I came up with.

By using me to raise money for something that I might need, I was put into a category not far off from begging. Consequently, my rights as a member of society were affected because I became a second-class citizen whose fate lay in the hands of my peers and their feelings of sorrow for me. Years later this would be given a good strapline within the disability political community, 'Rights Not Charity'.

At first, this might seem unrealistic to some, but the more I thought about it, the more it made sense. What are our basic rights within an inclusive society, and why is it better to be inclusive? There are many things people are asked to raise money for that should be paid for by taxpayers, and obviously, there are many things that shouldn't. In the US, health care is not seen as a right, while in the UK and much of Europe it is. Even so, sometimes though, some people's lives are left to hang in the balance of others who dress up as rabbits and run many miles to raise money for some specialised life-saving piece of equipment. The issue of rights is a complicated matter, but often the consensus that surrounds their acceptance comes from a place of compassion as much as it does political pragmatism. During the early 1900s, the West looked at the revolutions occurring around the world and thought it best to head them off in their own lands by legislating for more rights and care for the wider community before they took it forcefully.

1976 - Dislocated

Whether I consciously recognised this or not I started to become displaced in certain aspects of my life. Displaced from my peers on Roundshaw, not really included in Wilson's, and publicly advertised as being a second-class citizen within the local media and wider community. Unable to perform well academically at that point, I think I felt I had to get my feelings of significance from appearing clever to one set of people, tough to another, and as normal as possible whenever I could.

So, Mr Bassett got his free publicity, I got a typewriter which I never used, and a load of people got to feel good out of it. I'm not criticising them because they were acting out of the kindness of their hearts, but the politicians and businesses who use people to get cheap publicity, I don't have much time for them. As Ophelia said in Shakespeare's Hamlet:

"Take these again; for to the noble mind.

Rich gifts wax poor when givers prove unkind."

Part 2 - Angela

March 2014

I find my way to St George's Hospital. From my car I see Stephen standing near a window a couple of floors up. It's night, and his silhouette is surrounded by an orange wall behind him. He's on the phone to me, guiding me in. He comes down to greet me and then shows me to the ward where Mum is lying, her head slumped to one side. We both call out to her, but there's no response.

18th March 2014

Mum is asleep still and her breathing is laboured. The doctor wants to talk with us outside of the room in case she can hear us.

"It seems your mother has suffered an amount of hypoxia."

"What's that?" I ask.

"It's a lack of oxygen that affects the brain. She's certainly got some damage to the brain, but we can't tell until we do some scans and even with them, we won't be able to tell the full extent of the damage until she wakes up. I have done some tests on her and they indicate that the level of damage is severe, it's not the worst but it's still bad. I want to show you something, come with me."

We follow him back to the room where he digs his knuckle into the centre of Mum's sternum, as he does this, she brings her arms up, back of wrists first, to where he's pushing.

He stops and says, "That response indicates more of the brain is working than if her arms had straightened and she had arched her back."

Steve asks, "So is there any hope of recovery doctor?"

The doctor pauses a second, his eyebrows raise and his lips purse, "We really can't tell at this point. Let's do the scans and see how things go over the next few days."

Afterwards, we sit in the room talking as if she is asleep. Stephen says, "Mum, wake up, it's Stephen, I've come all the way over from Australia. Mum? Mum!"

But she doesn't respond.

In intensive care, each patient has a dedicated nurse to themselves 24 hours a day. Steve and I sleep on the floor through the night and start to take turns to be there. I do the night shifts. It all feels a bit surreal driving back to Mum's house to sleep in the morning, then back in the evening, with some food to snack on through the night.

1976 - The Writing's on the Wall

The night before we moved from Roundshaw to the new flat I wrote a message on the wall next to my bed to the new occupants. When I got to the new flat after school mum was really angry because she felt very let down when her sister had seen the writing. I guess that's when I learned that people tend not to appreciate seeing the writing on the wall after all. I never really got into graffiti, maybe it was a result of Mum's reaction to this little foray into it.

1976 - The New Flat

The new flat was on the second floor of a block on the main road. Once entered it had an L-shaped hallway. On the left was a bathroom, then on the longer bit of the L shape were entrances to two bedrooms on the left, opposite which was the kitchen and at the end was a large lounge. This was our new stage set for the next few years.

March 2014

After a few days of doing shifts in Mum's hospital room, I decided to go back to Eastbourne to get back some semblance of reality. Typically, the doctor called us in for a meeting to go over Mum's condition. I rushed back up but managed to get caught in traffic so came in at the end of the meeting. Stephen was very upset, as too was the doctor, which was a bit strange. I could pretty much tell what had been said, however, the doctor kindly went over it again for me.

The upshot was that most of Mum's higher brain areas had died and swollen, all that was left was the part that kept her alive, the stem. He then showed me the brain scans along with a diagram that showed what was still functioning. He added that the scans are not very precise so more of the brain may be functioning than might appear in the scans. However, we should prepare ourselves for the worst.

"What happens next?" I ask.

"Well, we'll take off some of the support systems and see what happens."

I look at him and ask, "How long do you think she'll have?"

"It's difficult to say, a few days, maybe a week, ultimately one has to hope that she'll get a respiratory infection such as pneumonia and gently, painlessly slip away. They used to call pneumonia the old man's friend."

I'm curious about her state of mind, "Do you think she has any consciousness?"

The doctor pauses, then says, "Yes, and no, not as she did before, but something, pre-words, probably no memories, no ability to make sense of her surroundings. More of a reactional state living in the moment, but not in any way that we would."

I interject, "A kind of primaeval consciousness?"

"Maybe, it's hard to know."

Steve joins in, "Will she stay in the intensive care ward?"

"For a day or so, then we'll move her to another one where she'll be kept as comfortable as we possibly can."

So, Steve and I continued our shifts. I would look into her eyes when she woke up, but even though there was a feeling that her eyes would lock on to mine if I moved my head off centre her eyes didn't follow. It was still Mum but she had changed. She would make noises in her sleep with her voice, but they weren't words, more like burps and groans and when the nurses cleared the back of her throat with a tube, she would clench her teeth and move her head away. I think we all felt that whatever was left of her could still suffer, so, we wanted her last days to be as pain-free as possible. As it turned out though, these weren't quite her last days.

March 2014 - One Side

One of Mum's friends was very involved during this time, but when I went to hug her goodbye, she didn't want to. I think I know why. At times in the past when Mum and I had fallen out as adults, Mum had confided in this friend and now she was judging me. But that was only one side of the story.

March 2014 - The Walking Dead

One night I was sitting next to Mum in the hospital and watching "The Walking Dead" on my iPad when I realised the sounds coming from Mum were a bit like the zombies in the program. I half expected to wake up to Mum biting me.

October 1976 - Cross Country

Our first sports field session at school was to send us out on a cross-country run. I think I got about half a mile when a fat kid, with a purple face, told me he was having an asthma attack. By this point, I too was having an asthma attack, and I don't even have asthma. It was then that I realised my running career was over, so I limped back to the school with him.

To some, it may have appeared our speedy return was due to us being exceptionally fast cross-country runners, so no wonder we looked so out of breath. However, given our teachers didn't ask either of us to join the cross-country team I think they had a handle on the reality of the situation.

November 1976

"I want a word with you," Mum says to me.

"What have I done!!!"

"What haven't you done, more like it."

"What do you mean?" (I've always hated the way some people like to keep the suspense up when it comes to persecution.)

"You know!"

My eyes look to the left and I shake my head pleading ignorance.

"How about homework, schoolwork, behaving well, not being disruptive, not showing off? I've just been to see your teachers and not one of them had a good thing to say about you. I couldn't be more ashamed."

My conscious mind probably thought, "So what", but deep down I didn't want to be a failure.

March 2014

Once we thought that Mum would only last a few days, we kept a 24-hour vigil and for a week life was put on hold. Steve only had a month till he'd have to return to Australia and during this time we had to start sorting things out, such as Mum's house. This may have appeared as a bit too pre-emptive, but we had to be practical.

As we spoke to the neighbours, we got an idea of what had happened from those who were there when she collapsed, and as we pieced this together, I found myself wondering more and more about the last moments of her previous self.

She knew something was wrong, and probably felt a bit scared, she could feel a pain in her neck and she felt herself getting dizzy, enough to tell her friend that she was "going to…" I presume she was going to say the word, "faint" and at that point lost consciousness. Between then and her brain not getting enough oxygen to survive, a window of anywhere between five and forty-five minutes passed. During that time, she may have experienced a few moments of consciousness. At one point she seemed to sigh; was this just air being expelled or was it her reacting to the situation? Did she go through a near-death experience which may be a byproduct of a lack of oxygen? Did she have an out-of-body experience? Did she feel herself being brought back and want to go back to the feeling of being absorbed into the light of love? Did she become aware of something going on but was trapped in a state of paralysis? Or maybe she didn't experience anything from the moment she collapsed until she became pretty much brain-dead. These thoughts haunted me, but why, what good does it do to go over possibilities that are never likely to be confirmed one way or another?

We focus so much on people's last thoughts, yet, given we may not have any more consciousness beyond them, how important are they? We hate to think of our loved ones suffering or feeling fear. Yet in life, they may well have felt similar feelings many times. It's the realisation that this is it, that's partly what haunts us because that same thought fills most of us with fear too.

Some people say they experienced an out-of-body existence as they nearly died. Is that real? Some people believe it is. Was Mum outside of her body when we were waiting for her to die? If there is a soul, does it take its memories with it? If not, did Mum become more of her essential self when only her brain stem survived?

Sitting in the hospital watching her exist as the same person but someone else I couldn't help but question what we are.

A week passed and I decided to go back to Eastbourne for a few days. Sure enough, the next day I got a call to say Mum might pass away in the next few hours. I rushed up the motorway and got there in record time, only to find that her breathing had calmed down and she'd stabilised.

A few days later her skin suddenly looked young, there were no wrinkles on her face. I had read that sometimes just before people die they tend to get a new lease of life, so I couldn't help but think she was just days away from dying, but a few days passed, and she kept chugging along. That heart of hers, the one that stopped a few weeks before, beat on strongly. That body that had knocked on death's door, kept going. No infections took hold, she just plodded on.

We started to think she might have to go into a long-term care home and enquired about stopping her feeding, but the hospital didn't want to do that. We all agreed that Mum wouldn't want to carry on living as she was, but there was nothing we could do but wait.

Steve and I cleared out the house, well actually Steve cleared most of it, I just ferried some of it for storage at my place and slowly we realised we were wishing that she would pass away soon.

I went back home for a few days and that night at about 4 a.m. the phone rang. I knew straight away it would be the hospital telling me that Mum's condition had deteriorated, and it was. I called Steve because he was nearer. He got up and started driving at top speed to the hospital. Typically, the police stopped him, so he told them what was going on. They then let him go on his way but followed him to the hospital to check he was telling the truth.

When he got there the nurse nodded at him slightly and said Mum had already passed away. We wondered whether Mum had passed away before they made the call because her hair was brushed, and Steve had only taken 20 minutes to get there.

We hadn't wanted Mum to die alone, but for me, she died when she collapsed in the Spiritualist Church, and at that point, she wasn't alone, in fact being where she was couldn't have been more apt in some ways.

Here it was, the moment had come, and Mum was no longer alive. She was 74, the same age as her mother when she died, the same age as John when he passed away, and the same age as Mr Bassett when he croaked. She died on April Fools' Day, like some dark joke, and later when I went through her things it was the same date her driving licence expired. All these things connected in my mind, they meant nothing, but I couldn't help but connect the dots.

April 2014 - Practicalities

That bit after someone dies, when you're dealing with officialdom and getting everything ready, it kind of acts as a buffer. We all thought it was funny that both the solicitors and the funeral directors were called "A Smith" which was Mum's name too. We prepared the funeral booklet, including a picture of Mum looking like a sexy film star when she was in her 20s. Then on the day of the funeral, I found myself sitting in the back of a limousine making small talk with her sister and Stephen. As the journey progressed, I watched the hooves of the horses drawing the carriage carrying Mum's body, glistening in the sunlight, and thought "Mum would have liked this." I felt tearful for a moment, but a funeral isn't the best place to grieve. It's like a show, and for this one, there was a large audience. As we approached the crematorium, a crowd had gathered outside, so, getting out of the car in floods of tears wasn't going to happen even if I had wanted to cry.

It's all very choreographed, these crematoriums work to a strict timetable, so in we went, dead on time. The place filled up so much that many people had to stand. The music we chose played without jumping (I had dreaded the CDs would have errors on them); after a long intro to Ave Maria, I looked around to check if the singer we'd booked was there, and just at the moment when I thought she wasn't, she started to sing.

When we all sang *Morning has Broken*, there was a hiccup when a verse unexpectedly repeated and nobody but me sang along, but otherwise, it all went to plan. Still, the whole event felt like a performance, constantly on show, from throwing the earth in the grave without falling in, to the greeting, meeting, and eating, it's not a time for grieving or for saying goodbye even. That all takes place for a long time after.

We had gone to see Mum's body in the funeral home a few times before the funeral, but something had occurred in the embalming process that caused Mum's neck to expand, and it didn't look like her. We also peeped through the curtains at the body next door, where an Indian man was laid out. I couldn't help but wonder if Mum was chatting to him and inviting him to her funeral.

Steve and I both wrote eulogies which were read at the funeral by Mum's brother-in-law, Edward, who's a priest, as well as her cousin Michael, who's also a vicar. I'll include copies of these at the end of the chapter.

I wondered if Mum would have preferred a spiritualist service, and there were some people I tried to get to come who couldn't make it, but overall, it was a fitting send-off. But who is a funeral for anyway?

Dream 1

Mum is in front of me, part of her face has decomposed. I tell her she is going to die and she tells me she doesn't want to.

Dream 2

I start crying because Mum has died and I feel like I will never stop. I wake up in real life and touch my eyes to see if there are any tears, but my eyes are dry.

1969 - Gran's House

I get into bed, the sheets are cold, but I quite like that. The room is dark but the door is open slightly. Mum pops her head around the door and says, "Good night, I love you."

Eulogies:

Simon's Words for Mum

Every goodbye echoes every goodbye. At first, when we say goodbye to those we love, we may be filled with sorrow and fear, but as we get older, we learn through experience that as painful as a goodbye can feel, somewhere behind it remains the gift of knowing.

From the beginning of our relationship, there were constant moments of separation. My mother would kiss me and go through a goodnight routine when I was a child. She would let me do a roly-poly on the bed, do some butterfly kisses on my face, Eskimo kisses on my nose, then switch off the light, and pull the door to. I would call out, "Don't turn the hall light off mummy", and she would say, "I won't darling, now go to sleep". Between the thousands of hellos and goodbyes, I came to know my mother and carry her in my mind and heart.

As Steve and I saw our mum for the last time ever, the final moments of experiencing her in this world were brought to a close through that process. But the shadows of those who have departed illuminate our inner world. Mum has passed away, but she is alive still in all of us who knew her. Very alive, not just in our imagination and dreams but in our actions too.

I first met Mum when she was 25, I don't remember much of those first few years, but I recall her clearly when she was about 28 to 29. She had an extremely pretty face, was proud of her looks and even at 74, her skin wasn't that of an elderly lady. She had a youthful quality about her, both in her appearance and her demeanour. In many ways, she was quite child-like and sometimes a bit naïve, and consequently she'd often ended up on the wrong end of advantage takers. Because of this we'd admonish her, and she would laugh sheepishly but at the same time, it was possible to see the disappointment, not just in herself but in humanity too.

There are as many Angelas, as the people who interacted with her, and then all the ones she knew in herself. To most of us though Mum had some constant traits. Her compassion, sensitivity, affection, love of animals, a desire to explore life and her artistic abilities, gregariousness, to love and be loved, and at times her ability to carry on in the face of great difficulty.

When she became pregnant with me, she didn't give me away as so many did in those days. Instead, she put up with the stigma of not only having a child out of wedlock but also a disabled child who, on top of all this, looked a bit foreign. Her compassion and love for me saved me from God knows what. She instinctively, or through empathy, connected with me and understood that it was not okay to abandon me just to keep up appearances. To her, other things were more important, namely the feelings of those she cared about, to be kind not only to her kin, her kind but also to humankind.

My version of Mum as a mother was very different to Stephen's, I have often felt like a witness to Mum's life. She was much younger when we met, and we existed in a different world then. The mum I got to know suffered at times, struggled and survived through some difficult moments. But she had many friends too and our life was often a very sociable one. Many of those people we interacted with are here today and will remember those times well. They too will know that Mum was a bit of a paradox, as most of us are. She was meek, and sometimes a bit too scared of confrontation, but she would fight for what she believed in, and though she often appeared as if she might not cope, she did. To be a single mum must have been very hard at times and while she yearned for love she still put me first and was lonely at times because of that.

When she met John and they married, her life entered a new phase, and she experienced a different and more stable world for a long time. Most of it was good but John's illness presented another period of difficulty. To watch one's partner fade away must be one of life's more painful challenges.

Recently though, the next part of her life seemed to be taking shape. She was planning on moving to Eastbourne where I thought she would have at least another ten years or more. So, while her collapse hopefully saved her from any long-term suffering or having to come to terms with a terminal condition, I still felt very sad for her.

Many of us here today carry with us memories of my mum that can't be summed up in a few sentences. But we can say her life was an interesting one, her personality was intricate, and while only God can know what the long-term effects of her presence in this world will be, we can say that she lived, she loved, she touched many of us, she felt deeply and laughed frequently, and all of us will carry a part of her with us way into the future. So, when we say goodbye today, it may be with tears, but it will also be with smiles and happy memories. And finally, for all that she did for me, I want to say, "Thank you and I love you."

The word Goodbye derives from the phrase God Be with you.

Goodbye Mum, goodbye, Angela.

Stephen's Eulogy

Mum Funeral Reading 15th April 2014 – By Stephen Hill (Son)

My mum was an amazing and generous lady. She did not have a bad bone in her body, always telling funny stories and forever laughing. She brought me up to be the person I am today, she taught me to always be polite, friendly, grateful, hard-working and, most importantly, how to waste lots of money on stuff I don't really need and then store it away for the next ten years. I wasn't sure who was worst between us, but after sorting through my mum's worldly possessions last week I think my Mum definitely won 1st prize. Well done Mum!

She was not just a great mum to both Simon and myself, she was also a loving mother-in-law, daughter, daughter-in-law, sister, sister-in-law, grandma, aunt, cousin, niece and of course a loving and devoted wife to my late dad John Anthony Hill, who sadly passed away last year. I think everyone who is here today will also agree that she was a great friend who would put herself out for anyone. Plus she was also good for a cheap haircut here and there.

We have been overwhelmed by the cards and phone calls that have been received since my mother was admitted to hospital four weeks ago. She undoubtedly has some wonderful friends and family who will miss her dearly.

It was just over one month ago when I last spoke to my mother on a video call, she spoke about how excited she was about her move to Eastbourne and how she was planning a few trips abroad in the next 12 months which included another trip to see myself and my wife Sarah in Melbourne. She had so much to look forward to, but tragically it was not meant to be.

I have so many fond memories of my mum, but my most recent happy memories are from her trip to Melbourne in December. I am so thankful Sarah and I got to spend one last Christmas with Mum, she had a great time. I even cooked the turkey on Christmas Day, which Mum was pleasantly surprised to see, as she'd never seen me cook before. She really let her hair down, we even got her singing karaoke in our living room on Christmas Day, she definitely would have given Robbie Williams a run for his money with her cover of Angels.

The highlight of her trip to Australia was spending the New Year on a boat cruising around the Great Barrier Reef where she got to see dolphins and whales. By the end of the trip, she had made friends with pretty much all 100 passengers, including the captain. We all know how my mum liked to talk to anyone and everyone, a quality that made my mum the wonderful person she was.

Although the last four weeks have been the most upsetting time of my life, I am still very thankful that my mother did not have to go through a long, painful illness, and it gives me great comfort knowing her last memories were happy ones. I will truly miss my mum more than words can describe and will always keep her close to my heart till the day we meet again.

May my dear Mum and Dad both rest in peace together.

———

Chapter 21
The Near Love Experience

Sonnet 129:
Th'expense of spirit in a waste of shame
BY WILLIAM SHAKESPEARE

Th' expense of spirit in a waste of shame
Is lust in action; and till action, lust
Is perjured, murd'rous, bloody, full of blame,
Savage, extreme, rude, cruel, not to trust,
Enjoyed no sooner but despisèd straight,
Past reason hunted; and, no sooner had
Past reason hated as a swallowed bait
On purpose laid to make the taker mad;
Mad in pursuit and in possession so,
Had, having, and in quest to have, extreme;
A bliss in proof and proved, a very woe;
Before, a joy proposed; behind, a dream.
All this the world well knows; yet none knows well
To shun the heaven that leads men to this hell.

When Shakespeare, or whoever it was who wrote this, they were looking at lust from multiple perspectives. Namely, before, during and after experiencing it. Now I am doing the same, only from a far more distant vantage point.

My journey with lust became more intense as I hit ten years old. From then on though, it became a major influence in my life, permeating much of what I did and it's only recently, in my fifties that it's begun to subside.

There's a line from one of my songs that goes, "If falling in love is a trick of the mind then why am I not laughing this time?" It's not as eloquent as Shakespeare but does illustrate how much my lustful actions tended not to result in the best of outcomes.

Still, Shakespeare did try to warn us about lust when he wrote in Sonnet 147:

> *My love is as a fever, longing still,*
> *For that which longer nurseth the disease*

To me, falling in love is just as tied up with our psychological issues, as it is our biological instincts and the net result of this being a melange of madness. Near the end of this volume, I'll be discussing love in far more detail, especially regarding how ancient societies saw Eros-type love, as something to be avoided given it would almost certainly result in pain. Hence Eros's arrows.

As a joke, I sometimes compare how we feel when someone who's acting strangely sits next to us on a bus, to being near someone who's in love. In both situations, it's not uncommon to get an overwhelming urge to move away.

Of course, if someone is in love with us and we don't feel the same, we can't help but want to get away from them. After all, we know they are a bit unstable, because let's face it, we know from our own experience of being in love that we were a bit mad then too. If we are in love with them too, then that's a whole different matter. In that case we no doubt feel both they and us are sane, although deep down we know we aren't. If we find ourselves in that situation then all we need do is brace ourselves and enjoy the madness till the insanity wears off.

There is a difference between loving someone and being in love with them; again, we'll look at that in more detail later, however, maybe we should be clearer about the words we use from the off. I guess though, we don't have a word that means "I love you in an insane way", for good reason, as it wouldn't go down well. Likewise, we don't write infatuation letters in which the words, "I'm so infatuated with you" are the main highlight. Instead, we use other, more acceptable labels, such as 'love letters', and being 'in love' and glibly tell people we love them with all our heart when we know it's not truthful in the slightest. Still, it gets the insanity juices going.

Anyway, from ten years old my sexual urges grew stronger and my ability to be insane when it came to love and lust increased dramatically.

Motivation

It's been a few years since I wrote the last chapter. The reason I started writing this book wasn't to leave my mark, to help others or because I have something special to offer. It was simpler than that. I was facing emptiness and it was a way to fill the void during that difficult time when Monica was leaving me. At the time I felt as if I was enveloped in a whole world of madness which I could barely cope with. That was 13 years ago, and now this project has gained a life of its own. As with many things in life, the reasons we start things are different to those which motivate us later.

23rd May 2017

I am not unconscious but all I can sense is darkness, and I am deep within it. It's all around me and it feels like death. I can see intermittent flashes of purple light and hear my name being called. Then I am in darkness again. That beautiful purple light is almost blinding and then it is gone.

Once again, I hear the voice that called my name. It's the anaesthetist who'd spoken to me earlier.

"We had to do the big cut. You asked me to tell you if we did, so I am just letting you know."

To me it was as if he was telling me it was Wednesday, it held little significance, and I couldn't feel anything. So, I nodded affirmatively. There were a few more moments after that, being wheeled on a trolley down a corridor and then dreamless sleep.

When I next regained consciousness, I was in intensive care. I wasn't very aware of myself and couldn't feel much, but as I started to see, I took in the scene. I was in a hospital bed at the end of a long desk-like nurses' workstation. It was daylight, noisy, and there was lots of activity.

A young Filipino man with spiky black hair and thick-rimmed glasses says, "Hi Simon, I'm Leo, I'm your nurse. You're in intensive care. We're keeping an eye on you, as your heart is a bit fast and we want to help you heal after your appendectomy. We also want to keep an eye on you in case the infection comes back. If you need anything, just call me, I will be close by".

I nod at him and ask, "Am I likely to have a heart attack?"

"Oh no, it's just when it's this fast we need to observe you. That way, if anything happens, we can react quickly."

I'd like to say I felt reassured, but just being in intensive care is a sign that things are not quite right.

The day before this I had driven to the local hospital after feeling ill for three days with what I thought was a kidney stone. Eventually, it got so bad I thought it best to go to casualty. The day before that, I'd spoken to a doctor on the phone and said, "I'm in extreme pain." They responded by saying, "Well, if it gets any worse, go to casualty". I'm not sure how much worse it could have got but anyway, I delayed going to the hospital for another day longer than I should have because of that.

When I arrived at the Accident and Emergency department, I was half expecting to be sitting around for four hours waiting to be seen. However, once the nurse started assessing me, she said my heart was beating so fast I had to be put into the resuscitation section immediately.

Over the next few hours, I had an intravenous line put into my arm which hurt, just as one would expect, but then as the doctor pushed it in some more, and a little further for luck it hurt somewhat more still. And then a while later I had a CAT scan which showed I had a perforated appendix.

The doctor informed me I was going to, "need surgery at the hospital in Hastings". "Shall I drive there now then?" I asked. "You're not driving anywhere!" came the reply. So, an ambulance took me to another hospital in full-blue light emergency mode. But once we arrived, we were made to wait for over seven hours whilst space was "bulldozed" (as the doctor put it) for me to have surgery. Without which, she said, I would "die that night."

For a month or so before this happened, I'd been feeling a bit clammy, especially after eating. On top of that, there'd been a few times when I'd woken in the middle of the night out of breath with my heart racing. I knew something was up, but had I known I had an issue with my heart I wouldn't have been peddling so hard on my exercise bike most evenings. I'd also thought a few times during that period I might be facing death shortly, partly because I knew something was up, even if it didn't feel serious enough to do anything about.

I've often said I didn't fear dying, but when I found myself lying in intensive care thinking I might suddenly have a heart attack, I realised I wasn't ready to die after all and as I imagine most people do, I asked for "just a bit more time please".

There were things I wanted to do before I died. Essays to write, music albums to produce, this book to publish, artworks to put out there, and of course, I didn't want to leave those I love and who love me. Thinking of them grieving made me even more upset. (OK, that might have been a little presumptuous of me.) Even leaving this autobiography in the air seemed like a betrayal to those who have spent the time and effort reading it over the years. And so, I bargained, just as most people do when facing death, "If you let me have some more time, I will focus on getting these things done."

For now, I have given myself five years to finish a set of projects, getting this finished to an extent, was part of the deal. I may think agnostic, but I feel spiritual; I expect lots of people do so too, especially when they think they might be close to death.

2022

Five years have passed and I'm still at least a year away from getting this book out. I've released a couple of albums but there are at least three waiting in the wings, and I have so many other projects I'd like to finish too. But if there's one thing facing death taught me, it's how unimportant a lot of things that seemed important previously really are. But more about that later.

1976 - Wallington, Surrey

In the last chapter I briefly described the new place Mum and I moved into after living on Roundshaw, but I don't think I mentioned it didn't feel like home, in fact, it would be a long time before I found a place I'd call home. The place on Roundshaw didn't feel safe, Gran's place had felt like home, but I wasn't allowed to be there continuously, and this place, Sycamore Manor, felt temporary.

I had already been delinquent for some time before moving off Roundshaw, and Mum probably hoped this would be a good move in terms of me being less so. However, during the next few years, I was to head even further downhill. Just before we moved from Roundshaw to Sycamore Manor something happened. What is strange though, is I don't remember it properly. I know it did though, because about a year ago I found some people on Facebook who I'd known on

Roundshaw then, a family who lived near me, so I sent them friend requests. The mother accepted my friend request and sent me a message asking how my mother and I were. The next day I went to reply but I couldn't send the message. She'd blocked me and her daughters had stopped me from sending them friend requests too. It was clear I'd done something to upset them, so I thought back and remembered the mother calling down to me as I was playing, and when I looked up at her she said I had an expression that looked guilty. She then laughed and said I wasn't in trouble. Even so, I recall doing something wrong, and it involved one of her daughters who was about a year younger than me. I am pretty sure it involved me asking her to take her clothes off, but I am certain it didn't involve penetration because I would have remembered that. But, if something else happened, I don't have any conscious memories of doing it. It could have been just getting her to undress was the actual misdeed, but I know she cried and that made me stop whatever it was I was doing.

I decided to write to her mother from another Facebook account to say that if I'd done something wrong then I would be more than willing to discuss it with them. After all, given their reaction I was worried I had traumatised her daughter and wanted to say sorry. Plus, I wanted to know what her daughter's memory of it was. I also didn't want a posse turning up to string me up for something I had done at age 11, about 42 years ago, which I could not even remember.

Although I didn't have intercourse till I was 19, there was a moment at around 11 or 12 with a girl of my age, who I used to play around with, and by that, I mean I used to put my tongue inside her, which she liked. I had seen it done in a porn magazine story, so, I thought it would be a good thing to do. Sadly, it didn't show me what a clitoris was so I imagine it must have been quite frustrating for her. On this occasion, she and I got into a position where my penis was pushing against her vagina but as I pushed, it hurt me. I didn't realise till years later that I would have to have some surgery if sex was not going to hurt as the skin that attaches the foreskin to the penis was almost tearing. Even though penetration didn't take place I felt an overwhelming feeling, one I hadn't felt before, and without knowing what was going on I ejaculated over her stomach and groin. She was angry about the mess I'd made over her and from then on, besides a few more sessions of me kissing her between her legs, or rubbing my penis on her thigh, our sexploits came to an end.

***

2018 - Memory

I am currently on beta blockers and blood thinners. I'm not sure if they have a side effect on memory but for the last year, I've struggled to remember words. Also, sometimes people recall incidents that involved me too, but I have no memory of them. Maybe it's the initial stages of dementia but it got me wondering if a person was to suddenly lose a lot of their memories would they essentially become a different person?

270

Even a word we might think of could have a different significance to us if memories relating to it disappeared. Memories may well define who we are but let's say as we die we let go of all our memories and just the essence of who we are moves on into the hereafter, would our essence have changed because of the experiences we had, or would we be the same as we were when we first existed?

It is quite difficult for most of us to accept our memories will almost certainly disappear when we die, yet, if we think about it, we've forgotten most of our life already and what we don't remember we don't miss. So, maybe, it's the thought of losing memories before they go that feels so devastating.

2017 - Dying to Know

As I lay in intensive care, I felt I may suddenly pass away at any moment, especially given my heart was constantly beating at around 156 bpm. I have spent quite a bit of my life thinking about the moment of dying. Maybe it's a way of subconsciously dealing with it because there'll be no time to do so afterwards. But the problem with this attempt to pre-empt what might happen means having to deal with an almost infinite range of possibilities.

The most likely experience of death most of us will have is a non-experience. The majority of people pass away in an unconscious state and even getting to that state is often via a process where there won't be a moment of, "This is it, here I come". Conversely, a lot of people who survive close calls often say they thought they were about to die, and obviously, lots of us will be conscious when we take our last breath. I kind of hope my dying thoughts will be along the lines of, "Thank you for letting me exist, what a miraculous opportunity it was." But I get the feeling it'll be more like, "Fuck!"

It's only natural to worry about suffering, pain, and panic and to believe that what will kill us will be more painful than the pain we may have already felt in our lives. However, in a way, it's being alive that scares us, not death. There are plenty of ways to die that are painless, people who nearly died from breathing in only nitrogen say they didn't even notice losing consciousness, and of course a lot of the time when we're first injured, we don't feel the pain. However, for all this reassurance, dying, and the process of dying, take up a lot of mental space for many of us, especially as we get older.

When I was young, I was preoccupied with sex, and when I became much older, I started to spend a lot of time thinking about dying. There's a connection, of course, procreation is nature's way of dealing with death too, and meditating on death is a way of coming to terms with it. Death, in many ways, is at the heart of most of our endeavours.

During my hospital stay, I ended up watching loads of films and TV programmes on my iPad. One program I watched a lot was the new version of "Cosmos", a series about Science, Space, and the Universe. A message it kept on about related to humans possibly, in time, moving out to other planets. It kind of struck a chord with me, that whilst religious beliefs are a matter of faith, the idea that humans may go on for thousands, if not tens, or even hundreds of thousands of years, searching for truth was a highly possible and meaningful aspiration. I mean, just mucking up one planet is a bit of a limited ambition when it comes to the human race.

I was also struck by the kindness, not only of the staff in the hospital but friends and family. Even my dentist came to help me with a problem with my tooth, and can you believe it, for free! So, to brush up against this world of kindness, a world that permeates many walks of life, drove its importance deep inside me and became a world I wanted to be a part of.

Anyone who knows me will tell you I'm hardly a part-time saint, so don't worry I'm not going to go all "goody-goody" on you, but being touched by kindness had a profound effect on me. That's not to say I haven't come across genuine kindness many times in my life before, but up till this moment, I had never been on morphine at the same time.

2016 - The Care Act

British society is, relatively speaking, quite generous to people with disabilities. Over the years though, a lot of people took advantage and claimed benefits even though they were not as disabled as they made out. People involved in the politics of this would argue that the numbers misclaiming were not significant, and they may well be right. However, even if the public perception was incorrect, the result was the government overly tightened the criteria for claiming benefits, especially around people's inability to move around.

After Mum died and her house sold, I received an inheritance. It wasn't enough to pay off my mortgage, but it helped make my home more habitable. Not only did I use it all up doing the work on the house, but I ended up in even more debt than I'd started with.

I told the authorities about the inheritance, and they wanted evidence of what it had been spent on, otherwise, I would be losing my benefits for a considerable amount of time. Given I work, my disability-related benefits are not much, but I get money for carers, and it was that which was mainly under threat. I was very worried about losing this so spent a month collating the evidence, which consisted of two large files full of spreadsheets, receipts, and explanations relating to the Care Act 2014.

When I met the officer dealing with the case, I asked them if they had read The Care Act. They told me they hadn't and with a rather perturbed look on their face went off with all 750 pages of information I provided for them to assess my case.

I'm telling you about this because there is a belief that if you look after people then they will feel an allegiance and in turn help others in society too. A bit like what I described in terms of my reaction to being cared for. But this doesn't happen as much as it should, partly because of what I call "relative poverty". For instance, a person living in the Third World might well look at a very poor person in the UK and think, "Wow, they live like royalty. They get health care, opportunities for education, money to buy clothes and food, shelter, clean water, electricity, television, fridges and so on." However, people in the UK will say, "Well, we're not that well off really, not compared to the rich people who live here." Again, that's right too but because we have a tendency to only compare ourselves to those who are better off than ourselves. The downside of this is we naturally veer towards feeling resentful because we see ourselves as being "relatively poor". Even a millionaire may feel resentful when faced with a billionaire's fortune. Not everyone feels this way, of course. Many people are thankful for what they have. But if you were to set a bar that represented a level of comfort, some people would be happy with that while some would still feel resentful. So, it's not just about being touched with kindness, it's also the personality of the subject and their reaction to others' good fortune that will determine if they'll appreciate their lot.

Thesis

I did my thesis for my degree on "Beauty and Evil", and what stuck in my mind after writing it was how, when St Augustine was watching babies suckle, he believed he could see that even at that early an age, some babies were greedier than others. If parts of our personality are already positioned before our first few weeks of life, then it's probably always going to be an issue that some will appreciate what they have and some will not, no matter what they do or don't have.

There's a reason I'm pointing this out: it's because I believe that when you're dealing with humans you should never forget that some of them are very fucked up and will not hesitate to treat others awfully. So, if you want to argue against any political system, just add real humans to the mix and watch it disintegrate. Greedy bankers, corrupt politicians, big companies that don't care about anything but making money, and people claiming money when they shouldn't, all come to mind. I think you get the picture.

When I got ill, it was by no means the first time I came in contact with genuine kindness, but when one is that ill, possibly facing death, then what becomes important is connection, love, and goodness. It is a way of thinking that comes from an emotional position set within an interdependent network. I had thought it before, but I hadn't felt it so intimately until then.

2016 - The Decision

A few weeks after I submitted my 750-page argument the decision came back. They accepted my points and my care package remained intact.

2018 - Ablation

A few weeks ago, I had some surgery on my heart where they performed an ablation. This involved a very small hole being made in my upper thigh/groin area, and special cables and cameras being passed through the arteries to my heart where some nerves were destroyed that had been causing arrhythmia. Afterwards, they stopped my heart and luckily, for me, started it again.

During this process, I was sedated, which means that I should have been semiconscious, but at one point I woke up, to find a load of nurses around me stopping my leg from bleeding out. I was oblivious to how serious it was and just thought, "I'm sure you'll sort it out" and went back to sleep. This would have all been fine if the nurse looking after me in the theatre hadn't asked after I woke up if I remembered what happened. I replied, "No, what happened?" He laughed and said, "It's probably better that I don't tell you".

Yet again, another moment of my life where my behaviour was memorable to others but not to me.

1977 - Shower

My mother tells me to get into the shower with her so she can help me wash. For the first time, I noticed her breasts. I'm curious about the veins that seem to map them, and about how big they are. I'm not getting aroused, but I notice them.

"Stop looking at me like that," she says sharply.

"I'm not."

That was the last shower we took together.

1977 - Comedy and Horror

When I think about this era the majority of memories I have are pretty much all delinquent ones. I shall list a few for your entertainment below but don't forget, there's a thin line between comedy and horror.

Soon after we moved from Roundshaw, I started to get into the practice of playing truant. I had an electric typewriter so, finally got around to using it to write a letter supposedly from my mother, forge her signature and get out of school for the day. In the morning, I would wait till my mum got off to work then come back home, watch TV, listen to music and have snacks till Mum returned. But one morning I saw Mum drive towards my school, so at top speed, I took all the short-cuts I knew to get there before she did but just as I arrived, she was walking out.

She looked annoyed. "Why aren't you in school?" She shouted.

"I had a puncture," I replied exasperatedly as only those caught in the act can.

I got away with it, but it scared me enough to not do it again.

After school, and during the holidays, I would get friends from Roundshaw to come over to our new place. Franny was a bit younger than me; we'd once had a few secret cuddles in the park and on one occasion she mimed the whole of, "Hopelessly Devoted to You" to me at the youth club disco. The problem was, whilst she was very pretty, the age gap between 10 and 13 proved too much, even for me. When the difference was 9 and 12, though, I thought I might get away with it. So, she'd come over sometimes and I'd want to have a kiss and cuddle with her, and that's all it ever was, much to my disappointment. The only thing was, she'd want to chat and try on my mother's jewellery, which was in the dressing table in my room. Maybe Mum was hoping I'd turn into a drag queen. It was the beginning of my learning that girls and boys are very different in many ways.

During the holidays, a couple of friends would come around to play on the telephone with me when my mum wasn't there. We'd ring people up, tell them we were a DJ on Capital Radio and they were live on air. At that point, they'd get very excited. We'd then play them a song from the record player, which was nearly always, Teddy Bear by Elvis Presley, which they'd have to guess the title of. Of course, they'd always get it right, and we'd promise to send them a Capital Radio T-Shirt, which we didn't, especially as we didn't wait around to ask them for their address.

Sometimes we'd be a bit cruel and ask people if they had a cat, and when they'd say yes, we'd ask what colour it was. When they replied, we'd say it was now very, very red, and dead. At which point they would start screaming at us. Back then, there was no caller ID, thankfully.

We would also run around the flats with air pistols firing at each other, and though we'd wear goggles to protect our eyes, we'd think it very clever to play dead when someone came in. To add realism, we found sucking on red aniseed balls allowed us to make it look as if blood was coming out our mouths. Unfortunately, one day a pregnant woman pushing a pram, came in and, unsurprisingly, was rather concerned and asked, "Are you alright?" In a much calmer manner than one would normally expect. At which point I jumped up, because even I knew this wasn't that funny after all, and said, "Yes, we're just playing". I'm sure she grumbled something at me as she parked her pram under the stairs. From then on, we thought it best to forget that prank too. Nowadays, it'd end with a police gun team getting involved but back then in the 70s, guns were rarely touted by criminals or the police.

I also saw myself as a bit of a Robin Hood. Well, the stealing from the middle classes bit at least, and decided on a couple of occasions to steal orange juice cartons from outside other people's flats and give them to my mother as a present. I really should have joined the Mafia with that kind of moral code.

For a short while, I thought it would be worth a shot at looking through people's letterboxes as I knew their bedrooms faced the front door and was hoping to see a woman naked. This came to an abrupt halt when I opened the letterbox only to see two eyes looking back at me. I shot back startled and shouted sorry. Nothing happened, the door didn't swing open, just silence. So, I backed off and decided it wasn't worth the risk. I realised later it was a reflection I'd seen, but it did the trick, and I didn't do that again.

I would still hang out my window at night, just as I had done on Roundshaw, looking out to see if any women were going to get undressed at their window. Hope obviously does spring eternal because I never saw anything except in the last weeks of living there after two years.

Then there was the woman upstairs who was married to a man who had no hands and wore artificial arms. He would often give me a bit of a look of disdain which I thought might be to do with me not covering my stumps as he had, but it was probably more likely because most days I would knock on their door to ask her to take my keys out of my trouser pocket. I would then use this act of kindness as an opportunity to look down her top as she never wore a bra. She would often take quite a while to find my keys and sometimes push herself against me. Maybe it was nothing, maybe I was just imagining it, but every day we'd do this little dance till eventually, I would get a key put on a piece of string around my neck. From then on, I would have to get her to do my shoelace up for me instead, which I couldn't ask to have done every day, so our dancing days just petered out.

1976 - Nosedive

My first two years at Wilson's continued to take a nosedive, that lack of basic skills kept tripping me up along with me trying to be tough when I wasn't. Any fight I got into around this time, I nearly always lost and with it my confidence. In every class, I mucked around, even in Art, which I had a flair for. I was more interested in seeing what would happen if I poured powder paint into a fan heater than actually painting or drawing. Although, in a way, I was ahead of my time, as no doubt a fan heater blowing paint onto a canvas would probably have got into the Tate Modern at some point pre-post-Modernism. Unfortunately, I used the teacher's back rather than a canvas to project it onto.

I was also a slow reader and still am, hence me not reading my previous chapters to check what I've already covered. Yes, there is a plan... Somewhere. So, reading books for school was a trial, even though I liked it. Nowadays I get my Amazon Alexa to read me my Kindle or Audible books when I get up in the morning, or my iPhone to read them if I'm driving far. Technically speaking, I'm no bookworm.

Evenings could be rather dull. After tea, I'd watch a bit of TV, have a bath, play around with my hairstyle in front of the mirror, occasionally write a letter and maybe listen to an album of music in my room alone. For all our attempts to fill the empty spaces, for both me and my mother there was something of an aloneness and that meant a change was coming. So, when one of Mum's friends thought it would be a good idea for Mum to go on a blind date, she did, and that's when she met John.

1977 - John

Before I bring John into the story in more detail, I'm going tell you what I thought of him. When he first appeared, I wanted him to be the father I never had, but even so, I probably set him up to fail. As time went on, we clashed a lot. But later on, once I left home, I started to feel for him. I recognised a lack of confidence in him, which I felt too, so whilst at times he was infuriating for me, (I think we all know he must have felt the same about me.) I did learn to have some empathy for him, eventually.

1977 - Blind Date

When Mum came back from the blind date, I asked her how it went.

"Well, he's not my type, he's not very tall, although he's very polite and courteous. But I'll see him again if he wants. Anyway, your mother's getting on a bit, I have to take what I can get." She laughed and so it began, they started to date and within a few months he proposed to her, and a wedding day was set.

"Oh, I can't wait till we get married," Mum said, then half laughing added, "he won't have sex till then." Mum, as you probably know by now, was not great on boundaries.

John, Mum and I did a few things together as "a family", like going to watch Star Wars at the local cinema or having a meal out. It was exciting to think I might have a new father figure but there was an unease between us from the start.

John was about 5 foot 6 inches tall, slightly built, always wore a suit, spoke with a posh accent and came over as very well-to-do. His father had been the local mayor, as well as being active in politics and business. His brother was a priest, his sister, who was very down-to-earth and friendly, had a large family, and his mother was a powerhouse. In later years, I'd come to the opinion that having such strong people so close to him would've caused a sense of self-doubt for John. It was safer to speak in terms of clichés or to repeat the lines he'd heard his family speak than to ever contradict them. So, when push came to shove, he couldn't logically argue with people. Faced with a delinquent child of 11 going on 12 he had no chance.

Things didn't go well between us when they found the first photograph they'd taken together had had the eyes pierced out with a compass needle.

"Why did you do that?" Mum said, shaking the photo at me

"I didn't!" I exclaimed as only a lying 11-year-old could.

"Of course you did," Mum shouted.

"That was our first photo together," John added with a touch of dramatic sadness. Going for the guilt card was a good strategy as I probably felt like crying when he said that.

"Why did you do it, eh, why?" Mum said, throwing the photo at me.

Had I had a few years of training in psychology, I might have been able to come up with some victim-riddled reason, but as it was, I didn't know why I'd done it at the time. There was a photo in front of me and I thought it would look better with eyes you could see light through. I didn't consciously do it as an act of violence towards them, but obviously, I didn't think it through either.

During this courting stage, I turned 12 years old, which as anyone who has 13-year-old kids will know means the intensity of irrationality goes up a notch on a dial of ten, to, well, twelve. The disagreements became more regular and the arguments all the more intense. But when John tried to put his foot down, Mum would take my side, which put a wedge between them.

To a child, there might be a sense of power that comes from that dynamic, but at the same time, possibly a measure of guilt too. Even if I thought I was doing the right thing by showing her John might not be right for her or me, deep down I must have known that I was making her unhappy, and although I may have wanted that on some subconscious level, there would have been a price to pay, and that price may have been me feeling even more isolated.

Possibly in a desperate attempt to get some time alone with John, Mum booked me on a load of holidays, including another school trip abroad. This time it was to be in Italy, and interestingly, possibly because the price of chocolate had skyrocketed, the school endeavoured to find a way for me to be included. But maybe, maybe it was because Mum, out of kind, loving feelings, wanted me to experience something she thought might stay with me all my life.

1977 - Changes

The night before the wedding John came around and they had an argument during which John looked at Mum and said, "There's going to be some changes around here after we're married".

"Well in that case maybe we shouldn't bother." She shouted back at him.

But they did, and there was.

1977 - The Wedding

Mum, who was extremely proud that I had got into Wilson's School, thought me wearing my school uniform for their wedding would be somewhat sophisticated, possibly even trend-setting. She'd bought me some new trousers but didn't get time to alter them, so, in all the wedding photographs I appear in from that day I looked like I had elephant's feet. Flares were still all the rage back then, but this was taking it literally one step further.

On the journey to the church, the chauffeur decided it was imperative he show me he had a finger missing, which, I admit, did create an immediate allegiance between us. This meant we chatted quite a bit, probably because I didn't want to be there. Not so much because it was Mum and John's wedding, but I disliked being on display. Outside of saying hello to the cousins, it was the same questions from the adult relatives as always, who probably didn't want to ask them either.

"How's school?"

"Shit" – I thought. "Good" is what came out.

"What's your favourite subject?"

"Fucking about" – okay, what I actually said was, "Art".

To which they'd say something like, "Well it's worth doing well in other subjects too, then you can become a lawyer or doctor and be very rich."

At which point I'd be tempted to reply, "Thank you for your insightful career advice but I'd rather rob a bank, it's quicker" – Okay, you're getting the hang of this now... The reality was more like, "Oh, I don't think I could be that clever."

There'd then be a pause while we all agreed that was probably very true.

"Oh, I'm sure you are," and off they'd wonder, probably thinking, "No chance".

But at least that day I had the all-unimportant job of being a page boy. This meant standing around feeling embarrassed and doing nothing useful.

After the ceremony, we went to the Cavalier Pub, which was situated next to the shopping centre car park in Wallington. The best bit of the proceedings for me was getting the barman to give me a couple of cherry brandies. Initially, he refused to serve them to me, but then I told him I was the child of the woman getting married. He obviously took pity because he gave me two double shots.

Mum and John were driven off to the cheers of the well-wishers, whilst I went to stay with Mum's sister, Yvonne, for the duration of Mum and John's honeymoon.

7th September 2018 - Tragedy

Last night I wanted to find a photo from the wedding to show you just how bad my trousers were. Once I found the wedding photos, I put a load of them on Facebook for family members to see. Quite a few of the comments on the photos were about those relatives who'd passed away, and how now, it is just us standing first in line on that conveyor belt to who knows where.

For the last few days, my heart rate has been very arrhythmic. One of the main dangers this poses is having a stroke because the top and bottom parts of the heart are likely to be beating at different speeds which means some blood might not pass through the heart and, if it pools, it may coagulate thus causing a clot. Hence, I now take blood thinners daily.

When I first got ill and thought I might die, I did think if I was to do so now, aged 53, I had had a good run and should be thankful for all I have experienced, and it would not be a tragedy compared to those who die at a young age. Somewhere between 40 and 50, there is a point where dying is less tragic. Of course, that depends on other factors, for instance, if you still have young children.

A few years ago, a friend of mine called Valerie, who's about the same age, sent me a few messages which were a bit flirtatious. My reaction was to not engage, so I didn't continue messaging her after that. About a year later I found out she'd committed suicide by breathing in exhaust fumes from her car. I have no idea why she killed herself, one can only assume that she was feeling very mentally unbalanced at that moment, especially as she left behind a ten-year-old son. But, still, I felt a twinge of responsibility. Had I made more of an effort to engage with her when she sent those photos, then maybe she'd have turned to me for support. Anyway, it hit me hard and still does, as I think it was a big loss to lose her at such an early age.

At 53 I can think of quite a few people I've met who died young, (nothing to do with me). So, whilst I don't want to pop my clogs just yet, I am still grateful for the time I've had and any time I may have left feels like extra time.

August 2018 - Spiritualist Church

My brother suggested we go to the Spiritualist church where Mum collapsed. It wasn't far from where she lived, and it was more about getting an idea of the setting where it happened than trying out a session of spiritualism. In both our minds, when we described to each other how we imagined it, we agreed we thought it would be quite church-like. Dark with wooden benches. When we got there it was a house that had had its back room and front room knocked into one and then had the front window blocked in leaving just three thin upward windows of stained glass. With its yellow walls, fluorescent light and plastic chairs it had more of a feeling of a waiting room from the 1980s, than a church.

Being new visitors, we sat at the back, but sure enough, we were the speaker's initial prime target. What she said to us didn't seem to apply though. Three of us had sat together and what we thought afterwards was that had her messages been switched around between us, then they would have been more apt. The closest match being a person who was murdered and another who committed suicide. That would have fitted with Theo, the guy I mentioned a few chapters back who killed his drug-dealing mate and then killed himself. But it's easy to find connections with hindsight, so we went away a little disappointed but glad to have got a more accurate vision of the place.

Psychic Matters - Ian Fletcher

It's very easy to dismiss psychic phenomena, likewise, it's also easy to accept them unquestioningly. A few years ago, I got in contact with one of my old medical doctors from Roehampton Hospital, his name was Ian Fletcher. When I met up with him, he was 92, so I picked him up in Trafalgar Square, just near Admiralty Arch, and from there we drove to The Chelsea Arts Club for a meal. At one point, we got on to the subject of telepathy and ESP and whilst I'm paraphrasing somewhat, this is very close to what he said to me.

"I spent many years debunking so-called psychics. I was in the magic circle for 70 years and knew many techniques that were used, but after all that time looking into this subject, I concluded that what most of us would describe as telepathy does exist. James Randi had offered a million-pound reward for hard evidence of psychic abilities, and while I realise that for now there is no consistently provable evidence, I do believe that one day we will be able to understand this phenomenon more fully."

He then told me of a few examples he'd experienced. But still, he accepted that to anyone with a scientific leaning, there is no hard evidence. Yet often in our lives, we come across situations that seem so improbable that we can't help but wonder if there are other factors at work beyond coincidence and for me, this happens a lot of the time.

I will give you a couple of examples that stick in my mind. A few weeks ago, I went to see some friends in Cornwall. At one point, we spoke about someone called Pino who lives in Italy. I haven't heard from him in years. Within an hour of that conversation, I noticed a message from him on my WhatsApp messenger saying, "I bet you don't know who this is?". Well, my app kind of gave it away because his name was on it as his number was in my phone book already. He's not on Facebook or other social networks, he just thought about contacting us at almost the same time the three of us in England were thinking about him.

In 1996 I felt very depressed and decided to try out a free psychic healing offer. During the process of the session, I was put in a darkened room whilst a woman passed her hands over me. As this went on, I went into a kind of trance-like state. The first thing that happened was I felt as if I shot up into the sky and was suddenly looking down over London. I then felt myself move to where I lived. I could see my girlfriend, Eileen, so said hello to her, then moved off again. A few other things happened after that: firstly, I went to where a house, road, and woods were, and then I had a vision, almost like a film where frames of a comic are shown in fast sequence. In this series of frames, I saw a plane crashing into a bay as the sun set.

Afterwards, I went home and the first thing Eileen said was, "Did you come back earlier and call me? I came down to see where you were, but I couldn't find you."

I spoke to her about the other bits of my trance and this could be more a case of her making tenuous connections but when I drew out the layout of the woods, the roads and the house she said it matched exactly where she had lived before she came to London, and of the comic strip imagery she said she had been to a bay where there was a monument to a pilot whose plane had crashed there. As I say, they may be coincidences, but Eileen hearing me call her, which she still remembers to this day, 28 years later, was less tenuous.

What was interesting about all this though, was later when I decided to study a bit about parapsychology, I realised there was a parallel between the process I went through and the development of the Spiritualist movement and Mesmerism. The mesmerists believed they could heal people by passing their hands over them without touching them and, by putting them into a trance, could transfer energy to them. Something akin to modern-day Reiki or Chinese medicine involving Chi and Chakras. Sometimes during this process, people would go into a trance and supernatural powers, precognitive visions and instances of telepathy seemingly occurred. It was so popular at the time that a leading medic, Professor John Elliotson, was sacked from his post at University College Hospital for daring to suggest there may be something in it. In fact, Charles Dickens, who saw himself as an authority on Mesmerism was one of Elliotson's biggest defenders. From these "supernatural" episodes the seeds of the Spiritualist movement were sown.

I'll give you one more example. I was sitting at the bar in The Chelsea Arts Club eating some supper one evening. A woman I had spoken to before came up and started talking to me, as she did, she began to tell me something about her son and I said, "You've told me this before, he fell out the window and landed in the bushes but was still seriously injured." She looked at me aghast. I thought, "Shit I've said something wrong now." As she went pale and started to shake a little, she said: "I couldn't have told you that, I haven't been here since it happened." But to me, there was a real memory of her telling me about this.

I don't conclude anything from these kinds of things, but it does make me wonder if there are other dimensions in which consciousness can exist without the mechanics of the body and mind, or at the very least some telepathic abilities might be real.

***

Many people reading this will have a complete belief that there is life after death, conversely, many others will believe that we simply switch off and are no more. I am agnostic on this subject. I accept it is entirely possible that before us was an eternity, in which we did not exist, and beyond us is another in which we won't exist either. If that is true, then given one's life is not full of suffering, then, within a caring community, one can find a piece of heaven on earth. Amos Oz wrote something along the lines of, a little evil and people are hell to each other, but with a little compassion and generosity, people may find paradise in each other. It's like the Chinese version of Heaven and Hell where both places are the same, everyone has arms that are chopsticks. In Hell, everyone starves, but in Heaven, everyone feeds each other.

I also accept that there may well be consciousness after life. Indeed, given I can barely remember a lot of my life and have complete black spots in my memory, as well as watching the memory of dreams disappear before my eyes, I can accept it's possible I existed before this life but have no memory of it. But then I would say that, given I don't have any memories of it.

Even if we say this is it, this is our one shot at existence, then, for those of us who do not live in continual pain or extreme deprivation and suffering, then for us, to have existed in this universe, on this planet and especially during such a magical time of technology, communication, and interactivity, what a gift our lives have been.

To be able to sense the world, to feel so many things, to have connected on so many levels with others. What a blessing that is. When doing the simplest of things, for instance breathing in fresh air or eating, one can take a moment to savour being alive. I am not advocating hedonism, in fact, the opposite. Service to one another, whether there is a God or not, and wanting to serve others is what it is about, but it should come from a feeling, not a thought.

***

The first day after the surgery was not so bad. I wasn't in much pain considering my stomach had been cut open from just above my groin to just under my solar plexus. A few months down the line after the swelling had died down the scar was not as long as it had first appeared. Even so, I wasn't in that great a shape, I could hardly move and felt like I had a big metal plate attached to my stomach, which was probably apt given 70 staples were holding my stomach together. I had 5 tubes coming out the right side of my neck, a drainage tube coming out a hole in my side, and a catheter attached to a bag at the end of the bed, which when moved gave me the feeling that my penis was going to be torn off at any moment.

I wasn't allowed to eat or drink or anything, so my mouth was very dry. Occasionally, the nurse, who was a very flamboyant man from the Philippines, would dab a small sponge filled with water on my lips as he danced and spun gracefully around my bed. In the evening, a few friends popped in, which at first made me feel a bit tearful as it was a reminder that in many ways, I was a long way from home and normality. Then at one point, someone on the ward started to be sick which made one of my friends turn pale and look quite ill. As they looked towards the person being sick and shook their head in disapproval I started to laugh, "Don't make me laugh, it hurts," I said. Of course, this made them laugh too and for a moment, there was normality.

After they went, it was back to the process of healing, but as the evening became night I started to vomit constantly and was unable to sleep. Not that I would have got much sleep anyway as the Intensive Care ward was constantly noisy. The next day, the doctor explained that because my intestines had slowed down so much, the liquid in my stomach, which is created as a by-product of digestion, had nowhere to go. They were scared that it might start filling up so much that it would enter my lungs which in turn would cause further complications. The solution they suggested was to put a pipe up through my nose and then down into my stomach to act as a drain. I agreed to this and soon after a nurse came over to fit it.

The initial feeling of it going up my nostril was quite uncomfortable, but as soon as it hit the back of my throat, I started to be sick and retch violently. "Just try to relax and swallow," the nurse instructed in a typical exercise class manner. Somehow it seemed to go into position. It was uncomfortable but at least we got there. The nurse looked at me, nodded her head from side to side and said, "I don't think it's in properly."

"Really?" I croaked. I wanted to ask if she had X-ray vision.

"I am sure it's not in the right position, we will have to try again."

She pulled it out, which wasn't the most joyous of experiences either.

The second attempt was far worse, I was so sick that she had no chance.

The doctor who'd done my surgery came in, gave me a verbal warning, and said they would try again tomorrow.

So, another sleepless night, full of being sick and then came the third attempt. This time a young male doctor came over with a tray of equipment including anaesthetic gel. "This should make it a lot less difficult," he said. He covered the tube in anaesthetic and started pushing it up my nose and down my throat. Again, I started retching violently and loudly, at this point a large blonde woman opened the curtains and said, "It's very important to relax and swallow", Fortunately, I was in a choking not joking mood.

"There we are, all done." the doctor said.

I tried to speak but I couldn't as my mouth was full of the pipe which had wrapped itself around into a mess in there. I looked at him and opened my mouth. He looked a bit surprised and started to pull it out again. I had had enough.

"I'm sorry doctor, but I would rather take the risk of getting sick in my lungs than continue trying this."

"Okay, we will leave it for a day and re-assess things then."

I could see in his eyes both a look of sorrow and failure.

At this point I hit a low, and in a rare move posted on Facebook that I was feeling bad and that in some ways it had been one of the worst times in my life. I think when the blonde woman stuck her oar in it took me back to being in institutions where I had no control and had felt completely at the mercy of people who didn't care, so, as a way to get some balance, I wanted to connect with people for some support.

Maybe my retching was disturbing others or maybe I was recovered enough to be taken off the Intensive Care Unit, either way, I was moved to The High Dependency Unit, which was about ten metres away and this time there was one nurse for two patients.

I didn't get to sleep till about 4 a.m. and at one point I had to ask the nurse to move one of the square syringe bins because, I said, it looked like a "Robotic Fertility Earth Mother". A bit later security had to be called when one of the patients became aggressive. He couldn't talk, I think he had something like a tracheotomy and was very emotional and restless. On top of all of this, a temporary filling was disintegrating in my mouth and felt like fine hairs touching the back of my throat.

When I finally did get to sleep between bouts of vomiting, I had a couple of dreams which seemed to signal to me that I was going to turn a corner in my recovery. They felt almost magical and even now I feel like I can't reveal them to others as it might negate their healing properties, which sounds mad, I know, but I don't even want to take the risk of betraying those dreams, even now, a year and a half afterwards.

Sure enough, the next day I stopped feeling sick and was able to start eating. After a few more days, I was put into a room of my own in another ward. I kept myself to myself, and in time yearned to go home. Throughout that week they pulled the tube out of my side and left it to heal. The catheter had failed on the High-Dependency Unit so they didn't bother replacing it, which was a relief when I saw them pull about half a metre of tube out. No, I'm not trying to make up for having a big car.

My legs had become so weak I could barely stand, so over the last few days, the physios prepared me to return home. On the final day, they took out my staples, which didn't hurt much but felt strange, and I half expected my stomach to split open and an alien to pop out. The last thing was to have IV lines pulled out of my neck; again, I worried it would hurt, or suddenly I'd pass out as blood gushed from the wound, but I didn't feel anything and there was very little bleeding. I was free to go. A porter wheeled me and my bags to the ambulance at which point I said: "I've just had Munchausen, what am I saying, I've just had an appendectomy". I could almost hear him think, "Mentally and physically disabled."

Just like a horror movie, there was more to come. The ambulance driver was obviously on his last run and drove like a maniac which was quite hard to stomach. Once home it was a while before there was any semblance of normality, with nurses coming in to re-dress the wounds and check my vitals. Even so, being back home felt wonderful.

After a week or so my medication came to an end, but about a week later I ended up back in casualty with a very fast heart rate. They put me on beta blockers and blood thinners which have quite an impact in terms of side effects. I won't go there though.

I waited a while for an appointment to see a coronary consultant and after some waiting, I called the hospital who informed me that I was correct an appointment should have been made, however, they had forgotten to make one but eventually, I got one.

The healthcare we have in the UK is a miracle. In most other countries if you get ill, you die, especially if you are not financially well off. One of the nurses said to me that in a staff meeting, they had said how I was so easy to look after that they wanted to put me in their pocket and take me home. As a child, I had been very difficult to look after, but now, touched by kindness, I wanted to think about their needs too. Even when I needed help in the toilet, (I could barely move so I really did need help), if a young nurse came in, I would say, "Look I wouldn't normally do this on a first date, but could you just wipe my arse... and please, could you use those expensive wipes if you don't mind?" See, I was 'consideration', personified.

Before I got ill, as I mentioned earlier, I thought I might die soon, I had been feeling off-colour for a while. In a way, I was right because, after ending up in hospital, my life would never be the same again. In fact, even now it feels like a race against time to finish some important things in case my time runs out.

Sometimes, you wake up and find it wasn't a dream, but at least you woke up.

Chapter 22
No More Heroes

26th Sep 2018

Before I write these chapters, I often hear parts of them in my mind. So much so that sometimes I'm sure I've written some of it already. To make sure I haven't though, I do a quick check. I also have a structural plan, listing out what's in the chapters already, as well as what's to come. Although a lot of what I focus on tends to be about incidents that occurred, the people involved often come back to me as if I'd met them in a dream where they no longer have faces but still, there's a feeling of who they were.

Before the Internet and mobile phones became commonplace, if you met someone and wanted to stay in contact there'd possibly be a brief opportunity to ask for their address or phone number. There'd be a bit of tension between imposing oneself or risking never seeing them again. Deciding which way to go would have to be based on working out whether the other party wanted to stay in contact too, and often that wasn't clear. Still, there was a sadness when details weren't exchanged, but in a way, it was a sweet pain that could sometimes haunt people for a lifetime.

Nowadays, it's much easier. One asks an acquaintance if they don't mind being added to whatever social network their age group uses, and then, if you do send a message, it'll merely be a "good to meet you," type one, and often, that's that.

In a later chapter, we'll be looking at romantic love and yearning in more detail, especially in terms of it being set out as a type of decorum. However, even now with all our ways of connecting, we're still prone to feelings of yearning and loss. It could be as fleeting as looking into someone's eyes as they pass on a train, or maybe someone who you share moments with for a while, only to find they are gone without a trace. Are we taught to connect and yearn, or is it something we naturally can't avoid?

I'm often struck by how accurate our intuition can be when first meeting people and knowing well before talking to a stranger if we'll click or not. Of course, there may well be plenty of subconscious cues involved but sometimes the amount of information is so limited that it leaves a bit of room for other, more ethereal possibilities. There are plenty of times my antennae got it wrong too, but that tends to happen less so.

1984 - Therapy

The Therapist asks, "Do you think your childhood experiences could have affected how you are today?"

"No," I answer.

Summer 1977 – Butlins Holiday Camp - Bognor Regis

I am at the front of one of the big amusement arcades. The whole facade is made of glass doors and windows with aluminium frames around them.

I'm singing along to something on the Tannoy. A girl with blonde hair looks at me. She's about my age, I can't recall her face, but she has a kindness about her. She's looking after a young child, but I don't think it's hers.

She smiles at me and says, "You've got a nice voice."

I didn't know I was singing loud enough for her to hear. I smile and thank her, but I feel embarrassed. I know I'm turning red. I'm so embarrassed, I don't stay to chat and walk away.

Later that day, it's night-time and my friend Peter and I are on the way back to our chalet. We pretend to be drunk and loud. We are only 12, fooling around, staggering and shouting, "We're drunk." The same girl sees us, and looking worried, she tells the child she's looking after not to worry. I hear her say, "They're just being silly." She rushes off but has stayed in my mind for close to 5 decades.

1989

My friend Ian Owles and I are walking near Tottenham Court Road in London. He's about 46 but looks a lot younger. He's got lots of curly hair and a rock-n-roll demeanour.

"The first rule of love," he says, "is, those you want, they won't want you, and those you don't will".

"What's the second rule?" I ask laughing.

"The second rule of love is this," he pauses and smiles, "When you're alone no one wants you but when you're with someone you get loads of offers."

We're getting into my Saab. A couple of women pass by, and one says to Ian, "I love Saabs." This was fortuitous because I was trying to get Ian to buy it and after she said that, he did. He was buying a dream, whilst I was trying to get rid of the reality, the cost of running it, which at the time was a bit of a nightmare.

1975

It was the last year of junior school, and our class was taken to the swimming pool at Wilson's School every week. There was a girl in our class called Debbie who I was in love with. On this occasion, she was standing at the other end of the pool in a green bikini. If this was a film then there'd be a slow-motion sequence of her climbing up to the diving board.

For the first time, I looked at her and saw her as a goddess. Long black hair, a beautiful figure and long, long legs that went all the way to the top. After school, I asked her if she fancied a lift home on the back of my bike, and she said yes. The rest might have been history, (okay, that's highly doubtful) if only I had been able to peddle and steer the bike with her on the back, but I couldn't. So, we swapped positions, and she cycled while I sat on the back instead.

Probably from the age of nine till about fifteen I had a massive crush on Debbie, but no matter how much I tried to let her know I couldn't. Even when she asked me outright if I fancied her because let's face it, it was obvious to everyone anyway, I still denied it. And the reason why I did that was I didn't want to face reality. You see, deep down, I quite liked yearning for her and hearing her say no would have meant I'd have to find someone else to yearn for.

When I got older, I came to see this situation as a valuable lesson and learnt that it's better to tell someone if you fancy them, obviously when the time is right and if it's appropriate of course, and better to be rejected than to waste years yearning unnecessarily.

By the way, if anyone reads this, takes my advice then ends up getting married because of it, then please let me know. However, if you end up in jail, I probably won't want to know, but then again...

As the joke goes: "My girlfriend says I'm a stalker. Well, she's not exactly my girl-friend yet."

1977 - Wilson's School - Laughing Stock

I was waiting outside a classroom with a load of other kids. Somehow, I got into a fight with a boy called Paul. The other kids started chanting as I took a few steps back, then ran towards him. I leapt into the air to do a flying kick (I was always useless at jumping so probably went downward immediately). He stepped side-ways, I landed on the floor, and he restrained me. Everyone started laughing, including him.

The teacher turned up soon after, so everyone acted as if nothing had happened, but as we walked into the classroom one of the other boys taunted me about losing the fight. I pushed him which caused him to stagger and fall backwards over a chair. The class laughed at him spread-eagled on the floor and for a moment, I found a modicum of redemption.

1977 - Wilson's School - Tuck Shop

Every school day at 10:30 there was a break between lessons. Downstairs on the ground floor in the foyer, a large metal hatch opened in the foyer wall. This was where a couple of parents volunteered to sell sweets to us.

I tended to go through phases of buying the same sweet every day until eventually, I'd get bored. One week it'd be a peanut Yorkie, the next a Lion Bar, but this week it was 50 aniseed balls. They'd take a while to count out, which didn't go down well with the queue behind me.

There are two types of people in the world, those that divide the world into two types of people, and those that don't. You can also divide people into "biters" or "suckers". "Suckers" take their time with a hard-boiled sweet, whereas, "biters", no matter how much they try, can't stop themselves from crunching their teeth down upon their prey.

Some people, okay, it's me saying this, say it's because "biters" feel less nurtured, so tend to be a bit more eager to devour, whereas "suckers" are more content deep down and don't need to possess the sweet so quickly. And yes, I'm a biter.

292

1976 – Roundshaw Park - Franny

Roundshaw was covered by low-hanging grey clouds as I made my way to the park. Franny, the girl I mentioned in the previous chapter who'd pop around and try my mum's costume jewellery for size, was playing on the swings nearby. I thought she was pretty but there was a three-year age gap between us, and at that age, that was a significant difference.

I sat on the swing next to her and after chatting for a few minutes asked her if she wanted to see the den some friends and I had built a few days earlier in the woods. She laughed and said, "Okay then." So, we made our way to it which involved crawling through some bushes. Once inside I took off my parker coat and laid it on the ground so we could both sit on its orange lining.

"Do you want to kiss me?" She said.

"Yes," I said, slightly taken aback by her being more forward than me.

I can't remember what kind of kissing we did but we ended up lying on the coat side-by-side. I liked kissing her, but I didn't want anyone to know. That age difference, even then, was a bit much. Just as I started thinking, "Now, how am I going to make sure no one finds out we've been kissing without annoying her," a group of friends cycled past, pulled up and through the foliage shouted.

"Hello Simon, Hello Franny... Ooooh, what are you two doing then?"

She looked at me, and said, "So, do you want to be my boyfriend?"

"Nope," I said.

"Why not, don't you fancy me?"

"Yeah, but you're too young."

"Well, I ain't too young to kiss, am I?"

I was tempted to say she was but thought that might not go down well in court in 30 years. So, I said we might have to wait a few years.

Still, there were times when I'd want to see her, so, as mentioned in the last chapter, I'd get her to pop around, or we'd bump into each other anyway at the youth club. I think the last time I saw her was in 1979, all I can recall was having a kiss with her near some garages. I didn't mind her passing me her well-chewed chewing gum as we snogged, but when she lit a cigarette and started to smoke. I said I didn't like smoking, and that was the end of it.

2018 - Franny

I thought it might be a good idea to get in contact with Franny to get permission to use her name in this story. It didn't take long to find her on Facebook. She still has the same pretty face and looks happy with her husband and kids.

When I messaged her, she told me the memories she had of me were nice ones. I couldn't help but wonder if she'd got me mixed up with somebody else.

2017 - Archetypes

When I was ill in hospital, I felt like I was submerged within an archetypal type of reality that felt heavy, dark, threatening and unavoidable. At times I imagined I was in cloisters and the people moving around me were archetypal nurses, doctors, and religious figures, which is not surprising given some nurses are called sisters, which derives from nuns being curers and carers in the past.

I was heavily sedated at the time and felt close to death, so it was as if many layers of my day-to-day existence had been stripped away. The thing was, it scared me to recognise those around me as archetypes, which most likely came about because archetypes lack humanity with their fixed personas. This is probably why many people fear clowns too, after all their expression barely changes and that makes them appear as not being human.

Archetypes are programmed to behave in a set manner, and no matter how much you try to appeal to them, they can only react as their role permits. They also symbolise the frightening reality that everything is programmed. From DNA to our daily routines, to our inescapable destiny. Archetypes remind us we are part of a programmed system that can't be avoided or bargained with, and at times, especially when humans lose their humanity, they too can't be appealed to.

1977/2018 - Elvis

Franny's sister, who's now a friend of mine on Facebook, recently shared one of my posts, so I went to her page to politely like the post as one does. The post above it was about Justin Sandor who's an excellent Elvis impersonator. I can do a good impersonation of Elvis's voice, but nowhere near as accurately as Sandor can. On August 16th, 1977, Elvis Presley died. At the time, I didn't pay much attention, I don't think it even registered with me. At the age of 12, the adult world, the evening news, and even pop music were barely of any interest to me, but within a year Elvis and his music started to play a big part in my life and would eventually have a profound effect on my life. At about the same time as Elvis passed away, my childhood did so too, but I wasn't aware of that then either.

1977 - Hi-Fidelity

Mum had some money left over from her mother's inheritance and decided to spend it on some furniture and a HiFi system. This meant I could have her old stereo in my room. Each night before going to sleep I'd listen to a side of a vinyl LP through big bulky headphones. Tom Jones, Neil Sedaka, or the latest Top of the Pops albums would take me halfway to sleep. The Top of the Pops albums were cheap compilations of popular songs recorded by cover artists. To my untrained teenage ears, the songs sounded like the originals and any quality issues were more than compensated for by the soft porn covers and life-size posters of women in bikinis. No doubt some people fell asleep next to them too, but mine were safely blu-tacked to the wall along with posters of the Wombles and David Cassidy. Just so you know, it took a lot of soul-searching for me to admit I had a poster of David Cassidy to you.

2017 - Archetypes

"To everything, there is a season and a time to every purpose under the heaven:
A time to be born, and a time to die; a time to plant, and a time to pluck up that which is planted;
A time to kill, and a time to heal; a time to break down, and a time to build up;
A time to weep, and a time to laugh; a time to mourn, and a time to dance;
A time to cast away stones, and a time to gather stones together; a time to embrace, and a time to refrain from embracing;
A time to get, and a time to lose; a time to keep, and a time to cast away;
A time to rend, and a time to sew; a time to keep silence, and a time to speak;
A time to love, and a time to hate; a time of war, and a time of peace."

These famous lines from Ecclesiastes will touch many of us deeply while simultaneously scaring us too. For me, they remind me that no matter what I write, sing, paint or photograph, one day it will all disappear forever and no matter what I do, or how much I appeal for mercy, there will be a time to lose, break down, and die.

When I brushed up against archetypes in my hospitalised state, I felt the same intransigence. Their mask-like expressions were fixed as was their raison d'etre. But still, their season of reigning was an ancient one, reaching back to the beginning of humankind.

Carl Jung stated there were, "identical psychic structures common to all," influencing all of us in how we experience the world. What this meant is whilst different cultures or individuals create varying symbols or characters, there will still be a commonality between them. This is because the psychological makeup of humans will always create them. For instance, the feelings we have for our mothers, fathers, authority, ourselves, strangers, water, the moon, the sun, the stars or that which we believed created us; all these things, will nearly always fill our inner worlds in similar ways, wherever or whenever we come from.

2018

We all know everyone is capable of being good or bad. The same goes for archetypes, each of them will be one face of a two-sided coin because it's human nature to be split between opposing desires. The paradox of explaining the human psyche using archetypes though is, whilst they touch us with their ability to illustrate reality, they are unrecognisable as humans. Real people switch between various archetypal roles all the time, whereas archetypes take on only one and stick with it forever.

In addition to our cultural archetypes, our individual experiences will result in us creating our personal ones too. So, if for instance, we look at our dreams to get an insight into our inner world and limit ourselves to interpreting them via cultural references only, then we'll miss out on our individual symbols and archetypes. That's why a psychoanalyst will often ask, "What does it mean to you?"

None of us can deny we are programmed to some extent, whether it be by nature, society, family, environment or other experiences and on top of all of those, our instincts will still play a large part in defining who we are. So, whilst there have been many attempts to reprogram people to act and think in certain ways, whether it be via religion, ideological dogma, education, hypnosis, or the media, there are still limits. Try to program people not to fall in love, not to feel turned on, not to feel jealous, and not to fear loss. If you do, there'll be errors that lead to a "crash" straight into the wall of our subconscious. There's been a lot of talk lately about 'enhancing' our psyches via genetic reprogramming. However, if that were ever to happen, then one could argue our archetypal structures would also change and then even our archetypes would find they have a season too.

2018 – Punch and Judy Program

Newsreader: "Barry Island has banned the performance of "Punch and Judy" amid fears it is too violent and contains, "inappropriate hitting". The show which portrays an abusive relationship between Mr. Punch and his wife Judy has been claimed by one councillor as treading a fine line. The Punch and Judy Fellowship argues that by their logic Shakespeare and Tom and Jerry should also be banned. Several other councils have banned the show too."

The belief people can be programmed seems to be popular within some circles and to a point it it may be possible. But deep down, we all know many other factors are at play, and some of those include the ancient archetypes that inhabit our inner worlds. From what I can tell though, they're not that keen on the scripts our current stage directors are handing out.

2018 - Dream - The Sea is Breaking

I look out my window, the sea is breaking hard against my house. I can also see hundreds of battle craft along the shoreline, some of which are semi-submerged. It's scary and awe-inspiring at the same time but as the dark waves swirl, I wonder how long my home will bear the battering. After I wake up, I try to analyse the dream. My initial interpretation is the sea is my feelings and desires, crashing up against my home, which symbolises security. The battle craft represents my own resources, conscious and subconscious, to either defend or attack myself or others. Thinking about it like that, made sense and reminded me to be cautious, to keep in mind I'm never far from the parts of myself that can be very self-destructive. All that said, I did check my house insurance covered flood damage, you know, just in case it was me being a bit psychic.

1989 - Carmen Jones - Hi-Infidelity

I'm in the stalls in The Old Vic Theatre in London. I'm watching an opera called Carmen Jones. I feel nauseous. There's something about the character of Carmen that makes me feel very anxious. Maybe it was seeing one of my archetypes in the flesh. She being the woman who is not faithful to me. On the one hand, it may relate to feelings about my mother, while on the other, does she represent who I've become too? I have a propensity to be unfaithful and if I am like that, then I can't be a good partner, and if I can't be a good partner then maybe I'll be alone forever, trapped in a world of unfaithful relationships. Carmen reveals a part of myself that scares me to the core.

1984 – South Kensington Underground Station

I'm waving goodbye to a woman called Carol. We'd met a few weeks previously at Roehampton Hospital where we'd got chatting and seemed to hit it off. We arranged to meet up, so she came to visit me for the day. We had had a lovely cold Autumn afternoon walk in Battersea Park, talked, and laughed for hours, then cuddled up in my room and kissed till it went dark and she had to go. In a matter of hours, I had fallen in love with her, well it wasn't really with her, was it, and I knew it.

As the train pulled away, I waved and bowed my head to say goodbye. In this underground world, I had a moment of understanding during which I knew something was wrong with me. It didn't seem appropriate to have such strong feelings for a stranger, even a perfect stranger. This wasn't the first time either. I'd met this archetype many times in both my dreams and reality, but in my dreams, I could never remember her face.

1984 - Oh Carol, I Am Such a Fool

As the days passed after our romantic afternoon, I started grieving for the loss of a relationship that didn't exist. Realising something was amiss I decided to talk about it to Roger, our student services advisor, at college. As we sat in his dark and cluttered office, he asked me a few questions about what had happened and suggested I try out an offer of 4 free counselling sessions in the adolescent department at a well-known therapy centre. So, I called them and booked a session.

1984 - First Therapy Session

I'm in a plain room, there's a desk near the window, a grey metal filing cabinet, a small sofa, a couple of chairs, and some prints on the walls. A middle-aged woman, whom I've immediately warmed to, has brought me here from the waiting room. She introduced herself to me. I'll refer to her as the therapist. We sit opposite each other. She doesn't say anything. I feel a bit uncomfortable with the silence. Eventually, I get what's happening, so, break the silence with, "I'm here because I think there's something wrong with me." She nods her head and quietly says, "Aha."

"I recently fell in love with someone, it didn't feel appropriate as I'd only just met her and my reaction after we parted was as if I was losing someone I'd been more involved with than I had."

"Aha."

Silence.

More silence.

Yep, more silence.

Finally, she asks, "Why do you think you have reacted as you have?"

"I don't know, that's why I came here."

She smiles, "Well, can you tell me a little about your life?"

I shrug, "There's not much to tell really."

She nods slightly and smiles again, "Well, tell me a little about it anyway".

"Okay," I say.

1977 - Disco 45

I came across a magazine called 'Disco 45' which not only had articles about some of the pop stars I was beginning to take an interest in, but it also had the lyrics to many of the songs I liked too. This meant I could sing along to them. Somewhere in my house I still have them all. I know hoarding isn't something I should show off about, but as they say, if you've got it, hoard it... or something like that.

One of these magazines had the lyrics to Elvis's *The Girl of My Best Friend* so I started to sing along to the song and discovered I could sound a bit like him. Not only that, but the song was also filled with archetypal yearnings that resonated with me as much as the music did. Even within Elvis's image, there were archetypal characters I longed to be. The hero-lover, the warrior and the eternal boy for a start.

October 1977 - No More Heroes

I'm in another fight. This time the other kid grabs my lapels and throws me to the floor. I get up, he throws me again. I'm not hurt much but I am aware more than ever that I'm no hero. Given the song, *No More Heroes* by the Stranglers was in the charts at the time, I could have tried to take some consolation from their anti-hero stance, but I was a rocker, not a punk, so that didn't help me one bit.

1977 - Italy Trip

Mum had sent in a form to the school to say she wanted me to go on the school trip to Italy, and this time they decided to raise the funds for another boy to come with me to act as my carer. In real terms, he hardly had to do anything, because by this point, I could take myself to the loo, and wash and get dressed independently. Even so, the school thought it a good idea to have one person who could focus on me if the need arose.

To raise the money for his fare and board, a local appeal was made to a charitable organisation. I couldn't help but feel uncomfortable being used as a begging bowl and maybe that made me even more determined not to use his help.

There's always a price to pay, especially in terms of feelings of self-worth and status when it comes to raising money for people. For this Italy trip, there was a mention in the local paper about how the money had been raised and the good cause it was going to. Just like the typewriter bought for me via charity, though, I got the feeling someone was gaining something at my expense, whilst I was gaining something I didn't want or need at a price I didn't want to pay.

One good thing that came from all of this was this trip demonstrated to the school I didn't need a helper, so on subsequent trips, there wasn't ever an issue of bringing someone along to help me. So, maybe in this instance, it was a price worth paying after all.

1977 - Great Art

I was bored, it was a Sunday, so Mum gave me an oil painting set. First, I painted a landscape, maybe it was a copy of a photo, then before it was dry, I painted over some of it to make it look like a cabin on a boat with a window through which part of the original landscape was still visible. Then I painted a severed hand on the windowsill of the cabin with some blood coming out of it.

"Oh, why did you have to ruin it, Simon?" My mother's tone was rather desperate.

I had no words to say.

She walked out huffing.

"Some people just don't appreciate great art," I thought to myself.

1977 - Inside Out

When I'd go out to play I'd often call on a girl called Jackie who lived around the corner. She and her parents had their quarters on the top floor of a small suburban house, whilst her aunt and their family lived on the bottom one. There was no dividing door between the two areas. It was a world away from my home.

Jackie was skinny, looked like a boy and acted like one. She and I would roam the local neighbourhood where we'd sometimes link up with a couple of brothers whose dad was known to be violent. They looked a bit like him and were already beginning to act a bit aggressively. Another boy befriended us too, he must have been a bit older and had an electric guitar, so we'd sit in his room and listen to him play. There were also a couple of girls I met who lived on a posh road in South Wallington. They were very pretty and their father would always come out to play and chat with us.

I'd often feel I didn't know many people in this area so would sometimes head back to Roundshaw, but Jackie wasn't allowed to go there with me. So, when I did frequent it, I'd be alone. In time I stopped visiting it so much, and even though I partially took the boy out of the estate, I'd never be able to completely take the estate out of the boy.

1977 - School Routine

The second year of school began to feel more routine. The highlight of most mornings would be singing popular hymns loudly and avoiding strategically placed hymn books positioned by the person sitting behind me, which if sat on would end up ramming my anus. This little dance would normally garner a great deal of attention from everyone else who'd managed to sit down safely. Consequently, even now I always look behind me when I sit down.

After assembly, there'd be a rush to get to class. It would either be a double lesson or two individual shorter ones, then a break for some refreshments at the tuck shop followed by a further lesson that'd take us to the lunch break. If you think reading this list is painful, I can assure you, doing them was far worse.

The smell of lunch would fill the air and then there'd be an hour of what was often close to anarchy. Not in a chaotic sense, but more in the Wild West/Lord of the Flies way. Dangerous things could happen suddenly before a teacher or prefect could intervene.

The corridors were lined with grey metal lockers, the lighting was white fluorescent, the flooring was grey, the walls were yellow brick, and the students were in black uniforms with yellow and white highlights. It was a colour scheme based on wasps, which in many ways was very apt.

After lunch, it was a slog to work and digest food simultaneously. Then after two hours of toil, there'd be ecstatic relief felt by all, as we were saved by the bell. People escape terrorist incidents slower than pupils exiting school at the end of the day.

1977 - Ginny

One day I got home after school to find my cat had been killed. She'd been run over. I was in shock so didn't react much right away. That night, though, I could hear another cat she'd often played with at the back of the flats, calling out long droning meows.

The next day on the way to school someone told me what had happened. Ginny had run across the road and was clipped by a car which stopped. Her back legs were no longer working but she tried to crawl across the road back towards where we lived. Someone picked her up, took her back to the other side of the road then slammed her head against a wall to, as he put it, "Put her out of her misery."

When I got to school, I was still in shock but as Mr Shaw took the register, I could feel I wanted to cry. As I went to ask him if I could go to the medical room, I couldn't speak clearly so he asked me to repeat myself, but instead, I burst out crying. Somehow, I managed to communicate my cat had been run over, so he got one of the other boys to escort me to the medical room where I lay down and wept.

I think the elements of tragedy, her attempts to get back to our side of the road, the frustration of being taken the wrong way, and then being killed rather than being taken to a vet, all added up to an overwhelming feeling of sadness and anger.

There were also other elements to this. My feelings for her were more connected to a real sense of love and compassion compared to the selfish "in love" feelings I'd previously mourned for. And on top of that, there was a feeling of disconnection going on at home, so, in some ways, this felt like another nail in the coffin.

Milan Kundera wrote that one of the reasons we love animals as we do is because we recognise in them the innocence we lost when Adam and Eve left the Garden of Eden. I doubt he meant it in any literal sense, but there's an innocence we attribute to animals that when set against our darkness, fills us with a sense of sadness.

1977 - The Eyes of the Needle

I'm in our form's classroom, this is where we would meet at the beginning of each school day for five years. A couple of boys have placed a large needle in the cushion of the teacher's chair. It's pointing vertically straight up. Mr Shaw, our teacher, walks in and sits down. There's silence. Suddenly there's a startled look on his face. Some of the class start to laugh. Still, Mr Shaw doesn't say anything but leans forward and takes out the compass needle, which is at least two inches long. I don't remember laughing, I think I was one of the boys who thought it must have hurt a lot. "Who put the needle in my chair?" He said firmly. The boy who did it put his hand up immediately. I can't remember what the punishment was but if there was one, I doubt many of us would have complained. For all my delinquent behaviour, moments of compassion were beginning to surface too.

1984 Therapy - The Invitation

Therapist: "We've had the four sessions offered by the scheme. I was wondering if you would be interested in going further and undertaking three sessions per week. I can sense in you that there is something I can work with, which I hope may help you in some way?"

"Yes, I'd love that, thank you."

And so, my journey into the realms of psychoanalysis began.

1977 - Wilson's School - My Enemy's Enemy

There must have been something about maths that brought out our aggressive tendencies. I didn't even see the beginning of this fight. Paul, the guy with whom I'd done my unspectacular flying kick was being held down on a table by a boy called Jim. Jim had the blackboard rubber in his hand and was bashing it on Paul's head. By this point, Paul was a bright purple colour while Jim was looking calm. There was a kind of conversation going on between each whack of the blackboard rubber. Something along the lines of, "Do you submit?" To which Paul was nodding in affirmation. However, Jim, obviously doubting his sincerity, continued hitting him for good measure until he got a more convincing answer. I couldn't help but admire Jim's brutality and was especially pleased to see my enemy's enemy in action.

1977 - Jim

I don't know how it was that I then managed to get into a face-off with Jim a few weeks later. I know I'd been extra abusive to him because he had already said he didn't want to fight me because I was disabled, which made me angry. I think my taunts had been rather feeble, something along the lines of him smelling bad, but they did the job, although I'm pretty sure he didn't need too much persuading anyway.

A bit later, I was in the loo and one of the other boys told me Jim wanted to fight me. I said I was on the loo so it would have to wait. There's always a difference between a fight just breaking out and having one arranged. The waiting allows for a certain amount of fear to develop. I was scared, and probably rightly so. Jim was tough, and in time I'd get to know him more and see his whole direction in life went along a path that would put him in the top band of tough people in society.

Years later he told me I was the only person in school he had some concerns about fighting because he wondered if one of my kicks might catch him. But I think we both knew I wouldn't have stood a chance.

1977 - Enemy and Empathy

There were only a couple of other fights I experienced at school and both involved a degree of guilt and empathy on my part. The first was in the music class when I kicked a small table out of the way and then kicked the legs of the boy until he started crying. He was quite big so there was a feeling of accomplishment, but I could see in his tearful eyes he wasn't a fighter and that sapped any joy I might have had. Then there was the fight I mentioned in Chapter 16 where I cornered a boy in a porchway. On both occasions, though I ended up feeling sorry for my victims.

Something was changing in me.

Chapter 23
My Right Foot, Archetypes, Programming and McDonald's

1975 to 1978 and 2018

> *"All the world's a stage,*
> *And all the men and women merely players;*
> *They have their exits and their entrances,*
> *And one man in his time plays many parts,*
> *His acts being seven ages".*
>
> *Shakespeare*
> *As You Like It Act II, Scene VII, Line 138*

1975 - The Presence of Nightmares

Soon after going to live on Roundshaw, I'd often have nightmares where I'd feel a malevolent presence approaching me. The dreams would start with a tiny dot in the distance which would get bigger as it got closer and eventually, I'd feel I was being suffocated by it. From the moment I'd see it in the distance, I'd be filled with dread, and no matter how much I'd try to wake myself up, I couldn't.

One evening as I watched a TV programme, there was a figure standing behind a door, its face couldn't be seen, but the sound of its breathing continually increased in volume. As I watched I became filled with fear, just as I had been in those nightmares.

2018 – Archetypes

For this chapter, I'd been thinking about the Commedia de l'Arte, which was a form of theatre that originated in Italy and from which Punch and Judy was derived. I couldn't help but wonder if it had possibly developed due to Italian society having very recognisable archetypes within its culture. Even now, Italian culture has a feeling of being larger than life, exaggerated and emotional.

While the wearing of masks goes back at least as far as 40,000 years, the Commedia de l'Arte, which became more established in the mid-1500s, was a relatively new advocate. The oldest surviving mask in the world today is around 9,000 years old and was most likely worn during rituals and ceremonies as a representation of dead ancestors – which in its way is a kind of theatre, and not creepy at all.

In Rome, the word persona meant "mask", as well as meaning "a citizen of Rome". The Greeks also used masks, especially as theatrical devices, and even today the commonly accepted symbol for the theatre or acting is the image of a happy and sad mask, the Greek Muses, Thalia (the muse of comedy), and Melpomene (the muse of tragedy).

Is it possible that as a society becomes more sophisticated it recognises its archetypes more readily, and as a consequence uses them more, especially within myths, storytelling and theatre?

In the UK, we have largely lost our connection with traditions which pushed us up against our archetypes. However, some vestiges remain. Close to where I live, there is a chalk fertility figure of a man, where ceremonies dating back hundreds of years take place each year.

If we look at other cultures around the world, they often still have a sense of community underpinned by traditions often involving masks and archetypal figures. In much of the West though, we've let go of those practices for a myriad of reasons, but has the consequence of doing so resulted in a sense of alienation from both each other and ourselves?

Recognising the archetypes present within us can be one of many ways to help us understand who we are. If I look back at my six-year-old self, marching around dressed up as a Roman soldier, I can't help but see the presence of an archetype. Still, while it might be easy to identify what archetype is with us at a certain point, maybe the more important question is, why is it there, then? If someone plays the fool, or conversely the sage, then what are they telling us, and why do they want to be seen that way? That's not an easy question to answer, no matter how well-qualified we are in psychology. Carl Jung, the psychoanalyst, realised in many ways he was in the same mental state as many of his patients, especially in the sense of being fragmented, divided, and ruled by unconscious dynamics. Similarly, nowadays many psycho-therapeutic theories revolve around seeing humans as programmable devices; however, as with computers, there's only so much a programmer's code can do. The hardware will always be a limiting factor, and if we're hardwired to have archetypes within our internal world, we may well risk our sanity if we ignore them. If the Greek Myths helped people to understand themselves for millennia, why have we turned our back on them? The answer can partly be found in the dominant ideologies that came to the fore during the last century, some of which I'll be looking at in the second volume of this series, but for now, I wanted to touch on the subject of archetypes given they play such an important role in helping us understand who we are.

The other day a friend asked, "So, what archetype am I?"

The answer is all of them. Not all at once, but different ones at various times and often we can switch between them seamlessly, sometimes flipping from one to its opposite within milliseconds.

A few weeks ago, I was talking with two female friends, and one was complaining her husband wants her to talk dirty to him, but she feels too self-conscious to do that and can't let go sexually. The other friend looked at her and said, "You need to get more in contact with your inner whore." When the other one stopped laughing, she said, "You're right, I probably need to, but how?" When it comes to archetypes, they're not so easily summoned and have a life of their own, way beyond our conscious mind's control.

1977 - The Honeymoon is Over

After Mum and John returned from their honeymoon, our routine continued as it had done before, but as John tried to take on a more fatherly role, I became increasingly resistant. A pattern of conflict regularly resulted in full-blown arguments during which there'd be a moment where I'd consciously decide to flip. I'd feel it coming then choose to go into a meltdown.

On one occasion, I walked out and hid in the bushes to the side of the flats. I could see John come out to find me and heard him calling, but stayed still and enjoyed the power of being camouflaged. Eventually, as it got colder, I had to go back. Mum answered the door and without saying anything I made my way to my bedroom. Mum came in a few minutes later and said, "If you can't behave, we'll have to stop your pocket money."

I looked at her and not wanting to calm matters hissed, "Well, you would say that wouldn't you, you fucking Jewish cunt," Then, thinking that wasn't quite hurtful enough, I thought I'd go for the jugular, so, added, "And by the way your cooking is shit, all you can cook is chips".

Like you, possibly, there's a part of me that'd like to beat that kid into submission now. At least you don't have to live with the fact that I was that little... Unfortunately, in terms of classic storylines, this wasn't the lowest point of the arc of my demise by any means, there's plenty more to come. However, the seeds of my arc of salvation were also beginning to take root.

When people ask what it was that made me change for the better, there isn't one answer. There were lots of factors, including many beyond my control, amongst which my genetic predisposition, the archetypes dominating my hidden internal mindscape, the kindness, and maybe cruelty of others, and all those coincidences that lead us to a multitude of life-changing intersections, all these things played a part.

1977 - Record Rendezvous

On days when I was bored or restless, I'd often cycle to Record Rendezvous, a record shop on Stafford Road in Wallington. A man who was balding, with greased-back black hair and a penchant for purple cardigans, owned it. He was in his 50's or 60's, although to a 12-year-old anyone over 30 looks at least 50, so he may have been a lot younger.

Across from the sales counter, there were several booths where customers could listen to their prospective purchases and find sanctuary from grey cloudy days and normality. Music tends to be very important to teenagers. Maybe it's because it helps fill the empty spaces with an almost trance-like meditative state of mind, or perhaps it's because it allows them to see their feelings are universal, which in turn helps them feel connected and accepted by others.

1977 - A Pregnant Pause in Hostilities

Within six weeks of being married, Mum became pregnant, but wouldn't realise until sometime in November. I was struck by the feeling of how strange it would be to have a brother or sister and for a while the dynamics changed between the three of us, partly because a protective circle tends to be drawn around pregnant women, and on top of that, Mum and John started to look for a new place to live which allowed us to focus on something together. Change was in the air.

1977- Trip to Italy

Around the time Mum became pregnant, I went to Italy on the school trip.

I had never flown before. On the aeroplane, I sat next to Mr Jefferson, the teacher who'd given me the chocolate bribe not to go to Germany. He was also a clergyman and insisted on wearing his clerical collar because, as he said, he was, "closer to his boss". We were also flying in an old Russian Aeroflot plane which had green flock wallpaper. Mr Jefferson was quite nervous, whereas I loved flying from the outset. Both the taking off and landing thrilled me, and back then, we were allowed to visit the cockpit. Even the turbulence was exciting.

As we disembarked in Rome there were soldiers and armed police around us, whereas in England, guns were rarely seen, so that along with the night air being so hot, this wasn't so much another country as a whole new world to me.

When we got to the hotel, even the bathrooms had strange devices in them. I'd never seen a bidet, and when it came to breakfast, it wasn't like anything I'd experienced before. As we sat on a large open-air balcony, the hazy morning sun warmed the air. A waiter introduced himself to us as Joseph as he passed us bread and jam, drinking chocolate and coffee. (I couldn't believe that there were no eggs and bacon on their way). I don't remember Joseph's face, but he made us laugh, especially if any of the boys annoyed him. If they did, he'd grab the top of their arm between his thumb and finger and pinch it so hard they'd be in pain for quite a while, but still, they'd laugh at his audacity. On our second day, one of the boys threw a thin sheet of cheese over the balcony and about 20 minutes later the police appeared because it had landed on one of the Russian Embassy security cameras below. I probably shouldn't mention that, after all, we don't want to give terrorists any ideas. Back then, even being told off by the cops was interesting.

This was the 1970s and school trip accommodation was rough. The bathroom was dirty when we arrived, the beds were uncomfortable and when I threw one of my shoes at one of the other boys in my room it bounced off him and hit the curtains which gracefully fell.

Twelve years old was a bit young to appreciate what we were experiencing. Rome was beautiful, but to many of us, it was merely a backdrop to us playing around. In the Sistine Chapel, we were blowing out candles, in the hotel we were playing dare with Joseph and his cow bite fingers, and when we went out alone, we'd end up in cafes drinking cappuccinos and playing songs on the jukebox. In one I tried to get it to play "Yes sir I can boogie" but instead it played an Italian song which seemed to make a few of the older customers happy. To us, the smell of chocolate, coffee and the feel of the Rome afternoon air was magical. There were even big posters up all over the city for a film called Star Wars but of course, they were in Italian. We hadn't got Star Wars in our cinemas in the UK yet, so we had no idea what all the fuss was about.

After a few days in Rome, we journeyed to Sorrento near Naples. Our hotel was right next to a church bell tower. We got the hotels normal customers wouldn't go near. Even so, this one was a bit cleaner. On our first evening, some sparkling red wine was given to us by our female guide who'd joined us. She taught me how to eat spaghetti and for once the wine was so sweet and rubbish, I liked it. After a few glasses I joked with her I might come to her room later, to which she stated clearly her door would be locked. Somehow as we made our way back to our rooms, I ended up trying my key in her door just to show her I could get in anyway. We all knew I couldn't, however to both our amazement, it worked. I imagine she pushed a wardrobe up against the door that night.

Some of the boys discovered "bangers", AKA "firecrackers". So, along with the church bells at 5 a.m. and the bangers cracking till the early hours, very little sleep took place. Some of the boys met up with girls from other school parties and snogged them in the street, much to my utter disgust, envy and disappointment. As for the touristy stuff, we visited Pompeii, where the sculptural casts of figures who died almost 2000 years ago made a big impact on me, not as much as the ash clouds had on them though. Still, for many years afterwards, I was haunted to such a degree I created artworks based on them.

I didn't take many photos but bought sheets of ready-made for tourists slides. They were so over-colourised that in their way, they too were artworks in themselves, albeit somewhat garish ones and again, years down the line maybe they subconsciously influenced me to make my photography lean towards paintings.

When we visited Vesuvius one of the teachers told me years later that I'd sat on the edge with my legs dangling in towards the crater and didn't realise the earth was giving way beneath me, so, he grabbed me. He says he saved my life, but I don't remember that at all.

Nowadays, in 2018, I regularly visit a Neapolitan café in Eastbourne called Mamma Mi. I've always thought I'd like to revisit Italy, but so far, my daily café jaunts are as far as I've got.

The Priests, the soldiers, Joseph the clown-like waiter, the naughty boys, the statues of death, the ruined cities, and the old men in the cafes. Now they are just faceless characters in my memory where, for moments, I visit them, vividly, even now, 41 years later.

1977 - Summer Plans

When I got back from the school trip, Mum and John's house search was in full swing. Every house we visited I liked, except for the one they chose. It was on another main road, and I was worried that any cats we'd have would get run over.

I wasn't going to be around when the move was scheduled to take place as Roehampton Hospital wanted me to come in for surgery to have my right foot amputated. All in all, I was booked in to stay in hospital for six weeks, so, this meant I wouldn't be home for both the move and the birth of my new sibling.

1984 - Therapy

Therapist: Do you think you planned to have the amputation at the same time as the birth of your brother so you could compete for attention when the baby was coming? Maybe you were saying something like, "Look I'm going through more suffering than you, Mum?"

Me: I don't think so, I didn't choose the dates, it was the hospital.

Therapist: Well, it's possible that even if you didn't make it happen, you may have had those kinds of feelings anyway.

Me: I don't remember feeling like that.

Therapist: Well, it might be worth thinking about.

1978 - My Right Foot - Roehampton Hospital

There was a long corridor that ran across the top edge of Roehampton Hospital. As Mum and I walked along it towards the ward I'd be staying on, it was empty. It must have been late because it was July, and it was already dark outside. It felt like a dreamscape. The emptiness, the long corridor and walking on a foot that wouldn't exist in a few days.

Mum kissed me goodbye on the ward after stopping for a cup of tea and left me in the company of the night nurse and a teenage guy, called James, a wheelchair user who I hit it off with immediately. This was going to be my home for some time, but that night, I felt a long way from home. I didn't realise it consciously, but this was an echo of my past, you know, the one that didn't have any effect on me.

The next day was a normal one on the ward. I got to chat with loads of the staff who I already knew and pretty much all my conversations ended up around the subject of how much the amputation was going to hurt. They all reassured me I'd be okay, and it wouldn't be that painful.

The next day came around quickly and this time I didn't fight the nurses when it came to having a pre-med. I probably behaved myself because the nurse who'd been assigned to look after me was Sandra, the same person who'd been the carer in Pastens. The one whose head I'd thought about kicking until she warned me of what would happen if I tried. I don't think her opinion of me had improved especially as, the day before, I told her I could see her underwear whilst she sat on a bench near me. I thought it was hilarious, but the rest of the world thought it was rather crass and immature. Still, behind my comment was probably a feeling of attraction towards her which was a bit kinky really, although fortunately, it had been absent when I was six.

She came to the operating theatre with me and my last memory before passing out was trying to resist the anaesthetic and looking up at her face which was spinning around just the way it does in movies. After a few seconds, it became too much to cope, with so I closed my eyes and as I did, I heard a buzzing noise get increasingly louder until it stopped suddenly. I opened my eyes again and realised I was in the recovery room. I looked at a picture on the ceiling, then drifted back to sleep. When I woke up, I was in a bedroom on the ward near the sister's office. John's parents were standing at the bottom of my bed while a nurse sat on a chair next to me reading a book.

"Sorry, I can't chat much," I said, "I'm feeling very sleepy,"

Connie, John's mum, chuckled and said, "Don't worry, we've just come to check you're okay. You go to sleep."

So, I did.

I woke a bit later and asked the nurse sitting next to me if they'd done the surgery because I could still feel my foot so wondered if they'd tried to straighten it instead. She told me they'd cut it off, which was reassuring and frightening at the same time. I must have drifted off again because the next thing I felt was a lot of pain coming from my leg. I'd managed to kick a big heavy metal frame that was keeping the covers off my legs, and it landed on my new right stump, just where the cut had been made. The nurse was no longer next to me, so I cried out for help, and seconds later, a nurse ran in and helped me.

1978 – Roehampton Hospital - Initial Recovery

The next few days were spent in bed, being sick as I always am after a general anaesthetic, and slowly coming around. A few visitors popped in, mainly Mum, John, John's parents, and his brother, Edward.

My leg constantly felt as if someone was squeezing my foot hard. The next day, I said to one of the staff, "I thought you said it wouldn't hurt."

She looked a bit annoyed, "I was just trying to make you feel better. Of course, having your foot cut off is going to hurt. What did you expect?"

"Well, I just wish you'd been more honest," I said indignantly.

"Listen, Simon, if I'd been honest how would you have felt?"

"Scared."

"And would that have made you feel better?"

"No."

"Well, stop whining then!"

I'm surprised she didn't say those famous Jack Nicholson lines:

"The Truth? You can't handle the truth."

But then again that film hadn't come out yet.

A few evenings after the surgery a couple of nurses thought I ought to get some fresh air, so, they took me down to a pub in Roehampton. Every crack in the pavement reverberated up through the wheelchair, which hurt, so I was very glad to get back to the ward and my bed, no matter how cool it was to go to the pub with some nurses. Once I started to feel a bit perkier, I was moved to a room in the teenage department. Mum and John brought my stereo over, along with loads of my records and a painting by-numbers set which I painted over, completely ignoring the numbers and outlines, instead, I offered up my own version. Even back then, painting was never a numbers game for me.

It didn't take long to start feeling at home on the ward. Maybe compared to the isolation I felt when I was home this was a welcome relief. There was also a turnover of people staying on the ward most weeks, so, I'd get to meet some old friends and make new ones too.

One guy who came to stay had short arms like mine and no legs. One day a pretty girl who was on the ward came to my room and this guy came in too. I don't know how we got into this position but within minutes we were all on the bed together. I was snogging the girl while this guy, who I'll call Colin, was on the other side of her to me. God knows how he got there.

So, there I was merrily having a snog with the girl, while "Colin" was undoing her top which had a kind of shoelace design. I was interested in his progress because, well, she had breasts, and I was 13 and wanted to see them. Slowly, using his mouth, he pulled the laces backwards out of their holes. When I say slowly, I mean fast, because obviously for Colin this was going to be a ground-breaking moment. Finally, he'd undone the laces as far as was necessary. He looked up at me, I stopped kissing, smiled and nodded affirmatively at him. At that very moment, the door to the room swung open and all of us looked towards it.

Sister Gwen Mears glared at us, assessed what was going on, and bellowed, "What do you think you're doing?"

Colin looked at me, he had the same look on his face that the squirrel who almost gets the nut at the beginning of the Ice Age films has.

"Well?" Sister Mears demanded.

"Nothing," I said.

Colin's head bowed as he murmured, "Shit."

Within about five seconds Sister Mears had Colin back in his chair which she then shoved down the corridor, the girl off the bed and out the room and her finger wagging in my face.

Other tellings-offs I got included playing my music too loud, which I thought was a tad unfair. After all, as far as I was concerned, there's a duty to make sure the whole world is made aware of the brilliant music they're missing. Just like an evangelical preacher I wanted to spread the songs of Elvis to the heathen masses trying to work on the ward.

I also got a stern telling off for telling the physiotherapist to "Fuck Off" when she was trying to get me to stand up. To be fair, the pain was excruciating when we tried. It felt like a burning heat and a scary build-up of pressure, and given I tend to live by the maxim of 'a problem shared is a problem doubled,' I thought if I was going to feel pain, then so was the physio.

"Listen," she said, "you won't get better if you don't stand up, remember, no pain no gain".

I looked at her and said, "I have a better version of that saying".

She looked at me quizzically, "Really, what's that?"

I smiled, "No pain... Good!"

I eventually decided to lower my leg and learn to stand on my one and only foot in my own time.

1978 - The Unravelling

I was beginning to get frustrated about being in a wheelchair, so the people who made artificial limbs said they could make some crutches that'd have sockets attached for me to put my arms into. Once they made these, I was able to propel my wheelchair by using them to push along the ground. As I started to get more confident with them, I stood up and began to move quickly. Unfortunately, at one point when I entered the lounge, James thought it would be funny to throw the contents of his teacup at me which got me in my eyes. This resulted in me landing on my stump and a few minutes later a small amount some blood started to show through the bandages. The next day a doctor checked it out and concluded my recovery had been set back a week or so.

There were advantages to not walking, for instance, being given a bed bath. One nurse who was probably in her late 50s, decided to give my penis a good wash. When I realised I was going to come, I got all shy and insisted I finish washing it.

I don't think she was being inappropriate, at 13 it only takes three up-and-down passes and it's all over. Once I got older I could manage five unless I was in a hurry, then it'd take ages.

A week after falling on my stump, sister Mears wanted to take the bandage off so she could remove the stitches. She took me into a room where she got me to lie on my back then grabbed my stump firmly at which point I yelped. She then started to unwind the bandage which there was a lot of. As she got about halfway through, the material became completely sodden with blood. I am not one to feel faint at the sight of blood, but I don't think I've ever seen so much of it in my life. It just went on and on until near the end there were mainly big black clots which had to be peeled off my leg. (I do hope you're not eating). Eventually, it was all off, Sister Mears, who wasn't particularly gentle, grabbed my stump again so she could have a closer inspection and removed the stitches. I think I shrieked, but I don't think it registered with her. Still, at least I'd reached the next stage of healing.

1978 - Hospital Holiday

Aside from my guests, a few volunteers kept me and some of the others company when visited the ward too. One of them was a man I liked a lot. I wanted to be suave like him. It was the '70s, and suave was cool then. He had flecks of grey hair near his temples so I'd put talcum powder in my hair to get the same effect. He was friends with a woman who owned a boutique shop in Putney, and she invited a couple of us to a tea party there. One of her other guests that afternoon was an actress called Penny Irvin. She'd played one of the busty secretaries in a very popular series on TV called, *Are You Being Served* and was also a frequent topless model on the *Sun's* page 3 feature. I was in my element, sandwiches, fizzy drinks, cake, sweets, and cleavage. I can't remember much from that meeting except they were all very sweet and friendly to us.

I also had another volunteer visitor called Shirley. She was probably about a year older than me. We ended up having a snog, and after she went, I fell in love with her. We wrote a few letters, probably in which I announced my undying love for her. She kindly kept writing back now and again, and then one day I realised we'd stopped writing to each other, but that was alright because I'd probably snogged someone else by then, and I think even I knew it wasn't going to go anywhere. Oh yes, and she told me she had a boyfriend, and that helped too.

There was kindness all around me. My mum's cousin Paul and his wife, Ann, would come to see me a lot even though I hardly knew them. My form teacher Mr Shaw visited and brought along a card from my class which included taunts, but I laughed with them this time. In many ways, I was having a lovely summer holiday in the hospital.

1978 - The Birth

One evening, I got a message relayed to me that Mum had given birth to a boy, and I felt elated. I didn't know at the time but she'd had a very difficult labour which included having an emergency caesarean because the umbilical cord had wound around my brother's neck. When Mum was under the anaesthetic she had a few nightmares, one of which felt like the film *2001 A Space Odyssey*. A few years later, she told me she was so traumatised by it all, she didn't want to have any more children.

One of the social workers on my ward was concerned I ought to visit my mother and see the new baby as soon as possible, otherwise, I might feel left out. She kindly offered to take me to visit Mum the next day while she was still in hospital. The sister in charge of the ward my mum was on made it very clear she didn't want a disabled person coming in and upsetting the mothers-to-be, so, I'd have to be brought in covertly with my arms covered up. The social worker was livid, but I don't think I felt anything about it. I hadn't got in touch with my disability politics archetype yet.

It was good to see Mum and the new baby who they named Stephen. Whilst I was there a photographer came around with a Polaroid camera. He took a photo of me with Mum and Stephen and left the instant photo with her. Later, when John turned up, he was annoyed I was in the picture and he wasn't and after a few minutes of him grumbling, I was glad to go back to the normality of the hospital ward.

About my healing and getting back on two feet, things were beginning to move on. A provisional prosthetic leg was being made and a couple of weekend home visits were arranged to allow Mum, Stephen and I to connect.

1978 - Yorkshire Lee

Near the end of my stay on the ward, I got to Lee, you may remember I mentioned him earlier, he was the one who lost part of an arm and his foot in an incident involving a train carriage. Well, we immediately got on very well especially as we had the same interests, namely, breaking the rules and flirting with girls. He and I would hang around the psychiatric wards and chat the nutty/vulnerable pretty women up when they came out for a smoke. Sometimes, we'd get invited into their rooms until one of the nurses would kick us out.

Lee told me that one of the girls on our ward (so she wasn't a psychiatric patient) liked kissing and having her breasts played with. The girl was called Lu-Ann and was very willing to play around. One day I said to Lee, "Are you going to see Lu-Ann tonight?"

He shook his head. and said, "Nae Simon." [He was from Yorkshire]

But a bit later I could hear him hopping up the corridor to her room. The last few hop-steps didn't sound right though, more of a slop than a flop. Then I heard him shout, "For fook's sake". He'd hopped right onto her urine bag which burst up his leg. I imagine some people would pay extra for that kind of experience, but for Lee, it was a step too far.

1978 - Moody Blue Peter

There was another guy on the ward from Barnsley, the same town as Lee, called Peter. There had been a program on TV about him titled "Our Peter", which was partly made because of the severity of his disability and how well he coped with it. Peter and I had always clashed a bit and whilst we were civil with each other (sometimes), there was always a bit of a distance. That didn't stop us from buying and selling things to each other over the years. This time I sold him my Elvis Presley blue vinyl limited edition LP of *Moody Blue* for £5 as I wanted to buy an LCD digital watch. For years, afterwards, Peter would tell me how much that album was worth, just to taunt me. So, just before writing this, I checked online and they generally go for about £10 on eBay, not that that's important of course, but then again LCD watches aren't too pricey nowadays either.

The weekends on the ward were very quiet, so, when I was just about to go back home for one, I asked Mum if Lee could come too, and she said yes.

When I introduced them to each other I felt I had to warn her he smoked. She looked at him and said, "Do you want one of mine?"

"Aw, thanks very much Angela," he said.

27th September 2018 - Recognising

Tomorrow I'll be driving almost 300 miles to see Lee. fort years have passed, and we are still good friends. You never know when you're meeting a friend for life but in a way, you do, because you don't find friends, you recognise them.

1978 - God, Give Me Patience and Give it To Me Quickly

Whilst we were there for the weekend, John's brother Edward, the priest, helped me walk to the record shop in Carshalton, as I was using crutches. He was very accommodating, well that was until I started taking ages to choose a record. "Come on Simon, I haven't got all day," he said, chuckling the way one does just before one loses one's temper.

Feeling rushed I opted for a pink vinyl Elvis album, which I thought was an expression of the trauma I felt having suffered an adult not understanding the complexities of choosing an album.

1978 - Playing Ball

The next time an adult took me out and didn't play ball, things went a bit differently. One of the volunteer visitors offered to take me out to an adventure playground for disabled children in Bishop's Park in Fulham. When we got there, it was closed. I don't know what I said but for some reason, he thought it'd be a good idea to try sticking a bit of holly down the back of my T-shirt. My reaction was as expected. I lifted my shoulders and arched my back. Unfortunately for him, my crutches, which were attached to my arms, went upwards too and one of them caught him in the balls. He dropped to the floor and writhed around in agony. I apologised profusely, whilst feeling quite proud of myself.

January 2018 - Edward and the Burger

Thirty-nine years after Stephen was born, he and his wife had their first child. I'm pretty sure John was 39 when Stephen was born too, as was Boris when I came into the world. As we get older our minds can't resist seeing patterns in our family histories, just like we can't stop seeing faces in patterns, symbols in the stars, animals in the clouds and echoes of the past in our present.

Stephen and his wife Sarah have just held a Christening for their son George. On the way there I was to pick up Edward, John's brother. He's now a Monsignor in the Catholic Church and lives in a retirement home for clergy. I made my way to the reception where a nun was sitting. She smiled at me, "Hello, how can I help you?"

"I've come to pick up Edward," I replied.

She stopped smiling, "Don't you mean Monsignor Father Edward?"

"No," I said, "Uncle Edward."

I laughed, she didn't, maybe she'd taken a vow not to laugh.

After the Christening, I drove Edward back. The food at the event was finger food so we were all a bit hungry still, so, I decided to stop off at a McDonald's en route and asked Edward if he wanted a burger too.

"No, I'm fine thank you," he said very poshly.

"Are you sure?"

"Well," he paused, "go on then, thank you."

He stayed in the car whilst we got the food. When we came back, we passed him his cheeseburger, which he cautiously unwrapped, then tenuously took a bite of.

"Oh, my goodness," he said, mid-munch, "it's delicious, it's lovely!"

Me and my kids looked at each other thinking, "It's just a cheeseburger", but maybe in old people's homes, the food is healthy, with barely any salt or sugar added to it, and anyway, it'd probably been years since he'd experienced the joys of rubbish food. I'm not saying McDonald's is rubbish, but you know what I mean. I felt proud to have reminded him of a world he'd been protected from for far too long. Remembering the pink record incident though, I was a bit tempted to tell him to hurry up and say, "C'mon Edward, we haven't got all day", but even I'm not that cruel.

1978 - First Steps

Six weeks after the amputation, I took my first steps with a prosthetic foot. It fitted on by sliding my stump into a socket made of leather which in turn slid into an outer metal shell that had a foot on the end of it and stayed fixed to my leg by a strap that tightened above and around my knee. It took a bit of time to get used to walking again and I couldn't help but worry my scar would split open, at which point I'd bleed to death. But in no time at all, I was almost back to normal, although I couldn't skateboard anymore, which for a teenager back then was a major disaster. Still, buying another Elvis album helped me get over that trauma very quickly.

1978 - The House

Our new home was a standard suburban house. It had 3 bedrooms and a bathroom upstairs, a kitchen, a front and back living room downstairs, and a garage to the side. This one was slightly odd as it had been built on a corner plot so had a small triangular rear garden with some more garden to the side and front. The man who had lived there beforehand was a keen Do-It-Yourself practitioner so in the back room there was a massive brick feature around the fireplace, and false beams on the ceiling, plus mock wooden panelling in the hallway and, best of all, furry flock wallpaper. I would sometimes stand there stroking it to make our new "old" cat, Shreddie, jealous. When we met the man during the house-buying process he'd seemed very nice, whereas his wife came over as a bit of a battle-axe. One evening, soon after we'd moved in, we were watching TV in the back room when the window swung open, and the curtains billowed about in the wind for a few seconds. Mum said, "Ooh, that was just like a ghost coming in, you know, like the way they do in the movies." Later that night there was a knock on the door. Two police officers were there and informed Mum and John that the previous owner had just killed himself by driving into a bridge at speed. The car was still registered to our address so that's why they'd come there. Recalling the window incident sent shivers down our spines and from then on, I'd often wonder if his spirit was in the house. If it was, I hoped he was happier with us than with you know who.

2018 - My Right Stump

The weather is turning cold. Autumn is almost upon us. When the sea mists come in, the temperature drops and my leg stump gets very cold. A few years ago, I fell on it which caused some permanent damage. That in turn caused a lump to develop which had to be removed, which then took three months of not walking to heal. I've recently been diagnosed with micro-vascular disease, which in time will affect the bigger vessels in my limbs too. What this all means is that I may well have to have a bit more of my leg cut off in the not-too-distant future.

Time's Up

The archetype for time is not a clock, especially as it has a face that changes. There is, of course, Father Time, but for me, I reckon my archetype for time doesn't have a face, it doesn't give much away at all. It's like one of those mad revellers who didn't want to be recognised so covered their face in soot or a mask.

Chapter 24
Waiting

1978 - *Grease*

During most of my stay in hospital recovering from the amputation, songs from the film *Grease* were being played regularly on the TV and radio. What seemed to be making the biggest impact were the clips from the film accompanying the songs. Music illustrated by images goes back a long way. A magic lantern projector had shown images to audiences while a song called *The Lost Child* played in theatres back in 1894. Later, during the 1930s, Screen Song films were produced where lyrics were animated so audiences could sing along to them, a bit like modern-day Karaoke. Disney cartoons and popular musicals were all further steps along the way to a winning formula that would soon be jumping from the cinema to the TV. From the Elvis, Bond, and Beatles films, to Bob Dylan's *Subterranean Homesick Blues* clip to Bowie's *Ashes to Ashes* video, The Monkees TV show, and then Queen's *Bohemian Rhapsody*, the combination of images and music became a powerful tool for marketing both artists and their wares. In the 70s we were being groomed by the media moguls, and it worked. By the time they'd finished with me, I had the clothes, the haircut, the albums and the cinema tickets.

I went to see *Grease* in a cinema in Croydon, South London. I'd never seen an audience so involved in watching a film. There were people dressed up like the characters, dancing and fighting in the aisles, whilst many others acted out parts simultaneously with the actors. There were cheers and boos and rapturous applause, all of which created a sense of communion between us, and that was something that had been absent in many of our lives.

I wouldn't experience anything like this again for another six years when I went to a cinema in Gibraltar where the kids, who probably felt constricted living on that small rock, were wild. There was dope being smoked openly, people dancing in the aisles, and things, including lit cigarettes, being thrown all over the place. It was pandemonium verging on a mass group 'primal scream' therapy session therapy session.

1985 - Hammersmith Odeon

Dire Straits, one of the biggest rock bands in the '80s, was performing at The Hammersmith Odeon which wasn't far from where I lived then. I didn't have a ticket, so, went there on the off chance of buying one from a ticket tout. I saw someone I knew selling some. She used to sell papers with her grandmother at Fulham Broadway Station and I'd often say hello to them both as I'd pass. She said she had some tickets for sale, so I bought one. When I got to the front of the queue I was taken aside and informed the ticket I had was a fake, so, I had to do the walk of shame past the long queue back outside. I hung around for a while looking for the woman, but she was long gone and from then on, unsurprisingly, I never saw her selling papers outside the station again.

Whilst hanging around, a young bloke came up to me and asked if I was trying to get in. When I said I was, he told me to wait near one of the doors at the side, which I did, along with about 20 other people. The doors opened an arm came out and beckoned us to enter quickly, so we did. Once inside he said, "OK, I want £20 each, once you go upstairs try to find an empty seat and if possible, go to the front of the stage, and if you get caught don't grass us up." So, we did as instructed, carefully infiltrating the audience. A few of us recognised each other through the night and gave knowing nods and smiles.

As the concert got going, a lot of people made their way to the front of the stage but because my legs couldn't stand standing for long periods, I found a seat. There must have been a lot more infiltrators than the 20 I was with because both the seats and aisles were filled with people dancing during the fast numbers and swaying during the slow ones. At one point I was mesmerised by a man dancing near me. He repeatedly moved the weight from his front leg to his back one, while standing in a running position with one foot on one step and the other on a lower one. It was like watching one of those looping animations of someone running. Thirty- three years later that man is animated in my mind still and probably in yours too.

These worlds where people became more anarchistic tend to take place in the semi-dark, coloured light, hidden spaces of theatres and concert halls where ceremonies are performed, and our more primaeval selves enter and genuflect before exorcising their inner shadows and light.

1982 - Tunnel of Love

I am walking in the rain listening to *Tunnel of Love* by Dire Straits on headphones. I suddenly feel an emotional high because of the music. I hadn't felt anything like it before, this was my first aesthetic experience.

1984 - Contemporary Art

I'm talking to a college technician called John.

I say, "Modern art is just a load of people pretending to see the emperor's new clothes, it's just pretentious bullshit".

He looks a bit taken aback, "I wouldn't say that, some of it has some substance." He says.

I curl my lip a little and shrug, "Well, I can't see it."

A few days later I am in The Tate Gallery on Millbank in London. I walk into a medium-sized room with big, purple-coloured paintings on every wall. I sit down because my legs are aching and look at the paintings. I feel an overwhelming sensation coming from the depths. I feel connected with the artist. The paintings were Mark Rothko's works and couldn't have been more abstract.

2018 - Pop, Pop Music

When it came to music though it was another story. Through it, I could not only connect with some deeper aspects of myself but with others too. As I grew out of adolescence, I started to recognise how youths were manipulated for commercial gain and most of the music targeted at them was neither nurturing nor deep in any spiritual way. Instead, the whole process seemed to be aimed at training us to get hooked on cycles of materialism which in turn would lead us to be even more ardent adult consumers. People complain our environment is polluted with plastic, but so too are our psyches.

The pop world may help teenagers deal with the trials and tribulations of infatuation, breaking up, and a bit of politics, but it rarely deals with the deeper concerns that we may face in life. I too have been guilty of playing safe when it comes to writing songs, and that's partly because in our society there are very clear limits to what's acceptable within the pop/rock arenas. Maybe that's partly why I write this too because I can cover a wider spectrum of subject matter.

2018 - Story Telling

I once heard an Amazon rainforest tribal storyteller relating a traditional tale. His story was filled with details I doubt we would generally find acceptable in our society. His audience consisted of all ages while his tale contained the intricacies of women's genitalia, complicated emotions relating to incest and a few other taboo areas such as lust and faithfulness. These were subjects that were also included in the Greek Tragedies but are now almost forgotten beyond a Hollywood treatment of one of those tales now and again. Even our own traditional stories have been replaced with sanitised versions, and yet mental health issues, addictive behaviour and suicides are on the increase. And yes, I think there's a connection between these taboo issues and our urge to deny a more honest portrayal of life, especially to adolescents. In later chapters, I'll go into this in more detail, and trust me you'll probably be shocked by what you read, especially when it comes to Snow White.

2018 - The Music of Tears

This evening, before writing this, I came across a video of a child, maybe around two years old, listening to Moonlight Sonata. As he listened, he was crying, seemingly as a reaction to the music, however, when it comes to kids, he could have been sad about not being allowed to bring his cuddly toy. You might be able to see it using this link.

https://www.youtube.com/watch?v=DHUnLY1_PvM

1978 - Wilson's School - Rob

There was a kid at school in the year above me; he was most notable for having a school blazer that looked black indoors, but in direct sunlight had a turquoise-green sheen to it, so, along with his copper-coloured hair, he stuck out. On top of all that he had an Elvis-style hair cut which meant I knew we had something important in common.

It's hard to remember the weaving process that takes one from acquaintance to friend but in the latter months of 1978 this other Elvis fan, his name was Rob, and I started to spend a lot of time together.

His father, an ambulance driver, was a big bear of a man called Jim, had a lot of grey hair and a white beard, and his mum was round and friendly. There were three other kids and a big Old English Sheepdog called Blue, who all lived in a little cottage of a house around a green in a housing estate in Wallington. On the walls were prints of paintings including a crying child and a scantily clad woman with

324

long black hair leaning against a tree. Images that I'd later think were naff but at the time found rather appealing.

In this dark, messy, overcrowded home was something I knew I didn't have. The experience of a big bustling family. As an adult, Rob would work on submarines for months at a time. Maybe, having a childhood like this was the perfect training for such a job.

Rob's family accepted me and included me in meals, and outings. In fact, his parents even told me off if I was being a bit out of line. One could see it as me playing the lost child, which probably had some truth to it, but at the same time, I was gravitating towards what I felt I needed.

1978 - Waiting

Even though I now only lived a few miles further away from Roundshaw, I started to visit friends there a lot less. This meant I spent a lot of time wandering around, calling on friends and meeting new people, especially in the parks. It was the beginning of learning to live with an often overwhelming sense of loneliness.

I don't think we'd studied *Waiting for Godot* at school yet, but if we had, I'd have probably recognised the experience of the main characters as my own, especially while waiting for the 157 bus that would take me to school for the next five years. As with Godot, there was a cut-off point when, if the bus wasn't coming, it would be worth walking about half a mile to where other buses were available too. I'm surprised I didn't grow up to be a compulsive gambler given the amount of adrenalin rushing through me whilst I decided whether to walk to the next bus stop or not. If I did, I'd be continually looking over my shoulder in case there was an option to run back to the previous or on to the next stop if the bus appeared.

325

I wasn't the only one, Sunil, who lived near the bus stop would often be there too as he went to another school near Wilson's, so we shared the same routes and dilemmas. Not only was the bus stop a good place to make friends, but the bus itself became a bit of a social club as well. There'd often be the same people on it, so, we'd chat with them, and over time became friends, even to the extent of visiting their homes, whether they wanted it or not.

The accountant I have used to tell me how poor I am for three decades now. Well, I met him 37 years ago through a woman on the bus who was his girlfriend. He still charges me the normal rate though.

Aside from meeting at the bus stop, Sunil and I would go to each other's homes too. He was from a family of Indian heritage and whilst his mum would react with sympathy about my arms, she would always be very welcoming. There were not many Indian people living in the area then and probably because of that, there was a lot more assimilation going on, especially with the younger generations.

I have advocated for a long time that the best education is integration, not only in terms of ethnic-related issues but also with disability ones too. It would be a few years before I'd start to become more politically aware but even so, experiences were going on in my life then that were stirring some kind of understanding, even if it was somewhat blurred.

Sunil and I would go to the local park which backed onto Westcroft Sports Centre. As we started to get to know other kids there, we'd use the sports centre to either go swimming in or just hang around the café with the other kids there.

Some of those we mixed with were a bit older than us, had either skinhead style haircuts or were dressed as Mods and made it clear they didn't normally like Rockers, although on this occasion they'd make an exception for me, and Sunil, who also looked a bit like Elvis. Some of them carried weapons, dealt drugs and were prone to violence. These were definitely on course for a time in prison and I hated the way they'd punch unsuspecting kids and soon felt this was a world best avoided.

At one point one of them called a national newspaper and informed them there was a bomb in the sports centre, which resulted in everyone, including all the shivering swimmers, being evacuated. I wanted to belong to a network of friends, but I could tell they weren't for me.

Some people believe that gangs act as an alternative to families for those who don't have a good family life, but in many ways, there is no comparison. The world of gangs is scary and insecure, it lacks trust and magnifies feelings of detachment. Oh, okay then, on second thoughts, there is a bit of a link after all. Anyway, gangs tend to reproduce the feelings of an absent or highly dysfunctional family, so maybe it feels like home to those who come from broken homes, as it's what they know. Still, while there may be honour amongst thieves, I doubt there's much love.

1978 - Argy-Party

One of Rob's friends invited us to a party that was to be held in a cricket pavilion in one of the big parks nearby. This friend's dad offered to drive us all home at midnight, but when I asked Mum and John about it during our Sunday dinner, John said I'd have to be home by 11. When I pointed out it would be safer for me to be brought back at midnight in a car than to walk home alone through a park and along roads around the time the pubs closed, John insisted I be back by 11.

I am not sure if it was the hatred of being controlled or the sense of injustice that triggered me, but I lost my temper and kicked a chair. Instead of it going flying, it remained where it was, but the seat part went flying up into the air. John got up and went for me. My reaction was to kick him, which by chance caught him right between the legs. He dropped to the floor. I stood there whilst Mum shouted at me and a short while later John stood up, pushed me back onto the armchair, pulled my artificial foot off and slapped me around the head. I can remember thinking, "Erm, I didn't kick you with the artificial foot, I think you're being a bit unfair", but I stayed quiet.

1978 - The Party - Watch This

The party in the park was probably the first adult one I'd gone to by myself. I tried drinking some beer but didn't like it, so, I thought it would be funny to spit it out. I was talking to a big black guy on the upper balcony and said, "Watch this". He was probably expecting something highly entertaining to happen, so might have been a bit disappointed when all I did was take a mouthful of beer and then whack my bloated cheeks with my arms to create a beautiful fountain of beer. He laughed, probably politely, thinking "Aww, he's mental as well, poor guy." Unfortunately, the guy below didn't think it was funny and came rushing up shouting, "Who just spat beer all over me?" Before I was able to come up with a plausible excuse he punched and knocked out the guy I'd just been talking with. The beer-soaked guy went back downstairs, whilst I frantically apologised to the guy as he came around. He looked at me and said, "Don't worry, I've been looking for an excuse to get him." At which point he went downstairs and knocked the beer-soaked bloke unconscious.

When I got home at 11, as instructed, Mum asked if it had been a nice party.

"It was okay," I said, "a few drunk people were being stupid though."

I didn't bother telling her there'd been a sober one too.

327

1978 - Allegiance and Betrayal

It was very rare that Mum'd exert any control over me, which must've wound John up. When I look back on it now, I feel a bit sorry for John because there was an allegiance between Mum and I against him at times. This would normally take the form of withholding information about things we'd know he'd disapprove of or agreeing not to do something to his face but doing it anyway. John probably reminded Mum of her own father, so, she tended to identify more with me than him, and consequently, he must have felt quite hurt and betrayed about that.

1978 - Hair Today

Sunil and I befriended a boy from an Irish family who lived down the road. I'd been mainly drawn in by him having an Elvis hairstyle. You can probably see a bit of a pattern emerging here. One weekend I went around his house and watched TV whilst one of his cousins, who was visiting from Ireland, got a bit drunk and told us about her sexual experiences. I was sure I might be in line to become one of those experiences if I hung around long enough, so, decided to stay the night. Nothing happened, and no I'm not going to make something up to keep you happy. The only thing I got was her putting a load of Brylcreem in my hair and giving me a proper rocker hairdo.

I knew Mum was going to be a bit surprised about my new look but when she opened the door, I wasn't quite prepared for the wrath that came my way. Within two minutes my head was under the shower as she washed the oil out of my hair. Even Mum had her limits, and being a hairdresser, Brylcreem in my hair wasn't so much a hair-do, but a hair-no-you-don't.

1977 – Chess Club

Next to the main crossroads at the top of Wallington High Street, there was a big church. It's now replaced by a supermarket, which just about sums up our culture. But back then, my only contact with it was to go to the chess club which met there every week. I had learned to play chess at about eight or nine years old and although I liked it, I wasn't particularly good.

My memory of the venue is almost surreal now; it was as if we were in a large hall whose ceiling was so high it couldn't be seen. The floor was made of long yellowing floorboards, the radiators were green, the members all wore sepia-coloured clothes, and the leader of the group had a large aged-yellow beard. A line of tables

328

were perfectly centred through the length of the room, each with a chessboard, box of chess pieces and a clock placed on them.

I only ever played the old man with the beard once and I won. Maybe he was being kind, or possibly my little arms moving the pieces around and me writing down every move in a little chess notation pad distracted him. I wasn't a strategist; I would just take as many pieces as I could and then try to overwhelm my opponent. Against a good chess player, I wouldn't stand a chance.

The main highlight of the evenings was the break time when tea and biscuits were served, in the winter months, the hall was so cold the tea was more a heating aid than a beverage.

There were a few other kids there who I'd end up going outside into the dark car park with and having a chat. We'd often be joined by two other girls who weren't from the chess club, they were from another world. Given the car park was a no man's land it was safe to meet there, plus we'd bring them hot drinks to warm their hearts and hands, which as you'll see later, came in use one dark day.

2018 - Borders

I was discussing with a friend recently who believed borders shouldn't exist given we're all one race with similar needs and rights. I couldn't help but disagree. For me, there is a link between all humans, that bit is true, and most of us have similar core aspirations and desires, including having compassion for our fellow human beings. But I also recognise differences, differences that cause varying levels of allegiance towards different groups of people. The notion of seeing past these differences is a noble aspiration but it might also be a self-destructive one too. What would you choose, being right and virtuous or surviving? Sometimes you can't have both.

For me, there are natural borders, especially around language, where differences can be perceived between not only speaking different languages but also varying vocabularies, and regional and class accents. This doesn't mean I can't feel someone very different from me is just as human as I am, but I can't help but keep in mind our allegiances tend to be aligned with kinship, so, people are more likely to be kind to those with whom there's more common ground. First in line are those that we love along with our close family and friends, then those we share our cultural values, ideological and religious beliefs with, possibly our local community, our region, or our country. Many also identify with others based on whether they look like each other. This tends to go hand in hand with genetic pools, which many see as "race". Although race is probably not the best word to use. Still, even those who say there's no scientific basis for the term are quick to point out racist behaviour against people of colour, although they might also add the notion of "otherness" to their definition. No matter how much people tell me we are all one race, I can still feel difference does influence how we feel about each "other". Yes, it's something to contend with, but I doubt we can have it programmed out of ourselves completely. Again, this is an area I'll come back to later, partly because it's such an uncomfortable one to deal with.

1978 - Saved by the Girl

I wore a blue Parker coat most of the time during the winter. One of the pockets on the right had a hole in it, which at first was annoying, but then I realised I could use it to make things disappear, especially from shops.

My main target was acquiring sunglasses. One week I went to an optician in Wallington High Street, tried on a few glasses and when they weren't looking pocketed a few. At one point the old woman serving me asked where I'd put one of the pairs, she'd just shown me. A cold fear ran through me, "I put them back on the shelf," I said. She grabbed a few pairs down and luckily for me, there was an exact same pair amongst those she'd chosen. But I'm sure she gave me a suspicious look.

The next day at school I sold them all for a highly reduced rate, and demand was high, so, on the way home, I popped into a chemist in Wallington High Street. The cashier was one of the girls from the chess club car park. She helped me go through a few pairs and then left me and my accomplice to look through the carousel. I think we took about seven pairs all in all and then walked out of the shop. As we walked off the girl came out of the shop and ran up to us. "Simon!" she said, "I saw what you just did then, I saw you take those glasses, don't ever do that again, next time I'll call the police. Don't be stupid."

I could see my days as a criminal mastermind were numbered, so I got a new coat with shallower pockets and decided to try getting a job.

1978 - Gradual Moments

I was mixing with violent people, being violent at home, stealing from people and only curbing that because I feared being caught. If ever there was a need for an axis point in my life, then this would have been the ideal time. But I'm not sure, even now, if one can talk about a moment of change, that doesn't feel real to me. When I meet people who tell me that one moment changed their life around, I can't help but feel a bit doubtful. Generally, big change tends to be gradual.

330

1985 - Therapy

Therapist: Why do you come to these sessions?

Me: Because I want to be cured.

Therapist: Do you think therapy will cure you?

Me: Yes, if not, what's the point in coming?

Therapist: I don't know if you can describe it as a cure, that would mean the problem doesn't exist anymore, like ridding a body of a virus. But these feelings you have, they might not ever go away totally. Maybe therapy will help you to deal with the feelings, or it will help you not to behave in ways that make them worse, but I can't promise to cure you of them.

2018 - Am-Dram Archetypes

I doubt very much that we normally have archetypal characters speaking openly to us in our minds, although sometimes they may do so in dreams. Still, it's a good way to dramatise how our psyche operates. If we are going to represent the inter-actions of different parts of ourselves then using theatrical devices might work well. For some situations, it could be a theatre production, other times a suspense thriller movie, others a piece of performance art, or maybe a musical, and so on. But at the age of 13, it's probably going to be a shit amateur dramatic scenario, with occasional intervals for a quick porn film.

Inter-mission – A play in One Act

There are large badly painted grey clouds hanging above the stage. The background is full of more grey skies. A character who's dressed as an artist is spraying the words "Boring Sunday" across the backdrop in big black letters as the lights come up.

Another character dressed as a beatnik walks in from the left holding a little black book. He turns to the audience and says in a posh accent.

"Who would want to come to see a play about a boring Sunday?"

He nods affirmatively to the audience.

There's a sudden burst of canned laughter, and then he lays down on his back, raises his arms and legs to the sky and snores a little.

"Poets!" says the artist, "They're so pretentious. They can't even speak properly."

"What are you doing artist?" The poet shouts.

The artist spreads his fingers and arches his back as if he's hearing the screech of chalk on a blackboard.

"I am using illusions to help you see the truth".

"No, you're not," says the poet, "You're just using your skills," he pauses and laughs, "to get attention, mainly female attention."

"Hypocrite" shouts the artist.

The poet lowers his limbs into a starfish position, "Oh, I don't deny it. I think my poetry is codswallop, it's just I have a knack for saying something that doesn't make any sense in a way that sounds like it must do.

Hold,

On,

I can,

Hear

Somebody."

The artist laughs, "Exactly."

The poet shouts, "Shhh!"

They both go quiet.

A young pretty woman in a light blue chiffon dress steps up from the audience and climbs onto the stage.

"I couldn't help but hear what you said," she says, "you know about art and poetry and I have to say I was very touched by your honesty."

332

The artist and the poet nod at each other.

Someone from the audience shouts out "It's a bit sexist, you need to get yourself up to date."

The woman looks at the audience, sighs, then says, "Look it's 1978, the only thing he knows about feminism is that they burn their bras. Anyway, I quite like playing these parts. It's my choice and I get paid loads of money."

Both the poet and artist say in unison, "Do you?"

There's a moment of silence.

All three characters stand up together in a line and look out toward the audience.

"All I can see is emptiness," says the artist.

The woman says, "I can't bear it."

She raises her finger to the poet's mouth.

A man walks on wearing a very large codpiece and says, "Did you know, pubescent boys think about sex nearly all the time?"

"So do girls," says the woman.

"Then why don't they let us have sex with them?" Asks the codpiece wearer.

The poet answers, "Because it's not true... sometimes OR they just don't think you're attractive."

He pauses and frowns, "Anyway, I would just like to point out that there is no way that this is a representation of a thirteen-year-old's mind in 1978, it's more like a 53-year-old's in 2018. I'm just saying."

A white man and a woman in a burka walk across the stage pushing a pram. Followed by a white boy and a black boy holding hands. Followed by a black woman in a wheelchair wearing a bridegroom's outfit and holding the hand of a man dressed in a bridal gown.

The poet picks up a clipboard with BBC written on the back and ticks off boxes as each group passes.

All the characters stand quietly, their eyes looking left and right, their mouths pursed.

A trap door opens, and a chair with a teenager sitting in it rises to the stage. The boy has headphones on and is blindfolded.

All the characters start shushing each other.

The boy holds out a remote control and pushes a button.

The woman says, "Remote controls weren't in common usage in 1978, what idiot put that in?"

Suddenly there's a sound of a car approaching. The actors mime watching a car passing over the stage hotly pursued by several police cars.

The poet starts to commentate on the chase.

"The police are going full throttle. They are catching up. One of the officers is leaning out the window. He's firing his gun. The rear window smashes as one of his bullets hits it. They are approaching a railway crossing. A train is coming. Oh my God, the train's hit the car they were chasing, and the driver's been thrown from the car and... he's possibly been decapitated."

"Oh no he hasn't. has he?" Asks the artist who is holding a can of paint and a brush and is painting a red line around his neck.

"No, unfortunately not," says the poet in a very disappointed tone, "As usual he got away".

The artist puts the paint can and brush down and sighs.

"That looks very Avant-Gard," says the woman pointing at the red line around the artist's neck.

"Do you think so?" Asks the artist proudly.

"Yes, I do," nods the woman. At first, she nods affirmatively then switches to a no. Then adds, "You do know that this is just your fantasy, and I don't really fancy you, don't you?"

"Yes, I know", he says sadly, "I really shouldn't get carried away."

A good-looking man enters stage left and walks across the stage combing his hair. He says loudly, "There's never a mirror when you need one" and exits stage left.

The poet says, "He could have used the pool of tears I cried, caused by jokes so cruel."

The boy in the chair stands up. The man with the codpiece goes down on all fours in front of him. The poet looks at the woman and nods towards the boy. The woman gives the poet a look of, "Don't go there." Which involves a cocked eyebrow and shaking her head. The codpiece man manoeuvres himself backwards until he is under the boy who then sits on his back.

"I'm bored," the boy says in exasperation.

The codpiece man passes him a novel. The boy throws it over his shoulder. The poet catches it.

The boy shouts, "Giddy Up!"

The codpiece wearer looks at the audience and mouths "Giddy up? What a wanker." But still rides him slowly towards the woman.

The boy says, "Hello? I can smell someone near."

The woman quietly steps backwards and looks up to the ceiling then says: "I'm getting very tired of this objectification. I know it's meant to be 1978 but we all know you're writing this after hashtag 'me too' and all of that."

A very good-looking topless man walks onto the stage, in one hand he's pushing a hoover, and in the other, he's holding a Kafka novel (The book is large and has Kafka writ large on it). The woman asks him which Kafka book he's reading and follows him off-stage.

A priest enters, stage right.

"I just want to say that sex before marriage is not for you. It's for good-looking sporty chaps, so you'd better get a grip of yourself."

The codpiece wearer smiles at the audience.

"No," says the priest "It's very bad to do that".

"Why?" says the codpiece man.

"Because you are killing," his voice is drowned out as some very loud music starts playing.

All the characters start dancing, and the woman and man re-enter the stage, dancing across the stage in a ballroom style. As they do, disco lights flash and an image of a woman in a bikini fades into view on the backdrop. The artist stops dancing and pulls a sheet from an easel to reveal a painting of the woman in a bikini. He bows ostentatiously, then beckons the audience for praise.

The music fades. There's a clatter of cutlery and crockery being loaded onto a table in the distance. Then a woman's voice calls out, "Thank God for that, I couldn't hear myself think." All the characters nod in agreement. She adds, "Anyway dinner's ready. Hurry up, it's getting cold. What are you doing?"

A clown walks onto the stage, shouts "I'm coming" then does a handstand, between his legs is another head, so he walks off stage on his hands. The woman looks at the audience and says, "I know, it's all so bleeding obvious now, but in a few years, it will be so much more sophisticated."

There's a moment of silence then she gesticulates a motion of mocking disbelief with her hand and mimes some uncontrollable laughter. The codpiece man lays down flat on his front. The boy walks around with his arms out feeling for something to guide him. The beautiful man starts doing push-ups at the feet of the bikini image. The priest prays whilst following the boy on his knees. The poet throws the book he caught. The artist puts a for sale sign on the painting. The canned laughter roars for a few seconds and fades as the lights go out. The "Boring Sunday" words on the backdrop shine out under ultraviolet light. Slowly the grey clouds and backdrop morph into beautiful colours.

Over the Tannoy, a voice says, "Please return to your seats, the programme will continue in 5, 4, 3, 2, 1."

1978 - Looking For

When I was 13 there was a feeling that there must be more to life than this. The empty spaces of time and places dominated this era for me, so, I'd wander the streets looking for connection and significance. I wasn't so much lost, but I hadn't found what I wasn't looking for, and as Bono hadn't yet sung about the same quandary, I felt even more alone.

1978 - Wilson's School

I came into school late (as normal) so had to wait in the foyer until assembly had reached a certain point. Whilst the kids were singing a hymn, I got talking to a new supply teacher. It didn't take long for me to realise that something was up with him. Within a few minutes, he was telling me how our materialistic society doomed us to a cycle of behaviour that dealt with psychic pain via a process of analgesic consumerism that may help us ignore that pain in the short term but ultimately, it made it worse. All of what he said rang true, but even I recognised the conversation was inappropriate and he was on an evangelical mission. It was okay for me to eagerly promote whatever I was obsessed with but revealing the crack in society's structure to a 13-year-old was probably a sign of madness. Sure enough, a few days later the teacher wasn't invited back, but still, in the interim, he'd managed to tell me, "Nothing is everything and everything is nothing," Whilst I thought that didn't make much sense, the poet in me never forgot it and used versions of it on many occasions thereafter. Often resulting in a response such as, "You're so deep". At which point the artist, poet and codpiece wearer nodded at each other.

January 1979 – Westcroft Sports Centre

I had no conscious notion I was seeking out an alternative family, but maybe at 13, given my home life felt somewhat detached for me, I was being adopted by some of the families of friends, well at least on a part-time basis.

One evening I was at the sports centre, sitting in the café area and across the room were a couple of men dressed in karate suits. I went up to them and asked if I could join their club. "I don't see why not," one of them said.

"I can do some kicks," I said as I did one. Unfortunately, I'd over-straightened my leg and almost broke my knee.

The karate man tried not to laugh.

"Why don't you come to our class?" he asked.

"Really, are you sure it'd be okay?"

"Yes, come along."

A week later I asked if I could go to a karate lesson and John said no, citing me possibly using it to bully other children (which wasn't something I had a history of). Although, of course, he may well have had his concerns about me being violent towards him. Mum, however, thought it might be a good idea.

It was 6 pm, and I took the 157 bus. I got on it where I normally got off it after school. This time I was going on a journey that would last a lifetime and would, as many books promise, change my life.

Chapter 25
The Master and the Fool

November 1979

The bus pulled up in front of St Hillier's Hospital on the Rosehill Estate. True, much of the housing was situated on a hill but it certainly wasn't very rosy. The hospital was white and so large it could be seen from many parts of London given its position on the rim of the artesian basin surrounding the River Thames.

I thanked the driver and got off.

This was the hospital where my brother Stephen had been born a year or so earlier. Right in front of it was a park, although back then it was more of a large expanse of land where dogs would do their business. Walking across it was always done at great risk to one's footwear, and required a clear focused mind and body to navigate it safely. The beginning of the famous 70s martial arts series, *Kung Fu*, starring David Carradine, often showed the hero walking across rice paper as a test of stealth. Walking across this park without getting dog shit on one's shoes was far, far harder, although, admittedly far less cinematic.

The place I was aiming for, Tweeddale School, was a few hundred metres along a road to the side of the 'park'. So, to avoid traversing the poo-mine field, I took the long cut. I wasn't one to live dangerously when it came to dog poo. Even so, in the 70s, dog poo was rarely cleared from pathways, which resulted in getting to know certain poos over time as they tended to stay in position for many months, sometimes years even. They'd become almost reassuring in their continued presence, like homely landmarks. There were a few I'd come to know that had a kind of poetry about them. We'd witness them getting old, turning white with age and finally, disappearing; at which point we'd feel an admittedly slight amount of grieving, for a second or two. Sometimes a little faint stain in the paving acted as a long-term memorial and after all these years, there are some I still remember fondly. Even dog poo can fill one with nostalgia.

When I got to Tweeddale school, there was no sign of anyone there. Unperturbed, I carried on investigating and found a wooden gateway at the back that opened to reveal a few more buildings. I felt I was on a quest and being tested. As I closed the gate behind me, I heard noises coming from one of the buildings nearby. In front of me was a gym with windows around it, and inside I could see people kicking a kick-bag and moving around in karate suits. The man I had talked to in Westcroft Sports Centre was there too, so, I went in and asked him if I could join in. He smiled and said yes, then told me to stand in the back row and follow the others.

For all my resistance to John's authority, there was still a yearning in me for father figures and discipline. Either consciously or not, I recognised Karate could offer not only that but also the chance to learn to fight more effectively. What I was not aware of was it would also help me become more acquainted with the world of men, and as we shall see, women.

In most cultures, the beginning of moving from being a child to an adult occurs around the age of 13, and the need to display some kind of symbol to mark this transition is often common too. When I looked at those coloured belts, I wanted one. I wanted to be recognised for accomplishing something because, so far, I felt I hadn't accomplished anything that could be seen as worthy.

April 1979 - Grenoble – France

If this was a film, the frames would slow down, freeze, and then rewind quickly to earlier in the year.

I'm on a bus in Grenoble in France. One of my teachers is trying to help me get my bus ticket out of my pocket, I'm almost insisting he doesn't.

"It's ok sir, I can do it," I say.

I lean over and try to get the ticket but there's a paper bag in the way.

"Oh, let me help you," he says.

As I cry, "No!" his hand is in my pocket removing the paper bag and even before he gets to the ticket, a flick knife falls to the floor. He looks at me, and his face turns to thunder. After we get off the bus, he tells me he'd trusted me when I said I couldn't join the group because my leg was hurting. Really though, it was just a ruse so I could buy the knife. He then drops the knife down a drain. I didn't lose my temper, but I felt so angry with him for throwing something away I'd spent my money on, that I was adamant I'd never forgive him. forty-three years later and we've been friends on Facebook for years.

April 1979 - Grenoble – France

As part of our French studies at Wilson's, we were encouraged to be part of an exchange programme which meant going to Grenoble. Grenoble was a big city near the foothills of the Alps in France. The idea behind the scheme was to spend a couple of weeks living with a family and attend a school there, and in return, the child we'd been paired with would come to stay with us. When we arrived in Grenoble we were paired with our counterparts; there was a look of contempt from one of the kids and the more I hoped we were not going to be put together, the more I knew we would be, and, of course, my gut feeling was right. Whilst his family and I got on well straight away, he and I did not connect. The only thing I wasn't keen on, outside of his dislike of me, was the big black family dog that also seemed not to be too keen on me either. Whenever I was in its presence it growled and followed me around, its teeth visible. I also got the feeling my fear of the dog was the source of my exchange victim's greatest pleasure for that fortnight.

Most of the kids from Wilson's didn't come from a council estate, so it was ironic we ended up living on one as part of our exchange. Even though this was a newish one called the Villeneuve, it was already known as a hot spot for tensions between youths and the police. The stairwell and lifts smelt of piss, and although there was a lack of dog poo, I felt very much at home there; it was as if I was back on Roundshaw. In those days the Villeneuve emitted an air of hopefulness for a dream of a brave crap world, what with its multicoloured tower blocks and a school filled with classrooms with no corners and, and... well that was about it. But maybe there was a subconscious logic in the architect's vision after all. While the children played on the grass areas encircled by the blocks of flats, and orange spotlights allowed playing till after the sky had disappeared, it was almost as if the architects wanted them to feel at home; I mean when they'd eventually end up in prison.

1979 - A Grassy Play Area in the Villeneuve

Some boys in our group were play fighting, showing each other how to get out of certain "self-defence" situations. A Vietnamese boy, who looked a bit like Bruce Lee to the untrained eye, was living up to our racist stereotype expectations of him being a martial arts expert. At this point, I hadn't done any martial arts training apart from my childhood karate sessions on Roundshaw and looking at some Bruce Tegner self-defence books. So, as he demonstrated a stranglehold that would be near impossible to escape from, I told him I could definitely get out of it. He took the challenge, grabbed me around the neck from behind, and applied some pressure. I dug my chin into the crease of his elbow, pushed his elbow towards his fist then whacked my head backwards into his face. There was a crunch and a gasp from those watching as he let go and fell to the ground. I turned around to see what the fuss was about; his lip had split apart and quite a bit of blood was oozing out and dribbling from his chin. He nodded approvingly.

I was still in the mode of trying to be a hard man, even though, you, me and most of the kids from my school know I wasn't.

One of the kids from Nigeria, and, "not that it matters," but he was black, came up to me and said, "You should meet my brother, he does Taekwondo."

"I'd love to, can he teach me some?"

"I'll ask him," he says smiling.

"Thanks, do you do it?" I ask.

"A little," he says.

He jumped in the air, spun and did a kick which I was very impressed by. So, the next day I went to his apartment. It was visibly a male-only flat. Sparse, just a table, cooker, and some metal chairs and there was something unnerving about the place, it had the feel of a lair. When his brother came in, he said, "My brother tells me you want to learn some taekwondo", I nodded affirmatively. He then kicked the kitchen door with a high roundhouse kick. There was a loud bang as it slammed shut.

"Come here," he said, "I'll show you something".

I stand up.

"Try to kick me," he shouts excitedly, "try to kick me in the balls,"

"I can't, I don't want to."

"Go on, try!" he ordered.

So, I kicked toward him. He spun around me, threw a punch to my head, kicked my leg away, and then grabbed me so I didn't hit the floor.

"That's amazing," I said, "will you show me how to do that, please?"

So, for the next hour, he made me practice it repeatedly until I started to get it.

Afterwards, I felt invincible, the rush of delusion felt incredible.

2018 - Karate - Part 1

There's something that Karate and psychoanalysis have in common. It's related to bringing people to a more honest understanding of themselves. Our society has created generations of people who have very little understanding of their true physical limits because they have never been tested. It was no coincidence that as National Service ended, football hooliganism increased massively. Young people want to know themselves because without doing so they will be filled with self-doubt. They posture, copy lines they've heard in films and enjoy the thrill of delusion that acting out a part can give you. But ultimately, a virtue untested is no virtue at all, no matter how much comfort it gives us. In many ways, our society created generations of excellent actors and I was heading for a leading role.

1979 - Grenoble

The father of my exchange victim was a small thin man with a humped back, glasses and a President Lincoln-type beard. The mother was chubby with dark wavy hair. I immediately connected with them and felt at home.

Each morning we'd have chocolate with loads of sugar lumps to drink, cereal and croissants, so, for the rest of the day I'd be bouncing off the walls, and in the evening, there'd be a lovely multiple-course meal.

I probably could have stayed a lot longer if I'd been allowed, but one day I was in their bathroom looking at the wall-size photograph of a forest, trying to work out if it was my eyes or could foliage really be that luminous when for a moment, I missed home, the grey clouds and rain, I even missed John, a tiny bit.

1979 - Grenoble

Wherever I went in their apartment that fucking dog followed me growling. For special moments it would bark at me ferociously. I tried to make friends with it, stroked it, fed it, and showed it I was genuinely terrified, but it wouldn't let up. If I was desperate to go to the loo at night it was like running a gauntlet, as he would bark and growl, waking everyone else up. After a while, if I woke up wanting a pee I'd be filled with dread. I'm sure my exchange buddy trained him to hate me.

2023 - The Fate of a Fool

When I start to write these chapters I make notes about things I want to cover, write down ideas on my phone, and research old diaries, books, and the Internet. After some time, themes start to emerge organically. Once I get to that point my mind will focus on those issues a lot, so much so, I can't get to sleep thinking about them. As I thought about this chapter, especially about Karate, I was struck by how often people ask what grade I am. The simple answer is I wasn't a high grade, and I was never any good. Even so, I loved it, training from 14 up until I was 59.

When people start doing most new sports they dream about success, maybe winning a competition, being respected for mastering something, teaching it to others, and so on. In reality, though, these things become the by-product of the activity becoming a way of life, a process that one loves being involved with.

I gained qualifications in painting, I am naturally competent at it and love doing it, but I love doing music more. I don't have any qualifications in music and doubt I could ever achieve any because what I have learned has very little to do with the formal learning route. However, to me, that's not important, because I love doing it anyway.

I have qualifications in other things, but that was about proving to others I could work in those fields. Whilst I still like teaching, I wouldn't want to do it all the time; likewise, I'm qualified in computer science and can work in it to some degree too but preferred to only do it part-time. I don't have qualifications in photography, but I worked as a studio photographer and enjoyed it. So, this made me wonder about our obsession with focusing on qualifications.

Anyone who is considered an expert by others will nearly always agree that other experts in their fields will disagree with them on many issues. Being an expert, having qualifications, or having martial arts belts, doesn't mean you're the fountain of knowledge. If anything, expertise teaches us humility, because we've come to realise our limitations.

In a deck of Tarot cards, there is the image of the fool. The archetypal fool can represent the ability to bring about new ways of doing and seeing things. From the moment we are born, we start to play with things and want to master the world around us, not just because we want to control it but because we love the process of learning, discovery and knowing.

Qualifications may be a way to feel significant, but playfulness and mastering things are a part of loving life. I don't want to criticise our need to feel significant because I think in many ways that's important too, but perhaps our greatest ambition should be to enjoy doing things for the love of it.

1979 - Grenoble - Flick Knife

I had been walking around Grenoble with the rest of my schoolmates and a couple of teachers. We'd got close to the Bastille, which was a fortress that was high on a hill when I spotted a shop selling flick knives. I told the teacher that, my legs were hurting, and I couldn't make the walk up the hill, so they let me wait for them there. That's when I bought the flick knife from quite a concerned-looking shop-keeper. He probably thought I'd lost my arms because of not handling one properly in the first place. It would have all gone to plan had I remembered to put the bus ticket above the knife in my pocket. But I must have had a guardian angel watching over me that day.

1979 - Tweeddale Karate Club

The film pauses again and fast-forwards to November.

I stood in the back row; I knew I didn't know what I was doing. The teacher was strict, and I obeyed. I was the same age as my father when he joined the army. I didn't know that then, as we hadn't yet met, but now when I think about it, it seems it was in our DNA to make way for our warrior archetypes to show their faces at 14.

16th October 2018 - Mastering

The word "Master" has its roots in the Latin noun "magister" which means, "one who has control and authority." More recently it came to mean "to acquire complete knowledge of." As one gains more knowledge one realises that it's very rare for anyone to acquire a complete knowledge of their discipline. Even in the more measured fields of science, there tends to be disagreement regarding the higher theoretical areas. Consequently, it becomes hard to accept something as a scientific "truth" when somewhere down the line someone else proves it's not 100% accurate. If we didn't think of mastering as "to acquire complete knowledge of something" but instead went back "to acquire a great deal of knowledge of something" then I think the definition would be far more accurate.

In 1981, Gwynne Thomas, who was one of the top civil servants under Margaret Thatcher, said to me, "Don't ever trust people who are labelled as experts. A load of so-called experts just designed a new train for the London Underground and the carriages are too big to fit in the tunnels safely." Whilst that stuck in my mind, I was still star-struck by the martial artists I came to meet, even into my twenties. It wasn't that they didn't deserve a lot of respect, it was my desire to idealise them that was a problem, mainly because it just wasn't realistic.

As we get older or even just progress through the journey of studying something in depth, we start to recognise in others, the different stages that we have passed through previously. At that point too, we are passing through yet another stage, but I doubt many of us would believe we have learned all there is to know.

At 53 I can still feel the warrior archetype has a big role in my internal world. I still train regularly and at times can feel my violent desires, especially if someone pisses me off. That doesn't mean I would do anything, even if I could, but I am willing to accept that part of who I am is driven by primaeval influences.

For the last few days, I've been watching Season One of *Vikings* and was struck by how many people in our society style themselves in a similar way to how we perceive Vikings looked, and how popular tattooing has become. It's as if the more sophisticated we are, and the more sociologically engineered we feel, then the more we are drawn to reconnect with our primordial selves.

2018 - The Fool and the Master

I have mentioned before that when it comes to humans, they can't be reprogrammed completely. Living in a world where we can program computers and some genes, many believe we can program humans too. Behind this belief lies the issue of idealism versus realism. Even in the world of Martial Arts, this debate rages too. Some martial arts end with the word "Do", as in Ju-Do, which roughly translates as the "art of doing something", whereas others use the word Jitsu, as in Ju-Jitsu which tends to be translated as "realistic" or "true". In other words, the practical way of doing something.

Throughout our lives, we'll probably recognise this issue in many areas of life, especially in politics, as in, is it "idealism" or "pragmatism" that we mostly hold our faith in? These are fundamental values that in some instances may decide our survival or destruction.

The fool and the master circle each other but neither are sure who is who.

1940 - Vernon

In the early days of World War 2, Vernon, who was brought up in Barnsley in South Yorkshire and had a strong Northern accent, was asked to attend an interview by the Secret Intelligence Service (SIS). He was already well known in academic circles for his papers on French education and for being something of a specialist regarding all things to do with Belgium. During the 1930s he'd travelled

346

widely around Europe, especially France and Belgium, where he picked up some of the local accents to such an extent he was now being considered as an agent to work behind enemy lines. One of the interviewers asked in a very plummy accent, "Do you think your Yorkshire intonation might come through in any way?'

"I doo 'ope not," he said smiling.

After some training, he was covertly taken to Brussels where he helped coordinate the local underground resistance. This mainly consisted of publishing pamphlets and disseminating information. One day one of the young teenage boys came to him to say his father had found out he was delivering some of the pamphlets and had beaten him for doing so. Vernon told him it would be okay to stop but the boy wanted to carry on.

For Vernon, his job primarily required fitting in as a local and most importantly not sticking out in any way. Outside of reporting information between England and the underground members, life was quiet and in time, he settled and befriended a woman with whom he felt very connected. During his time there, he knew he was living a lie and that meant not getting too close to those around him. So, as the war in Europe came to an end and the celebration party for the members of the underground proceeded, he felt a bittersweetness.

The father who had beaten his son turned out to be the editor of the underground pamphlets. He apologised to his son, explaining to him that it was because he was the editor, he'd been so determined to put him off. Not only did he not want his son to be in danger, but he was also worried they might all end up being discovered.

The relationship between the woman and Vernon did not blossom into a romance. Maybe seeing she didn't really know him, or he could so easily take on another persona, created a wedge between them, but even so, they kept in contact for the rest of their lives. She eventually married someone else while Vernon returned to the world of education. As the years passed, he'd often visit the woman and her husband who he became friends with too. In time they had children, one of whom was born with an absent lower arm. Maybe this was the son Vernon never had, the one he would have had, or maybe in a way it was a symbol of himself, a boy with something missing. Either way, he felt very close to this child and because of this relationship, he became interested in how children with disabilities were dealt with in the education system.

When I was 11, Mum and I visited Vernon for the first time. He was already in his late 60s but was busy writing many books and still working in academia, both as a professor and dean at a major university.

Every year Mum would send me to stay with him in his flat in Walmer, near Deal in Kent. He was one of the many father figures that affected me. He tended to be quite direct. If I told him something I didn't like about my mother, for instance, he'd tell me she was right and why he thought so, but I didn't mind. He would explain himself which was one of the many things I liked about him. Somewhere in those stays, he planted some of the seeds of my redemption. I needed male mentors, and he was a good one. He would tell me stories about Graham Greene, who he knew and didn't like, and Ian Flemming, who he knew as well, but resented somewhat for using the word "Spy" in his 007 novels, as they were not spies.

One day he told me about a fellow professor whose main interest was geology. "He had no formal qualifications, but he loved the subject so much and wrote so many great papers on it that the university made him a professor. Nowadays he wouldn't be allowed into the university; he wouldn't have been able to pass the entrance requirements. Who is the education system for? If it's ultimately for the advancement of society then it's not doing a very good job is it?"

I could be impressed by the men who could roundhouse kick a door in Grenoble but there was something I knew to be more nourishing in the likes of Vernon or Grant my new karate teacher.

In his later years, Vernon bought a gold Ford Capri which rather impressed me because I didn't expect him to have that kind of car. He was also friends with Ian Fletcher, the doctor who I mentioned in an earlier chapter, the one who was in the magic circle, well, he also had a very fast Nissan Sports car. Both, it seems, had a penchant for fast cars. Maybe they'd learned to only let their warrior archetypes out between work and home.

Vernon.

September 2018 - Dream

I'm in a strange triangular-shaped living room; on one side there is a balcony that overlooks the sea where a young girl is, she's probably in her teens. I go out to her, and say, "Hello". She's a guest in this kind of hotel which I am the owner of. She says "Hello," quietly.

I walk back into the living room and there is another window looking out onto the sea too. I can see big waves coming towards us, so I say to her, "Look, have a look at this." We both do so, and she says, "It's a bit dangerous living so close to the sea". I say "Well, this property has been here a long time, but I guess there is a risk that I could be in trouble in the future. Especially with global warming and all that."

Her parents walk into the living room. I realise they have been guests before. I remember a previous conversation we had had. It had been about her father looking like he was a teacher, when in fact he wasn't. It's such a real memory that later when I woke up, I wondered whether I had actually had a dream with them in previously or was it simply a memory made up within that dream.

At one point, I hear his wife whisper something like, "I think he is an unsuccessful artist who's become a teacher."

I say, "Are you talking about me?"

She says, "Yes."

So, I ask, "Well, what do you count as a successful artist? Is it someone who has made lots of money and is recognised by their peers?"

They both say, "Yes."

I ask another question, "What if they are very unhappy, what about if they don't even like doing art, are they a successful artist then?"

The husband says, "No, not completely," and his wife nods in agreement.

I then put to them, "What about if I enjoy doing art?"

I can see that the other people in the room, other guests are nodding in agreement, they get what I'm saying. I look at the couple and say, "People are defined by their peers. They can say they are an artist, but if no one else agrees then they tend to be seen as deluded. But success is another matter, that can be measured in all sorts of ways."

When I wake up, I realise the dream is telling me something, it's telling me not to be a hotelier.

1977 – Aged 12 - Beat the Intro

I was sitting at the main terminus bus stop on Roundshaw. It was dark, but the air was still hot from a summer's sunny day. A car pulled up across the road, someone was smoking in the driver's seat and their window was down. They had their car stereo on loud. Some guitar notes were playing, quite long ones with big spaces between. Suddenly the drums kicked in along with a rhythm guitar and then the bass line thumped through the air. A voice sang out about surrendering on the quayside, hiding in the shadows and counting numbers down... to the waterline. The car's front wheels spun and then shot off fast.

I didn't know it then but that was my introduction to the music of Dire Straits.

1979 - Grenoble to Dijon

During the middle of our stay in Grenoble, the family I was staying with took me to one of their extended family parties in Dijon. Outside of getting me a bit tipsy on champagne, I don't remember much (maybe I was tipsier than I thought), but at one point, one of the guys there took me to a room and insisted on playing me an album of music which he said was fantastic. When I listened to it, it didn't grab me. I knew one of the songs from the radio and recognised the first track, it was the one I'd heard at the bus stop a few years before. It was the first album by Dire Straits, a music band that would become a big part of my and many other people's lives in a few years.

1979 - Survival of the British

Mum had put a camp bed up for my French exchange "survivor"; needless to say, he was less than impressed. To add further to his woes, I had a big tropical fish tank in my room and his head was positioned at the end of it for maximum distur- bance of sleep patterns. Not only was he homesick but he didn't like anything about England. Admittedly Mum's food was not the finest example of English cuisine but who doesn't like chips? I mean they're called French Fries for God's sake. Okay, not by French people. Anyway, he hardly ate anything, nor did he get much sleep, the weather was bad and we didn't get on. I don't think he ever came back to England and imagine he was one of the many Europeans who cheered when the Brexit vote came through.

At one point, he said something that annoyed me. I had a hairbrush on a stick that looked like a lavatory brush, so, I threw it at him. I couldn't understand his French but I'm sure it was something along the lines of, "How much worse can life get?"

I would have felt sorry for him, but the memory of his dog was still raw and, as you're getting to see, I wasn't a very nice person.

October 2018 - Connecting

Over the last month or so I have been working on the previous few chapters, initially because a piece of my music-making equipment needed repairing, so I thought I'd use the time to not only write but get some space from the music album I was working on. During this time as people have come to mind, I have searched them out on the Internet and tried to get back in touch. Overall, it's been a touching experience and helped to bring back many memories.

I haven't heard from a lot of these people for between 30 to 40 years. I know you might be thinking they were trying to tell me something, but just in case they weren't, I sent them a message.

For most of them, our last communication would have been by letter. There was a ceremony around corresponding by post, and whilst I wouldn't want to go back to it, it had some elements about it I miss. Waiting for a reply and its subsequent arrival had an emotional resonance and writing a letter by hand had a measure of romance that linked back to hundreds of years of tradition.

Every week I would probably write two or three letters and that went on right up to around 1996 when the Internet became a big part of my life. From then on communication involved looking at a screen and typing or putting a piece of plastic and glass to our faces to make a call. Previously a heavy home phone receiver pressed against our ear whilst we spoke into a mouthpiece, and apart from being heavy, the cost of calls tended to limit the length of chatting too.

Lee, (the guy I met in hospital when I had my foot removed), and I stayed in contact quite a bit. Lee was in a boarding school so had plenty of time to write. We also figured out a way of calling each other for free. We would go to phone boxes near where we lived at a pre-arranged time agreed in a letter then one of us would call the operator and request a reverse charge call, (collect call), to the other public pay phone. The operator would call that number and ask whichever one of us answered if we were willing to accept the charge, to which we'd say yes, and then we'd chat without having to pay for hours until it got too cold, or a queue of people grew outside the phone box. It was during some of these calls and letters, we arranged to meet up at a holiday camp for disabled kids during the summer.

1979 - Holiday Campsite for Disabled

George and Clive had no legs, they were bouncing on a trampoline on the lawn just outside the reception area when we arrived at the campsite. My heart sank because Clive was the guy who had given me a black eye in hospital when I grassed him up for smoking. George was just plain dangerous and Veronica, the girl who'd held my legs down as he punched me, was there too and there was something about her that scared me also.

Lee, who'd got the minibus with me from the hospital was less filled with dread. Instead, Clive was wary of him because once when they'd come to blows, Lee had unattached the hook from his artificial arm and thrown it at Clive's head catching him just above the eye. At that moment, their relationship was defined with Lee being marked as, "dangerous".

The campsite, which was a big field surrounded by trees had a main meeting hall, a toilet/shower block, a cookhouse to one side of it and tucked into the hillside, just below the main camping area, was an outdoor heated swimming pool. Lee and I were allotted a tent at the edge of the field near the drop to the pool. Another kid whom we hadn't met before was allocated our tent too.

The first evening went as most introductory events go, but from the outset, we made it clear we were aligned with the bad kids. For all the hassle we might get from the adult world, it wouldn't be as bad as the risks involved in going against George or Clive. Whilst they were in their mid-teens, they had an edge of violence about them that scared us, but even being on their side came with its risks.

On the first night, Lee, Clive, Veronica, George and I crept down to the swimming pool for a swim. It was eerie because a lot of steam was coming off the pool while all around us came the sounds of animals doing what animals do at night. We quietly slipped into the pool, whispering, and swimming as silently as we could. Suddenly I felt a hand grab my hair and push me underwater. Even in the darkness, I could tell it was Clive. I struggled, but couldn't escape, I thought he was going to let go of me, but he didn't. I struggled more, kicking off from the bottom of the pool, but I couldn't get above the surface of the water for a breath. I started to punch at his hand, I was feeling desperate, thinking he was going to kill me, I twisted frantically, then his hand was gone and I came to the surface. As I gasped for air both Clive and George were laughing.

"You could have killed me," I said.

"We were only having a laugh, what's the matter with you?" he said.

Veronica, who was sitting on the side of the pool could hear what had happened, "Leave him alone Clive, stop being a cunt," she said in her strong London accent.

Lee put his hand on Clive's head and pushed him down, but Clive batted his arm away.

"Fuck off Lee," Clive barked.

"Ya Don like it whan sumone duz it t'you, d'ya?" Lee said.

"Just watch it, Lee," Clive warned.

"Fuk off," Lee said disparagingly.

We slunk out of the pool, then made our way back up the hill to our tents. Still wet and shivering we got into our sleeping bags, had a chat then slept.

When I woke up it was to the sound of Lee complaining about something. There was a strong smell of shit. The boy sharing our tent had a colostomy bag which had leaked and due to us sleeping on a hill, he had slid towards Lee, who was now daubed in poo. When it came to urine or colostomy bags Lee was obviously not well-fated. After Lee got cleaned up and the tent had been sorted out, we asked if we could not share the tent with the guy anymore. Our wish was granted. The downside to this was the kid then told on us for swimming in the pool, so we were hauled in and given a stern warning that we'd be sent home if we did it again. A bit later, we watched the kid heading to his new tent, we checked for staff, then both of us ran past him and kicked his crutches into the air so he fell back. As we picked him up, we warned him that if he crossed us again there'd be hell to pay. He cried and we walked off feeling very self-satisfied. To him, we were as bad and frightening as Clive and George were to us.

1979 - Campsite

Relatively speaking, my misdemeanours were quite mild at this point, but I was certainly heading in the same direction as Clive and George. Clive eventually ended up doing time in prison, then after a period of substance abuse became a beggar. The last time I saw him he was begging outside a station in Richmond. I don't know what happened to him after that. As for George, I think he ended up in prison; he was extremely violent and even though he had no legs he was a formidable fighter. I don't know what path his life took either, but he certainly identified a lot with his own warrior archetype.

1979 - Campsite - The Drowning

For a day or so there was a truce between us, even so, Clive thought it was funny to try drowning me again but this time I fought back and started to lose my temper with him. At that point, he swam off. A few minutes later there was a bit of a panic, then we realised that one of the kids was being hauled out of the pool. As a couple of people applied mouth-to-mouth and cardiac resuscitation, we could see he was in a bad way. His eye sockets and lips were a purple-blue colour, and he was coughing up leaves and a bit later he died. He wasn't supposed to have gone into the pool as he had epilepsy. There would, of course, be an inquiry, and changes would be made, but for this child, it was all too late.

Clive had lost his legs whilst playing on train lines, Lee had lost his hand and foot playing between train carriages. Some kids, if they get the chance, will take deadly risks.

1979 - Campsite - Deserved Punishment

From that point on a sombre air permeated the camp and a few days later a memorial service was arranged for the kid who died, which his mother would be attending. All of us were summoned to attend the ceremony which was held around a tree in the centre of the site. Although Lee and I sat at the back and were out of view of the mother, our decision to get the giggles didn't go unnoticed. One of the older male organisers put his hand over my mouth, his other hand on the back of my neck and marched me away from the service, then pushed me to the ground and quite rightly gave me a full-throttled dressing down. He then placed me in the main meeting room and informed me I would be sent home.

After the formalities of the memorial service ended, people were milling around outside. I could see some of the other kids talking about me whilst Clive, George

354

and Veronica observed from a distance.

The main door slid open and two of the organisers came in.

The man who had pinned me to the ground said, "I think your behaviour has been disgusting, you don't deserve to be allowed to stay here, but Dennis here, he thinks you should be offered a chance at redemption. He thinks you should be allowed to stay if you work in the cookhouse till the end of the week. Do you want to do that?"

I sorrowfully nodded yes.

The other man interjected "Well?"

"Thank you. I'm sorry" I said.

"We've offered the same deal for your mate too and he's agreed to the same terms," Dennis said.

I continued the regretful act but knowing that Lee was going to keep me company in our punishment, filled me with joy.

1979 - Campsite - The Spotted Cow

Working in the cookhouse meant cleaning the pans used for cooking, some were so big that I could sit in them whilst I scraped off the dried porridge. It also involved serving food and dealing with selling sweets in the tuck shop. True to our Robin Hood selves we served big portions to those we liked and not so big ones to those we didn't, and when it came to selling sweets, we gave more change back to our chosen flock than they gave us in the first place. So, over a few days, we cemented more allegiance from a few of the kids, and because we got on with our duties so dutifully, the management felt we were taking our punishment seriously and were at least learning a lesson.

What this also meant was that outside of our chores, we were free to do what we liked. So, one evening we went for a walk to the local pub, The Spotted Cow. We were 14 years old, and the legal age for being in a pub unaccompanied was 18.

"Just be confident, walk up to the bar and calmly ask for a drink," Lee said.

So, we walked in and approached the bar. A blond woman with short hair said, "Hello Gentlemen, what can I get you?"

Lee said, "Half a shandy Luv," (look it's the 1970's).

"And you sir?" she said tilting her head at me.

"A snowball please," Outside of a Babycham, it was the only alcoholic drink I liked.

She almost burst out laughing but kept a straight face, "Would you like a cherry on that sir?"

"Yes please," I said smiling.

"Take a seat, I'll bring them over," she said.

The pub was empty.

"Ayup," said Lee, "They've got a one-armed bandit, d'ya wanna have a go, Simon?"

"OK," I said.

"Don't worry, I'll 'elp ya, I play one like this all the time up in Barnsley."

So, I put 50p in and didn't win a thing, and that was the end of my gambling days, (excluding doing the lottery). Losing 50p back then was quite a bit, but in its way, it was a very cheap lesson.

"You are over 18, aren't you?" The bar lady asked.

"Yes, I'm 19 and he's 18," Lee said. Then he reeled off our dates of birth as previously prepared.

"It's ok," she said, "I'm just checking."

"Aw don't worry, we're always being asked, aren't we Simon? We look young for our age." Lee said with yet another well-rehearsed performance.

I nodded in agreement.

She knew we were underage, but in those days, especially in country pubs, it wasn't a big deal and as long as she asked us if we were over 18 and we gave the correct answers, it wasn't a problem. Well, that's what I planned on telling the judge.

1979 - Campsite - My Enemy's Enemy

It wasn't all plain sailing over the remaining days. Lee and I were seen as being delinquent, especially by the staff, and there were quite a few people who wanted to bring us down a peg or two.

At one point one of the Scoutmasters went for me, I can't remember why, but I expect he had good reason to. He pushed me down and with his hand around my throat said something like "Either he goes, or I go!" Yes, I definitely must have said something bad, and it probably didn't help matters when my reaction to his ultimatum was to say, "Bye then, do you need help packing?" At that point, he lifted his arm to thump me but within a second Clive was by his side, grabbing his arm and saying. "If you touch him, you'll have me to deal with." Which probably allowed him to pull back from his anger enough to back off. From then on Clive was much friendlier towards me as I had become his enemy's enemy.

A bit later, one of the men who worked in the kitchen with us told me I couldn't hurt a fly, that I hadn't defended myself against the Scoutmaster's attack. So, remembering what the Taekwondo guy had taught me in Grenoble I suggested he try kicking me in the balls. This must have been an odd response because he looked a bit perturbed. He probably thought that if he hurt me, he'd be in trouble and if by some miracle I managed to hurt him he wouldn't look good either. For some reason, he too became a bit friendlier towards me after that. I was beginning to sense there were complicated codes of allegiance and respect that I hadn't come across before, probably because men start to recognise that at 14, boys are beginning to no longer be children, although they certainly aren't men either.

1979 - Tweeddale Karate Club

I had been going to the karate club for about five weeks when Grant couldn't take a session. Instead, one of the brown belts called Martin took it and "not that it matters" but he was white. Within about five minutes, he told me to sit in the corner because I had been talking when I shouldn't have. I knew I had to do what I was told but was still cursing under my breath. After about 20 minutes he said, "Do you think you can behave yourself now?"

"Yes, sir," I said sheepishly.

"Well get in line then."

And from then on, at least in the karate dojo, I did.

Dedicated to Vernon Mallinson born 27 February 1910 and died 1991 –
Awarded the Ordre de Leopold II

And to Chris, the boy who died at the holiday camp.

Chapter 26
Significance and Emptiness

2018 - Dream

There's a group of us, men and women, in black paramilitary uniforms, carrying guns, running along a road in the city at night. Someone gets shot at, so we dart into an old hotel, as we enter, we realise there's no one in it.

We run up a couple of flights, then through a long corridor to a large room. I turn the lights off as we all take defensive positions around the room and back down the corridor. Near the end of the corridor, the lights from the foyer just about illuminate the semi-silhouetted figures against the wall, their guns are at the ready. A couple of spotters stand to the side of the large windows as they try to work out where the shot came from.

One of the spotters quietly calls out, "Someone's entering the building, I think it's just a civilian."

I'm suspicious, so reply, "I'll go check them out,"

I make my way to the lobby where I can see a woman, wearing a long beige heavy coat, is walking up the stairs. She exudes grace, her hair is in a 1930s style, and she's wearing a dark burgundy beret.

I point my pistol at her, and say, "Excuse me".

She smiles, and seductively whispers, "That's not very polite."

I lower my gun. She walks slowly back down the stairs toward me. As she gets closer, she points a gun at me, so I raise mine. It happens in a moment.

"What do you want?" I ask.

"Why did you stop me?" She asks.

I get the feeling she is going to shoot me. But I'm feeling very connected to her. We're looking into each other's eyes. Even so, I am still trying to squeeze the trigger of my pistol, my hand is shaking slightly with the strain. I'm wondering if the bullet will stop her from firing her gun too. It's imperative I shoot first and pull the trigger without her realising what I'm attempting to do, but no matter how hard I try I can't squeeze it hard enough. I hear a gun go off in the distance, I wonder if it's hers, but we are both still standing, guns pointing at each other.

I'm aware there's a man now standing to our side.

2018 Universal Dream Studios - Part 1

A voice over the Tannoy calls out, "Okay everyone, that's a wrap".

The woman in the beret hands her gun to the man opposite her who takes a camera contraption from his forehead.

"When does your shift end?" He asks.

"I've got a few more hours left then I'm off. Why, what are you thinking?" She says.

"Do you fancy coming out with me and Dave, we're going swimming in the back-drop sea later?"

She smiles, "Sure, I'll see you there."

The group of soldiers amble out along the corridor, some are smoking, and some playing with their guns.

There are a few oohs and ahhs coming from them as a figure comes out of one of the rooms. It's a Queen Elizabeth II look-alike holding on to her crown and running to get downstairs. "Sorry everyone, it's a busy day, night, whatever," she says. She grabs a cigarette from one of the "soldiers", takes a drag, and says, "Thank you, sweetheart," as she mounts the banister rail in a side saddle position and slides down it while waving regally. Everyone cheers.

1979 - Karate - Part 1

John didn't want me to do Karate so when I came home, I'd put my karate uniform, called a Gi (pronounced like the word "key" but with a G), into the boot of Mum's car. She'd then wash it for me, ready for my next session a few days later.

1979 - Wilson's School

Art at Wilson's back then was not a priority subject. The woodwork and metal-work rooms were bigger than the art room and on top of that, the art department was positioned as far to the rear of the school as possible. Mr James, who was our art teacher, wasn't too bothered though. He had a job, he did what he had to do, and as long as he was left to his own devices there wasn't a problem. At one point, I pushed my luck too far with him, so he took me into a side room and, whilst giving me a pep talk, he wandered up and down the room, whacking a cane against his hand. I didn't pay much attention to his words; I just heard the thwack of the stick against his skin.

As much as people disagree with corporal punishment, I have to say that moment did affect me. It scared me and definitely caused me to modify my behaviour. Consequently, over the next few months, I started concentrating on drawing, but one day, without looking up, he barked, "Smith! Come and see me at the end of the class."

1979 - Wilson's School Dinner Hall

I've gone back to the dinner ladies to ask for seconds. If there was any food left over, they were happy for it to be used up. I mean it wasn't as if they were going to take it home with them. For me though, having spent so much time in hospitals and institutions, I had a palette perfectly suited to school dinners, so I often asked for seconds. They probably thought my mum didn't feed me so were always obliging, plus of course, it was a compliment to their cooking.

On this occasion, though, I decided to show one of the dinner ladies a poem I had just written. Instead of saying, "What a load of crap", which it was, she started showing the others there and saying how sad it was. "Oh, that's beautiful Simon," they said. Even now I can, shamefully, remember the start of that poem. It was a poem about looking for somebody to love me, someone to fill a hole inside me. I think it started "This poem is to somebody, but to nobody it seems, I write with all my heart this time to the person of my dreams". It would take years for me to realise the significance of those words, maybe that's why the dinner ladies reacted as they did. It wasn't a good poem, but it struck at the heart of many people's dilemmas. When it comes to relationships, the elusive romantic illusion that we yearn for, and the reality of relationships are often very hard to come to terms with. But it was also a call to be loved, rather than to love, and that would be something I'd eventually have to come to understand were very different things.

1979 - Home

By 14, if Mum ever tried to hug me, I'd wince and move away. I was very much detached from home life as it was no longer a place of great connection for me. Even though Mum and John's acts of kindness existed they were largely unappreciated by me.

Life mainly took place outside of home. I also had familial connections with others, such as Rob and his family, or my Mum's cousin Paul and his wife, Ann. There was also another couple who'd spend time with me too; they were neighbours also called Ann and Paul. There was karate, and my friend Peter who shared an interest in tropical fish with me, and of course other friends too. But for all of that, there was a feeling something was missing. At the time, I thought it was because I didn't have a girlfriend, but that was just a dream.

2018 October – An Italian Café Eastbourne

I'm chatting to a friend over a coffee who I've bumped into in the café. She's waiting for her husband.

"I'm reading Nietzsche again," she says.

362

"Why's that?" I ask.

"I don't know, maybe it's to make my mind work in a more focused way. I did my degree in Philosophy," she says.

"Sometimes people read philosophy because they are trying to find answers to things about their psychological issues," I say.

"Yes, that's true," she nods.

"I don't think philosophy or religion can fill you with meaning," I say, "Because feeling meaningful or buoyant is a feeling. If you don't feel it, then the question is - why don't you feel it now when you did previously?" She's looking at me and glazing over a bit, I'm on a roll so I carry on regardless. "The answer to that isn't probably related to philosophy or metaphysics."

With a look of, "finally," on her face, she interjects, "Yes, not only that, a lot of people do philosophy or psychology to try to solve their own problems as well, but they won't find their answers there either."

"It's funny," I say, "I got into Psychology and Philosophy but what I needed was psychological help which I got through therapy."

"Did it work?" she asks.

I make a gesture of presenting myself as a perfect specimen.

(As an aside, chapter 27 came about because of this accidental meeting of our minds.)

1979 - Secrets and Lies

Most of my friends and their parents were sympathetic when I told them about the arguments between John and myself. Of course, they were only getting my side of the story and probably knew that too. So, when I told one of John's close relatives that Mum was secretly washing my karate suit, she decided that instead of going to Mum first and maybe sorting out the issue with her, she'd go straight to John who was, predictably, very angry. Consequently, a big argument ensued, at the end of which Mum persuaded John to give me a chance, especially as over the last month or so, my behaviour had improved, which, she suggested, was partly to do with the karate lessons.

Whilst the truth was out, and in some ways, things were resolved, the fracture between John and Mum was even bigger than it had ever been.

Mum was also very angry with me because I hadn't been wise enough to keep my mouth shut. Still, she agreed that she was very surprised this relative had grassed her up too. From the outside, it's easy to see that secrets and lies often cause bigger problems in the long run. But there are times when it's better to lie, especially if you're a secret agent of course.

2018 Universal Dream Studios - Part 2

As the woman, the soldier and David drank cocktails by the sea, her eyes caught David's for a moment, and they looked at each other longingly.

Her phone bleeped so she looked down at it.

"Hey, Sylvia, did you hear what happened to June?" David asked.

Still looking at her phone, she said, "Hold on, I've got one coming up."

Just as she was going to answer David, a man passed by with one of those camera devices strapped to his forehead. Sylvia looked at him, squinted her eyes slightly then turned away. At first, he kept looking toward her too but once he was out of earshot, another guy nearby shouted, "It's okay, he's gone". She waved a thank you at him and went to continue the conversation, but the sky darkened, and a fleet of alien spacecraft flew over.

She sighed, "Never a dull moment hey?"

1979 - Karate - Part 2

There are many different styles of Karate. Normally a style comes about because a student of one style becomes very successful then, either because the teacher they followed dies or there's a disagreement between them, they branch off. From that point, variations of the original techniques occur over time so eventually, distinct differences develop. Most people do not join a style of Karate based on working out which is best, they join for other reasons, such as its locality or a friend recommending it.

Like most ideologies, religions or political positions, the main reason we choose them is rarely based on logic alone, but on time and place. It's where we find ourselves at a particular moment in relation to their availability.

You might think advertising is there just to convince you to buy something you haven't already got but does it not also reassure those who've already purchased the item? The same is true within the martial arts world, practitioners tend to believe whatever they are doing is the best, but the truth is far more complicated.

There were two symbols sewn to my karate suit. The first was the Kanji calligraphy, which was written vertically near my left chest area (no doubt placed near the heart on purpose). Unbeknown to me at the time it was shaped like a Samurai sword safely held in its scabbard.

The second symbol was the Kanku. This was sewn on the left sleeve halfway up the upper arm, which was lucky for me considering if it had been lower down, I'd have had to grow my arms longer.

Zen monks would put their hands together with an opening between their thumbs and their forefingers so that they made a circle through which they could gaze up to the sky and meditate. There are lots of other meanings ascribed to the symbol such as the outer circle representing continuity or cycles of life, while the smaller circle in the middle represents the universe. There was also a more graphic interpretation whereby the symbol represented hands where strength was where the wrists were and peaks where the fingers met.

The reason I wanted to spend so much time on this was to show that within Karate, a discipline that appears initially to be just about fighting has other layers that most of us can connect with too. After all, do we not all look to the stars through our limited field of vision, and wonder what it's all about?

I knew the poetry I showed to the dinner ladies was somewhat lacking in, well, poetry, but in every move and turn of Karate, there were lines and verses that resonated with a kind of poetry deep inside me.

1979 - Poetry, Sketchbooks and Photo Albums

At 14 I started getting into writing poems; the first one I wrote was inspired by one I'd read in a newspaper about Elvis. Although I tend to cringe at most of the "poetry" I wrote during this time, this one was no exception. Nowadays, I find it hard to understand what initially acted as a catalyst for me to start writing them in the first place. I probably found the process cathartic and I may have thought if I was suffering then maybe the rest of the world could suffer too by having to be subjected to this rubbish. After all, a problem shared is a problem doubled. Mum would often say, "They're very deep," which roughly translated as, "What the fuck was that about". However, I would have still taken that as a compliment. As the months went by, I wrote enough poems to fill a hard-backed exercise book, on which one of the kids at school drew a skull and crossbones. Even that filled me with pride, so I left it on.

To help me carry my poetry and sketchbooks I acquired a holdall which resembled the official karate sports bags that people had at the karate club. I couldn't afford one of those, so, to let the world know I did karate I wrote BKK British Kyokushinkai Karate in capital letters using Tippex type correction fluid; which I have to say, looked rather incompetently scribed, but to me, aged 14, I didn't care. I'd saved a lot of money. I'm sure one day we'll find a hormone that causes delusion, and when we do, we'll realise that teenagers are full of it.

A few months later one of the other boys at school photographed me doing some karate moves. Given I had only been practising it for about nine months and had just got off the second white belt onto a blue one, I think we can safely say it was rather grandiose of me to be doing any kind of demonstration, but I was besotted by Karate. It filled my every waking moment and the guy taking photos was just practising his photography skills. To be fair, he mainly wanted to photograph me breaking some tiles with my arm, which he did, and then he got me to jump off a bench and do a flying butterfly kick where both legs kick out sideways simultaneously. In the photo, I looked like a plane coming into land which was apt because a few weeks later I was brought down to the ground when I overheard a couple of the other karate guys at the club saying, "Did you see Simon's photos? He'll be ok, as long as there's a bench nearby?"

As much as I was upset by being slagged off it was a good lesson. In the adult world, pretence is not looked upon well, but sadly that still didn't stop me from carrying my karate photos in my bag of tricks. A pleasure many an unsuspecting stranger would have forced upon them at any opportunity.

These days I have Facebook and my website and this to show off on, so that saves me carrying a bag.

2018 - The Respect I Yearned For

When I look at teenagers, I often see them as cockatoos, strutting about with lots of plumage. I had no confidence in how I looked when I was a teenager, so I probably thought I could be attractive in other ways. But the thing is, I don't think a lot of what I was doing at that point was about attracting girls, it may have been more about trying to gain some respect from adults. I knew that compared to other kids at school I wasn't as academically capable. I also realised that in the world of karate, I was nothing, but for my age, I was quite good at drawing, and to my mum, I had a talent for poetry (which I didn't), but I could feel that being good at things might get me some of the respect I yearned for.

1980 - Raynes Park Karate Club

Shihan Arneil 7th Dan (he's now a Hanshi, a 10th Dan) used to teach kids on a Saturday morning. This day he took us out to the field.

"Take off your Gi tops," he said.

So, we all folded our tops as we had been taught and tied our belts around the rolled-up garment. He then took us through one of the katas.

"Listen," he said, "You can't make your Gi make a noise, can you? You can't try to impress people with a trick. You are like parrots who have lost all their feathers. All they have is their song."

1987 - Therapy

Therapist: So, you're feeling very regretful?

Me: Yes, I feel awful. I know people say we shouldn't regret anything, but I do.

Therapist: Why shouldn't we regret things? Surely that's a motivation to improve ourselves.

1980 - Significance

Perhaps I wanted to feel significant because I keenly felt a lack of expectations from others due to my disability. On the bus from school one day, I passed two old ladies whom I then sat behind. As they spoke, I overheard them saying it was such a waste of time sending me to a good school like Wilson's as I would never be able to do anything useful with that knowledge. No doubt such low expectations would have got to me, but after meeting my father many years later, I could see wanting to shine was in my DNA. Maybe it's in all of us to desire significance in the world and while it's easy to see it as precociousness, and no doubt it was, that energy or drive to do well in the world is both a cause for good and ill in many of us, not just someone with a disability. Even at 14, I understood that others saw my disability as the main drive and influence in my life whereas I saw it as a part of who I was, but it certainly wasn't the only one.

1979/80 - If Only I Had

At 14 I had become aware of the importance of significance in the adult world and was also conscious of an emptiness inside. It's not surprising that people call their partners "my significant other," especially in a world where the notion of a well-functioning partner is seen as the main route to happiness.

As children, we hear, "And they lived happily ever after," repeated on an almost nightly basis, but as most of us come to find, our relationships generally do not automatically bring happiness. In fact, for many, they stir up deeply uncomfortable feelings which can often be a painful experience. The expectations around relationships are so high that it is no wonder that many of them flounder. At 14 though, I was sure a relationship would solve all my troubles and life would feel complete... if only I had a girlfriend.

In a way, I probably held on to that myth emotionally throughout my whole life, even if I was aware it wasn't true. Indeed, when I first started writing this, I was desolated at the thought of losing Monica and later, Miss Lovelight, worrying I might be alone for the rest of my life. That isn't to say companionship is not a large component of what makes us happy but to see any single component as a panacea is not realistic for most of us.

Cardiff – Italian Restaurant with Monica

I'm in a restaurant in Cardiff with Monica. The waiter is a short stout Italian man in his 60s. He's making us a Zabaglione and as he stirs it, he says, "You know, when I came to Britain over 40 years ago, I had no expectations and I have had a wonderful life."

He pours the zabaglione into two long-stemmed glass dishes.

"There," he smiles proudly.

"But you know," he sighs, "my children, they expect everything, and they are never happy. If they get something they don't appreciate it, and if they don't get something, wow, then we hear about it."

Given what he said I felt slightly worried about expecting it to taste okay, but luckily all he heard from us was how lovely it was.

2018 - Universal Dream Studios - Part 3

David looks at Sylvia, "Do you ever wonder how big Universal Dream Studios are?"

Sylvia, confidently answers, "It's all in the creator's mind, it doesn't have any dimensions in the sense you're thinking about. If he wants a new planet or a galaxy, it's there immediately."

There's a pause, then David says, "Yes, I guess you're right, but still, he must be in a space, and how big is that?"

Sylvia laughs, "Who said he's in a space?"

1980 - Peter and the Ghost Train

Peter who was the kid I'd got lost on Roundshaw that first day we visited it, shared an interest in tropical fish with me. We'd grown up together because our mums were friends but now in our teens, we'd meet up independently of them. Sometimes we'd go to the tropical fish shop together. We'd then have to get back to our homes within a certain time so the water didn't get too cold, or the air wouldn't run out in the sealed plastic bag. It must have bought out our maternal archetypes as we'd have to nurture our new pets, keeping them close to our hearts inside our coats all the way home.

On other occasions, we'd go swimming together and, for the life of me, I can't understand how it came about, but we'd travel to Crystal Palace Sports Centre, especially when we had other pools much closer by. One of the things that drew us there was a secret abandoned platform in the station that could only be accessed by crawling past a panel. It was as if we'd entered a dream world or a film set. We'd climb down to where the tracks had been and play on the lines, only worrying about the possibility of a ghost train coming. We'd look at the old signs and posters and feel the presence of those who had frequented this place. It was empty, but it was full of ghosts to us, and for that, it was truly magical.

1979 - Sutton Market

There was a big market at the bottom of the high street in Sutton. Sutton was the nearest large town to where I lived. Like most outside markets there were lots of stalls where a very wide selection of goods was sold.

I'd often end up talking to the guy who owned the leather goods stall, his name was Jack and he'd come all the way from Ascot to Sutton to sell his wares. I'd gone to him originally to buy a belt with a big buckle, the kind Elvis wore in his later years. The one I chose had written on it, "The Right to Bear Arms", which I no doubt thought was slightly funny in a "post-modern" way.

What was special, to me, about this stallholder was he'd seen Elvis perform at a couple of college concerts before he was famous. "You know," he said in his slightly Anglicised American accent, "Elvis wasn't that special at that point, it took him a while to develop into what you know as Elvis, to us he was a lot like the other kids performing."

One day I brought an oil painting to him I'd done of Elvis. It was still a bit wet which pissed him off when he got some on his clothes. However, he was so impressed, he tried to sell it on his stall. It didn't sell, but when I'd come to check on its lack of progress, he would get me to mind the stall for him, a chore he'd pay me for with items from the stall. In a way, it was my first job, and I liked the feeling of being accepted and useful.

One day, I told him I hated "Punks", or something like that. He looked at me for a moment and very seriously said, "Hate is a strong word, you must always be very careful about using it for a group of people. It's how the Nazis got people to agree to kill millions of innocent people. Don't let me hear you say you hate people again, okay?" I was a bit taken aback and nodded. But his words have never left me. Nowadays I say, "I have a bit of an issue with such and such," but we all know what I mean.

One cold day he got me to try selling a box of cheap plastic belts by calling out something like, "Come and get your cheap belts here," but I only managed to sell two. He probably hoped I might get some sympathy sales, but the belts were so rubbish even I didn't stand a chance. Whilst I was doing that, my mum's sister-in-law walked past, stopped and said hello, so we chatted and being proud to have a job I told her I was working in the market. (Kind of).

It was a very cold day and after my brave attempts at selling rubbish, Jack gave me a sip of brandy. I didn't like the taste but a few minutes later my whole back got hot. I'd never experienced such a sensation. It was yet another introduction to the secret world of adults.

When I got home, John told me I'd been spotted in the market, and how ashamed he was I was working there, mixing with the lowest of the low. "I better not find out you're working there again otherwise I'll cut your pocket money, do you understand?"

"There's nothing wrong with people who work on the market," Mum said indignantly, at which point John stormed out of the room.

"Don't take any notice of him, he's had a bad day at the bookies, and he's had a couple of drinks. If he cuts your pocket money, I'll give you some," she whispered.

I continued visiting the market and given it wasn't technically a job I'd just socialise a bit, help a little, and get given some food and drinks but slowly, over time, I stopped going there as much. Then one day Mr James the art teacher barked at me to see him later.

1979 - Meeting with Mr James

After the class, I stayed behind as ordered but couldn't help but wonder what I'd done wrong now.

"Sit down Smith," Mr James said nodding at a seat. So I did as I was told for a change.

"I've noticed you've been working on your drawing skills lately and I was thinking you might want to try life drawing classes at the local college."

"What, with real naked models?" I asked in shock.

"Yes," he said, obviously wondering if he was making a mistake.

Feeling beyond relieved I said, "Yes, that would be great."

And so, a couple of weeks later I enrolled in the Sutton College of Liberal Arts Life drawing Saturday morning classes and from then on, I didn't have time to work at the market anymore.

1979 - Sutton College of Liberal Arts - Life Drawing

Right next door to Sutton Library, and joined by internal doors, was Sutton College of Liberal Arts. As I entered the building there was a reception area, then a staircase up to the first floor where the canteen was situated, and on the floor above, there were the art rooms. When I walked into the art area, a scruffy man with curly hair and a big smile of yellowed teeth asked what I was there for. I nervously said, "Life drawing," so he pointed me to a doorway at the end of a concertinaed dividing curtain. I went in and there were a few people in the room sorting out their sketch pads and pencils sitting on little wooden contraptions, which I'd later come to know as donkeys. The teacher came up to me smiling and gently asked if I was there to do life drawing. I said yes, and she asked me where I wanted to sit. "I prefer to sit at a desk please". So, she helped pull a table into place and put a chair in position and then I got myself ready. The man in the room next door was being loud and funny but our room had a serious solemnness about it. I was obviously in the real art room.

There was a changing cubicle in the corner from which a woman came out in a blue dressing gown. I started to feel a little nervous. She was young and looked pretty.

"Hello class," the teacher said very calmly, "My name is Melody, and I am going to be your teacher for this term. In a minute, I shall pose the model. I would like you to draw what you see, and I shall come around and help those of you who wish to receive help."

She sounded and looked a bit like a character from a Janet Austen novel. She had long brown hair tied back in a bun and her features seemed very delicate. Everything about her came over as considered, and there was a serenity about her, which was something I had never come across before. In a way, she was everything I was not.

"Jean," she said, "if I could get you to lay down here, please."

The model took off her dressing gown. My eyes passed over her, and then something unexpected happened. I suddenly lost all interest in her as a sex object. There was no feeling of titillation, just a feeling of wanting to get on with the drawing.

I still have that drawing somewhere, it wasn't very good, but it showed promise and somewhere in that first session Melody and I made a good, "student-teacher" connection. I was not only struck by her demeanour, but I could tell she had a lot to offer in terms of technical expertise. I was filled with respect for her, and I think she had a real desire to help me develop.

As the model got up from her pose, I could see some deep indentation in her chest where her fingernails had rested. They were a message from her to us that no matter how hard we looked, there was a whole universe unravelling within her, within the stillness portrayed before us.

1983 - Chelsea Art College - Life Drawing Class

I very rarely ever felt sexually or romantically interested in the models in our life drawing classes, not that that stopped me from trying to chat them up given any opportunity. This time though, in this old room, with the autumn light hard upon the walls, I was immediately struck by the beauty of the woman modelling for us.

I sat on the floor, my sketchbook on my lap, trying to capture whatever it was about her that was stirring in me. There wasn't enough time though, there never could be. After she went, I felt a sense of loss. A few days later she was posing clothed for another of our classes. I wanted to ask her if she'd like to meet up, maybe for a coffee; I even wrote that on a small piece of paper, but, uncharacteristically of me, I knew it wouldn't be the right thing to do, so, I didn't do or say anything about it.

A few weeks later she was in the canteen so I asked if I could join her. We got talking and as the conversation developed, I realised that she was very political, especially in terms of women's and anti-establishment issues. By the time we'd finished talking, I was almost petrified as one wrong word might have been my last. But still, the conversation rolled naturally and so we arranged to meet up at her squat in Brixton for dinner one evening.

After that, we saw each other a few times, just as friends. Although, when she told me she'd written a poem about me my heart rushed but, try as much as I could to get her to show it to me, she wouldn't. The next time we spoke she told me she'd met a man who she felt was 'the one'. By then I no longer had any aspirations that we'd ever get together, especially given in terms of politics and intellect, she was so much more advanced than I.

A year later I was at a friend's house, and we were talking about life drawing when my friend's uncle said, "That's strange, I've just read a poem about someone with short arms drawing a naked model. I've got it with me, do you want to read it?"

As soon as I set my eyes on the page, I could see the model's name. The poem spoke about the feelings she had when we first met. How she felt my desire and the contrast of her beauty against my imperfections. At one point, she described my finger as "horrible", and I realised that's why hadn't wanted to show me the poem. When I called her to tell her I'd seen it I think she felt a little ashamed, but of course, I was bowled over by having a poem written in a book of poetry about me. As you can see, I'm easily bought off. But then with lines that spoke of my breath being on her face, and her flesh being stirred, who could blame me?

1980 - Equal Footing

Within months of starting life drawing classes, I realised when it came to Art, I'd be able to compete on an equal footing with others. In terms of karate, even if I had fantasies of having success in it, I understood I had my limitations. There would always be the possibility of teaching, but that would sit too close for comfort to the saying, "There are those that do and those that teach."

So, at 15 I found I was able to gain a bit of self-respect when it came to drawing, but at the same time was happy to be involved in practising karate even though I'd never be any good. Those two directions became important throughout my life. One may be good at something, and one may love doing something, even though one isn't that proficient at it, but choosing which one to focus on can often be an interesting quandary.

In my mid-20s, I decided to focus on music; it's something I had no formal knowledge of nor was I ever likely to be successful in, but I thought that the pleasure of doing it was so great it made it worth concentrating on.

At thirteen I had lots of empty space around me, but by fifteen I was beginning to fill that space with things I could be good at or at least feel passionate about. I began to experience the pleasure of living.

In my thirties, I worked in substance abuse centres and could see how a lot of the clients had lives that solely revolved around drugs or drinking. Half the battle for them was to start living again and to see the pleasure in life. The thing is though, even when you do that, you'll still have to face emptiness and psychic pain at times. There's also a danger of going too far in the other direction, I mean by "living" life too much to the full, so much so that one doesn't have time to feel the sadness, loneliness, and emptiness which we must all feel sometimes, even in the best of situations.

At fifteen I didn't turn to drink or drugs, however; either I'd feel depressed and not know how to cope with it or would focus on finding a girlfriend to solve all my problems or worse still, get involved with girls I didn't want to be with, just so I could distract myself.

1986 - Therapy

Simon: I hate feeling depressed.

Therapist: Do you not think it's important to feel sad at times? I mean depression and sadness are a bit different. There are lots of different versions of sadness and depression but trying to get away from it could be a bit like not facing something that must be faced if it is to be less dominating. Perhaps it's a part of you crying out to be heard.

Simon: I see what you're saying but I still don't like feeling like no one cares or feeling lonely.

Therapist: I don't think it's as simple as that. Let's say someone keeps telling you they care for you. Do you think you might still feel those same doubts?

Simon: No.

Therapist: [Laughing a little] I think you know what I mean. These feelings are coming from you, from a part that feels like it is punctured, so no matter how much air is pumped in, after a while you will keep feeling deflated.

Simon: So, let's say we find what's punctured me, will working that out suddenly fix me?

Therapist: It's more of a slow process, it's not so much about intellectually recognising something and then it goes away, it's not like in the movies. It's partially about understanding yourself as well as experiencing the relationship with your therapist, me.

Simon: I don't understand, it's not like a real relationship, I mean you're paid to talk to me, you might care a little, but it's not the unconditional love that I want. I can't see how that could work.

Therapist: Do you not think it's interesting that you see me as someone who is like a stone, someone who is just here for the money? It must be hard to feel cared for if you can't accept there's any care here. Are you interested in trying to find out why you think and automatically feel like that?

Simon: Yes, I suppose so.

1986 - Therapy

Therapist: Have you ever heard that saying, it goes something like 'The knife that carves out pain leaves a vessel for joy to run through', I think there's a lot of truth in that. In time, you may come to see pain as less of an enemy than you're seeing it now.

2018 - Joy and Sorrow

I just looked up that quote, it's from Khalil Gibran's chapter, "On Joy and Sorrow", from his book "The Prophet". If you can, it's worth reading. I shall reproduce it below.

> *Then a woman said, "Speak to us of Joy and Sorrow".*
> *And he answered:*
> *"Your joy is your sorrow unmasked.*
> *And the self-same well from which your laughter rises was oftentimes filled*
>   *with your tears.*
> *And how else can it be?*
> *The deeper that sorrow carves into your being, the more joy you can contain.*
> *Is not the cup that holds your wine the very cup that was burned in the*
>   *potter's oven?*
> *And is not the lute that soothes your spirit, the very wood that was hollowed*
>   *with knives?*

When you are joyous, look deep into your heart and you shall find it is only
that which has given you sorrow that is giving you joy.
When you are sorrowful look again in your heart, and you shall see that in
truth you are weeping for that which has been your delight.
Some of you say, "Joy is greater than sorrow," and others say, "Nay, sorrow is
the greater."
But I say unto you, they are inseparable.
Together they come, and when one sits alone with you at your board,
remember that the other is asleep upon your bed.
Verily you are suspended like scales between your sorrow and your joy.
Only when you are empty are you at a standstill and balanced.
When the treasure-keeper lifts you to weigh his gold and his silver, needs must
your joy or your sorrow rise or fall."

"On Joy and Sorrow"
From "The Prophet" by Khalil Gibran

2018 - Dream

I'm walking through a crowd of people on a beach. I catch a woman's eye, she looks familiar. I feel an overwhelming feeling of love and pain. I look towards her again but she's looking away. I feel like she's scared to look, if she does, I know we will be in danger. I decide it's best to look away and keep walking.

The phone rings and wakes me from the dream. It's the garage wanting me to book a time for my car to be serviced.

I go back to sleep.

I'm on a bed with a woman. I feel like we love each other. I want to kiss her.

The phone rings and I'm woken again!

I sigh, "Oh fuck it! I might as well get up, I guess it just wasn't meant to be."

376

Chapter 27
The Meaning of Life

The Ripples Her Breath Caused Moved Through Time and Space

For most of these chapters I write about something I experienced and then reflect on it, but this chapter follows a theme and from it, incidents came to mind.

I hadn't initially planned to write this chapter as it is, but the conversation I mentioned in the last chapter, the one in the Italian café, helped bring it about.

She blew on her coffee to cool it down and the ripples her breath caused moved through time and space to me, and from me to you, but you are not the end of it.

When people ask me if I'm religious I say, "I think agnostic but feel spiritual", but it's a bit more complicated than that.

The Meeting of Minds – Part 1

In the world this story is set, curbing people's curiosity, especially around subjects of significance, has been one of the most successful ways to discourage dissent. Making people feel information ought to be simple and complicated ideas are just a means of obfuscation or, at the very least, boring you into submission, has led to a society where just showing two pages of writing causes nausea for most 'readers'. Even this paragraph is a bit of a struggle.

The best things in life are not "things", but to many people, even though they didn't use 99% of the things they possessed, they still sought more. From cradle to grave, they would crave, crave., crave... But after all that, they still couldn't feel satisfied, so with credit cards in hand, they'd soon be back for more, and more, and more.

There were some though, who didn't buy into that way of living, and many of them wanted to meet with others to discuss their ideas and beliefs. But these meetings, these meetings of the mind, were viewed by the authorities as dangerous, so that meant going to them was too.

The Meeting of Minds - Part 2

I'm in a long room with tables through the middle of it, men and women are ambling around. On each table, are books and candles. This isn't a dream, but it is somewhere in your imagination though.

When people say they are not creative, I point out to them their imagination and dreams. Within a milli-seconds, their minds can design beautiful rooms and land-scapes. So, as we move through these spaces, I'm not sure who is guiding who. Maybe it's partly you, partly me, and partly those walking around the room.

Around the first table are a couple of women, one is a rabbi, and the other is a Christian bishop. Nowadays, even symbolic imagery has to follow inclusive guide-lines, which in this situation makes no difference, because they are all reading from the same book anyway.

The bishop clears her throat and the room falls silent.

"We are gathered here tonight to discuss the Meaning of Life. Simon is our guest and shall be writing about the proceedings as well as asking questions from a layperson's perspective, your identities will be protected.

So, without further ado, I shall put the case from my point of view, which is just one of many differing Christian perspectives. I believe that Humankind is made in the image of God, but the "Fall of Man" caused the offspring of Adam and Eve to inherit Original Sin and its consequences."

There are a few voices of dissent. "What do you define as God?", one asks then another adds, "Why did God let them fall in the first place? God must have known all the suffering that would cause."

The bishop looks irritated, but continues, "Please, I would like to finish, then I shall answer your questions."

"So much for turning the other cheek," a voice from the back shouts.

378

"Shh, shh, let her speak," comes another and finally the room quietens.

She takes a breath and looks at me, "So I take it you want to know what Man's main purpose is?"

I nod.

"Well, the answer, for me, is, Man's chief end is to glorify God and enjoy him forever. And, before you ask, God made us to know Him, to love Him, and to serve Him in this world, and to be happy with Him forever in heaven."

I'm a bit confused so ask, "Do you mean that metaphorically, as in whether we believe God exists or not as long as we accept God is in us, even just as a function of our brain, then we will be happy?"

She looks at me a bit sternly. "Well, I can't see how you can love and worship God if you only believe God exists in your mind. That sounds narcissistic to me."

I look back at her and try to explain, "Well for me, I can separate different parts of my mind, I can say I can't prove God exists, but I can also accept a part of me feels a God-like entity exists, at least in my psyche."

Her bottom lip pushes her top one into an upside-down smile, "That sounds like you're being disingenuous if you ask me," she says. "Listen, St. Ignatius of Loyola stated that the human person is created to praise, reverence, and serve God Our Lord, and by doing so, to save his or her soul. You seem to see the soul as a by-product of your brain, whereas I see our brains as a by-product of our souls. To me, God is real, whereas to you, God is just a figment of your brain."

I want to know why she feels so definite in her belief, so ask, "But can you prove the existence of God, or souls, or heaven, or everlasting life? Because, if you can't, that's a big problem to me."

She comes back with, "Romans 11:33 states: 'O the depth of the riches both of the wisdom and knowledge of God! How unsearchable are his judgments, and his ways past finding out!' You see, we cannot understand God, but God knows all."

I feel like we're getting somewhere, "So are you saying we can never really understand?"

She smiles and says, "Yes."

So I ask, "So, do we have to take all of this as the Gospel Truth without any evidence, to be guided by blind faith?"

She nods like she's been understood, "Yes."

I'm not giving up, "So, how do you know it's his word?"

"I believe it to be."

I sigh, then ask, "So is every word in the Bible the word of God?"

She pauses, puts her hand to her mouth and taps her fingers above her upper lip, "It's complicated, there are mistranslations, different opinions on the interpretations and historical context to take into account."

"But some people interpret it very literally," I say.

She replies, "Their interpretation is theirs, not mine, I can only speak for myself."

A quiet man is standing just behind her, listening in. He's not very tall, wearing glasses, and has a slightly greying beard.

He coughs, half puts his hand up but speaks without being invited, "I can't relate to theistic arguments anymore." He says, "It feels like something from a bygone age. I think if people enjoy it, that's good, but I doubt most people can truly relate to it now. But, to me, that's a good thing. That way people can relax and drift more into real spiritual experiences. Theism has tended to downgrade the universe to a mere collection of objects that we can't relate to, it's something people often use and abuse as they wish. Theism and galloping technology are twins. Theism is very male and rationalistic; it is part of the story but needs the feminine to balance it. In these centuries of war and consumerism, we've lost our compassion." He laughs, then says, "End of sermon".

The bishop asks him if he's a clergyman.

"I was", he says, "a long time ago."

Psychic Events

You might think I am being a bit harsh or blinkered but given I have experienced lots of "psychic events", I am open-minded about the possibility of there being more than just this physical existential dimension that we call the universe and life. At the same time, my logical side knows no one can prove there's a "God".

One may ask, "Who or what created the universe?" hoping the answer is God, but that question can be turned on its head too, "Who or what created God?"

Some may argue, "God is timeless and has no beginning or end," but again the same could be said of the universe, or at least what caused the Big Bang. Maybe time and the universe have no beginning or end either. However, because we are bound by beginnings and ends, it's almost impossible for us to truly understand existence as having no cause or beginning.

Scientists may argue time did not exist before the Big Bang, but we can't help but ask what caused the Big Bang, what was before?

The Meeting of Minds - Part 3

Distant police lights flash through the windows outside.

"Quickly", the bishop says, "Follow us."

We exit as fast as we can through a door into a dank thin tunnel where only small dim lights along the walls illuminate the passageway. When we come to a stop, we're in a commercial kitchen although there is no one working there. It's immaculate.

"Do you want some tea?" the bishop asks.

"Yes, I'd love some, thank you. What happened just then?" I ask.

She frowns. "We don't take any risks."

"Surely, it's not that bad?" I say.

"I'm a female bishop, having women priests has split the church. There's a consequence to sharing opinions and there are consequences to those consequences. Maybe you should speak to the rabbi while I make us some tea." She motions me toward her.

"So why do you think we're here?" I ask the rabbi.

"I don't think I'm going to be any more persuasive," she says laughing a little. "I think we are here to elevate those in the physical world and prepare for the world to come, the spiritual afterlife. We are not so focused on personal redemption, but instead on the salvation of mankind as well as ourselves and God."

I am not sure if I took all that in but feel like I got the gist of it. "I kind of get that helping others is a good thing to do, I also get developing ourselves is beneficial as well, but I still wonder why God made us go through all of this, and so much suffering. I get it that it's important to suffer too, especially in terms of developing ourselves, but the pain so many innocents have been forced to endure and the billions of people who have had awful lives, not just now, but throughout history, I find all that hard to fathom. Why, if God is so powerful, did he or she bother making us in the first place especially if she or he knew there would be so much suffering? What is there at the end of all of that that makes it worthwhile?".

"Paradise!" she smiles, "If you or anyone you loved could live in paradise forever, then how much suffering do you think would be worth it?"

"I don't know," I say, "But I also don't know if we'd want to live forever, and why not just make everyone perfect in the first place, I mean so perfect they wouldn't sin, just create them and stick them in paradise forever. Surely that would be kinder, and anyway, do you have any proof there's everlasting life?"

The bishop hands me some tea and says, "I'm sorry, but do you need help holding the cup?"

"No, I'm fine," I say as I put my arms out ready to dock with it.

"You're amazing, the way you cope. I'm very impressed." She says, "Anyway, as we were saying, the apostle Paul said in Romans 8:18 'I consider that our present sufferings are not worth comparing with the glory that will be revealed in us'."

I interject, "By the way, thank you, for the tea." I feel self-conscious because everyone is watching how I hold the cup. They're more interested in that than what we're talking about.

"So, you're not thanking me for my very apt quote?" she laughs. I laugh too, "No, but I can if you think I should, but about your quote," I say, "Well, it still relies on evidence of an afterlife."

There are a few "hear hears" from those listening in.

Her eyebrows are raised, "You do realise that this is faith, we know we can't explain everything, but as Isaiah says, 'As the heavens are higher than the earth, so are my ways higher than your ways and my thoughts than your thoughts'."

"So, again, it requires blind faith," I say, "and in a way, there's no point arguing because there's no conclusive proof one way or the other?"

"Exactly," she says, "how's your tea?"

"Heavenly," I say. "That's good" she smiles, "I think we are going back up, you can take your tea with you, do you want me to carry it?" I show her the empty cup, but my mouth is full of the last gulp. "Oh, you've drunk it all, that was quick. You should have savoured it."

1979 - Magical Thinking

I'm walking to the bus stop about half a mile away as I just missed the bus I normally get to go to school. I'm thinking that if I can get past the next lamp post before that blue car coming towards me passes, then there will be an alternative bus at the top of Wallington High Street that'll get me to school on time. I'm beginning to do a lot more of this lately, making deals with fate or is it, God? It's like asking fate to bring me good luck, it's almost a kind of prayer. As I get to the end of Park Gate Road there are a load of very small shops. One of them was a junk merchant. About a year beforehand I was taking jewellery I'd stolen from my mother's jewellery box there and selling it, telling him my mum was desperate for the money and was too ashamed to bring it herself. I didn't count on the guilt at the time. I just counted the money, even though I was well aware what I was doing was wrong. From then on, that shop served as a constant reminder to me of my trespasses for many decades afterwards. Telling you now is a kind of confessional process, only it's not that confidential.

The Meeting of Minds – Part 4

We're back upstairs and I'm talking to the bishop. "For all my doubts about God's existence and there being an afterlife, I do think the essence of many religions have a lot to offer in terms of living in a way that has meaning. Even just in terms of understanding human psychology, they are very important. But I have to say I tend to cherry-pick from religious texts, and I have a lot of issues with organised religions."

"I don't think you're alone in those beliefs," she says, "Most members of any religion will argue with each other especially as interpretations can vary so much. But still, like you, they are trying to find the truth."

"Are you sure?" I ask, "Do you not feel the truth is only sought when it supports the dogma, otherwise, it tends to be rather inconvenient."

2018 - Seaford - "The Grumpy Chef" Café

I'm with a few friends. We're talking about this chapter. They aren't religious nor do they believe in God, well not in any traditional sense. One of them is saying what many of us say, that religion has caused too much suffering and it's hard to justify its existence in light of that.

"But," I say, "there are many good things related to religion that we're lacking now."

"Like what?" Liz says.

"Communion, being with others to discuss spiritual-related matters." I say, "People haven't got many places they can go for that kind of discussion now, especially if they want to consider different ways to live their lives. It's like people have been abandoned. Okay, they can go to church but that is often very dogmatic and based on unprovable principles. But in terms of spiritual matters, no one has filled the void left in the space where religion existed."

Liz says, "My father was very big in the church, but he was a terribly cruel man."

I agree, "Yes, you see that kind of thing a lot in organised religions."

"Normally," Liz says, "I can't bear to speak about religion or politics at the table, but today, I feel comfortable doing so in our little group here."

I was tempted to jump across the table and attack her, but I didn't think she'd see the funny side.

The Meeting of Minds – Part 5

I'm looking at the bishop and the rabbi, they're talking to an Imam. They're all being very chatty with each other, but I know that although their religions stemmed from similar Abrahamic roots, their interpretation of the texts varies greatly, even in the way they see God, and which words they believe to be true. Behind the joviality are the ingredients that have caused so much suffering throughout history. But I'm also thinking about the historical and current attempts to purge the world of religion and I'm wondering why, for instance, was it so important for the Soviets to get rid of religion, was it just because, as Marx said, it was "the opium of the people"? On the surface, they said it was because they thought religion was backward and was often used to exploit and stupefy the working classes. However, power and control were probably just as much the main reasons. The Soviets killed, persecuted and imprisoned tens of millions of people in their attempt to rid society of religion and were just as adept at exploiting and propagandising as any religion had been. For them, it was more about getting rid of the competition.

Many religions depend on a belief in an omnipresent and all-powerful God, the existence of the soul, Heaven, and Hell, and that their ideology is the only true one, passed to them directly from God. I find it hard to accept those principles, but for those who take that leap of faith, there's a strong sense of "Meaning" that comes from those ingredients. This often becomes manifested firstly, through the belief they are part of a quest that is full of ultimate meanings. Secondly, a promise of life beyond death. Thirdly the presence of God means they're no longer alone. And fourthly, they are part of a large group they can identify with. Paradoxically, such aspirations are also at the core of most non-religious approaches to finding meaning in life too.

The Meeting of Minds – Part 6

Another priest comes up to me, and speaking in a Scottish accent says, "I over-heard your conversation about suffering. You see it as a reason to doubt God, but I see it as a reason to believe."

"Why's that?" I ask.

"I see this world as a preparation for another life. That life will be without suffering but it requires we reveal who we are in this world so God can see if we are ready. If he just stuck us in paradise we would not have been tested, it would be as if we'd never become ourselves."

"Then why didn't God just make us as we will be after being tested, in the first place?" I ask.

"Maybe God thinks this is the most truthful way to make us," he says. "If you had a child, would you just want it to suddenly be a ready-made adult or would you want it to grow and become itself through the struggle of life?"

It depends," I say, "it depends on how much suffering they'd have to endure. I think some beings suffer so much that it would be better if they had never existed. It's a matter of degree."

"So, are you saying there could be a formula that could be used to work out when too much suffering meant life was no longer worth living?" he asks.

"I suppose so, yes. After all, some destinies are considered to be a fate worse than death."

He shakes his head. "You know, God has felt all our pain, God has suffered every moment of pain that has ever been experienced. Just as a parent would rather suffer than let their child suffer, God has suffered with us out of love."

"That doesn't justify all the suffering to me," I say.

He looks at me with an air of pity, "Maybe if you knew God's plan, it would."

I ask him, "Maybe I would, but I don't, do you?"

"Do you want to rid the world of suffering?" he asks.

"Not really," I answer. He looks a bit shocked, so, I try to explain, "We need some but it's also hard to justify some too. It makes me wonder whether God is as all-powerful as you say or maybe even a little bit cruel?"

The priest is looking a bit disbelieving. Maybe he can't understand my lack of understanding.

I go on anyway. "I mean if he allowed Satan to cause the Fall of Man then that shows either he was complicit or he was not as all-seeing as you say. I mean after the flood in the Noah story God said he felt regret. Some say he regretted the sinfulness of mankind, and some say he regretted killing nearly all of humanity. Either way, it indicates he was not as all-seeing as we are led to believe?"

"Maybe you are not as all-seeing as you wish. If you were, you might accept there might be other possibilities," he says in an exasperated tone.

I'm feeling the same way too, "I can only go on what I know," I say, "I have come here for knowledge but you're telling me I have to accept not knowing."

"In your heart, you know," he says.

1973 – Matlock Swimming Pool

I started to cough and splutter and then I felt myself relax and looking down at the bottom of the pool I said to God, "I didn't think I was going to die this soon, but if that's your will I'm ready". I started to blank out, everything went fuzzy, my vision went speckly and just as I thought that was it, I felt myself being dragged and lifted. The lifeguard pulled me out and asked if I was alright.

2018 - Neurotheology

I could hear a voice in me that some might say is God, and whilst I am willing to accept it could be I can't prove it either way, so I won't pretend I know. Just like archetypes, our brains are built to have a relationship with a god, whether we believe it or not.

Neurotheology is a contentious field which attempts to unearth neural links and mechanisms of religious experience. Those working in this area suggest that the human brain has a systematic tendency for such experiences, and living without using them may cause an imbalance in the psyche. I have a bit of sympathy for that idea.

After decades of the Soviets attempting to eradicate religion, and propaganda too, many Russians were quick to re-embrace it when they were finally allowed to.

The Meeting of Minds – Part 7

So far, it's all felt like a bit of a dead end to me. Maybe Dead Ends are the real motivation behind a lot of this. We don't want to die so we invent a possibility of everlasting life. There's an interesting book which I have half-read recently called The Worm at The Core. Its main argument is our concerns about dying fuel nearly every human endeavour. In some ways, the question might be more appropriately put as, "What is the meaning of death?"

The priest suddenly looks at me with a startled expression on his face.

2018 - The Meaning of God

There are between 200 billion to 2 trillion galaxies in the known universe, and the variation in numbers is a debatable point. Either way, there are a lot of galaxies in our Universe. Even though it's scientific methodology that brings that information to us, it is still a matter of belief that what we are told is the truth. Still, the fact a scientist will attempt to provide evidence when called upon, to me, holds a lot of weight.

When I think about some of the religious-based "meanings of life", even if they are about a way of making ourselves spiritually purer, there is something in me that searches for meaning beyond that and even beyond ridding the world of "evil". I want to know if there is a bigger quest and if there is a meaning for God to exist too.

The Meeting of Minds – Part 8

"You have to get out of here, quickly," the priest says. "Follow the bishop."

I do as he says, again passing through the same passageway we took before. I ask her what's going on and she semi-whispers breathlessly to me, "We are splitting into two groups, some of the people are staying behind so that we can get away. We have to hurry, please, be as quiet as you can."

When we get to the kitchen someone is holding open a mirror which also serves as a door. One by one we step into a far darker, damper passageway. I hear the mirror door close behind us.

2018 - Feeling Meaningful

Even though we might think that there is no clear meaning to life, we can still feel very happy to be alive. There is a separation between our thoughts and our feelings. If we feel happy we don't tend to question the meaning of life but for most of us, there will be testing times when this issue becomes extremely pertinent to us on an emotional level. It's probably a good idea to recognise this split because one path leads to philosophical debate, whereas the other route has more to do with asking, "What has caused this emotional state?"

The answer will rarely be a clear one, but it probably won't be helped much by philosophy either. Not only does philosophy not come up with any clear-cut and simple answers, but it rarely deals with deep psychological issues that might be behind such feelings. If anything, a good therapist might be more beneficial.

Loss can be through death, separation, disconnection from others, or a sudden change in our own or someone we love's health. We can lose our familiar world, our work, unfulfilled ambitions; all these and many other painful aspects of life can easily provoke feelings of meaninglessness.

Some philosophers and many religious people will see these as situations that allow us to grow emotionally. But even so, God, or no God, they will be a harsh test of faith. A test that may well be made easier or harder depending on the personality of the person going through these experiences. Some people can bear almost anything while others will fall at the slightest hurdle.

One could argue then, that the feeling of meaningfulness may well be just as much about internal resources, such as our DNA, childhood experiences, and other influences behind our attitude. My point is, when dealing with feelings of meaning-less caused by emotional issues, personality may play a far bigger part than religion or philosophy, even if philosophy and religion may help to some extent and affect our personality too.

It's quite easy to think that if religion helps people who can't normally cope with life's difficulties, then that's a good thing, but there are aspects of religion which I think are extremely dangerous too. If religion was just about love, caring for others, developing ourselves and being less selfish, then I wouldn't have an issue outside of doubting its core "beliefs" as previously mentioned. But there are so many damaging and dangerous dogmas that fuel hatred, war, persecution, and death that I can't help but wonder if the payoff is worth it.

I am not advocating the Soviets' approach of getting rid of religion but one can't help but wonder if Jesus, Abraham, Buddha, Mohamed or Krishna would have wanted so much suffering propagated in their names.

Even now, so-called witches are still being burnt to death, women are taken as sex slaves, and homosexuals are persecuted throughout the world. All these things can be justified in religious texts, not just in Christianity but in Islam and many other major world religions too.

As you can see, I have very mixed feelings about religion.

The Meeting of Minds – Part 9

We find ourselves in an underground chapel, it's been carved out of the rock. Candles are flickering on the altar.

A bald man approaches me and puts his hand on my shoulder.

"Not all of us here are religious, some of us have other views," he says. "There might be supernatural elements to life but I decided long ago to focus on what I could change."

"What do you mean?" I ask.

"Well, if you can't change the world change yourself, and if you can't change yourself change the world," he says smiling.

"I don't understand that, it doesn't make sense," I say.

"Surely it does if you think about it. I mean you can't completely change the world, can you? So, in that case, it might help you to change yourself. Likewise, you can't completely change yourself, therefore, you could try your best to change the world, even just a little."

"Why didn't you say that in the first place?" I ask.

"Well, the shorter version fits better on Twitter and makes people think about it more, plus I heard it in a song once," he says.

"So, what is your main reason for telling me?" I say.

"Everything comes to pass right?" he says.

"Yes," I agree.

"So, what can you do about that?" He asks.

"Nothing," I say.

"Are you sure?" He says.

"Well, I can't stop it from happening," I say.

"That's true," he says "So, why is it a problem?"

"Because I don't want to lose the people I love, the health I have, the world I feel is home."

He smiles, "So if you didn't fear that, would that help?"

"I don't think that's very realistic for most people. I think part of being human means fearing and grieving loss. It's a part of life. I can't see how we can switch off our natural emotions."

"I agree," he says, "But how you react to the loss may well affect the meaning of your life. If you recognise everything will be lost sooner or later, doesn't that make you appreciate it more while you still can?"

I bite my top lip, the thought of losing everything is very hard to accept and fills me with dread.

He pauses and bows his head slightly, "When people die, they change and the people who loved them change due to their death as well. But accepting that this is the way of the universe may help people become more loving. They can choose to fill themselves with love or fill the world with hate."

I am touched by his words and can sense some truth in them, but I can also see that it must take a great deal of struggle to react to life in that way. It is almost saintly.

I tell him the oft-used line I stole from a Mark Knopfler record about being a part-time saint. "What if you're like me, only a part-time saint, how do you deal with the less saintly aspects of your personality?"

He starts to walk off but as he does, he says, "Whichever one you focus on will be the dominating influence, there is an element of choice in the matter, even though that choice might be very limited."

I thank him.

I hear another voice from behind me, I turn and there's a man with a walking stick, he's in his 60s, with black oiled hair combed back, and wearing an old-fashioned tweed suit.

"What he said, it's kind of what I believe in too." He says. "I'm what you might call a secular humanist. We believe in evolution. We don't believe we were made by a supernatural being. We still believe in following ethical guidelines through life though. To us, it's about not only fulfilling ourselves but also humanity overall. We call it enlightened self-interest. By helping others, we help ourselves and by developing ourselves we help others. Do you not think most of those gathered here are similar to each other in that way? Can you see the connection?"

I'm just about to agree with him when another man says, "We don't, we believe in enjoying life as much as we can. As long as we don't directly hurt others."

There's a woman with him who says, "I think this is the only life we have. I agree you can't just ride roughshod over others, mainly because they'll probably kill you if you do, but I can't pretend to care about things when I don't. I have had a good life and I have suffered too, it's just I try to enjoy what I can, while I can. I think a lot of what people go on about in this group can't apply to everyone, different strokes for different folks and I think we should live and let live."

"Hear hear," says the man in tweed, "Although I do wonder if deep down you would be happier if you paid more attention to others."

She looks at him, "I can't pretend to feel what I don't feel. You'd prefer me to be honest, wouldn't you?"

"Yes," he says, "I agree that each person may find meaning in things other people might not and vice versa, I think that's just subjectivism. I remember a Taoist once telling me that through introspection we can attempt to find our innermost reasons for living, he felt the answer is within ourselves. Some people are searching for bliss while some aim to help others live with less suffering."

"I'm not being rude, or anything," the 'honest' woman says in a kind of vaudeville insult tone, "but for someone who's not a priest you're very good at mansplaining, I mean preaching."

He laughs, "I suppose," he says, "that there's a big crossover between many of our points of view because nearly all of us recognise that we are linked to others, so if we hurt another person, it somehow hurts us too. Even though you say you just want to live and enjoy your life, you still don't want to hurt others. You say it's for self-preservation reasons, but I wonder if it's also because you have compassion too."

Her eyebrows are cocked, "Maybe, but while I don't think I'm anywhere near as caring as others in this group, I sometimes wonder how caring they really are. I mean, are they just trying to get a golden ticket into Heaven? Anyway, there are plenty of psychopaths in the world who don't care if they hurt someone. I think you're all being a bit idealist."

I am still worrying about whether we're going to be caught. "Do you not feel worried?" I ask.

"About what?" The man in the tweed suit asks.

"The police finding us."

The woman nods her head. "Nah, we'll be okay. This is always happening. The ones we left behind will be questioned but they'll be okay. They're raising money for the poor or druggies."

"Actually," the humanist says smiling slightly, "maybe I'll take that bit back about you having compassion."

She shrugs as she says, "I can't pretend to love everyone equally like some of you say you do. My family and friends come first to me. I wouldn't feel right in myself if I didn't put them first. I'm not a hedonist, I'm more like an Epicurean."

"Are you sure?" says the man in tweed, "I thought they abstained from sex and other sensual pleasures. They did try to avoid pain including mental anguish, but I get the feeling that you're not as strict as they were."

Irritated, she snaps, "I was referring to them in terms of them not believing in an immortal soul, they believed in a soul, but they saw it as a physical part of us. I'm not stupid."

"Do you think you're referring to your consciousness when you say, soul?" He asks.

If there was a clear-cut definite meaning in life, then it would probably be written in the stars or our genes and it wouldn't be a debatable issue. If you firmly believe in God, you will probably think I have been foolish to speak as openly as I have done here, but I imagine many of us have similar thoughts and if there's a God then God will understand (I hope).

To me, the main questions remain unanswered. What is the endpoint we are aiming for? What is God's purpose? What possible good reason did God have to create so many lives that are so full of suffering they would rather have never lived? And besides all of that, how can you prove that this is the will of God anyway?

To me, as time has passed, our view of the universe has changed which in turn has altered our perception of the meaning of life. The ancients looked at the stars and built religions around them, then later their gods changed, but still, humans were at the heart of religious meaning. But as we started to get a clearer view of space, we realised we were no longer at the centre of the universe, so our place in the order of things changed too. As science became more able, the question "why" became somewhat interchangeable with "how". If a scientist can prove life occurred because of this or that happening, then is that "why" we were created? If there was no superintelligence involved, then was there no greater meaning than us being a by-product of evolution? Is "how" we were made the same as "why" we were made? There's often a very thin line between them.

I once heard someone define themselves as a traditional Catholic. I didn't know what that meant, but he said that as far as he was concerned there could never be a conflict between science and religion because both should be primarily concerned with the truth. But what if science could ever prove there wasn't a God? I admired him for his focus on the truth but, as I mentioned earlier, history has shown over and over that people who follow a strong ideology tend to ignore the truth if it doesn't coincide with their beliefs.

———

There was an imam, a rabbi, and a priest. God says, "This better be a good joke." However, by the time they'd finished killing each other in God's name, no one was laughing.

———

Do you remember that friend of mine, the one who bought my Saab, Ian Owles? Shortly before he died, he said to me, "The stars are souls waiting to experience living, life is a miracle." And I kind of knew what he meant.

When I think about how good my life has been so far I can understand that idea, it's just, when I look around and see people suffering for a lifetime through no fault of their own, or whole lives that are racked with pain and torment, then if I believe there's an all-powerful God involved in that, I see a harshness that is hard for me to understand.

———

Leap of Faith

One way to assess the strength of a "meaning of life" could be to think about whether that meaning would still hold value to someone who finds themselves in a very difficult situation; would the meaning help them through? Let's say, someone had lost their family, their home, and job. Would they be able to use the meaning in question to help them carry on living? When we are in desperate situations we may turn towards desperate measures, especially to nullify the pain. Hopefully a worthwhile "meaning" would help a person avoid turning to such dangerous things.

Plato once defined humans as 'A being in search of meaning'. Even without the bigger, supernatural, or lofty aspirations to help others or develop ourselves, people will often find meaning in all kinds of things, for instance fulfilling an ambition, being creative, or mastering something. Even our biology provides meaning, after all, are we not driven to find a mate and create a family? Then there are feelings of significance, they too may offer a sense of meaning. Hence people strive to become famous or infamous or even anonymously significant because their work must remain a secret. And yet even if all of our desires prove significant, we will

392

never know the true extent of our significance, good or bad, because we can never know the ultimate consequences of our actions and our mere existence.

There's an irony in that idea because even people who feel they are the least significant, for example, substance abusers, compulsive gamblers, or the homeless, provide meaning for those who want to help them. It might not be a meaning they want to be part of, but nevertheless, they are significant. Even those caught up in a cycle of consumerism are providing meaning for everyone in the retail and production chain plus all those people dealing with the consequences of consumerism, (waste disposal, anti-pollution activists, anti-slavery activists). I realise I'm being a bit provocative, but you can get a sense of our interdependence from such examples.

The angel says to the demon, "Thank you".

I was thinking about my point about the meaning of life tending to be a more pertinent question to those in a more anxious state, and wondered if we would find it acceptable to deal with it medically. For instance, what if we could take a pill and our emotional focus would move to the real issue that was upsetting us?

Most of the time that might work, but would it be somewhat like a drug addict escaping their pain or would it be more akin to therapy? Drug misuse tends to be about not facing the truth whereas this imaginary medication would be about focusing on the true cause of our pain, not so much about escaping it.

Victor Frankl, who was a psychoanalyst, spent a lot of time as a prisoner in the Nazi concentration camps and wrote a very famous book called, "Man's Search for Meaning", as well as developing a school of psychoanalysis which in part focused on meaning. He asked his fellow therapists, how they could label a patient as being mentally unwell because the patient felt life was meaningless, especially given the "meaning of life" isn't provable without blind faith. There is, of course, the possibility that some causes of anxiety are linked directly to thinking about meaning, especially things like facing one's death or the death of loved ones.

2017 – May – Hastings – The Conquest Hospital

When I was in intensive care and told I was very ill with a heart condition and life-threatening infections from the burst appendix, I thought I might die at any moment. Whether that was true or not, that's how I perceived it. I wasn't in a lot of pain although I was uncomfortable, but had I been in agony I may well have wanted to end it all.

I did feel though that there could be more to life, and this was a situation that would pass. I promised myself, and God, if there was one, that whatever time I had left would be used to help others via my creative endeavours. Just as others' creativity has helped me.

I realise to some that it's arrogant to think we have things to offer that might help others, and maybe in a way it is. Still, we can but try to help, and that's probably the best we can do.

———

Victor Frankl, who I mentioned a bit earlier, also felt people should cease endlessly reflecting on themselves and instead try to engage in life as much as possible. That way questions about the meaning of life would tend to fade. He still thought it would be a good idea to question oneself regarding why we may neglect our loved ones, or block our enjoyment of life, and to seek to be honest about ourselves as best we can, but that focusing on the "why" would rarely produce a definitive answer.

Studies relating to people being engrossed in the process of doing something consistently suggest that humans experience feelings of meaning and fulfilment when mastering challenging tasks, and it's not so much the choice of the task but more the way tasks are approached and performed.

The more we lose ourselves in an activity or helping others, the greater the sense of meaningfulness we experience. It's not an ultimate quest-like meaning but on a day-to-day level, it's probably one of the many things that help many of us get through.

———

2017 May - Hastings Hospital

As I watched the series *Cosmos* I could see that venturing out into space to other worlds to live on has become our latest meaningful quest; well, that and searching for the truth and finding God. Even if it's futile, it feels worthwhile. Plato would have probably approved, as attaining the highest form of knowledge was very much wrapped up in meaningfulness.

———

When people speak of the impossibility of travelling through space due to the distances involved it's always worth keeping in mind the paradox of travelling at speeds close to the speed of light. While impossible now, who knows what the future will bring, but let's say humans could ever travel close to those speeds, then a person travelling millions, if not billions of light years, could do so within a life-time. For those they left on earth, the journey would have taken millions or billions of years, but for those travelling close to the speed of light, time slows down massively.

394

My point is, whether it is impossible or not for us to ever travel at such speeds, just the possibilities it could offer may provide many of us with a meaningful quest to pursue.

A teacher says to her class, "In 100 million years the sun will enlarge and engulf the earth."

One of the pupils asks, "Excuse me, Miss. Did you say a million or 100 million years?

The teacher says, "A hundred million years".

"Phew!" says the student "That's a relief".

The Meeting of Minds – Part 10

"It's time," the bishop says, as she clicks off her phone. "The coast is clear, so we are going to make our way through the garden and out to the boat. There is a small party going on in the garden if any of you wish to disperse into it."

"I'll have a bit of that," says the woman who prefers to be honest about not caring much.

So, we make our way through another door along a passageway that inclines to a door to the outside. It's dark, but the stars are brightly filling the sky.

Once we are all out the bishop says in a slightly raised voice, "Okay, those of you who want to go to the party follow Father Peter, those of you who wish to take the boat, follow me."

I quite fancy going on a boat ride, although a party sounds fun too. However, I think it'll be safer to get the boat. It will drop us off in the harbour and from there, it's an easy journey home.

There are about 18 of us in the boat group, the other group consists of around eight who walk with us till we get near the party. We can hear talking, music and laughter but can't see the people as we are slightly downhill from them and the main house, when I say house, I mean stately home. It's big with many rooms and stories.

We walk on toward the jetty where a small ferry boat is waiting for us. We are helped on by the crew and within minutes the electric engines silently glide us away. As we move out toward the sea, we can still hear the party and from a few hundred metres away we can just about make out the illuminated marquee. Everyone on the boat is silent, taking in the stars, the house and party.

The marquee suddenly goes dark, and then within seconds, there are a few distant crackling sounds and a couple of thuds. I thought I could hear a scream, then high above the house a beautiful neon blue rocket-type firework bloomed, illuminating the sky. As we moved away, we watched the display as it got smaller and smaller until it faded away.

Søren Kierkegaard, a Danish philosopher who lived during the 1800s, recognised an absurdity about our search for meaning. Firstly, there were those who might wish to escape existence, but that didn't seem viable. Then some would lean towards religion or other supernatural beliefs, but to do so would require letting go of rationality and to many philosophers that was tantamount to philosophical suicide. So finally, at least to him, what was left was the absurdity of continuing to live without any true understanding of significant meaning.

Sometimes though, you will hear a piece of music, or look out at the world or the stars, and you can feel meaning even if you cannot put it into words. In fact, maybe it's words, with their ability to hide the truth, that prevents us from understanding what we've always known.

The Meeting of Minds – Part 11

We are getting near the end of our journey. The bishop comes up to me, puts her hand on my shoulder and says, "It's been a bit of an unexpected adventure."

"Yes," I say, but it's been interesting, it's given me lots to think about."

I can hear a strange noise coming from the other end of the boat. I look around, but it's so dark I can't see anything. It sounds like muffled voices. Then everything goes very dark and I feel cold.

Do you feel, do you feel like you need to know? Is it time for you to know or are you willing to accept you can't?

The Meeting of Minds – Part 12

I'm in the water, I feel like someone is holding me under. It's pitch dark, I feel paralysed and can't resist.

There are hundreds of archetypes and each of them has a script they follow. Do you know the main archetypes that dominate your internal world, do you know if their script has a happy ending? Do your archetypes stop you from finding meaning?

The Meeting of Minds – Part 13

I don't want to be alone in this cold darkness. I want to be with those I connect with, singing, talking, laughing, crying, and living.

I feel myself come to the surface, biology is in control, and I am gasping for air and coughing. I still can't see anything, there's a mist all around and I feel it cold upon my face.

For me, life has been beyond good, even with the suffering I have experienced. I accept things might change and maybe my suffering might become overwhelming. But for me, existing has been a miracle and I don't want to die yet. And in my story, there have been so many kind individuals or groups who helped me to live such a life and many of them I'll never know or if I did, I may not remember.

One translation of the word "Religion" is "Re-Connected". (ligo "bind, connect", re- (again) + ligare "to reconnect,"). One of the biggest meaningful aspects of life for me is connecting with others who I feel a "connection" with.

The Meeting of Minds – Part 14

I let my legs come up to the surface and float on my back for a while. I can hear others nearby. Were we attacked by some of the people in the group or did something else happen? Could the boat have exploded? I am feeling confused and frightened. I am scared to call out in case it was an attack.

There's only so much time I will last before hypothermia will set in. I also worry that some massive sea creature will attack me. The mist starts to clear a bit and I can see the stars again. I recognise some of the constellations. They feel like old friends. Cassiopeia, Andromeda, Cygnus, and Pegasus are right above me.

I feel something push against my head. I panic, thinking a sea monster is just about to pull me under. Then I recognise it's the side of a dinghy and hands are grabbing at me. I can't see much, there's a bright light shining on my face. I feel myself being pulled into the boat. Even if it is the police I would rather it was them than a monster. I realise I can't hear properly, just a dull sound of voices.

Once I'm hauled into the boat I'm kept lying down and something is put over me. I'm shivering uncontrollably. Whoever these people are they are being kind. I feel like I'm in the world of good people and start to cry. Someone starts to talk to me, but although I can't hear them, I feel their hand stroking my face. I look at them but don't recognise them. We've never met but I know we will be bonded by this moment forever.

Thank you, for connecting.

Now, back to life, back to reality.

Chapter 28
Empty Spaces
1980 and 2018-2019

2019 - Empty Spaces

This page was blank a moment before I wrote on it, and before it was a blank page there was an empty space that it came to fill. In time, it will disappear, and there will be a space where it had been, but here, right now, it has a life. When it comes to empty spaces, we tend to either avoid or fill them, because just living with them can often be almost intolerable.

For much of my life, I felt compelled to fill the empty spaces around me. There were times when the consequences of doing so were positive but there were also plenty of others when they were not. Part of my life's lesson has been learning to differentiate which was which and whether it was better to face the emptiness or not.

1980 - The Bridge

The year 1980 was a bridge between worlds for me, maybe at the time it didn't feel that way, but now I can see a transition took place, one in which I started to fill my time with more meaningful exploits.

1979 - Standing At The Bus Stop

I was feeling heartbroken, I'd fallen in love with a girl called Anne, but she told me she wasn't interested. As I made my way home, I felt an emptiness where my dreams of being with her had been. No one else was at the bus stop so I sang *Sandy* from *Grease*, replacing the word Sandy with Annie, (which was fortunately rather fitting). The car lights shone on me as if I was on stage, and the rain poured down. I wanted to suffer as spurned lovers do, and in its way, it was a little magically filmic, which I thought was a nice touch. Then the bus came, so, I went home and wrote a poem.

1980 - Spring

Rob, the boy from school with the green-tinted uniform, loved listening to Elvis, just as I did. Most of our peers weren't into Elvis, so, to them we were outcasts, but we liked it that way. I didn't need to do anything to become an outcast, I was automatically one due to how I looked. Rob though had his slightly off-black blazer and this, along with his short red hair, assured him his place as an outsider too.

I would don a uniform of sorts, jeans and a T-shirt. It was an anti-fashion state-ment that stated clearly, I didn't want to use my clothes to make a statement about myself. We were Rockabilly rebels from head to toe, except Rob also loved listening to Blondie, so we did make exceptions. But, as with most teenagers, we weren't just listening to music, we were hearing the call of allegiance. It's as if our adolescent brains were primed for us to take our place in the tribe.

1980 - Summer

During a trip on a double-decker bus to the seaside with Rob, his family, and about 50 other locals, I decided that trying to drop an empty fizzy drink can from the top deck on a child as she ran past was very funny. I soon found out that everyone else thought I was stupid and ignored me for the rest of the trip. Nowadays people might try to blame the additives in the drink for my idiocy, but back then it was a simple case of me having no bounds until everyone applied some, and I can assure you that had an impact on me.

Through the summer months, there was a feeling of Rob being in a no man's land. Busy times were interspersed with sunny day breaks, but as the holidays drew to their end, these gentle times merged into one long quiet before the stormy seas.

Rob's house was part of a ring of properties that looked over a circular area of grass with a road around it. We'd spend hours with other children there, but we also felt we were getting a bit old to be with them anymore. One moment we'd be talking about our friend's mothers, one of whom would wash her car in a bikini whilst we looked on, and the next we'd be part of a gang of kids whose ages ranged from 11 to 15. But for Rob, who was a year older than me, his world was just about to change from our dry grass, days of play, to the dark cramped world of a submarine. For me too, I might not have been sure where I was headed but I knew my life wasn't going to be the same for much longer.

1980 - October – Wilson's

Wilson's School changed its identity when it moved from Camberwell to Wallington, and similarly moving away from Roundshaw allowed me to partially reinvent myself too. Whilst you can indeed take the kid out of the council estate but can't take the council estate out of the kid, karate was a good channel for the part of me that wanted to be a warrior.

One day as I walked across the playing fields in front of St Helier Hospital to Tweeddale Karate Club a guy ran up to me. He was one of the kids I'd had a fight with on Roundshaw some years before. The conversation started cordially enough, but within seconds we were both lining up for another fight. Nothing came of it, but I certainly hadn't lost my eagerness to get into a fracas.

The school encouraged the teachers to set a lot of homework, often three or four hours' worth per night, and that was enough to keep even the likes of me out of trouble most of the time. I was going to be facing exams in less than a year and a half, and these would change the direction of my life. But it wasn't just about working for the sake of my future, I also came to enjoy the process of studying. There was the comforting reason and problem-solving of maths, the wonder of physics, the artistry of English Language, and the entertainment and analysis of English Literature. Each of them had something to offer in their own right and the more I came to appreciate studying, the more I let go of seeing fighting as a means of gaining respect from my peers.

1980 and October 2019 - Radio Homework

Each evening after dinner I'd sit in the back room and slowly trudge through my homework. The radio would play in the background, and John would tell me to turn it off, saying it would distract me. Mum would then intervene and it'd get left on. Of course, it was a distraction, that was the point, but it also offered a sense of communion with the other kids at school as they'd be listening to the same programs too. This meant the next day we'd laugh together about the phone calls, especially to the sexual problems programme on Capital Radio, or talk about some of the new music John Peel played.

Now, as I write this in 2019, I've got Spotify playing a random playlist, *Perfect Day* by Lou Reed is on right now, and Facebook sitting in the background in case I start feeling a bit lonely.

1980 - Winter

I had spent a lot of time with Rob, but he'd already left school, and I knew our time was limited which added a preciousness about it. He was going to wait till after Christmas before basic training commenced. His parents told me I could pop around whenever I wanted once he was gone, but I knew it wouldn't feel right if he wasn't there. Rob's crowded house and intense family probably prepared him well for life on a submarine; maybe for him, it would be a kind of home from home, but for me, the prospect of Rob leaving left a space in me that both he and his family had filled.

The space someone leaves when they're no longer around can't just be re-filled and healed, and to think it can be is not just a mistake, but it dishonours the relationship that filled it. Instead, while there will be sadness for the loss, and an appreciation of how the relationship enriched us, recognising the new opportunities to connect with others in different ways, to go on further adventures in the empty space of time that's now available, could be of some comfort too.

I once read a religious text that spoke of a similar situation with a person losing the love of their life. It proposed that when God takes away our greatest love, the space that's left is there to remind us that God's love remains. As you know, I'm not religious, but in the later chapters about love, the significance of that idea, even outside of a religious context will become far clearer.

402

Darkness

When Simon and Garfunkel sang of darkness being an old friend, they may have partially seen darkness, sadness and loss as things that bring gifts to us, just as friends do, even if they're wrapped in so much pain it's hard to see their value at the time.

I later learned that there was an Internet myth about that lyric which suggested it came about because of a friendship Garfunkel had with a blind man called Sandy Greenberg with whom he referred to himself as Darkness. While that did happen, given Paul Simon wrote the lyrics, there's no credible evidence that the lyrics ever related to that friendship. However, as stated in an interview with Paul Simon, it's more likely they were inspired by a memory he had of practising guitar in darkness in his bathroom. Ultimately the song's theme was about our inability to truly communicate with each other, as in hearing without listening. So, are you listening or just hearing? I'm sure when I listen to audiobooks, I'm only hearing most of the time.

August 2019

A couple I know, Ali and Brian, have met up with me in the Italian café in Eastbourne. It's very sunny on the street, it's 4 pm, but dark inside. There's the smell of coffee, chocolate croissants, and a bit of political discussion. Everything is Brexit right now; it has been for almost four years. But there's a bit of a respite when Ali looks at me and tells me she's been reading most of the chapters from this that I've already put online.

"It's very interesting, but lately it feels like you've left something out, like a bit of story has ended without you talking about it."

"Is it because I am not writing about my love life?" I ask.

"It might be, I'm not quite sure, it just feels like something is missing."

2019 October

The slowness of 1980 for me isn't going to make for a tense psychological drama, there wasn't much action either. I could try to do a big build-up about my exams, I mean for most 15-year-olds that's the big story, along with their love life, or lack of it. I could try to paint you a picture of what it felt like to be alive then, after all this was still an exciting time, especially in the music world. But it's probably the same with any era. When we look back, we get to see the great things that occurred during it in a very concentrated way. For instance, we might say the 1800s had so many great painters, but in reality, if you average out the number of artists we still recognise as "great" over a hundred years, it'd probably result in about one or two per decade. Mind you, the legendary music that came out between the 1950s to the 1990s far outstripped what was to come in the following three decades. So, it's not so much that there are not richer eras, it's just at the time when these things occur, they don't tend to feel particularly out of the ordinary. If we wanted to portray a life, what would we do with all the empty spaces? We'd most likely omit them as they'd bore the audience, but the moments of interest are often a consequence of endured empty spaces.

1980 - December

I'm sitting at the table doing my homework. You're viewing this image as a camera would. The camera pans around me, and as it does the room fades to black so all you can see is me sitting at the table. Slowly I'm getting smaller. Roxy Music's 2HB plays...

Here's looking at you kid.

The screen fades to black.

Hard white light fills your eyes, everything is out of focus, then the image becomes clearer, and there's ice on the windows. The camera pans around to me sleeping.

The clock radio shows 6:30 am. The radio switches on.

"This is the News. John Lennon is dead, shot several times by a young American as he was going into his home in New York"

I pull the duvet over my face and cry.

When someone dies, they don't just leave an empty space where they existed, but, if they meant something to us, we become filled with emptiness. Paradoxically though, we are also filled by their presence reverberating through us, and even beyond our internal world, beyond our memory of them, beyond our own lives, something of them will continue to influence this world far further into the future than we could possibly appreciate. The emptiness that people leave is completely different to the emptiness they once filled. You may think some people might be excluded from such a notion because no one ever knew them, but their possible existence was in the minds of their forefathers just as those people who will exist in the future are in our minds too. The interconnection between us isn't just amongst those around us as we live but goes forward and backwards in time too. We are innately significant even though we can't help but think we are not.

Saturday 24th November 2018 - Light Eras

I'm visiting a friend called Gregory, he needs some help with his iPad. I've gone through the main entrance doors to the block he lives in and I'm approaching the lift which is one of those old-fashioned ones where there's an inner concertina cage-type door. As I approach it I feel like I'm being taken back decades in time. It's nothing mystical it's just the subdued yellow lighting.

Many things define the look of an era, but lighting tends to get ignored. Clothing, textile designs, paint colours, wallpapers, furniture, cars, and architecture are most likely to take precedence over lighting, but all those things get bathed in artificial light once the sun goes down and just like a varnish over a painting, they give it the colour of an era.

We are now in the era of LED lighting, which can be almost any colour, but the way it radiates is different to other types of lighting. It has a very bright core that will hurt your eyes even if you glimpse at it and a lovely soft light radiating from it. If we go back 10 years there were low-energy bulbs, and for quite a few decades before, we were still acting out our lives under the warm yellow light of incandescent bulbs. Neon lights also had their cold light era, especially in the 1970s, and before them, there were the yellow tungsten bulbs and going back further, there were gas lights and various types of lanterns and candlelight. Of course, way back when there were fire and fire torches, and failing a dry supply of kindling, the moon and starlight.

1980 - Descriptive Passages

At school, in 1980, we started to study books for English Literature which contained long descriptive passages aimed at setting the scene. I'd often have to read the same paragraph over and over before I could take in the words properly. In a lot of contemporary writing, there's a more minimalist approach, which is something I tend to do too. Instead of painting a detailed image with words, a key line is given instead, such as "I entered the dentist's waiting room" and immediately, with barely any effort, by either the writer or reader, the image is complete. This technique does, of course, rely on the reader having some experience of a dentist's waiting room, and even then, the reader's version of one probably doesn't bear any similarity to the one the writer was referring to.

Post-Modernism has infiltrated many disciplines of Art and tends to be more concerned with letting the onlooker control their perception of an object rather than the other way around. It's also possible that people nowadays have a far more extensive internal library of other scenes from life, partly because of film and TV, whereas writers before the mass media era had to present a scene far more vividly.

There's still a temptation to evoke a scene when writing, especially about the past, it's both a sign of literary prowess and can, at times, create a reassuring backdrop.

But the reality is one can only do that by looking back at an era from our present-day perspective. The problem with that is if we view our past settings from such a vantage point, we can't see it as we did. For us, back then, our environment felt pretty much as it does now. Every day normality felt, well, normal. There are moments, of course, when one can perceive our surroundings so intensely that not only do we feel as if we've viewed that moment from outside normality, but it was such a powerful experience it stays with us for the rest of our lives. But generally, our everyday world feels as normal as any other normal moment in our life, so if you want to know how things felt in the 1980s, well, they felt the same as now. It's only when we look at a photo from those times that we're confronted with just how different the world was back then.

I have recently been watching a series on TV called *Peaky Blinders* which is set in my grandparents' era, and it struck me that it wasn't so much the look of the clothes that were worn, but their meaning. They were uniforms that spoke of class and wealth, power or even a disregard for power. Nowadays those uniforms are not conformed to, so they're no longer reliable signs of status.

1980 - Real Rockers

One weekend I asked my mum if I could stay at a friend's house just down the road. Once there we stayed up all night lounging on their orange and brown woolly sofa, with the gas fire lighting up the room as their female cousins, (who were over from Ireland for a week), told us what they could do, (sexually), with a bottle. This understandably resulted in us spending hours trying to persuade them to demonstrate this to us, which no matter how drunk they got, they weren't up for.

In the early hours, as the sun came up and bits of dull blue sky appeared in the cracks between the curtains, the girls decided we'd all look great with Bryl-Cream in our hair. That way we could look like real Rockers. Deprived of sleep I walked back up to my house, knocked on the door and waited for Mum to be impressed by my new hair-don't. She took one look at me and said, "Are you stupid? Get upstairs and wash that out now." I didn't know what all the fuss was about, but I went upstairs and washed it out anyway.

1985 - Therapy

Therapist: You have holes in your clothes, do you think that means something?

Simon: I hate buying clothes, it's a lot of hassle trying them on, and then I have to get them altered, and I prefer spending my money on records.

Therapist: Aha, [she nods and waits for more]

Simon: I think because I look different, dressing up in good clothes would come over as pretentious as if I believed they could make up for my disability. It might even accentuate my disability and I think people would think I was deluding myself. [I think of a line in a book we studied for English Literature, "Clothes maketh the man".]

Therapist: How do you feel people perceive you when you dress so scruffily?

Simon: I don't care what they think. Why should I worry, they are going to make lots of incorrect assumptions about me anyway, so I feel I can't rely on them judging me on how I look.

Therapist: But your look isn't neutral, it's a clear statement.

Simon: Really? I don't think I'm saying anything beyond I don't care much about what I look like.

Therapist: I think it's almost as if you choose to look like a street urchin. As if you had no parents to look after you. It's not so much that you don't care about what others think but quite the opposite, you want them to think you are uncared for.

Simon: I think that's more your thoughts than mine.

Therapist: Maybe, but have a think about it.

2019 - Scruffy Like A Millionaire

My artificial leg has a buckle on the outside of my knee it's made a hole in every pair of trousers I own. I haven't covered the buckle, which would be an easy fix for future pairs of trousers. I still dislike buying clothes and a big part of me, even now, doesn't want to get involved in dressing up nicely. If I see pictures of myself in a suit, I think I look ridiculous. In my mind, I don't look anything like I do. Once someone told me I looked so scruffy they thought I must be a millionaire, I kind of liked that.

1980 - Light Eras and The Streets of London

When I was 15 the world I frequented was often tinted in either a harsh greenish-white fluorescent light, yellow tungsten or the flickering light from the TV, all of which were also often accompanied by a veil of smoke. Once outside though, the sun, clouds, rain, night sky, moonlight, and starry skies cast light upon me just as they do so now.

Sometimes, back then, I'd be very aware of just how empty the streets were. Even up in London, one could be close to the centre and the streets would be empty. I often imagined myself inside a surrealist painting of empty streets, hard sunlight and long shadows. Those same streets now, for instance, Millbank, near the Tate Britain Gallery, seem to always have a constant stream of people passing. It's as if even London couldn't bear the empty spaces, so, filled them with lonely people.

2019 - Stage Sets

Not only are the eras in our life defined by the design of the world we live in but there are whole stage sets in which much of our life takes place. There are the buildings we live in, the schools and colleges in which a lot of our early life plays out, then there are our surroundings and the modes of transport we use to travel. These backdrops often envelop us, often for many years, and then one day we no longer enter them. Of course, these stages and set designs are also filled with people, many of whom we'll interact with for years, yet eventually, we'll scarcely remember most of them.

A friend of mine sent me one of those Internet posts that do the rounds, it was about a person asking someone what they owned. Everything they listed was shown to be transitory, except in the end only the present moment was accepted as something we can own, albeit only for a moment. To me, it missed the point partly. Everything indeed comes to pass and contending with that is a difficult thing to cope with. Yet, if we are fortunate enough, we will get some time to play our parts in the world, and for a brief period, we can savour life and our connection with others. Likewise, we think we own land and properties, but we are merely spending some time experiencing them or at least using them as a means to experience other things in life, even if it's just to experience feeling significant.

2019 - Interesting Times

If we had been born a few hundred years ago, or earlier, for most of us, our lives would have been far less interesting than now. Even going back to 1980 I felt bored and lonely a lot of the time. Part of that has to do with me, but nowadays we have 24-hour TV, Instant News, social media, and the ability to talk and see those we're connected with instantly anywhere in the world. On top of that, no matter which direction we come from politically, none of us can complain that what's going on is dull. Whether it's Brexit or Trump, we know we're living through a momentous era.

1980 - The Intimate Touch of Stigma

I was telling a friend about a mutual friend's mum washing her car in a bikini. My friend looked at me and informed me that she'd told him my arms made her feel very uncomfortable. To me, she had never shown anything to give me that impression, if anything it had been the opposite because her son had a very small disability on his hand, and as far as she was concerned, I'd helped him feel a lot better about himself. But the friend who'd told me about her had no reason to lie.

I also had another similar experience around the same time. I'd often chat with a girl on the bus and one day she invited me to her home, warning me before we went in that her mother had mental health issues. Everything seemed fine, so much so, that a few weeks later I was nearby and knocked on their door. My friend wasn't in, but her mother seemed more than happy to invite me in for a cuppa.

A few days later the girl told me not to go there again because her mother found it upsetting seeing me. I'm not sure now if it was because of what I'd said, my arms, or was my friend just making it up. But either way, I was beginning to see that some people will find my arms difficult but won't show it outwardly.

There were many other similar incidents, so it was no surprise that over time I grew expectant of people rejecting me whilst at the same time trying to hide it. It was the intimate touch of stigma, and I learned to recognise it a mile off.

2019 – Political Policy Think Tank Panel

Someone mentions Diversity.

"Would it surprise you if I said I have a big issue with diversity?" I asked.

The person looked a bit shocked.

"I fully support inclusivity," I said, "But when it comes to Diversity, I think we spend all our time looking at the benefits but are too scared to look at the costs."

They still look shocked.

"Have you ever looked at the costs?" I ask.

"Surely, whatever the costs, they're worth it?" They say.

I look them in the eye, "Well until you've looked at the costs, how would you know? Maybe if you did you might have a different opinion."

The person who invited me to the panel told me they wanted diversity of thought just as much as any other type of diversity. If you have people who look different but share the same mindset, then what good is that? So, I guess I proved my point, there's always a cost to diversity, in this instance, it was them not feeling comfortable, but then isn't that how most people feel when faced with someone different?

––––––––––

1980 Summer - A Lesson In Feminism

It's hard to know when boredom ends and loneliness kicks in. I would wander for miles calling on friends to see if they wanted to come out to play. My desperation may well have put some of them off, but many probably felt the same way too. So much so, that even if you didn't like someone, you'd go out somewhere with them just because it was better than nothing. It's the equivalent of not receiving any emails for a few days, in time you'll start appreciating spam emails.

I can't even remember how I met Roberta, but not only did she seem to take a shine to me, but she also did Judo, which okay, wasn't karate, but it was close enough. I don't think much happened, maybe a gentle kiss goodbye, I'm probably even imagining that, anyway, I think there was an indication that we were seeing each other. Well, we were until we went to the Carshalton Hall disco where we had a slow dance together. This should have been an epiphany given she was about a foot taller than me, but maybe I thought this was an advantage from my vantage.

When I came up for air, I noticed my friend Jack was looking longingly at Roberta and when I looked up at her, she seemed to be doing the same to him. A bit later she told me she had to go home early; I offered to accompany her but she preferred me not to. I then looked for Jack, but he was nowhere to be found either. It was then that everything clicked. I was so angry that a bit later, during a group dance (when did I learn those moves?), I deliberately stepped on another kid's foot. He looked at me and said sorry. 'For fuck's sake, I thought, 'I can't even redistribute my pain without feeling guilty'. I came out of the dancehall onto Carshalton High Street, it was still sunny, and the world was merrily going on as it does when we're pissed off or dying, even if it's just from heartbreak. I felt the wide empty space of rejection and single-dom ahead of me so went home and, you guessed it, wrote a poem. The next day Jack called me to tell me he was sorry, but this was true love and he hoped I'd understand. "It's okay, the right people should get together," I said, hoping it wouldn't last long and sure enough it didn't.

At karate, the following week I was telling Jan, one of the women who trained there too, what had happened. She was very sympathetic until I referred to the girl I'd previously been a bit in love with as a slag. That's when I got my first lesson in feminism.

"Hold on Simon!" she said, "How comes she's a slag when if a bloke did the same thing, he'd be cool?"

I wanted to say, excuse me, but I think you'll find we were talking about me and how hard done by I was... but instead what came out was, "Erm, I'm sorry, I didn't think."

She knew she had me on the ropes so added, "I'm very disappointed in you Simon, I thought you were better than that."

I tried my best to look sorry, but that didn't cut it. So, she continued, "I'm sorry, it's not okay. Just think about how unfair you're being." And then she walked off in disgust.

I was probably a little tempted to make a high-pitched, "oooooh" sound, but even I wasn't that stupid. So instead I did a bit of stretching in the corner.

1980 - A Cure for Drudgery

Life started to take on a slightly repetitious nature by the time I hit 15, which in some ways was good, but there was still a lot of empty "between times". My days would mainly consist of getting up too late, rushing to get to school, and having fun with some of the regular passengers on the bus. Then there was the mixture of boredom and lawlessness at school, life drawing classes twice a week, karate 3 times a week, homework, chores, eating, arguing with my parents, watching TV and seeing friends.

Throughout 1980 and for quite a few years onwards I would write a page-a-day diary and as I write these chapters, I'm reading through them.

Sometimes the repetitiveness of my daily routine almost felt like the film, *Groundhog Day*. But when faced with such drudgery, many people, including me, try to inject a bit of 'magic' into their mundane existence whenever possible. Even on the bus to school, I would read my latest poems to a group of women that Sunil and I would chat with. One of them was called Penny, she had long copper-coloured hair and liked to wear green. According to my diary, she was quite up for telling me which poems she did or didn't like. On one occasion she told me she thought "To What" was better than "Weekends", which was very diplomatic given they were both rubbish. She was also very happy to discuss equal rights and other political matters. Nowadays any discussion of politics, on public transport would probably cause a riot within seconds. But back then we were desperate to break the routine, no matter the risks involved.

Even the bus driver had a similar mindset. One day he pulled up and got off the bus. A woman approached him, and they kissed passionately for a minute while we all looked on. (Was this a precursor to dogging?) He then got back on the bus and drove off to a round of applause. He took his cap off and gave us a little bow. Nowadays every driver is probably tracked and filmed; it's as if humans are being forced to act like robots until the automation era kicks in, at which point robots will try to be as human as possible, only without the dodgy humanity that we all love deep down.

As the world has become more technologically adept and correct procedures have become the main requisite of managerial agendas, people gaze into their phones where indeed, in the private circles of "friends" they can laugh at inappropriate things, discuss what they truly think about politics and look for the magic of the world that ironically, is all around them anyway.

2019 - Egg Shells or Assertiveness

I was in the Italian café the other day and one of the very young waitresses came in on her day off to chat with one of the good-looking waiters. She sat on a stool at the bar leaning towards him and laughing. Then an old man who I'm pretty sure has some mental health issues came and sat right next to her. It was all a bit awkward, and in time she moved away. After a while, he walked off.

"I felt so uncomfortable," she said.

I looked at her and said, "If that happens again, get the person's attention and say, "Excuse me, but you are in my personal space, what you're doing is inappropriate." Then, if they don't move, shout, "FUCK OFF!".

She laughed but looked horrified, this was not just a clash of how different personalities deal with things but also of different eras.

During the 1970s and '80s assertiveness classes were very popular. Women especially, recognised they were rarely taught as a matter of course to stand up to inappropriate behaviour, (especially within certain class strata), so these courses helped to redress the issue. So, three decades later, it's hard to fathom why that hasn't become part of the school curriculum. Instead, the onus is put on everyone not to do anything that might offend others, but let's face it, that's a quagmire that'll lead to everyone walking on eggshells because how can you second guess everyone's sensitivities? I'm all for thinking about others but training people to be assertive too would also be helpful.

1980 - IBM building East Croydon

As part of our studies, we were encouraged to join a scheme called, "Young Enterprise". The idea of it was to show us how a business worked. Working in a group of kids from a few other schools we would have to come up with a product, work out how to produce it, sell shares in our "company", sell the product and distribute the profits, as well as do the accounts. IBM was happy to host it in their building near East Croydon station. So, for three months we'd go there once a week.

Our group came up with a stunning product, a spoon rest, which one could, surprisingly, rest a teaspoon on. What was underwhelmingly different about our spoon rest was that they were made from Perspex. This meant we could personalise them by putting a photograph in the spoon rest. "This time next year, we'll be millionaires" we all didn't think.

It was like being on *The Apprentice* programme, so, after two or three meetings of listening to the group arguing over how they were not going to go about things, I decided to explore the IBM building. During my reconnaissance mission, I discovered two major attributes. The first was the staff canteen which was open throughout the night. The serving counter was brightly lit and gleaming, while the rest of the canteen was in darkness, but best of all, and to my amazement, the food was free. The second discovery was the photocopy room where not only was I able to copy 300-page karate books I'd borrowed from the library, but I could bind and laminate the covers too. By the time I'd finished, I'd saved myself, (okay, mum and John), about ten evening meals and I'd copied seven books which would have cost me hundreds of pounds in today's money. So, all in all, it certainly taught me how to be enterprising as well as how to photocopy my face, which was possibly my artistic side breaking through.

1980 - All in All

Although much of this period of my life was set within the walls of Wilson's School, you may have noticed I've barely focused on the staff or other students there. There were plenty of interesting people and no doubt many a tale to tell, but I did not come up against any awful persecutors and was not aware of any salacious goings on, (although there may well have been plenty behind the scenes). For me, school was just as much a part of the mundane world as was most of the other sections of my life.

In 1979 Pink Floyd's album *The Wall* was released and whilst most of us focused on the hit record, *We Don't Need No Education*, there was another track that held an equally pertinent message. The song was *Empty Spaces* and consisted of a list of things people do to fill the empty spaces they can't bear and included things such as seeking adulation, substance abuse, possessing things or people, going to war, and fighting. A few years later I would become one of the many millions of people captivated by *The Wall*, but I still didn't find a solution to the issue of empty spaces.

2019 September - Contentious Friendships

I've just cancelled my Netflix subscription for a few months as a protest because they cancelled finishing a series called *The OA* which I had invested 20 hours of my life watching. So now I only have Amazon Prime to watch, and just like that Bruce Springsteen song about there being 57 channels and nothing's on, I spent quite a while searching for something to watch and ended up watching a program about Pink Floyd's album *The Wall*. As I watched it, I saw a friend of mine who I sometimes write songs with. He'd been part of the live version of Pink Floyd for *The Wall* tour. When Brexit came about, we stopped working together, possibly because we took different sides in the debate, and whilst that is only one of several reasons, one can't help but recognise just how divided society has become.

That same thing that brought us closer together, the Internet, also allowed us to recognise we are quite different too. I know this is a bit political, but to me, it seemed the same people who were telling me we should see what it is that unites us are often the main protagonists when it comes to avoiding those they don't agree with.

At my birthday meal earlier in the year, my guests were pretty much split equally between those for or against Brexit. Fortunately, it didn't turn into a brawl, but when you start scratching the surface you get to see that people are generally not as tolerant as they'd have you believe. Right now, in 2019 all you have to do is mention any of the following to see people get quite agitated: Brexit, Trump, Corbyn, Jacob Rees Mogg, Boris Johnson, (politicians in general), transgender issues, Islam, mass immigration, racism, and of course, environmental issues. Now if you're reading this years later, you'll probably have completely different contentious issues, but these are the ones that divide and rule us now.

1980 - Racism

On Saturday mornings, I'd go to a life drawing class at Sutton College of Liberal Arts (SCOLA). Afterwards one of my fellow students, Margaret, would give me a lift home. One day we got on to the subject of black people coming into Britain, her position was that there were too many. I got very angry and said something like, "Well, if you don't like it maybe you should go live in another country". There was complete silence for the rest of the journey and I'm not sure if I ever got offered another lift. Even now, almost 40 years later, the emotional intensity around the issues of immigration and race is very high, although thankfully things are a little better than they were then.

1980 - Daily Routine

As I read through my diary for this period there would rarely be an entry in which I hadn't recorded the adventure I had getting to school. It was only by seeing it in relation to trying to make my day more interesting that I understood I was purposefully creating a drama. The consequence of getting up late wasn't just being late, it was about creating a struggle, so if all else failed, at least there would have been one highlight to the day. Living uneventfully was proving to be somewhat of an anathema to me.

2019 - Daily Routine

In my mid-50s I get up late because I like working into the early hours, there are no distractions then and I don't feel the urge to socialise late at night. Consequently, I normally get up quite late but still don't get enough sleep. Once up and breakfasted I'll often go to the Italian café and chat with some of the regulars, after which I'll do some paid work, and then get on with my creative projects. It's humdrum too, but I like it this way.

2019 - Marketing Music and Van Gogh

A couple of months ago I finished a music album I'd been working on for several years called *Dangerous Things*, I then spent two months promoting and marketing it. During that process, I discovered the current way of marketing music is to release every single that'll eventually end up on an album individually as and when they are ready, in other words before the album is completed. This is done to maximise the way streaming services like Spotify automatically share new releases. If I release an album Spotify will only put one song from it on their "New Music" playlist, whereas if I release ten singles I will get on that playlist ten times, thus getting me far more exposure. This will affect how other artists make music too but in a year or two, the system will change yet again and we'll all be forced to dance to a different tune, but at least we'll be dancing.

I tend to find promotion and marketing a bit soul-destroying. There are a lot of people competing for attention, (about 24,000 song releases per day), so most of my efforts just hit a brick wall, but I feel that if I'm going to create things then I have a duty to get my work out there so people who might appreciate it can find it. Although it's a bit arrogant to think people might ever be interested in it, to just hide away for fear of appearing arrogant seems a bit self-centred too.

People think they define who they are to others, but it's the other way around, our peers decide if we should be seen in a certain way. So, it's no wonder reputation is so important now. For instance, I could think I'm going to be a doctor, but there's a long process that determines if I would be allowed to be. Likewise, with art and music, I can put my stuff out there, but if people don't react to it positively in enough numbers, then I would be seen as being delusional. The problem is, there's only so much room for people to be successful on a commercial basis, and most artists will not earn enough from their art to live from it. So, if one doesn't earn a living from one's art but can still sell some, are we technically professionals, or must we sell at least 10,000 albums before we can earn that title? Then you get someone like van Gogh who was not recognised properly until after his death. So, even if someone's not successful whilst they're alive, they can still hang on to the notion that one day they'll possibly be posthumously recognised. It's no wonder so many people in the art world feel doubts about themselves, and alternatively why there are so many deluded people in the art world too. A few weeks ago, I went to the Tate Britain in London to see the van Gogh exhibition and one of his *Starry Starry Night* paintings was on display; it was the one across the bay. The difference between seeing it in real life and seeing a print was astounding, I was blown away by the colour and feelings I felt while viewing it. I loved it so much that I came up the following week to see it again just before the exhibition ended.

Just as we can't ever know the consequences or significance of our lives, the same goes for the things we create, especially when it comes to artistic creations. To a point, we have to be defined by our peers, but it's never an absolute definition. The thing is, so much of what we do is us connecting with everyone else across the empty spaces between the intimate and infinite.

1980 - Stylistic Development In the Music World

From the age of about ten, I'd been listening to music on my headphones before I went to sleep. Probably for a lot of people, there was a ritual when it came to listening to music in their room in the dark, for it was there where a transcendental journey would take place, moving them between their outer and inner worlds.

The Sony Walkman had been released the year before but was quite expensive, so I put together my version by using Michael's (Mum's psychopath boyfriend from a few years back) cassette recorder that he'd left behind. I bought a 5-pin din to female 3.5 jack adaptor from Tandy's (the high street shop for all things technical and rubbish quality electricals), to which I connected my headphones, which were also rubbish ones I'd bought from Tandy. The cassette recorder was quite big but came with a shoulder bag, so along with my bag full of poetry books and karate photo albums I rarely travelled light, but at least I had a soundtrack to the world.

Technology changed the music world dramatically at different times throughout the 1900s, whether it was via new ways to record music (e.g. multitrack recording), or new types of instruments (electric guitars, synthesisers and samplers), to new ways to distribute it, (radio, vinyl records, 8-Track, cassettes, CDs, Mp3s, and streaming services), but from the 1950s to the mid-90s, the most dramatic stylistic developments occurred. By the late-1990s there were very few new great advances, and even now, 25 years later, it's hard to hear anything that hadn't already been done during the earlier four decades. What this all meant for me at 15, was my world became even more enmeshed with music, I was filling the silence with something that was nourishing (overall) and doing it so much that I started to appreciate silence.

Even though the 70s had been more intense when it came to stylistic innovation, especially with punk rock and rock, and all their spin-offs, the music world in the 1980s was still heaving with great music and interesting artists. If you were a teenager, then you'd probably remember just how significant it was. Nowadays music is still very important to young people but there's a lot more formulation going on. If anything, as a metaphor for the world we seem to be living in now, there's a sense of sanitisation, both in terms of style and content. Ironically though, the people in charge of society now mainly consist of those who were teenagers in the 80s. It's as if they've distilled their past and are feeding the kids of today a more purified, more profitable version.

1980 - Wilson's Karate Club

As I began to go up the belts in karate, I came to realise teaching might be an area in which I could perform on an equal footing with other people. I was far from qualified to be doing this and in time I would get into trouble for doing so, but for a few years, I ran a karate club at school.

It started with me showing a couple of kids how to do basic techniques in the corridors. Whilst doing this we'd get loads of other kids watching, both curious and taunting us. One day, Mr Parr, who was one of our very old teachers, (he was about 80), told us it was unacceptable for us to do this in the passageway, so, not to be discouraged, I asked the sports master, Mr Sollis, if we could use the gym to practice in and if that was being used, then could we use the storage room. He gave us permission, so from then on, we trained every lunch hour for 30 minutes, and after school some days. The club grew but had a core membership of about eight dedicated practitioners. We eventually ended up doing a demonstration for The Duke of Edinburgh at Hever Castle as part of The Duke of Edinburgh Award scheme, after which he spoke to us, and we received a big round of applause as well as ending up in the newspapers.

1989 - Wilson's - Empty Stigma Spaces

I was recently chatting online about this time with one of my fellow pupils at Wilson's, Lee P. He said: "I saw you 100 times eating alone in the dining room, I never joined you once, I'm still ashamed of myself for my shallowness." I reminded him I was quite difficult at the time, so I didn't blame him for not approaching me. But maybe I was a bit more aware of the empty spaces because there was an element of me being avoided by others, partly because of my personality, but also because of some social stigma relating to my disability.

Empty Spaces

People react to empty spaces differently. They not only perceive emptiness differently but their reaction to their perception will vary considerably too. Some might experience it as boredom, some as loneliness, some as an existential threat, while for some it may even be an opportunity for peace, introspection and spiritual development.

I have a theory about adolescent loneliness, which was something I experienced a lot. When we're children we can be left to our own devices and will probably enjoy playing and not feel bored. But as soon as we hit puberty our reaction to being alone is far more acute. This might partly be because our nature is driving us to find a mate, therefore we feel bad either because we aren't getting on with the job in hand, (although I'm sure many were), or we feel we are failing to do so because we believe we are inadequate. It's a base way of looking at it but it probably has some substance to it.

418

On a deeper level, we associate empty spaces with death, and worse still empty spaces mean we have to face 'being by ourselves'. If we are literally with no one else but ourselves then there's nothing to distract us, but what is it about being with ourselves that we find so difficult? Maybe it's our unresolvable thought patterns or the many dark feelings, that without the help of others, are so hard to face alone. Then there's all that internal clutter we've been avoiding that's so overwhelming we just don't know where to start. Okay, it might not be that bad for most of us, but being happy by ourselves is a skill that can help us but does take time to master. Don't worry, or worry, I'll be coming back to this in the later love chapters.

The Poetry of Words

Sometimes, well actually lots of times, when I was alone and feeling lonely, I would write a poem, maybe it was a way of feeling less alone because I was communicating with others. Later, I would become more interested in the artistry of poetry, and how words can be used to communicate ideas or feelings, but it started as a means of escape.

Now, as I write this in the early hours, I'm thinking about you, wondering what you're thinking and what your life is like. When I'm writing this it's as if we're together in some way.

2018 - Addicted to Games

For decades now there have been growing concerns about addictions to computer games. I have been through it myself, (that will have to wait for another chapter), but it's easy to see how they've become so seductive. They can take a player out of their humdrum world straight into an exciting, magical one that triggers all kinds of powerful primaeval feelings while also satisfying our need for significance, for there in front of the player stands their archetypes in virtual flesh and blood.

When Keats wrote "Ever let the fancy roam, pleasure never is at home", he wasn't wrong. Fantasy becomes even more attractive when we're faced with stark reality. At the same time, online players are connected not just via the Internet but in many other ways too. It's no wonder they're so popular.

2018 - 2nd December - Suburban Adventures

My friend Gregory has popped around to see me. He's quite tall, with white hair, thick-rimmed round spectacles, a long coat and a hat. He's sprawled across my little sofa.

"I had to go to audiology the other day," he says in his strong sing-song Northern Irish accent. "I asked the bus driver to tell me when to get off. But when I thought it seemed to be taking us a long time to get there, I asked him how far we had to go. He told me he'd shouted out to me 20 minutes ago. I don't think he knew what I meant when I said I was going to audiology. Anyway, I got off the bus and found I was in the middle of suburbia. I mean it was completely void of human life. Not a soul could be seen.

Eventually, a car pulled up with an old couple in, I mean they must've been old if I thought they were. I asked them if they knew a number for a taxi firm so they gave me one which I tried dialling but couldn't get through, and they tried too, but to no avail."

"Did you dial the local number?" I asked.

"No," he replied, slightly perplexed, "were we supposed to?"

"Yes," I said.

"Well, they did the same thing. Three old people and a mobile phone are not a good combination. Anyway, they asked where I was going and when I told them they offered me a lift. I would love to send them a thank you card, but I could never find their house again, they all look the same in suburbia."

And to the untrained eye, they do, that's true.

But even in that story, I could feel their offer of a lift was just as much benefit to them as it was to Gregory. When you live in suburbia and an opportunity for adventure arises one learns to grab it with both hands (or paws in my case) — anything to break up the routine.

1980 - Front Room at Home - Wallington

An episode of *Hill Street Blues* started on the TV. As I listened to the music and watched the opening credits, I could feel an overwhelming sense of sadness and joy. The images showed a police car pulling out onto the cold grey rainy streets of a Chicago-like city. The music was full of sadness and heroism whilst the characters, who I'd come to know and love, were introduced one by one. In that opening scene, I recognised part of my internal landscape, one of grey skies and connections.

2019 - Love Life

When someone asks me how my love life's going, I say "Fantastic". They then ask, "Why, what's happening" and I say, "Nothing, that's why it's fantastic".

I'm 54 now, and my feelings of lust have been waning for some years. They haven't completely gone, and sometimes when faced with a bit of time to kill I can feel not so much a desire for sex, but more a feeling of wanting to do something that's self-destructive. When I was younger, I wouldn't have hesitated at the opportunity to get myself into a difficult situation, but now, it's a different story.

2014 - Needs and Desires

I was still with Sue in the spring of 2014, but I knew what she needed wasn't me. I wasn't with anyone else, so said she could stay with me until she found someone else if she wanted, the choice was hers. I didn't want to abandon her, I felt a lot of responsibility regarding her feelings, and something in her resonated in me too, but in the same way, I felt what she desired was desire, what she needed was a need, but I didn't feel those things anymore.

One day she said she'd met someone and was going to go on a date with them and was I sure I wanted her to go. I said yes. But after she went, I cried hard tears, not because I didn't want her to go, but because I didn't want her to feel rejected.

This happened just before my mother died, so by the time the funeral came, things had become more defined between us. We were no longer together.

The space in my story that Ali noticed in the café was the sudden lack of focus on the subject of my love life because, where there had once been desire, there was now an empty space, well to be more accurate an emptier space.

There was some flickering at first, an Internet relationship that became too complicated and developed into a relationship about connection but wasn't going to come to live in everyday life, and after a while, I realised I was happy with the companionship of a friend, someone to cuddle up to and share life's experiences with.

I once wrote in a song, 'If falling in love is a trick of the mind then why am I not laughing this time," because to me there's an element of nature coming into play within the infatuation process, but from that experience, we can connect with someone on other levels too, and the main ones to me are compassion and friendship, as well as finding them attractive. There were many times when I thought I loved someone, but I wanted to keep hold of them so I could keep myself "happy".

But loving someone may well mean having to balance out both of your needs even if it means losing them.

This story is not about a finale or a destination, it's about a journey and what was learned or reflected on during it.

When I write, I can feel you too, your needs and desires, and even the disappointment of there not being a happy ending or conclusion, but there's a lot more to come so don't feel too despondent. Have nostalgia for the future. I can feel my time fold upon itself. This moment in my life touches a moment in yours. I feel the connection even if you didn't exist when I wrote these words and I no longer exist as you read them now.

Sometimes the feeling of loneliness resonates with the idea that we are not significant in the minds of others. Especially those who matter to us. That we aren't loved, or our feeling of purpose has diminished. It is as if the part of us that helps us feel buoyant is punctured so we end up feeling empty.

The empty spaces that we face in life often come from inside of us. Sometimes, they are caused by our behaviour, and it's that which needs to be dealt with. Philosophical or religious ideologies may help you feel less isolated and inflated for a while, but it'll just be a temporary solution if you don't deal with the main cause. This was the journey of understanding that I started when I sat opposite the therapist and stated something was wrong, even though I didn't know what it was. Of course, it's more complicated than this, but this is a good starting point.

1986 - Therapy

Simon: I was reading a book on meditation, and it said that if someone feels lust then they can move that energy upwards to their mind and higher spirit.

Therapist: Is that a bit like avoiding living?

Simon: It might be useful if you can't cope with lustful feelings.

Therapist: If they are that strong, maybe there's a reason that, if identified, could help lessen them.

Simon: But in the meantime, it might be useful.

Unfortunately, I didn't get to meditate my lustful feelings away and consequently, I got myself and others into a lot of trouble. Maybe living a full and interesting life involves some amount of trouble though, well that's my excuse.

2019 - Leonard

My Alexa smart speaker is reading a biography of Leonard Cohen to me. It's telling me how he'd spent ten years in a monastery, but even then, he would sometimes go home so he could be truly alone. There have been long periods in my life when I have suffered almost debilitating loneliness, but often, even though those periods would come late at night, I would then become creative and after a while feel content. The next morning, I would wake up, feel okay for a few seconds then feel a sense of dread and for the rest of the day, I'd feel down or eager to escape feeling that way, until once again, late at night, I'd start wanting to be by myself so I could be creative. In time those dark times went away, but even now I tend to work from 10 pm to 3:30 am.

After ten years in the monastery, Cohen decided to live in the outside world and share his gift of a golden voice. If part of our inner significance comes from helping others, then sometimes these might be good reasons to vacate the empty spaces we hide in. It's probably good for others if we develop ourselves, spend some time outside of our normal life and understand ourselves more. Emotionally rather than intellectually, but ultimately one must enter life and feel it deeply to know it.

After my foot had been amputated, I used crutches to allow me to move around until I had healed enough to wear a prosthesis. Likewise, as we heal and grow emotionally there are good crutches that allow us to do exactly that and then, of course, there are crutches that trip us over, injure us and stop us from ever healing. These often manifest themselves as addictions or self-destructive behaviour. It would take me years to stop damaging myself and even now there is often a temptation to do so, but maybe because my feelings of lust have waned so much as I've aged, the temptation is far more subdued.

1980 - Retail Therapy with a Spiritual Dimension

If in 1980 I'd known how much of an adventure my life was going to be I probably would not have written so much poetry, which to many might have been a blessing, but for me, it was good training. If I had been more content, then would I have listened to the words of songs with the same eagerness to find solace? On Boxing Day (the day after Christmas day) I took a bus to Croydon, went to WH Smith's and sold my Book Token presents to people at the cashier till at a reduced rate. Then with the money, I bought a Roxy Music record. It was already getting dark, it was cold and wet, but the whole mission was imbued with meaningfulness. I knew that when I got in I would put the record on, plug my headphones in and in the darkness meditate on what I would discover in the music, and in turn myself. It was both a shallow retail therapy type experience as well as having a spiritual dimension.

1980 - The Dance

Just before we broke up for the Christmas break there was a school disco where some of the parents turned up too. At one point one of the mums who had been drinking a bit too much grabbed me, pulled me onto the dance floor, and held me to her bosom, which was actually quite flat, but I was still very grateful. (I'm only mentioning that to keep it real for you). Even though I was sure she was only doing it because she felt sorry for me, I was prepared to forgive her because as a male I would do anything for some female attention. I could feel people looking on, was it with amazement, incredulity, pity, glee, or laughter? But within her "cleavage" I felt a moment of connection because even if she was feeling sorry for me there was some kind of dialogue going on between us. Whilst I would have preferred it not to have been pity, I felt her compassion and felt sorry for her too.

Even now, when people feel sorry for me, I feel sorry for them because I know they're suffering a little and it's unnecessary. Later, when I would become more immersed in the disability-issue-based political world this double-view approach would help me avoid the "us and them" dynamic that typifies so much of these arenas. However, although there were a few exceptions, what was significant about this approach was it came from a feeling rather than a thought.

2019 - Choice Cuts

Some friends and I went to the Hydro Hotel in Eastbourne the other day for after-noon tea. In 1980 much of my time would have been spent with friends too, especially on very sunny days like this. But back then time alone felt far more lonely, desperate at times even. Whereas now, there are things to get done and the world is far more entertaining, all one has to do is reach for one's phone to feel some connection.

This meeting wasn't one in which we sat staring at our phones, as is very common nowadays, but instead, Fred, who is a friend's 20-year-old son did not agree that we have any choice in our lives. He believes what defines us, our species, genetics, experiences and all that makes us who we are, causes us to make the choices we do. His point being, we cannot control those factors so whatever we choose to do is simply a result of them.

I argue, "Well, doesn't this come down to how we define the 'you' or the 'I'? If I accept we have no choice, do we not, well, at least most of us, still end up in a position where we can make some choices at least, even if those choices are highly influenced by things beyond our control?"

"Yes, but you don't get it", he says exasperatedly, "You believe that the choice is yours, but it is determined by so many influences beyond your control it can't be seen as your choice. If a computer is programmed to make a choice based on certain parameters, can you say it has a choice?"

"But part of our programming is built on moral codes, and our reaction to how we make others feel, so to a point we have some choice," I say.

"No, not really, you just don't get it." He says.

1980 – Tough Choices

At 15, I was beginning to have to make some tough choices in my life. There were exams coming up that would act as a gateway to the next level of education, and/or the world of work. There was Karate, Vernon, my school, the other students there, friends and family, all of which played a part in giving weight to the importance of studying, but perhaps the most important factor was I enjoyed studying too. We were often set a lot of homework, so once back home there was a bit of time to eat and relax, but then I would sit in the back room with the radio on and work through my homework. Again, a routine set in, and it was one I liked. I'd listen to the programmes about relationship issues on Capital Radio, then music programmes, whilst problem-solving, trying to learn things and writing. Instead of wandering the streets looking for company, I'd found a good way to fill some of the empty spaces I so disliked.

If ever there was a single factor that I could identify as being the main reason I didn't go completely downhill in my life it was this. I enjoyed living and learning and I recognised the significance of connecting, not just with others around me but with humanity, the world, nature and with some kind of notion of "God", even if I didn't believe in "God".

1986 - Therapy - Choice

Therapist: Do you not think that doing this, causes you to worry?

Simon: Not really, I don't think about it.

Therapist: But you tell me you feel alone a lot of the time, don't you think that the way you act contributes to how you feel? It's easy to rush towards something to escape inner pain only to find that what you rushed towards just makes things worse. I mean, if you were undernourished and went into a food store you might grab a doughnut or a burger but if you took more time and effort would it not be better to buy some healthy food, take it home and prepare a good healthy meal? Sure, it would take longer and require more work, but all that effort and time could be seen as caring for yourself.

Simon: I can see what you're saying is right, but I often feel compelled to do what's not good for me.

Therapist: Well, that's partly why you are here, to try to find what it is in you that doesn't want to do what's best for yourself. It's not just laziness, it's a deliberate choice.

2019 - We're Complicated

When I was ill, I was touched by the kindness of those around me, and it reminded me of how important it is to decide which side to try to be on. Such things are never simple because, for instance, we may help one person but it may be at the expense of another.

I started writing this for reasons I've explained in the past but now I probably write it for other ones. In the same way, we fall in love with someone for reasons that are often different to the ones that cause us to stay together. I liked John Lennon because I liked The Beatles, then I listened to his solo albums and I liked him for those, then he got killed and I felt sorry for him. Then I found out he'd been terrible to one of his wives and I have to admit I still liked his music, but now I realised he was a weak person, as most of us are at times. He wasn't very nice in some ways but was incredible in others. The same could be said about many of those we see as heroes including the likes of JFK, Martin Luther King Jnr, and Churchill, who were all imperfect heroes too.

There's something in society at the moment that isn't willing to accept that nearly all great people have very bad sides to themselves as well. It's as if we can't accept ourselves, both ourselves and others. It reminds me of Soviet Art, it could only show one version of the world, and anything else was intolerable.

At 15, the way I viewed others was probably limited in many ways because I hadn't even confronted my dark sides. It never crossed my mind that for some people seeing my arms might cause psychological distress, and given that information, I could choose to react differently to it than just feeling rejected. I hadn't quite taken on board that people, well, all of us, are complicated.

Chapter 29
The Miracle In Our Eyes

FORWARD TO CHAPTER 29

The Miracle In Our Eyes

Today's the 23rd of May 2020, it's been three years since I ended up in the Intensive Care Unit for a burst appendix and sepsis. During my recovery, I was very aware of how little time might be left, and what I wanted to do with whatever remained. Faced with possible impending death most of us will wish for more time, and even though I truly felt wonder for having existed in the first place, and gratitude for the time I'd already had, I still wanted more. There I was, thinking I might switch off at any moment and now, three years later, not all that extra time has been used as wisely as I'd promised.

When we look at what happened to bring us to this present moment, it's probably also worth considering all the things that didn't happen that were involved too. This may seem a bit of a strange way to look at things but think how many times in a day we decide not to do things. It might be as simple as not getting up when the alarm goes off, waiting a bit longer before getting out of the shower, or not replying to a message. There may also be far bigger choices, for instance not having another child, not taking a plane, not accepting a job offer, or not telling someone how we feel.

I once wrote a song called *For What We Didn't Say* which focused on how our lives may be stifled due to our inaction, especially when it comes to following up on a feeling of connection with someone. The same goes for all those who came before us, we are just as much a result of what they didn't do or say as what they did. Of course, just as with our actions, we cannot know the ultimate consequences of our lack of them either.

When that German soldier bent down to help my grandfather and chose not to kill him, he couldn't possibly see that one of the consequences would be you reading these words now. If there is an all-seeing being, then they're probably aware of miraculous consequences all over the place, and likewise, tragic ones too. Whether there is such an all-seeing being or not, in many ways, given we can remember so much of our lives, we become a witness to our own life, albeit a very selective and limited one, and with the perspective time allows, we may come to recognise meaning in our actions and inactions that could never have been apparent at the time.

3.5 Million Years Ago "Little Foot"

Between 3 to 3.5 million years ago, one of our possible ancestors, a female hominid, classified by us as an Australopithecus Prometheus, walked on two legs, had similar proportions to present-day humans and stood at around 1.35m (4ft 5 inches). She was most likely middle-aged, her hands were very similar to modern-day humans, whereas her feet had extended big toes that were used for tree climbing. She may have spent her days foraging and nights sleeping in the trees.

One day whilst out searching for food, she didn't notice a hole in the ground surrounded by foliage, as she started to lose her balance, she tried to save herself, but couldn't and fell ten metres into a cave. Her injuries were so severe she probably wasn't able to call or crawl out and it was there, alone, she died.

In 1997 some of her bones were discovered and over the next 20 years, many of her bones were excavated and reassembled by Prof Ron Clarke and his team. Her skeleton allowed scientists to gain incredible insights into the study of human evolution.

2020 - 16 Years of Not-So-Quiet Desperation

I started writing this book in 2004 which is around 16 years ago now, so it seems appropriate that this chapter is about my 16th year. By 16 I started writing a page-a-day diary, so, what that means for you is that there's going to be a lot more to this, and the following chapters. As I read my diary from 1981 there was a "not so quiet desperation" within the lines and a resigned impatience for escape.

The Lack of Story So Far

If you've managed to get this far then you're either enjoying or tolerating my digressions and you've possibly come to realise I've partly approached this as a metaphor for the experience of living. Sure, there's a direction this book is going in, but this is about the journey, not the destination. I have read many books which took me on journeys that end in reunion and forgiveness, and yes, annoyingly they make me cry (a little). Both writers and readers will often give great importance to the ending of a story and rightly so, a disappointing ending can take a lot away from an otherwise well-told tale. But there is also something rather belittling about merely seeing the end of someone's life in terms of entertainment or a brief emotionally charged kick for a host of onlookers.

In therapy, we once spoke about people wanting to leave a legacy, to feel that they would be remembered after their death, but who is it that people remember, probably no one resembling the real person? There was something about the process of therapy itself that brought about a feeling of being known, just as we might experience it in a "functional family" to a degree, and maybe that is far more important than leaving a legacy. For many of us, there isn't just a need to be known during our living years, but also a desire to connect with others. So, maybe it's a lack of fulfilment in those areas that drives some to focus so much on their legacy.

There was a lack of connection in my life at 16. As I walked the empty streets resembling ones I'd seen in surrealist paintings, I found myself looking for an open door to a house full of love and connection. Now, almost 40 years later, in my mid-50s, I'm sitting in a house next to the sea, (which I can hear in the distance), it's 3:25 am, and I feel connections all around me, and I know I've said this before, but it includes you.

CHAPTER 29

1889 - Rēzekne, Latvia

Winter was drawing in. The ground was sodden and the roadway was turning from dry to wet. Three children, wrapped in shawls and clothes that matched the colours of the road and surrounding foliage, shuffled along, occasionally stopping to jump over puddles. A girl, in her late teens, was ahead of them and shouted without looking around, "Come on, we're going to be late". The three of them hurried, exaggerated a waddled gait for a short while, giggled and then forgot their mission of obedience. The day was almost over, the sky was blue, the sun bright and low, and the air cold. The girls marvelled at the length of their shadows as they danced and spun their way.

These were kids from the Jewish neighbourhood, but then most of this town was made up of the poor or the Jews. During the latter part of the 19th Century, Latvia was a rich country comparatively speaking, and Riga, its capital, was as grand as many of the other beautiful Eastern European cities. Its wealth spread out along the railways.

The preceding 30 years had seen the construction of the Moscow-Ventspils and Saint Petersburg-Warsaw railways which transformed Rēzekne from a small country town with a bloody past into a city of distinction. Even so, it's hard for us to grasp the sense of oppression that hung over the Jewish population here. Technically, most Jews had to live in certain areas in Russia, defined as the Pale of Settlement, and whilst just a few years before, Alexander II had expanded the rights of rich and educated Jews to live beyond the Pale, his subsequent assassination (which was falsely rumoured to have been at the hands of the Jews), led to not only stricter adherence to the restrictions on where Jews could live but even more persecution, such as the rights of peasants to demand the expulsion of Jews in their towns and occasional pogroms (basically killing sprees).

Plans had been made for just eight blocks of houses to be specifically for Jews when the new city of Rēzekne was being built, but by 1889 a large majority of the inhabitants were Jewish. So, as the three girls walked with their older sister to the station, they didn't feel the oppression keenly, but they did know they had to behave.

They got to the train station a few minutes early, the platform was full, but there was silence. Everyone was listening for the sound of the train vibrating the lines long before it, or its steam, could be viewed. As soon as it gave its strange-sounding warning, people started to talk and within 30 seconds, the steam puffed above the trees in the distance and a few seconds later, the train appeared. At first, it was urgent then as if it sensed all was not lost, it slowed, blew its whistle then came to a stop.

The girls and their older sister stood back as people waited to disembark or board. The carriages were so high above the platform that steps had to be put in place but for the daring or impatient jumping the queue became a sport. The girls were here to meet their father who'd received a dispensation to go to Moscow. Once he climbed down, he rushed over and picked up each child one by one, kissed them on their cheek and told them how much he loved them. As he did, they laughed and kissed him back. The older sister handed him a piece of bread, he surreptitiously popped it in his mouth and then smiled innocently at her, which made her laugh too. As they walked back home, he told them of his adventurous stay in Moscow, which of course, involved fighting off a few dragons and trolls, "Well, mainly trolls," he said, "The place is full of them, due to the number of bridges there."

1981 – Sixteen

Sixteen is a significant age in the life of a teenager, but in a way, it's just an arbitrary age our culture has decided on as marking the delineation between childhood and becoming an adult. In other cultures, 13 might be the chosen age. Whatever age is decided on, it's mostly related to the approximate age when puberty occurs. The problem is, not only do many people go through puberty at widely varying ages, but their response to it is often markedly different too. So, when people face coming-of-age rituals based on their age rather than their physical and psychological development it may well result in some being overwhelmed and unfairly burdened. Likewise, not recognising that certain children go through puberty at a far younger age means they tend to get labelled as being sexually delinquent or precocious.

When I had my 16th birthday it was just our society's view, that on that day, I was somehow to be treated differently. However, knowing society now had expectations of me, probably triggered further changes, beyond those caused by my physiology. At 16, I was told I was no longer a child, but not an adult either.

1889 - Rēzekne, Latvia

As they approached their home the three young girls ran ahead, so, when their father neared the house, his wife came out to greet him. She looked at him, and he at her, but when he shook his head very slightly, her eyes lowered for a second, she smiled and reached out to him, and he took her hand. She looked at the girl who had led the three to the station, "Chaya, can you go in and set the table while I speak with your father, please?"

They stood in front of the house. It was made of wood and painted green. Just as all the other houses nearby were, they all had a door on the gable end, a window above it and another to the right. You would have thought of them as single-storey houses from the outside, but the window above the door lit the sleeping floor. The ground floors were not wooden, instead, they were packed with earth and stones with threshing strewn across them.

These eight houses had been built and bequeathed to this man, Boruch Berzin, by his father, which afforded him an income but with so many mouths to feed they had to live frugally. Having a large family would be seen as irresponsible nowadays, especially if you're poor, but back then, it was the responsibility of families to go forth and multiply, especially for those of a religious nature and Nechama, his wife had always felt a close affiliation to her faith.

The evening light had almost gone, the air was cold and damp, smelling sweet with rotting leaves.

"It wasn't so bad," he said, "I have some extra orders, but I don't think anyone is going to get permission to leave here for a long time, not without a lot of money".

She paused and said, "Come, let's eat".

He touched the back of her hand, "We are blessed, Nechama. Even here."

As they entered the house the children quietened, except for the baby who murmured. Boruch and Nechama sat down, bowed their heads, and the children followed too.

"Blessed are you..."

2020 - Negative Space

If I draw 3 dots your mind can't help but form a

.

.

.

We naturally fill in the spaces.

But emptiness itself also informs us of what else is there, or at least what may be there. As I started to study Art more, I realised the importance of negative space, which is the gaps between or around an object that suggests its shape. A prime example might be the inside of the handle of a cup or the space between the legs of a chair. If you look at something now and look at what's around it, then imagine the thing itself disappearing, would the things around it give you a clue as to what had been there?

So, one of the themes of this chapter is the importance of something not existing or not happening. For instance, when I start writing these chapters my mind becomes filled with thoughts and ideas relating to them, but if I don't write them down, they rarely get remembered. Just imagine how much more you'd have to read if I was disciplined enough to note them all. So, sometimes, by something not happening, something occurs that wouldn't have.

1889 - Rēzekne, Latvia

When Boruch had made his way to the station in Moscow he had two options for his route, they were both the same distance but one passed a bakery, and knowing he would be tempted to buy something to eat, he chose to go the other way. Had he gone past the bakery he would have heard the newspaper seller calling out the headlines. Had he heard the headlines, then his future would have been very different.

1986 - Therapy

Simon: I often feel lonely. Like I'm of no significance to anyone else.

Therapist: But do you think that's true, that no one cares?

Simon: Well, I know my mum cares about me, but that doesn't count. And I know some of my friends care a bit. But I feel like I need someone to make me feel loved.

Therapist: Do you think that there's a part of you, that no matter how much love you received, it would never be enough?

Simon: Yes, I do, but how can I change that? I feel like I'll always feel a bit lonely.

Therapist: Well, do you not think there's a difference between an understanding that we are individuals that are interdependent, and feeling lonely? When you are happy, I could tell you that we are all separate and you wouldn't give a fig, but when you are lonely, no matter what anyone says, you'll still feel lonely. As I have pointed out to you before, we are not dealing with the rational part of you, but your deeper feelings. Where do they come from? You can't rationalise away a feeling.

I thought for a moment about what she'd said, but I didn't feel anything consciously, and even though I agreed with her, I still believed finding someone to connect with would help me escape my loneliness. What I wasn't aware of then though, was a part of me yearned to feel lonely and would even be willing to scupper relationships to feel that way.

1981 - Retail Therapy

I had often enjoyed getting toys, as most kids do, but when I hit 16 Mum allowed me to keep some of the weekly disability benefit money for myself. This meant I'd be responsible for my karate subs and art-related purchases. But this also marked the start of me having a bit of an issue when it comes to retail therapy. As soon as I'd got the money from the post office, I'd often buy a music album or treat myself to a cuppa in the local café. It made me feel a bit better for a short while, but it was always at a cost because it got me into a pattern of not saving, but instead giving into my impulsive feelings. When Pink Floyd sang *Quiet Desperation is the English Way* I recognised someone who understood something of my world. So, I just had to go out and buy the album.

2019 - Retail Therapy

Nowadays I keep a list in my notes app of things I'd like to buy and by doing that it takes some of the urgency from my desire to buy them there and then. It allows me to window shop, which is tantamount to retail therapy porn. Last November I'd made a list of things I'd wanted to buy over the previous few months and waited till the Black Friday sales came. Sure enough, lots of the things I wanted were reduced in price, so I convinced myself that I had to buy them. They were all related to music making except one thing, a robotic vacuum cleaner which was so much cheaper than normal I knew I'd be able to resell it if it was of no interest, (which as it happens is what I did). Still, within 24 hours I'd loaded an extra £1000 onto one of my credit cards. There was a hum in the background, like a distant foreboding train that I could barely hear, but because I didn't want to hear it, I didn't.

434

1981 - January 1st

The first page of my diary for 1981 listed some of my hopes for the year. Among them were, doing well in my exams and karate, showing off less and improving my relationship with Mum and John. All of these were admirable enough, but it ended with a cringe-worthy, "because I will not lose my integrity."

I think we had recently read "The Crucible". A play by Arthur Miller (you know, the playwright who married Marilyn Monroe) and the play was about a man's journey regarding his integrity. Being an impressionable 16-year-old, this had stuck in my mind. As things go, it's not such a bad thing to be impressed by, but there is something about the scripts that people latch on to that can still be deeply disturbing to witness. It's as if we're watching someone detaching themselves from reality and falling into a world of pretence, and when that happens, it can lead to all kinds of trouble. Of course, the scripts we latch on to say a lot about who we are, or at least who we'd like to appear to be to others. But even so, it's still.... Annoying.

2020 - January 1st - 6:30 am - Mark the Lodger

I was woken up by loud voices coming from the room below me. It's a room I'd rented out to someone called Mark, but after he hadn't paid his rent for several weeks and ran up an extra £1000 electric bill over the last 3 months, I went through the process of evicting him. His leaving date had been December 28th but because I felt sorry for him, I said he could have an extra month provided he didn't fall any further into arrears, use any more electricity beyond acceptable normal use, (60 kWh/week), didn't bring back strangers from the pub again and didn't cause any trouble.

The night before this incident, New Year's Eve, he told me he was going out for one drink, so I told him not to bring anyone back from the pub. He was staying on as a guest and was on borrowed time. So, when at 6:30 am I could hear a group of people in his room I rang him to find out what was going on. The phone rang, he didn't answer and the loud voices continued. So, I got up, went downstairs and knocked on his door, but there was no answer. The voices were very loud and given kids were sleeping in the room below, I pushed the door open and said, "What the fuck do you think you're playing at? You're disturbing the whole house and it's 6:30 in the morning."

I was confronted by three people. Mark, a woman, and a man with a beard who were all a bit drunk.

"Mark, you promised you wouldn't bring anyone back," I said.

He looked a bit sheepish, sat on his bed and bowed his head. He was obviously the worst for wear.

"You can't do this," the woman yelled at me, "It's illegal."

I said, "It isn't, he is no longer a lodger, and even if he was, I'd have the right to enter his room to stop this."

The woman continued to shout that I couldn't do this, and how her sister is a solicitor, so she knows, "it's illegal." I stood my ground and repeated my point. However, after about the fifth repetition, I added that she was an idiot, which didn't go down well at all. It was then she put her face up to mine and continued shouting. I was tempted to give her a little kiss and say, "Happy New Year", but I didn't think that would improve matters.

She had screamed "It's illegal" so loudly and so many times that the next day the kids downstairs repeated it to their dad, "Apparently, it's illegal Dad." "What's illegal?" he asked. "I don't know, but it is, the woman said so."

Anyway, back to the night before. The man with the beard was trying to pacify things, Mark was sitting quietly on the bed, the woman was still in my face, and I'm sure was lining me up for a kiss too. I decided to show them I was recording them on my phone, which I wasn't, but it allowed me to get my phone out and start the recorder. At that point Mark insisted they go home, so the man and woman left the house, but not without pretty much waking the whole neighbourhood too.

As I walked away from Mark he said, "Do you want a fight?"

I probably should have thought about this a little more, but instead, I said "Yes".

1981 – January 4th

The house we lived in was on Park Lane, which followed the North to South Wallington, Carshalton boundary line running straight through the middle of the road. Our neighbours across from us lived in Carshalton whilst we would wave to them from Wallington. I once stood on one side of the street whilst rain poured just on the other side. Even nature seemed to respect the local boundaries, well at least once it did. Park Lane became a lot more honest as it went up the hill because, at a certain point, it became Boundary Road.

It was the first Sunday after the New Year, Stephen, my little brother, who was now three years old, was trying to get in the covers with me, but the cat was already there and given it was so cold wasn't moving for anyone. The night beforehand I'd stayed up very late drawing a few pictures and writing a poem, so I was not particularly enamoured with the idea of having to share my cosy nest with any other beings. In the end, the cat and I made way, and Stephen, who was very bored got in the covers and decided I wasn't going back to sleep.

When I got out of bed I grabbed the duvet and wrapped it around myself leaving both the cat and Stephen on the bed looking rather out manoeuvred. Stephen got up and started using me as a kickbag whilst I looked on. The sink, half full with slightly soapy water had a film of ice over it. I pretended it was a tile, and in slow motion brought my arm down on it, enjoying the sensation of it cracking. Stephen looked on, then started whacking it a bit too hard. At this point the cat, caught a few icy drops, jumped down from the bed and walked off, stopping a few steps later to lick her shoulder three times in disgust, then continued downstairs.

"Is John in?" I asked Stephen.

"No."

"Where's he gone?"

"To the betting shop."

This was my cue to go downstairs in my pyjamas. Mum wouldn't mind but John would always have a go.

As I got downstairs, I could see Mum was looking comfortable watching the TV.

"Can I have some breakfast please Mum?" I asked.

Laughing she said, "You know where it is. Can't you see I've just sat down!" Then in a resigned tone, she half whined, half shouted. "Oh, don't worry, I'll do it in a minute after I've finished my cigarette."

I think she intended for me to feel a bit guilty, but I didn't. Stephen, who was still upstairs shouted. "Dad's walking up the road." So, I darted back upstairs and got dressed quickly. A few minutes later I heard John's key in the door. I was just about to thank Stephen when he shouted down to John, "Simon was downstairs in his pyjamas Dad, that's not allowed is it?"

"Was he now?" John said loudly, he laughed the kind of laugh the cat in Tom and Jerry laughed when he'd caught the mouse. "I'll be having words with him a bit later then."

"Stephen", I said quietly, "you're not meant to grass me up. We're meant to be a team, and THEY are the enemy."

Stephen laughed.

"Don't worry," I said, "You'll see, and then you'll understand."

As I started to walk down the stairs I felt a book hit my leg. It was Stephen throwing one of his ladybird books at me. At the top of the stairs was a giant hard-backed illustrated Bible. The temptation was there, even the image of Stephen laid beneath it, with just his arms and legs protruding from under it was egging me on, but I was hungry and the smell of bacon had a stronger pull. So, I threw it anyway.

"What's going on?" John shouted.

"Stephen's throwing books up and down the stairs, and one of them is the bible," I said

"Stephen!" John shouted.

June 2019 - Mark the Lodger

Things were going well with my lodgers, they all seemed very happy. I had even thought that they might stay several years, which was great as they were helping me pay my bills and mortgage which meant I didn't have to work as much and could concentrate on my music. But I should have known not to think like that because, within a few days, one of my lodgers said she was going to have to leave.

So, now, instead of having a couple of hundred pounds extra each month I was going to be in the red by a couple of hundred. I got an advert out for a lodger and sure enough, no one enquired. Well, not for a couple of weeks, at which point I started to worry. When someone did get in contact, I met them straight away and thought, "Well, they're not perfect, but as long as they keep their head down and pay the rent, what's there to lose."

A week later Mark moved in. A week after that he told me he couldn't pay his rent on time that week, but he would be able to catch up soon.

———————

1889 - Rēzekne, Latvia

When there are 15 children and one baby under one roof, then there has to be a lot of discipline. Boruch was too soft-hearted, so was used as an abstract threat, whereas Nechama was made of tougher stuff. There were routines, responsibilities, and rotas. The three older children were bringing in money and were itching to fly the nest. The way to freedom was viewed as marriage; the irony will not be lost on those who have been. Then there was making money or having some special skill or talent that might also lead to gaining an income. But these were just dreams to most people and the children of this world knew from very early on the difference between dreams and everyday life.

They were also keenly aware of their place as Jews, here in Rēzekne, which meant there was always a threat of danger. Even, surrounded as they were, by a large Jewish community, they became alert from an early age that one wrong word or action could be their last. Each layer of the community was there to cushion them from the next. Parents, siblings, family members, neighbours, and the local community, were part of the protectorate, then the Gentiles, the non-Jewish townsfolk, the country people, the rulers, the Russians and so on, they were dangerous.

Boruch was talented when it came to building, especially with wood, not just for building but carving ornate features. For these reasons, he was in demand, but with 16 children, even working all he could, they were still poor.

———————

2019 - Mark's Retail Therapy

Over the next few months Mark would continue to play catch up with his rent, some weeks he'd be ahead for a few days then he'd get two weeks behind. He'd tell me he was feeling ill, then spend two weeks in his bedroom recovering. This would become part of his regular pattern of behaviour. Get a new job, work for a week, get paid, then be ill for a week or two and lose the new job. It didn't take long to see the coincidence of him getting paid and then feeling ill. He was either binge drinking or taking drugs. After a couple of months of this, I asked him to start looking for somewhere else to live. He agreed but didn't take it seriously.

There's something about having someone in your house you'd rather not, it makes you feel insecure. After another fortnight of not getting rent, I phoned him to tell him I was going to have to give him notice to quit as he was eating too far into his deposit.

"Stop hassling me. I'll give it to you when I'm good and ready. Get off my fucking back!" he shouted.

"Are you downstairs?" I said, "Because I'm coming down to see you now".

So, I went downstairs, and said outside his door, "I want a word with you".

"OK," he said.

I opened his door and said to him, "Don't fucking talk to me in my own house like that. If you want a fight that's a sure way to cause one. You should be apologising to me and thanking me for not kicking you out already." [Lodgers can have notice equivalent to their rent payment intervals, which in this case would be one week.] "Instead, you're giving me lip."

"Sorry mate," he said in his Australian accent. ("Mate," said in such circumstances generally means "cunt" or "wanker") "but my aunt's just died and my mum is calling me all the time, it's stressing me out."

I looked at him and said in an incredulous tone "But you'd told me your mum had died last month and that was stressing you out then!".

He shrugged and said he'd get the rent by the end of the week.

1981 – The Not-So-Secret Diary

The first part of 1981 was dominated by mock O-level exams, which would be followed by a further four months of preparing for the real ones. The importance of these exams was not lost on me. Whichever path I wished to follow required a good handful of O levels. So, my life centred pretty much entirely on schoolwork, studying at the local art college for my art-related exams, Karate three nights a week, and a little bit of socialising or letter writing in the evenings. There was a lot of letter writing back then, and even now I think many of us write lots of emails and texts each day so not much different, in fact, many of us probably write a lot more now. Oh, there was the poetry writing of course and recitals on the bus to school. And each night I'd write my diary which nearly always included a line or two about meeting a girl on the bus, "who was quite divine".

I am sure when Sue Townsend wrote her book called The Secret Diary of Adrian Mole, a lot of people may well have thought that somehow, she had spied on their very own diary. But, whilst there is some crossover between her writings and mine, I never came across entries in her's that, as you will read below, quite matched the finesse of mine:

21/4/81

We had a hard-ish lesson, in which we did a load of fighting. There was a bloke from a Taekwondo club, he got chosen as a substitute for the team, the cunt. He was a right old cocky sod.

8/6/81

On the way home, I saw Susan K, wow! She's still divine. She's hoping to become a hairdresser, and when she said, "Well I've taken 12 O levels," I said, "I'm taking 9."

7/3/81

I felt quite lonely today, but there are no poems.

25 April 81

John didn't go to church as Stephen was wearing odd socks.

14/6/ 81

I read a load of good stuff on contraception and the woman's vagina (??!!). I then settled down to murdering about 100 ants in our garden and kitchen.

[An analyst would have a field day with that one]

11th March 1981

At the bus stop, someone had stuck some racist National Front Stickers on the bus post. Sunil took them down for me. [Ever the white saviour] On the bus, I saw Penny, we carried on our discussion about equal rights and politics. I said I didn't think that there should be seats just for disabled people on buses. I thought all the seats should be available for anyone with greater needs.

10/7/81

On the way to hospital, an Arabic man stood next to me and just stared – The ignorant cunt.

9/8/81

I went to see Bill and Gee on Powell Close, they seemed very racialist.

12/8/81

While drinking my coffee just a moment ago I saw a white cloud in it, so if I suddenly stop writing, I've been poisoned.

440

13/10/81 John tells me my photo of a kid having a pee was disgusting! – what does he know of true art?

3/12/81

To be faced with eternal loneliness is the ultimate horror. The day was normal. There was nearly a fight on the bus between two women over a window being opened.

Okay, maybe Sue Townsend did sneak a peek after all.

1889 Rēzekne, Latvia

Winter was moving in slowly, and with seasonal change, the daily routine would slowly adjust too. Routine was both constraining and reassuring, qualities the children, and parents, both associated with family and religion. Life for them was full of constraints. It was as if when babies were swaddled, they were being readied for life. But for each of them, there was also the desire to escape, to run away from each other, or with each other, away from this house, town, land, and life. Each day when they said, "One day Jerusalem", what they were also saying was, "We need to Escape".

As the children slept Nechama stroked them gently. But as they became older, she stopped and instead exerted tighter control on them. She knew the power of desire, and the struggles she had endured, so as her children became sexualised, instead of giving them more freedom, they got less.

1970 - Middle-Named

I have a memory of my mum telling me my middle name. I was about five years old and sitting next to her in Gran's front room drinking from my light blue beaker and trying to delay being put to bed. On the television, there was mention of someone having a middle name.

Mum stroked my hair and said, "You have a middle name, Simon".

I couldn't help but feel as if this was a prestigious gift being bestowed upon me, so, I regally awaited the blessing.

"It's Mark, your name is Simon Mark."

I gracefully bowed in thanks and for years afterwards believed that was the moment she'd middle-named me.

When I met my father, he said he'd influenced the name Mum chose because he'd asked her to use his father's, Samuel Moses. Whether Mum was influenced by this or not, I don't know, but there is a similarity.

———————

2020 January 1st 6:45 am - MARK

My middle name doesn't feel like it's my name, however, "Mark", relates to Mars, the god of war. So, it's apt in some ways. As you may have noticed, I have a bit of a bellicose streak and am too quick to react sometimes. So, when Mark asked me for a fight, I didn't back down.

"So, Mark, you want a fight then?"

There was a long silence, as I waited to see what he would do.

We both stood on either side of his doorway. At first, it felt a bit playful, and as he was quite drunk, I didn't feel very threatened. He was quite a bit taller than me, so when he feigned a movement, I parried his arm and put my foot gently to his stomach.

"Careful Mark," I said, "You're not going to win this."

"You reckon?" He slurred.

I could sense his mood darken.

There was another long pause and then I could feel his arm move towards my head. I didn't see it, but automatically turned my face away, and pushed my left arm upwards to block his punch. As my phone was still recording, I was able to listen back after and this all happened within about 1.5 seconds, but my memory of it was more like five seconds.

As I pushed my arm up I imagined I was pushing a bag up into an aeroplane's over-head storage compartment. But what happened was my arm went straight up into Mark's neck which brought him off his feet. I then turned towards him to deliver a strike and, even now I can recall deciding on whether to deliver a fast penetrating strike to his torso or more of a push. I went for the latter.

The next image I have is of him staggering backwards and falling on the floor, dazed, and almost unable to right himself. During this bit, my adrenalin kicked in and I shouted, "Do you want some fucking more Mark? Cos, if you do, I'm gonna kick you in the fucking head!"

"That's assault," he said, "I'm gonna call the police".

"You do that, and I'll play the cops the recording of you throwing the first punch," I said, my voice much calmer. "Just go to sleep and we'll talk about this tomorrow".

As I walked off his door shut.

Even though he was drunk, and if as he claimed the next day, he hadn't gone to punch me properly, I was pleased my karate training had kicked in.

Mark did try reporting me for assault a few days later, but when I told the police about it and played them the recording they couldn't stop laughing, which kind of made it all the more worthwhile. They then informed him that it was going on record that he had committed a common assault on me as he had thrown the first punch. However, they did suggest to me that when he asked for a fight, I should have sidestepped the issue.

So, all's well that ends well. Although, as we'll see, it didn't.

1981 - Routine

When I say my routine in 1981 resembles the one throughout much of my life, what I'm talking about is the outer shell of who I am and by 16, it had already taken on a clearly defined form. Inside though, my inner core was by no means anywhere nearly as "developed" and probably wouldn't be so for many decades.

The paradox of these separate identities is whilst the outer shell was mainly a front, it would often keep the inner part of me afloat during some of the bad emotional times to come. When my inner self collapsed, my outer shell would continue to operate, especially in its creative pursuits, and in that way, I would be able to ride the waves of desolation.

Even before ever coming into contact with psychoanalysis, I had experienced different levels of consciousness in myself. Not in any mystical way, but simply by looking up into the sky and seeing things floating in my vision, small chains of dots that I could chase around as I moved my eyes, and then there were voices in my head that seemed to be independent of my conscious thoughts. It wasn't anything like schizophrenia, just in my half-sleep moments, I'd be aware of my inner world existing. As you may recall at 4 years old I'd hear some of the voices saying, "The wolf", repeatedly as I tried to sleep in the dormitory in Barnardo's. As much as I pleaded with them to be hush, they seemed to have a life of their own. Later, when I was seven or eight and mum had her violent boyfriend, Michael, my night terror dreams of wanting to escape the impending train crash or sinking ship, felt like films playing out in front of me. I felt I was watching from a near-long distance but, try as I might, there was no way of waking up or escaping them.

I once heard in a film about Freud that he'd stated we struggle in life to avoid manifesting the negative aspects of who we truly are, yet for most of us, it is unavoidable. I was never able to substantiate if he said that, but it did resonate with me, in fact, it scared me. I have lived my life worrying that the anger in me could be so strong that it would destroy me, especially through an act of rage.

When Mark faced me off, I was just as worried about what he might do to me if we fought as what I might do to him if I lost control. As he hit the ground, I looked at his head and had he appeared to me to continue being on the attack I would have kicked his head with force. Fortunately, he didn't.

1986 - Therapy

Simon: I had a dream about being on a train that was running people over.

Therapist: What do you think it means?

Simon: I don't really know.

Therapist: Can you remember anything else?

Simon: I felt disturbed by it. I was on the train in the dream, and when I woke up, I felt relieved it was just a dream, but I still felt a bit depressed by it.

Therapist: Do you think you felt guilty, after all, it was your train that went over them.

Simon: Well, I didn't choose to do that.

Therapist: But it was your dream. Maybe you were trying to tell yourself something. Do you think it might be reminding you we can sometimes be a part of something that has dire consequences for others, and that's what we find difficult to cope with?

Simon: I think that's true in a lot of ways, even being part of our society means people suffer as a consequence of our gains.

Therapist: But on a more personal level, can you see any parallels?

Simon: Like the tracks?

Therapist: It's interesting that you make that connection.

Simon: Are we playing railway metaphors?

Therapist: You like to use humour to avoid the feelings brought up by this dream.

(I would come back to this dream in a few artworks and songs. It was the beginning of understanding that my behaviour would sometimes cause me to feel lonely or depressed. Even so, it didn't stop me from behaving that way.)

1981 - After the Exams

After taking my O-levels, a two-month break from school sprawled ahead of me and beyond that, I knew going into the 6th form would be very different. I could feel the touch of freedom and loved it.

In the first week, I sat out on the concrete paving in the back garden and tried to read Shakespeare's Romeo and Juliet. The white of the paper was so bright in the afternoon sun, that my eyes watered. I closed the book and thought about how I could fill this time.

On the last day of term, I went to one of my school friend's places and when we got there, he showed me a camera he was selling. It was a Chinon CS SLR 35mm camera with a built-in light meter and fully manual override mode. It was one notch up from the bottom rung Russian-built Zenith, but I knew I had to have it. That marked the beginning of my interest in photography. Once we'd secured that deal, he tried to sell me a synthesiser, but "what was I going to do with that, I can't make music," I thought. And until computer-controlled music became available, I was right.

Even so, during this break, there was a moment when I came in contact with the songwriter in me. One of the other boys in my year, Daniel, was a very proficient musician for his age. He had heard me imitating Elvis and said I should come around to try recording something with him. So, we met up and whilst he played on a guitar, I ad-libbed lyrics and vocal melodies which we recorded on to cassette. What I came up with wasn't any good but being able to come up with lyrics on the fly as well as melodies is something I still utilise sometimes to get ideas for songs nowadays. So, by 16, I'd already discovered an interest in songwriting, writing, photography, painting, karate, and studying, which is pretty much what I still focus on now.

1889 Rēzekne

Although religion figured heavily in nearly everyone's life in Rēzekne, many Jews were not part of the Orthodox church. Consequently, they dressed similarly to their Christian neighbours, and likewise socialised, danced, went to the theatre, were entertained by musicians and singers, and tried to live their lives to the fullest as best they could, but it was a precarious truce.

Life was dominated by work, family, and the traditions of Jewish culture. Families would meet up, the children would play whilst the mothers would look out for possible matches, and when their children became young adults, they'd either choose each other for marriage or the decision would be made for them. This was the outer shell of their world, but their internal worlds were filled with dreams. During daylight, people were acutely aware they could be seen, but at night, on their sleeping floors, there were silent stirrings that were never to be seen in the light of day.

1981 - Summer

Peggy Waites had been a helper at the riding school for disabled children I'd attended and had taken an interest in me and Mum over the years. She was also the widow of a building tycoon. One afternoon she invited my mother, John and me for tea. Whilst they chatted in the house I swam in her outside pool. There was no one else around, so I swam a few lengths underwater, lay on my back, looked at the sky, took in the deep colours of the trees, then realising that this wasn't so much fun when alone, so I went to the dressing room and started to change.

A minute or so later the door opened and a woman, probably aged between 45 to 50 walked in. "Sorry," she said "Do you mind if I come in? Don't worry, I've seen it all before."

"Yes, I don't mind," I nervously answered.

She started to chat to me as she undressed. My heart started to race but I was soon disappointed to find she already had her bathing suit on under her clothes. I, however, had my towel strategically, yet precariously positioned. She kept chatting and looking towards me. She even asked me if I needed any help and I stupidly said, "No I'm fine thanks."

I couldn't help but feel a bit turned on, there was a part of me that wanted to be physically desired, and the notion of that was arousing.

"What's your name?" She asked.

"Simon," I said.

She smiled "I'm Jean, pleased to meet you".

I asked her where she lived and found she didn't live far from me, so I asked for her phone number and said I might visit one day if that was okay.

"Yes, that'd be lovely. You can come and meet my husband and my children, they're about your age. I'm sure they'd love to meet you."

This wasn't going the way I'd hoped it would.

1985 - Therapy

Simon: I feel that women have the power when it comes to relationships.

Therapist: What do you mean?

Simon: Well, a man might want to go out and have sex but unless he finds a woman who wants him, it's not going to happen. Unless of course, he rapes someone.

Therapist: That's an interesting connection you've made there.

Simon: What do you mean?

Therapist: Well, you've connected rape to a man not getting their way.

Simon: Well, I didn't mean that's an option I'd consider.

Therapist: It's worth noting the connection though.

Simon: What are you getting at?

Therapist: I'm wondering if the idea that you're powerless in some ways causes feelings of anger in you. In a way, it's an echo of most children's experiences. Won't they, at least at some point, experience having a tantrum when they don't get their way? Even in adults, you can see this happening all the time when people have road rage.

Simon: I suppose you have a point, thinking women have most of the power in this situation does make me feel a bit resentful.

1999 - The Gangster Who Went Straight

One of my clients was quite a famous journalist and TV personality. I won't say his name as I don't want to be prosecuted for misquoting him but before he was a journalist, he was a gangster, so I'll leave it up to you to work it out.

One day he and I were chatting about women's sexuality. He started telling me that when men witness women's unbridled sexuality, they find it threatening. Not only does their orgasm look far more overwhelming than a man's, but to see in a woman an equal amount of relinquishing control to nature makes them realise that they are up against a formidable foe. If a woman is free to do as she pleases then anyone who connects with her will fear where her desires may take her. The same could be said about men, and that's what scares them. They don't want women to have the same freedom they have.

Afterwards, I thought about the irony of men transferring responsibility to women when it comes to dealing with the aftermath of their desire. In other words, a man may blame a woman for the way he feels, or what he does, when really those feelings and actions are his, and his alone. So, on one hand, men want to curb women's sexual freedom, and on the other, they want to blame them for causing their own lust.

Now, this might come over like I'm virtue signalling in an area of politics which isn't my domain, but I'm partly bringing it up because as time went on, I became very aware of just how central this theme was to me personally.

My mother had seemed to abandon me, and maybe in my subconscious it was for another man, so I was possibly more primed to feel jealous and possessive than most. Then, as I got older and became interested in sex, not only did I realise I was powerless to a large degree when it came to attracting women, but I understood that some women might be just as unfaithful and lusty as myself. To make things worse, if I were to try to tie a woman down then that would destroy the relationship, and the final icing on the cake was, a lot of women felt the same way as I did. On top of all that, some men were just as attractive to women as women were to men, men who could pretty much pick and choose who they wanted, and worst of all I wasn't one of them.

Unfortunately, no one taught me about those dynamics, I had to learn the hard way that if I felt the need to exert control, I'd already lost. If I couldn't let go of my desire to possess then everything would slip from my grasp. If I couldn't love someone enough to just let them be who they are, then I didn't love them at all, and likewise, if I felt I couldn't accept they might not stay forever, then these might not be feelings of love either.

All these ideas went completely against my instincts or inclinations. I can't blame anyone who feels such feelings too, as, for many of us, this is how we experience love. But the point is, these feelings are probably just as destructive as the things we worry about, so it's worth paying attention to them if you think they might be your undoing.

This desire in me to control and possess, wasn't just a socially learned way of thinking, nor was it just a primaeval biological process, it was also a result of the way I'd reacted to my relationship with my mother and absent father. Please note that I would like to emphasise the words "the way I had reacted" because who I intrinsically am is part of all this too.

2007 - What If

In one of my poems, I wrote, "What if what I do, kills the love of me in you".

1981/2020 - Letters and Emails

In 1981 I would often write letters, and now in 2020, I write emails and send messages and texts as most people do. But lately, I've been delaying my replies to some people to bring back something of the delay of letter writing I'd experienced before the Internet came into my life. If you haven't tried doing it, it's worth a go, but of course, let the person know what you're up to beforehand otherwise they'll probably call the police to check you're okay.

When email became popular it changed the nature of writing. The speed at which a reply would come back meant the nature of the communication changed too. In some ways, it was a bit oppressive, or at least it felt demanding. Instant messaging isn't so bad because it often doesn't require a reply or if it does, it can be concise. But writing a letter requires time to reflect more deeply upon the feelings, words and thoughts being sent.

2020 - Gurdjieff and the Essential Self

When I think about my outer shell becoming more distinctive at this point in my life, I'm reminded of the philosopher George Gurdjieff, whose work was very focused on trying to find our essential selves. He believed that the soul we are born with gets trapped by personality and is kept hidden and unexpressed, leaving us not truly conscious. For him, there was an onus to free our souls. I mention this because no matter how happy or oppressed we find our lives to be, there will often be a desire to escape. It might be something obvious, like pain, but then it could be death and for some even, life.

As the seconds pass us by, we don't initially notice the erosion or build-up of that which covers who we are, but in time we recognise the changes. We see what is and what was, and the more we lose our self the harder it is to be connected with who we truly are.

2020 - Looking at a Photo of Esther

I'm looking at a photo of my grandmother Esther Berzin, she's probably in her 40s in it. There is something disingenuous about old photographs of our relatives, they look so staid and posed, yet if they were to jump down from the photograph into our life now, we could see them as the animated humans they were, we could see that in so many ways they're just like us.

When I look into Esther's eyes in this photo, I see her pain, I don't feel it, but I can see it's there. There must have been many moments of happiness too though.

Looking at her in her mid-40s she looks so weighed down that it's almost impossible to see her as a young, hopeful, laughing, in love, lusty woman. She would come to have five children, were they borne of love and lust or duty?

As she got older, she'd enjoy growing produce she'd sell from a table in front of her house, just as her mother had done too. Her life in many ways was simple, but even a simple life can be filled with complexities and suffering.

As the Nazis grew ever more powerful, she knew she would have to leave her homeland. Even though she had yearned to leave it for so long, leave behind all the hatred towards her and the whole Jewish community there, when the time finally came to step upon the boat, with her sons, Eliezer and Boris, by her side, she looked back, and all she could see was herself standing on the dock, waving goodbye.

I don't think it's any coincidence that many people fall ill with cancer around a year to 18 months after suffering a psychological trauma. Even the word Cancer connects to the notion of a crab, just like it does in astrology, but in medicine, it's partly because there is a hard-outer shell to many tumours, partly the sensation of being pinched or gripped by a painful unyielding force, and partly the protrusions appear just like the legs of a crab. On top of that, crabs will often seek out empty dark areas to inhabit.

The reason I'm ramming this home, possibly, a little too harshly, is to bring attention to the physical repercussions of psychological trauma. One might argue whether it's a good idea to burden someone who is recovering from a difficult time emotionally, but to me, just being a little bit more vigilant during such times is probably a good idea.

As Esther approached her death, she cried out for someone to kill her. My father would often say to me that he'd have done it for her, but he wasn't allowed to, and this was way before palliative care was available to the likes of Esther.

2020 - The Crow - Part 1

I can hear the noise of a bit of debris falling down the chimney, I'm on the first floor, and it sounds a bit like an animal is moving around in there. Like there's a struggle, but I'm not sure. Later, I am in the room below. I'm sure I can hear a sound, but it's quiet and repeats twice, it's almost computerised. I pull out the tumble dryer which sits below the chimney stack (the bottom part of the chimney was taken away years ago). I get my mobile phone and take a photo up the chimney. I'm a bit scared. If there is an animal up there it might attack me. But there's no noise, and the photo doesn't show anything out of the ordinary.

The night before I'd dreamt I was speaking to a crow, but maybe it's all in my imagination.

1981 - Voluntary Work

I knew I ought to fill some of the summer holidays doing something worthwhile and because I'd applied to do my Duke of Edinburgh Award I went to the local volunteers' association and asked them if there was anything I could do. By the way, I never completed the Duke of Edinburgh Award due to the expedition section of it becoming a bit too difficult for me, plus I had a very bad attitude.

I got a phone call from the woman at the volunteers' association, and she said that I could go to the patient's classroom at the hospital to meet the teacher there who would discuss with me some possible work.

1981 - Queen Mary's Hospital for Children - Carshalton

It was a hot June afternoon when I visited the woman who ran the classroom. I'd turned up topless, my T-shirt in my bag, my bag flung over my shoulder. It didn't even go through my head that this might be inappropriate. The woman was called Janet, she was slightly big built and had copper-coloured hair that stopped just above her shoulders.

We got on straight away and made a plan for me to come back over the next few weeks and help paint cartoon images on the windows. Which I did. The pictures came out far better than I thought they would, and when we finished, I asked if there was anything else I could do. So, Janet called a few of the wards to see if they had any opportunities but when I called back to find out if there were, she said that the hospital had refused my offer because they were worried that due to my disability, I might get injured, and they couldn't take that risk. After our conversation ended, I called the volunteer association and spoke to the woman in charge. Before I managed to get a word in, she told me she was very shocked and disappointed to hear that I had turned up topless for my interview. "Shit", I thought "you've got me there... And thanks for grassing me up Janet, don't come begging on your knees for forgiveness when I'm a famous painter and you want your portrait done!" When we finally got past that minor faux pas the volunteer association lady said there was nothing she could do and put the phone down on me.

I was so annoyed I walked down to the Art Shop in Carshalton High Street, which had kindly put my rubbish portraits of Charles and Diana in the window to sell; well actually they weren't that bad, but I had made Diana's teeth look like she'd been chewing liquorice, so needless to say, they didn't get the price I'd hoped for or, indeed, any price at all. Anyway, I often chatted to Charles, the owner of the shop, not the prince who was just about to get married to the wrong woman. So, I thought I'd get his opinion on the whole issue of not being allowed to help because of my disability. The thing is, for people who haven't spent a lot of time pondering these issues, it's hard for them to offer anything unexpected, so I came away just thinking that this is the way of the world, and life's not fair. But I knew it wasn't right, so I went home and wrote an essay about it. I was beginning to take on board that society can choose to make provisions for all kinds of human needs, and it's less about natural law and more about what we believe society should be about.

Here are a few lines from one of my early disability-issue-based songs:

> *We don't live in a jungle*
> *We're here to live by the law*
> *We're here to give and to gain*
> *But who is all of it for?"*

This was still an era when single women trying to get a mortgage for a house had to get a male to sign for them, but it was also a time when things were beginning to change. In 1982 the mortgage laws changed so a male signature was no longer required, and the disability rights movement began to make headway on its long road towards legislation.

2020 - MAY 22nd - The Crow - Part 2

In the room where the tumble dryer is, there's a door to the backyard. As I walked back in through that door, I was sure I heard that noise from the chimney again. Was it the freezer? I tried to imitate the noise, but nothing came back. I wasn't certain but I got the feeling there was something trapped in the chimney. That night I looked online to see how to deal with trapped animals in the chimney, the solutions either involved big costs or putting up with unseemly odours and guilt for some time. I thought the chimneys had cowls on them, but the winds are strong here so maybe they'd been damaged.

1981 - Queen Mary's Hospital for Children - Carshalton

During the days I'd been painting at the hospital I'd gone to the staff canteen to eat and it was there I met a few nurses (I know what you're thinking) and a few other volunteers. So, after I'd been informed my services were no longer required, I popped back in to share my good news and to say goodbye. However, one of the nurses I spoke to was a sister on one of the wards and she told me she hadn't been asked and would be more than happy for me to come on to her ward and play with some of the kids there. So, over the next few weeks, I popped in and helped break up the monotony for some of the long-term patients, who I also became quite attached to.

After these sessions, I would go to the staff canteen for some cheap hospital food which I liked due to my years at Roehampton Hospital and befriended a couple of the staff members there, especially one called Jill. During my "work" on the ward, I became friends with one of the other volunteers as well, who had bright red hair and was called Lisa. Both Jill and Lisa would feature in my life a lot over the next few years and through them, I'd get to meet other people of significance too.

1981 - Ann And Paul

I have already mentioned Ann and Paul to you. Ann became a second mother not only to me but to many other people too. She was the one who'd visited me when I'd had my foot amputated and years before then I'd met at the crocodile pond party. She also had a naked photograph of herself on the bookcase in her front room that I would spend time studying whenever the coast was clear. Sometimes she'd catch me and laugh, "Oh sweetheart, what are we going to do with you?" I had a few suggestions, but I kept them to myself.

It was probably around this time in my life I started to visit them more frequently. They lived a short walk away from the hospital where I was doing the "voluntary work", and outside of feeding me, they were very happy to either listen to my tales of woe, admire my artworks and poetry, (just for that they both deserve saint-hoods), and then they'd drive me to my local friends or home afterwards. (I don't think I put reading my poems and suddenly being offered a lift home together at the time).

30th July 1981 - The Commission

One of the boys at school, Cameron, told his mum that I was becoming quite good at Art, so she asked me if I'd be willing to be commissioned by her to paint a land-scape of the Gower Peninsular. I agreed to it, so she came to the art shop with me and bought £9 worth of materials, which was quite a bit of money back then. The thing is, I couldn't do it. For some reason, I just put it off and it never got it done. Letting them down still haunts me today, so much so that almost 40 years on I feel I ought to do it now. I'll let you know if I ever do.

1889 - Rēzekne, Latvia

In Britain and other Western European countries, people started to move away from the countryside and into the cities. For centuries, if not millennia, people had lived a life of subsistence, but in the more industrialised countries, farming was becoming industrialised too. While this inevitably led to fewer opportunities for land workers, it also meant there was more surplus food which in turn meant greater opportunities for people to follow other careers. But in Rēzekne, the Berzin family's paths were very much set. Instead of learning to read, the children learned to forage, not just for food but also for medicinal bark, herbs and plants. Instead of doing sports, they were physically exhausted by the end of the day from dealing with the family's smallholding or delivering goods to local customers.

The family had acquired a few musical instruments over time; some of the flutes had been carved by Boruch, and a battered fiddle and bow had been a family heirloom. The children had all, at some point picked them up enthusiastically, but after a few minutes of nothing sounding good, put them down, much to the relief of everyone else. Boruch lived in the hope that there would be at least one child who would persist and magically learn to play by ear, but it didn't happen.

Boruch's large family was very unusual, most Jewish families had three to four children during this period, so just by their size, they were well known in Rēzekne. Boruch was popular and given Rēzekne had such a large population of Jews, there was generally a sense of them being safe.

In Riga, the capital city, the Jewish population had secured some rights, which was in some small way, progress. Especially because during Nicholas I's reign, 600 laws over 30 years had overly regulated Jewish people's lives.

Whilst the Jews in the countryside mainly focused on providing essential goods to each other as well as non-Jews, the development of large-scale trade and industry was more the domain of those who lived in the city. Wood industries, flax processing and even alcohol production were particularly successful. One Jewish merchant built and ran the largest match factory in Russia. While others focused on the buying and selling of grain. By the end of the 19th century, ten banks in Riga were owned by Jews.

However, after the murder of Alexander II in 1881, there were outbursts of political and economic anti-Semitism followed by anti-Semitic riots, during which over 40 Jews were killed, and hundreds of women were raped. On May the 3rd, 1882, Alexander III demanded that any Jews in Riga, Jelgava and Liepāja who did not work in officially registered professions had to leave the cities. Even four years later, the newspaper "Dienas Lapa" wrote:

"[Jews] clearly show us how a small and despised people can become strong. Their example overtly shows what people can achieve through care, patience and a strong community."

So, to be able to live in relative peace, when such hatred was only a train ride away, was a gift that Boruch and Nechama did not take for granted.

2020 - Mark the Lodger

After Mark moved out, he left his belongings in situ. Legally, I had to give him 14 days to remove them. I got a few people in to clear out the room, all of which had to be videoed as evidence in case he was going to make a claim against me for any losses, but after 14 days, the law states that the belongings can be sold or given or thrown away, if not kept. Any revenue collected from sales must be kept for six years, and small expensive items should be kept for the same duration too. A night after he'd moved out, he called me at 2 am insisting he pick up his medicine, and if I didn't allow him to do so he might die, then I would be responsible for his manslaughter. I was up anyway, so let him in and as I sat and watched him get a bag full of pills, he told me they were illegal drugs, prescription opiates that he'd bought from dealers. "I'm a dead man walking," he said.

"I'm sure that's not true" I replied, hoping I was wrong.

For the first few days after he'd left, he came back to pick things up, it was then he'd ask me if he could take a shower. I relented, but a few days later he also asked to do his clothes washing. I told him that after that there could be no more showers or use of the facilities. Maybe it was that which set him off, but he decided to pick a fight about cleaning the microwave, because, as he put it, "someone else had used it."

When I told him he was wrong, that he was the only one to have ever used it, he called the police because I wouldn't leave him alone in the room. When they turned, up they spoke to both of us separately, then told Mark that he must organise getting a van to take all his belongings in one go. He agreed to this but when it came to it, didn't do anything. So, after a week of not hearing from him, we emptied his room, put his stuff into boxes in another room, and started the clean-up job which was costly and disturbing. There were blood stains on the bed and lots of other unsavoury things to be dealt with.

During the clear up it came to light that Mark was on migration bail, which means he'd overstayed his visa but was awaiting trial. He'd been prosecuted for trying to blackmail a woman with a video he had of her doing something sexual. Plus, he was charged with beating her as well. He also had two drunk driving prosecutions and another for a racially aggravated attack.

About a week after we'd cleared his room he telephoned and threatened me, but I didn't record the call so the police said there was nothing I could do. Three months passed, and during this time his belongings ended up being put in the backyard, which was accessible to him so he could pick them up, but outside of a few bags, he didn't bother.

And then in mid-April, he called me and threatened me again because he believed I had stolen some diamond earrings from him. I was recording the call this time so asked him what exactly he meant by his threats, to which he said, "Well you've only got one head and I'm gonna cut it off." So, once again I went to the police. This time they said that they couldn't do anything because I had goaded him by asking exactly what he meant. Since then, I have received a few more messages, mainly insisting on his diamond earrings, and being certain I've taken them, to which I have informed him I have not.

1981 - Summer – Exam Results

It was a beautiful sunny summer day. It was the day before my exam results would be posted. I sat in the park and thought about my life, and what would happen if I'd failed them.

———

2020 - The Crow - Part 3

I had a client over; we were talking about setting up her blog. When I went to set it up, I found we'd already started this process a few years ago but she hadn't got around to posting anything on it. I hardly had any memory of doing it, but I could see by the way it was set up that I'd done it. As we approached the end of her session, I suddenly heard the sound I'd heard in the chimney, but this time it was much louder.

"Excuse me for one minute please," I said.

"Sure, is everything okay?" She asked, a bit startled.

"I think I've got a bit of an emergency. I'll be back soon."

———

2020 - Stories Told a Thousand Times

Most days I spend a few hours watching something on one of the streaming services, and when I get up I either listen to talk radio or a book on my Alexa. I think most of us love to listen to stories, it's a way to get to know people and be reassured by tales we have heard thousands of times already.

———

Between Goodbye and Hello

When I felt like I might be dying three years ago, I imagined if there is to be a life after death, then, if we're lucky, there might be people who will surround us with their love as we leave this world and loved ones waiting on the other side to welcome us. The idea that the story ends abruptly is almost inconceivable to us.

———

Chapter 30
Woods For The Trees

June 2020 - Those Days Are Gone Forever"

I was driving home today. The sun shone hard on my arm and face. The music app on my phone was set to random and started playing Don Henley's, *The Boys of Summer*. He sang of seeing his lover's skin shining in the sun, and how his love would last beyond the time when boys of summer had gone.

Stories of the Past, Stories of the Future

Stories about the past tend to have a nostalgic air about them, even when it's clear people's lives were exceptionally difficult. Meanwhile, futuristic stories, even dystopian ones, are often technologically and materialistically rich, but emotionally and spiritually empty. Perhaps it's just storytellers who require tension to make things interesting, or could it be we're 'hard-wired' to believe physical comfort will lead to emotional suffering? After all, is this not a major tenet of most religions? Of course, these beliefs haven't stopped humans from seeking more and more convenience, luxury and material wealth. Is this based on another, far more popular belief, that the greater the physical comfort, the higher our spiritual development will be?

One day in 1981, the local library was selling off some of its old books. I bought one called *Chastity, Poverty and Obedience: The True Virtues*. I wasn't drawn to it with a view to suddenly becoming religious but was intrigued by the philosophies it advocated. At the same time, I bought a few other psychology books. It was as if I recognised that my unhappiness required a two-pronged approach. One involved exploring the universal issues we all must face, whilst the other sought to address matters that were particular to me.

As I began to move towards adulthood, I realised I was embarking on a journey which involved making significant choices. These would not just be about qualifications and career, but also which values should take precedence in my life. Amongst these were: money, relationships, spiritual matters, emotional well-being and political concerns. What I didn't consider though, was just how many of those decisions would be taken by the more irrational parts of my mind, no matter what I decided on a conscious level.

1997 - Therapy

Simon: Sometimes I try my best to behave in a certain way, but the next moment I'm unable to stick to my principles.

Therapist: Going through life is like riding a horse bareback. You can point it in a certain direction, but outside of that, you'll barely have any control.

Simon: Now you tell me. Can I have a refund, please?

Therapist [laughing]: No.

The Future (Part 1)

The words we use to communicate with each other are stories in themselves, handed down to us from our ancestors. Stories of the past, history, must be one of the most interesting and important subjects in the school curriculum, yet you'd never know it from the version we were taught. Instead of being told stories that'd touch our hearts, which in turn may have made us want to learn the copious lists we were supposed to remember, all we got were the lists. There's a hint for teachers in the phrase 'learn by heart'.

I didn't sit history O-level, instead, I studied British Constitution. This was a subject that sold itself and was interesting to me from the outset. It mainly covered the basics of law and how our political and legal systems worked. Even though our teacher was massively overweight, so much so, he'd occasionally have a trickle of urine showing on his trousers, he made the subject interesting. Also, unlike a lot of school subjects, this one came to my aid many times throughout my life, especially when challenging parking tickets, thinking about legal issues and arguing about politics.

In my forties, I became re-acquainted with history and the etymology of words. Words are not only the building blocks of stories but are individual time capsules full of stories in themselves. Of course, it's not just words that were handed down to us by our ancestors, but also their dreams. For instance, someone once imagined a house, had plans drawn up and had it built. Now, 130 years later I live in such a building, a house of someone's dreams. Likewise, every law, every piece of art, in fact almost everything created by humans started as a thought, realisation, feeling or dream, which once materialised led to further ones.

For thousands of years, people were barely able to subsist let alone come up with revolutionary ideas. For them, staving off hunger, creating shelter, and protecting themselves from violence or conversely, acquiring food, shelter and wealth through violent means, were their main preoccupations. However, around 600 years ago things started to progress at a much greater pace. There wasn't a single catalyst that brought this about, but instead, a whole set of factors that resulted in people looking way beyond their own horizons.

Improved optics led to new ways of seeing the world and space, printing presses led to newspapers and the distribution of books, and the knowledge and the dissemination of different ideas meant people's thoughts, dreams and imagination were broadened too. It's the same today. Nowadays we know of the existence of atoms and consequently, we dream of controlling them, and at the other end of the spectrum, we've discovered the existence of billions of galaxies, so now we dream of exploring them.

―――

At first I didn't know I didn't know
Then I knew I didn't know
Then I knew I knew
Then I didn't know I knew

―――

The Crow

I left my client in the front room as I checked out the commotion at the back of the house. I realised the loud noise I'd heard was coming from the room where strange sounds emanated these last few days. As I got closer, I saw a black bird standing in the middle of the room. It was motionless except for a slight eye movement. Before it could panic, I shut the door.

The room it was trapped in also had another entrance that could be opened from the outside and I realised by opening it, the bird could escape. Time was of the essence, as there is no end to the carnage a scared bird can inflict on a room. I went outside via another door and got there as quickly as possible then slowly opened the door. There, standing on a bucket was the bird I'd just seen and next to it was another. Without getting into confusing details, the route these birds had found to escape the chimney was technically impossible, but somehow, they'd managed it. Whilst officially, they were not blackbirds or crows as mentioned in my dream, they were pigeons that were either very dark or had been covered in soot from the chimney. I stepped back out of view and within a few seconds, they flew out of the room, settling on another chimney across the road.

Had birds ever learned to tell folk stories, there would be a tale about 2 stupid birds who showed off just how high their chimney-top nests were. The horror of the pigeon pie that they became would have stuck in the mind of any baby birds who ever heard this tale and consequently, for the rest of their lives, they'd have avoided building nests on chimneys. Given birds talk so much you'd have thought storytelling would have been an evolutionary certainty, but as this pair's behaviour suggests, it wasn't.

Rēzekne 1889 – Ruth

A few days after Boruch returned home, Nechama sent Chaya and one of the younger girls, Ruth, to forage for wild vegetables and herbs. The day was unusually hot for this time of year, so they wandered down towards the lake. Chaya wanted to teach Ruth what to look for, so she picked two similar-looking mushrooms and asked her if she could smell the difference between them.

"This one is sweet, and this one is like wet wood," Ruth said, pushing the mushroom to her nose.

Chaya pulled the mushrooms away from her, "One of them is dangerous, can you tell which?"

Ruth, again went to pull the mushrooms closer, but Chaya's grip became even firmer. Ruth took a guess and pointed to the one on the right.

"Yes," you're right," Chaya said smiling, "Did you just guess that, or did mamma show you this one already?"

"I just guessed," Ruth laughed.

"Well, here's the basket, try to find some more, and I will look over there. Don't wander off, keep where I can see you." Chaya's words were as firm as her grip. "Don't go near the water, there are fish in there that will eat you with one bite!"

Ruth looked worried and nodded. Chaya tried not to laugh, then ambled across to where the woods met the lakeside and carefully loaded her basket.

"Chaya! Come here," a voice loudly whispered from nearby.

Chaya looked in the direction of the sound, "I can't, I'm watching over Ruth".

"Then I shall come to you. I need to hold you."

For a moment Chaya became lost in his words.

"No! Don't!" Chaya almost shouted. "Not now."

Ruth looked up to see what was going on.

"What Chaya? What is it?" Ruth shouted across the 50 metres between them.

"It's nothing, carry on," Chaya shouted back while flipping her hand in a go-away motion.

"I didn't do anything," Ruth shouted back.

Chaya looked to the ground and then whispered loudly, "Just go away, Kristian. I will try to see you another time."

Kristian, no longer whispering, said, "I miss you, Chaya."

Chaya smiled and looked at him, "I miss you as well, but it's too dangerous!"

Chaya wanted to rush into the woods and steal a moment with Kristian, but she knew this was the script of many a folk story she'd heard. So, she remained where she was, focusing on her job and keeping an eye on Ruth.

1981 - August - Exam Results

When the results of my 'O' level exams came through in August I was surprised by how well I'd done. Although I'd failed English Language (Don't ask!) and Engineering Drawing, I'd still passed seven which was more than adequate to get me into sixth form at Wilson's to do 'A' levels.

I was beginning to consider a career in social work, but I hadn't thought it through at all, still, the idea of helping others appealed to me. Maybe I desired to become what I felt I needed for myself. But, with hindsight, I don't think I was cut out for that line of work at all.

_____

January 2020 - Ann

I have already mentioned my Mum's cousin, Paul's wife Ann. She would almost become a second mother to me and was kindness personified. But I'm going to start at the end with her because it was during the months this chapter was written that she died.

I had gone to visit Ann and Paul, as Ann had been seriously ill with breast cancer over the previous six months. Each time she told me of her trials with the National Health Service I was filled with anger. Initially, she'd gone to see her doctor with an abscess on her chest and on seeing it, the doctor told her it was serious and referred her to her local hospital which then did nothing for a further two months. By then it had spread to her lungs. This miracle of social evolution, The National Health Service, in this instance failed, but Ann seemed to take it in her stride. Normally she would be the one fighting for other people's rights, but when it came to her own, she didn't want to be too much trouble. When I visited her that last time, she insisted on cooking dinner even though she couldn't breathe well. She wanted to live as normally as possible, for as long as she could.

As I left I said, "I better not hug you as there's all this talk of a virus and I don't want to give you anything," but she put her arms around me and gave me a little squeeze. I did my best not to breathe on her and as I walked out to my car, she came outside to wave goodbye. I said, "Don't stand out in the cold, I'm going to be a few minutes getting the satnav set up."

"Oh, ok," she said and then mumbled something to Paul who'd also come out. At the time, I didn't pay much attention to what she was saying to him, but later I realised it was something along the lines of her not seeing me again. I said I'd be coming up in the next week or so, so I'd see her then, but I was wrong.

A few days later she had her final escapade with the National Health, this time she was made to wait to be seen for seven hours in casualty, and when she was, they put her straight into a ward. Over the next week, as much as they tried to drain off the fluid building up in her lungs and around her heart, all they could do was try their best to make her last days less uncomfortable. Then one morning Paul called me and said, "It's bad news I'm afraid."

_____

Rēzekne - The Lake

Ruth was cautiously smelling each mushroom she came across and in time it became a game to her. Every now and again she would check on Chaya to see if she was still in sight, which she was.

"Have you seen this?" came a voice from about five metres away, just close to the edge of the lake.

Ruth turned and saw a man in a big dark coat and wide-brimmed hat pointing over the reeds towards the lake. The man seemed old to her, but he was most likely in his 40s. He was bearded, a cross between someone with money and a traveller.

"What is it?" Ruth said, slightly scared but curious still.

"It's a family of otters, look, the babies are having their first swim."

Ruth stood on her tiptoes. "I can't see them."

"Hold on, I'll show you," the man put his arms out offering to pick her up.

Ruth nodded, so he did.

"Oh yes, I can see them, I've never seen a family of otters before, they're so sweet." She savoured the sight and the thrill of being held up high.

"I know," the man laughed, "They are wonderful."

She looked over her shoulder at him, "How do you know it's their first swim?"

"You are a clever one," he smiled, "you're right, I don't know for sure."

"Ruth get down." Chaya's shouted, "Get down now!"

"But I'm just looking at the baby otters, Chaya!" Ruth protested.

"Get down now! I am sorry sir, but she should not have allowed you to pick her up." Chaya bowed to the man as she spoke.

The man lowered Ruth to the ground whilst she held on as long as she could.

"I suppose you are right," he said, "but she didn't come to any harm, I wasn't going to hurt her."

Chaya shook her head, "I can see that sir, but she didn't know that, and she has been told never to talk to strangers. I'm very disappointed Ruth. Get your basket, it's time to go home."

"But we haven't finished yet!" she cried.

Chaya, still looking downwards continued, "I'm sorry sir, thank you for your kindness."

Then swivelling around, she stared at Ruth who was stamping steps of anger. Chaya grabbed her hand and said, "Come on, we're going. Come on now!"

The man lowered his head and apologised as they passed him.

Chaya turned, and looking back at the man asked, "You're not from here, are you?"

He pointed westwards adding, "No, I'm just passing through."

Chaya, who wasn't one to be shy, looked at the man sternly, "Around here men do not speak with women they do not know. It's forbidden. I'm sorry but we must leave, and sir I would ask, please do not speak to us any further."

The man stood aside, took off his hat and bowed his head as they passed. He gave a little wave at Ruth who waved back at him. As they walked off, he watched them until they were out of sight, then he turned in the other direction and stopped for a moment as he realised there was someone else nearby watching. He placed his hat back on his head and walked towards the woods.

The Wild, Wildwood

Most of the languages that influenced English were very likely to have stemmed from Proto-Indo-European languages about 6500 years ago. Anglo-Saxon, from Northern Europe, and Latin and French from Middle and Southern Europe make up about 84% of present-day English. The majority of our single-syllable words are derived from Anglo-Saxon, whereas most of the multi-syllabic ones are Latin, French or Greek based. So, the word 'wood', being mono-syllabic, derives from the Germanic family of languages.

A long time before humans ever populated Europe, our pre-Homo-Sapiens ancestors lived in forests and jungles. The trees were their home and even now, somewhere in our DNA, we are deeply connected to the world of trees. There is also much of our physical structure that is tree-like (dendritic) too. Our brain, nervous, lung and venous systems are all dendritic. Even on the outside, we look like trees. We have a trunk, a crown with foliage on top and branches. If we don't have a full-length branch, then what remains is often referred to as a stump. Such thoughts are nothing new, the Celts, for instance, believed we were descended from 'The Great Oak'.

As we've become more cultivated and less involved with nature, or should I say, tame, the thought of the woods for most modern humans is a scary place. For us, the woods are the wilds, and the wilds are an unknown quantity. For our ancestors 6500 years ago, and for much of the ensuing time, the wilds were very well known. The Germanic word 'waldes', was equivalent to the present-day separate words 'wild' and 'wood'. But when we think of the word 'wood' nowadays, we no longer associate it with its wild past.

1972 - Roundshaw

The name Roundshaw means a circular group of trees, but I doubt many people who lived there were aware of that. I certainly wasn't. Soon after we'd moved onto the estate, I opened one of the new cupboards in the front room, put my head inside it and inhaled deeply. I loved the smell of the wood, it was heaven to me.

Almost 50 years later we are still heavily dependent on trees, but people now would rarely consider spending any time treating the wood in their house. Instead, we'd prefer timber that's been reduced to a form of chippings or dust which then requires toxic chemicals to bond it. Consequently, it barely lasts a fraction of the time well-seasoned timber would have. But then, to keep furniture for decades also means not keeping up with the trends and that, for many, would be sacrilegious. As a child, I felt the presence of wood all around me. At night, I would look into the grain on the wardrobe doors in my bedroom, see scary faces and quickly close my eyes. Maybe wood reminds us of reality and that's why we're so keen to banish it from our modern world.

The Wood and the Cross

Tree worship, known as dendrolatry, has been featured in many religions throughout the world, and the cut-down version of a tree, the cross has been a spiritual symbol for many thousands of years right up to today. The symbol of the crucifix was not introduced into Christianity until centuries after Jesus's death. Whilst the Bible states Jesus died on the cross, its design was not described, so, could have been a number of different shapes. Whatever type of crucifix was used to kill Jesus, it would have been a shape used by previous religions, so there was no way of avoiding the link between old religions and this new one. The cross was connected to wood and trees within early Christianity, and even before then, the Old Testament mentions it in Hebrew as 'êç,"(wood). According to some Christian legends, the upright part of The Crucifix was derived from wood grown from a branch of the Tree of Knowledge. However, other legends contradict that. The thing is trees, woods and wood continued to play a part both spiritually and metaphorically within Christianity. Noah, for instance, used a wooden stronghold to protect wild animals and even the word paradise, originally meaning a 'walled garden', is a metaphor for bringing the wild to order. After all, is that not what gardens are? Even from the outset 'The Tree of Knowledge' figured as a central theme, as did the first mention of paradise, The Garden of Eden.

For many pagan religions, there were further astronomical connections to the cross, including marking out the sun's pathway in relation to the horizon, as well as time-related patterns too. Within old stone circles, there were cross-shaped patterns that predate Christianity by millennia. Some people argue that when Constantine chose the shape of the cross we currently use, he did it partly as a means of bringing together the symbols of pagan beliefs and Christianity. The cross itself can be additionally symbolic, in terms of him bringing together two faiths of opposing directions. Whether that is true or not there is something poetic in the image of pagans seeing the crucifix as a tree, whilst simultaneously Christians seeing it as a highly significant symbol.

In many societies, apart from religion, the symbolism of trees, forests and the wild was prevalent. When Vikings or Anglo-Saxons cast out wrongdoers, they would often end up living in the forest. As opposed to visiting it as a resource. The trees came to demarcate the boundaries of the civilisation, so, to end up living there meant a loss of honour. In Old English, the word wōd also came to mean 'mad', 'senseless', or 'blasphemous' and even now the term, someone 'went wild' connects with similar notions. Fortunately, we haven't completely forgotten the importance of trees. After all, trees still form a central pillar within our modern-day belief systems, especially with them being recognised as the lungs of the world and our very survival being tied up with them.

1981 - Back to School

I was a little excited about returning to Wilson's after the summer break. It was almost as if I was starting at a new school. Our uniform was slightly different, we had powers over the younger boys which we hadn't had before, and there was a whole area set aside for us to relax and study in which even had its own kitchen. We would also have fewer lessons because much of our studying was to be done in our own time. I was set to take three academic 'A' levels and two Art ones. This meant that some of my time would be spent at Sutton College of Liberal Arts, (SCOLA), which is where I'd been doing my life drawing studies for the last few years.

SCOLA

I've already mentioned Sutton College of Liberal Arts, SCOLA, being a part of the same building complex as Sutton Library. At the time it was built, the library was seen as cutting-edge architecture, okay that's pushing it, but it was a bit modern, but when it came to its sister building, SCOLA, there was nothing to write home about. If I think about how to describe it to you, the first thing that comes to mind is the dark orange nylon carpeted areas, especially in the café, which was large, probably twenty-five metres by ten meters with big windows that looked out onto the main road and the backs of shops. It's possible the carpet wasn't that colour at all, but either way, that's the impression it left on me.

The classrooms were spacious but had a harder, more utilitarian feel. There was a trace of the 1930s in their design, especially the black metal framed windows, white walls, and grey tiled floors. While the architects were going for a hint of Bauhaus minimalism, that was put a stop to by the clutter of real life which mainly consisted of art materials; equipment; and rubbish art left leaning against the walls by students till the next week's lesson.

I often got the sense that their work had been positioned in the hope that someone of influence in the Art World would pass by and be blown away by their interpretation of their cat. But, unless the Art World's scout was looking for a toilet, it was very unlikely they'd ever be sauntering through in the first place. I am not saying this to disrespect SCOLA, but as I became more acquainted with the Art World, I came to recognise the divisions that existed. Those same people who headed the Art World and would make art all about class war and social justice, couldn't help but look down their noses at the lower-class artists.

1981 - Backdrops

The sixth form centre, Sutton Library, SCOLA and Tweeddale Karate Club were going to be the main backdrops to my life for the next two years. Whilst this had already been so for the last two years there was a different texture to them now. I was, without realising it, becoming part of 'the establishment'. This came about at first when I got asked to provide some artwork not only for the school magazine but also for the national karate magazine.

The Future (PART 2)

When we look at the fundamental problems humankind faces today, most of us would agree that a far smaller world population of humans would help matters. For a start, we'd have less pollution, there'd be less need for resources, and greater social cohesion because everyone could have what they needed. However, paradoxically, we might also say it would be good if we could live longer, stay youthful, and not have to suffer. If possible, it'd be perfect if we could live forever or at least till we decided to die. These may have been the aspirations of all humans throughout history, but the difference is, we are on the precipice of being able to do these things. These are the dreams of today, and many of us believe they will be the realities of tomorrow's world.

Rēzekne - Supper

When Chaya and Ruth returned home, they explained to their mother what had happened with the man, and that was why their baskets were only half full. Nechama was happy they were safe and said she'd tell her neighbours about the stranger.

"What's father doing?" Chaya asked.

"He's making a surprise for tonight, why don't you see if he wants any help?"

So, Chaya and Ruth wandered slowly towards where he sat in the sunlight.

He looked up at them, "Ah, what good timing," he laughed, "You can help me cut and peel these vegetables."

1980 - The Competition

Grant, my karate teacher, was very inclusive when it came to me. So, when he asked me to enter a kata competition I was touched and said yes. In karate, there are sets of movements, a bit like dances, and these are called katas.

On the day of the competition, a few of us met up outside the karate club at 7 am, then bundled into Grant's VW camper van, and after an hour or so's drive to the other side of London, we entered the sports centre and nervously waited for our turn. Kata competitions are judged on how well the katas are performed which is a bit like *Strictly Come Dancing* but not so romantic.

Grant brought a black and white video camera with a separate video recording unit, which at the time was very high-tech, and said this was going to be useful for us to look back on how we did.

When it came to my go, I was put up against another kid and won that round, but in the next, I lost. I was already aware that in a way it was unfair on the other participant because lots of my techniques were changed because of my disability. Whilst such things as power, timing, focus, balance, and speed could be compared between me and someone with a full set of limbs, there was a lot that couldn't be.

As I watched myself back on the video, I was faced with something I've always found very hard to deal with, and that is being confronted with what I really look like. For most people, this is normally quite difficult anyway, but for me, it was, and still is, especially so, because in my mind I look quite different.

"You know Grant," I said, "I don't think it's fair on those who go up against me."

He looked at me quizzically, "Really? Why do you say that?"

So, I explained what I thought, and he said, "Well, as long as you know, it's your decision, and if you ever want to compete again, I'll happily support you."

And so, from then on, I didn't enter a competition again. Even for fighting ones, it would have been too complicated. My artificial leg is a dangerous weapon, striking with elbows isn't normally allowed and when it comes to arm strikes, they are my primary weapons. I also have to wear shoes, which is an advantage too, and then there'd be the psychological disadvantage an opponent would have as they'd most likely think, "What would everyone think if I hurt him, or even worse if he hurts me?"

I was beginning to come to terms with some of the complexities of disability-related issues. Sometimes people would be too quick to prohibit me from being included unfairly, but there was also a responsibility for me to understand when it might not be appropriate that I do certain things, even when people would be happy for me to do so.

When it came to getting into scraps on the street, however, I was far less concerned with what the other person thought. I didn't go out looking for fights, but I wouldn't back down if an opportunity arose either.

1981 - The Lost World Within Me

Although things were going well in my outer world, inside I still felt something was amiss. For many decades, I would continue struggling with such issues, as I am sure many other people do too. I truly felt as if there was this outer me who did okay, but then there was a whole other sense of who I was that felt empty and lonely a lot of the time. The other strange side effect of this was I didn't enjoy my successes much, and even though I came across as very egocentric, I didn't and still don't feel much in those terms. Where I mostly felt my emotions, was in the lost world within me.

Even writing this now I am aware that some people might feel I have some kind of psychological hero complex, that I have to write my version of history in which I come out looking good, even if that's done by making myself look bad. But, as I've mentioned before, the feeling of connection with others is my main driving force.

1981 November 11th - Courage

A few weeks after starting back at school our careers advisor asked me if I'd like to be entered into a Triumph Over Adversity Awards scheme organised by Barnardo's. Even at 16, I was very aware that firstly, my existence didn't rely on me being courageous, secondly, even if it did, courage was more of a predisposition rather than a choice, and thirdly, by accepting such a reward it would make me feel as if I was not trying to live a normal life. It reeked of a double standard to me, and whilst being a hypocrite doesn't normally stop me from getting myself into all sorts of difficult positions, in this instance, it made me feel uncomfortable enough not to go for it.

At 16, when it came to disability issues, I didn't have a cohesive approach or clearly defined understanding. On one hand, I would follow scripts, for instance doing things because people expected me not to. On the other though, I would expect discrimination, yet subconsciously encourage it in the way I approached situations. For instance, I could sow the seeds of doubt in others so that they might feel confused as to whether to allow me to do something or not. Had I known better I could have approached such matters in a more positive way which would have inspired confidence in others. Here's an example of what I mean. When I was about 19, I was looking for a room to rent so I called a number I'd seen in a paper advertising one. A friendly guy answered and when I mentioned my disability, he said, "No problem." Instead of just going to meet him I then listed all the reasons why it might be difficult, so, by the end of the conversation, he became a bit doubtful it would be suitable for me. Maybe just hearing me being negative, was enough to put him off. But, looking back now, I can see there were times when I played a significant part in the rejection process.

There were other occasions though when I was ahead of the times. One evening, John's Mum and Dad came around. John had obviously primed them beforehand because, within a couple of minutes, they were making it very clear they thought people who modelled naked for artists were the lowest of the low and I should not be mixing with them. When I said that one of the models was a fireman and another was a yoga teacher, they wouldn't have it. Seeing that they were not persuading me, they went for another tack. The issue of Mum letting me have my benefit money directly instead of pocket money was 'checkmate' as far as they were concerned.

John's mum laughed, "Well you say you want to be treated the same as everyone else, but you're quite happy to take money from the state."

His dad nodded and added, "When we were your age we were already going to work. You can't have any pride in yourself taking benefit money."

In a way, I respected them for not making an allowance for me, but I genuinely felt that there were far fewer opportunities for me to work than for others. So, I saw the benefit money as compensation for society's lack of accommodation for people with disabilities. On one hand, society would be praising me for being brave but on the other, there was a sign that clearly stated "No Entry". I explained this to them but there was just an uncomfortable silence afterwards.

Mum walked into the room and recognised the same atmosphere created by the cats after they'd been fighting, so quickly intervened, "Does anyone want another cup of tea?" She smiled a big smile but looked me in the eye, a look that said, "What the fuck have you been up to now?"

I was already recognising that disability tended to be experienced in both a physical and social way. Later I'd come to learn this was titled the medical and social models. This means that whilst some things are made difficult because of an 'impairment' (the medical model), it's also possible society could make things less disabling (the social model). For instance, a wheelchair user may find stairs a barrier but a ramp useful. So, are they disabled by their impairment or the choice their wider community makes as to whether a ramp is provided?

1997 - Corfu

I was sitting on the beach, and my partner's white skin was shining in the sun. I'd tried to read but couldn't get comfortable and was feeling bored. I watched people paragliding, so, I walked over to the guy who was in charge of the rides.

"Hi," I said smiling.

He nodded, the way someone who's owed money nods.

"I'd like to have a go at paragliding?" I said as if I was ordering a drink from a bar.

He looked me up and down. "I'm not sure if my insurance would cover you."

I was tempted to look myself up and down too and say, "Oh, don't worry, it's not as bad as it looks," but what came out was, "Don't worry, if I die, I die".

He paused for a second, then shouted at one of his workers to fetch the harness.

Had we been in the UK, a letter from my doctor would have been required, disclaimer forms filled, and probably someone else would have had to accompany me. But within five minutes I was running along the jetty as the boat sped off and the cables quickly pulled into position. I got the biggest jolt of my life, as they took hold and flung me forwards and upwards.

"Fuck!" I semi-yelped, and the air got knocked out of me for a second. Within seconds I was rising higher and higher. The boat looked very small, and the people were little dots on the beach. It was slightly windy but silent. It crossed my mind that at any point I might fall to my death, but I felt calm, in a way too calm. A bit of fear may have given it more of an edge, but I hung there in the sky, happily alone, waiting to be reeled in and back to the noise.

After they'd dropped me into the sea, I thanked the guy for letting me on with so little fuss. If anything, having my opinion of my capabilities taken seriously meant as much to me as the ride itself.

When I got back to my partner she asked where I'd got to - Okay, that bit's not true, she took photos of me, however, what came out was a few pictures of the sky with a little dot in the middle that was me.

2018 - November - Netflix

I got a message from a production company that makes documentaries for Netflix. They were interested in making a programme about me. At first, I was a bit taken with the idea, not so much because of the flattery of it but for pragmatic reasons. By raising my profile, I could build up my career more, but, after consideration, I realised if I got involved with it, it would be at a cost. After a few days of email discussions, I stated that if I had already had some success in at least one of my creative pursuits, then it might make sense to also do a programme that touched on my disability. But as I haven't had much success, then outside of my disability, why would they want to do a programme about me? I realised if I went ahead with this project then I'd be going against one of my fundamental principles, which is my artwork and music should be judged on their own merit and not measured with a different yardstick because of my disability, because in my mind that would be no success at all.

Even writing this book had me questioning whether my disability would become its main focus. However, I felt that while, of course, it's a part of it, there were many other matters that I'd be covering too as you may have noticed.

1981 - Karate

Although I'd come to accept it was difficult to include me when it came to kata and fighting competitions, I was still very interested in passing my belts. Having a high grade in karate acts as a warning to others to keep away whilst at the same garnering respect. These might not be good reasons to go for a karate belt, but they are probably many people's true initial motivations. The paradox was, the higher a grade I became, the more I realised that belts have very little to do with proficiency at fighting. That isn't to say many high grades are not good fighters, because a lot are, but it's not as simple as A plus B equals C.

The more I learned about fighting the more I realised I was never going to be as good a fighter as I'd like to be. So, I had to ask myself what the point of training was, and the conclusion I came to was, that in the unlikely event that I may need to protect myself or others, I ought to be as well prepared as possible. That wouldn't mean I'd ever be a great fighter, but instead, having some confidence I could deliver a powerful enough blow to knock someone out or at least stun them as well as being able to fend off an attack. Having those skills would be better than being a helpless target.

Karate means "Empty Hand", so for me to choose to focus on doing it probably involved some subconscious ironic humour. Also, a great deal of karate does indeed focus on hand techniques, so it was not lost on many people that I was at a big disadvantage. The way people reacted was either they didn't want me there, or they backed off because they didn't want to hurt me, or they gave me a good whack to put me back in my box.

Diary Entry: 11 Sept 81 Neil Kicked me in the head at karate.

The reason Neil kicked me was because I deserved it. Just beforehand I was fighting a guy called Tony who was in his 50s. I decided Tony would be a good person to practice my spinning kicks on. Neil, who was instructing that day told me off afterwards and said I was to fight him next. Instead of being apologetic I immediately did a fast-spinning back kick and got it through Neil's defence. I think I laughed. The next thing I knew I was seeing stars and getting up off the floor a little bit dazed. Not only was it a lesson learned but I was grateful for not being treated differently, and judging by the number of kickings I got, I was generally being treated similarly to most of the others. That's not to say they abused me, but they certainly liked to give me regular, not-so-gentle, reality checks.

1981 - Martial Arts Teaching

Over the last 40 years, the way martial arts are taught has changed significantly. Whilst some aspects have done so for the worse there have also been drastic improvements. In 1981 there were still a lot of people teaching who were abusive both physically and psychologically. Whilst it is possible to argue martial arts require hard discipline and some physical pain, what I started to witness as I looked into other martial arts was something akin to the baddie in the film 'The Karate Kid'.

Diary Entry: 19/8/81

"This evening we watched a Kung-Fu class. It was a beginner's one. The teacher was a young bully of a black belt. It was like watching a dark comedy film."

People recognised in the ensuing years, not just in the martial arts world but in teaching in general, that the personality of the teacher was extremely influential in terms of both the success and failure of the students. What this led to was an attempt within the mainstream education systems to take the teacher's personality out of the equation.

Teachers were taught to look at how students learned best and adapt their teaching styles to match accordingly. In other words, just as computers began to dominate our world, the idea of turning teachers into 'computers' became a big part of the ideology. This may well have been in the service of ultimately replacing teachers with computers. But, will these computers recognise those pupils who want the teacher to be a bit renegade too, will they bring personality back into the equation, or instead, will it be a sterile learning environment?

2000 - Teaching

When I was teaching computer classes for beginners for the local authority in Fulham, London, I would split the lessons up into several sections. The final one would normally be about the fun aspect of using computers. Amongst other things, it might be playing online games with real people, talking to AI chatbots, or accessing music or videos. One lesson I'd give would be about playing online Karaoke songs. To start that section, I would play a song and break out into a singing and dancing routine much to my students' hysterical laughter or horror, I wasn't always sure which. If a computer were to do the same, I get the feeling it wouldn't be quite the same, plus I doubt those programming the teacher-bots would ever consider anything out of the ordinary in the first place.

2020/2021 - Mark

Mark continued his demands for his earrings, so I sent him a copy of the video of them being packed and the CCTV video of him picking up that bag. Things went quiet for a while, until one night, drunk, he messaged me to say he was coming to pick up all his belongings and had booked a van. I informed him that only a few items were left so a van wouldn't be necessary. He insisted the van couldn't be cancelled and he would come as soon as possible. His belongings were placed in an accessible place but of course, he didn't turn up. He then continued his threats, so I told him not to call again unless it was to arrange to pick up the remaining items.

A year later, he contacted me again, by this time there was just a box of his bits left. He paid for a courier, the parcel got picked up and I hoped that was the last I'd ever hear from him.

To some, Mark's a victim, both of circumstances and himself and no doubt he has a tragic story behind his addiction. For me, though, protecting myself from his madness was my main priority, because, let's face it, he may well be the cause of one of those unlikely events that I've spent so much of my life training for. You can try to understand and feel sorry for someone who's threatened you as much as you want, but it won't take the threat away.

Rēzekne – Supper

When the children came to take their places for dinner, they were confronted with a big saucepan on the table which wasn't normal for them at all. Once the blessings were said Boruch lifted the lid and tilted the open pan to each child, one at a time.

"Go on, take one each,"

"What are they?" one of the boys asked.

"You will see in just a minute."

"I know what they are," Ruth said.

Her father laughed, "Well of course you do, you helped make them."

Each child held a vegetable that had been carved.

"Now," he said, "they will not last very long so enjoy them while you can. Put the smaller end in your mouth and blow."

Within a second there was a cacophony of shrill whistles. Both Nechama and Boruch joined in too, laughing and whistling, whilst also trying to cover their ears. Ruth got off her chair, walked over to her father and made a big gesture of wiping a tear from her eye while simultaneously showing him her half-eaten carrot whistle. He pulled her close, gave her a comforting hug and handed her his.

1981 - Baby Driver

One day Gwynne, the civil servant I mentioned a few chapters ago, called me to ask if I'd like a driving lesson on a private track. I was still too young to get a provisional licence so was not allowed to practice driving on public roads. To get around this, he came all the way down from central London to pick me up, then drove me to another county, and after giving me a lesson brought me back.

Gwynne had a bit of an obsession with amputees, (I didn't particularly understand this back then, but such people are known as "Devotees"). However, even then, I sensed he might have some ulterior motives but didn't care, I was going to get a free driving lesson and without it, it was going to be a very boring Sunday.

When we got to the track it was an area with a load of roadways laid out which aimed to emulate normal roads. There were traffic lights, give way signs, and speed limits. Gwynne started me off by getting me used to keeping the revs to a certain level, and then we set off. After a while, I began to feel very comfortable so decided to take a sharp bend at 30 mph and that was when the lesson came to an abrupt end. Had I known about his passion for stumps I probably could have bartered another 30 minutes out of him for a stroke of my arm, but I didn't, so it ended there.

I wouldn't drive a car again for another five years but when I did, I started taking corners at much higher speeds. But that's another story. However, Gwynne's words, "Good driving goes unnoticed" stuck with me from then on. Not that I adhered to them though.

1981 - Three Parts to a Conversation

Gwynne once told me he believed there were three parts to a conversation. One was when one person spoke, the other was when the other replied, and the third bit was when both parties thought about what had been said, before speaking further.

He then looked at me with a slight frown. I thought for a minute but stayed silent. He just shook his head and raised his eyes to the heavens.

1981 - The Quiet

From September to December my life seemed to plod along nicely. I enjoyed studying, practising karate and socialising, it was also during this time we did the karate demonstration for the Duke of Edinburgh. But maybe it's because I have a subconscious desire to sabotage myself that I've come to recognise these periods as the quiet before a storm. Even though my diary was peppered with melancholia during this time, it was manageable. But there was a part of me that wasn't happy unless I wasn't happy, and it was only willing to be silenced for a while.

476

2020 - Politics

Although the last few years have been politically turbulent, what with Brexit and Trump, 2020 has exceeded all other recent times with COVID-19 and its combination of the above plus issues relating to racism. I will try to keep away from the political issues just listed because no matter what I say it will alienate some readers, and just like them, I get very pissed off when an artist I like starts pontificating their political beliefs, especially if I don't agree with them. Some artists brand themselves as political mouthpieces from the outset, for instance, Billy Bragg, so I don't feel let down by them. But outside of a few areas such as disability issues, it's probably best I don't get involved here with some of the more contentious political subjects. I hope you'll forgive me.

2005 - London – A40/A406 - Racism

It's rush hour traffic, autumn early dark sky, I'm trying to get around a large roundabout on the North Circular near Wembley. A flashy large white car cuts me up causing me to slam my brakes on. It then continues to do the same to a few other people. A few minutes later, I catch up with the car, put my window down and say, "You're being way too aggressive."

The guy, puts his window down, he's black with short dreadlocks, and shouts, "What did you say?"

I said, "You're driving very aggressively."

He sneers at me and shouts, "Fuck off you white cunt".

I disapprovingly shake my head from side to side slightly, and shout back, "That's a bit racist".

He pauses for a second then shouts back, this time with a little more forethought, "Fuck off you cunt".

"That's better", I say, this time moving my head more approvingly, and for a moment, all was right with the world.

1981 - Protest Songs

In my mid-20s I attended quite a few disability issue-based demonstrations and protests but the first protest I ever joined was at school. A few months into being a sixth former we were told that playing music in our department was no longer permissible. A petition was drawn up which everyone except one student signed, there's always one and it's normally me, but this time it wasn't. Then to make our voices heard we congregated in the main foyer near the headmaster's office and sang two hymns, *Jerusalem* and *To Be a Pilgrim*.

I don't remember if we got a formal change of the rule, but music was heard at times, if at a somewhat low volume. Fortunately, technology came to the rescue as personal stereo cassette players started to become affordable.

1981 - The Hungry Heart

One evening we had Speech Day at school which was a ceremony we had to attend involving, you guessed it, lots of boring speeches. A few years previously my mum had come to one of them, fell asleep and snored loudly. So, for everyone's sake, she didn't attend anymore.

Afterwards, we all gave a sigh of relief that it was over and congregated in the main foyer where one of the younger boys introduced me to his older sister, Joanna H. There was an immediate spark between us that both of us felt (for a change). As we bantered and laughed, we arranged to meet up again soon, and just as we were about to part, she kissed me, I described it as a salty kiss in my diary, but that was probably because I was very hungry.

When we met up next it was at her house where her mum invited me to stay for dinner. Maybe Jo told her she sensed I was hungry when we kissed. We all got on well and there seemed to be a promise of a relationship in the air. But, instead of feeling happy, when I woke up the next day, I felt depressed. Without her saying anything I'd picked up subconsciously that the promise of more was probably a little ambitious. Even so, later that day we met up at Sutton Library, did a bit of homework together then went to MacDonald's for something to eat. I should have realised Pizza Hut was the way to a girl's heart in 1981, but I liked the Hot Apple Pies that MacDonald's served so I thought she'd feel the same too. I should have listened closer to Joe Jackson's hit single, *It's Different for Girls*, but I was probably too busy still listening to Elvis. As we walked back to her place, she told me I'd upset her when I mentioned something about her teeth. When I got home I wrote in my diary I was devastated by my lack of tact, and I vowed to make an extra effort to be more diplomatic with everyone from then on. Needless to say, that invaluable rule was to be broken countless times throughout my life. But at least now I can blame that wayward bareback horse my therapist mentioned.

Jo and I met up a few more times over the next few weeks. She told me she didn't want to get involved and preferred to remain free. I read between the lines that she was waiting for a 'past love', whereas all I needed to do was read the neon writing on the wall, which funnily enough was the same as what she'd said to me, which was, "I don't want to get involved with you".

1981 - Sutton Library

Sutton Library was one of the biggest libraries in Europe at the time. It had five floors, but Level 5 was a bit like a balcony that sat above and overlooked the level below it. All along this top floor were desks that faced the open area. This is where we would go to study, it was also a good place to meet other students (girls). As time passed, I got to get to know the regulars and would often do a circuit of the fifth floor first to see who to sit next to and not do any work with. Usually, after half an hour of pretending to study, we'd all decide to go down to the café, where I'd sometimes get a cup of tea, a microwaved sausage roll and an Eccles Cake. Once in the café, there'd be other people to join up with, so we'd push the tables together and before long it'd be a mini party. There aren't many libraries in the world where girls and boys would get dressed up to go there, but for us, that was normal.

The Future - Part 3

To solve the issue of an overpopulated planet without killing billions in one go, the governments of the world decided on a softer approach. By encouraging people via financial incentives to only have a maximum of two children, populations began to reduce significantly within 50 years. This was partly because not every couple had children plus a lot of individuals opted for cyborg partners. Within 200 years, the world population was lowered to just over three billion people and was still decreasing.

Technology had advanced to the point where to an extent, for those who could afford it, there was an option of eternal life, of sorts. For those who couldn't, an offer of resurrection was made on the condition a copy of them would be part of a mission to search for other habitable planets.

Not surprisingly millions chose not to have any children but send themselves into the future instead. Once signed up, their atomic structure was assessed and saved, and it was that record of them, which would be sent into space. Meanwhile, their original selves would live out their days on earth where they would die, as normal.

During the two centuries that passed whilst these plans came together, several offshoots of the human genus also developed. The main one was a much stronger regenerative, almost everlasting one, only available to several hundred leaders. The second type was edited to be as divine as possible. They didn't feel anger, lust, hatred, or violent impulses, in fact, they barely felt anything that we'd recognise as desire. As computer-like as they were though, they could feel love and compassion.

On every craft, atomic records of all the new human types were kept as well as the normal humans. So, whilst the humans of all three branches knew they were seeking out new places to live, they were also aware they were pursuing the ultimate meaning of life. Meanwhile, though, they were enacting biology's primary purpose, survival.

As long as the ships had access to energy, they could not only use their atomic rebuilders to resurrect their recorded "occupants", but they could create new ships, new rebuilders, and copies of the recorded archives. In time, trillions of humans came to explore the universe.

Without getting into technicalities, some ships could apply an acceleration that felt similar to the gravity we feel, and by doing so they reached phenomenal speeds within a few years. To keep the sensation of gravity they'd oscillate between accelerating and decelerating for long periods of time. As you may remember, I mentioned earlier that as we approach the speed of light, we experience time much more slowly than someone observing us who was not going at such a speed. For those live humans on the ships, millions of light years could be covered in decades. As you already know, most of the travellers were just digital records of people, but having a few live humans was seen as a way to deal with things the A-I's and robots couldn't.

For some, the option of choosing everlasting death became appealing, but they knew they'd never know if another version of themselves lived on in the universe and that thought would leave them wondering if there was such a thing as a soul and, if so, how would it cope with having multiple mortal coils?

1981 - SCOLA – The Unknown Beginnings of Journeys

Just as with the library, the lessons in SCOLA became a social event, especially during the breaks. I was going in at least twice a week, mainly for life drawing, and was beginning to become part of the furniture as I'd been going there for over three years. Whilst I tended to behave in Melody's classes, I would muck around quite a bit in the others. I held Melody in high esteem, as she had studied at the prestigious Slade School of Art and was a working illustrator. Her work was exquisitely delicate, beautiful and precise, just like her. There was also something about her vulnerability that made mucking about too much of a betrayal for me to bear, so, I'd just get on with drawing in her classes. Okay, I still chatted up the female models or any girls sitting near me, but for me, that was well-behaved.

One Saturday, early in December, after Melody's morning session, I spent the afternoon in Sutton Library with four others I'd met in the college. On our way out of the college, I started running to the office so I could ask the model for her address. (Yes, like you, I am sitting here shaking my head in disbelief). Unfortunately, my artificial foot came off, so I went flying. I was more embarrassed than anything. My new-found friends were worried for me, maybe a little impressed too, in fact so much so they may well have thought it worthwhile waiting to see what my next trick would be. Either way, this was a meeting that would be the root of many other connections and journeys far beyond that time in my life.

My four new acquaintances consisted of Scarlet, who was Canadian, Dee, who was half Italian but sounded American, Juan who was English whom I thought might have a learning disability, but only because he was even more inappropriate than me, and Jules who was quite reserved but laughed at my jokes, so I liked her. We went record shopping in Sutton High Street, then back to Scarlett's place to chat, where we had some tea and biscuits and listened to one of the albums they'd just bought, The Police's 999.

After all this excitement, I went back to Jules's family home where we chatted more. Jules was a little taller than me, she had brown hair, big brown eyes, and an air of stoic sadness about her, but she was quick-witted and funny too. That evening she played me the album she'd bought. It was Bruce Springsteen's "The River". I didn't register it then but that was when I first discovered an artist who'd be a part of my life even till now. That was the day I lost my 'Bruce Cherry'.

I also got to meet Jules's parents and brother. They lived in a well-to-do area, and I immediately got the feeling I was being assessed rather than warmly welcomed. At 16, when visiting a girl's house that tended to be the stock reaction, so, it almost went unnoticed by me. Jules and I had a good chat and said our goodbyes, there wasn't any romance in the air, but I genuinely liked being with her.

When I got home it was late, but not so late John and I couldn't argue. Even then, the day was not over for me. I grabbed my karate kit and said I'd be back the following day. My Karate club was holding a 24-hour sponsored marathon training session, split into shifts. So, I got the bus there, where we trained and took turns sleeping till Sunday night. When I got back home, I was aching and tired, but John was still gunning for me.

I couldn't wait to leave home. Home to me was somewhere else out in the world that I'd have to discover later, although there were times when I could see it in the eyes of perfect strangers, the laughter of friends, or the echoes of my karate kias. (Pronounced like key-eyes). Home was to be found in the freedom of my possible futures.

1981 - The Blizzard

We were experiencing the worst snow blizzards for 30 years, house lights stayed on all day, and barely any drivers dared to risk the roads in this monochrome world. We got sent home early from school so made our way on foot. As we slipped and fell on the icy pavements we laughed at each other, our arses wet from the not-so-soft icy landings, our faces burning from being hit by snowballs. Once home, the windows were like big screens showing a faded grey and white movie. It was a cold world out there, but I wanted to be out in it and as soon as the buses were running again.

1981 - National Theatre

I'd bought tickets for Joanna and me to go to a play in London that our English Literature teacher had organised for our class, but Joanna called me a few days beforehand to say she couldn't come. Had I not just met Jules, I'd probably have been a bit pissed off but, being rather fickle, the thought of inviting Jules seemed a far better option given Jo had told me she didn't want to get involved. So, I called her and she said yes.

Going to the theatre, even if it was technically a school trip, seemed a very grown-up thing to do. The venue was the National Theatre which was a modern building on the South Bank of the Thames. Once inside there was a dark feeling about the place. It was almost as if we'd entered a slightly dreamy world.

I was the only one in our group to bring an outsider. Even so, my classmates didn't show off particularly or make a move on her. Instead, they may have wanted to help me get a girlfriend. Either way, they were a little curious to see what the nature of our relationship was.

When I look back on this time, I see how unaware I was of what Jules might have been thinking or feeling. I don't want to be too hard on my 16-year-old self because most 16-year-olds are pretty stupid, and at any age, it's hard to know what's going on in someone else's mind and very easy to think someone else may react similarly to how we might. That's known as projective identification in some psychoanalytic circles. Paradoxically, the more I've become aware of how others think, the more I realise I don't have a clue, but still, being concerned about how those around us feel is a worthy pursuit even if it has its limitations.

1981 - Transition

I liked Jules a lot, and although we got on very well, I didn't push for a relation-ship. When I missed her calls, I didn't feel bad. To me, she was a new friend, and anyway, it was a busy time with the lead-up to Christmas, with its parties and socialising. All the same, there was a lighter feeling running through my veins. Maybe it was because I sensed Jules was interested in me, even if it was just as a friend, and that was new to me. She'd call when normally it was me doing the call-ing. She invited me over to her place, sent me a Christmas card and even gave me a peg that had "Hello" written on it. Meanwhile, Joanna asked if we could still be friends even if she didn't want it to go any further, which I was more than happy with. Getting over rejection is so much easier when someone else of interest is interested too. This became more apparent when Jules came to visit me one evening and told me her parents had asked her not to get involved with me. The way she said it though, sounded like 'getting involved' was on the cards and their concerns were even more reason to do so.

I didn't realise this then, but I would come to recognise a pattern in many of my relationships in time. This generally involved me feeling aloof during the initial period, which possibly caused the other person to become proactive in terms of developing a relationship with me. Then there'd be a time when I'd become equally interested in them too and then, just like a ball thrown in the air, there'd be a moment when it seemed to hover, and that was about the length of time that there was true equality between, but from that point onwards the balance shifted. It's hard to tell why and when this happens as it does, and what causes the shift, but once it does, it's a downward trajectory from then on.

1981 - Christmas

By the time Christmas came, I started thinking about Jules all the time. So much so that I couldn't enjoy Christmas. In my diary, I wrote:

> *"I didn't really enjoy today. There was a lot of tension in the air. Mum was in a hectic-go-happy mood".*

It is Mum and John I now feel for as she wanted things to be joyous, but John and I weren't going to let that happen. John couldn't forgive her for not being the good wife he'd dreamt of, and I wouldn't forgive her for not being the mother I'd wanted. We didn't know that consciously at the time and neither of us attempted to love her for who she was.

1981 - First Kiss

On Boxing Day, the day after Christmas Day, Jules asked me to come over. It was snowing still and only a few buses were running, I must have been desperate to see her as I even paid a taxi to take me on the last leg of the journey.

Her parents said I could only stay for a short while, so we sat on the floor in the front room and listened to Bruce singing about Mary. As we did, I passed Jules a letter I'd written which told her I had strong feelings for her. I lay next to her while she read it and should have stuck my paws in the air like a submissive dog, but instead, I lay as still as possible on my side waiting for her reaction.

Maybe I should have whimpered a bit, but fortunately, such displays weren't necessary. After reading it, she leaned down and kissed me. Unfortunately, I'd got myself into such a strange position that I was very uncomfortable but not wanting to spoil the moment I put up with it. She most likely thought I was shaking because of nerves, but it was mainly muscle strain. Her parents became aware of the 15 minutes of silence, so they got her brother to knock on the door, who offered me a lift home. I probably could have floated home anyway, but after paying £4 for a taxi I thought it prudent to take him up on his offer anyway.

The next day Jules came around to my place. We lay in the front room kissing, at one point the cat climbed the Christmas tree which then fell on us. I was intoxicated by the whole situation, and even though her parents reiterated to her not to get involved, she told me she loved me, and we met up every day over the following week. When we did, we'd kiss and she'd hold my arm wherever we went. When we were together I felt happy, when we were apart I'd feel a little low. I told myself off for feeling so infatuated, but in the next breath, I'd be convincing myself I would love her more than myself.

1981 - The Looming Break

Just like in the scenario with Monica and Kate, there was a time looming when she'd be going away for a week, and just as in those situations, I dreaded it because I knew it would bring out a darker part of me.

Therapy - How Many Psychoanalysts Does It Take

During my psychoanalytic journey, I didn't have just one therapist. As things turned out I had to end the first therapy prematurely because there was a time limit imposed on both the patients and the therapists as it was funded by the National Health Service. A few years after I finished the first therapy I went through a year of tears. If I ever write the next tome you'll get to hear more about that. Anyway, I called my original therapist to ask if I could see her. She gave me a session but said she couldn't offer me anything more at that time, however, she could refer me to another therapist who I'll call Diana. Soon after, I went to meet Diana and even though she was quite old, we clicked and for the next 11 years, I would visit her three times a week, so it was somewhat intense at times. If you know anything about psychoanalytic psychotherapy, you'll probably have heard of a process called transference. Principally, what happens is the presumptions and baggage you bring to many of your relationships can be observed by what you think and feel about the therapist. This tends to rely on the therapist being an empty canvas upon which you can project these thoughts and feelings. So, with that in mind the less you know about the therapist the better. Of course, though, there's a lot you pick up about someone, even if you can't see them because you're lying down and they're sitting out of sight, especially when they start snoring.

2015 - Fifty, The Beginning of The End

When I hit 50 years old, I was certain this was the beginning of the end. Fifty is very likely to be way past the midway point of most people's lives, indeed for most of us, the halfway marker is more likely to be somewhere between 35 and 44. But, there's something about 50 that makes it a significant milestone. If 16 was the end of being a child, then 50 is the beginning of being old.

There is something very compelling about endings. Many of us will spend a lot of our lives considering and preparing for our finale. Likewise, when it comes to relationships, the very thought of their endings may dominate one or both partners during the relationship and paradoxically bring about, or at least hasten its end.

When it comes to storytelling, I've often felt very disappointed by bad endings, even ones that were otherwise very well told. Just as a title can be a key to the meaning of a book or a film, a story's ending is the fulcrum upon which its meaning is balanced. It's the same with most jokes too, the punch line must always be remembered before embarking on its recounting, no matter how well the rest is told. So, when it comes to telling a tale, the storyteller will most likely fare far better if they start with their ending envisioned before the first word is ever spoken or written, and yes, I do know how this book ends, it happens on Battersea Bridge, or at least that was my plan.

The Future - Part 4

For millions of years, the explorer crafts moved throughout the universe at great speed. Although a few humans existed on board, everything was mainly controlled by artificial intelligence, but to those who were resurrected, it was as if they had closed their eyes for a second.

As each planet was arrived at, the AI would work out if it was feasible for humans to live on it, and if not, the mission would move on to the next way station. Even when planets were seen to be viable, the main craft would eventually move on to the next "venue" after dropping its payload, and creating a new population where it would set off to repeat the same process.

One of the things the AI would occasionally report to the travelling humans was far faster craft had passed them millions of light years beforehand, leaving messages that they would be venturing far deeper into the universe than these crafts could ever go. The immediate query that most of the humans asked was why hadn't the more developed humans passed on their technology to them.

2020 - The Covid-19 Virus

There had been news items from before Christmas that mentioned a virus in China. We'd had MERS, SARS and Bird Flu during the past decades, all of which came and went without affecting our lives, but by February this new virus was rapidly spreading around the world. People, including me, were playing down its death rate, or at least comparing it to a bad flu epidemic. In the UK, some health experts were warning it might kill up to 500 thousand people in Britain alone, whilst others said if we started to practice social distancing procedures it might be as low as 20 thousand. By the time we got to March the death rate was escalating in other countries and with that, a sense of panic started to move through the population. I'd often hear people say they felt they were in some disaster movie as a surreal quiet before the storm settled all around us. With each passing day, the government spoke of new restrictions, people started panic buying, and society braced itself for what looked like a possible Armageddon.

1981 - Camaraderie

I began to recognise that friendships often helped alleviate my feelings of being disconnected from myself. But I also found that seeing people just for the sake of it, especially when there wasn't a good connection, sometimes resulted in me feeling even more lonely. It's hard to put one's finger on what it is that makes us feel more connected to some rather than others.

When people say they only have a handful of true friends in life, that doesn't mean all their other friendships are meaningless and only distractions to help them pass the time. There are many levels of friendship and it's quite possible to feel a wave-length connection with people we deal with even on a superficial level. We may never become any more than acquainted with them, but all the same, there is something of great value in these connections. With some of those I spoke to on the bus, there was something significant, an understanding, or recognition of a similar light that shone in them too. And at school too, certain students, teachers or other members of staff, made the world a far less lonely place. All around us are people who want to connect with us just as we wish to with them.

2020 - Camaraderie

During the first week of lockdown, a call to applaud the health staff and key workers was made on social media. So, at 8 pm every Thursday, people would come to their front doors, balconies, gardens and windows to clap, bang pots and pans or just cheer. For many people, this was the only contact they'd have with others during this time so there was a strong feeling of camaraderie in those two minutes. But after a few weeks, there were also murmurings about those who didn't appear to join in, and after a few more it lost its sense of meaning, it became part of a routine ritual. There was something of the coercive spirit of the Soviet era starting to accompany it too. After all, to not clap was tantamount to not appreciating the great sacrifice of the workers, and that, as we all know, is a no-no.

2020 - Covid 19 March to July

For a lot of people, it was the end of the world. Up till now, July 1st there have been possibly around 60,000 people who may have died as a result of catching COVID-19 in the UK. For many of those who died and their loved ones, it was also made worse because they were not allowed to be together in their last moments as the possibility of infection was so great it was deemed too dangerous.

By March 23rd, most of the economy was closed and people were ordered to stay indoors except for an hour's exercise and essential journeys, such as shopping for food. Meanwhile, the government made provisions for some sections of society to help them ride the economic downturn. Each day there'd be a governmental briefing on TV. At first, that was the highlight of the day, but in time it became so repetitive and uninformative that I, and many other people, stopped watching it. Meanwhile, the media came over as so partisan that it was barely worth watching the news. In time the daily routine of getting up late, being creative, watching streaming services, eating, going for a cycle ride and sleeping became quite pleasurable. Outside of meeting friends, I didn't seem to miss much of the life I'd known before lockdown, so, by the time the government started to lift the restrictions, my immediate response was to continue isolating.

2020 - May 28th Nobody on The Road, Nobody On The Beach

I look out from my balcony to the sea. It's a very hot sunny day. There are lots of people walking around, sitting on the beach, meeting up with friends, and buying ice cream from the ice cream van. It's like a typical summer's day but it doesn't feel right. Nothing has felt right for a while.

The government has relaxed restrictions here slightly, but many people have seen this as a green light to go back to normal. Meanwhile, the virus is still out there, so, people are predicting a second wave. Of course, if the elderly and vulnerable continue to isolate then it might not be so bad. After all, most young people will only get mild symptoms and very, very few have died from it so far. Maybe this is the way we should have approached it in the first place. But when it first started spreading so little was known about it the authorities were rightly fearful. It's easy to look back now and say, "What was all the fuss about," but whilst hindsight is a wonderful thing it's also useless.

1889 - Rēzekne

Had Boruch taken the other route to the station, he would have heard the newspaper seller heralding the arrival of a new deadly pandemic and that would have given him several days' extra time, which might have made the world of difference. But even when news of it did manage to travel ahead, a million people still died because of it.

I could focus on the passing of Ruth and Chaya, as many storytellers would. Even though we know it's a bit of a cheap trick, we still find something touches us deeply when we witness the passing of the innocent. But there's something disrespectful to me about using their deaths to entertain you. Ruth and Chaya (Although their names were slightly different), were two of the thirteen children in my family to die from the Russian Flu. You may remember me mentioning this incident in the first chapter. Chaya was the first to show symptoms, she felt like cold water was running down her back and legs, and then she would flit between feeling very hot, and a bit later cold again. Her sense of taste and smell diminished and soon after she lost all her energy. When Chaya stopped breathing all her siblings had entered the final stages too. Nechama, Boruch and the doctors who visited could do nothing to help. Over the next few days, each one took their last gasp for air, except one of the older boys, another sister and Esther. Her brother lived long enough to witness the Nazis and local collaborators systematically kill most of the Rēzekne Jews in the same woods where Kristian was murdered by the man in the coat. It's always possible to see some silver linings, even in the worst of tragedies, not that that negates the loss. But for Chaya, news of Kristian's murder was something she wouldn't have to bear. Had she lived, his death would have driven a fault line through her entire being, so, she'd never truly love another man properly and had this virus not appeared then, Ruth would have been Kristian's killer's next target. Together though, the virus and Ruth brought the psychopath's reign of destruction to an end. When he picked her up, she passed the virus on to him and as he became ill, he found a hollowed tree, climbed in and died there.

It's no consolation to Esther's 13 siblings that they avoided whatever other tragedies they would have had to face. For them, just like us, they would rather have lived and suffered. We cannot expect not to suffer if we choose to live. This is the unsaid deal all of us have to accept.

Nechama and Boruch prayed to be taken instead of any of their children, but neither of them showed any symptoms, they could only ask the same questions any parent would, why would God do this to their sweet innocent children? What had they or their children done to deserve this? If there was a silver lining for them, they couldn't see it. For Esther, though, there was one. When the Spanish Flu appeared in 1918 most older people were immune, possibly because many had acquired some immunity after surviving Russian Flu, although this is merely conjecture. While she would never remember having the virus, she carried the weight of being one of the few survivors. She was painfully aware from an early age that she was extra precious to her parents, and while at the same time she felt some guilt for surviving she also felt a pressure to be worthy of that survival.

The ghosts of her siblings, these brothers and sisters she'd never got to know, accompanied her throughout her whole life. In her last days, she pictured Ruth and Chaya and the others standing by her bed and took comfort from their love and presence.

When I look at the photographs of Esther, there is a heaviness weighing down upon her, so it was no surprise that when Boris came along exhibiting the lightness of his being, she could only try to beat it out of him. But in those last days, her inner and outer cores became more differentiated, as they often do for many when they endure extreme pain. But, still, she felt some relief as she came to recognise the importance of both the weight and lightness within us. Just as my grandmother reached out to me to ask for forgiveness, Esther reached out to Boris. It wasn't the forgiveness borne of duty, but that which comes from the truest love and understanding.

The Future - Part 5

Initial opinions had given the universe another six billion years to go, and this may have sounded like a fair amount of time, but six billion years can go by in a flash when you can be kept on file for hundreds of millions of years and travel close to the speed of light. Even though some humans lived thousands of lifetimes, many of which they'd enjoyed on one planet and then another until the local star or stars became unstable, but for all those lifetimes, they knew eventually there wouldn't be anywhere to run to.

This was why the more developed humans had not tried to help them, they realised that even though, to a point, they were immortal, it was what they were, what they were made of, that wouldn't allow them to go to the "next stage", and that was because the next stage could only be accessed by a completely different being. How can a human that has evolved within a universe of certain laws of physics enter another where those laws do not apply?

Those streaks of light that passed the original explorers millions of light years previously hadn't found the meaning of life but instead developed themselves to search for it in another universe. Did they find God, or did they become God, even they were not sure? But in this new universe horizons and dreams did not exist and as they entered it, there was a moment, almost like waking from a dream, where they felt all their memories of the old universe slipped away. The experience of existing or being conscious in this sphere was not comparable to our universe and because it was so different it is pointless trying to describe it. How could we understand a thought that does not exist in time?

If there is a God then maybe God would be laughing because in this new universe they entered, everything that had lived and existed in our universe connected with them. Humans had pretty much defeated death to get there, but it turned out that death was the quickest way to enter it anyway.

2020 - Ann's Funeral

Ann's funeral was held in a large glass room in the middle of a field. Her son spoke about her and reminded us of her many qualities. She had started her own life surrounded by fields in a valley near the Welsh border. Her parents were dysfunctional, so she was brought up by her grandparents who'd let her roam the countryside alone. As an adult, she was very independent, practical, ferocious when it came to dealing with injustice, extremely creative, and did everything possible to nurture others, especially via food. There were not many high-end chefs who could have outdone her when it came to style and taste. One day I said to her that I thought she'd become what she'd always needed. She looked at me and said in a slightly sad tone, "You're probably right darling". Then she jumped up and said with a giggle, "Right there's some cake that needs eating, do you want some?"

2010 - Rēzekne – Stories

After Boris died in 2010, I went to Latvia for a short holiday. One day I decided to visit Rēzekne which involved a long train journey. I could only stay there for a few hours as I had to get back to Riga that night. I had the name of the road where my father had lived as a child and sure enough, when I got a local minicab driver to take me there, there were a few of those traditional houses still standing. The story I've told about my ancestors in Rēzekne is partly true, 13 of the 16 children did die of Russian Flu, but the rest of it was mostly something pieced together, just as history predominantly is. That's why the word "his story" is so appropriate. If my memory is so full of gaps, as is probably true for most people, how can we hope to recall things that are not affected by our internal narratives and desires? In that way, we become a story, created in part by the influence of so many other stories, including less obvious ones such as our genetic, evolutionary, family and dream ones.

As I stood on that dusty dried-out mud track I thought about those children and Boris's grandparents. I wondered if they could see me come to say hello. Since then, I have often wondered that if there is an afterlife, would my ancestors come to greet me upon my arrival, maybe even my descendants would come too if it's a timeless place.

As I research these chapters I often read through my diary, and even though I know what happened I'm still interested to read the next page. Stories underpin our culture, our history, and our ethical and moral principles, and help pass away the hours, especially nowadays with multiple streaming services and TV stations.

In the twentieth century, many artists tried to veer away from creating narrative art, instead, they wanted to focus on the medium itself. So, for instance, abstract art became about paint and mark making, poetry became about the sound of words and filmmaking, the image. But for all that, every one of those artists loved a good story.

Rēzekne 1889 - Before the Russian Flu

When a reading from the Torah was to be the highlight of the service at the synagogue, only the elders and a few dedicated worshippers would turn up. But when parables were conveyed the attendance would be very high and at the end of each tale, people would nod their heads, whilst murmuring in appreciation of not only being entertained but also being shown a glimpse of truth.

I tend to watch a movie on my iPad most evenings, and what's funny is how unmemorable most of them are. Sometimes I'm halfway through a film when I realise I've seen it before, but a good story gets lodged in your memory for a lifetime.

I remember hearing this next story when I was young and it's stuck with me ever since. I'll warn you now, it's disturbing, so if you're feeling delicate maybe jump to the next page. As with so many dark folk tales, they are echoes from our ancestors and often reach back thousands of years. This one is known as The Faithful Hound. Versions of it range from *Lady and The Tramp* to *Old Shep*, and *The Tale of Gelert*.

There once was a king who had a dog he truly loved; they had grown up together and were inseparable, but as the dog reached its final days, the king would leave it behind to help guard the queen and his firstborn child. But this day he came home to find his wife was nowhere to be found and when he went to check his baby's cot there was a pool of blood around it. In his panic, he called his dog's name. The dog came to him but to his dismay, the dog's mouth and teeth were covered in blood. At that moment, he realised what had happened so pulled out his sword and raised it above his head. The dog knew what was about to happen and whimpered, but it was no good, the king brought down the sword, the dog yelped and was killed. There was a cold silence but then from behind the bed, the king heard his child cry out. He ran to where the noise was coming from and there was his baby, completely safe, while next to the child lay a dead wolf. When the king realised what he'd just done he became full of remorse. Even though the ceremony he put on for the dog was a lavish one, he could not stop thinking of his betrayal.

By the way, given we now live in a very caring world, allegedly, I would just like to point out that no animals were hurt in the telling of that tale, and even though a wolf was used to illustrate a point, most wolves are very nice, fluffy and very scared of humans, so are not as much of a threat as people think. However, if you're a sheep, please do take care. If you're not a sheep though, you should be okay.

Finale

You're at a theatre.

The curtains open, and the auditorium lights fade.

[In the centre of the stage is a young good-looking man posed and decorated to resemble a tree. There's a rope tied around his waist that goes off in two directions and disappears on either side of the stage.]

[A king and his dog walk on stage. The king raises his sword. The dog seems to wince and cower.]

King: Stop milking it, I've already said sorry a million times.

[The King throws him a treat. The dog catches it and looks happy with himself. He then trots merrily towards the tree.]

King: Let the competition commence!

[The dog pees on the tree.]

King to the tree: I'm terribly sorry about that. He's in therapy.

The Tree: Don't worry, I'm used to it.

[The king throws a treat at the tree man who catches it in his mouth and mouths, "Thank you" to him.]

[There is the sound of men groaning and heaving. A few druids appear on the left side of the stage holding the rope whilst some bishops emerge on the right side also pulling their end of it. The tree slowly starts to move towards the bishops.]

[The lights gently fade down whilst another spotlight shines on Ruth in the sky. She is holding a vegetable flute. She nods her head as she counts herself in.]

[There is the sound of a beautiful whistle which plays the music for *To be a Pilgrim*]

[Another spotlight shines on the bishops who start to sing the words of the hymn. As they sing, Chaya and Kristian appear next to Ruth and join in playing the music.]

[The sound of a church organ plays, and as it does another spotlight illuminates Ann sitting at an organ in the sky.]

[A few seconds later the black background disappears and is replaced by a multiple mirror system which makes all those in the sky have infinite reflections behind them.]

[Four astronauts slowly float down towards Chaya, Ruth, Kristian and Ann and proceed to move them upwards above the stage and out of view.]

[The music fades, and the lights dim.]

[A spotlight shines on the centre of the stage. The man in the hat and coat from the lake stands motionless for a second then shouts, "No one is completely good or evil." He throws off his coat. His torso is bare. He has a beautiful athletic body.]

[As Bruce Springsteen's *Brilliant Disguise* plays, the man dances gracefully in a Ballet/Flamenco style to it. As he does so, the audience is illuminated and can see their own disjointed reflections in the mirrored background too.]

I'll paraphrase the song for copyright reasons.

Bruce sings to his woman, he wants her to see he's struggling to do everything right, but when he does, everything falls apart. He knows he walks in wealth but still feels like a lonely pilgrim and doesn't know if it's his woman he can't trust or if it's just himself. So, he warns her, when she looks at him, it'd be best to look twice, because is it him or just a brilliant disguise?

[At the end of the song there is silence.]

[The man from the lake takes a bow, looks at the audience and applauds them, some of the audience join in. He bows once more and walks off stage.]

[The lights remain on so the audience can continue to see themselves in the infinite and disjointed reflections.]

[Slowly the curtains close.]

You hear the teenage couple in the seats next to you talking. You look to your right and see Teenage Simon sitting next to you, and beside him is Jules.

Jules asks Simon, "So, what did you think of it then?".

Simon lets out a slightly exasperated sigh, then adds, "Well, I liked the Springsteen song."

As they prepare to leave, Teenage Simon looks at you and smiles a hello smile.

Chapter 31
First Love

First Love

It's hard to work out which relationship was my first love. Was it Jackie, when I was seven, Sue when I was ten, or Jules when I was sixteen, or should I only count the more adult affairs in my 20s? For me, it was the one with Jules because in a way it created its own universe which, with a bit of focus, I can still enter and feel a touch of its emotional intensity. Of course, there were other serious relationships which still hold powerful emotional resonances for me, and each of them also exists in their universe of time and space.

Perhaps, if there are multiverses, in some, we were together for a lifetime and that's why we couldn't stay with each other in this one. However, less romantically, I ought to add that there were also quite a few solar systems, shooting stars and meteor showers, but it's probably best not to dwell on those too much, well, at least not now.

I did wonder whether spending time writing about my first love would be of any interest to you, but the more I read my diaries and the love (and not so love) letters from around this time, the more apparent it became that there were indeed significant universal issues wrapped up in this story.

It is no wonder there are so many songs about first love, whether it's, *The End of the Innocence* by Don Henley, or *Puppy Love* by Jimmy Osmond. Okay, I'm joking, I'm not including that one. And then there are the more cynical, but highly amusing ones, such as *Walk Away Renee* by Billy Bragg, and *Jilted John* by Graham Fellows AKA John Shuttleworth.

My older self, i.e. me now, would have chosen Bill Bailey's *Love Song* to illustrate my reaction to this relationship. It's a dark, but extremely funny look at a less-than-mature reaction to a breakup. My younger self, however, would have seen some very definite parallels in Dire Straits' track, *Romeo and Juliet*. However, if I'd have had to bring those two opposing parts of me together then I think they'd have seen a connection with the film *Donnie Darko*. In it, the main character gets to see the outcome of various scenarios concerning the girl he loves, and [Spoiler Alert], he finally realises the best thing he can do for her sake is to sacrifice himself. So, here, almost 40 years later, I look at a glimpse of Jules's life, and I'm thankful, for her sake, that our relationship ended when it did because, in so many ways, she was much better off without me.

Jules – 1981/2020

The night we first kissed in 1981, I could not sleep, and when in 2020 I found her again it was like plugging in a connection that went back 38 years and took me directly to that time. I was a ghost of the future looking at our story, knowing what was about to happen but still wanting to see it again. It was like watching a film I'd loved a long time ago but this time I noticed subtleties and hints of what was to come, which first time around I missed.

In 1981 I'd fallen in love with Jules, and my mind was exploding with all the possibilities of what was to come. But in 2020, it was compassion, and a sense of sorrow, for both Jules and me, and the story I knew, that filled my thoughts and feelings.

The Shock of Love

As soon as I started to get involved with Jules, I felt a sense of dread. I knew it wasn't going to last, and instead of thinking, "Fuck it, let's just enjoy the connection", I ended up trying to hold on as tightly as I could. I also felt dread because this type of relationship would not only reveal the multiple layers of myself to me but also the lack of control I had when it came to dealing with them.

When faced with the reality of being involved with someone romantically, most of us are likely to feel quite unprepared. There are, of course, a few who seem to have an easy ride when it comes to relationships, but in my experience, most of us don't. Someone once told me, "If you want passionate love, you can't have peace too."

Expectations

Most of us have expectations of what a loving relationship should entail. In some ways, this is surprising, given fairy stories only ever went as far as, "And they lived happily ever after". So, where do these expectations come from?

As part of my 'extensive research' into this matter, I was talking with a friend the other day, and she said some of our expectations might come from our parents, but for me, my parents certainly did not act as positive role models, conversely though, they did show me what to avoid.

It's quite obvious that our community, culture, media, as well as the religions and ideologies that we come in contact with, will all have an influence. But often, they are merely an echo of what beats deep inside us in the first place.

For all the political shifts in the 70s and 80s, Bruce Springsteen never wrote a song about Mary drawing up a rota for housework. Had he done so, there might have been a lot fewer arguments about washing up, but I get the feeling his record company and fans wouldn't have been too enamoured about his 'New-Man' direction. In the same vein, had I had this relationship six months later, I might have listened to the album *The Lexicon of Love* by ABC, and may have had a more realistic expectation of love. Yes, you're right, I doubt it too. These external cultural influences may only have a slight effect compared to what's already stirring within us. We may like to think our rules for life come from our higher ideals, but just below the surface, it's biology that controls much of what we do and expect.

When it comes to 'the romantic illusion', an idea I've mentioned before, it's very tempting to believe it developed via millennia of trial and error, but is it not mainly a by-product of our survival instinct? In this illusion, our love for another will be revealed, at first sight, we will be compatible in every way, and no one else will tempt us or break us apart. While this may sound very romantic, is it not just an elaborate mating ritual?

There's a very long poem by Adrian Henri called *Words Without a Story* that lists all the things the writer does to win the "heart" of his beloved. Once they have "made love" he loses interest in her, and she is left distraught. This is probably a very familiar experience for many on both sides of the dynamic.

When we first get involved with someone it's as if we are dealt a handful of picture cards. The romantic lover, seducer, whore or lothario, the mother, father, true one, or betrayer may suddenly inhabit our subconscious view. So, for instance, that 'getting to know all about you' part of a relationship could also be seen as a 'figuring out which archetypes you are?' stage. We tend to hope and expect our partners to be similar to positive archetypes, but any hints of them being otherwise tend to leave us feeling very anxious.

If You Want a Happy Partner, Choose a Happy Person

Given the amount of grief most of us experience when it comes to relationships, you'd think we wouldn't bother. However, biology is not going to take such rational thinking lying down and add to that our individual psychological dynamics, all of which are desperate to have their moments too, it's no wonder many of us feel doomed when we get involved with someone.

There are some who prefer not to have relationships, and thanks to them the hobby industries are booming, but maybe the opposite is true. After all, those who live a fulfilling life are more likely to feel less desperate to have a relationship. Consequently, they are less likely to treat a relationship as a crutch. For them, it's something extra to add to an already happy life.

When we make a relationship too precious, the fear invoked by the possibility of losing it would be akin to the "my precious" ring in Lord of The Rings, and likewise may destroy us.

1981 - Loneliness

At 16, I felt lonely a lot of the time. I wasn't happy at home, and even though I got on well with Mum, in fact so well John would complain we chatted too much, I would often go in search of companionship elsewhere. There I was, completely unprepared for a relationship but desperate for one. Not only that but my past experiences and genes – and yes, I do blame my mum and dad for them – added even more complications.

For me, relationships were never going to go smoothly, well, not for a long time. However, I like to take some consolation in Carl Jung's words, the tree that reaches up to heaven must also have roots that reach down to hell.

Perfect Imperfect

I've said before we probably spend more time choosing which tomatoes to buy in a supermarket than we do selecting a partner. In a perfect world, we'd meet someone, recognise some kind of attraction, and spend time getting to know them before moving on to the next stage. In reality, our biology says, "We haven't got time for all that crap, let's just get mating." In a perfect world, well, things would be so much different.

If you dwell on the past, you'll lose an eye, but if you don't dwell on it, you'll lose both eyes.

1982 January – Jules

Jules had gone away for a few days with her parents, but to me, it felt as if she'd taken a year's sabbatical in Siberia. She was actually near Pevensey, so that wasn't too far from the truth. While she was away, I filled the empty spaces with activities that still involved her. Firstly, I used my new camera equipment to photograph our photo booth photos, and then I wrote a long letter to her.

Maybe because I knew my love for her wasn't based on really knowing her, and likewise, I knew she didn't know me either, I was ready to doubt her love for me from the start. So, when I wrote in my diary, "Sometimes I wonder if she loves me as I love her?" I was both reading from my internal drama of not being lovable and touching on something truthful about all new relationships: the love isn't real.

On the fourth day, I, along with some other school friends visited part of London University to check out their psychology department. Whilst being shown around I got hooked up to a heart and perspiration monitor machine which suddenly went a bit haywire when I looked into the eyes of Lorna, a girl from my hometown who I'd chatted to in the lunch hour. "That wasn't supposed to happen," I thought to myself, after all, I only have eyes for Jules. But it did. Lorna saw it too and figured it meant something. You may remember my friend, Ian Owles, telling me that if the first rule of love is those who you want don't want you, then the second rule is, when you're single no one wants you, but when you're with someone, people will throw themselves at you. Well, this was my first taste of them.

Lorna and I journeyed back to Sutton together and got on well. There was a spark between us, which confused me, but I sensed if I did anything with her it would be contaminated by my feelings for Jules and vice-versa. Even so, I still felt tempted. This was something I hadn't even considered as a possibility, but as I was soon to find out, this was a dynamic I was going to have to contend with for the rest of my life. The pattern throughout my early years had been to look for comfort wherever I could find it. Whether it was the carers in the homes when my mother left me there or the other families I visited because my own family was dysfunctional. They were all a part of the same coping mechanism. So, if I already felt that our 'love' was mainly imagined and possibly short-lived, it's no wonder I was very willing to gather around me possible substitutes. What I didn't factor in though, was that the carers would never love me as my mother would, the alternative families were not going to offer me a home long-term, and by looking at substitutes I was saying to my mother and Jules, 'See, you're replaceable', when in fact they were not.

There was also another factor to consider. Does being a male mean I'd be tempted no matter what my upbringing was? Not all men are philanderers, but it does tend to go with the territory for a lot of them. Of course, plenty of women act similarly too. So, what is it that makes some people more prone to cheating than others? The answer, as usual, is most likely multi-layered, but then that might mean my genetics and history have less to do with it than I presume.

Theatre

You're in an old theatre, the lights are very low, it's almost pitch black, and there are slight murmurings which fade out as the lights rise. The stage is on two levels. The bottom half has some American cars surrounding an American 50s-era diner bar with stools positioned along it. The upper stage is a cross-section of the top floor of a house. To the right, there's a balcony with a wall and a vined trellis going down to the lower stage. The room that links to the balcony has a bed in it, some posters of a young Bruce Springsteen on the walls, and a desk. To the left of that room is a hallway, and to the left of that is a master bedroom in which there's a four-poster bed and some classical ionic columns in the corners of the room. There is another door that goes to another room (off-stage) to the far left.

Jules is lying on her front, on her bed. Her feet are crossed in the air.

There's the sound of people climbing the stairs. Her mother's voice calls out, "I hope you're revising in there Jules." Jules, a bit panicked quickly jumps off her bed, switches her handheld transistor radio off, and throws the magazine under the bed then sits at her desk just as the door opens.

She twists around to look at her mother.

Jules's Mother: Oh, you are such a good girl, working so hard.

Jules: I think I ought to take a break, I've been studying for hours.

Jules's Mother: Oh, you poor thing. I'm going to make dinner in a minute anyway, so come down when you're ready.

Jules [hesitatingly]: Mum?

Jules's Mother: Yes darling.

Jules: Can I ask you something?

[Jules gets up and sits on her bed. Her mother closes the door, sits next to her, and holds her hand]

Jules: You know Simon, the boy you met the other night?

Jules's Mother [warily]: Yes.

Jules: Well, I like him and would like to go out with him. You know, as a friend, nothing serious.

[Jules looks at the audience]: I don't think now is a good time to tell her I love him.

[Her mum looks at the audience]: I knew it, she's fallen in love with him!

[She looks back towards Jules and puts both her hands around Jules's hand]

Jules's Mother: Erm... I know he's a very nice boy, but he's obviously been hurt enough by life, and I really wouldn't want to see him getting hurt anymore.

[Jules looks at the audience]: Aww, my Mum is so sweet. She obviously really cares about him too. My Mum's the best!

[Her mother looks at the audience, licks her finger and makes the "I just scored one point" sign]

[She kisses Jules on the cheek, leaves the room and is heard walking down the stairs]

[Jules goes back to her desk and grabs a sheet of paper and a pen. She speaks as she writes]

Dear Mum,

I'm going to go out with Simon on my own or with friends. As far as I'm concerned if you don't trust me now then it's your problem, not mine. I trust myself and I know what I'm doing. When you think about it, I could be legally married in six months, yet you are trying to keep me in like a little kid!

[Jules looks at the audience]: Yes, I know. I'm a fast writer.

[She continues writing the letter]

If you say I'm not to go out with him then I will but you won't know about it, that's all. Don't you think it would be nicer for you to know exactly where I am and nicer for me to not have to lie to you about where I'm going?

I thought about what you said about him being hurt and keeping it casual. I told him and it's agreed that when it all flops apart we'll still be good friends.

Don't get cross Mum.

You're a great Mum but give me a chance!

[She puts the letter into an envelope, then goes to their bedroom, places it on their bed and walks downstairs]

[The lights fade down on the upper floors but are brightened on the lower level. Simon walks onto the stage from the right]

Simon: Wow, what a cool set.

[Simon looks off stage]

Hey, do you mind if I have a cool actor play me, please?"

[There's a puff of smoke and standing where Simon had been standing is John Travolta dressed up as Danny from the movie *Grease*]

[Simon's voice comes over the intercom] "No... Cooler."

502

[Danny, looks incredulous, sticks his finger up at the 'voice in the sky' and struts off as only cool 23-year-old teenagers do]

[The lights fade down, and a spotlight hovers over the right of the stage. Elvis, in his 68 Special leather suit walks on]

"Treat me like a fool, treat me mean and cruel, but love me."

[Simon's voice over the Intercom]: "That's better."

[Elvis smiles a little coyly]

[The music continues as the lights fade]

Stages of Development

I began to become more aware of stages of development in many aspects of life around this time. It was probably as I started feeling myself moving through various ones myself that I became truly aware of their significance.

As I got better at art, I started to see other people doing things I'd done previously, and ahead of me, I could see others doing things I couldn't understand. There are varying stages of relationships too. I may have understood that cognitively then but not emotionally. We were very young so it would seem appropriate that at least for some time our relationship would only exist within a certain framework.

At seven with Jackie, we had tea together and a kiss goodbye, then at ten with Sue we had one kiss, I wrote a few letters and I looked at her photo a lot. At sixteen, going any further than spending time together, holding hands, and kissing could easily end up with us derailing our lives, but that still didn't stop me from wanting it all.

1982 January - Jules

As soon as Jules got back from being away, we'd meet up every day. The more I saw her, the more I wanted to see her, and she seemed to feel the same way. We'd meet at the library where we'd do our homework together for about 20 minutes then chat for the rest of the time. We'd bring each other letters we'd written when we were apart, and little presents such as poems and small affectionate keepsakes. Fortunately, I didn't bring her all my poems, as I think one called something like 'The Pain of Love' may have worried her slightly. As things were, she would tell me off for being a bit too possessive anyway. Maybe I thought showing someone I wanted to be with them all the time was something they'd appreciate, but I hadn't learnt yet, people not only need a little space to feel their own feelings, but also there is something far more attractive about someone who's happy with life and still wants to see you. In contrast, someone seeing you as their saviour because their life is empty without you can be a little off-putting. Fortunately, in time, I did take that on board, although that was about 30 years later.

Theatre

[The lights fade up, Elvis walks towards the trellis, he gently plays his guitar and sings *Love Me Tender*. Jules gets out of bed and walks to the balcony. She closes her eyes and swoons a little. Simon walks onto the balcony]

Simon [Whispering]: Hey Jules.

Jules [Shocked]: Oh! How did you get up here?

Simon: There's a little lift just off-stage.

[She nods but looks a bit confused]

[Elvis starts singing loudly]: Up above my head there is music in the air.

Jules and Simon: Shhhhhhhh!

[Jules's parents sit up in unison, turn their bedside lamps on, look at each other, shrug their shoulders then slowly turn their lights off and lie down again]

Simon: Is everything ok?

[Jules grabs Simon, hugs him and runs her fingers through his hair – Yes, I had hair back then]

Jules: I love you and I missed you one hell of a lot, but I don't want it to get too serious too soon if you know what I mean. I hope you understand.

Simon: Yes, of course, I do.

[Simon looks at the audience and shakes his head in confusion.]

Jules: My parents are very worried about how serious it might get, and therefore they aren't going to be overly sociable or jolly in the hope we notice and finish it off because of them. They've really annoyed me.

Simon [Angrily]: Fuck 'em!

[Jules looks anxious]

Jules: I hope you're not serious as that will just make matters worse. I think if we continue to be friendly then in time, they'll be friendly to you. I've seen it before with my sister.

Simon: Yes, you're right, it won't help if I'm like that.

[Jules pulls Simon towards her and gives him a big kiss. She pauses]

Jules: Hold on, I'm just going to change the music.

[Elvis looks at the audience and shakes his head in disbelief and despondently walks off stage]

[The spotlight goes to the same place to the right of the stage as before, when an eerie harmonica wails as Bruce Springsteen appears, he starts singing, *The River*. The volume and lights fade]

Bruce: Man, that's the shortest concert I've ever done.

Reasons To Be Fearful

I couldn't be sure exactly why Jules' parents took against me; however, it wasn't inconceivable that it had something to do with my disability. Maybe they felt that Jules just felt sorry for me and wanted to protect her from herself and there might have been other reasons, but I don't think they were particularly being malicious towards me. For them, it was about protecting their daughter's interests.

1982 January

Jules thought it would be a good idea to try a bit of aversion therapy on her parents. The plan was to get them to have a bit of contact with me, and hopefully, in time they'd be a bit more amenable to the idea of us at least being friends. When I entered the house, I wiped my feet on the mat at least 30 times until I noticed a slight nod from her mum that I'd shown enough respect. I was then led to the kitchen where Jules made me a cup of tea and we had a good laugh together. Perhaps it was the laughter that did it. Maybe they knew that laughter was far more dangerous than kissing or silence. After less than an hour, I was asked to leave. We were both fuming but deep down we knew this was the death knell of our relationship.

I was so angry that on the way home I called Lorna and asked if I could pop around. When I got there her mum and dad welcomed me to stay for something to eat and afterwards, I sat on the sofa with them and watched TV. As I left, Lorna went to kiss me goodbye, as our mouths touched it felt wrong. I told her I liked her, but I loved Jules and I didn't want to hurt either of them. I felt awful because I didn't want to reject her and had we met before Jules and I had, then maybe we would have got together. But it was too late.

When I got home, I asked Mum if Jules had phoned, but she hadn't so I went upstairs, got into bed, and listened to the radio. I knew Jules would be listening to the same programme. There was always a phone-in competition at this time called Beat the Intro. The caller would have to recognise the song being played before the singing started and this night it was an easy one. The song was *Don't You Want Me?* by The Human League. After the song finished, I read my poster of Desiderata which I'd put up above my tropical fish tank so was lit by the neon-glow light.

"What amazing words," I thought, but I still felt shit.

I didn't see or hear from Jules for a couple of days, but when I did, she told me her parents had ordered her to stop going out with me.

When I got to school the next day one of Lorna's friends told me she'd cried after I'd seen her the other night. She said that even though she didn't want to go out with me, she was touched by me being so straight with her. I don't think I was as straight about it to Jules though. I thought to myself, "I'm sure God's having a bit of a laugh at my expense right now."

Our first lesson that day was geography. We had a new teacher, Mr Hay, who had a big biker beard and resembled a massive wrestler. He looked at me and said, "You okay mate?" The class went very quiet as this wasn't normal. I said, "My girlfriend's parents won't let us be together". He nodded very slightly in understanding then added "That's heavy man".

For another two days, there was radio silence between Jules and me, but on Saturday we had our art class. She was there and afterwards, she kissed me and said she still wanted us to carry on seeing each other. We spent the afternoon together, but then she was gone, and I fell into a depression again.

On the way home, I popped into Cameron's house. He was one of my school friends. His parents were one of the few very happy couples I'd ever come across. I talked to his dad about the situation and asked what he thought I should do. He told me I was being selfish, and I should think about what was best for Jules. So, when I got in, I wrote her a letter saying I'd understand if it was too much for her and we could end it if that'd help. When I got into bed, I knew the end was approaching and cried.

The next day Jules called me, but to get some privacy I grabbed some coins and ran to the nearest phone box. When I got there, there was already someone using it. I made it clear I was waiting to use the phone by queuing in their line of sight which probably made them take longer. Couldn't they see that this was a matter of life and death? Jules's parents were only out for half an hour, and I had at least two letters to read her!

As the person came out of the phone box, they huffed a little whilst looking me up and down. I smiled and said, "Thanks". I got through just in time and was able to read my resignation letter to Jules.

"They're back, I've got to go," she said, "but I don't want to split up, I'm missing you so much, I love you." And then the phone clicked off.

For the next few days, all I could think of was Jules. She tried to call me once when I was out. But then a letter from her arrived for me and in it, she wrote:

> *"Lying to my parents isn't going to bother me that much because I've already warned them I would do so. In time, they won't be so against it. You must admit this problem does add a bit of spice (or at least try to convince yourself it does) I miss you and I love you, but you know that anyway."*

She was willing to fight for our love and once again I was filled with energy and hope. On the way home from school the next day some kids from another school started a fight at the bus stop. I lightly kicked one of them in the head and as I went to kick another, he looked at me in recognition. He was the younger brother of a friend from my junior school, so I stopped myself. He looked shocked, maybe even horrified, or confused even. It was a strange moment of revelation, and he ordered the others to stop.

Afterwards, I made my way to Sutton Library where Jules was waiting for me. She gave me the biggest hug. We couldn't spend long together but I breathed in every breath she exhaled and then she was gone.

The next day her parents were going to be out, so she invited me over. As I came out of school there was a roar of cheering from the kids at the bus stop who'd witnessed the previous day's fight. I smiled but my main priority was getting to the other bus stop down the road so I could get to see Jules on time. When I got to her place, I lay in her arms whilst we chatted and laughed but all the time, I couldn't help but listen out for the sound of a car pulling up or keys turning in the door. "It's okay," she said, "they won't be back for ages". And fortunately, she was right.

A week had passed since her parents had laid down the law. There were going to be some sacrifices but at least we were still together.

The following Saturday afternoon I went with Jules to get her ears pierced, she'd told her Mum she was going with her friend Scarlett. Her Mum called Scarlett's mum to check they were together and luckily Scarlett's Mum covered for us.

The next day I didn't hear from Jules, but Mum brought me a letter that had just dropped through the letterbox:

> *"Dear Simon,*
>
> *So, I'm afraid it all boils down to the fact that we're going to have to reach an agreement that we'll both be happy with. Either it finishes and we stay just as very good friends, or it carries on but we keep it from my mum and dad (which would be hard). What I don't want is a full-scale argument and then we never speak again. I couldn't stand that. I'm sorry Simon but I can see that life is going to be hell for as long as they think I'm going out with you. Why can't they love you like I do?*
>
> *Thinking of you and missing you*
>
> *Your kiss is so gentle... I love you.*
>
> *Jules –x"*

Had I had any sense I'd have made my exit then, but I obviously wanted to suffer. In fact, over the next few days, I did everything possible to make matters worse. Firstly, when she took the risk to visit me at my place, I tried to push things further, sexually. Then afterwards, I wrote two provocative letters, in one I said I doubted she was truly in love with me and in the other I complained she didn't try very hard. I knew what I was doing, I just didn't know why, but I couldn't stop myself.

1982 - February

I hadn't got myself into this situation by accident, it took careful choreography by my subconscious to not only provoke some of the rejection that was beginning to come my way but also to remain in a position of vulnerability. So why did I have a part of me that wanted to put myself in the firing line? Was it because, as some psychologists hypothesise, we recreate difficult situations in order to gain a different, more positive outcome, or is it because this is what we know and understand to be 'home', what we believe is normal?

For me, what I knew of love was yearning. The drama of, 'Will she leave or rescue me?' was very much the distilled version of how it felt to me to be put in care as a child. So, was I trying to recreate that emotional scenario again? The thing is, this situation was also very close to how other people who were not abandoned as children, feel when they fall in love for the first time too.

Some psychologists might argue, that sometime during the early development of a child they realise they're a separate being from their parents, especially their mother in most cases, and at that point, they'll feel insecure and become clingy. So, even for people with a 'normal' upbringing, there may be echoes of separation anxiety evoked in their first experience of 'love'.

Theatre

The lights fade up.

[Simon is lying on a sofa that is in the shape of a naked woman, his head rests on her breasts. There is a therapist covered in a golden sheet sitting near Simon's head.]

Simon: I was just reading about people with separation or abandonment issues.

Therapist: I am sure that your past has had some effect on you, but what makes you think you have that kind of syndrome?

Simon: Well, whenever I fall in love, I feel like I become obsessed, and it feels irrational.

[The therapist seems to lose control for a second]

Therapist [raised voice]: Oh, what poppycock!

[She calms herself, and straightens her golden sheet]

Therapist: Isn't that how most people react when they fall in love? Does that mean that all the great poets and artists were mental, [she corrects herself] I mean had mental health and abandonment issues?

Me: Yes. I mean, I would like to think that I could have a more reasonable reaction.

[The therapist laughs a big laugh]

Therapist: Yes, you and the rest of the human race. Falling in love is not noted for being a state of rationality.

The lights fade down.

1982 - February – Sutton Library

Jules and I had been going out with each other for about five weeks, and although her parents had ordered her to stop seeing me, she disobeyed them and tried to meet me as often as she could. Sutton Library was our main meeting place, and overall, it was a safe place for us. However, we did get told off for having a snog in the children's library, and soon after that got a further warning to change our ways after I thumped a bookcase which made a big bang. This had been my reaction to an old woman hissing at me "You make me sick" when she came across Jules sitting on my lap in one of the comfy reading chairs.

1982 - February

Most days, I would bunk off school a little early so I could get the bus that would take me to Jules's school on time to meet her as she came out the front gates. If we only had a short time together, we'd go to the American Café, in Cheam, where we'd have a cappuccino, chat, hold hands and be affectionate. Although it wasn't perfect, we both liked it and some days, if we had a bit longer, we'd go to Sutton and either go shopping or do our homework in the library. There were a few times when Jules managed to come to my place. I'd put my head on her lap, while she'd hum and stroke my hair. When we weren't together, we'd chat on the phone or send letters to each other.

There were times when the gaps between seeing each other might be longer than a few days, that's when the doubts would set in. I'd feel forgotten and focus on the end.

1982 - Human Geography Lesson

Our lessons with Mr Hay were becoming more entertaining with each passing day. He was able to mix a bit of learning with having open and frank discussions with us about life. Especially our love lives. We loved it and looked forward to his lessons.

One day I gave him one of my poems to read and the next day he returned it with some humorous comments added. Just to have been given some attention meant something.

At the end of the lesson, he told me he had a girl coming around that night, which, though inappropriate, opened my eyes to him being human too.

The Look of Love

There is, of course, a big difference between what we learn on a cognitive level rather than on an emotional one. Even at 16, I was completely unaware of how I should treat someone I supposedly loved. When Jules and I told each other we loved each other, we meant, "I love how you make me feel". But what we heard was some kind of commitment to a duty of care. For me, it was partly about never leaving me, for her, being cared for. Either way, both of us were on a journey of discovery about love, it's just we didn't expect the first few miles to be as fraught as they were.

1982 - February – Geography Lesson

The last thing Mr Hay had told me the week before, was he was going out with a woman on Valentine's Day, but as we entered his class there was a new teacher, a middle-aged woman who introduced herself as Mrs Ballantyne. She informed us that Mr Hay had had a mental breakdown and she'd be our new teacher. I automatically assumed he'd had a breakdown because of something to do with his relationship with that woman, but there was no evidence to support that.

Our new teacher sent us out to do a survey of local shops so we could see how property types changed as they got further away from the centre of the town. I was partnered with Phil who agreed with me to stop at as many cafes as possible en route, where we'd have a cup of tea and snack whilst we just made up the data because we knew it would never be checked. In a way, it was our way of honouring the loss of Mr Hay.

1982 - February – Near Missing

Over the next few days, Jules and I met up twice, the first time was to go to a party. We arrived separately so as not to arouse suspicion from her parents, but as her dad was dropping her off, I had to dart into someone's garden so he wouldn't see me. No matter how careful you are it only takes one mistake to set the alarm bells off.

Two days after the party Jules came around to my house. She'd told her mum she was going swimming at Westcroft sports centre which was around the corner from where I lived. A short while after Jules arrived the phone rang, and John called out that it was for me. "It's Jules's Mum, she wants a word with you." He said.

"Hello Simon, can I speak to Jules please?" she asked.

"She's not here," I said as calmly as I could, then I added for effect,

"Is she ok? Has she run away?"

"No, of course, she hasn't run away! It's just she said she was going swimming around the corner from you and she's not there."

"Oh, well she's not here, sorry," I said,

"Oh ok, thank you." She said. I'm sure she wanted to add, "You're not as good at lying as you think you are buster!", but instead, she politely said goodbye and put the phone down.

This was about 12 years before mobile phones were commonplace, so I automatically presumed she was calling from a nearby phone box. I walked to the front room looked out the window and was certain I could see Jules's parents' car parked across the road. That meant she was at the telephone box around the corner, so she was likely to be outside within seconds.

I went to the back room where Jules was still oblivious and ready to resume cuddling up, but as I told her what had gone on, we both knew that that was probably our last ever kiss as girlfriend and boyfriend.

I suggested calling my neighbours to ask them if Jules could climb over their fence and make her way back to Westcroft before her mum did. Jules thought it best too, or at least played along with my genius idea. I called the neighbours and they agreed to help with our version of The Great Escape. Remember, this was suburbia, so any excitement was always more than welcome. They helped Jules over, escorted her to the main road and gave her directions to a back route so her Mum wouldn't see her. She did everything to plan, but her mother was one step ahead of us. As Jules entered the sports centre her mum was waiting for her.

1982 - Dear Simon

The next day Jules asked me to meet her in the library. I knew what was coming as she solemnly passed me an envelope and shook as I read its contents. I felt cold shudders of fear as I read the words which I had dreaded right from the beginning.

The letter said:

> *Dear Simon,*
>
> *I really shouldn't be writing this. I should say it to you. If I did I would choke up with tears... You must know what I'm going to say. I should've said it was over when you gave me the chance a couple of weeks ago, but I guess I thought it could have worked out... This hurts like Hell. On Jan 16th, you asked me to promise not to chuck you on account of my parents. I suppose I didn't wholly keep that promise. The tension at home is unbearable and I can't stand it.*

I will keep your letters, poems, bracelet and picture on my wall. Most of all I will keep happy memories of you. Just keep in touch and try to remain great friends.

I walked with Jules up the road. She held my arm and kissed me goodbye at the junction of Mulgrave Road and Bridge Road (Oh, the symbolism!), and then we went our separate ways. I looked over my shoulder and could see Jules was crying. I couldn't believe what was happening, so I went around to Lorna's and spent the day there in shock.

You would think that I'd have gracefully bowed out at this point but instead, the next month was still fertile ground for my dynamics to have their way.

Theatre

In the therapy room.

Simon: I feel like dying without Jules.

Therapist: Have you heard of the five stages of grief?

Simon: No

Therapist: Well, let me enlighten you.

[The stage goes dark except for a spotlight on the therapist]

She stands up, the golden cover slips off her to reveal a beautiful belly dancer. She continues to dance as she sings the following lines to the rhythm of Middle Eastern drums.

Therapist: I want you to think D.A.N.G.A. Did you get that, baby?

Simon: Yes

Therapist: D is for denial as you won't believe it's true, is that right, am I wrong, baby is that you?

Simon: Yes

Therapist: A is for Anger because you're gonna feel rage. But take my advice, try not to engage.

N is the negotiation you're going to try. You'll probably beg for the end not to be nigh.
[She looks at the audience] Who writes this shit

[She looks back at Simon]

G is for gloomy, that's how you're gonna feel. If you don't feel that then it's not the true deal.

And A is near the end when you Accept what's real.

You got that baby, does it feel true?

If you want to heal your heart,

It's something

You're gonna have to do.

[The therapist sits back down and covers herself]

[The spotlight fades down]

1982 - March

Sure enough, the first few weeks were full of denial, anger, bargaining and depression. However, I don't think there was much, if any, acceptance.

At first, Jules phoned each day, and it was as if nothing had changed. I still couldn't believe it was over. But when I asked her if we could get back together, she just went quiet. Jules would tell me of her arguments with her parents, and because I knew she still cared and missed me, I seriously believed we might reunite. When she'd write, she would end each letter saying how much she missed me, but rather than seeing it as her simply letting me know she still had strong feelings, I took it to mean there was a chance. After a few weeks, she didn't budge and the anger kicked in, at that point my letters to her became accusatory. My dynamics tended towards seeing the person who was supposed to love me as not loving me properly. So, I huffed and I puffed until all the walls came down.

When I next saw Jules, she told me her parents had grounded her until after her exams in the summer. She held my arm as she told me as I gently stroked my nose against her face, but we didn't kiss, except to say goodbye. Even then though, I thought we might, somehow, get back together.

Over the next two weeks, I began to come to terms with it being over. However, I stayed in contact with three of her friends, maybe because I couldn't let go, but one of them was Dee who I'd met when we all met for the first time, and it felt like a genuine friendship which I had the right to pursue.

Jules and I met one more time, she held my paw and even invited me to come to her house, but her parents found out, revoked the invitation, and banned her from art classes too. From this point on there was no more intimacy and I went back to my old ways of seeking comfort from friends and slowly disengaged from Jules. Well, at least to a point. On my birthday Jules sent a card. In it, she said:

> *"You know that I loved you in my own valentine way and you must know how much I'm missing you. I still love you in my way although I feel what's happened is for the best.*
>
> *Don't contact me...remember me. I'll always remember you.*
>
> *Goodbye Simon —xx–*

We would occasionally bump into each other at the lessons after her parents lifted the ban, but she told a mutual friend my jovial insults were beginning to make her sick and tired of me, and in time we stopped talking to each other. But it was the kind of silence that said quite a lot.

Love

Jules valued family far more than me, I was more of a street kid who felt abandoned by their family and sought allegiances with other street kids. The love of the family is partly based on compassion and unconditional love whereas the gangs are held together by mutual advantage, as well as honour and fear. In real terms though, I was more of a part-time street kid, because most of the time I sought out other families to spend time with and let's face it, I hadn't been totally abandoned.

To me, true love meant that I was possessed by the person I loved. They were in my mind all the time and were the most important 'thing' in my life. Conversely, I expected them to be possessed by me too. The story of Romeo and Juliet was where I was at. So, when Jules didn't want to go against her parents, as Shakespeare's lovers did, I felt betrayed.

Whilst it's true that when someone gets married their parents should be secondary to their married partner in many ways, I was completely oblivious to the notion of stages of development and couldn't see there was a big difference between just getting together and being married. Someone should have told me that relationships are like an English Breakfast of eggs and bacon. The chicken is involved, but the pig is committed.

Before I met Jules, I'd prayed to have a girlfriend to connect with, get to know, kiss, cuddle and share experiences with, but instead of being grateful and savouring every moment, I wanted more and didn't appreciate the gift I had been given.

Jules - Legacy

The first song I ever wrote was based on what happened with Jules. It was called *Johnny Talked to Sue* and told the story of a woman going out with a disabled man and her parents stopping her. It's not a good song particularly, but interesting that I chose that subject matter as the first thing I wanted to sing about.

The other legacy of this experience was from then on, I was always nervous about meeting my partner's parents. Sometimes I would get on very well with them, but even so, I saw them as a possible barrier.

The Last Words

A year later I got a letter from Jules in which she said she just wanted to talk with someone, and I was the only one she could talk to openly, but still, she thought it better not to reply. She also asked me not to forget her.

We did speak once more, a year or so later, on the phone. I don't remember much of what was said but I felt awkward. There was so much I wanted to say, but I could no longer remember what exactly the words were, so all that came out was rubbish.

Now, though, 38 years later, there are two things I want to end this chapter with. One was something I wrote to Jules in one of my last letters to her and it made me laugh when I found it the other day, it was this:

"One day, if either of us is famous and 'This Is Your Life' does a programme on one of us, I will greet you and cuddle you for so long that I'll only let go once your husband punches me."

And the other thing I wanted to say, is, of course, I will never forget you.

1982 - Retail Therapy

I stood in WH Smiths in Wallington High Street, looking for a record to buy. One cover caught my eye. It was completely red except for a thin light blue strip on one edge. It was the Dire Straits album *Making Movies*. I looked at the song list and there were only seven tracks listed, but I recognised one as a pretty song I'd heard on the radio called *Romeo and Juliet*. I thought I'd give it a try and bought it.

When I got home, I put it on the turntable in the lounge. No one else was in. The afternoon sun filled the room, so I cranked up the volume and sat back. By the eighth minute of the first track, I realised that there was more to life than boy meets girl, and art and beauty can touch us to the depths too. But then, by the end of the second track, I was reminded that relationships are very much at the core of my meaning and happiness.

In under 15 minutes, I'd taken a ride to another world and returned holding a tiny but invaluable piece of emotional understanding. I was blown away. Suddenly the music went off. I opened my eyes. John had come in and switched the HiFi off.

"It's a bit loud Simon!" He said, his irritation was palpable, "Are you deaf?" He scratched his head vigorously for a second.

However, like a kid caught smoking marijuana I wasn't quite in the zone, so instead of arguing back, I said. "You should try it. It's amazing."

But he didn't.

Theatre – Musical Outro

[Lights fade up]

Simon is standing under a streetlight on the left of the stage.

Jules is on her balcony. She doesn't look towards Simon.

On the right of the stage, a spotlight appears.

Mark Knopfler walks on with a big silver National Guitar.

He performs *Romeo and Juliet*.

Both Jules and Simon listen to it.

[Lights Fade down]

———

2021 – Jules

Since getting back in contact with Jules, we still message each other a few times a year, and soon after writing this chapter, we chatted for over an hour on a video call. After all these years there was still that easy-going, chatty connection we'd had right at the beginning.

———

Chapter 32
Divergence
1981 to 1982

Poem to Jules – 2020

You pull back your curtains
Birds blur the clouds
The scent of wet grass fills the air
Time and space
Separates
Our unhurt laughter

1982 - Jules

For a few months after Jules and I split up I continued to feel emotionally raw, and even a year later when we'd bump into each other, there'd still be a bit of a charge between us. Generally, though, the trajectory was towards recovery where both of us moved on and lived our lives without each other.

1982 – Recovery After Jules

There's often a temptation after a relationship ends to seek solace in the arms, or legs, of someone else, even when we know doing so won't ease the pain for long. In fact, sometimes it just accentuates it. During the first few weeks after we parted, I turned back to Lorna who'd just split up with her new boyfriend. I'm not sure whether it was something physiological or just me telling myself not to do it, but when we kissed, it felt wrong, and this caused me to back off.

Lorna was very pretty, we got on well, and she liked me. It would be tempting to say it was a pity I reacted as I did, but I get the feeling I'd have done so whatever the extenuating circumstances. As you may have already guessed, I was probably more attracted to rejection, so if someone wanted me, that was the kiss of death. It didn't take long for Lorna to realise I wasn't investing much into the relationship, so, each time we met up, things became a little more dislocated and within a week or so it was over.

Untrue Love

People might complain girls are taught to wait for a Prince Charming to rescue them, but likewise, boys believe a fair maiden will bring them true happiness. I wanted to believe in a narrative of love and romance, but if there was anything to take from these times it was the revelation that who I was, did not match up with the dreams I wanted to be a part of.

The question that still perplexes me though is, did I corrupt the path to true love because of who I was, or was my vision of true love too idealistic in the first place? Maybe it was a bit of both?

Leonard Cohen Live in London

If you've never heard Leonard Cohen's introduction to *Ain't No Cure for Love* on the *Live in London* album, then I'd recommend you have a listen. If you'd rather experience what he says afresh without the following 'spoiler' then please skip to the next section. Otherwise, read on.

In the introduction, he tells the audience that it's been a long time since he last performed on stage in London, that it was about 15 years ago when he was 60 years old, just a kid with a crazy dream. The audience laughs. He then discloses that since then he's tried a lot of medications including Prozac, Ritalin, and Focalin as well as studying deeply in the religions and philosophies of the world, but cheerfulness kept breaking through. Nevertheless, there's one thing he says can't easily be contradicted, there ain't no cure for love, and at that point, the band start playing.

1982 – Seventeen

In 1979, a band called The Regents released a song called *Seventeen*. Its first lines declared being seventeen meant not yet being a woman. In a way, the same went for boys, this was still an in-between age. Throughout my teens, I felt as if I was waiting to live, whereas now in my 50s there's a sense of waiting to die.

During the early years of the 1980s, there was a change for good in the air. The music scene was vibrant and outlandish fashion styles danced their way through the streets. Even in Sutton Library, people talked of androgynous guys called Marilyn and Boy George whom they'd met in clubs in London's West End.

After the library closed for the night, those who didn't want to go home right away would head to the Whistle Stop pub which was a short walk away. It was a shadowy place, even on bright sunny afternoons. Daylight barely got two feet through the door before being subdued by darkness, and by sundown, it would often feel as if a dark sea of people was swirling around within. As it turned out this was rather convenient given most of the customers were underage and practically speaking it was Sutton's version of a late teen youth club. The police probably let it be, as it kept the kids off the street and at least it meant they knew where most of the delinquent kids could be found.

1982 – Meeting Julia

Once I'd had my seventeenth birthday my world enlarged. I'd regularly have to take myself up to Roehampton Hospital to get my leg repaired or have fittings for a new one and it was during one of those visits I got talking to a nurse called Julia who invited me to a party she was having at her place that weekend.

A few days later I cycled to Morden Underground station, took my bike on the Tube to Fulham Broadway and then through a cold, rainy Friday night, followed the route I'd marked out in my A-Z map book up to Shepherds Bush Green.

I met up with Julia in a pub where she worked to make ends meet, and at 11 pm she, along with some of her friends and I went to a Chinese restaurant. After the meal, we piled into her place where we chatted until the sun came up, at which point we went to sleep. There wasn't even an inkling of a romantic spark between Julia and me, but she welcomed me wholeheartedly into her world.

In Wallington, my hometown, I was constantly looking for company and was conscious I was a bit of a pest, at least in some people's eyes, but as I was driven by a desperate loneliness, that didn't stop me. A year or so later I'd move away, which allowed me to reinvent myself a little, or at least cast off some of that feeling of being a bother. Someone once told me the famous singer George Michael would often come around to her house when he was a teenager because he felt so alone and needed company. Had I known that when I felt the same, I might not have felt so bad. I may have believed I was doing these less-than-grateful people a favour by ringing their doorbell unexpectedly. After all, if I was to ever become famous, they'd have looked back and been glad of the imposition.

The Fear of 1984

After World War 2 ended, the late 1940s and 1950s were periods of recovery, where the emphasis was on rebalancing the world. For some, there was an aim to take it back to how things had been before, but for others, this was an opportunity to build a brave new world.

By the late 1950s, the pendulum hovered, motionlessly hung in the air for a moment, then through the next decade swung so far in the opposite direction it became known as the swinging 60s. Okay, that's not what that phrase means, but for many people who lived through that period, the '60s saw more social and cultural changes than any other decade in the 20th Century.

As we shall see, from this era onwards there was no going back. Culture wars were declared and through the '70s and beyond the battles continued, however, by the time we got to the '80s, the direction had become much clearer. There was a general acceptance that solving social issues was of paramount importance. The '80s also saw the onset of technology and computers entering our homes and everyday lives. Still, for all the hope that things were changing for the greater good, now, almost 40 years later, there's a sense that something went awry and some of the things forewarned in Orwell's book *1984*, had now come to exist. Somehow, all those roads we'd paved with good intentions had led us to a dangerous arena of division and fear.

1997 - Therapy

Therapist: When they pulled up the tram lines in London, it felt symbolic to me. It was as if the clear guidelines that society followed disappeared too. It was both frightening and freeing at the same time. It was as if we were entering an unknown world.

524

1982 - Wilson's School – General Studies

After my O-level results had come through in the summer of 1981 some of the teachers were just as surprised at how well I'd done as I was. One of them whom I particularly liked, Mr Jenkins, said of my success, "I guess miracles do happen after all."

The headmaster, who had always been somewhat aloof, not just to me, but to everyone, decided to take a small group of us once a week for General Studies. This could be on any subject, so for instance, one week we might be looking at architectural styles, and the next the issue of the global North-South divide. In one, we looked at cryptic crosswords, which I aptly renamed Kryptonite crosswords because I would fall to pieces as soon as I came into contact with them.

One of the lessons he taught us that came in very useful and stuck in my mind ever since was about ideologies. His main theme that day was the assumptions made within the foundations of most ideologies, once accepted, make arguing against them very difficult. Therefore, it's these initial assumptions that should be most focused on when trying to assess an ideology's value. He also pointed out that most systems when put into practice meet challenges their creators never envisioned, and consequently, they tend to fail in many ways, especially when they start trying to "fix" those challenges.

1982 - On the Buses

Between school and home was the bus journey. Unlike other bus journeys, this one not only included other kids from Wilson's whom I wouldn't normally have interacted with but also pupils from other schools. Highview was a school situated a few hundred metres from Wilson's, so there'd be a few co-travellers with us from there. One called Brenda would often sit with me and have a chat on the way home. There were a few times when to a chorus of "ooh" from my schoolmates she'd give me a snog. Maybe she felt sorry for me, maybe she just liked kissing me, I wasn't too worried about her motivations, there was never any promise of anything more, it was a 'this is happening now... enjoy it' moment.

As the bus journey would get closer to Wallington High Street loads of girls from Wallington Girls School would jump on, and there'd often be continuations of previously abruptly paused conversations from the day before, the giving of Christmas, Birthday and Valentine's cards as well as the resumption of the occasional feud.

While we connect eras in our lives to certain buildings, it's easy to forget how often transient settings act as backdrops to our lives too. Buses, trains, tubes, bus stops, platforms, waiting rooms, cars, parks and streets all play their part. These were our 'between worlds'.

Some of the buses and most of the trains we rode were of old stock that still had the feel of the 1940s, although the buses we took to school were quite modern at the time. You'd get on at the front, show the driver your pass or pay for your journey then get off via the middle doors. But as you got closer to the centre of London it would be far more likely you'd hop on an old bus via the continuously open doorway and platform at the back. Once on, you'd be bathed in yellow light from little bulbs which had a theatre dressing room feel to them. Soon after sitting down, if you could, a bus conductor would sway in front of you, maybe dance a few steps to keep their balance, and as they took the money, they'd give back a ticket in return from a steampunk-like machine strapped to their torso.

Diary entries:

Tuesday the 2nd of March 1982: On the way home from Roehampton Hospital, the bus conductress looked me straight in the eyes, it sent a shiver up my spine. She gave me a lovely smile.

Tuesday the 4th May 1982: On the way to school, I saw Penny and Hazel, and as usual, we had a giggle. Well, it's better than admiring dirty windows or looking at one's reflection.

1982 - Lessons in Belief

In one of our English literature lessons, our teacher told us we were naive because while we could criticise our government, what difference did it make? We all nodded in agreement. But now, in 2021, my opinion has settled somewhere between his and our naïve ones. There are indeed lots of barriers to changing our world, especially the political one, but things do change, both dramatically and not so. Some for better and some for worse, and partly because of or despite our actions. While we were naïve back then he may also have been somewhat jaded.

Although teachers were not supposed to bring their political or religious beliefs into the classroom, by the time we hit the sixth form they certainly did. Whether this was because we became more interested in politics and therefore provoked such discussions, or the teachers felt freer to bring up the subjects, it's hard to know. Either way, politics and religion became common topics within our daily lives both in and out of the classroom.

One day, in another English Literature class, we were studying a section of Virginia Woolf's book, *To the Lighthouse.* The bit we focused on was about religion. Woolf was an atheist and at one point in the text we were reading, it was inferred that believing in God was something one should grow out of. This stuck in my mind, not because it was logically argued well but because it made me think that anyone who believed in God was immature, at least academically.

Even though our teacher, pointed out that logic and faith by definition can't always come together, spiritual belief is probably in our blood. After the lesson one of my friends, Cameron, and I discussed some of the central issues around belief. Even though I felt I was winning the logical arguments, he told me he wanted to become a Church of England priest. Now, four decades later, I'm still a "think agnostic, feel spiritual" person and he's a bishop.

After school that day I stopped off at one of my friends who lived on Roundshaw. My friend wasn't in, but her mum invited me in for a cup of tea. At one point, she mentioned God, so, trying to sound clever and mature I said, "Surely, we've all grown out of believing in fairy tales such as God".

My friend's mum, I'll call her Paula, looked at me and then in a raised voice said, "I don't know what they teach you at that school. How can you talk in such an arrogant way?"

I was a bit shocked and knew this was not going to bode well in terms of my chances of ever going out with her daughter, who I had fancied since I was eight. I stuttered, "Well, I didn't mean to be arrogant, it's just there's no way there's an old man in the sky, or a Heaven in the clouds, or Hell beneath the earth, or Adam and Eve starting off humanity. And, and..." I hesitated slightly as I could see these arguments were not helping matters, they were not helping one bit. Her face was red, and she shook as she glared at me harder than I ever thought was humanly possible.

"And," I bravely or stupidly went on, "if there is a God, why would he allow such suffering just so he can get us to become perfect again?"

At that moment, my mind went ahead to the wedding I'd always dreamt of between me and her daughter, and there on the main table Paula did not look happy about our union, in fact, she looked like thunder. I came back to reality, and the same thunderous face was still looking at me.

I was rather hoping for a calm counterargument, but instead, she asked me in an "I'm still really angry with you, tone", "If you're so sure about there not being a God, then how do you think the universe got started? And if you're so sure there's not a God, then prove it to me, you can't, can you? Just because the Bible stories may not stand up to scientific scrutiny, doesn't mean there isn't a God, does it?"

Trying to calm the situation I conceded, "Well I can't prove it, that's the point, it's about belief."

"Exactly!" she exclaimed, "So, if it's about belief why are you trying to make it sound like only idiots believe in God? I'm disgusted by what that school's done to you Simon, I'm so disappointed."

I hated anyone using the, "I'm very disappointed in you" line, mainly because it was easily the best way to get my eyes to well up with tears. Well, at least it did so until I became so bad that I was more disappointed with myself than anyone else could ever be. For a moment, I wanted to explain that Virginia Woolf had made me say it, but I didn't think that would help either. So, I went quiet and left soon after.

About 30 years later I met up with Paula, her husband and their daughter, the love of my early teenage life, for a reunion meal. Near the end of our meeting, I started to tell a joke then interrupted myself with, "Maybe I shouldn't tell this as you might not get it as it's for people who have had therapy."

Paula leaned back slightly, nodded then encouraged me with, "Go on, try us".

"Okay," I said, "Okay, how many psychoanalysts does it take to put a light bulb in?"

"I don't know," she said.

"Two," I said, "One to put the bulb in and the other one to hold my cock, I mean my mother, I mean the ladder."

They laughed politely and we carried on chatting. As we walked to our cars, I looked at the woman who'd been the girl I fancied. She was a lot taller than me and just on that level, I realised my teenage ambitions had been a little too lofty, let alone all the other reasons I'd have never been the one for her. I remotely lowered the roof of my car, but no one was impressed.

A few years after that I sent them all Facebook friend requests which were never accepted, although one of her brothers, whom I was always very fond of, as I was of all of them, did. But I knew, okay I believed, that somewhere in all of that was the remnants of that argument and how I'd become quite unlikeable in their eyes.

1982 - Girl Friends

The types of relationships I had with girls and women varied greatly during 1982. Firstly, I stepped away from trying to have intense romantic connections. Yes, it was my choice, okay it wasn't my first choice, but, okay then, it wasn't my choice at all. Secondly, I began to develop a few non-romantic friendships and thirdly, I started to get involved in sexual situations with girls/women who I realised either before or after things happened, I didn't want to get emotionally involved with in any serious way, whether they did or not. In the poem I mentioned in the previous chapter, *Words Without a Story*, by Adrian Henri, the narrator describes all the things he'll do to capture the heart of his beloved, but once they'd 'rolled amongst the galaxies' he becomes aware of a 'distant star', and soon after, rejects her. This was the place I found myself too, I was lost in space where yearning for someone and then no longer desiring them after we got up to something, was new to me. Even though I knew it didn't help in terms of gaining a long-term deep and meaningful relationship, nor was it particularly nice for the other party, especially if they wanted more. None of that stopped me from getting caught up in the same dynamic repeatedly for years to come. Was it because there was something wrong with me, or was this the way of the world? It's true there are probably a lot of dynamics going on within the process of falling in lust and then pulling away. And there might be a dark side to them too, but I can't help but think of the Woody Allen lines about casual sex being a meaningless experience, but as meaningless experiences go, it's a pretty good one. And you wonder why I ended up in therapy.

2021 - From Paris with Love

I'm listening to Melody Gardot singing her song, *From Paris with Love*. She sings of lovers falling in love like they fall out of bed.

Interested In

When someone says they're "interested in" someone, the primary meaning of this phrase is they're interested in developing a romantic/sexual relationship with them. Consequently, this involves showing an interest in who they are, and what they say, do, think and feel.

With Jules, I hung on to every word she uttered. But was I genuinely interested in her? I may have been, but then how could I know given I was so 'interested in her' romantically?

Of course, this is probably the same for most of us, but once we begin to realise this is going on we can admit to ourselves that a more realistic relationship between us and our lovers may take some time to get to. Likewise, when we lose interest in someone, it may not mean they're no longer interesting, but instead, no matter what they do, we will not be interested, especially if we've become 'interested in' someone else.

July 1981- Photography

I've been interested in taking photographs since I was five years old. There was something about capturing an instant that seemed deeply important to me. Even now if I meet someone I connect with, albeit very slightly, I find it almost unbearable not to have some way of getting in contact with them again if ever I'd like to. It was the same with memories and moments in time, photography became a way to hold on to them.

As I began to become more involved in art, I realised that just like telling a story, it's the way images are presented that makes them interesting. So, everywhere I went I took my new second-hand, bottom-of-the-line, Chinon CS SLR with me and to top it off, to the untrained eye, it made me look like a photographer who knew what they were doing.

1981 - Anya Part 1

I had originally considered placing Anya's story in an earlier chapter as it started in the summer of 1981. However, given it illustrates my divergence from a more romantic path, it made it far more relevant for this chapter.

The main part of Anya's story started about four months before I met Jules. Looking back on it now, my life changed considerably during those six months. At 16, I could still frequent playgrounds and act in a far more childlike way than I could at 17. It was as if the relationship with Jules was the watershed between feeling wholly disconnected and yearning for a relationship to save me, and realising that there were other connections to be made in life that were just as significant in their way. Even so, in my new incarnation, there was still plenty of scope to make connections in not-so-meaningful ways too.

Meeting Anya – Tuesday 18th August 1981

Sunil and I had gone to the recreation ground in Carshalton Park where we met his friends Colin and Paul. Colin had a perfect Elvis quiff, every time I looked at it, I felt a bit of quiff envy. He also had a big Rock n' Roll Jacket, it wasn't leather, but he still looked the part. Paul was very tall, well-built, and had bright ginger hair. He seemed a bit of a gentle giant, a little depressed and slightly dislocated, but then none of us seemed to fit together outside of being misfits. We were a gang of slightly too old teenagers hanging around the playground and would've normally had little time for each other, but the empty spaces around us pushed us together. Having my camera with me seemed to set me apart though, it made me feel like a not-present observer. My arms probably set me apart a little too, but I'd forgotten all about them.

Nearby a couple of girls were sitting on the children's roundabout chatting while slowly pushing it around with their feet. A small child waited patiently for them to get off, but they weren't going to, so, after a few minutes, he got on anyway and started to push it faster. The girls pushed their shoes to the ground to hinder his efforts while nonchalantly chatting.

Sunil knew one of the girls and nodded knowingly at one of them while quietly saying, "See the one with ginger hair, she's up for it."

Quiff Boy Colin quipped, "How do you know? Have you got off with her then?"

"Nah, mate," Sunil laughed as if he wouldn't touch her with a barge pole.

"Well, how do you know then?" Colin asked again.

Sunil nodded sagely, "I hear things."

We could've been in an American teenage gangster film if the sky hadn't been so overcast.

"I'll call them over. You'll see."

Sunil then shouted, "Hey, Jacqui, come over here!"

"Fuck off!" came the reply.

Sunil leapt off his swing, "Let's go and chat with them."

So, we coolly dismounted from our swings too and ambled towards them.

"You got a fag?" Sunil asked.

Jacqui flicked ash from her cigarette. "I don't smoke."

He smiled. "I don't either".

We all climbed on the roundabout and started to push it in the opposite direction. It came to an ominous stop for a moment then started to move.

"Don't go fast," Jacqui shouted.

The little kid's eyes lit up as he barked, "Go fast, go fast!"

We all held on tight and put our heads near the middle to make it more bearable while Paul and Sunil pushed it faster. I could feel a slight sense of nausea.

The other girl a bit angrily shouted, "Fucking hell, I feel sick, can you stop please?"

As it slowed down, she looked at me. She was tall, had long dark hair, and was slightly Indian or Middle Eastern looking.

"What's your name then, Mr photographer?"

I looked up at her.

"Simon. What's yours?"

"Anya."

I took a photograph of her and the others.

"Oi! I didn't give you permission." Her voice was raised enough for me to be a bit worried.

I paused for a second, "I don't need it, we're in a public place." (The finer points of the law might have pointed out that the land was council-owned, but I didn't want to get into that.)

Frowning a little she pointed at me, "Well it better look good or else I'm gonna sue you."

"How could it not look good?" I replied.

She laughed, "Such a charmer." She squinted slightly as she looked into my eyes. Then she looked up at everyone and asked, "Do you lot wanna come back to my house, my mum's not going to be back for a few hours, we can have some toast?"

The little kid shouted 'Yes", to which nearly all of us said, "Not you!" in unison. And so, with the little kid looking at us like a forlorn abandoned pet fading into the distance, we made our way to Anya's.

1981 – 18th August – Anya's Place

We all crammed into Anya's bedroom, the walls were cluttered with posters and pink and blue tiny flower-patterned wallpaper. A few minutes later Jacqui and Anya come in with some mugs of tea, a plate full of white bread toast soaked in butter and a jar of marmite.

Now before we go any further, I just want to point out that if you find the following dialogue a bit naff, it's not a weakness in my writing skills but is accurate to the kind of conversations we, as slightly socially dislocated teenagers who'd watched too much of the TV programme Grange Hill, had in the 1980s.

Sunil pursed his lips, and cocked his head up slightly, "So, you got a boyfriend Jacqui?".

"Yeah, I 'av."

"Wa's 'is name then?"

"Why, don't you believe me?"

"Yeah," he paused, "just wondering if I know 'im."

"Nah, you won't know him, he's at college, e's a man, not a boy."

Paul, who had been silent since we arrived, made an, "ooh" sound, then went quiet again.

"I'm a man," Sunil, irritated paused again, "I'll prove it if you want."

Jacqui laughed, "Yeah, you'd love to try. I bet".

"Don't flatter yourself," Sunil said, raising one side of his top lip. As he looked a little like Elvis, albeit an Indian one, I had a slight moment of curled-lip envy.

Anya decided to take things on a different tack.

"I just got a new guitar, can anyone sing?"

"Simon can do a good Elvis," Sunil said laughing as he offered me up for sacrifice.

Colin looked a bit put out, to my delight.

"Oh, that's good, I've got an Elvis song in my guitar book."

She pulled out a 'Start Playing the Guitar' pamphlet and strummed a few chords from, *Can't Help Falling in Love*. Her playing was stilted and slightly out of tune, but I sang a few lines, while at the same time eating toast.

Big Paul started clapping, demanding an encore.

So, we did.

I grabbed my camera and took a photograph of her playing.

"Wow," Anya looked at me, "you're brilliant, don't you think so Jax?"

Jacqui politely nodded in a direction not discernible by the naked eye. Anya stood up and started clearing away the plates and mugs, and along with Jacqui took them downstairs. After they'd been gone a while Sunil turned to Colin, "Well, what do you think then? I don't like the look of your one mate."

Colin laughed, made a face back at Sunil and said, "I don't like the look of yours".

"No mate," Sunil shook his head, "Can't you tell, Jacqui's well inta me."

Colin looked incredulously at Sunil, "Yeah right, you're fuckin well deluded".

"Who's deluded?" Anya asked as she came back into the room unexpectedly.

"Sunil is, he thinks he's got a chance with Jacqui." Paul chirped in.

Anya nodded her head from side to side, "Hold on, I'll find out."

She walked out of the room and shouted down to Jacqui who was still in the kitchen. "Has Sunil got a chance of getting off with you Jax?"

Jacqui shouted back laughing "Yeah, I'd give him one, one in a million."

Sunil smiled optimistically, "See, you heard her, she'd give me one."

Shaking her head even more vigorously this time, Anya sighed "Yep, you're deluded, mate". Then gesticulated for everyone to get up, as it was time to go.

"Anyway, c'mon, my mum's gonna be back soon so you better all go otherwise she's gonna have a right ol' go."

As we all got ready, and the others went ahead, Anya asked me for my phone number, which was a bit of a new one for me. "Why don't you come round and we can do some music together." She suggested.

"Yeah, that sounds like a good idea," I said smiling and feeling buoyant. I went home. It'd been a good day.

1st September 1981 - Anya – Night Out

A few weeks later Anya and I met up.

"What do you want to do?" I asked.

"Let's go to the cinema," she said excitedly.

So, we went to the one in Sutton, where a film called "Outland" was on. After about 15 minutes Anya leant towards me and quietly whispered. "This is shit, let's get out of here."

I nodded in agreement and as we walked out, I asked what she fancied doing.

"Let's go up to London," her face beamed a big smile.

"And do what?" I asked.

"Walk around a bit then come back home." She looked like a prisoner who'd just escaped.

"Okay," I said while thinking, "Well, it's not like I've got anything better to do."

We took the bus to Morden Tube station then the Underground up to Leicester Square and just as planned, we walked amongst the crowds and the dodgy street vendors. After an hour of sitting on benches, and walking and talking, we headed back home on the Underground. As the train swayed us from side to side, Anya, who was sitting opposite me, told me all about a great new band called The Jam who she'd seen a few times. As she talked wildly about them, she put her foot gently between my legs. I didn't feel any in-love feelings towards her, but she turned me on.

1981 - Don't Listen to Me Fa Fa Fa Fa Fashion

I hadn't listened to The Jam because I was a rocker and that style of music belonged to The Mods who were technically Rockers' enemies and had been for decades. The '60s, '70s and '80s were especially full of rivalry and conflict associated with musical styles. Was it partly because once army conscription ended, the pent-up energy and anger of young men had to be redirected somehow, or was it just due to tribal tendencies? Whatever was behind it, the music world was extremely demarcated into style-related camps, of which you were only supposed to choose one, and from then on, all others were off-limits. Well, at least that was the rule for teenagers. The rules would come to change as you got older. At that point, you'd be allowed to like a variety of styles, but even then, some were still off-limits. If you listened to them, you were very, very uncool.

The world was much more demarcated back then. For Catholics or Protestants going into each other's churches was still a big issue. It was the same in the art world where similar snobberies existed, maybe even more so. In turn, they partly related to education which also relates to class. If you were working class, ballet, opera and classical music would most likely feel alien as would conceptual and abstract art. Similarly, listening to music your parents listened to was also a no-no. Music was, and still is, a fashion victim, no matter how great or rubbish it ever is or was.

In the late '70s and '80s, there were a lot of developments in the music world. It was partly driven by technological advances (synthesisers, drum machines, samplers, digital recording and music technology becoming available to more

534

people). But by the mid-1990s there were very few new significant stylistic developments within the music world. Other things had a big effect, such as home studios, MP3 files and the Internet. But since then, while there have been many fantastic artists, I can't think of any great new musical styles. Can you?

In the early '80s music was a big part of people's lives, there were loads of new sounds and even I started to allow myself to listen to many other artists apart from Elvis and Dire Straits. Music would continue to fill my life, not just for the sake of filling an empty space but because it was full of nourishment for body, mind, heart and soul. Even if music echoed the pain in us, it also made it clear that such pain is an important part of our lives and shouldn't always be avoided. Music was, for many of us, our 'safe space' where we could open our hearts to our deepest joys and sorrows.

September 1981 - Anya – Shouting Quietly

A few days after our night out I spoke to Sunil who told me Anya wanted me to be her boyfriend. I knew he wasn't joking as she'd made it quite clear to me already, however, even though she had a fantastic body and was good-looking looking it didn't feel right to me.

I wondered what it would feel like to her if I were to say I didn't want to go out with her. I knew what it was like to feel rejected and didn't want someone else to feel the same way. Even so, I decided that the next time I saw her I'd tell her. The only thing about that was, I hadn't considered she'd be with her friend Jacqui. So, instead, I ended up inviting them both in and we had lunch together, after which they went off without me. By this point, I was almost in a state of despair, so I phoned Anya and asked if she'd pop around the next day. She said she would but when the time came, she called to cancel. I squirmed when she said, "Don't worry my love, I'll see you tomorrow." Well, she probably didn't say those exact words, but whatever she did say, that's what I heard.

Finally, a few days later she invited me around to her place. I went there ready to deliver the 'bad news' and just when I got the courage to tell her, she started snogging me, which I found quite a turn-on, so I thought to myself, 'Well, c'mon, there's no rush is there?' and didn't attempt to push her away.

Of course, I kicked myself for not telling her when I got back home. 'What was I playing at?' I shouted to myself, very quietly. This was going to be a conversation I would end up repeating many times throughout my life. Still, I vowed I'd tell her the next time we met. What I didn't count on was that she didn't get in contact with me for another month, by which point I couldn't see the harm in meeting up. Part of me, yes, we know which part, hoped she might like the idea of meeting occasionally for a snog and not want any more commitment than that. This time though, things were a bit different.

Instead of trying to have a kiss she just wanted to chat. Just as I got ready to go, I thought, 'I won't bother coming again', but then she asked if she could borrow my poetry book, saying she'd return it a few days later (which she didn't). However, a week later she phoned to see if I'd like to go to London with her again, but my leg was very sore so I couldn't. Another week passed, and this time I called her and asked if it was okay for me to pop around to get my poetry book back. She said yes, but when I got there, there was no answer. As you can imagine I was a little pissed off. I walked back home and called her to find out what was going on. She said she couldn't have heard the doorbell. I was adamant that next time I saw her I would blank her.

A few days later I was in Carshalton High Street, and just as I came out of the bank she passed by. I so wanted to blank her but instead, I merrily said, "Hi Anya."

"Oh! Hi Simon. Sorry about the other night, I can't believe I didn't hear the doorbell. I bet you were annoyed. I am sorry."

I smiled, "Oh, it's okay, these things happen. Don't worry, I completely understand."

About a week later I went to her place where I drew a picture of Paul Weller, the lead singer from The Jam. We had a good chat, and she gave me my poetry book back and showed me a letter from a friend of hers saying they liked some of my poems. And that was the last time I saw Anya until I decided to get in contact one lonely day six months later.

March 1982 - Anya

At the beginning of March, I was still yearning to hear from Jules and hoping against all odds that she'd come back to me. In my diary, there were pages of my angsty bullshit, self-pity and even more self-delusion than I tell myself nowadays. But for all of that, it didn't take me long at all to firstly approach Lorna, and then Anya. It wasn't that I was trying to replace Jules, I was just trying to avoid the pain of grieving by creating periods where I could forget her. I started to use sexual behaviour as a kind of analgesic, just as someone might do with alcohol or drugs. It was a cocktail of socialising and sexualising. Previously I'd just been a habitual user of the socialising drug, but now I'd moved on to this harder combination.

Halfway through March, I met up with Anya, who I probably bored stiff talking about my break-up and how upset I was. She was very sympathetic and had her mum's boyfriend not been in the room next to us, may have consoled me further with her beautiful breasts. But nothing happened. A week later I called Anya, and she said I could come around but as she was going to be out for a little while would leave a key out for me, so I could let myself in, which I did. After a few hours, she

536

still hadn't turned up, so I went home feeling annoyed. I called her the next day and had a go at her which she didn't react well to. "I've just about had enough of her mucking me about," I thought to myself.

The next time I felt I needed a distraction, I didn't bother calling Anya, instead, I went to see Lorna. Things between her and I soured quickly once we both sensed there was a dislocation. So, after a couple of weeks, I finally recognised I had to be strong and face the situation head-on and start to heal or be weak and keep finding solace in the arms of an analgesic situation. So, one Friday evening at the beginning of April I decided not to go to karate and instead visit Anya. Things didn't go to plan though as she had some friends pop around, so, it ended up as just a social event but as consolations go, I was happy with that. The distraction had been enough to help me get through a difficult evening. Still, for Anya, this may have come across as me being interested in a boyfriend/girlfriend relationship with her because a week later she invited me around in the daytime when her mum was out.

When I got to her place, Anya greeted me wrapped in a purple towel. "Sorry," she said, I'm not quite ready."

"Oh, okay, sorry about that," I said.

She started walking upstairs, looked over her shoulder and said, "It's okay, you can come upstairs."

So, I obediently followed her to her room. She started drying her hair while talking with me. I couldn't hear what she was saying properly, so she stopped the hairdryer and walked over to where I was sitting on her bed. She let her wet hair touch my head and face. I looked up at her. She then leaned down and kissed me.

"Do you want to see my body?" she whispered.

Trying not to sound too eager I whispered/stammered, "Yes," Then, trying not to show I was going to gulp, I gulped.

She stood upright and slowly undid her towel.

She had very long legs and large breasts. She kissed me again and then lay down on her bed. I stood up took my T-shirt off then as quickly and un-seductively as possible took off my trousers and my prosthetic foot. I don't think she was too bothered about any of that though. I lay down next to her, and we started to kiss and touch each other. This was my first fully naked experience with a woman. Even though she was 17, as far as I was concerned, she was a woman.

For many of us, there's a change in our lovemaking as we become more experienced where the focus on what we're doing changes into what I would describe as entering a lower conscious dreamy world of connection. It's hard to describe it, but it is as if we enter a dimension in which our archetypes live, but instead of being scary it's enrapturing. Well, this was not one of those occasions. I wanted to lose myself in kissing her body, but instead, I tried to be a good lover. So, I kissed her between her legs because I was sure that's what a lot of women would like, even if I wasn't aware of the finer points of such things. Fortunately, for both of us, she reacted well, telling me how lovely it was and after a while, she told me she'd come. She then pulled me up to her, so we were face to face. "Do you want to fuck me?" She said wrapping her legs around me. I said yes.

Slowly I pushed my penis towards her vagina. But instead of it going in I felt a painful sensation, so stopped pushing. "I don't think I can," I said.

"It's okay, it's okay," she said. "This is nice, just hold me."

We started to kiss again, and I rubbed my penis on her thigh.

"Let me hold it," she said.

So, I sat up and she placed her fingers around it and gently pulled downwards on it.

"Ouch," I flinched.

She let go. "What's wrong?" she said looking at me like she'd done something awful.

I wasn't sure but I suggested that if she didn't pull my foreskin back it shouldn't hurt.

"Like this?" She asked as tenderly as her fingers touched me.

"Yes, that's nice," I said, moving towards her to kiss her again.

Within a short while, I ejaculated and some of the semen fell right between her legs. I immediately panicked and as romantically as possible grabbed her pyjamas which were lying on her bed and tried to wipe it away.

Within that moment of coming my whole being seemed to change. Firstly, I was worried about even the slightest risk of getting her pregnant, and secondly, I didn't want to be close to her anymore. It was as if someone had pressed a button and my real feelings had been released while those pretend ones, the ones that feigned interest, evaporated into the universe, forever gone. Only, as I would find out in time, they were never gone for long and often I'd come to wonder which set of feelings and thoughts were my true ones. But at this moment, I was introduced to just how split I was when it came to these sexual situations.

These wouldn't be the only type of sexual scenarios I would find myself in, but they were ones I'd repeat continually throughout my life. There were many other times when I didn't want to pull away after I'd orgasmed, but as I was to find out later these would most likely be with women who I'd want to be with properly, only to find that they weren't into me as much as I was them. So, maybe subconsciously I'd picked that up, so it allowed me to feel connected because I knew it was still part of the pursuer-distancer dynamic which I seemed so attached to. Or it could be something else, for instance, maybe deep down I did believe they were the one, but I would later come to sabotage the situation as I couldn't deal with such a balanced relationship.

Anyway, this was my introduction to a part of myself I hadn't previously known existed, and it did not fit neatly with my beliefs about romantic relationships, at all.

April 1982 - Regret

For the next week, I felt very worried that I might have impregnated Anya. No matter how unlikely it could be, there was still a microscopic chance, and that played on my mind. "From now on I'm going to be damn careful," I told myself. Okay, it's easy to laugh now, but at that moment I meant it. I hadn't got my head around just how easy it is to go against our principles when lust raises its head.

I wrote in my diary, 'If she's pregnant I may as well have no legs either as I won't be going anywhere. I'd be damned on earth.' I was so worried that for a few days, I flagellated myself (metaphorically speaking – I'm not that kinky). I went to the park and thought hard about not only being more careful but putting more important things ahead of sex, which no longer seemed worth the hassle. 'It's time to move on.' I wrote 'Get that Brown Belt, finish unfinished work, practice painting, and focus on my schoolwork'.

About two weeks later, I spoke to Anya on the phone. She wasn't pregnant. It was then I truly understood the significance of the grand celebrations at the end of some of the Star Wars movies, as well as how people felt when they reached for the heavens in films and shouted "Freedom." Five days later Anya asked if I wanted to come around. I said yes. We ended up in bed. But this time I made sure I didn't come anywhere near her vagina. That night though, her mother rang me up. I wasn't in at the time, so Mum took the call. Anya's mother said I wasn't to see her anymore. Anya had left some incriminating evidence which meant her mother worked out what we'd been up to, and that I was a bad influence. My mother said, "It takes two to tango," and things got left like that. Yet again it was the parents who brought one of my relationships to an end. But this time I was slightly relieved. It gave me an excuse to get out of a relationship I knew wasn't good for either of us. Without rejecting Anya directly, it also gave me a bit of kudos, at least in my deluded mind, and Mum's, who thought it was quite funny. Still, I felt bad for Anya, so I wrote her a letter and asked one of her friends to pass it on to her. Her friend asked me why I got off with Anya if I wasn't that interested in her. I replied, "I don't know, I ask myself the same question." The simple answer was because I'm somewhat of a prick, but, well there may be other reasons too, but that'd be a whole other book, and the prick answer does the job for most people.

Last Call for Anya

About a month later Anya called me, she told me she loved me and asked if I felt the same. I said I didn't so she told me to fuck off and slammed the phone down. That was the last time we saw or spoke to each other, well, at least, for the next thirty-three years.

2015 - Anya

I was scanning some of my old photographs and came across the photos I took of Anya the first time we met, the ones in the recreational ground, and the one of her playing the guitar in her room. It didn't take long to find her on Facebook. She's got grown-up kids of her own now, in fact, she has grandkids too. When I first contacted her she wrote, "Your name doesn't ring any bells but it was a long, long time ago. LOL". I then described what I looked like and she remembered me. She's still very involved in listening to music but I'm not sure if she'll ever listen to the songs I didn't write about her or even remember not to forget me again.

April 1982 - Anya – Poem

Here's a poem I wrote about Anya back then:

In her arms
I may lay using
And in hers
I will dream
The most precious meanings
Catch me
On black and yellow days
Such as these

Moving On – Girl Friends (Part 2)

By late April I had recovered from the emotional wreckage of being in my version of Romeo and Juliet with Jules. Outside of what had gone on with Anya, I tended to be mainly interested in girls for friendship. Some people believe that it's very difficult for men and women to be friends, however, if at least one of the two is uninterested in the other then that makes the possibility of friendship far greater. Most of the time the girls I became friends with were the ones who were uninterested in the other person (i.e. me). But that often did the trick as far as I was concerned. As long as they didn't show any interest in me, I wouldn't get my hopes up, well, not normally.

Jackie and Other Girl Friends

In one of the life drawing classes I went to at SCOLA, there was a girl called Jackie. She was very polite, considerate and pretty. She was also very careful not to show anything but friendliness towards me. One day, after the class finished, she invited me to her home where I was welcomed to stay for dinner. At the table was her father who was a university professor, her very friendly mother and her two extremely characterful sisters, plus a few other family friends. This was something that I could only dream of in terms of an image of family life. Of course, I didn't know what their life was really like, but in terms of an image, it was ideal.

Maybe because Jackie had a boyfriend that made it even easier to see her as a friend only. In terms of building up a pool of "girlfriends" who I wasn't romantically involved with, Jackie was one of the first who I'd see quite a bit and have a relaxed relationship with. It wasn't a big friendship, but there was a sense of being comfortable around each other, and this added a dimension of connection to my life that had been lacking previously.

When it came to female relationships the graduations between the types that existed in my life started to become much subtler. Previously, after I hit puberty, there had been girls I was interested in, most of whom were not interested back, pen friends, girls I chatted to on the bus, and, girls I'd known as a child who I thought might be worth chatting up but soon found out that they felt very let down when I did. So, while a part of me used women for my sexual gratification, other parts started to have genuine friendships with them. As these new relationships became a bigger part of my life, I realised the value of having opposite-sex friendships, but, as I was to find out in time, not everyone would be comfortable with that.

1982 - Voyeurism

One night as I went to close the curtains to the front room, I noticed the new neighbours across the street in their un-curtained bedroom. I quickly switched the lights off, came back to the window and pulled the curtains almost shut, leaving a gap between them big enough to look through.

The new neighbours seemed to have forgotten they were potentially on stage to the likes of me. I waited, hoping to see the woman getting undressed. Given I must have seen tens of women naked in real life already, especially in life-drawing classes, you'd have thought I wouldn't be interested in seeing another one, especially from such a distance, but I was.

At one point the woman switched off the light, much to my disappointment, but there was still some light coming through the doorway from their hallway. As she came out of the darkness, I could see her in silhouette. My heart rushed a little even though I wasn't sure if she was naked. As it turned out, I wasn't the only one wondering. At that very moment, the boys who lived two doors up from me turned on a very powerful torch from their attic room and pointed it straight at the silhouetted woman's body.

I'm not sure if she noticed. But I didn't see her moving into view again. I couldn't help but burst out laughing at the audacity of my watch-tower neighbours, even if it was just their way of welcoming the new neighbours to the hood.

Summer 1982 - Routine

My life followed an almost regimented routine by 1982. I'd get up late, as usual, chat at the bus stop with Sunil, get the bus to school, and talk to loads of people on the bus. At school, there'd be an assembly, then I'd go up to the sixth form centre, have a cup of coffee made with coffee mate milk powder and loads of sugar, then off to a class if I had one, or spend time either studying or chatting if I had a free period. In the mid-morning break, I'd probably help keep order near the tuck shop and demand a few sweets from those who'd bought too many for their own good.

The second half of the morning would follow a similar pattern to the first, but during the lunch hour, there'd be a 30-minute karate training session, usually in the gym storage cupboard. The sessions were intense, often including a thousand kicks or something else that'd test us, and then we'd all go for a quick lunch together.

The afternoon would be a repeat of the morning, bar the tuck shop break but if there weren't any lessons, I'd get out of school early. Then I'd either go home, or to WH Smiths in Wallington to buy a record, or to Sutton Library for a bit of social-ising studies, or to SCOLA for an art class.

At least twice a week I'd go to karate at either Tweeddale or Westcroft. The latter had a bar, so after the training session, I'd join the other trainees there for a drink of orange and soda water and a chat.

Outside of this routine, I'd meet up with friends, or stay home where I'd listen to music, watch TV and most likely argue with John. Sometimes an opportunity to break the routine would arise, such as going up to London to see Julia, the nurse I'd met at Roehampton, and it was during one of these adventures I went from being a boy to becoming a...

15th of May 1982 – Eileen S

Julia lived in Sinclair Mansions, which was a red brick tenement-style building on a quiet road at the back of Shepherds Bush Shopping Centre. Once through the main ominous door, I'd have to go up a couple of flights of stairs to a flat Julia shared with three other people.

This time I rang the doorbell and a short while later a stranger opened the door. There was a sudden sound of music, chatting and laughter. A guy with spikey hair stood there, looked me up and down and said, "Hi, are you here for the party?"

"Yes," I said, "I'm a friend of Julia's."

"Oh, come in sweetheart," he said while grabbing and pulling me in.

"Julia, Julia," he shouted, "You've got a visitor."

Julia came over, cuddled me and said, "C'mon I'll get you a drink and introduce you to a few people."

She poured me a plastic cup of cider, which I made last a few hours, (I hadn't quite got the knack of wanting to get drunk) and spent the night chatting with everyone I could. This was a whole new world to me, but in a way, I still felt more like an observer than a participant.

There was music, but not a lot of dancing, it was more a case of small groups of people standing and chatting together while wriggling to the beat. There was one woman there with blue hair and loads of dark makeup around her eyes. To me, she was stunning-looking. For this, I could probably blame the film, 'Carry on Screaming' in which Fenella Fielding played a vamp comic femme-fatale. From the moment I saw her in it I had a bit of a thing for vamp-looking women... I had my camera with me so took a few photos of the party including one of the blue-haired woman, but either I was too scared to talk to her, or she wasn't having any of it when I did.

One of my other enduring memories from the party was chatting to a bloke and his wife, then a bit later watching him pass his number surreptitiously to another woman. I couldn't help but feel sorry for his wife. I was still quite idealistic when it came to relationships even though I was already witnessing my fall from grace.

The party went on till about 5 am, at which point there were just a few people left. I was supposed to have slept in one of Julia's flatmates' bedrooms, but all the occupants' bedrooms were otherwise engaged, so, I was shown how to set up the sofa bed and left to my own devices.

I started to get the bed sorted out when a woman came out of the bathroom. She was about 34, my height, had long black hair and wore a long hippie-styled skirt and a light loose-fitting blouse. She looked at me looking at her.

"Do you want me to help you with that darling?" she asked.

"Erm, okay, I was only shown how to do it a few minutes ago but I've forgotten already."

She laughed, "Have you had too much to drink?"

I stood up straight and turned towards her. "No, I don't drink".

She came over to the sofa bed instead of helping to unfold it sat down and patted the seat next to her.

"That's a bit strange, not drinking I mean," she said, "What's your name then?"

"Simon, what's yours?"

"I'm Eileen."

We chatted for a while, and then without any warning, she gently slid towards me so her back came to rest at my side. We both went quiet. She pushed her head towards my face. I gently stroked my nose and lips against the back of her head.

"That's nice," she said, "Really nice."

She then turned around, so she was facing me and slowly brought her mouth to mine. We kissed gently for a while and then the kisses got deeper and more passionate.

Suddenly she stood. "Let's turn this into a bed then."

I stood up too, "Okay."

So, we pulled out the mattress and threw the bedding over it. Eileen stood up, kicked off her sandals, and took off her shirt so she was bare-breasted and with her skirt still on, she lay down. I on the other hand took all my clothes off as quickly as I could. At that point, Julia came out of her room to go to the loo. On the way back she looked at me as if to say, "What the fuck are you doing with her", which might mean that Eileen wasn't as good-looking as I remember, but for the purpose of this story, she was stunningly beautiful.

After a few minutes of us kissing and me spiralling my face around her breasts towards her nipples then back out again – something I'd read in a book was supposed to be a good technique – I still hadn't got to the point, nor would I for a long while, where technique would be less focused on.

I said, "Can you take your skirt off, I want to feel your legs?"

This wasn't the whole truth, but I was sure she'd understand what I meant.

"Okay", she said, "but I've got my period so we're not going to have sex this time."

"That's okay," I said while thinking, "Thanks for mentioning periods."

I had a bit of an issue with periods, partly because Mum occasionally left her used sanitary towels in my room because she'd come in to get things from the airing cupboard and then forget to take them to the bathroom to be disposed of. Plus, I also had some issues to do with blood that would be talked about in therapy a few years later. But back then, thinking about periods was a bit of a problem for me.

Anyway, it couldn't have been that much of an issue because I was still up for it. What I hadn't counted on though was her underwear was made of a rough golden sparkly material which had similar sensual properties to sandpaper. She grabbed my penis and started rubbing it against her golden vulva of death, at which point I began to think this wasn't quite going to plan, and my penis thought the same.

She stopped grinding my cock and pushed me onto my back. Putting her head near my groin she started speaking as a children's presenter might start talking to a glove puppet.

544

"Oh dear, are you feeling a little shy? Do you need a kiss hello?"

Part of me wanted to answer, "No, he just doesn't like having his head reshaped by your sandpaper knickers," But instead what came out was, "Yes," and an accompanying realisation that TV presenter voices were, surprisingly, quite a turn-on.

She then put my penis in her mouth, "Finally, I thought, a real blow job, this is going to be fantastic... Here goes", but then all I could feel were her sharp teeth digging into me. Within seconds, I lost my erection and realised that my belief that blow jobs were one of the most pleasurable experiences in life, turned out to be a fallacy.

She then guided me on top of her, where she got me to position my hip between her legs.

"Just push there darling, just rock gently there, yes that's it."

I did as I was told. We kissed and stroked each other, and even though to me as a 17-year-old, she was quite old, she looked beautiful (remember, this is my version, okay?). I began to feel something of a connection with her. That was until she decided to dig her sharp nails into my back.

"Ouch!" I yelped, "That hurts."

She paused, looked at me a bit sternly and said, "Do you want me to carry on?"

"Yes," I said a bit doubtfully.

"Then stop being a baby," she said as if she was talking to a child, which unfortunately again was a bit of a turn-on. "How old are you?" she asked.

"Seventeen," I said, slightly hesitantly, wondering whether adding "and a half" might help matters.

"Don't be seventeen with me," she said, then repeated it about five times, looking slightly disturbed. Which again added a slightly seductive quality to the situation.

Eventually, I came, and she said she did too.

"I always feel very horny when I'm having my period," she added.

"That's so nice to hear," I thought.

"Listen," she said, "I'm going to go off now, do you want my number?"

"Yes definitely," I said.

The morning light was coming up. She gave me her phone number, kissed me goodbye and as she let herself out whispered, "I'll see you again."

If I were to write a song about this experience, it would be one where at the beginning of the night I was a boy, and by the end of it, I was a mouse. I expect for her too, this may have been a memorable experience for all the wrong reasons.

I knew we weren't ever going to live happily ever after together, or apart, but for a 17-year-old boy/man/mouse, it was a pretty cool experience, even if I did feel a little depressed about it the next day, which was probably because I realised that none of this was in the service of me meeting the love of my life.

Nowadays she'd probably be locked up for abuse, but back then it wasn't seen as such, because it wasn't.

Diary Entry 17th May 1982

I told the blonde girl on the bus, Phil, Cameron and Allen the caretaker about Eileen. Her words were echoing in my head. She was like a witch. I reckon that's why she turns me on. I phoned her today. I hope I'll see her soon.

1941 – Moshe and Battiya's Story Part 1

My father was the youngest of five. Bettie was the eldest, she stood with a straight back, would look anyone in the eye when they spoke, and had an inner strength about her. Then there was Rue, acting responsibly was his guiding principle, no doubt a reaction to his father's failure to do so. He would eventually become a successful businessman and world-class long-distance desert runner. Battiya was the middle child. She had eyes full of sadness, but still, there was a fortitude in her weakness. After her came her two brothers, Eliezer, the artist, and then my father, Boris. Boris and Battiya were opposites in their approach to life and personalities, but they were still very close.

Moshe was from the same hometown as Boris and his siblings. He was one of the few people who'd beaten my father in a fight. Boris was always quick to remind me that they were "just kids then, and anyway, Moshe was older and had cheated by using a stone to bash" him into submission. When it comes to childhood fights it's hard to forget the ones we lose. Moshe and Battiya had known each other since their early childhood often sitting next to each other in their classes in Rēzekne. As they grew up, they lost contact but in their early twenties, in a social club for young Jewish people in Riga, they reconnected and later, fell in love.

By 1941 the war had engulfed much of the world and Riga was just about to become one of the latest flashpoints between Germany and Russia. The encroaching threat of death posed by the Nazis focused the minds, and hearts, of all those who lay in its path. This wasn't the best of times to get married, but for Moshe and Battiya, the perilous nature of their existence tilted the balance, so, with just her sister Bettie and a couple of friends, they made their vows and became husband and wife.

Barely a week after the ceremony the Soviet authorities ordered Moshe to relocate to Siberia. The German army was just days away from occupying the city, and the future was terrifying for all the Jews who remained. Siberia was known as an ice-filled version of Hell, but to anyone trapped in Riga, it was a Godsend.

With just one hour's notice to get to the station, Moshe and Battiya packed whatever essentials they could. What becomes essential when you're only allowed to take one small case each? If you had to make that choice right now, what would you choose?

For their wedding, Bettie had given them a set of three small matching cases. Grabbing them, Battiya packed warm clothes into one, while Moshe crammed money, valuables, paperwork, and a couple of tools for work into the other. After one last check, Moshe picked up his case and then went to pick up Battiya's.

"No," she said, "It's okay, I'll carry mine," she picked it up, "and anyway, it's light, see?"

"Yes, I know, you're a lot stronger than you look," Moshe said smiling.

They hurriedly left their tiny apartment and made their way to the station.

As the last train out of Riga prepared for the journey ahead, they stood side by side in the queue on the platform. Battiya half knelt to double-check her case.

"Oh no," she said looking up at Moshe. She opened the case wider so he could see that it was filled with scarves and handkerchiefs. Somehow the cases had got mixed up.

"I thought you'd put the ones we were taking together?" She said.

He shook his head, "I just grabbed the case nearest the door in the bedroom and put it in the hallway."

Battiya started to cry, "No, I told you, the one I packed was on the bed!"

Moshe now exasperated, said, "I didn't see it, I thought you said it was in the bedroom. I just grabbed the one nearest the door."

There was a moment while they were tempted to continue blaming each other, but Battiya looked down at the case and put her face in her hands.

"Please Moshe, run back and fetch it."

Again, he shook his head, "I can't. We'll miss the train and they said there won't be another after this one."

She looked at him in disbelief. "There'll be another. We are going to die without our winter clothes. You have to get them."

Moshe crouched beside her, he wanted to console her, but his anger was getting the better of him. "We'll be okay, it won't be that cold for months. I'll make sure we get some winter clothes before then."

She could hear the reassurance she yearned for in the words he said but couldn't feel it in their tone. They both went quiet, looked away from each other and bit their lips.

"I can't believe this," she said.

"Don't worry, I'll deal with it somehow."

Under her breath, Battiya said, "Don't worry he says".

Moshe was just about to approach one of the guards to ask if he had time to get the other case when the guard pointed at them, "Hey, you two, yes you, quickly, it's time, get on."

They stood up and walked towards a carriage, the guard barked at them to hurry up. Moshe helped Battiya up the steps first, where a man inside reached down to help her, and then passed the cases up. As Moshe grabbed the step rail the man pulled him up too. Slightly out of breath, Moshe smiled, put his hand on the man's shoulder, and thanked him. Moshe looked at Battiya because, to them, there was something unnerving about this act of gallantry.

Above the sound of the train preparing to set off came the screeching sound of a plane approaching at speed. Those still queueing on the platform ran for cover. Moshe and Battiya were still in the doorway. They were not paralysed by fear but instead entered a different dimension of time. Everything moved at a tenth of normal speed. Moshe pulled Battiya towards him and turned her as if they were dancing, he wanted his back to face the platform hoping this might offer her some protection.

A rally of bullets ricocheted nearby as the pilot tried his best to disable the train. A couple of Red Army guards shot back, while the train driver released as much steam as possible in a futile attempt to create a kind of smoke screen. The pilot flew off into the distance, there was a moment of relief, but then he turned around and approached once more.

Chapter 33
A Story of Love
Ideologies of Love

Moshe Shruster   Batya (Basya) Shruster (Rachailovich)

*Moshe Shruster and Battiya Shruster (Rachailovich) Image used by kind permission of
Eduard Shruster.*

This chapter will change your life. Even if it's just because you'll never get the time
back again you spent reading it.

Ideologies of Love Part 1 – There's More to Love Than Eye meets I

The problem with this subject, no matter how much I write I won't be able to do it justice. So, please forgive me if I don't cover areas you think should be included. Hopefully, though, I will give a good enough outline, even if it's with very broad strokes. Throughout the sections on love, I'll be referring to 'Idealistic Love'. This is mainly based on the writings of Aristotle and Eric Fromm. In contrast, I'll be using the term 'Romantic Love' to loosely refer to various widespread Western contemporary notions about love.

My life, and probably yours too, has been profoundly entwined with many aspects of love, even if, at times, it was the lack of it. Chuck Spezzano, the author of numerous books on relationships, states that nearly everything we do can be traced back to a desire to be loved, even acts of hate. Given love is so pervasive, it feels as if it's solely borne of instinct, but it's not.

Ideologies of love not only affect the circumstances in which we experience love, but they also change the nature of how we experience it. Different generations, cultures and countries all vary in their approach to love, especially when it comes to who's considered desirable, how people become involved with each other, and the prescribed paths that relationships ought to follow. However, it goes a lot deeper than that. If, for instance, we consider sex as being one of the many ways that love is expressed and experienced, then how open a society is to it will have a profound effect on its citizens. For instance, the Japanese have penis festivals in which people of all ages dress up in penis costumes, and suck and lick penis-shaped ice lollies and sweets. For the Japanese, there is far less guilt, shame and taboos associated with sex, however, paradoxically they're also a far more sexually passive society than many others around the world. Maybe it's a case of forbidden fruit accentuating sexual desire in those more inhibited but sexually active countries.

In many Western, so-called, liberal cultures an erect penis is taboo and at the time of writing this in 2021, it was still against the rules for an aroused one to be shown on television in the UK. That might partly be because less than well-endowed men don't want women to see what they're missing out on, but it may also link to our society's unbalanced focus on male sexual needs ahead of women's. In contrast, the overt focus on women's breasts in most Western societies not only echoes this disparity but also connects sex to our more child-like feelings of being at one with another human. Women's breasts have been a powerful multilevel symbol in most cultures throughout history, but then so too have male phallic symbols. So, why have things become so unbalanced?

Ideologies around sex and love connect to the heart of our society's deepest issues, as they do our own too. At one end of the spectrum, some cultures see sex as being solely for procreation; at the other, sexual experiences are the be-all and end-all. For some, good sex will bring about a more harmonious relationship, for others, a good relationship will pave the way for better sex, and of course, many think it's a bit of both.

In some Chinese cultures in the past matchmakers would examine people's facial features to work out what size their genitals were. They would then match couples based on those criteria, figuring that good sex would create good relationships. Given this method is not a popular feature on most dating websites nowadays suggests it was probably just a load of bollocks.

Beyond basic human nature and cultural influences, there are people's individual motivations which are often tied up with their own personal history and psychological dynamics. So, it's no wonder the range of sexual persuasions tends to be far more all-embracing than most of us could imagine. Likewise, when it comes to assessing whether some ideologies are better than others, a lot comes down to the values of the individual assessor. For some, what matters is whether those doctrines make people happy, but even happiness can mean different things to different people. For others, happiness might not be important at all. They may, for example, make their judgement based on the effect relationships have on others, such as children or the wider circles of society. Alternatively, others might go for a utilitarian approach, where a balance of the most pleasure is set against the least suffering. Then there may be some who see the survival of their 'group' identity as the main guiding principle. So, not only do we have different ideologies, but there are countless ways of judging them too. Perhaps this is why people tend to feel so ill at ease when it comes to dealing with this 'challenging' subject.

Elvis and Joe

I was having a cuppa with a friend of mine, Joe, a few weeks ago. We were talking about how most of the very famous rock legends probably had sex with girls who were technically underage. Then Joe said, "Elvis was supposed to be a bit of a paedophile, wasn't he?" There was silence for a second. "Really?" I said, "I've never heard that before." Joe nodded his head as if he'd just scored a point, "Well didn't he go out with a 14-year-old girl when he was 24?" I laughed. "That doesn't make him a paedophile. Firstly, she wasn't prepubescent and secondly, Priscilla always maintained they didn't have sex until she was 21. And even if they did, then that would have been statutory rape, depending on that state's laws. But," I paused in anger at such an accusation, then added, "that's still not the same as paedophilia." Again, Joe had a victorious look on his face as he said, "Yeah, but they shared a bed from when she was 14, do you believe they didn't get up to stuff," I shook my head and continued, "Back then and even now loads of US states don't specify an age limit for marriage and apparently, more children under 14 are being married nowadays than back in Elvis's day." Joe's mouth turned down at the corners a little, "Really, I'm surprised to hear that." There was a bit of a change in the mood, so I added, "Yeah, there's a drive to stop it, but it's an uphill battle." He still looked serious, "Do you not think 14 is a bit young to be getting married?" I shrugged, "Personally, I don't think people should be allowed to get married until they're 21 at the very least." Joe laughed, "Why do you say that?" I laughed too, "Because they're idiots, we all were, even at 21, maybe 32 would be a safer age." Then we both looked at each other and shaking our heads in unison said, "No, still too young." While we were talking, I looked up Google about this issue on my phone. I started reading what I'd found, "Younger brides tend to lose out in terms of their education, physical and mental health, as well as being more likely to live in poverty and become victims of sexual, physical and mental abuse." I took a big breath and looked up at Joe, "So, yeah, I agree with you, but I'm not accepting that Elvis was a paedophile."

I then called out to my smart speaker "Alexa, play the song, *Baby Let's Play House* by Elvis Presley.

The Complications of Complying

Hopefully, you're getting the gist of what I'm on about regarding ideologies affecting our approach to love. One of the ones I find particularly good at illustrating this is the notion of soulmates. I'll come back to this idea in more detail later, but if you consider the belief that only one person will be right for you, then surely that will affect your relationships. After all, if someone doesn't fit perfectly with your ideal fantasy then won't that result in you being very intolerant? And what if you lost someone who you thought was your one and only soul mate, would that mean it would be impossible to let someone else into your heart?

Given the complexity of the subject as well as all the philosophical opinions accumulated throughout human history, you'd think our societies would have made the subject of love part of the school curriculum by now. Sure, there's sex education, but paradoxically, ideologies of love are far more contentious than sexual ones, hence their exclusion. On some levels, this lack of 'training' could be part of an ideology of love too. After all, people don't normally hesitate when it comes to laying down social rules. Yet, outside of most of the romantic illusions coming out of Hollywood, most people keep very quiet on the subject, unless they're religious, in which case they have their own set of rules too. My point is, so far, no one has come up with a clearly defined and realistic approach to love that is not beyond reproach. Some may believe they have, but they haven't. Even for those who manage to strike it lucky when it comes to matters of the heart, and of course, there will be some, there may be times when they too feel the ideology they believe in doesn't quite ring true completely.

If love is as dark as I portray it, you might wonder why people search it out in the first place. The answer lies in the alternatives. Without love and connection, we're left with isolation and loneliness, and besides, we're still programmed to connect, even if it's just to mate, let alone be intimate.

Even without social conditioning, we're born with some innate expectations about the love between ourselves and our parents. We call out and expect a positive response. Later our feelings and thoughts about love become extremely complicated, especially as we separate from our parents. At that point, many of us go out into the world, with scarcely any education about love, and through trial and error, try to find our way.

At 17 I was full of ideas about love, but I soon realised there was a mismatch between what I'd come to believe and 'reality'. This led me to ask if these beliefs were so unrealistic why were they perpetuated so widely, and are there any others which may be more realistic? I looked for the answers in books of philosophical and religious texts, but most of what I came across didn't ring true to me either and even years later, I felt just as lost. By then though, I'd accepted things were way more complicated than I initially thought and given humans vary so much, trying to apply a one-size-fits-all doctrine was never going to work.

The first stage of determining an ideology's veracity involves testing it against our more irrational, primaeval and dreamy sides. Whether it's anarchy or no sex before marriage, human nature is going to be THE major factor that'll determine an ideology's success, and for those with any experience of human nature, the chances are likely to be very low.

It's no wonder then that many traditional and religiously based approaches to love will fixate on our irrationality, and consequently aim to avoid temptation at all costs. While they have a point, one can resist everything except temptation, so these dogmatic approaches by their, or our, nature tend to be met with resistance. In turn, this makes those who can't comply feel guilty, or worse still, leads to them being severely punished. Even for those who do, there's a high chance they'll end up with someone they don't connect well with and given connection often requires the glue of passion, without it, a relationship may merely feel like a lip service. Without the bond that passion reveals, passionless relationships may well lead to depression or the motivation to seek out what is missing elsewhere.

It's not surprising these opposing approaches exist, after all, human nature is contradictory. For a start on many levels, we are animalistic. We react to molecules we can neither see nor smell and are driven by hormones aimed to do what all life-forms do, pass on our genes. At the same time, though, we have other desires to consider. We may want someone we can share our life with, who we not only like being with but with whom we share similar aspirations and values. At one end of the argument, there's the belief that suppressing our natural inclinations causes more harm than not doing so, while at the other, there's a conviction that it's better to do so as it prevents even greater suffering.

Moshe and Battiya's Story Part 2 – Visit to Riga

When Battiya was about three her brother, Eliezer was born, and a short while after that, Shmuel (Samuel), my grandfather, told her they were going to Riga to visit her aunt. She hadn't been to a city before, so felt honoured to be allowed to join her father on such an adventure. The train journey from Rēzekne to Riga took 12 hours, so by the time they got there, it was already evening. Her aunt, who was very pleased to see them both, made supper then put Battiya to bed. The following morning, Battiya came down to breakfast, but only her aunt was at the table. Battiya asked where her father was. Her aunt told her he'd had to go back home urgently and would return in a few days, but as the weeks passed Battiya realised he wasn't coming back for her.

Five years passed before she would see her parents and siblings again and when she did, she politely accepted their reasoning. They explained they couldn't afford to look after her, but in her heart, it was beyond her that they could do such a thing to a child. No matter how much she tried to forgive them, their betrayal cracked her to the core. Maybe it was a coincidence that Moshe (Moses) was the name of the man Battiya chose to marry as it was also her father's middle name too, or maybe it was a light within him she recognised and connected to.

Ideologies of Love Part 2 – A Serious Affair

> *When love beckons to you, follow him,*
> *Though his ways are hard and steep.*
> *And when his wings enfold you yield to him,*
> *Though the sword hidden among his*
> *pinions may wound you.*
> *And when he speaks to you believe in him,*
> *Though his voice may shatter your dreams*
> *As the north wind lays waste the garden.*
>
> *From On Love – The Prophet*
>
> *By Kahlil Gibran*

I'm going to spend a bit of time looking at some of the idealistic and pragmatic ideologies of love, especially those, as I mentioned earlier, set out by Aristotle and Eric Fromm. However, just as with most other ideologies, things start to go awry as soon as humans get involved, so no matter how well-considered these theories are, they're not going to appeal to everyone.

Most people accept the Nazis caused WW2 which killed close to 85 million people, Communism over 100 million deaths, and Capitalism at least 100 million. Meanwhile, religions are said to have killed over 195 million throughout recorded history. But when it comes to ideologies of love are the death figures comparable?

If we consider the deaths caused by depression due to rejection, physical, mental and sexual abuse, forced and non-forced marriages, not being with the right person, infidelity, and unhappy parents who stay together or separate, the numbers will indeed be very high. Then, of course, we can add the victims of direct killings caused by things such as jealousy, humiliation, and betrayal. When it comes to ideologies of love, it's a far more serious and deadly affair than we were first led to believe.

It's no accident that the word mad is linked to romantic desire. Antony and Cleopatra, and Romeo and Juliet, are held up as the epitome of romantic love, but given their tragic endings, you'd think people would see this as a warning, and not something to aspire to. The ancient Greeks saw romantic love as something to avoid, in fact, they feared it. When it comes to romantic love there's an implication that it involves extreme behaviour, and sure enough, people have committed the most horrific crimes in the name of love. Killing someone out of love is not an example of 'loving too much' but instead of love going wrong when absolutism and extremism, rather than conciliation and accommodation, are the guiding values. So, while it can be argued that it's not love that causes all this suffering, it's hard to deny the ideologies related to love do play a big part in it.

1941 - Riga Station - Moshe and Battiya's Story Part 3

When the plane first approached the station, Battiya felt Moshe's arms tightly wrap around her, his chest against her back, shielding her as best he could. Somewhere in this grip, there was a reassurance of love. Had this been her last moment, then it would have been one she would have chosen. However, as the plane flew away, they checked each other for wounds, and there weren't any. Then the aircraft approached again, and this time they moved further into the carriage, Battiya curled in a ball in front of the only available seats, and Moshe positioned himself over her, pulling their cases over both their heads for protection. "See, this case isn't so useless after all?" he joked, though his breathless words were fragmented with dread. She laughed, shook in panic and cried as they waited for the plane's bullets to pierce the roof. The carriage shook violently, and then there was silence.

Ideologies of Love Part 3 – Just one word – Love

As far as the ancient Greeks were concerned, romantic and erotic obsessions were clearly defined as a particular type of love. For us though, here in our 21st Century Western cultures, the word 'love' has so vague a meaning, that most of us can't define it, let alone categorise its various forms. However, the reason we use just one word is a story in itself.

For the Greeks and Romans, there were six main categories of love. There was Eros, the Greek god of love and fertility who they perceived as a dangerous, irrational influence centred around sexual passion and desire. For those who entered Eros's realm, no one would survive unscathed by his deeply wounding arrows.

In contrast to Eros, there was Pragma. This love came about from the deep understanding that may develop between long-term married couples. However, it also required, as we shall come to see, selfless love. Pragma was principally focused on making a relationship work long-term and involved compromise, patience, tolerance, and having realistic beliefs about one's partner and oneself. It also required supporting each other's needs and was chiefly nurtured in the service of providing a stable and secure environment for children to grow up in.

Although the Greeks were also very interested in the other forms of love such as brotherly love, true friendships and the love between parents and children, the ones I want to focus on here are 'Agape',' Ludus' and 'Philautia'.

Agape could be described as a love for all humans, no matter what their connection to us is. It relates in part to our idea of charity, (in its purest sense), and is very much the backbone of ideologies such as socialism and humanism, and religions such as Christianity, Buddhism and Confucianism. Primarily, it's unconditional love given without any expectation of reward. However, as we will see later, being altruistic still offers rewards of sorts.

While the types of love we've looked at so far have a gravity about them, 'Ludus' could be said to be the love of the lightness of being. It's a playful type of love, that may, for instance, involve having fun with friends, courtly rituals, flirting, and dancing. Although it's a love with very little substance its purpose is to help us get through the tedium of life.

The last of the three is self-love, 'Philautia', and comes in two forms, one negative and the other positive. The former is mainly concerned with satisfying our selfish desires to gain personal pleasures, riches and status whereas the latter serves to equip us to help others by understanding and caring for ourselves too. In the tale of St. Martin, a Roman soldier encountered a half-naked beggar, so he cut his own cloak in half and shared one half with the beggar and kept the other for himself. Later the beggar revealed himself to be Christ to the soldier who was later beatified for his troubles.

Before going further it's important to recognise that when we talk about past cultural norms, we keep in mind they were not as clearly defined as historians portray them to be. There were large swathes of people in Europe who lived very separate lives from the higher echelons. For those without property, there was rarely any need for arranged marriages, so for them, marriage, love and sex didn't necessarily follow the same rules as the middle classes and aristocracy. To think for one second that people back then didn't kiss passionately, marry for love, fall in and out of love, and have extremely diverse types of relationships would be highly inaccurate.

Anyone who's read Chaucer would know he had a lot to say on the subject. Likewise, it didn't take the distribution of ancient Chinese, Indian, Greek, or Roman images of sexual positions for people to find their way around each other's bodies. Just as it is for us, there were common consensuses about love, as well as other more peripheral ones. Therefore, when we speak about cultural norms, remember, they were not the only ones to exist at any given time. The reason I mention this is I came across a lot of misinformation as I researched, most of it seemingly directed by current political agendas. This included the belief that Europeans lived awful lives until foreigners showed them what they were missing out on. Somehow, according to one writer, Europeans didn't even know how to kiss passionately until Arab invaders from Spain gave life to the notion of a kiss. The fact that passionate kissing had been written about in Europe for thousands of years previously must have slipped that writer's mind. My point is, don't believe everything you read, unless, of course, I wrote it.

So, let's have a brief look at how Western cultures came to amalgamate all those different types of love into one word. Our story, and it is a story, possibly begins with a thousand tales around 1000 years ago. The Tales of the Arabian Nights helped perpetuate the idea of love being a combination of Eros and the fusion of the lovers' souls. Even if it wasn't the first to do this, these notions possibly travelled from Spain to other European royal courts, where they certainly affected attitudes about Courtly Love.

When it came to European royal courts and aristocratic circles, strict rules acted as guides to live by for those in such privileged positions. Given their marriages tended to be loveless, the rules around Courtly Love allowed love to be expressed and experienced at least to some degree. It was during this period that Eros and Agape were combined within rituals of gallantry, chivalry, and heroic deeds. The object of the man's attention would normally be another member of the aristocracy, however, one of the most surprising rules was she was never to be his wife or a possible future one. Mixing up love and marriage was considered a bad combination given the latter was, for all intents and purposes, a business arrangement.

For those involved in these Courtly rituals, relationships were supposed to remain chaste. Whether the 'object' of desire was of a higher social rank or was only to be revered from a distance, the intended result was a yearning that heightened the passion and eroticism of the situation. Maybe it was the thrill of the chase, or should it be chaste? Nowadays, unrequited love is still a major factor within our romantic narratives. Why suffer settling for someone you can have when you can suffer far more by yearning for someone you can't? For many people, the sweet pain of romance is what it's all about, no matter how much they deny it.

During the 17th Century marriages within the middle and upper classes started to evolve from being principally pragmatic relationships focused on bringing up the next generation, to ones in which both the husband and wife not only introduced companionship, a form of love known as Philia, but Eros too. Sex was no longer simply an act of procreation but also a pastime in which couples could share in the pleasures of each other's flesh and heart. On the surface, this may seem a happy turn of events, but men still kept much of their erotic life away from the marital home, so let's not get too weepy-eyed just yet.

Between 1800 and 1850 the Romantic movement was at its peak and the importance of Eros, Philautia and Ludus within romantic pursuits became paramount. Three central themes dominated the depiction of true love. The protagonist would fall 'madly' in love, the love should be unrequited, and as a consequence, it would lead to a tragic end. Nothing new you might say, after all, Shakespeare had written Romeo and Juliet centuries earlier, but still Goethe, Shelley, and Keats all based much of their work on these narratives.

Whilst these writers had approached these themes as a warning, the explosion of tragic romantic art and writing resulted in thousands of people playing out these roles, many of whom subsequently committed suicide. What's more, even today, we are still peddling the same storylines as the embodiment of true love, sometimes with similarly tragic results.

Even though both the Greeks and the Romantics tried to point out that being led by Eros would result in madness, destruction and unhappiness, we continue to take no heed. Add to this our obsession with finding a soulmate, which is paradoxical given our society has detached itself so much from religion, and it's no wonder that love and mental health issues go together like a horse and marriage.

So, here we are, armed with one word, very little education about love, a pout, a narcissistic selfie and an expectation that we can find everything we need in just one person. What could possibly go wrong?

Mummy, Why?

"Mummy, what'll happen when I get married, will I live happily ever after?"

"Oh, little one, well, there will be some good times, at least I hope so. But..." she sighs, "there might be lots of arguments, jealousy, rubbish sex, depression, drinking and infidelity."

"Mummy, you're joking, aren't you?"

"Well, for some people it's a lot better or so I've been told. Here's a tissue, come on cuddle up to mummy. Aww, darling, come on now, there's no need to cry, well not yet. You know what sweetheart, I'm sure you're going to live happily ever after."

"Fuck that mummy, I'm joining a monastery".

558

"Oh well, at least you'll get more sex there."

Moshe and Battiya's Story Part 4 – Enemies of the People

A few months before Battiya and Moshe were ordered to evacuate from Riga, around 15,500 'Enemies of The Soviet State', including 2400 children, were forcibly deported from Latvia to Siberia. These deportees were predominantly made up of the families of people in leading positions in the government, economy and culture. The same railroad carts that'd transported those families were now attached to the back of the passenger carriages of Moshe and Battiya's train. This time they were filled with materials destined to be used for those on the front lines as well as a lot of desperate passengers who'd paid the guards bribes to allow them on unofficially.

Once everyone was on board it became clear that even if this wasn't the last train out of Riga, everyone believed it was. All the seats were taken, the aisles were full of people and those unofficial passengers in the cattle trucks made very little effort to conceal their presence.

As the Germans approached, the divisions in Latvian society between the Jews and non-Jews became abundantly clear. Even though no one had any idea what the Nazis had in store for them, their imminent conquest was seen as liberation by most Latvians. As far as they were concerned the Nazis were going to push the Russians out, and for the Latvians that couldn't come soon enough. But, for the Jews, Gypsies, those with Jewish spouses, and communists, it was a different story.

The main Nazi plan for the Baltic States, known as the Generalplan Ost, was to colonise the conquered territories and deport two-thirds of the native population to labour camps. As for the remaining third, they were either to be liquidated, used as slave labour, or if deemed sufficiently "Aryan", Germanized. After this, hundreds of thousands of German settlers were to be relocated into the area.

During a conference on 16 July 1941, Hitler clarified that the Baltic states were to be annexed to Germany at the earliest possible opportunity. With this in mind, some Nazi ideologists recommended integrating the Baltics as German provinces, titling Estonia as Peipusland and Latvia as Dünaland.

Had the non-Jewish Latvians known about this they might have been far less inclined to see the Nazis as their liberators. Instead, not only did they relish the Nazi occupation, but they also tried their very best to out-Nazi the Nazis, especially when it came to brutally persecuting and killing their Jewish countrymen and women.

Anti-Semitism wasn't a unique characteristic of the Latvians, most of Europe had deeply held anti-Semitic views and had done so for centuries; however, when it came to acting on those beliefs many in the Baltic states excelled, and even after the war, it didn't end there.

1995 – Café in London

I went into a café on a side road near West Kensington Station in London and ordered an English breakfast. I was by myself and didn't speak to anyone except the waiter. I got out a book and became a part of the background. There was a collection of people of different nationalities at another table near me who started to speak about Jews unfavourably. They openly made it clear they thought Jews were the dirty descendants of pigs who controlled the world, Wall Street, Hollywood, the Central Banks, the Media and Governments. There was no discussion about Israel, it was just plain anti-Semitism. At the time, I couldn't believe the vitriol that was pouring from them, but a year or so later the Internet became a big part of my life and from then on such hatred became something I'd witness on an almost daily basis.

Ideologies of Love Part 4 – Broken Hearts

After all the millennia we've been evolving, one would have thought natural selection would have made us far better equipped to have happy lifelong relationships. Unfortunately, evolution is only concerned with us breeding and surviving. Happiness is irrelevant unless it affects our survival, and given hope springs eternal, it didn't need to worry.

If sex tends to lie at the root of most of the crimes against ideologies of love, then we are victims of our own success. Even between couples who are bumping (and grinding) along quite nicely, sexual infidelity wreaks havoc at the most unexpected of times. If you reacted to that last sentence, thinking, "Well, there must have been something wrong for one of them to stray," then maybe that illustrates part of your own love-related ideologies. You probably believe that when all is running well, neither party will go elsewhere, unless, of course, one of them is psychologically damaged. But maybe that's just it, maybe humans are generally emotionally broken. So, to be a good partner you're going to have to be a good person, and for most people, if that's even possible, it's going to require a lot of work.

The Call of Regret

A friend of mine was having a drink with one of her friends who told of getting a call a few years back from a woman informing her that her husband had been cheating on her. This was the catalyst that ended their marriage in divorce. "You know," she said, as she looked at the light glinting through her wine glass, "Sometimes I wish that woman hadn't told me. I knew Pete might play around but as far as I was concerned, if no one knew about it, including me, I wouldn't have cared," she took a sip and swished the wine between her front teeth, "but once that woman called," she paused for another sip, "the events that followed took on a life of their own and there was nothing I could do to stop it. Oh, God! It wasn't as if I had been squeaky clean either, but at least I made sure he never found out. I regret that call far more than I do his infidelity."

Therapy

In therapy, the issue of holding back before getting involved with someone came up a few times. Especially during my 20's (30's and 40's). There was one session where we spoke about this and I might have misinterpreted what she said, which can happen a lot in therapy. However, to me, she seemed to be pushing for me to be more cautious. Of course, that was good advice, but I generally didn't take it. "There's a reason it's called Making Love," she said, "You can very easily create a strong bond even though you are unsuited to one another." Maybe I wanted to bond with unsuitable people as, even if the relationships were awful, the sex was good, well for a while, and the suffering was maybe exactly what my internal love doctor ordered.

My therapist came from a different world, one where people formally dated, got engaged, married then had sex. Admittedly many people strayed from the approved path back then, both before and after marriage, but it was also an era where people stayed unhappily together forever and ever. So, as much as I could see the sense in waiting to get to know someone before jumping into bed, where was the place in that ideology for someone like me who could resist very little temptation?

Therapist: Do you think you're split when it comes to relationships?

Simon: Kind of, even when I feel completely in love, I still have desires for others too.

Therapist: Do you think being tempted to stray has anything to do with your childhood?

Simon: Probably, but aren't we all a bit split?

Therapist: Have you read Faust?

Simon: No.

Therapist: Faust is a fictional character in a play by Goethe, one of the things he says might strike a chord with you.

Simon: Oh, what's that?

Therapist: "Two souls, alas, are dwelling in my breast. And one is striving to forsake its brother." Do you understand what he meant?

Simon: I think so, he feels like he has different parts of himself that are at odds with each other.

Therapist: Yes, that's it. But why are people, why are you split?

I don't think my therapist meant for me to leave that session feeling as if I was broken, but I did and, in a way, I was, but I'm not sure how much control I could ever have had. Therapy would help me a lot, but my hormone level lowering as I got older had a significant effect too. Was I broken, or was the ideology of love that says don't rush into having sex, itself broken? As sensible as that ideology was, it felt unrealistic to me.

Moshe and Battiya's Story Part 5 – Journey to Siberia

At around the same time that Battiya and Moshe's train passed Rēzekne, Moshe's parents tried to flee the town. As they approached the border between Latvia and Russia, they were attacked by a German patrol plane, so, were forced to return home. Their next-door neighbour was less than pleased to see them come back. So, as soon as the Germans were entrenched in the region, he was quick to inform the Nazis they were Jewish. As a punishment for not surrendering themselves when all the local Jews were supposed to have done so, Moshe's father was tied to a horse and dragged through the streets until only his legs and spine remained attached to the rope, while Moshe's mother was taken to the forest where she was murdered out of sight.

The neighbour who informed on them took Moshe's family house for himself and stayed there until the end of the war. Soon after, he sold the property and emigrated to Australia. After the fall of the Soviet Union, there was never any serious attempt by the Latvian government to find the descendants of those whose property and lives had been stolen. As far as they were concerned this was blood under the bridge.

The carriages were unbearably hot in the day, freezing at night, the atmosphere suffocating, and there was a pungent, nauseating smell of too many bodies in a closed-in area. Occasionally there was some respite when the train stopped at stations. During those times the passengers could alight for a short while to collect food rations and buy items from the locals who gathered on the platform to sell their wares. Rations only consisted of 100 grams of bread, a ladle of oily porridge, some tea and a canister measure of water. Getting extra provisions became essential for survival.

On the platforms, the passengers would chat a little. Those in the cargo wagons spoke of etched graffiti all along the lower parts of the inside of their trucks that listed the names, ages and dates of death of those who'd died a few weeks back, along with pleas to remember them. There were even descriptions of farewell notes scattered along the full length of the journey. What they didn't know, but probably surmised anyway, was very few of these ever reached their intended recipients. It would be years before it was revealed that 8500 of those 'enemies of the State' had been separated and executed soon after the journey began.

Even though Moshe and Battiya's carriage was nowhere near as insanitary or overcrowded as the cargo trucks, it didn't take long for people to start dying. The first person to do so was a man in his 50s. There was no sign that anything was wrong with him but on the third day, someone shook him to tell him they'd stopped for their daily rations, and he didn't react. Once people realised what had happened a short struggle broke out between a couple of men wanting to relieve the dead man of his clothing and valuables. As the train was at a standstill and the Soviet guards were nearby, it didn't take long for them to intervene. The body was then taken away with only its coat removed.

After the train set off, one of the men who'd helped break up the scuffle, Valdis, said loudly that the next time someone died who didn't have any family with them, their personal belongings and clothes should be removed and shared with those most in need. The people in the carriage murmured their opinions on the matter for a few minutes, then it went quiet again. No one dared argue with him though because they couldn't help but wonder if he was a guard in disguise.

The places where people settled in the carriages were partly defined by their allegiances and friendships and partly by a lack of options. For those who didn't have any friends though, it was simply a gamble based on an initial feeling. In the first few hours, everyone assessed each other to a point, working out where best to settle. But, once they'd taken their positions, that was it, that's where they stayed for the rest of the journey.

Apart from the hostility of the squabble over the dead man's clothes, there was very little friction within the carriage, but that was more indicative of widespread guarded isolation than a leaning towards peace. Outside of people taking turns standing near the windows to breathe in the fresh air or queuing patiently for the makeshift toilet near one of the exits, there was very little connection between strangers. If this had been full of British or other Europeans there would have been plenty of playing cards, checkers or chess, even if they had to do it with makeshift boards and pieces. And when darkness fell, there'd have been a lot of chatting, some music, singing and the telling of stories and jokes. But in this Soviet world, where families couldn't trust each other, let alone strangers, everyone was aware that on a journey to or from Hell, acts of kindness could bring a touch of heaven to their world; but on this train, in these lands, there was no room for heaven.

As the weeks progressed more deaths occurred, it was predominantly the elderly, very young or those who'd fallen sick from a lack of nutrition who succumbed. Valdis's wishes for a fair redistribution of wealth went unheeded. For the most part, there were very few who died who were completely alone, but when they did, those nearby quietly stripped the body of its clothes and belongings, then when the train stopped, the close-to-naked corpse would be removed by the guards and thrown in a cart.

Although Moshe and Battiya had brought the wrong case they did have all their money. This meant they could buy extra food and items of clothing from the platform sellers. About 20 days into the journey there was a two-day stop-over at Kuibyshev. Those who could afford it took rooms in the local residents' houses for the night. This gave them the chance to clean up, get a good night's sleep and eat some cooked food. Moshe and Battiya stayed in a house belonging to an old man.

When they woke up, they realised all their money had been taken whilst they slept. After desperately searching for it, they could only determine it had been stolen by the old man or someone he knew. It was there before they went to sleep but now it was nowhere to be found. There was no point in calling the police. For Jews, involving the police would have made things worse. Even confronting the old man might have ended with them being strung up, there was nothing they could do.

Maybe the host felt guilty, but as they left he passed them a bucket of potatoes. That was it though, he gave nothing else, just a slight smile as they walked off. Fortunately, they managed to sell a few of the potatoes in the market on the way back to the station, as well as keeping some to eat in secret on the train.

Moshe and Battiya now had barely any money or belongings and over the next few weeks, they became very weak, spending most of the time huddled together keeping warm and conserving what little energy they had.

Ideologies of Love Part 5 – Ideal Love

Before setting off on this journey, I wanted to make it clear that for many people the notions of love, ideal or otherwise, that I'll be referring to may not ring true or resonate in any way. If that's the way you feel about them, I hope you'll accept my apology. There are many types of love and just as many ways of living that are not touched on here. However, these were the kinds of love that I was interested in for most of my life, hence my focus on them.

―――――

Lovable Products

Are you looking for a good match, do you want to be loved, are you doing everything you can to make yourself more lovable, so Ms or Mr Right will want you? If so, then stop right there. As far as Fromm's Idealistic love goes. You're going about it the wrong way.

It's hard to avoid seeing ourselves in the context of the world we live in, and we live in a very commercial one, full of consumables and consumers. When we think about finding a long-term partner, we expend a lot of resources on making ourselves 'lovable' and attractive, whether that be physically, sexually, socially, economically or personality-wise. The emphasis is placed on us to position ourselves so the right person can find and love us, or at least the image of us we've created.

One of the problems with focusing on making ourselves into a lovable product, apart from us not being our genuine selves, is just as with commercial products, standardisation comes into play. Unless we're a high-end, one-of-a-kind, exclusive artefact, it's safer to make ourselves into an acceptable standard item. It's not surprising then that so many people look alike. Similar clothing, hairstyles, and bodies are not just directed by fashion but by the zeitgeist of standardised love-ables. As with all production lines, there's a quality control and grading system that'll categorise our level of attractiveness between luxury, run-of-the-mill, bargain basement and wonky. This, as with most commercial systems, means people of similar value can be traded against each other. Terms such as meat market, being in the market or being left on the shelf have been commonplace for decades. I'm not saying that this way of thinking is primarily a symptom of our consumer era, but I can't help but think there's a bit of a link.

The thing is, relationships are based on far more criteria than just appearances, so while determining someone's core values might be possible to a degree by assessing their looks, it has its limitations. When Marilyn Munroe got together with the playwright Arthur Miller it might have shocked some people but generally, they accepted other values were coming into play in that union.

―――――

The Look of Love

I was acutely aware of the significance of looks at 17. My body didn't fit our society's notion of normality, so I knew for some I was never going to be of any interest no matter how successful, clever, sexy, funny or caring I was. But I was also aware some people found me attractive. That still didn't stop me from going for the ones who didn't want me. It was the era of the New Romantics, so I'll place part of the blame on their stylish shoed feet, after all, *Don't You Want Me Baby* was the anthem of the day and that along with ABC's *The Lexicon of Love* album, pretty much told me, heartbreak was the way to go. But then so had Elvis. I was a sacrificial lamb to the god of romantic love and didn't stand a chance from the start.

For most of us, we see love as a feeling, a feeling that may come and go with the wind. When we think of a lifelong commitment, we wonder how that could ever be possible, especially when we doubt our own feelings lasting, let alone anyone else's. On top of that, what we believe makes us, or others, lovable is transient too. Our bodies, personalities, careers, wealth, and health are all likely to change over time, so how could love remain constant? Furthermore, there are our deeper darker thoughts and feelings, which at times we feel completely at the mercy of. How can we trust others when we're not sure if we can trust ourselves? We are surrounded by the belief in happiness ever after, but it's our doubts that truly guide us.

Love is a Verb

The notion that being attractive will improve our chance of experiencing 'true love' illustrates perfectly the difference between Idealistic and Western Romantic ideologies of love. Both Western Romantic cultures and those that place their faith in arranged marriages, share the same belief that all you need to do is bring the right ingredients together, and from then on everything will fall into place. In this way, the process of love is perceived as a response to a stimulus.

In the Idealistic Love ideologies of Fromm, it's the other way around. Sure, there must be good ingredients, but the main emphasis is on the process. Romantic love focuses on being loved; Idealistic love emphasises learning how to love. One is about an immediate arrival. The other is about recognising potential and building on it.

For most people giving love rather than receiving it is problematic, especially if they feel starved of love in the first place, because for them, there's very little love to give. Being loved might be the aim of Romantic love, but if so much of who we are gets lost within the process of becoming attractive, is it really us being loved? Romantic narratives say we'll see each other in the look of love, so, as we gaze into each other's eyes we will see the depths of our souls. But in practice, these initial connections are likely borne of fantasy and whichever way the relationship goes will be more a matter of chance than spiritual connection.

Fromm's Idealistic Love ideology takes a very different approach. As far as it is concerned finding ourselves and being strong enough to show others who we are is one of its primary objectives. This doesn't just mean we say, "This is me, take it or leave it." It's part of a much larger process that involves a lot of self-development, especially by becoming less narcissistic and more caring towards others.

Yours Pragmatically

In previous times, there was very little romance or care in long-term relationships. Even up to quite recently, such relationships were widely viewed as pragmatic arrangements that were for the sake of the children. They also kept people busily involved in what felt like a meaningful pursuit, and possibly, more importantly, helped society remain stable. Keeping most of the male population busy was one way of stopping them from getting up to no good, which, let's face it is what tends to happen when they're left to their own devices.

In turn, this all helped create an environment in which industry could capitalise on a ready-made workforce. Whether it was under the guise of Capitalism or Communism, the family unit provided workers with a support system and a constant source of workers for industry. However, even though some stability was brought about because of this, it would take clam-like social rules to keep these families together. Forcing people to remain with each other when they shouldn't have, resulted in a lot of abuse, particularly towards women and children and of course, some men too. There were, after all, a lot more murdered husbands back then.

The Power of Love

From the 1950s onwards, the image of the family unit began to collapse, leading in turn to both new opportunities and a whole host of other problems. Possibly the biggest development in our society that directly offered a better way forward for relationships was the fundamental change in women's roles within Western societies. As far back as the Roman era, women were viewed as the property of their fathers and then their husbands. It was around that time that the word 'obey' was introduced to the wedding vows and it took close to 2000 years for it to be renounced, and even then, that was only in some quarters. In 1922 the Episcopal Church voted to remove the word obey from the bride's wedding vows; however, many other denominations of Christianity continue to incorporate it today, and in most weddings, fathers still give their daughters away.

There may, of course, be plenty of women (and men) who like the feeling of being owned or bound to someone else but in terms of a relationship based on equality, such dynamics are not helpful. If you're going to attempt developing love between two people, then one cannot hold more power over the other. All relationships involve power dynamics, so, to a point they're unavoidable. However, if one person cannot be themselves out of fear of the other, then that is a very different matter.

Aristotle, George and Margaret

I once went to a philosophy meeting about friendship. It was held in a room above the Rose and Crown, an old-fashioned pub that stood alone, surrounded by large blocks of flats in Colombo Street, London. In this room, with its swirly grey carpet and an old wooden bar in the corner, one of the speakers talked about some of Aristotle's ideas about friendship, including his resistance to the possibility that men and women, especially husbands and wives, could have what he termed, 'perfect friendships'.

Aristotle's main argument was when there is a role between two people such as a parent and child or boss and employee, certain restrictions act upon their relationship. For instance, could a husband or wife be entirely honest, in the same way they'd be to a close friend, especially about feelings they might have for someone else? In most cases, the answer would be no. For this reason, they can't truly be themselves in each other's company, so for Aristotle that meant their relationship had limits to it.

When I mentioned this to one of the very few couples I know who I believe have had a close-to-perfect marriage, they looked dismayed. George, who'd been a police officer, shook his head and said, "Margaret's my best friend, I could tell her anything", then Margaret, who was a woman of very few words said, "That Aristotle doesn't know what he's talking about." Perhaps there was some truth in what she said, after all, when Aristotle considered these matters men and women were not equal at all. Maybe, for George and Margaret, there had been equality between them from the outset but for most people, this is a far more recent phenomenon.

Moshe and Battiya's Story Part 6 – Ishim

In present-day Europe, there's a route called the E22. One end of it starts in the United Kingdom, then passes through the Netherlands, Germany, Sweden, Latvia and Russia, where it terminates at the city of Ishim in Siberia. This too was the end of the line for Battiya and Moshe. They were over 2000 miles from Riga, and after four weeks of travelling, they were undernourished, weak, sick, and despondent, but at least they were still alive. Hand in hand, barely able to walk, they

568

waited on the platform while a couple of guards allocated the new arrivals places to stay.

Ishim was an administrative centre in Western Siberia. The middle of it had a few grand buildings situated near the river. There was a station, a market, and an industrial area to the northeast, but apart from that, the main roads and dirt tracks that radiated from the centre had very few buildings along them. There was a surreal wretchedness about this place.

The sudden influx of several hundred 'essential foreign workers' was met with mixed reactions. In terms of the Soviet system, these were 'fellow comrades' whom the locals were ordered to take in and receive rent from for their trouble. However, they were 'comrades' who didn't speak their language, so, they certainly couldn't be trusted, but then people didn't trust their own family members, so this wasn't anything new. The upshot of all of this though, was they were not welcomed into the local community.

The word Ishim, whether it's related to the town's name or not, also refers to a class of angels in Judaism that were said to be closest to the affairs of men. The angels themselves were composed of fire and ice in equal measure. Their primary raison d'être was to extol the virtues of God and give advice to and pray for humans. But the only bit of Heaven in Ishim would be between those who trusted each other, and they were few and far between.

Some of the newcomers ended up in provisional barracks, while others, including Battiya and Moshe, were offered rooms in local residents' small log cabin homes. It was luck of the draw as to whether they were allocated a good proprietor. Fortunately for Battiya and Moshe, theirs was a kind-hearted middle-aged man who welcomed them, and their rent. He was a widower so the promise of a bit of company and help around the house made him a little more amenable. He also let them have a patch of the garden where they could grow food, although he expected a share of the yield for doing so, and to help them get started he gave them some seeds.

The house had no upper floors and just one small communal area with a couple of bedrooms off it. There was no bathroom or toilet, just an outhouse for anyone brave enough to use it in the winter and the smaller of the two bedrooms became Moshe and Battiya's new home.

For the 'Enemy of the Soviet State' family members who survived, it had been a very different story. They'd been 'settled' in towns not so far away, but when they arrived, they were left in a field for several days. During that time, severe storms left them soaked, cold and unwell. Those who survived were offered shelter on condition that they signed trumped-up confessions and accepted a 20-year conviction to remain in Siberia.

At first, they were housed in long wooden overcrowded barracks which were unsanitary, freezing cold, and disease-ridden. So, when farms and factories were offered as alternative places for the children to stay, their mothers agreed to them being placed there even though it meant they would be separated from each other. Essentially these children became slaves. For some, walking cattle 60 miles to the slaughterhouses was one of the easier posts, although none of the meat was ever intended to come back to those who lived in this region, however, unofficially, it did. For the workers, nice food only ever appeared in dreams and nearly everything nutritious was either sent to the front lines, the cities or the local more equal, equals in charge.

For Moshe and Battiya there was no respite either. Only one day after moving in they were told to come to the factory where they had to start working straight away. Whilst they were not confined to a Gulag, they were forced to work for most of their waking hours while being fed and paid very little in return. For all intents and purposes, they were slaves. It's true that the place they got to sleep in wasn't as bad as the Gulag barracks, but they were extremely undernourished, forced to work for 14 hours a day, with no days off and on top of that, they were inadequately clothed for the -40 degree temperatures. So, it was no surprise that for many of the workers, their bodies started to falter.

Outside of working at the factory, Moshe got requests from people to do jobs in exchange for food and clothing. The United States had donated lots of tools to help Russia in its war effort, so the factory and consequently Moshe acquired quite a few of them. As most of what he did revolved around working with metals, his expertise became sought after, so, from the moment he arrived at the factory till late at night he worked.

One of the food hall managers asked him to patch up some of the pans. Moshe was a bit wary of him, he looked like a boulder that might fall upon him, but still, Moshe knew he couldn't refuse especially as the manager had ties to the local Communist Party. After Moshe completed the job, he expected the man to pay him in kind with some food. Instead, nothing was offered at all. Moshe stood there waiting, but the man just looked him up and down.

"What are you waiting for?" he said.

"I thought we had a deal," Moshe said.

The man shook his head, pushed his lips together into an upside-down smile, and said, "I don't think so."

Moshe wanted to clout him one, but he knew nothing good would come of that, so he stayed silent. This was what happened when you came up against a more equal, equal.

The next day Moshe had to go to work early, so, it was still dark and no one was on the street except him. As he passed the food hall, he felt overwhelmed with anger, picked up a rock and threw it at one of the windows. As it flew through the air, he half hoped it would just bounce off, but instead, the whole pane came crashing down. For a second, he was frozen to the spot, then realising what he'd done, he ran down an alley and made a detour so he wouldn't be seen. Later that day a police officer turned up at his work and went into one of the manager's offices. A short while later he came out looking as if something was troubling him. Moshe tried his best not to look at him but as the officer passed, their eyes met for a second, so Moshe bowed his head.

When Moshe got home that night, he didn't tell Battiya about the shop window. He knew it was going to come back on him and didn't want her to be culpable in any way. This was a world where you were obliged to tell on your husband or wife if they did anything wrong. As he walked in Battiya made him some tea.

"That food hall manager, you know he's not going to pay you now," she said.

Moshe felt slightly faint, "Why? What has he said?"

As she passed him his tea she loudly whispered, "He's not saying anything, well not to anyone in Ishim. He was rounded up and sent to the front line today."

A feeling of relief travelled from Moshe's head to his toes. "Do you know why they took him?"

"Why are you asking? You know, no one knows why. One thing I can tell you though is, he must have upset the wrong person."

Moshe wrapped his hands around the metal cup, sipped his tea and said, "You're right, I won't get paid then."

Battiya sighed, "Yes, I had a bad feeling about him."

"So did I," Moshe said raising his eyebrows.

At that point, their landlord walked into the room from his bedroom.

"Who did you have a bad feeling about?" he asked.

"The man who got arrested today, the one who owns the food hall," Battiya said.

"Ah him, yes he has a lot of enemies." The landlord checked himself. "Is there any more tea left in the pot?"

"Yes," Battiya said, then poured him a cup.

"Hey," the landlord was suddenly animated "Do you want to try some of my Samogon?"

They both nodded and smiled but deep down they knew this homemade alcohol was dangerous, not just because it could poison you, but also because it might lead to letting things slip.

He poured the Samogon into a couple of mugs and lifting his own, toasted, "Let's celebrate the corrupt manager being caught."

They only had one drink, thanked him then retired to their room, where not a word was spoken.

Ideologies of Love Part 6 – Ideal Love – Preparations

> *For even as love crowns you so shall he*
> *crucify you.*
> *Even as he is for your growth*
> *so is he for your pruning.*
> *Even as he ascends to your height and*
> *caresses your tenderest branches that quiver in the sun,*
> *So, shall he descend to your roots and*
> *shake them in their clinging to the earth.*
>
> *From 'On Love' – The Prophet*
>
> *By Kahlil Gibran*

The Patient Patient

A list of instructions on "How to have a good relationship' would be welcomed by most of us. That way we could follow them, just as a computer does a program. However, the directions laid out by Fromm might better be thought of as a guide to creating an environment in which love can grow. To make matters worse, the suggestions he makes require lots of preparation and training. If you're after a quick fix, then you're going to be very disappointed. Right from the start, you're going to need a degree of patience, and when I say a degree, I mean a very big one. I'll be straight, this is probably going to take years and there'll be plenty of setbacks. However, if you're tempted to throw in the towel straight away, I'd suggest reading on as a lot of what he proposes is worth considering anyway, and even if that doesn't tempt you, keep this chapter in mind just in case one day you find yourself all out of love for the Nth time and can't see any way forward.

Of course, if you feel you lack patience you can always say this prayer,

"God give me patience and give it to me quickly".

It probably won't work, but at least you asked.

Self-Sufficiency

At the heart of preparing ourselves for love is self-sufficiency. Fromm believed that being self-sufficient will stand us in good stead to not be with others merely because we can't bear being by ourselves. However, there's a big difference between filling our time with distracting activities such as watching films, playing computer games, getting drunk or stoned, or even becoming a workaholic, and being happy in our own company.

The problem for many in our society is we've been brought up with the notion of constantly being entertained, so, the things Fromm suggested will seem alien to most people. However, they're still worth considering, and indeed, if you feel anxious about letting go of activities you've relied on for so long it begs the question, why?

The kind of things Fromm believed might help us be by ourselves included meditating, reading, listening to music or talks, and amongst many other things, studying subjects we find interesting. The aim is to provide a sense of peace and structure to our lives rather than excitement and distraction. For most people, the idea of trying to instigate such a big change will fill them with nausea, but it's possible that even after just a short time, this new way of living may be pleasurable.

If you're someone who finds it hard to be alone it might be worth trying to work out if it's because you can't stand being with yourself, and if so, why? Of course, it's not that you're meant to put yourself in solitary confinement for months, but at least starting with small periods of peaceful time alone might be worth trying and in time extending it further. Once we're able to spend time happily alone we won't feel so driven to be with someone just for the sake of it and that'll mean we'll wait to find a person we want to be with.

Considerate Reactions

The next fundamental principle of this system requires us to become less self-absorbed, and more considerate, caring and altruistic. This includes not seeing people primarily as resources, but instead, as individuals with their own needs and problems. If we use others for our ends, then we'll probably think they're doing the same with us. If, however, we approach relationships with some degree of care and recognise the humanity in others, we may enter a world where we too feel genuinely cared for, or at least recognised by others as human with our weaknesses, strengths, vulnerabilities and abilities.

Reactivity – It's Not About You, It's About Me

It's very easy to perceive others' behaviour as somehow relating to us. For example, if someone's actions have an adverse effect on us, we may immediately think they either set out to hurt us intentionally or just didn't consider us at all, and for many, either reason is enough to feel anger. When we come up against such a situation it's tempting to want to "teach them a lesson", however, this risks things becoming far more explosive.

Alternatively, we can approach difficult interactions with the aim of trying to understand what is really going on. If we do, we may find we played no part in their actions at all and that'll help us see they're calling for love and understanding. Alternatively, if we focus only on our needs being considered then we're likely to end up treading a destructive path; after all, most of the world doesn't consider us, so we better prepare for being constantly at war.

The same applies when it comes to our more intimate relationships. We can choose to take everything personally or seek to understand what's going on in those we care for. If we take the latter path not only will we nurture a more peaceful atmosphere, but those we love will most likely be touched by our consideration.

Unfortunately, in my case, it generally was because I had actually pissed them off, and when I suggested that it was anything but me that might be the cause, well, that didn't help matters either.

Extra Punitive

If we are prone to taking things out on others, even though logically we knew it was completely our fault, then we probably have a propensity to be extra punitive. If we don't check ourselves for such reactions, we can all too easily, and unfairly, take things out on those around us. This too requires us to consider other people's feelings, and personalities. I often find myself quick to think this way, but I've found I can consciously tell myself it's not someone else's fault, and that tends to help a little.

The same is true if we're primed to believe people will let us down. If we think that way, then we'll be far more likely to see others as unreliable, whether they are or not. Being aware of our presumptions and expectations can help us to stop continually jumping to the wrong conclusions. Still, this kind of awareness may take years of study and self-analysis to develop and no matter how hard we try to be objective, we should always keep in mind that we only ever have a partial picture of what's going on in others and ourselves.

In many ways, this caring approach lies within the realm of Agape-type love and requires truly loving others, recognising their essence as humans, and understanding them as best we can, even when they are being difficult. This doesn't mean losing ourselves by falling into them but holding both ourselves and them in a light of love and care. Now if you believe you can't feel for others at all, that you have no empathy or sympathy, then again this may require years of work, but at least recognising it's an issue will be a step in the right direction.

Self-Discipline and Commitment

If we're serious about having real love in our lives, then we must be prepared to put in the effort. Any attempts to change ourselves will have to be backed up by self-discipline, patience, and commitment.

Concentration

Concentration will also be essential, not just in terms of learning and thinking, but also when it comes to dealing with others. Being able to concentrate means we can focus more fully on our friends and loved ones. Again, this will be an important skill when it comes to loving someone, as we learn to listen more carefully, we'll be able to hear what people are telling us and pay attention to their needs.

Values

Reassessing what characteristics in ourselves and others resonate with our own core beliefs will help us identify what values we'd like to develop as well as the negative ones we ought to work on. Even just thinking back on our past experiences we may remember people who touched us in a good way. The more we do this, the more we'll be able to find ourselves, and the more we do that, the greater confidence we'll have.

Confidence

The consequence of becoming more focused on seeking the truth will be having a conviction about what we believe is right. This doesn't mean we can't accept we're wrong, quite the opposite, if we seek the truth then we must welcome adjustments. However, instead of blindly following the herd and believing something just because everyone else does, we can spend time rooting out the truth.

Faith in Others

The more genuine confidence we attain, the more faith we will have in others, including our loved ones. When we recognise in them their passion for the truth, then we can let them make their own decisions, knowing that they are doing so with the best of intentions. This doesn't mean they won't get things wrong or there's never going to be a risk of betrayal, there will be. The thing is, we're going to have to make leaps of faith when it comes to love, and accept no matter how well we know someone, there will always be the possibility of them letting us down. But, when we know we can be trusted, we'll recognise this virtue in others too.

If we believe we can't be honourable, then we'll find it very hard to have faith in anyone else. What's more, when others sense our trust in them it will inspire them to flourish, whereas if they sense our distrust then they will most likely stumble.

For those who don't have faith in others, there will be a temptation to take control through domination and power, but this kind of forcefulness is the result of fear. If we are to love, then we must have courage and accept the possibility of pain and disappointment. Apart from being anxious about the dangers we may face as individuals, just loving someone will mean we're also concerned with them too. If we're going to love someone, we have to accept it won't always feel good.

Fear

When we say, "We're scared of not being loved", we ought to remember we are also scared of loving and all the risks it involves.

Did you get all of that? I will be writing more about it a bit later, but if you want to read more about this in-depth you may find Eric Fromm's book "On Love" of interest.

Moshe and Battiya's Story Part 7 – Winter – Ishim

During the autumn months, the landscape turned from green to brown. Many people lost their shoes in the thick, muddy fields, so to cope, they bound their feet with cloth which soon became sodden and cold. For some, it would be years before they would ever wear shoes again and in the meantime, their feet would become permanently damaged.

Before the snow fell, people collected as many nettles and shrubs as possible for the soups they'd make through the winter. The rations weren't anywhere near close enough to provide the calories and nutrition required to keep people working, so pilfering and bartering became essential for survival.

In a land of nothing, something extra had to come from somewhere or someone, otherwise, everything would have collapsed. So, it fell to the more equals, the local police, soldiers, and officials, to provide that extra little bit of something, and to turn a blind eye when it suited them. This put them in extraordinary positions of power and furnished them with quite a bit of wealth. For those who were chosen to be caught though, the punishments were severe. One mother took two cabbages and got six months in prison. No doubt her real 'crime' was her refusing the advances of a more equal, equal. Her children were then left to fend for themselves. There were no social services or goodwill, especially to the offspring of the criminal classes.

As the landscape turned to white, this first winter was especially cold with temperatures dropping as low as -40 degrees. Moshe and Battiya's extra shifts and work on the side meant they could 'acquire' good enough clothing to survive. But the lack of rest and nutrition saw Battiya's immune system start to weaken, so much so, that one day her body gave up and she fell ill. Their landlord recognised the symptoms immediately, he'd seen it before. The stiffness in her joints, the spinal abscesses, and the paralysis from the waist down. He beckoned Moshe to come out of the bedroom and whispered, "I'm sorry, but I'm pretty sure It's skeletal tuberculosis. We have to get her to the hospital."

Moshe looked at him and asked, "How do you know?"

"Because," he paused and looked down at the ground, "Because my wife had it."

Moshe frowned, "But you might be mistaken."

The landlord pulled his top lip in between his teeth, then nodded slightly and said, "Yes, I hope so."

It was impossible to get her to the hospital there and then, the weather was vicious and there were no horses or carts available. Battiya's condition worsened with every passing hour and by the morning she had fallen into unconsciousness. None of the neighbours had vehicles, so, Moshe ran to the factory where he asked if one of the drivers would help. "I can't," came the reply, "not without the manager's consent." So, when Moshe approached him, he wasn't surprised when he'd only agree to do so on condition Moshe worked 30 extra hours the following month.

What he meant by that was Moshe would have to pay him the wages for those hours and do the extra work.

The Soviet health care system far exceeded that of the pre-civil war Russian Empire. However, the Second World War had already taken its toll, so, while Battiya was given medical attention soon after arriving at the hospital, the responsibility for feeding her fell on Moshe.

Moshe had to work 16 hours a day, not only to pay for Battiya's ride to the hospital but to make up for the shortfall in their wages. There was no sick pay, so, no work meant no income. After leaving the factory he'd buy food, or procure it through barter jobs, then make his way to the hospital, after which he'd return home to sleep for a few hours. Then he'd repeat the whole process over again.

The main 'cure' for tuberculosis back then was rest, a good diet and fresh air. This had been the principal approach since the 1880s when research showed this had a positive effect.

One evening Moshe came to the hospital to find Battiya's bed empty. A man's voice called from behind him. "Mr Shruster, Mr Shruster?" Moshe turned around. A doctor was standing a few feet behind him.

"Yes," Moshe said.

The Doctor looked at him. "I'm afraid I have some very bad news".

Ideologies of Love Part 7- Ten Things That May Help Love to Develop

Like sheaves of corn he gathers you unto himself.
He threshes you to make you naked.
He sifts you to free you from your husks.
He grinds you to whiteness.
He kneads you until you are pliant;
And then he assigns you to his sacred fire,
that you may become sacred bread for
God's sacred feast.
All these things shall love do unto you
that you may know the secrets of your
heart, and in that knowledge become a
fragment of Life's heart.

From 'On Love' – The Prophet
By Kahlil Gibran

So, with the preparations explained above, here's a list I've collated from the writings of Plato and Fromm, regarding some of the higher ideals that may help develop true love.

1 Accepting our initial feelings are not grounded in reality allows us to resist making commitments too early. For instance, by not rushing to get married, buying a property or having children together.

2 Letting go of the belief that love will come from 'enjoying' the experience of each other. I can love ice cream but I'm not going to marry it, although one brand of salted caramel flavour was a contender. Separating these two things will help us focus on what love is truly about. In other words, we should avoid seeing those we love as a source of pleasure, a means to an end.

3 We must allow ourselves to be truly who we are and not hide behind a facade. Unless of course, you're a psychopathic killer, in which case none of this is going to help much. Likewise, we should avoid becoming a clone or seeking one out, but instead spend time working out what we value in others and ourselves. Even if our work is pushing us more and more to act as automatons, being able to be ourselves is an important factor in our relationships with others and ourselves. It's better to be disliked for who we are than liked for who we are not.

4 Apart from dealing with the traumas and stress that life deals us, we should aim to be as happy as we can, to love ourselves unselfishly while helping our friends and loved ones to be themselves too. This may involve us connecting with our deeper creative parts, whether that be via the arts, cooking, decorating, fixing cars, you name it, there are probably many things that you like doing in life. This is part of being yourself but also makes space for you to help others be themselves too.

5 Avoid approaching a relationship as a deal. Seeing one another on an equal basis is of the utmost importance. That doesn't necessarily mean you should both share everything equally. It's about recognising and respecting each other's strengths and weaknesses and, again, not seeing the other person as a means to an end.

6 We hear a lot about being independent, but maybe interdependency is a better way forward. An interdependent individual acknowledges the value of vulnerability and is able to create emotional intimacy between themselves and their loved ones. They also hold dear a sense of their self and their loved one's self, allowing each other to be themselves without any need to compromise who they are, or their values.

Once again this is more about creating an environment in which things can grow, whereas when you feel dependent you're more likely to have expectations and demands. Ultimately, being dependent will lead to you not getting what you want, so instead, try to let go and give, but give without expectation.

7 If we focus on giving to others when it's needed, we allow ourselves to feel a greater pleasure than when we take. So, in a selfish way, giving can make us feel happy and potent. On a slightly less selfish note, we can tap into our more empathetic capabilities and by making others happy, feel happy too. Whether we choose to see giving as a selfish or altruistic undertaking, either way, it lies at the heart of love.

8 By trying to understand ourselves more, and yes that is no easy task, we can love others in two main ways. Firstly, we can recognise when our destructive patterns come into play, and secondly, we can try to understand our loved ones because we realise they are prone to being irrational, just as we are at times too. By stepping back, being less reactive and more considerate in our dealings with others we can help bring about a more loving environment.

9 Respect. The word respect comes from the Latin to look back at. When we look at or see those we love we should strive to see them for who they are. We must become knowledgeable of them to their core, but with a motivation of care, not power. We should know them as much as we can, inside out.

10 Having faith in our loved ones doesn't just mean trusting them not to betray us. It also means trusting them to do what is best for themselves. Likewise, trusting ourselves to do what is best for us and them too. Our attempts to help them develop must not be for our sake, as in we mustn't mould them to our taste, but help them be who they truly can be.

Many of us, including me, may well have tried to control our partners, to prevent them from going off with someone else or getting involved in something that we believe might not be good for them. Without our trust in our loved ones, we will more than likely damage if not destroy love. In other words, there is no choice. One must have faith in others and ourselves, and accept if they or we act against the relationship, then so be it, we'll have to cross that bridge and see what it means then.

I'm going to take you on another detour, don't worry, we'll be coming back.

Ideologies of Love Part 7 Continued – Betrayal

> Your pain is the breaking of the shell that encloses your under-
> standing.
> Even as the stone of the fruit must break, that its heart may stand in
> the sun, so must you know pain...
> ... Much of your pain is self-chosen.
> It is the bitter potion by which the physician within you heals your
> sick self.
> Therefore, trust the physician, and drink his remedy in silence and
> tranquillity.
> For his hand, though heavy and hard, is guided by the tender hand of
> the Unseen,
> And the cup he brings,
> though it burns your lips, has been fashioned of the clay which the
> Potter has moistened with His own sacred tears.
>
> *'On Pain' – The Prophet by Kahlil Gibran*

There's a story about a father teaching his child to be more courageous. He gets the child to jump from the first step of a staircase into his arms. He does this again, this time the child jumps from the next step up, and then again until the child is on the fourth step. At this point, the father steps back so the child lands flat on their face. The child gets up, their nose is bleeding and they cry from the depths of their soul.

It's very hard not to react to this story as an act of child abuse. That's the way I felt about it when I first heard it. Even though the point of this act is to teach the child those you trust and love can literally let you down, it's almost unbearable to think of our children being treated this way. Still, this story has value. It isn't just about treachery, it's also about learning to deal with our falls, even horrific ones. And accepting that our children's biggest lessons in life will most likely be painful ones.

There are many paths we can take when reacting to the blows life deals us. We can feel victimised, persecuted, and full of anger, or we can learn other ways to react. Amongst these are trying to accept that often these things have very little to do with us and we were just unlucky. Equally, there may be times when we have played a part in our demise, and by coming to terms with that we can improve ourselves.

In some ways, this story is similar to the fall of Adam and Eve in the Bible. Surely God knew they would eat from the Tree of Knowledge and therefore fall from Paradise. Was God being cruel for cruelty's sake, or was God laying the ground for humans to realise that putting our trust in the earth beneath our feet, to have blind faith, is a mistake? Was God's love in the Old Testament the conditional love of a father, which at times can be cruel, and the New Testament one of unconditional love, the love of the mother and holy mother? Both types of love have their negative and positive sides, but somehow, it is unconditional love that seems more divine.

I've mentioned before the word Religion relates to a notion of 'reconnecting' and is generally seen in this context as relating to God, but it may also include reconnecting to ourselves. When we understand the betrayer is not just out there but in us, we get to be more self-aware and understand others more clearly. By accepting our potential to betray we discover a truth about ourselves which in turn makes us feel better known and therefore less betrayed. The more we deny who we are the more we betray ourselves, and others. Therefore, once betrayal is seen as a part of ourselves, life and love, the more prepared we are to heal the wounds we must bear when confronted with it.

There have been times when I have been betrayed and had I lived in a world where I thought betrayal should never occur, I think I'd have been broken by those experiences. But there have also been occasions in relationships when I have betrayed and felt the bitter taste of doing so. And then later, to find I was repeating the same mistakes, even though I'd vowed I wouldn't, was a further betrayal, but this time, of myself too. When we betray others, we betray ourselves, as they betray themselves when they do it to us.

When we experience betrayal, we may be tempted to exact revenge, and ironically this vengeance may involve acts of betrayal. Maybe all betrayal is vengeance for previous betrayals. But as we are often reminded, revenge may incur a heavy price upon us psychologically, a further self-betrayal. If forgiveness will set us free, why do we so readily choose vengeance?

There are many costs to vengeance, one of them is we no longer see the person who hurt us as multi-dimensional. If we only see them as evil, then we can't allow the part of them we loved, if we ever loved them, to exist. In other words, we will have to reject an uncomfortable part of reality if we deny they are human.

Likewise, if we don't accept we were too trusting too quickly, then are we not ignoring a part of who we are, a part that had we been more conscious of, would have meant we'd have been more careful in the first place? If so, then denying our role in our self-betrayal is yet a further self-betrayal.

We may well view the father in this story as being cruel, yet deep down, for all the ways we try to make learning pleasurable for our children, we know that the greatest lessons are likely to be painful ones and if we do not prepare them for this, then would that not be a betrayal in itself?

What depth of love will they experience if they believe the arms they leap into will never let them down, what meaning would there be, what would be the point of leaping? The same goes for life, if we believed we would live forever, would love and life, feel as precious as they do? We may see death as the ultimate betrayal, but is it not also a gift that tells us not to waste our lives?

Moshe and Battiya's Story Part 8 – Sacrifice and Betrayal

"Your wife is in surgery; we're going to have to remove two of her ribs."

There was only one question Moshe wanted to ask right then, and he did.

"Is she going to die?"

The doctor bowed his head slightly.

When the doctors removed two of Battiya's ribs, both Moshe and later Battiya, had a similar thought, was this some kind of payback for Adam sacrificing his rib to help create Eve? The sins of the parents get handed to their children, and sometimes it's with added interest.

Carl Jung spoke of 'quandaries' that are passed down through generations in families. For him, I think he was referring to more philosophical questions than personal psychological ones, but even so the same can be applied. Just as we may seek to resolve issues in our own lives by repeating difficult scenarios, ever hopeful that one day we will bring things to a more preferred conclusion, maybe some issues get passed down through family lines. The idea that one generation seeks to escape the bondage of the previous one is nothing new. Whether it's escaping poverty, abuse or abandonment, it's precisely those things that cause the next generation to experience the same things too.

In my family, the women seemed to suffer far more than the men, and probably because of them too. Boris's father, Samuel, who'd been damaged by World War One, may have been predestined to be a gambler, womaniser and irresponsible father. Was this caused by genetics, his parents, or something else, we'll never know. Both Esther and Battiya suffered as a direct result of Samuel's behaviour, and who knows if the other children were affected adversely too. Boris certainly took on some of the same traits as Samuel, as I did as well. Were these betrayals caused by betrayals or was it already in our nature?

Ideologies of Love Part 8 – For Better or Forget It

There's someone I know, they're not a friend, but a relation (through marriage) of a friend. This person married a man a good bit older than herself. They both went to church and liked to appear as upstanding members of the community. But when in his late 80's he fell ill, all she could do was complain to him that he was ruining her life, that she never had a moment to herself, and all he ever did was call to her for help, and she'd had enough. This was despite there being a live-in carer and plenty of other support.

He had been a good provider, and they were certainly not short of money, so, as he got progressively frailer, they also paid for an extra nighttime carer. Now there was close to 24-hour help at hand, but still, as he became more and more scared, he'd call out for her, and she would just shout at him to stop. Then she started shouting at the carers for not doing their job properly. Consequently, after a few weeks, she'd gone through most of the agency's employees as she'd either sacked them or they'd left as they couldn't stand the abuse. Then one day he became very disorientated and kept whispering the word, "help."

His wife said, "I've had enough of this, I'm going out to get some space." Fortunately, the latest carer kept an eye on him and soon realised he was spiralling down very quickly, so she called an ambulance. The paramedics arrived soon after and within minutes diagnosed an infection. He was rushed to hospital where after a few days of antibiotics he was ready to go home.

"I promise to be good this time, tell me how I can help," he pleaded to his wife.

"I just need to have a bit of time for myself, that's all." She said, as he reached out his hand towards her and like a very sorry child anxiously said to her, "I love you."

"I love you too," she coldly replied.

Of course, within hours she was telling him to stop calling for her, at which point the carer went up to my friend and said, "She has no use for him anymore, now he is just a burden to her."

From the other room, he shouted, "I love you," and with a sigh, his wife shouted back, "Yes, and I love you too."

For a short while after that, things looked like they'd settled down a bit. A new routine began to take shape which mainly involved his wife having as little to do with his care as possible. Even so, she made it known that the little she did do was close to intolerable for any normal human being. There were times in the day when the carer wasn't necessary. This day the man's wife was tending to the garden. She hadn't left his walking frame near him, so he decided to make his way to the toilet. As he was on a mezzanine floor, he had a choice of either going up or down a few steps to get to the loo. He thought it would be safer to go up a flight given his balance was not good, but halfway up he fell backwards onto the wooden floor. It was sometime before his wife came in and by this time he was semi-conscious. She called for an ambulance and once again he was taken to the hospital.

His wife didn't want him back, she insisted that he mustn't come home because she couldn't bear him anymore, that she hated him and besides, all the savings were getting used up so she wouldn't be able to pay for any more carers. That turned out to be untrue, it's just she didn't want their money being wasted on him any longer.

When I looked at their wedding photo, they were an attractive middle-aged couple, she was grinning a big toothy smile and he looked relieved. They'd signed the legal documents. The deal had been done. But a certificate of marriage is not a certificate of love. For all her betrayal of him, he'd equally betrayed himself. I had only met her a few times but still got the measure of her, so I couldn't help but think he knew what he was getting himself into.

Moshe and Battiya's Story Part 9 – Love

During the first days after Battiya's surgery, Moshe wondered if his life would be worth living if she was to die. Then as she started to regain consciousness, he watched her body convulsing in pain and felt awful for her, but all he could do was gently stroke her face to calm her, wet her lips when they were dry, wipe the sweat away when the fevers came, and quietly speak so she'd know she wasn't alone. After a week, she became conscious of her surroundings, but then when he wasn't there it felt as if she was in an ocean of loneliness, and when it came to him going home, they would cry, not just because they were going to miss one another, but because they realised just how much love flowed between them. The day they married, they thought that would be the pinnacle of their love, but now they understood it grew greater with every moment. In this frozen wasteland, where one wrong word might be your last, where the State and those around you do their best to strip away even the tiniest modicum of trust, their love and belief in each other grew stronger.

Ideologies of Love Part 9 – Deal or No Ideal

But if in your fear you would seek
only love's peace and love's pleasure,
Then it is better for you
that you cover your nakedness
and pass out of love's threshing-floor,
Into the seasonless world where you shall laugh,
but not all of your laughter,
and weep, but not all of your tears.

From On Love – The Prophet

By Kahlil Gibran

Beyond the realms of Ideal Love, there must be innumerable other approaches, including alternative versions of ideal love. I thought I'd end this section by looking at various other ideologies, both good and bad. Again, it won't be wholly representative, but hopefully, it will help people consider these issues further.

For millennia marriages have been dealt with as loveless transactions. They were fundamentally deals, and that was it, and even now it's no wonder people still think of marriage as a deal. While deal-based relationships might not reach the heady heights of romantic or ideal love, they may still have value, especially when they're a key ingredient of a happy life, even if for some, it's based on a lie. Of course, for others, these relationships can be the cause of great physical and mental suffering. At that end of the scale, we're talking about the complete antithesis of ideal love, where one human is pouring evil onto another. Even if we see evil as a symptom of psychological dysfunction, it is still very hard to accept that so many of these relationships go unchallenged throughout the world. Up until relatively recently, rape within marriage and domestic abuse in the West was met with a blind eye by much of the public and the authorities. In the early 90s, I once called the police when I heard a neighbour screaming for her partner to stop hitting her. After the police left, one of my other neighbours told me I should have kept my nose out of other people's business.

Still, on a negative note, don't worry I'll end on a high, many people become resigned to a pragmatic relationship in which they are generally unhappy. While not on the same level as the more abusive ones, there is still a lot of discontent involved. There's a song by Paula Cole called *Where Have All the Cowboys Gone* in which the character's romantic notions of love are juxtaposed against the mundane aspects of an unequal and unfair deal-type relationship. She sings of doing the laundry if he pays the bills, of doing the dishes, while he goes to the bar. Meanwhile, she's left holding the baby wondering what happened to all those dreams of a perfect man.

From a psychoanalytic point of view, one might ask whether people sometimes choose the difficult situations they find themselves in. While it's tempting to brush that aside because for many there is no choice at all, many of us have issues that pull us towards painful relationships. Untangling our self-destructive tendencies requires help and skills that are rarely available or will take too much time to resolve for most. Still, for some at least, there may be ways to escape and move forward to a better life.

Given there's so little questioning about relationships nowadays, certain narcissistic tendencies seem to have become aspirations of modern love. One of these is the notion of possession. There were times in my life when I found myself believing that if someone truly loved me, they'd want to be possessed by me. The fact that they didn't, made me think they didn't love me. So not only did I want to possess them, but their love for me was my primary concern.

The other day I read this on a friend's Facebook wall.

"The most appealing thing to me is effort.

Somebody who really desires to converse with me,

See me, and make me a part of their day."

In a strange twist, one could argue that idealistic love does require a desire to converse and make someone else a part of one's day, but the difference is, that it wouldn't be demanded by either party. It might be natural to have such desires, but there's an expectation or a demand in those lines, and in that light, I hear it as a warning bell now.

There are other issues regarding possession that are worth touching on here because it's far more central to a destructive ideology than it first appears. In my more lothario times, there was a paradox when it came to possession. During the early part of a relationship, there would be a moment when a woman would make it clear she wanted me. At the time, I didn't pay much attention to it, but later, especially if I'd become involved with her, I would look back at that moment as extremely meaningful. There was something in the period when someone else wanted me that touched me to the core. Maybe it's the power of moments of submission to another that makes infidelity and seduction so addictive.

I probably don't need to point this out to you now, but wanting to be wanted, while very natural, has a somewhat narcissistic edge to it. The ironic thing about focusing on being wanted is, the person being desired is just an illusion, especially when people hardly know each other. Even so, illusion or not, for the participants, it's still filled with powerful emotions rooted in their psychological issues, biological nature and romantic beliefs.

There was a line in a drama I was watching recently in which one of the characters said that after he ejaculated, he'd either want to get away as quickly as possible or stay with that person forever. While the latter feeling might indicate the potential for a relationship to grow, there's something very self-centred in gambling on there possibly being a good outcome, especially given a bad one risks hurting the other. As I've already mentioned I was not averse to acting in this way. Had I known better would it have made any difference? There were plenty of times I got told I shouldn't have gone that far with someone if I wasn't sure. My answer to them was I never told them I wanted to be with them properly and they knew what they were getting themselves into. But maybe all of that was part of a dance and you know what they say about the Tango.

The issue of possession and wanting to be wanted cuts both ways when it comes to men and women, and again has its foundations in biological, personal and social motivations, but from wherever it comes it is not in the service of love. Yet, romantic love tells us it is.

Nietzsche wrote of possession:

> "He asks himself if the woman, when she gives up everything for him, is not doing this for something like a phantom of himself: he wants to be well known first, fundamentally, even profoundly, in order to be able, in general, to be loved. He dares to allow himself to be revealed. – Only then does he feel that the loved one is fully in his possession, when she is no longer deceived about him, when she loves him just as much for his devilry and hidden insatiability as for his kindness, patience, and spirituality."

Nietzsche's lines above challenge Fromm's ideas about true love. Not so much through their logic but their passion. I think for many of us, this passion is extremely seductive at times as it makes love seem exceptionally real, whereas Fromm's Ideological Love appears almost passionless. But doesn't this cut to the heart of the matter? We already know if you want romantic love, you can't have peace, but how much distress, anxiety, agitation and conflict can you stand? For those who want peace, then perhaps a more pragmatic, non-possessive approach is the way forward.

Alongside possessiveness, the issues of domination and submission also come into play. I'm sorry to be repetitious, but you may remember me mentioning Sam's ideas regarding domination in an earlier chapter. For him, the dynamics of dominance were integral to a relationship's success. While most of us hover somewhere between being dominant and submissive in different situations and with different people, he proposed that if both members of a couple were predominantly dominant or submissive, then the relationship was destined to fail. As far as he was concerned, it would be better if a dominant and submissive linked up, although even then, it would be essential for the dominant partner to be receptive to the submissive's needs. His definition of a dominant was someone who liked making decisions whereas the submissive wouldn't, but instead preferred to work in a more supporting role. I'm not advocating this, but it shows another ideology of love that many of us have probably never considered.

Moshe and Battiya's Story Part 10 – Back to Life

For close to 3 months Moshe followed the same routine. Then one day the doctor said she should go home. That night they slowly walked back to the house. As she entered, she started to cry and quietly said to Moshe, "I thought I would never come back." He drew her close and said, "There is a light here now, and that light is you." She looked up at him and gently touched his lips.

Ideologies of Love Part 10 – No Sex Please, We're Religious

I haven't spent a lot of time on religious ideologies to do with love. One might be tempted to point out that many of the leading religions practice sexual abstinence, with an ethos that couples should get to know each other before making any commitments. In some ways, this sounds similar to the direction Fromm's Ideal Love ideology takes.

The problem with no sex before marriage is one might love someone for who they are but when it comes to sex it might feel wrong. For some that would be an irrelevance, but there are many for whom it would be a problem. Just because we fit together in lots of ways doesn't mean we'll do the same when it comes to sex.

This might explain why some religions not only mandate no sex before marriage but barely any afterwards too. Sex might be allowed for procreation, but pleasures of the flesh are off-limits, and this may be because they don't want to risk destroying the pragmatic relationship, which could well be the result if either party felt they were not sexually compatible. While this might be an astute way of keeping couples together, it does so at a price. Again, for some, such things may be of no significance, but it's probably no coincidence that so many men of the cloth are commonly referred to as 'father'.

In contrast to this, there are those who are completely fixated on excitement and sexual pleasure, especially concerning the first stages of a relationship. For them, the constant repetition of seduction and ending will most likely weigh heavily in time and they'll seek something deeper. However, seduction is seductive, and no one is more perfect than a perfect stranger, so, until they change themselves, they'll keep getting pulled along by their patterns, unable to move on. Filled with the excitement of a train passing at speed, but never able to get on it and see what awaits beyond.

When Detective Frank Drebin states to his co-worker in the Film *The Naked Gun 2* ½ that he envies him having the same woman for 30 years and that having to have a different 20-year-old every night is somewhat of a hardship, audiences all around the world laughed uncontrollably, especially when they saw his co-worker in a state of apoplectic envy. We are, after all, only human and recognise that we are driven by many, many conflicting urges.

Moshe and Battiya's Story Part 11 – Endings and Beginnings

Within a week the factory manager ordered Battiya back to work. It was a time of war and people were dying in their millions, so she was of no significance to anyone but Moshe. There have been philosophical discussions for millennia about the importance of the collective's needs over those of the individual. During times of war, the emphasis generally tends to move more towards the collective, but for Battiya there wasn't even the tiniest gesture of care from her comrades in the factory. Likewise, her manager made no effort to make things easier for her.

When it came to exploiting workers, there was very little difference between the Capitalist West and the Soviet States. Even before the war, Stalin aimed to turn the Soviet Union into a ceaseless productivity machine. From 1941 all holidays were cancelled due to the war and the working week was seven days long with no time off, and any unauthorized absconding could mean sentences in the Gulag from five to eight years.

New Year's Day was the only holiday allowed. For Moshe and Battiya there was almost zero socialising and even invites to a New Year's drinks party to listen to a gramophone represented a deadly threat as far as they were concerned. They once went to one but felt on edge the whole time. No one tried to befriend them as everyone knew making friends was dangerous. Even their landlord couldn't be trusted, so, they were always very careful about what was discussed in front of him. They were cordial but kept a safe distance, as he did them.

The journey to and from work in the summer months was one of the few opportunities to walk hand in hand and chat quietly with each other, but besides that nowhere felt safe. All walls might have ears pressed up against them, so at home or in the factory, every word was considered carefully before being uttered.

One day, late in 1944 news of the Russians pushing the Nazis out of Latvia brought a glimmer of hope that one day they might be able to leave this god-forsaken place. Although World War Two would continue in Europe until September 1945, the Soviet Red Army secured the surrender of Nazi forces in Latvia during the first weeks of May. It had been more than six months since the Nazis were pushed out of Riga; however, they, and their Latvian regiments, held out in various areas of the Baltic states until finally the Russians, and their Latvian fighters, forced their hand. 200,000 Nazi troops were then deported to Soviet prison camps along with the 14,000 Latvian soldiers who'd fought alongside them. Tens, if not hundreds of thousands of Latvians, both civilians and soldiers, fled to Sweden and Germany from where many ended up in exile in places such as Australia, North and South America and various other countries in Europe.

I frequently find that my awareness of time is dramatically altered by my direction of travel. Often the return leg of a journey is far quicker than the outgoing one. Maybe it's because I just drive faster, obviously, if you're a cop, I didn't write that.

For Moshe and Battiya the return journey still took close to 30 days, but this time they were prepared. Their landlord, who was genuinely sad to see them go, helped them stock up on food for the journey and came to see them off from the station. As the train pulled away, they waved goodbye to each other as holidaymakers who were sad to go would, but in their quietly excited hearts, they were happy to see the back of Ishim.

They realised the Riga they were returning to would not be the one they'd left, but they still weren't prepared for the magnitude of devastation that confronted them. All the bridges had been destroyed, as had nearly every building. Some of their Latvian 'workmates' were greeted at the station by surviving relatives, but for Moshe and Battiya there was no one. They went to the place where her sister had lived but there was no one there. At first, they had no idea what had happened to their family members and friends, but rumours soon began to circulate that all the Jews had been taken away or massacred earlier in the war. Moshe and Battiya hoped in time that those who'd gone missing would walk up to them, hug them and tell of their adventures surviving. But in the meantime, there were practicalities to attend to, such as getting food and finding somewhere to sleep, albeit amongst the ruins. Even here, in Riga, every moment of the day was taken up with survival.

Latvia's population decreased by around 25% during the War. Hundreds of thousands of Latvians were killed fighting for both the Nazis and Russians, there were those who 'emigrated', and thousands were sent to the Gulag or deported as part of the Soviet policy of forced population transfer. Over the next few decades, hundreds of thousands of Russians were moved to Latvia, so, by 1991, when the country gained its independence, just 62% of the population were 'ethnically' Latvian. These actions were repeated throughout most of the countries in the USSR and would eventually come to be recognised as acts of genocide.

Close to a hundred thousand Latvian Jews were murdered by the German Nazis and Latvians during the war. Afterwards, a few hundred who'd escaped came out of the forests or homes of brave sympathetic Latvians where they'd been hiding. About 1,000 more returned from the Nazi camps, and several thousand who'd escaped to the Soviet Union also came back. All in all, around 97% of Latvia's Jews were murdered during the war.

After a few weeks camping out, Moshe was approached by a soldier. The soldier stood over him. As Moshe looked up his heart filled with dread.

"Are you Moshe Shruster?"

Moshe stood up and nodded.

"I hear you're good with building things. Is that right?"

"I'm okay," Moshe said tilting his head from side to side very slightly as if he were calculating something.

The soldier looked up at the building they were standing near.

"If you can fix this roof and make the place watertight you can have one of the apartments in it, anyone you want."

"Where will I get the materials from?" Moshe asked.

The soldier looked to his left, paused a second, then to his right and looked at Moshe.

"This is all the materials there are."

"Ah," Moshe said.

The soldier put his hand on Moshe's shoulder.

"Have we got a deal?"

Moshe nodded in agreement.

"Yes, we have a deal."

Moshe still had some of the American tools he'd got from working in Siberia. So, bit by bit he made the ladders and scaffolding. He didn't ask for any help. It was better for him to work alone, although Battiya did what she could. He was also aware the factory he was told to work in would want him working there very soon, so the window of opportunity was getting smaller by the day. Sure enough, just before he started on the last section he got called to the factory, as did Battiya. With no one to keep guard, not only was their temporary home at risk but so too were all the repairs he'd done. He asked for some time off, but his boss couldn't spare him. When they came back that evening, their shelter was gone, as were his ladders. Fortunately, he still had his tools, money and food. They stayed with him always.

That night, they angled a board against the wall and lay on the ground. As they tried to get to sleep, wondering if someone might slit their throats, Moshe said under his breath, "There's nothing sacred, nothing pure here." Battiya paused for a moment then kissed him gently. "Okay", he said, "There's a little bit of sacred and a tiny bit of pure." She tapped her finger on his nose and laughingly said, "What are you saying Moshe, are you saying I'm not pure?" He looked at her and laughed too.

A voice from nearby called out as if it was calling a pet, "Hello little rats, what are you laughing at?" Battiya froze, Moshe grabbed his knife and sat up, his back against the wall. Then again, the voice taunted, "I'm coming to do what Hitler should have done, here little ratties."

There was a thud then the ground vibrated a little.

In the darkness, Moshe could still make out Battiya's face. She was petrified. He positioned himself so if the board was moved, he could lunge at the attacker with the knife. Outside of a kind of "oomph" and the sound of something or somebody being dragged across some debris, there was just silence. After a few minutes, Moshe slowly poked his head out to take a look, but there was nothing to see. He stood up and walked to where he thought the voice had come from, but again, there was nobody, not even a trace of someone having been there.

The next day Moshe made another ladder, but from then on, he hid whatever he left behind. After work he'd rush back, the nights were getting longer, so he worked on the roof until he had to stop. Battiya sharpened his tools, and prepared and sawed the wood. It took a further three weeks, but finally, the roof was watertight and from then on they slept in the building, where they barricaded themselves in until all the doors and windows were completed. This Frankenstein monster of a building was ready, not just for them, but for other people too.

The soldier kept his word and provided them with the correct documentation and over the next 26 years, Moshe and Battiya lived in this apartment. The building served its purpose, it sheltered them, kept them warm and saw their two sons come into being, but the hatred that visited them that night was never far away. Besides the constant threat of falling foul of the Soviet system, there was the extra danger of being Jewish in a society that had done its best to rid itself of nearly every Jew living there. And all around, there were still plenty of people who wanted the job finished.

Even though Moshe became highly respected in his field, their two sons, Yakov and Eddie would grow up being constantly bullied for being Jewish. They too kept their heads down, studied hard and didn't cause any problems. But for some, their very existence was an abomination. While overt attacks occurred now and again most of the time everything was done in secret, that was the Soviet way. Things only went your way if someone in the background agreed to it.

Twice a year, fearing that one day something awful would happen to them, Moshe applied to emigrate to Israel. For eleven years, his application was refused, then in July 1971 permission was granted. They were given 21 days to leave, if they hadn't left by then they'd have to reapply again in six months. The emigration department looked at Moshe's finances and thought he'd have no chance of raising the money for the flights, but there was another secret world and after 11 years of applying to the Israeli embassy for a visa, they, the Israelis, let him connect to it. Moshe made it clear to them that he didn't have the funds to pay for the flights, but they said they'd lend him the money. This time Moshe and Battiya felt it was going to happen, that somehow, they'd escape.

When Yakov, their son, said he wanted to stay in Riga with his girlfriend, Battiya insisted that there was no way she'd split the family up. She would never be a party to doing what her father had done to her. Either they all went together, or they stayed. Yakov asked his girlfriend if she'd move to Israel too, and she said yes, but her parents wouldn't allow it. To him, this girl was the love of his life, and he didn't want to leave her. Moshe couldn't believe Battiya wouldn't let Yakov stay by himself. He didn't argue, but he couldn't speak to her for days.

Yakov knew that as much as he loved his girlfriend, he couldn't be the one to make his family stay, so he agreed to go to Israel too. For them, it was an escape but for him, it was a prison sentence, without her he didn't feel whole.

The day of departure came. They had to take a very long train ride to Moscow first and from there catch a plane to Vienna. When they got to the airport the guards took Moshe into an office where they interrogated him about the money for the flights. They wanted to know if he had got it from dealing in the black market. Moshe and Battiya had been warned by their Israeli contact that this might happen and were given a number to call if it did.

Battiya asked if she could make a phone call, but her request was refused. Yakov asked if he could go to the lavatory. The guard said okay, and pointed to where it was. As Yakov walked to the toilet block, he looked for a phone, but couldn't find one. A few guards were standing nearby chatting and smoking, they looked at him, then continued talking. When he got back, he made it clear to his mother he hadn't been successful and it was then, she knew in her heart the Soviets weren't going to let them go.

What they didn't see, was one of those guards near the toilet block saw what was going on and somehow sent a signal to somebody that things were awry. Within ten minutes another guard entered the office where Moshe was being interrogated and whispered something to the guard in charge. He then looked at the other guards and nodded to them. Moshe was free to go. As the saying goes, money talks, even if it's just in nods and whispers, and, as the guards soon worked out, interrogating people could certainly get money chatting freely, straight into their pockets.

On the 8th of July 1971, Moshe, Battiya and their two sons touched down at Tel-A-Viv airport. I asked Eddie, their youngest son, and my cousin, what his first thoughts were when they arrived in Israel. He said it was like going from a black-and-white world into a multi-coloured one.

It took a long time before they got used to not feeling as if someone was watching their every move but within nine years, they started to find their feet financially as well as socially. Yakov met a woman and settled down with her then found out that his girlfriend from Latvia had also made her way to Israel, but it was too late by then.

Eddie, like his father, became a kind of metal worker too, for him though it was as a sculptor and artist. By 1980 he was beginning to have exhibitions and started dating another artist, Miri, who would later become his wife. Life was finally coming together for the family.

One day Battiya told Moshe she didn't feel well and within a few months, aged just 60, she died of colon cancer. Just before she died, she and Moshe were in their living room looking out at their children in the garden. "There are so many things I wish had been different," she said. Moshe positioned himself behind her and slowly wrapped his arms around her shoulders and whispered, "I wish I could have been a better husband."

"You weren't so bad," she paused for a second then added, "We were the lucky ones. And look how happy they are now," she nodded towards their sons chatting in the garden, "They're free." She reached up to Moshe's hand on her shoulder and gently took hold of it. Their fingers interlinked. She looked up at him and smiled.

At my father's funeral, Moshe spoke when I had tried to say something, something I'd spent a long time working out beforehand, but as I opened my mouth to speak, I burst out crying and couldn't stop, so he kindly took over. He told us of his love for my father, how Boris would come to them when they lived in Riga after the war with suitcases full of contraband, and how, now, all these years later, he wanted to say sorry to Boris for banging that stone against his head.

Moshe died in 2011 a year after Boris. In 2008 his son, Yakov took me on a long journey and at no point during it did he let me know he only had a few months to live. For Moshe, there was a penalty to living a long life, it was watching those he loved die before him. So, when it came to his dying moments, it wasn't God he wanted to greet first but his wife, Battiya, his son Yakov, and his parents as well as many other loved ones.

I've often seen it written that God is Love, but maybe to most people, Love is God.

Moshe and Battiya's Story Part 12 – Epilogue

I asked my cousin Eddie to help me with this story about his parents Moshe and Battiya. He must have had a lot of patience because every time I showed him my initial drafts, he'd tell me that what I'd written barely scratched the surface of how awful it was to live under Soviet rule. As far as he was concerned the way I portrayed Soviet citizens was far too sweet whereas, in his experience, the system made them very dangerous.

594

My father couldn't find it in him to forgive the Latvians, which is not surprising. His family were persecuted both before, during and after the war by the non-Jewish Latvian population. When I told Eddie I thought a lot of Latvians nowadays were not anti-Semitic he got quite annoyed with me. He pointed out that there have been far-right anti-Jewish marches in recent years in Latvia, and just because I once visited the country didn't mean I had the insight or right to let modern-day Latvians off the hook. But there was something inside me that wanted to push towards a middle ground. To say, okay, there may well be a lot of Latvians with anti-Semitic views, but there might also be a lot who don't feel that way.

Then I spent a bit of time looking online and there it was, the division. The 'Zionists' this and the 'Zionists' that, and I realised that it's not just Latvians, it's the whole Western world that's building up its reserves of hatred again. It's the Jews, the Muslims, the far right, people of colour, the far left, the police, the politicians, the elites, the white middle-class men, the stupid masses, the deplorable, it's everyone that isn't us, it's them, it's the others. There's no middle ground for people to meet on, there's no sense of proportion, you're either totally with us or you're against us. If you hold even the slightest non-sanctioned views you are an enemy of the people. The Soviets may have lost the Cold War, but I can't help but feel I'm living in a world that's beginning to head in that direction.

Ideologies of Love Part 11 – Moshe and Battiya

Maybe for Moshe and Battiya, having grown up together, they knew each other well. Still, the Moshe and Battiya that they would come to know throughout their married life would be very different to their childhood images of each other.

For most people, even very connected couples, there may well be temptations, loneliness, hatred, anger, detachment, and, well I think you get the picture. As much as they loved each other, this was no fairy tale and there were plenty of times when Battiya would have left Moshe had she had her family around her, and maybe he felt the same way too, but they stayed together and knew something of love.

Given our lack of education about love, our problematic psychologies and our innate nature, it's a miracle that any successful marriages ever come about, but they do. For most people, romantic love might bring them together but how they cope with the reality of being with someone, especially when the romantic image falls, will be the make or break of their relationship. Beyond that point, there will be many other hurdles that, if the couple are caring people, will bring something of Ideal Love to their world without ever having read a word of Fromm or Aristotle.

So here we are, back at the beginning. We know that taking time, not being rash, being caring, responsible and unselfish are all very sensible ways to behave, but the immediate joys of temptation are so powerful they can barely be resisted.

Elvis sang of wise men not rushing in, but he couldn't help falling in love. What he didn't tell us was those wise men only got so wise after quite a few lessons, many of which were filled with pain, well that and a drop in their hormone levels.

———

Epilogue

I'd originally planned to release this as one volume, but as it grew, I realised it might be easier to digest as two. Also, as the chapters progressed it was clear there was a different emphasis between the first half and the second. The first focuses on my experiences of love, hate and knowledge, whereas the second revolves around belief systems and ideologies. Of course, those themes are still wrapped around the events of my life up till 18. I'd also planned to write a third volume covering my 20s and 30s, but I don't think that's going to be possible now.

———

June 8th, 2023

I'm ill, and I have to get to A&E. Well, that's what the advice is on the Internet. I haven't been to the loo for several days and now I'm vomiting. It's 2 am, Gill, my partner, says she'll come to the hospital with me. When we arrive, we're made to wait for about an hour before my blood is taken. After that, I'm left in the waiting area. I ask Gill to go home, that way she'll have more energy if needed later. I end up trying to sleep on the chairs in the waiting area. Every hour I vomit, mostly air and bile. At 9:30 the junior doctor who took my blood approaches me and says I can go home.

"No," I say, "You don't know what's wrong with me."

He shrugs and says, "We think if you take a laxative, you'll be okay".

Again, I rebuff him, "I've had doctors try to dismiss an illness before and I nearly died."

"What was that then?" he asks.

"I had a burst appendix."

He looks a little surprised, "Oh, I didn't realise you'd had surgery on your intestines before."

I can't help but feel a bit indignant, "It's in my records, plus I have already informed you I'm due for a colonoscopy next week which suggests all is not well with my colon."

The doctor says he'll have a chat with the consultant in charge.

A few minutes later I'm directed to another area. There are beds around the room, so I ask if I can lay on one as I feel so ill. The consultant who's in his 60s seems to take a dislike to me, as if I'm making a fuss about nothing, and tells me I'll have to sit in a chair, which I do. A woman is screaming in an anti-room, begging for pain relief, and another man with mental health issues is walking around ominously. I decide to stay seated and not make any more of a fuss.

About half an hour later I am taken to have a CAT Scan done, and about another hour after the consultant stands about six feet away from me and without any privacy or decorum, tells me I've got a tumour blocking my colon with raised glands around it and there are multiple tumour markers on my liver too. At the end of it, he says, "You'll have to be taken to another hospital to be assessed."

I'd been half expecting this news, though not so bad, after I got the request for the colonoscopy. At the time I'd felt dread as well as noticing a feeling in my side where it would later turn out to be where the tumour was.

Gill has been my partner for quite a few years now. I'd finally found a relationship where I could be caring and less selfish, likewise, Gill was very caring to me too. I let her know what was going on and a friend drove her to the hospital I'd been ambulanced to. It was there we were informed that there'd be no radiologists available to perform the required surgery until Monday as it was a weekend. And so, I went through three and a half days of puking up faecal matter every few hours, feeling a lot of pain, and getting very little sleep. When Monday came, I was taken to have a stent placed in my colon to open it up. The procedure took about 45 minutes, and I immediately felt a lot better. I wasn't allowed to eat for a few days which meant I managed to finally hit my target weight, something I'd been trying to get to for months, so at least that was one positive outcome.

It would be a few weeks before I'd get to see a consultant and when I did the first thing she said to me was, "The cancer you have isn't curable, and we can only offer you palliative care. If you don't have it, you'll most likely die within six to nine months, but with it, you may get to live three years, however, it's very hard to say, it may be less or more."

Gill and my sons had joined me for the consultation. There was a stunned silence after the consultant laid out the prognosis, but as she showed us the scan of my liver and pointed out the tumours she paused and stood up while saying, "Don't worry, we will do everything we can." I realised she was speaking to Gill who was in floods of tears and as I looked at her, I burst out crying too. The thought of leaving her alone felt worse than the thought of my death.

When I managed to recompose myself, I said to the consultant, "I know this may sound a bit strange, but I realise that it might be possible when looking at me to think my life is difficult and I don't have much to offer the world, but I love my life and I have a lot more to give, so if you ever think otherwise, please don't." Even though she reassured me that she wouldn't ever think that way, I still felt I had to make it clear.

Within a couple of weeks, I had a Port-Cath surgically implanted into my chest to allow the chemotherapy and blood to be more conveniently given and taken, and then the fortnightly chemotherapy cycles started. The first day tended to leave me feeling quite sick, and then for 48 hours, I had a pump attached that'd deliver more chemotherapy. Outside of it getting in the way and occasionally getting the tubes caught on things that'd then pull on the needle inserted into the Port, it wasn't too bad. I also had to have GCS-F injections that had a profound effect on me, including pain, nausea, fatigue, hallucinations, and tachycardia. Once that subsided, I'd get three or four days of not feeling too bad, so along with three days after the initial one, I'd feel well enough to work on getting this finished in time. I had four books all in all to edit as well as 70 songs I'd like to produce properly. However, I understood it'd be very unlikely I'd get time to do so, that there was a very real deadline coming up.

There were also practical things to get sorted, from photos, letters, creative stuff, Power of Attorney, my Will, and many other things, including tying up loose ends such as reaching out to others where some form of closure would help both myself and them. The problem was I became so focused on getting things dealt with, that I realised that although cognitively I was aware of what my likely fate was going to be, emotionally I was in a complete state of denial.

To me, I felt I was going to get through this and live till I was 85, just as my father had predicted. But then I wondered if he'd seen 58, and not 85, and not wanting to scare me, said 85. Given I'm now 58, if that was true, then there's only a matter of weeks left. And then I got the news my cancer markers had been rising every week for the last month and a half. That was the first time since the early days when I felt dread again and realised I was living under a very precarious sword of Damocles.

Most of the time I feel as I have done through most of my life, but I'll get pangs of dread hit me as well as some form of acceptance. Conversely, I feel resentment that I'd like to have another 20 or 30 years, but in the same breath, accept I've had a good life and hope my end won't be too painful.

So, for now, this is where I'll end volume one. Thank you for reading it and I hope you'll join me for volume two. Either way, you being there has helped me get through many a dark night over the last 18 years, so thank you for that too. And if I do pass away soon, then this connection will be among the many throughout my life which have helped me come to understand I wasn't alone after all.

About the Author

Simon Mark Smith is a published writer whose work has appeared in magazines and poetry tomes, including a Microsoft book and Christmas Card, don't knock it they paid him well. He has also published three other books.

Initially, Smith studied and received a BA in Fine Art painting at the prestigious Chelsea School of Art. His work has been exhibited in major galleries and he'd later come to work for the Arts Council's policy-making division, as well as for Microsoft, both as a writer and a public speaker. He has also worked as a writer, singer-songwriter, studio photographer, digital artist, computer consultant, property developer and teacher.

Smith's life was borne amidst difficult circumstances, including being born with no lower arms and deformed legs, being illegitimate, and living in care homes part-time until, at the age of 7, he moved in with his mother onto a rough council estate along with her psychopathic boyfriend. Smith says he became who he was not despite these issues but partly because of them as they too were also life-enriching experiences. Smith often says he's unique, just like everyone else, but the life he lived has brought perspectives to him that many would find thought-provoking and maybe even life-changing.

He now lives on the South Coast of the UK but was brought up and spent most of his life in London. He has four grown-up children.

To find out more about Simon please visit www.simonsdiary.co.uk

facebook.com/Simonmarksmith

x.com/simonsmith1

instagram.com/simonsmith1

Also by Simon Mark Smith

Simon's Diary Volume Two - Ideologies and Beliefs

Simon's Diary - The Travel Diaries

Poetry and Lyrics

Milton Keynes UK
Ingram Content Group UK Ltd.
UKHW052120310724
446306UK00001B/4